W9-APA-140

"I'm a lifelong fact-freak, a hopelessly obsessed lover of trivia games and crossword puzzles. So I'm utterly fascinated each year when this *Almanac* comes out. It's packed with the kind of info you can use to stump your friends. Which two 19-century winners of the Royal Gold Medal had the same name? (Smirke and Smirke, of course. A supercilious pair!) What percentage of students in Master of Architecture programs are women? (Not enough, but getting there.) What state has the most architects per capita? (Hawaii by a mile, but they've still got less than one for every thousand residents. Surely the world needs more of us architects than that.)

But the *Almanac* is much more than a gold mine of facts. It's quickly becoming indispensable for any public library, any design firm, and any school of architecture, landscape architecture, or interior design. And certainly for any architectural journalist. It's solid, reliable and remarkably complete. It's also handsome, clear and orderly. And it improves each year. In a world in which access to information is critical, the *Almanac* is essential."

From the Foreword by Robert Campbell,
Pulitzer Prize-Winning Architecture Critic,
The Boston Globe

The purpose of this *Almanac* is to promote quality architecture and design. It would have been impossible without the generous support of the following:

The American Institute of Architects
Architectural Woodwork Institute
Autodesk
CMDG
CNA Financial
The Durrant Group

AIA Hilton Head
AIA Minnesota
American Institute of Architecture Students
Armstrong
ASD
Beck Group
Counsel House Research
Design Futures Council
Disney Imagineering
Michael Graves & Associates
Hellmuth Obata + Kasabaum
Morris Architects
Society of Marketing Professional Services
Steelcase
The Stubbins Associates
Wimberly Allison Tong & Goo

ALMANAC *of*
ARCHITECTURE
& DESIGN
THIRD EDITION

ALMANAC *of*
ARCHITECTURE
& DESIGN
THIRD EDITION

Edited by
James P. Cramer and
Jennifer Evans Yankopolus

Foreword by
Robert Campbell

Greenway Communications
A Division of The Greenway Group

CMDG
Construction Market Data Group

Editors: James P. Cramer & Jennifer Evans
    Yankopolus
Editorial and Research Staff: Jan Akers, Austin
    Cramer, Corinne Cramer, Kerry Harding, Mary
    Pereboom, Beth Seitz, Bret Witter
Consulting Architectural Historian: Jane Wolford
Book Design: Lee Cuthbert
Index: Kay Wosewick, Pathways Indexing

Copyright © 2002
by Greenway Communications, LLC
All rights reserved. No part of this book may be
reproduced or transmitted in any form without
written permission from the publisher.

Greenway Communications,
a division of The Greenway Group
30 Technology Parkway South, Suite 200
Norcross, GA 30309
(800) 726-8603
www.greenwayconsulting.com

Publisher's Cataloging-in-Publication
(Provided by Quality Books, Inc.)

Almanac of architecture & design / James P.
    Cramer and Jennifer Evans Yankopolus, editors;
    foreword by Robert Campbell.
    -- 3rd ed.
    p. cm.
    Almanac of architecture and design
    Includes bibliographical references and index.
    LCCN: 2001095131
    ISBN: 0-9675477-2-5

    1. Architecture—Directories. 2. Architectural
design. 3. Architecture—United States. I. Title:
Almanac of architecture and design

NA9.A27 2002   720
                             QB101-201213

Distributed in North America by
National Book Network
(800) 462-6420
www.nbnbooks.com

CONTENTS

CONTENTS (CON'T)

CONTENTS (CON'T)

CONTENTS (CON'T)

CONTENTS (CON'T)

FOREWORD

Robert Campbell

I'm a lifelong fact-freak, a hopelessly obsessed lover of trivia games and crossword puzzles. So I'm utterly fascinated each year when this *Almanac* comes out. It's packed with the kind of info you can use to stump your friends. Which two 19-century winners of the Royal Gold Medal had the same name? (Smirke and Smirke, of course. A supercilious pair!) What percentage of students in Master of Architecture programs are women? (Not enough, but getting there.) What state has the most architects per capita? (Hawaii by a mile, but they've still got less than one for every thousand residents. Surely the world needs more of us architects than that.)

But the *Almanac* is much more than a gold mine of facts. It's quickly becoming indispensable for any public library, any design firm, and any school of architecture, landscape architecture, or interior design. And certainly for any architectural journalist. It's solid, reliable and remarkably complete. It's also handsome, clear and orderly. And it improves each year. In a world in which access to information is critical, the *Almanac* is essential.

It also makes you think about where we are, and where we're going. Looking back over the year 2001, and ahead to 2002, a couple of trends seem to stand out. One is the ever-growing globalization of design, otherwise known as the star system. In my own city of Boston, for example, there were no fewer than eight winners of the Pritzker Prize actively designing buildings in 2001 (you can check out the Pritzker on page 141). Only two of these eight were Americans. The others came from Austria, Japan, Spain, Italy, Britain and The Netherlands.

Why were these architects asked to come so far, sometimes halfway around the world, to work in my city? Because they are all international stars, of course. Why are they stars? Well, the first stars were, of course, the movie stars, which gives us the clue. Stars are a product of media publicity. And in a world in which the media are powerful, the stars become global. If you're a rock star in England today, you're automatically a rock star in Bangladesh and Singapore and Rio. It's the same with architects.

The more important question is this: Why do clients hire these stars, when there are, usually, perfectly good architects closer to home? There are, I think, two reasons. One, the media hype leads client to believe that the stars are really better, more creative, more competent. And sometimes, no doubt, they are. Two, the client often believes that labeling the building with the "brand name" of an architectural star will assure its success. Maybe the "signature" name will help with fundraising, maybe it will draw crowds to the finished building. Universities and art museums are especially susceptible to these two incentives. The model for them all is the Guggenheim Museum in Bilbao, Spain, by superstar Frank Gehry. Bilbao was in international sensation and drew visitors from all over the world. It did so, at least, in its first years. The roar of the crowd has now somewhat faded. The novelty is gone. Bilbao is now a large museum without a collection of its own, sited in a medium-sized and rarely visited city. It is doubtful that all those enthusiastic overseas visitors—of whom I was one—will ever pay a second visit to Bilbao.

Yet the initial success of Bilbao spurs other cities to emulation. Of a proposed museum in Denver, by star Daniel Libeskind, the New York Times writes: "Politicians and civic leaders have begun excitedly predicting that it will focus attention on Denver much as Frank Gehry's Guggenheim Museum has done for Bilbao, Spain." Well, maybe it will, maybe not. It sometimes seems the same twenty or thirty international stars are now being asked to design every important building in the world. Are clients buying quality, or designer labels? The stars can't do their best work if they're doing too much. Often, they don't have time to get to know the places they're designing for. The star system is a worrisome trend. It recalls the warning of the late Norwegian historian Christian Norberg-Schulz: "The institutions are becoming monuments to the architect who designed them, rather than expressions of common agreements and values."

As always happens with a trend, there's a counter-trend, working against the star system and against the globalization of which it is part. It's like politics. Just at the moment when nations are relaxing their nationalism and gathering into larger units (for example, the economic community of Western Europe), nationalism elsewhere is becoming more intense. In the case of Russia, Yugoslavia, Scotland, Quebec, it either splits former federations into smaller parts, or threatens to do so. Big is beautiful and small is beautiful at the same time. In architecture, the same thing happens. Just as everything seems to be in the hands of those global stars, there's a revival of interest in something more local. It's at its best in the Aga Khan Award for Architecture (see page 33). This is a program that awards prizes every three years to distinguished new works of architecture in the Muslim world. The idea is to encourage architecture that isn't an imitation of star-studded, Western-dominated global culture, a culture that is threatening to engulf the whole world. But at the same time, the Aga Khan program also discourages reactionary Disneyish stage-set copies of the Muslim architecture of the past. It seeks instead to honor buildings that respond to whatever is genuine in the geography, the culture, the climate and the building traditions of their locations. The Aga Khan, who is the spiritual leader of many millions of Muslims around the world, was present at the awards ceremony, held this year in Aleppo, Syria. His program is the wisest thing going.

Another trend that gets a lot of attention is the so-called information revolution. I'm among the few who think the importance of that revolution is exaggerated. Last year's *Almanac* printed a speech given by Dutch architect Rem Koolhaas, on the occasion of his winning the Pritzker Prize. He said, with his usual eloquence, that "brick and mortar have evolved to click and mortar...the domain of the virtual has asserted itself." But let's get real. The info revolution is not the sole property of our own era. It has been going on for a very long time. It began with the printing press, which author Victor Hugo predicted would kill architecture, just as Koolhaas is predicting the Internet will kill it today. Printing was the first cyberworld in which we began to communicate not directly but by means of coded signals. Later came the telephone, an innovation that surely transformed the world of communication as much as has the computer. Architecture is not going to be replaced by electronic imagery. Architecture is the art of making places. Real places, not web sites. Rooms, gardens, towns. Places for human habitation. As long as we remain physical beings, we will seek to inhabit physical places. It is the proper role of architecture to provide them. Architects should not be surfing the wave of media delight. They should be digging in their heels against it. One of the things I like best about the *Almanac* is the lack of images. In today's world, that's as daring as it is intelligent.

The real revolutions are elsewhere. Genetic manipulation, the possible cloning of human traits—now that is going to be a change, although not one that's especially relevant to design. The other impending change, however, is indeed relevant. It's the ongoing despoiling of Planet Earth by our species, a process that may, possibly, eventually render the world unfit for life. Human beings at their worst can be rather like cancer cells, multiplying and spreading out of control over the organism we call Earth, mowing down everything in their path. Koolhaas got this issue right in his Pritzker speech, when he spoke of "the disappearance of Nature." But the good news is that the healing response has begun. Throughout the United States and the world, there is concern about sprawl development, the kind that eats up forest and farm, depends on the automobile, and consumes a disproportionate share of the earth's resources. There's also—more in Europe than in the U.S.—a growing interest in the kind of architecture that doesn't damage the environment, that may even nurture it. This is the powerful so-called green movement, evidenced by some of the awards listed in this *Almanac*.

Planetary survival is likely to become the biggest political issue of the 21st century. It's one in which architects and other designers are crucially involved. We've got a long way to go before we can say we've halted the deterioration of the planet. Perhaps when Venice—arguably the greatest collective work of art ever created by human talent—disappears under the rising surface of the sea, as now seems likely, the issue will strike home with greater force.

If there is a single notable change in the United States in the last few years, it's the comeback of the city or the town, as opposed to the suburb, as a place to live. As noted, cities and towns are far more efficient than suburbs or rural areas in their use of resources per capita. They also support an interactive social life. People of different backgrounds, different ethnicities, different economic status get to know one another in towns, more than they do in the gated community of the suburb. They develop empathy for one another. They become members of a community. Of course there are other kinds of communities, the communities of shared interests that meet via the Internet. I think of myself as a member of such a cyber-clan, a worldwide community of architects, my friends and colleagues in almost every city. But I'm equally glad to be a resident of an actual physical city block that held, in 2001, its 25th successive annual block party. It's a mistake to believe that virtual communities and actual communities are in some way opposites. We need them both. To be a citizen of the world today is to be an occupant of both kinds of communities simultaneously.

What about architectural style? That's a topic one can only guess about. But it does seem safe to predict that we'll continue to live in a culture of many competing styles and philosophies. There will never again be a single dominant style in any given place, like the Gothic of the European Middle Ages, or the high modernism of the West in the middle 20th century. We live in a world that is too aware of too many options for that. In the U.S., we've recently seen a revival of classic Modernism, especially in architecture schools. The revival resulted, in 2001, in an enormous two-museum show in New York of the work of modernist Mies van der Rohe. But at the same time, other architects--member of the New Urbanist movement--are creating communities where both the planning and the architecture are a deliberate imitation of the American small town of the past. And still other architects are experimenting with never-before-seen shapes. Architects known as Blobmeisters create buildings that look like enormous lopsided candy apples (for instance, Frank Gehry's Experiment Music Project in Seattle). Architects known as Deconstructionists create buildings that look like tragic train wrecks (for instance, Daniel Libeskind's proposed addition to the Victoria and Albert Museum in London). Both blobs and wrecks are the result of a new tool, the computer. The computer makes it possible both to draw, and later to build, such irregular structures. Will they be good places to live, work, visit? Will they gather to shape good streets, squares, parks? Time will tell. What we can be pretty sure of is that in a world as self-aware as ours now is, no style, once established, will ever completely disappear. Even a revival of the Post-Modernism of the 1980s, so much deplored during the 1990s, may now be imminent.

The one thing you can say for certain is that design today is on the front burner of culture everywhere. People are arguing about it. They are visiting it. And in this *Almanac*, they will be learning more about it.

INTRODUCTION

The pace of change is exponentially faster than it has ever been – and architecture and design are not immune. The changes we are seeing in the design professions encompass not only linear innovation – that which you might plan for– but non-linear innovation in response to unanticipated changes.

The terrorist acts against the World Trade Center and the Pentagon were devastating and unprecedented—and define 2001 as much as any event has ever defined a year. The loss of human life was horrific, making the destruction of one of the world's great architectural works an unfortunate sideshow. But the damage to the American economy and cultural psyche, at least in the short term, is equally of note. September 11th marked a turning point in United States history, one all of us will be dealing with for years to come.

And yet life, and work, goes on. While many architectural projects were cancelled, others were created as security and safety became key elements in the design of new projects and adaptation of current buildings. Within two weeks of the terrorist attacks, the New York Real Estate Board convened a Tri-State executive conference to explore a regional strategy for rebuilding Lower Manhattan. From tragedy comes opportunity. The seeds of transformation are clearing the way for New York and other progressive cities to become "cities of tomorrow." This requires the skills, talents, and visions of architects and designers—now more than ever. It is possible to imagine a worldwide embracement of the "I Love NY" theme.

Things change with time. Ideas mutate in nature. The same is also true for architecture and design.

In this Third Edition of the *Almanac of Architecture & Design* we have assembled extensive research on the essential facts and trends in the design professions. Although we don't have a crystal ball, as the terrorist acts all too vividly remind us, our research over the past year has given us fresh insight into burgeoning long-term transformations in the design professions.

In 1897 the state of Illinois enacted the first architecture registration laws. That was the 19th Century. Today we are at the dawn of the 21st Century. A new industry is being created and with it demands for a new design profession that will be defined not only by government regulations but also by innovation in practice management, leadership, and design creativity.

In order to formulate a perspective on the current magnitude of change itself, just consider for a moment what's happening in medicine: the human genome, DNA tracking, new cancer vaccines, artificial blood, organ transplants, bloodless surgery, cholesterol lowering medication saving thousands of lives a year from coronary disease, and the creative prevention programs that have led to increased longevity unimaginable a generation ago.

In law, attorneys scramble to redefine their own professional practices as the size of the body of knowledge required to excel in a particular area precludes excellence across all areas of practice.

There will be radical new value propositions in architecture and design as well. New processes, new technologies, new business models, new strategies. And perhaps a new economic world.

Like everyone, architects and designers are closely watching economic indicators. They know that in the years ahead the economy in which they practice will be different—perhaps very different. Many of the benchmarks in this *Almanac* should be kept in perspective and, in certain cases, recalibrated in light of fluctuating economic trends. Some regions and areas of practice will be less affected, of course, but overall a softening of the economy is already underway. The duration of this circumstance is uncertain. However, the trends that many firms are now reporting tell us that their own three year growth plans are still just that—growth plans. Many firms are repositioning themselves in the value chain by offering both the richness and reach of new services, from interiors to consulting. The response so far has been positive, and there is considerable upside opportunity still projected by leading firms around the globe.

To the casual observer, it may appear that technology is taking a breather, but in reality new net platforms and hi-tech solutions will be bulking up in preparation for the next big wave of growth. Technology will be more invisible and more taken for granted – but it will also be disruptive to traditional industry practices. This will create new opportunities for design professionals willing to change the way they practice. Even today there is an increasingly seamless continuum between the conception and implementation of forms. Design processes are migrating from 2-D forward to 3-D, with some people talking about 4-D.

We should not fool ourselves into thinking that the Internet and technological breakthroughs are at an end. On the horizon, artificial intelligence will be imbedded into CAD systems that include building codes, costs, and even liability insurance aids. And instead of the traditional mouse tool, there will be real time feedback from every stroke of the CAD pen. The Internet is looming as an even bigger factor in the future of the design professions. The real power of the Internet lies in its ubiquity and simplicity. It has the ability to permeate and catalyze the new design economy in a manner comparable to the interstate highway system.

New value in the design professions is based, in many ways, on speed and efficiency. It is becoming somewhat of a myth that good design takes a long time. Our research indicates that, using the tools already available, typical commercial projects could be delivered in half the time. Currently, 20% of total delivery time on a typical office building is the design phase; through technology, this time can be decreased by nearly 60% on standard buildings. Diminished labor requirements, thanks to new robotics and other systems, will cut down on construction time even more.

In the future, building solutions will be pre-assembled at a large scale. Clients can already get customized small and medium scaled pre-fabricated buildings that almost appear like one-off buildings. At www.workstage.com you can see how an alliance between owners, developers, manufacturers, and designers is creating mass produced buildings that are customized to each owner and user with economic and time saving benefits. Joseph Pine Jr., co-author of *The Experience Economy* (Harvard Business Review) and a senior fellow of the Design Futures Council, calls this mass customization.

We do not know yet just how pervasive this experimental trend will become. In the near future, high-end design solutions could be pre-assembled, and Pritzker Prize-winning architects could design and redesign even low budget building projects like those boxy strip hotels you see on the way to the airport.

At the same time, building construction will become 20-40% more efficient in the next five to ten years. Better information and technical coordination is the best opportunity for value enhancement and greater efficiency. Architects and designers are moving from fragmentation to integrated solutions. Just as you used to have to buy twelve pieces of office equipment to have a home office, now you can simply go to Kinko's.

Integrated services beyond standard design-build services will become more common. Our research reveals that architects and their clients believe that advanced integrated delivery will become nearly 60% of all project delivery by 2008, as opposed to less than 30% today. And traditional service delivery including design-bid-build will actually decline from 59% today to approximately 31% in 2008.

Real innovation in design happens in context and that context requires highly collaborative processes. For instance, the myth of a split between "design architects" and "contractors" is becoming a charming artifact of the past. Where there is obvious binary opposition in this industry, there is also the greatest opportunity for breakaway new value propositions. Those firms that are taking a position counter to conventional wisdom are likely on to something that offers new and fresh value.

And just as there is a convergence of design and construction, there is a new vocabulary in use by architects such as: Balanced Scorecards, Benchmarking, Best Practice, Client Centric Solutions, Competence Alliance, Core Structural Capital, Economic Value Added, Innovation, Synergism, Value Creation, and Value Design Drivers.

On a broader scale, the public is coming to value and appreciate community aesthetics at new high levels. Good design is in vogue. Industrial designer Karim Rashid made his name with an eight-dollar trashcan and a stackable chair. He now has an impressive backlog of work unthinkable in the last decade. And celebrity architect-designed buildings are in demand now more than ever. You only need to visit any major U.S. city to witness either a recently completed or soon to be completed building by one of a handful of world-famous architects. There is a new point of intersection between popular and professional taste. We are entering a period where everyone wants good design. This phenomenon fosters globalization of design services. Go from city to city in the United States and you will see European and Asians taking the lead on design innovation, while American talent is being exported all over the world.

And yet, the economic conditions making for the delivery of these services is moving from elite to universal. Just a few years ago color printers cost $10,000; today, they are a tenth of that. Ditto designer buildings—they are not just for the patron clients anymore.

This also translates into greater success for the designers themselves. Take Michael Graves, the 2001 Gold Medal recipient. Not only can he get a wonderful fee for designing a building, but he can capture a royalty on each sale of his patented product designs at Target stores as well. With Target selling hundreds of thousands of items in its Michael Graves line, he will probably make as much from his alarm clocks and coffee pots as he will for his next building design.

A new world of design and intellectual capital is unfolding at a staggering pace. It stands to reason those firms with the best business skills and best design talent will have a marketplace advantage.

In our work with the organizations, publications, and firms who helped us assemble this *Almanac*, we discovered a profile of today's successful design firm. The following five characteristics are those most often mentioned by firms finding success and satisfaction today:

- Developing a coherent point of view about the future. No firm outperforms its aspirations. So the point of view should be very high – expansive – and motivating.

- Operating with a vision and a plan. Most often this includes a few non-linear futures invention characteristics. Their business plan is most often edgy—that is it doesn't just rely on last year's success formula.

- Extinguishing inertia in their organizations. They co-opt and neutralize the anti-change forces within their midst.

- Using a vocabulary of action and motivation. They don't acknowledge binary opposites very often; instead they build bridges using unifying business logic.

- Focusing on priorities and accountability. They are disciplined toward the renewal of goals and achieving them.

It has been exhilarating and sometimes exhausting for us to daily track developments for this edition of the *Almanac of Architecture & Design*. Nearly one hundred pages of new content have been added and every page has been updated and enhanced with the most current information. New sources have been discovered and the responses to our surveys have been bountiful. Thousands of people have helped us compile the information in this 3rd

Edition. We extend a special thanks to those organizations and their leaders who share with us daily the changes, updates, and latest information. We especially thank CMD, Autodesk, Armstrong, Steelcase, Architectural Woodwork Institute, The American Institute of Architects, and The Design Futures Council. Thanks to the Pulitzer Prize winning architecture critics Paul Goldberger and Blair Kamin for their thoughtful critiques and support of the Almanac over the years. And for this edition's foreword we want to thank Robert Campbell of *The Boston Globe* for his review of significant issues facing the design professions.

We value your comments. Both of us will be diligently working non-stop on the next edition, so we invite you to call (770-209-3770) or email us (jcramer@greenwayconsulting.com or jyank@greenwayconsulting.com) with your suggestions.

James P. Cramer
Jennifer Evans Yankopolus
Editors

Speeches & Essays

Acceptance speeches from some of this past year's major award winners and essays from recent architecture and interior design graduates can be found in this chapter. A list of these awards' past winners is available in the Awards & Honors chapter beginning on page 31, and additional student-specific information and resources are located in the Design Education chapter beginning on page 509.

Michael Graves. Photo: Bill Phelps.

AIA Gold Medal 2001 – Michael Graves

The 2001 AIA Gold Medallist, Michael Graves, delivered the following acceptance speech at the Accent on Architecture Gala at the National Building Museum in Washington, D.C. on February 16, 2001.

Thank you. Teaching at Princeton for 39 years has me programmed to speak for only fifteen minutes. Tonight they told me five or ten. You guys are so generous. I am overwhelmed, of course, because I think this is the only award an architect can get where only his or her peers vote for them. And you all are as competitive as I am, so I know how hard it was.

I was at the Institute today, and they had put my name, the firm's name, on the wall. It was truly overwhelming, I must say. It was humbling. There were some past winners that weren't mentioned by Bob Schieffer in his introduction. Just seeing Jefferson's name on the wall and Le Corbusier and Mies makes you feel that anybody that would have you in their club and give you the Gold Medal, you wouldn't ever join it, certainly. That's Woody Allen I think.

There was a moment today when I was looking at the archives of the Institute – and I would recommend it to all of you who love drawings – that I was told a story. I love telling stories, and I am going to try to tell you this story. I had somebody write it down for me so I wouldn't forget. I though it was an interesting – not comparison for tonight because one couldn't have a better night than tonight – but anecdote. In 1923 the Gold Medal ceremony was held at the Lincoln Memorial. It must have been warmer weather. All participants, all of us, were dresses in neoclassical garb, you're basic toga party. Henry Bacon was the recipient. He was seated on a barge with a golden putto above his head about to bestow a laurel wreath on his head. He was pulled down the reflecting pool, finally ending up at the steps of the Lincoln Memorial . He was met there by the President of the United States and the Chief Justice of the Supreme Court – are they here? – and members of the AIA, of course. After the ceremony they all dined al fresco on the Memorial grounds. Things have changed. Anyway, it's great, all of this.

I have no idea what I can say tonight that hasn't been said by Charles Herbert and by David Childs, how sweet that was. By my count, David, SOM

AIA Gold Medal 2001 – Acceptance Speech (Con't)

has won four of them – twenty-five year awards, I mean – and therefore you must be a hundred now. And they're all great projects, of course. But that's enough.

We as architects are so incredibly fortunate to get to do what we do. We all complain a lot. But to think that we get to make things and also make the contribution that all our parents told us we had to make or we weren't worth our soul– at least mine did. That is just an enormous gift. To think we could be podiatrists – it's amazing – and we're not. And we're dressed a little better too I'm sure.

I'm here tonight with several tables – I think five or six tables – of certainly all of the principles in my office and all of our collaborators in the office but also our clients, architects who have been associated with our firm in one way or another, and engineers – who I am absolutely glad do what they do so that I didn't have to do it because I couldn't, and they do it so brilliantly. They are so good at their craft. We also have a number of clients here tonight. They are just wonderful people because they became our friends, and that doesn't happen in very many institutions and instances that I can think of.

We have a client here who's been with us for 30 years, and I've only had my practice since 1964. Sam and Rosell Miller are here from the New York Museum and came from Florida out of retirement. He's my age, shouldn't I retire? I don't know, maybe. We have people like Bobby Cadwallader here tonight who really gave me my start in furniture design. I asked Bobby when he asked me to design showrooms for Sunar and SunarHauserman if I could also design furniture for them. He said, "well if you do a good job with the showrooms, we'll let you design furniture." He did let me do that. The showrooms were a sort of hit. People came in and looked at the showrooms and then they bought Doug Ball's furniture. So I learned what a loss leader was.

We have many clients. For instance, we worked on a corporate office building called Crowned American, and they said, "we want you to do everything." I had already been trained by that time by looking at the work of people

AIA Gold Medal 2001 – Acceptance Speech (Con't)

like Charles Eames and Saarinen and Le Corbusier and Mies and others who had always designed furniture and the interiors of their buildings, which I get questioned about all the time these days as if it's odd for us to do that. I always ask the interviewer to go talk to the people who are not doing that. The folks at Crowned America in Johnstown, Pennsylvania, said we want you to design our building, of course, our interiors, our dining room and everything in it – the plates, the chairs, the artwork, the murals, the whole works. What a gift we get to do all of this. And when we do it well there is no better reward, of course. We've been very fortunate in that the breadth of our practice has allowed us to do so many different things, from the buildings that some of you know to the things that often times fill them, the objects I mean. To think we have gotten to do things as far fetched as the Washington Monument and sets and costumes for the Joffrey Ballet. And speaking of heat, we did take heat for that one.

Nevertheless, when you think about character in architecture and you think about a room like this, you have to think of character, that's what we do. It may be tragedy one day and comedy the other, but most of the time it is somewhere in between. That breadth is really extraordinary in the kind of work that one finally gets to do in architecture whether it is buildings or a spatula for Target. That was a great day for me because, for me, working for Target has allowed me to see the modernist's dream come true. What Gropius and Joseph Hoffman and others wanted to have happen for design, and good design at that, to be affordable, is now finally coming true, not just by Target but a lot of different places. And that's another kind of gift that we have looked for. Now what we must all do is go after the other parts of the puzzle – housing, schools. I know some of you are extraordinarily gifted at that and maybe will get a chance to try as well.

And finally I just wanted to say that the most memorable evening for me that was like this one was when Philip Johnson got his Gold Medal in the late-70s. Because the first thing that happened when Philip found out that he had been awarded the Gold Medal or had been nominated for it, he called a lot of young architects, eight of us, and said, "I'm too old and crotchety just to get this by myself. I want to give it to you guys as well because you're the ones that will take the mantle from this point on." Philip,

AIA Gold Medal 2001 – Acceptance Speech (Con't)

always the cheerleader of architecture, said, "join me in Dallas." We were called the Dallas Eight—numbers were big in those days, there was a group called the Five as well. Philip said, "I'd like for each of you to give a talk at the Gold Medal ceremony." He'd convinced the AIA that this was a good thing. Although they really were not convinced, they let us do it anyway. We all gave a talk, some of you might remember it. The house was packed. My friends were there talking. Philip was this very generous figure who made sure, like some of the rest of us have tried over our lifetimes to make sure, that the young are brought up in a way that we think is appropriate and the best we can do. Hence my teaching. And Philip did what he did.

My teaching for all this time has been so extraordinarily rewarding for me. And I know that in certain instances, maybe not all, but in certain instances it has been good for the other side as well because some of my students are here tonight. Some of them are running schools, many of them have great practices. It is a little disconcerting when you are walking out of an interview or walking into an interview and your students are walking out and you're competing with them, as did happen to me two weeks ago in Richmond. But nevertheless, sometimes you win and sometimes you don't. But you're happy their practices are going well.

So, with all of that and with all of this tonight, I can't thank you enough. You are very, very generous. I'm just pleased to be among you.

Courtesy of the American Architectural Foundation

Herbert Lewis Kruse Blunck Architecture's
University of Iowa's Newton Road Parking Facility
accommodates 800 cars and houses a 5,000 ton
chiller plant as part of a complex master plan to
unite the isolated west campus with the rest of the
university. Photo: Farshid Assassi.

Architecture Firm Award – Herbert Lewis Kruse Blunck Architecture

The following was taking from Herbert Lewis Kruse Blunck Architecture's submission for the 2001 AIA Firm of the Year Award and reflects the firm's guiding design philosophy and commitment.

HISTORY

Herbert Lewis Kruse Blunck Architecture is the continuation of Charles Herbert and Associates, an architectural practice established in Des Moines, Iowa, in 1961. Over the past 40 years the Firm has evolved from small, private commissions to more prominent public and institutional works. Throughout this time, however, the Firm has consistently worked to create architecture of the highest quality; an architecture of substance carefully tailored to the needs and aspirations of each client and community. This pursuit has resulted in a portfolio of significant and enduring buildings and has garnered the Firm a national reputation for creating sensible and successful design solutions. Moreover, the body of work has helped elevate the design consciousness of architects and raised the bar for the region's practitioners. As a result, the Firm has been, and continues to be, a major influence on architecture in the Midwest. For nearly four decades, three core tenets have guided the Firm's development:

DESIGN QUALITY

The fundamental principle which drives Herbert Lewis Kruse Blunck Architecture is an uncompromising commitment to design and project execution of the highest quality. Design is the Firm's core competency, its marketing niche, and its near-religious conviction. Every project, be it grand or modest, is viewed as a design opportunity worthy of the best design effort. Projects are not viewed as good or bad but simply as challenges. The success of this approach is evidenced by the over 200 awards for excellence in master planning, architectural design, urban design, and interior design. Among these award winners is a $2,000 children's play space and a $25 million corporate office complex clearly indicating that this commitment to design obeys no boundaries of budget or scale. This quest for excellence has consistently transcended specific project typologies, evidenced by a port-

Architecture Firm Award (Con't)

folio of work that includes carefully crafted historical restoration, raw factory spaces, artist studios, sophisticated corporate headquarters, rigorous retail interiors, thoughtful landscapes, and complex urban master plans.

DESIGN EDUCATION

Of critical importance to the Firm and the profession is the education and mentoring of the next generation of practitioners. An operating philosophy which views all projects as "A" projects requires a staff comprised entirely of "A" players. Clearly, this can only be achieved through a commitment to both formal and informal learning.

In addition to the structured academic involvement, the Firm's office is organized to enhance lifetime learning among staff members. The open studio, in which experienced architectural professionals, top interns, and talented students work side by side, encourages a "cross-pollination" of ideas that has proven to be an effective and motivating mentoring environment. Integrated architect and intern teams are expected to carry out all phases of any given project from the earliest conceptual design through contract administration. This lack of specialization provides valuable continuity for each project and a wealth of practical experience for the staff. Herbert Lewis Kruse Blunck Architecture is a teaching office, bringing together architects who view the design process as an opportunity to listen, learn, and grow.

DESIGN LEADERSHIP

Members of Herbert Lewis Kruse Blunck Architecture are expected to be deeply involved in both their community and the profession and to work to "make a difference". Principals and staff serve as leaders on numerous public, institutional, and professional boards and have invested themselves in their community and profession. They bring their unique visual and organizational insights to lead both public and private initiatives -- many of which have been instrumental in changing the face of the region. In addition, the Principals and staff have consistently filled leadership roles for the AIA. From committee and convention chairs, to organizing speaker programs, editing the Iowa Architect, and serving on the Chapter's Board of Directors,

Architecture Firm Award (Con't)

Herbert Lewis Kruse Blunck Architecture has been instrumental in guiding this AIA Component to be one of the best in the country.

A COLLABORATIVE ENVIRONMENT

Herbert Lewis Kruse Blunck Architecture employs an inclusive design philosophy which views each project, regardless of scale, as a unique design opportunity. The Firm strives to balance the issues which confront all projects -- site, program, image, economics -- and coalesce them into a clear, elegant, comprehensive whole.

This holistic sensibility informs the Firm's practice methodology in which teams are empowered with shared responsibility for project performance at all levels -- both aesthetic and financial. Interns and young professionals play an important role in this strategy. The best students are drawn to the firm by its reputation. Upon arrival, they become integrally involved in projects and are given tremendous latitude and a commensurate level of accountability. The resulting accelerated learning curve is as self-serving to the Firm as it is effective for the staff, providing a rich, invaluable experience and a dynamic, collaborative work environment in the purest form.

ACHIEVEMENTS

Herbert Lewis Kruse Blunck Architecture has received 202 awards for excellence in architectural design, interior design, historic preservation, and urban planning, 87 of which have been won at the national and regional level. Included in this group is one-third of the awards given in the 26 year history of the Central States Region Honor Awards Program. One-third of awards presented in AIA Iowa's Honor Awards program have gone to the Firm as well. Most notable, however, Herbert Lewis Kruse Blunck Architecture has received five National AIA Honor Awards, including four in the last four years. This national recognition is testimony to the breadth and diversity of the Firm's expertise, representing a historical restoration, a factory, and advertising agency, a retail store, and finally, a complex urban project weaving together a parking garage, public transit facility, and a child day care.

Architecture Firm Award (Con't)

Projects have been completed in thirteen states, including new significant projects in San Francisco and New York City. These commissions have not been the result of an organized marketing effort; they are a testimony to the quality of the extensive and diverse body of work accomplished. Well-known and respected in both the public and professional realms, Herbert Lewis Kruse Blunck Architecture has a growing influence and reputation, spreading far beyond its humble Iowa roots.

The cumulative effect of this body of work has irrevocably changed the face of the Central States region. Architectural excellence, we believe, should know no boundaries of place or size or project. Our goal is simply to do common things uncommonly well. We seek to be an inspiration to one another, to our peers, to our community, and to our profession. We work hard to be consistent, never in terms of style, but always in the quality, clarity, and commitment we bring to the design process.

Courtesy of Herbert Lewis Kruse Blunck Architecture

Jacques Herzog (top) and Pierre de Meuron
(bottom). Photos: © Margherita Spiluttini.

Pritzker Architecture Prize 2001 – Herzog & de Meuron

Jacques Herzog, the 2001 Pritzker Prize Laureate with Pierre de Meuron, delivered the following acceptance speech at Thomas Jefferson's Monticello in Charlottesville, Virginia, on May 7, 2001.

Dear Mrs. Pritzker and all of the Pritzker family, dear members of the jury, dear friends, ladies and gentlemen, thank you for so many things. Thank you for your ongoing and uncompromisable commitment to architecture. Thank you for choosing us for this prize which we were longing for and hoping to get, like only children can wish to get things deep in their hearts. Thank you to our clients and friends, some of whom are here this evening, for their support and their willingness to dialog also in difficult phases of a project.

Thank you to those who have opened us the door at the GSD many years ago. That has proved to be a critical step for us into this country quite some time before we, actually, were given the chance to realize some of our best work here. Thank you to our partners, Harry and Christine, and to all our collaborators who have been working with us for many years with an unbelievable commitment.

In 1978, Pierre and I opened our joint architectural offices, but it was neither a historical decision nor a momentous founding event. During our last semester at the Federal Institute of Technology, we had already realized that we had a great deal in common. The fact that we struck out on our own was more or less an act of rebellion and desperation. What else were we to do?

The economy was not very rosy and architecture both at home and abroad seemed foreign to us. We had no idea what we wanted, we only knew what we didn't want. A few semesters with Aldo Rossi, who was forty at the time, had filled us with enthusiasm.

In his earliest buildings made of poorly processed concrete, we discovered an affinity, something that swung to rest between Pasolini and Arte Povera. And we loved his dry dictum "architecture is architecture" because it seems to be so provocatively simple minded and pinpoints something that is still vital to us today: architecture can only survive as architecture in its physical

Pritzker Architecture Prize 2001 Acceptance Speech (Con't)

and central diversity and not as a vehicle for an ideology of some kind. It is the materiality of architecture that paradoxically conveys thoughts and ideas. In other words, its immateriality. That's an old story, but it is more relevant today than ever before: architecture lives and survives because of its beauty, because it seduces, animates and even inspires people, because it is matter and because it can – if only sometimes – transcend matter.

But this anarchist and poetic side of Rossi, which we loved so much as students, was gradually assimilated into the postmodernist Zeitgeist. What remained was an academically rigid ideology of permanence and typology, and a sudden dominance of decorative historical elements of style, a kind of coming-out of the decorative, which had beaten an embarrassed retreat since the rise of Modernism.

In the fine arts, which are usually more critical, more radical and ahead of architecture in adopting artistic and social changes of paradigm, representatives of the Transavanguardia and the so-called Wild Painting came up with so many new pictures that in spite of or, perhaps, because of this inundation, there was no room left for our own. Nor did we see any latitude of this kind in deconstructivism; although we were fascinated by its chief philosophical exponents, we were bored to tears by its architectural advocates and their explanations. In the early years, we experimented with all kinds of forms and materials trying to subvert their conventional usage as if to squeeze something hidden, something invisible out of them that would breathe life into our architecture. Yes, that was what we wanted: to breathe life into architecture although we could not specifically describe what we meant by that, despite endless attempts to put it into words. There was no philosophy that we felt we could embrace unconditionally although phenomenological questions have always played a salient role, for instance, questions of sensual perception or of signified and signifier.

The artist Rémy Zaugg with whom we have often collaborated over the years relentlessly asks questions that address our concerns as well. Obvious perhaps and simpleminded, but all the more profound – what, where, how, who? Our designs became increasing minimal, radically minimal. Suddenly, the room for action became huge. At the beginning of the eighties, no one

Pritzker Architecture Prize 2001 Acceptance Speech (Con't)

used a rectangle as ground plan and section, that is, a box as the basis of design. We wanted architecture without any distinguishable figuration, but with a hesitant non-imitating analogy. We were looking for a hint of memory, of association. We did not want complete reduction or pure abstraction. We were not trying to simplify the world or to reduce it to so-called essentials. There was no religion, no ideology at stake.

We did not want a sect of Minimalists. On the contrary, we were aghast at the ravages caused by so-called Minimalism in architecture, which was linked with morals and perfection and had the imprint of latent Protestant zeal.

We in turn began to have more and more doubts about the dominance of the rectangle in our designs. It had become too confining. Paradoxically, the box, conceivably the simplest and most basic architectural shape, had acquired the value of its own like a stylistic device. And that was exactly what we always tried so assiduously to avoid.

But there may be another entirely different explanation. The reasons for the supposed breaks and changes of style in our work may not only be design-motivated, but also psychological. The supposed objectivity of the modernist formal canon may merely have served to simply the workings of our long-term cooperative venture and the discussion of projects; it may actually have held us together as a team. The fact is that we've worked as a duo since our youth and have in recent years involved two other partners, Harry Guger and Christine Binswanger, who are also here in Monticello today and rightfully so.

Possibly, co-authorship with Pierre and later with our partners, has in recent years yielded the startling realization that individually distinctive gesturally expressive forms and images for our projects are, indeed, feasible and are now surfacing all the more passionately in our work.

Working with last year's winner of the Pritzker Prize, Rem Koolhaas, on the project for Astor Place in New York shows that our experience of a complex team structure is capable of generating an even more complex architecture

Pritzker Architecture Prize 2001 Acceptance Speech (Con't)

than emerges from the hermetically sealed isolation of the single author. Precisely because Pierre and I have developed projects together for so long, we have been able increasingly to involve other people and other areas in our cooperative undertakings and therefore other forms and spaces as well. The sculptural and even seemingly accidental elements, the figurative and the chaotic, which have recently appeared in our work, are as much a consequence of conceptual strategies as our previously developed formal idiom and not the result of a singular artist gesture.

This conceptual approach is actually a device developed for each project by means of which we remain invisible as authors. Of course, this invisibility does not apply to the name Herzog and de Meuron which cannot remain hidden and even less so now, thanks to the Pritzker prize; rather it applies only to our architectural identity. It is a strategy that gives us the freedom to reinvent architecture with each new project rather than consolidating our style. It also means that we are constantly intensifying our research into and with materials and surfaces, sometimes alone, sometimes in collaboration with various manufacturers and laboratories with artists and even with biologists. We look for materials that are as breathtakingly beautiful as the cherry blossoms in Japan or as condensed and compact as the rock formations of the Alps or as enigmatic and unfathomable as the surfaces of the oceans. We look for materials that are as intelligent, as virtuoso, as complex as natural phenomena, materials that not only tickle the retina of the astonished art critic, but that are really efficient and appeal to all of our senses - not just the eyes, but also the nose, the ears, the sense of taste and the sense of touch. Much has failed and continues to fail because the large concerns that would set up the technological and methodological conditions for new developments show too little interest, because there is no market for such things.

Moreover, politically, demands for improving both the ecological and energy aspects of society have not been radical enough in addressing the construction sector of the economy. Does this wish to extend architectural research into major industrial concerns express a romantically transfigured view of the world, a kind of aftereffect of the ideas of Joseph Beuys whom we had the privilege of assisting for a brief period, or does this refer to a possible role of the architect in the twenty-first century? We are not interested in

Pritzker Architecture Prize 2001 Acceptance Speech (Con't)

making prophetic statements about the future of architecture. In this respect, however, one observation must be made: The rise of a global star system in recent years is indicative of the colossal battle of displacement in the world of architecture.

A narrow elite of author-architects stands opposite an overpowering ninety percent majority of simulation architecture, an architecture essentially without an Appellation controlée, as it is called in the world of wines. There is hardly anything left in between, only a few young people desperately seeking salvation in the few remaining niches and the largely hopeless prospects of design competitions.

Rampantly spreading simulation architecture is no longer projected on the world by an author but instead simulates, reproduces, manipulates and consumes existing imagery. Instead of passively letting ourselves be sucked into the maelstrom of this simulation architecture which not only absorbs all the imagery, but also any and all innovation in order to survive, we can actively deploy simulation as a possible strategy in our own architecture - in a kind of subversive reversal, as in biotechnology. And that may well be the most exciting prospect in architecture today and indeed in human society, this incredible latitude that leaves room for the most extraordinary achievements – and the ghastly ones as well. Thank you.

Courtesy of the Hyatt Foundation

Architecture Student Essay
Carlin MacDougall

The editors of the Almanac of Architecture & Design *asked a recent graduate from Cornell University, last year's Top School for Architecture (see page 559 for this year's ranking), to contribute an essay on design education and the future of the profession. Carlin MacDougall studied architecture at Cornell University and graduated in August 2001 with a Master of Architecture degree. She has also earned a Bachelor of Architecture and a Bachelor of Arts in anthropology from Cornell. Currently she works at Tecnikos: Architecture, Planning, Interiors in Seattle, Washington.*

The most common criticism leveled at the process of architectural education is that it does not adequately prepare students to be fully participating members in architectural practice. Students invariably do not gather all the skills necessary to create a work of architecture independently and must, therefore, endure a lengthy term of apprenticeship. Conversely, people new to the profession are commonly dissatisfied with architecture as it is practiced and most often cite the lack of intellectual and creative stimulation in the office setting as the greatest challenge in adjusting to the working environment. Interns are frustrated by their inability to grasp the entirety of the process of making architecture and are confused about the apparent loss of concern for the creative process within the profession.

In order to elucidate the nature of this confusion it is necessary to better understand the purpose of the separation of the educational process and apprenticeship. The clearest characterization of the role of higher education in the development of an architect is that it instills a set of values that will later inform his or her attitudes in practice. Subsequently, during the period of apprenticeship there is an opportunity to gather necessary technical knowledge. The ideals instilled in architecture schools combined with the technical knowledge to realize these ideals are the two components of successful architecture. Unfortunately, this distinction remains unclear to most students, who believe that they are gathering skills in the educational process, and to prospective employers, who are uncertain as to why interns do not know more.

Generally speaking, the values instilled in a student of architecture are the ability to recognize good design and, more importantly, to generate good design through a rigorous, logical process. In most schools this means dis-

Architecture Student Essay (Con't)

mantling preconceived attitudes about the built environment and reorienting the student toward a particular set of theoretical ideas and aesthetic parameters. This is logically the domain of higher education, traditionally the setting for the cultivation of intellectual pursuits rather than practical knowledge. A well educated student of architecture will be able to explain the importance of maintaining clarity of a generative idea in any design. He or she will want to create a controlled process to develop the idea, in which all aspects of the design are derived from the inspirational source. The process is interpretive and is the mechanism through which the student learns to understand the built environment and the creative process.

From the perspective of the architectural profession, it is important for educational institutions to instill values, because it creates a community of professionals who share attitudes about the goals of architectural design. It also serves to exclude those who have not had the training that cultivates such attitudes, and is, therefore, a vehicle for social stratification in the building profession. Thus, it is not surprising that the more emphasis on theory and aesthetic control, the more prestigious the institution, and the more attractive its graduates.

Students emerge from these institutions with the expectation that they have gained valuable knowledge for their careers as architects. It is common for interns to view the set of design values and methods learned in school as a set of skills, rather than an overall orientation, and to want to put their knowledge to immediate use in the professional setting. The desire to contribute to the generation of design is logical considering that design values are the core of their educational program and often reflect the sum of what the intern has to offer an architectural project. Unfortunately for many intern architects, conceptual design is a relatively small part of the total building process and is usually controlled by more experienced architects. Interns are given tasks to allow them to gather the mundane skills in their apprenticeship that were not a part of their formal education.

Perhaps the greatest conflict with instilling values that focus intensively on design and the role of the designer is the lack of emphasis on the variety of roles in the profession. Schools put little stress on the importance of draftspeople to the production of a building and also ignore the need for the collaborative involvement of other types of architects such as project managers,

Architecture Student Essay (Con't)

code and technical specialists, and specifications writers. Few schools, particularly prestigious institutions, will present such options for professional paths. It is not clear to everyone entering the profession that in many firms these roles are indeed separate tracks and the designer is only one of the players in a much a larger cast of characters.

Employers certainly use design education as an important criterion in the selection of junior architects but may only understand vaguely that their training has been about developing an orientation toward design and architectural ideas. Regardless of education, most interns are hired to do intense CAD drafting despite their design or intellectual potential. The tendency of architectural offices to exploit well educated junior designers as draftspeople is, in fact, encouraged by the idea of internship. The requirements for licensing and the Intern Development Program (IDP), for instance, ensure that the majority of experience earned will not be in design but in the preparation of technical documents that provide the real instructions for building. Schematic design, which is what most students are learning to master in school, requires only 15 credits for IDP, while the category of construction documents requires 135.

Despite what seems to be a remarkable lack of communication between the educational process and the profession, students do continue to enter the profession and become successful licensed architects. The system produces professionals notwithstanding the apparent inefficiency in the use of young designers and the frustration and confusion of people new to the profession. In fact, the profession has a vested interest in being able to hire interns as cheap, unskilled labor while maintaining the illusion that architects are the intellectuals of the building trades, given their superior education and defining values. For this reason, there is little pressure on the educational system to produce more highly skilled graduates. Eventually interns rise in the profession and are able to use the knowledge gained in their apprenticeships to create architecture. The real question is whether people entering the architectural profession do benefit from the values they learned in school. It may simply be misleading to teach students that architectural work is governed by a set of principles, principles which few people are able to fully implement.

Interior Design Student Essay
Sally Moeller

The editors of the Almanac of Architecture & Design *asked a recent interior design graduate from the University of Cincinnati, last year's Top School for Interior Design (see page 558 for this year's ranking), to contribute an essay on design education and the future of the profession. Sally Moeller studied interior design at the University of Cincinnati and graduated in June 2001 with a Bachelor of Design degree. She is currently awaiting the next leg of her design adventure. She can be reached at Moellesp@yahoo.com.*

My Perspective on Design Education

The past five years in design school have consisted of twelve apartments, 10 weeks homeless in Europe, drained bank accounts, internships in three different cities at three different design firms, four and a half years of hard work preparing for senior thesis, and six long months of senior thesis. At this point in my life (post graduation) it takes me less than an hour to pack all my personal belongings (mostly clothing) into three L.L. Bean duffel bags and be out the door. Looking back on it, no matter how hard or frustrating it was at times, I wouldn't dare change a thing. For me design education was not just about sitting in studio endlessly debating concepts and reworking drawings, it was about experiencing all the amazing opportunities that the world has to offer and how, ultimately, those experiences are traced back to design.

I entered design school not having an inkling about design; let alone what designers actually do. I decided on design school after two years of majoring in history and realizing history, although fascinating to study, would take me nowhere I really wanted to be. I needed a skill. I loved to draw and be creative, so design school became the obvious choice. The first day of class I was standing around with a bunch of strangers when in walks my first studio professor, looking like a respectful Hugh Grant. Without any introduction he immediately began talking design: why design is important, what does it mean to be a designer, does anyone know what the word 'Datum' means? As these ideas and questions bounced back and fourth in my mind during those endless first hours of studio, all I could think was, "what am I getting myself into?"

Interior Design Student Essay (Con't)

Let's face it, the most important aspect of a design student's education is the classroom. This is where professors lay the educational foundation. I almost think of it as entering the army. In the first couple weeks of school all my pre-conceived ideas on design were literally stripped away. Once gone, each professor began to build a new stronger foundation in its place. In studio we were introduced to the fundamental principles of design. History, theory and technology began to give these abstract principles shape—demonstrating to me for the first time that the design world came fully equipped with a dynamic and intriguing history and brilliant scholars fixedly dissecting, questioning, and revolutionizing theory and technology. In my first two years of design school I began to comprehend my professors' fascination with design. Design is not solely about buildings, environments, and other tangible objects. Design is about creating for mankind, and the only way to do that is to learn and understand through emotions, actions, geography, and culture. Designers are constantly trying to prove their understanding of mankind through the tangible objects they design.

After two and a half years of design education, my foundation was beginning to take shape. The next task of development was to combine my knowledge of the world with my education. However, at nineteen years old what did I know about the world? I had grown up in white middle class suburbia, considered pepperoni pizza an ethnic food, and couldn't even comprehend the possibility of owning a pair of red shoes. I was extremely naïve—and I needed to change all that as soon as possible.

Fortunately for me, the University of Cincinnati offers endless opportunities for educational experiences outside of academia. After two and a half years of the classroom experience, all design students must participate in the co-operative education program. This program gives students the opportunity to explore the professional world through a series of six required internships. Students are given the freedom to go anywhere in the world as long as the internships meet University guidelines. Upon realizing my need to break out of the "bubble," I took full advantage of the co-operative education program. I learned many valuable lessons on the way.

Most projects in my academic career had been individual projects. I developed the concept, I space planned, I selected the materials, I built and con-

Interior Design Student Essay (Con't)

structed the final presentation. It was my complete vision. The only other person immediately involved in the process was the professor who pushed for more, set boundaries, and constantly questioned my intentions. Practicing design is a different story.

It was on my first internship that I learned the value of my peers and the vital necessity of self-confidence. I was assigned to a team of designers and architects working on one project. Each person on the team had a specific role, collaborating together for a built outcome. But does it work? How do designers put aside egos and work together as a team? The few group projects I had encountered in school were always difficult because of hurt egos, members not giving a hundred percent, or members scared to share their ideas. However, at the end of this internship, designing in a team oriented environment proved its merit. Each person on the team, including me–the intern–had something very important to offer the project, a reflection of the group's diversity. Members included multiple ethnicities, economic backgrounds, religions and political opinions. Discussions about design always led to other topics related to the issues at hand and allowed individuals a chance to voice their experiences and opinions. Once the discussions came full circle, each member viewed the original topic differently. Ultimately, it was the group's diversity that allowed the project to become richer in theoretical meaning and aesthetics.

Back at school, this lesson allowed me to explore the diversity of my peers. I had previously viewed their opinions and insights as a resource but never fully utilized them. This is partly because of the insecurity and vulnerability I felt with my projects. Letting go of these feelings and allowing design to be explored by my peers made each project stronger and me a better designer.

Each internship nurtured my development as a designer. I've been given the opportunity to do everything from red lines on construction documents to setting up photo shoots. The more experience I developed interning, the more opportunities presented themselves to me. During my final internship, I felt I was no longer an intern but an employee. The firm gave me the utmost respect and responsibility, allowing me to be involved in all aspects of a project. I sat in meetings discussing concept development, where I not only listened but actively participated in the evolution of the project's solu-

Interior Design Student Essay (Con't)

tion. I was even given the opportunity to meet and present a project to a client. All this as an intern–it was an amazing learning experience.

However, it was not just the internships that aided in my development as a designer; it was also the cultural and geographical diversity I experienced along the way. I spent six months each in New York City and Chicago and three months in San Francisco. To top it off, I traded in my final work quarter for a travel quarter and managed to backpack all throughout Europe looking at art and design on $35 a day (yes, it can still be done).

Looking back, I don't think I fully comprehended what I was getting myself into. New York City compared to the rest of the country is completely foreign–bordering on alien. My life went from living in the peaceful Midwest to restless Alphabet City, driving in my comfortable car to standing shoulder to shoulder in the subway and thinking I was so stylish in my khakis to ...well ...realizing I wasn't stylish at all. But I absolutely loved everything about this foreign land. After New York, I went to the opposite coast. San Francisco was spent trying to understand how it can be so cold in July and how all the new "internet money" would transform the region. I also developed a love for sushi and wine tasting. When I got to Chicago, I finally bought my first pair of red shoes. But Europe truly offered the most amazing cultural learning experience. I was mesmerized by the glow of the Guggenheim Bilbao and the intricacies of the Alhambra in Granada. Berlin was reminiscent of a science fiction novel, complete with the most interesting and complex population I have yet to encounter. I touched the sky when I hiked the Swiss Alps and reached paradise at the Turkish baths in Budapest.

The cultural and geographical diversity that I have experienced is just as important as the theories learned in the classroom and the internships completed in the profession. I have seen parts of the world and met unique individuals that will stay with me forever, and it is these experiences that will help me understand the complexity of mankind. It is these experiences that will guide me in the design profession. In a couple days I will get my three L.L. Bean duffle bags out yet again and migrate to New York City. I don't have a job yet, but I'm not worried, something exciting always turns up–the last five years are proof of that.

Awards & Honors

This chapter outlines the scope and purpose of the major national and international awards – both design and individual recognition awards – and lists their winners. Historic preservation award programs can be found in the Design & Historic Preservation chapter beginning on page 411, and award and recognition programs for design students and educators are located in the Design Education chapter beginning on page 509.

Aga Khan Award for Architecture

Granted once every three years, the Aga Khan Trust for Culture's Aga Khan Award for Architecture recognizes outstanding contributions to the built environment in the Muslim world. The diversity of winning projects includes individual buildings, restoration and re-use schemes, large-scale community developments, and environmental projects. In addition to the physical, economic, and social needs of a region, this award seeks to emphasize the importance of cultural and spiritual aspects of a project. The Steering Committee, comprised of internationally distinguished architects and scholars, governs this complex three-year process of nominations and technical review in addition to the selection of the Master Jury, which selects the final winning entries. Eligible projects must have been completed within the past 25 years and in use for a minimum of two years. An award of US $500,000 is apportioned between each cycle's winners.

For more information about this award and photographs, drawings and descriptions of the 1998 award recipients, visit the Aga Khan Award for Architecture's Web site at *www.akdn.org*.

1980

Agricultural Training Centre
Nianing, Senegal
UNESCO/BREDA (Senegal)

Medical Centre
Mopti, Mali
André Ravereau (France)

Courtyard Houses
Agadir, Morocco
Jean-François Zevaco (Morocco)

Sidi Bou Saïd
Tunis, Tunisia
Technical Bureau of the Municipality, Planners
   (Tunisia)

Halawa House
Agamy, Egypt
Abdelwahed El-Wakil (England)

Rüstem Pasa Caravanserai
Edirne, Turkey
Ertan Çakirlar (Turkey)

Ertegün House
Bodrum, Turkey
Turgut Cansever

Turkish Historical Society
Ankara, Turkey
Turgut Cansever and Ertur Yener (Turkey)

Inter-Continental Hotel and Conference Centre
Mecca, Saudi Arabia
Rolf Gutbrod and Frei Otto (Germany)

National Museum, Doha, Qatar
Michael Rice and Co. (England) and Design and
   Construction Group (Greece)

Water Towers
Kuwait City, Kuwait
VBB, Sune Lindström and Joe Lindström, Björn
   and Björn Design, Stig Egnell (Sweden)

Aga Khan Award for Architecture (Con't)

Ali Qapu, Chehel Sutun and Hasht Behesht
Isfahan, Iran
ISMEO – Istituto Italiano per il Medio ed
   Estremo Oriente (Italy)

Mughal Sheraton Hotel
Agra, India
ARCOP Design Group (Canada)

Kampung Improvement Program
Jakarta, Indonesia
KIP Technical Unit (Indonesia)

Pondok Pesantren Pabelan
Central Java, Indonesia
Amin Arraihana and Fanani (Indonesia)

1983

Hafsia Quarter
Tunis, Tunisia
Association de Sauvegarde de la Médina de
   Tunis (Tunisia)

Darb Qirmiz Quarter
Cairo, Egypt
Egyptian Antiquities Organization and German
   Archaeological Institute (Egypt)

Sherefudin's White Mosque
Visoko, Bosnia-Herzegovina
Zlatko Ugljen with D. Malkin, Engineer
   (Bosnia-Herzegovina)

Residence Andalous
Sousse, Tunisia
Serge Santelli (France) and Cabinet GERAU
   (Tunisia)

Hajj Terminal, King Abdul Aziz International
   Airport
Jeddah, Saudi Arabia
Skidmore, Owings and Merrill (USA)

Ramses Wissa Wassef Arts Centre
Giza, Egypt
Ramses Wissa Wassef (Egypt)

Tanjong Jara Beach Hotel and Rantau Abang
   Visitors' Centre
Kuala Trengganu, Malaysia
Wimberly, Wisenand, Allison, Tong and Goo
   (USA) with Arkitek Bersikutu (Malaysia)

Great Mosque of Niono
Niono, Mali
Lassina Minta (Mali)

Nail Çakirhan Residence
Akyaka Village, Turkey
Nail Çakirhan (Turkey)

Azem Palace
Damascus, Syria
Michel Ecochard (France) and Shafiq al-Imam
   (Syria)

Tomb of Shah Rukn-i-'Alam
Multan, Pakistan
Awqaf Department (Pakistan)

1986

Social Security Complex
Istanbul, Turkey
Sedad Hakki Eldem (Turkey)

Dar Lamane Housing Community
Casablanca, Morocco
Abderrahim Charai and Abdelaziz Lazrak
   (Morocco)

Mostar Old Town
Bosnia-Herzegovina
Stari-Grad Mostar (Bosnia-Herzegovina)

Al-Aqsa Mosque
al-Haram al-Sharif, Jerusalem
Isam Awwad (Jerusalem) and ICCROM (Italy)

Aga Khan Award for Architecture (Con't)

Yaama Mosque, Yaama
Tahoua, Niger
Falké Barmou (Niger)

Bhong Mosque, Bhong
Rahim-Yar Khan, Pakistan
Rais Ghazi Mohammad, Patron (Pakistan)

1986 Honorable Mentions

Shushtar New Town
Shushtar, Iran
DAZ Architects (Iran)

Kampung Kebalen Improvement
Surabaya, Indonesia
Surabaya Kampung Improvement Program,
  with the Surabaya Institute of Technology,
  and the Kampung Kebalen Community
  (Indonesia)

Ismaïliyya Development Projects
Ismaïliyya, Egypt
Culpin Planning (England)

Saïd Naum Mosque
Jakarta, Indonesia
Atelier Enam Architects and Planners
  (Indonesia)

Historic Sites Development
Istanbul, Turkey
Touring and Automobile Association of Turkey
  (Turkey)

1989

Great Omari Mosque
Sidon, Lebanon
Saleh Lamei-Mostafa (Egypt)

Rehabilitation of Asilah
Morocco
Al-Mouhit Cultural Association, Patron
  (Morocco)

Grameen Bank Housing Program
Bangladesh
Grameen Bank (Bangladesh)

Citra Niaga Urban Development
Samarinda, Indonesia
Antonio Ismael Risianto, PT Triaco, and PT
  Griyantara Architects (Indonesia)

Gürel Family Summer Residence
Çanakkale, Turkey
Sedat Gürel (Turkey)

Hayy Assafarat Landscaping and Al-Kindi Plaza
Riyadh, Saudi Arabia
Bödeker, Boyer, Wagenfeld and Partners,
  Landscape Architects (Germany)
Beeah Group Consultants, Architects (Saudi
  Arabia)

Sidi el-Aloui Primary School
Tunis, Tunisia
Association de la Sauvegarde de la Médina de
  Tunis (Tunisia)

Corniche Mosque
Jeddah, Saudi Arabia
Architect: Abdelwahed El-Wakil (England)

Ministry of Foreign Affairs
Riyadh, Saudi Arabia
Henning Larsen (Denmark)

National Assembly Building, Sher-e-Bangla
  Nagar
Dhaka, Bangladesh
Louis I. Kahn with David Wisdom and
  Associates (USA)

Institut du Monde Arabe
Paris, France
Jean Nouvel, Pierre Soria and Gilbert Lezénés,
  with the Architecture Studio (France)

Aga Khan Award for Architecture (Con't)

1992

Kairouan Conservation Program
Kairouan, Tunisia
Association de Sauvegarde de la Médina de
Kairouan (Tunisia)

Palace Parks Program
Istanbul, Turkey
Regional Offices of the National Palaces Trust
(Turkey)

Cultural Park for Children
Cairo, Egypt
Abdelhalim Ibrahim Abdelhalim (Egypt)

East Wahdat Upgrading Program
Amman, Jordan
Urban Development Department, Planners
(Jordan)
Halcrow Fox Associates and Jouzy and
Partners, Feasibility Studies (Jordan)

Kampung Kali Cho-de
Yogyakarta, Indonesia
Yousef B. Mangunwijaya (Indonesia)

Stone Building System
Dar'a Province, Syria
Raif Muhanna, Ziad Muhanna, and Rafi
Muhanna (Civil Engineer), (Syria)

Demir Holiday Village
Bodrum, Turkey
Turgut Cansever, Emine Ögün, Mehmet Ögün,
and Feyza Cansever (Turkey)

Panafrican Institute for Development
Ouagadougou, Burkina Faso
ADAUA Burkina Faso (Burkina Faso)

Entrepreneurship Development Institute of
India
Ahmedabad, India
Bimal Hasmukh Patel (India)

1995

Restoration of Bukhara Old City
Uzbekistan
Restoration Institute of Uzbekistan, Tashkent,
and the Restoration Office of the
Municipality of Bukhara, Uzbekistan

Conservation of Old Sana'a
Yemen
General Organization for the Protection of the
Historic Cities of Yemen (Yemen)

Reconstruction of Hafsia Quarter II
Tunis, Tunisia
Association de Sauvegarde de la Médina
(Tunisia)

Khuda-ki-Basti Incremental Development
Scheme
Hyderabad, Pakistan
Hyderabad Development Authority and
Tasneem Ahmed Siddiqui (Pakistan)

Aranya Low-Cost Housing
Indore, India
Vastu-Shilpa Foundation, Balkrishna V. Doshi
(India)

Great Mosque and Redevelopment of the Old
City Centre
Riyadh, Saudi Arabia
Rasem Badran (Jordan)

Menara Mesiniaga
Kuala Lumpur, Malaysia
T.R. Hamzah & Yeang Sdn. Bhd. (Malaysia)

Kaedi Regional Hospital
Kaedi, Mauritania
Association pour le Développement naturel
d'une Architecture et d'un Urbanisme
Africains (Mauritania)

Aga Khan Award for Architecture (Con't)

Mosque of the Grand National Assembly
Ankara, Turkey
Behruz Cinici and Can Cinici (Turkey)

Alliance Franco-Sénégalaise
Kaolack, Senegal
Patrick Dujarric (Senegal)

Re-Forestation Program of the Middle East
  Technical University
Ankara, Turkey
Middle East Technical University, Landscaping
  and Planners

Landscaping Integration of the Soekarno-Hatta
  Airport
Cengkareng, Indonesia
Aéroports de Paris, Paul Andreu (France)

1998

Rehabilitation of Hebron Old Town
Hebron, Palestine
Engineering Office of the Hebron
  Rehabilitation Committee (Palestine)

Slum Networking of Indore City
Indore, India
Himanshu Parikh, Civil Engineer (India)

Lepers Hospital
Chopda Taluka, India
Per Christian Brynildsen and Jan Olav Jensen
  (Norway)

Salinger Residence
Bamgi, Selangor, Malaysia
Jimmy C.S. Lim (Malaysia)

Tuwaiq Palace
Riyadh, Saudi Arabia
OHO Joint Venture (Atelier Frei Otto, Buro
  Happold, Omrania)

Alhamra Arts Council
Lahore, Pakistan
Nayyar Ali Dada (Pakistan)

Vidhan Bhavan
Bhopal, India
Charles Correa (India)

Chairman's Awards

*On two occasions the Chairman's Award has been
granted. It was established to honor the achievements
of individuals who have made considerable lifetime
achievements to Muslim architecture but whose work
was not within the scope of the Master Jury's mandate.*

1980 Hassan Fathy (Egypt)
1986 Rifat Chadirji (Iraq)

Source: The Aga Khan Trust for Culture

**The problem of architecture as I
see it is the problem of all art –
the elimination of the human ele-
ment from the consideration of
form.**

Otto Friedrich Silenus

AIA Continental Europe International Design Awards

The AIA Continental Europe chapter's International Design Awards, sponsored by Herman Miller, recognize excellent architecture in Europe. Members of the chapter, European licensed architects, and U.S. AIA chapter members with a project located within the AIA Continental Europe chapter's territory are eligible. Projects completed within the previous six years may be submitted in one of the following categories: new construction; historic preservation, adaptive re-use and remodeling; interiors; or urban design and planning. A panel of U.S. and European professionals with expertise in all categories evaluate the entries, choosing as many awards as they deem worthy of merit.

For additional information about the AIA Continental Europe chapter and their design awards, visit their Web site at *www.aiaeurope.org*.

2001 Winners:

1st Prize:
Laboratório Nacional de Investigação Veterinária
Vairão - Vila do Conde, Portugal
João Álvaro Rocha, Arquitectos Lda. (Portugal)

2nd Prize:
Sports Hall
Magglingen, Switzerland
Bauzeit Architekten GmbH (Switzerland)

3rd Prize:
'Théâtre du passage' - A Regional Theatre
City of Neuchâtel, Switzerland
Architects Associated Walter Hunziker +
    Chi-Chain and Anton Herrmann-Chong
    (Switzerland)

Award of Excellence:
NOOS Shop - Internet and Telecommunications
    Room
Paris, France
Patrick Mellett + Christine Reinke-Rousseau
    (France)

2001 Jury:
Nicola Jackson, *World Architecture*
Gianfranco Franchini, Dott. Arch. Franchini G.+
    R. Architects
Wilfried Wang Architect (Germany)

Source: AIA Continental Europe Chapter

AIA Gold Medal

The Gold Medal is The American Institute of Architects' highest award. Eligibility is open to architects or non-architects, living or dead, whose contribution to the field of architecture has made a lasting impact. The AIA's Board of Directors grants no more than one Gold Medal each year, occasionally granting none.

For more information, contact the AIA's Honor and Awards Dept. at (202) 626-7586 or visit their Web site at *www.aia.org*.

1907	Sir Aston Webb	1968	Marcel Breuer
1909	Charles Follen McKim	1969	William Wilson Wurster
1911	George Browne Post	1970	Richard Buckminster Fuller
1914	Jean Louis Pascal	1971	Louis I. Kahn
1922	Victor Laloux	1972	Pietro Belluschi
1923	Henry Bacon	1977	Richard Joseph Neutra*
1925	Sir Edwin Landseer Lutyens	1978	Philip Cortelyou Johnson
1925	Bertram Grosvenor Goodhue	1979	Ieoh Ming Pei
1927	Howard Van Doren Shaw	1981	Joseph Luis Sert
1929	Milton Bennett Medary	1982	Romaldo Giurgola
1933	Ragnar Östberg	1983	Nathaniel A. Owings
1938	Paul Philippe Cret	1985	William Wayne Caudill*
1944	Louis Henri Sullivan	1986	Arthur Erickson
1947	Eliel Saarinen	1989	Joseph Esherick
1948	Charles Donagh Maginnis	1990	E. Fay Jones
1949	Frank Lloyd Wright	1991	Charles W. Moore
1950	Sir Patrick Abercrombie	1992	Benjamin Thompson
1951	Bernard Ralph Maybeck	1993	Thomas Jefferson*
1952	Auguste Perret	1993	Kevin Roche
1953	William Adams Delano	1994	Sir Norman Foster
1955	William Marinus Dudok Hilversum	1995	Cesar Pelli
1956	Clarence S. Stein	1997	Richard Meier
1957	Ralph Walker (Centennial Medal of Honor)	1999	Frank Gehry
1957	Louis Skidmore	2000	Ricardo Legorreta
1958	John Wellborn Root	2001	Michael Graves
1959	Walter Gropius		
1960	Ludwig Mies van der Rohe		
1961	Le Corbusier (Charles Edouard Jeanneret-Gris)		
1962	Eero Saarinen*		
1963	Alvar Aalto		
1964	Pier Luigi Nervi		
1966	Kenzo Tange		
1967	Wallace K. Harrison		

* honored posthumously
Source: The American Institute of Architects

The Western History Collection reading room of the
Denver Public Library (above), designed by Michael
Graves, uses a rich warm golden maple in its tables,
bookshelves and wall and ceiling panels. The room's
focal point is the timber derrick-like structure that
recalls the nation's westward expansion. Photo:
Timothy Hursley, The Arkansas Office, Inc.

AIA Honor Awards

The American Institute of Architects' (AIA) Honor Awards celebrate outstanding design in three areas: Architecture, Interior Architecture, and Regional & Urban Design. Juries of designers and executives present separate awards in each category.

Additional information and entry forms may be obtained by contacting the AIA Honors and Awards Department at (202) 626-7586 or by visiting their Web site at *www.aia.org*.

2001 AIA Honor Awards for Architecture Recipients:

Conference Barn,
Middleburg, Virginia
Sant Architects, Inc.

Rifkind Residence
Wainscott, New York
Tod Williams Billie Tsien and Associates

Queens Borough Public Library, Flushing
Branch
Queens, New York
Polshek Partnership Architects, LLP

The New York Times Printing Plant
Queens, New York
Polshek Partnership Architects, LLP

University of Pennsylvania Modular VII Chiller
Plant
Philadelphia, Pennsylvania
Leers Weinzapfel Associates

11th Avenue Townhomes
Escondido, California
Studio E Architects

McCormick Place South Building
Chicago, Illinois
Thompson, Ventulett, Stainback & Assoc., Inc.

Downtown Homeless Drop In Center
Los Angeles, California
Lehrer Architects

Natatorium at Cranbrook Educational
Community
Bloomfield Hills, Michigan
Tod Williams Billie Tsien and Associates

Hyde Park Branch Library
Boston, Massachusetts
Schwartz/Silver Architects

The Conde Nast Building
New York, New York
Fox & Fowle Architects

College-Conservatory of Music, University of
Cincinnati
Cincinnati, Ohio
Pei Cobb Freed & Partners Architects, LLP

Benaroya Hall
Seattle, Washington
LMN Architects

Reliance Building/Hotel Burnham
Chicago, Illinois
Antunovich Associates

Left: The new College-Conservatory of Music at the University of Cincinnati was created through a complex program of new construction and renovation of existing structures. The Corbett Auditorium, a 750-seat proscenium theater, underwent a $5 million renovation, fully updating it for opera, musical theater, choral, orchestral and wind concerts, ballet, and recitals. Photo: © Eric Schiller, Pei Cobb Freed & Partners Architects LLC.

Below: The Conference Barn, located on an 18th century horse farm in Virginia, houses a family foundation focused on environmental issues. The site plan integrates some existing farm buildings, and the design and orientation of the barn itself takes advantage of the tranquility of the landscape. Photo: © John Edward Linden.

AIA Honor Awards (Con't)

2001 AIA Honor Awards for Architecture Jury:

John Belle (Chair)
Lo-Yi Chan
Ginelle Desrochers
Sheila A. Dial
Mark W. Rios
Rebecca Swanston
Kit Tuveson
Edward Weinstein
Carol A. Wilson

2001 AIA Honor Awards for Interior Architecture Recipients:

Jacobs Residence Subterranean
Sherman Oaks, California
Patrick J. Tighe, AIA

Alliance Française de Chicago
Chicago, Illinois
DeStefano & Partners

Pratt Institute, School of Architecture
New York, New York
Rogers Marvel Architects PLLC

Lucent Technologies – Government Business Solutions
Washington, D.C
Group Goetz Architects

Fitch/O'Rourke Residence
Washington, D.C
Robert M. Gurney, AIA

Herman Miller National Showroom
Chicago, Illinois
Krueck & Sexton Architects

Jin Mao Tower
Shanghai, The People's Republic of China
Skidmore, Owings & Merrill LLP

Radio City Music Hall
New York, New York
Hardy Holzman Pfeiffer Associates

New York Stock Exchange Trading Floor Expansion
New York, New York
Skidmore, Owings & Merrill LLP

SoHo Loft
New York, New York
Architecture Research Office

Reactor Films
Santa Monica, California
Pugh + Scarpa

Detroit Opera House
Detroit, Michigan
Albert Kahn Associates, Inc.

2001 AIA Honor Awards for Interior Design Jury:

Barbara Hillier (Chair)
Mattias Z. Bergman
Randy Brown
Victor A. Saroki
John Vinci

2001 AIA Honor Awards for Regional and Urban Design Recipients:

A Civic Vision for Turnpike Air Rights in Boston
Boston, Massachusetts
Goody, Clancy & Associates

Flag House Courts Revitalization
Silver Springs, Maryland
Torti Gallas and Partners CHK, Inc.

The Downtown Racine Development Plan
Racine, Wisconsin
Crandall Arambula PC

Left: Albert Kahn Associates' $24 million restoration of the 1922 Detroit Opera House transformed it from an urban ruin back into an eclectic European opera house-style theater. Photo: © Hedrich Blessing Photography.

Below: The architects fused two historic buildings - one Second Empire and one Victorian - via a glass and steel walkway and courtyard and created a contemporary interior environment for the Alliance Francaise de Chicago. Photo: © Barbara Karant, Karant & Associates.

AIA Honor Awards (Con't)

Santa Monica Boulevard Master Plan
City of West Hollywood, California
Zimmer Gunsul Frasca Partnership

2001 AIA Honor Awards for Regional and Urban Design Jury:
Amy Weinstein (Chair)
Thomas E. Lollini
Weiming Lu
Elizabeth Seward Padjen
Stephen Vogel

Source: The American Institute of Architects

Did you know...

In the last 10 years, the following firms have won the most AIA Honor Awards:

Skidmore, Owings and Merrill – 14
Hardy Holzman Pfeiffer Associates – 7
Polshek Partnership Architecture– 7
Kallman, McKinnell & Wood Architects– 5
Shelton, Mindel & Associates – 5
William Rawn Associates, Architects, Inc. – 5
Herbert Lewis Kruse Blunk Architecture– 4
HOK Sport – 4
Richard Meier & Partners – 4
Studio E Architects – 4
Bohlin Cywinski Jackson– 3
Elliot + Associates Architects – 3
Gabellini Associates – 3
James Cutler Architects – 3
Lake/Flato Architects, Inc. – 3
Perkins & Will – 3
R.M. Kliment & Frances Halsband Architects – 3
Steven Ehrlich Architect – 3
Steven Holl Architects – 3
Tod Williams Billie Tsien and Associates – 3
Venturi, Scott Brown and Associates, Inc. – 3

Source: Design Intelligence

AIA Honors for Collaborative Achievement

The American Institute of Architects (AIA) annually presents their Honors for Collaborative Achievement award to recognize achievements in influencing or advancing the architectural profession. Recipients may be individuals or groups. Nominees must be living and may have been active in any number of areas, including administration, art, collaborative achievement, construction, industrial design, information science, professions allied with architecture, public policy, research, education, recording, illustration, and writing and scholarship.

For more information, refer to the AIA's Web site at *www.aia.org* or contact the AIA's Honors and Awards Department at (202) 626-7586.

1976
Edmund N. Bacon
Charles A. Blessing
Wendell J. Campbell
Gordon Cullen
James Marston Fitch
The Institute for Architecture and Urban Studies
New York City Planning Commission and New York City Landmarks Preservation Committee
Saul Steinberg
Vincent J. Scully Jr.
Robert Le Ricolais

1977
Claes Oldenburg
Louise Nevelson
Historic American Buildings Survey
Arthur Drexler
G. Holmes Perkins
The Baroness Jackson of Lodsworth DBE (Barbara Ward)
Walker Art Center
City of Boston
Pittsburgh History & Landmarks Foundation
Montreal Metro System

1978
Frederick Gutheim
Richard Haas

Dr. August Komendant
David A. Macaulay
National Trust for Historic Preservation
Stanislawa Nowicki
John C. Portman Jr.
Robert Royston
Nicholas N. Solovioff
Robert Venturi

1979
Douglas Haskell
Barry Commoner
John D. Entenza
Bernard Rudofsky
Steen Eiler Rasmussen
National Endowment for the Arts
Christo
Bedford-Stuyvesant Restoration
Charles E. Peters
Arthur S. Siegel (posthumous)

1980
Cyril M. Harris
Sol LeWitt
Robert Campbell
Committee for the Preservation of Architectural Records
Progressive Architecture Awards Program
The Rouse Company for Faneuil Hall Marketplace
John Benson

AIA Honors for Collaborative Achievement (Con't)

M. Paul Friedberg
Jack E. Boucher
Mrs. Lyndon B. Johnson

1981

Kenneth Snelson
Paul Goldberger
Sir Nikolaus Pevsner
Herman Miller, Inc.
Edison Price
Colin Rowe
Reynolds Metals Company
Smithsonian Associates

1982

"Oppositions" (Institute for Architecture &
   Urban Studies)
Historic New Harmony, Inc.
The MIT Press
Jean Dubuffet
Sir John Summerson
The Plan of St. Gall
The Washington Metropolitan Area Transit
   Authority
William H. Whyte

1983

The Honorable Christopher S. Bond, Governor
   of Missouri
Donald Canty
Fazlur Khan (posthumous)
Knoll International
Christian Norberg-Schulz
Paul Stevenson Oles

1984

Reyner Banham
Bolt, Beranek & Newman
Cooper-Hewitt Museum
Inner Harbor Development of the City of
   Baltimore
His Highness the Aga Khan
T.Y. Lin
Steve Rosenthal
San Antonio River Walk
Bruno Zevi

1985

Ward Bennett
Kenneth Frampton
Esther McCoy
Norman McGrath
The Hon. John F. Seiberling
Weidlinger Associates
Nick Wheeler
Games of the XXIII Olympiad
Cranbrook Academy of Art
Central Park

1986

Cathedral Church of St. John the Divine
Antoinette Forrester Downing
David H. Geiger
Gladding, McBean & Company
William H. Jordy
Master Plan for the United States Capitol
Adolf Kurt Placzek
Cervin Robinson
Rudolf Wittkower (posthumous)

1987

James S. Ackerman
Jennifer Bartlett
Steven Brooke
The Chicago Architecture Foundation
Jules Fisher & Paul Marantz, Inc.
Charles Guggenheim
John B. Jackson
Mesa Verde National Park
Rizzoli International Publications, Inc.
Carter Wiseman

1988

Spiro Kostof
Loeb Fellowship in Advanced Environmental
   Studies, Harvard University
Robert Smithson (posthumous)
Society for the Preservation of New England
   Antiquities
Sussman/Prejza & Company, Inc.
Robert Wilson

1989

Battery Park City Authority
American Academy in Rome

AIA Honors for Collaborative Achievement (Con't)

Eduard Sekler
Leslie E. Robertson
Niels Diffrient
David S. Haviland
V'Soske

1990
The Association for the Preservation of Virginia
  Antiquities
Corning Incorporated
Jackie Ferrara
Timothy Hursley
Marvin Mass
Mary Miss
Peter G. Rolland
Joseph Santeramo
Taos Pueblo
Emmet L. Wemple

1991
James Fraser Carpenter
Danish Design Centre
Foundation for Architecture, Philadelphia
The J.M. Kaplan Fund
Maguire Thomas Partners
Native American Architecture (Robert Easton
  and Peter Nabokov)
Princeton Architectural Press
Seaside, Florida
Allan Temko
Lebbeus Woods

1992
Siah Armajani
Canadian Centre for Architecture
Stephen Coyle
Milton Glaser
The Mayors' Institute on City Design
The Municipal Art Society of New York
John Julius Norwich
Ove Arup & Partners Consulting Engineers PC
Peter Vanderwarker
Peter Walker

1993
ADPSR (Architects/Designers/Planners for
  Social Responsibility)

Michael Blackwood
The Conservation Trust of Puerto Rico
Benjamin Forgey
The Gamble House
Philadelphia Zoological Society
The Princeton University Board of Trustees,
  Officers and the Office of Physical Planning
Jane Thompson
Sally B. Woodbridge
World Monuments Fund

1994
Joseph H. Baum
Beth Dunlop
Mildred Friedman
Historic Savannah Foundation
Rhode Island Historical Preservation
  Commission
Salvadori Educational Center on the Built
  Environment
Gordon H. Smith
The Stuart Collection
Sunset Magazine
Judith Turner

1995
The Art Institute of Chicago, Dept. of Arch.
ASAP (The American Society of Architectural
  Perspectivists)
Friends of Post Office Square
The University of Virginia, Curator and
  Architect for the Academical Village/ The
  Rotunda
Albert Paley
UrbanArts, Inc.
Dr. Yoichi Ando

1996
Boston by Foot, Inc.
William S. Donnell
Haley & Aldrich, Inc.
Toshio Nakamura
Joseph Passonneau
Preservation Society of Charleston
Earl Walls Associates
Paul Warchol Photography, Inc.

AIA Honors for Collaborative Achievement (Con't)

1997
Architecture Resource Center

1998
Lian Hurst Mann
SOM Foundation
William Morgan

1999
Howard Brandston
Jeff Goldberg
Ann E. Gray
Blair Kamin
Ronald McKay
Miami-Dade Art in Public Places
Monacelli Press
New York Landmarks Conservancy

2000
The Aga Khan Award for Architecture
Douglas Cooper
Dr. Christopher Jaffe
Donald Kaufman and Taffy Dahl
William Lam
San Antonio Conservation Society
F. Michael Wong

2001
Vernon L. Mays Jr.
John R. Stilgoe

Source: The American Institute of Architects

AIA Housing Professional Interest Area (PIA) Awards

The American Institute of Architects's (AIA) Housing Professional Interest Area (PIA) established the Housing PIA Awards to recognize the importance of good housing as a necessity of life, a sanctuary for the human spirit, and a valuable national resource. Awards are presented in four categories, at the discretion of the judges: single family housing, multifamily housing, community design, and innovation in housing design. AIA-member architects licensed in the U.S. are eligible to enter built projects located in the U.S. Winning projects are published in *Architectural Record* magazine and displayed at the AIA National Convention and Expo.

For additional information, contact Rashidah Martin in the AIA Honors and Awards department at (202) 626-7563 or email rmartin@aia.org.

2000 **Winners:**

Multifamily Housing

8th and Alexander
Charlotte, N.C.
David Furman/Architecture PA

Bridgecourt
Emeryville, CA
McLarand, Vasquez & Partners

Gateway Commons
Emeryville and Oakland, CA
Pyatok Associates

Jake's Run Condominiums
Portland, OR
Fletcher Farr Ayotte PC

Community Design Award

Jackson Meadow-Marine on St. Croix
Marine on St. Croix, MN
Salmela Architect/Coen + Stumpf & Associates

Addison Circle
Addison, TX
RTKL Associates

Swan's Market Place
Oakland, CA
Michael Pyatok, FAIA
Associate Architect: Y.H. Lee

Single Family Housing

No awards granted

Innovation in Housing Design

No awards granted

Jury:

William H. Kreager, Mithun Partners (Chair)
Robert Ivy, *Architectural Record*
Anne Lewis, architect
Rob Robinson, Urban Design Associates

Source: The American Institute of Architects

AIA/HUD Secretary's Housing and Community Design Award

Innovative, affordable and accessible building designs are honored each year by the HUD Secretary's Housing and Community Design Award, presented jointly by The American Institute of Architects (AIA) and the U.S. Department of Housing and Urban Development (HUD). The AIA's Center for Livable Communities and the AIA Housing Professional Interest Area, in partnership with HUD, created the awards program to recognize the best in residential and community design. Categories include Mixed-Use/Mixed Income Development, for projects that revitalize neighborhoods through a combination of residential and non-residential uses; Community Building by Design, to honor projects that rebuild poor neighborhoods; and the Alan J. Rothman Housing Accessibility Award, named in honor of the late HUD senior policy analyst, an expert on disability issues.

Additional information can be found on the AIA's Web site at *www.aia.org*.

2001 Winners:

Mixed-Use/Mixed-Income Development
  Swan's Market Place, Oakland, CA
  Pyatok Associates, with Y.H. Lee, associate
    architect

  Center Commons, Portland, OR
  Vallaster and Corl Architects and Otak
    Architects PC

  TriBeCa Pointe, Battery Park City, NY
  Gruzen Samton LLP

  East Lake Commons, Decatur, GA
  Village Habitat Design, LLC

Community Building by Design
  Arbolera De Vida, Albuquerque, NM
    Design Workshop and Studio E Architects

  Alan J. Rothman Award for Housing
    Accessibility
  Inglis Gardens at Eastwick, Philadelphia, PA
  Cecil Baker and Associates

2001 Jury:
  John K. Spear (Chair)
  Mark Ginsberg
  Gita Dev
  Michael Freedberg
  Carlos E. Martin

Source: The American Institute of Architects

Did you know...

The Colorado Court (Santa Monica, CA, Pugh Scarpa Kodama), a 44-unit, five-story apartment building, is one of the first affordable housing units in the United States planned to be nearly 100% green, by producing 92% of its own power and using energy-saving and environmentally benign devices.

The design for Center Commons supports a variety of housing types and age groups. Affordable senior housing overlooks a children's playground (top) located across the L-shaped courtyard from affordable family units. Community involvement was sought at all design phases, resulting in retail space along the main commercial street and its daycare and playground being opened to the entire community. Photos: Sally Schoolmaster.

Alice Davis Hitchcock Book Award

The Alice Davis Hitchcock book award has been granted annually by the Society of Architectural Historians (SAH) since 1949. It is given to a publication by a North American scholar, published within the preceding two years, that demonstrates a high level of scholarly distinction in the field of the history of architecture.

For more information contact the SAH at (312) 573-1365 or visit their Web site at *www.sah.org.*

1949
   Colonial Architecture and Sculpture in Peru by Harold Wethey (Harvard University Press)
1950
   Architecture of the Old Northwest Territory by Rexford Newcomb (University of Chicago Press)
1951
   Architecture and Town Planning in Colonial Connecticut by Anthony Garvan (Yale University Press)
1952
   The Architectural History of Newport by Antoinette Downing and Vincent Scully (Harvard University Press)
1953
   Charles Rennie Macintosh and the Modern Movement by Thomas Howarth (Routledge and K. Paul)
1954
   Early Victorian Architecture in Britain by Henry Russell Hitchcock (Da Capo Press, Inc.)
1955
   Benjamin H. Latrobe by Talbot Hamlin (Oxford University Press)
1956
   The Railroad Station: An Architectural History by Carroll L. V. Meeks (Yale University Press)
1957
   The Early Architecture of Georgia by Frederick D. Nichols (University of N.C. Press)
1958
   The Public Buildings of Williamsburg by Marcus Whiffen (Colonial Williamsburg)

1959
   Carolingian and Romanesque Architecture, 800 to 1200 by Kenneth J. Conant (Yale University Press)
1960
   The Villa d'Este at Tivoli by David Coffin (Princeton University Press)
1961
   The Architecture of Michelangelo by James Ackerman (University of Chicago Press)
1962
   The Art and Architecture of Ancient America by George Kubler (Yale University Press)
1963
   La Cathédrale de Bourges et sa Place dans L'archtietture Gothique by Robert Branner (Tardy)
1964
   Images of American Living, Four Centuries of Architecture and Furniture as Cultural Expression by Alan Gowans (Lippincott)
1965
   The Open-Air Churches of Sixteenth Century Mexico by John McAndrew (Harvard University Press)
1966
   Early Christian and Byzantine Architecture by Richard Krautheimer (Penguin Books)
1967
   Eighteenth-Century Architecture in Piedmont: the open structures of Juvarra, Alfieri & Vittone by Richard Pommer (New York University Press)

Alice Davis Hitchcock Book Award (Con't)

1968

Architecture and Politics in Germany, 1918-1945 by Barbara Miller Lane (Harvard University Press)

1969

Samothrace, Volume III: The Hieron by Phyllis Williams Lehmann

1970

The Church of Notre Dame in Montreal by Franklin Toker (McGill-Queen's University Press)

1971

no award granted

1972

The Prairie School; Frank Lloyd Wright and his Midwest Contemporaries by H. Allen Brooks (University of Toronto Press)

The Early Churches of Constantinople: Architecture and Liturgy by Thomas F. Mathews (Pennsylvania State University Press)

1973

The Campanile of Florence Cathedral: "Giotto's Tower" by Marvin Trachtenberg (New York University Press)

1974

FLO, A Biography of Frederick Law Olmstead by Laura Wood Roper (Johns Hopkins University Press)

1975

Gothic vs. Classic, Architectural Projects in Seventeenth-Century Italy by Rudolf Wittkower (G. Braziller)

1976

no award granted

1977

The Esplanade Ridge (Vol. V in The New Orleans Architecture Series) by Mary Louise Christovich, Sally Kitredge Evans, Betsy Swanson, and Roulhac Toledano (Pelican Publishing Company)

1978

Sebastiano Serlio on Domestic Architecture by Myra Nan Rosenfeld (Architectural History Foundation)

1979

The Framed Houses of Massachusetts Bay, 1625-1725 by Abbott Lowell Cummings (Belknap Press)

Paris: A Century of Change, 1878-1978 by Norma Evenson (Yale University Press)

1980

Rome: Profile of a City, 312-1308 by Richard Krautheimer (Princton University Press)

1981

Gardens of Illusion: The Genius of Andre LeNotre by Franklin Hamilton Hazelhurst (Vanderbilt University Press)

1982

Indian Summer: Luytens, Baker and Imperial Delhi by Robert Grant Irving (Yale Univ. Press)

1983

Architecture and the Crisis of Modern Science by Alberto Pérez-Goméz (MIT Press)

1984

Campus: An American Planning Tradition by Paul Venable Turner (MIT Press)

1985

The Law Courts: The Architecture of George Edmund Street by David Brownlee (MIT Press)

1986

The Architecture of the Roman Empire: An Urban Appraisal by William L. MacDonald (Yale University Press)

1987

Holy Things and Profane: Anglican Parish Churches in Colonial Virginia by Dell Upton (MIT Press)

1988

Designing Paris: The Architecture of Duban, Labrouste, Duc and Vaudoyer by David Van Zanten (MIT Press)

1989

Florentine New Towns: Urban Design in the Late Middle Ages by David Friedman (MIT Press)

1990

Claude-Nicolas Ledoux: Architecture and Social Reform at the End of the Ancient Régime by Anthony Vidler (MIT Press)

Alice Davis Hitchcock Book Award (Con't)

1991

The Paris of Henri IV: Architecture and Urbanism by Hilary Ballon (MIT Press)

Seventeenth-Century Roman Palaces: Use and the Art of the Plan by Patricia Waddy (MIT Press)

1992

Modernism in Italian Architecture, 1890-1940 by Richard Etlin (MIT Press)

1994*

Baths and Bathing in Classical Antiquity by Fikret Yegul (MIT Press)

1995

The Politics of the German Gothic Revival: August Reichensperger by Michael J. Lewis (MIT Press)

1996

Hadrian's Villa and Its Legacy by William J. MacDonald and John Pinto (Yale University Press)

1997

Gottfried Semper: Architect of the Nineteenth Century by Harry Francis Mallgrave (Yale University Press)

1998

The Dancing Column: On Order in Architecture by Joseph Rykwert (MIT Press)

1999

Dominion of the Eye: Urbanism, Art & Power in Early Modern Florence by Marvin Trachtenberg (Cambridge University Press)

2000

The Architectural Treatise in the Renaissance by Alina A. Payne (Cambridge University Press)

2001

The Architecture of Red Vienna, 1919-1934 by Eve Blau (MIT Press)

---

*   *At this time the SAH altered their award schedule to coincide with their annual meeting, and no award for 1993 was granted.*

Source: Society of Architectural Historians

The past should always be looked on as a servant, not as a monster.

Calvert Vaux

American Academy of Arts and Letters Academy Awards

The American Academy of Arts and Letters grants their annual Academy Award to an architect(s) as an honor of their work and an encouragement to their ongoing creativity. The prize consists of a $7500 cash award. Recipients must be citizens of the United States. Members of the Academy are not eligible.

For more information, contact the American Academy of Arts and Letters at (212) 368-5900.

1991 Rodolfo Machado and Jorge Silvetti
1992 Thom Mayne and Michael Rotondi, Morphosis
1993 Franklin D. Israel
1994 Craig Hodgetts and Hsin-Ming Fung
1995 Mack Scogin and Merrill Elam
1996 Maya Lin
1997 Daniel Libeskind
1998 Laurie Olin
1999 Eric Owen Moss
2000 Will Bruder
Jesse Reiser and Nanako Umemoto
2001 Vincent James
SHoP/Sharples Holden Pasquarelli

Source: American Academy of Arts and Letters

American Academy of Arts and Letters Gold Medal for Architecture

The American Academy of Arts and Letters grants a gold medal in the arts in rotation among painting, music, sculpture, poetry, architecture, and many other categories. The entire work of the architect is weighed when being considered for the award. Only citizens of the United States are eligible.

For more information contact the American Academy of Arts and Letters at (212) 368-5900.

1912   William Rutherford Mead
1921   Cass Gilbert
1930   Charles Adams Platt
1940   William Adams Delano
1949   Frederick Law Olmsted
1953   Frank Lloyd Wright
1958   Henry R. Shepley
1963   Ludwig Mies van der Rohe
1968   R. Buckminster Fuller
1973   Louis I. Kahn
1979   I. M. Pei
1984   Gordon Bunshaft
1990   Kevin Roche
1996   Philip Johnson

Source: American Academy of Arts and Letters

I've always been for grandeur... The history of architecture is the history of monuments. I don't think man lives by bread and bad housing alone.

Philip Johnson

APA Journalism Awards

The American Planning Association (APA) honors outstanding newspaper coverage of city and regional planning issues each year with its Journalism Awards. These honors are presented to daily or weekly newspapers in each of three classes: circulation below 50,000; circulation of 50,000 to 100,000; and circulation above 100,000. Papers in the U.S. and Canada are eligible to enter; nominations may be made by an editor, publisher, or any other person. Winning articles must render outstanding public service in their coverage, perspective, interpretation and impact.

Additional information is available on the Internet at *www.planning.org/abtapa/jrnlism2000.html*, or by contacting Sylvia Lewis at slewis@planning.org. Entry forms are available from the APA's automated Fax-on-Demand Service at (800) 800-1589.

2001 Winners:

Large Newspaper
"It Takes a Village to Raise a Fortune"
Orlando Sentinel, Orlando Florida

Honorable Mention
"Fate of the Foothills"
Idaho Statesman, Boise, Idaho

Medium Newspaper
"Crisis at Our Doorstep"
Cape Cod Times, Hyannis Massachusetts

Small Newspaper
"Plotting a Course"
Anderson Independent-Mail, Anderson, South Carolina

Source: American Planning Association

Did you know...

80% of architecture critics in a 2001 survey disagreed with the statement, "We can be proud of the new built environment we have developed over the last 25 years." Sprawl was widely sited as the reason.

Source: The Architecture Critic, *National Arts Journalism Program, Columbia University*

Apgar Award for Excellence

The Apgar Award for Excellence recognizes individuals whose interpretation and evaluation of America's built environment has heightened public awareness toward the importance of excellence in building and urban design, community revitalization, and city and regional planning. Established in 1998 by former National Building Museum Trustee Mahlon Apgar IV and his wife, Anne N. Apgar, the objective of the award is to encourage the communication of knowledge, experience, and ideas about the built environment among policymakers, professionals, and the general public through any form of print or electronic media. Nominations are reviewed by a panel of architecture professionals including journalists, academics, and practitioners. Recipients are awarded a $1500 honorarium and are invited to participate in public programs at the Museum.

For more information about the Apgar Award, contact the National Building Museum at (202) 272-2448 or visit them on the Internet at *www.nbm.org*.

1999 Samuel Mockbee
2000 Earl Blumenauer
2001 *no award granted*

Source: National Building Museum

Architecture Firm Award

The American Institute of Architects (AIA) awards its Architecture Firm Award annually to an architecture firm for "consistently producing distinguished architecture." The highest honor that the AIA can bestow on a firm, the Board of Directors confers the award. Eligible firms must claim collaboration within the practice as a hallmark of their methodology and must have been producing work as an entity for at least 10 years.

For more information, visit the AIA on the Internet at *www.aia.org* or contact the AIA Honors and Awards Department at (202) 626-7586.

1962	Skidmore, Owings & Merrill	1984	Kallmann, McKinnell & Wood, Architects
1964	The Architects Collaborative	1985	Venturi, Rauch and Scott Brown
1965	Wurster, Bernardi & Emmons	1986	Esherick Homsey Dodge & Davis
1967	Hugh Stubbins & Associates	1987	Benjamin Thompson & Associates
1968	I.M. Pei & Partners	1988	Hartman-Cox Architects
1969	Jones & Emmons	1989	Cesar Pelli & Associates
1970	Ernest J. Kump Associates	1990	Kohn Pedersen Fox Associates
1971	Albert Kahn Associates, Inc.	1991	Zimmer Gunsul Frasca Partnership
1972	Caudill Rowlett Scott	1992	James Stewart Polshek and Partners
1973	Shepley Bulfinch Richardson Abbott	1993	Cambridge Seven Associates Inc.
1974	Kevin Roche John Dinkeloo & Associates	1994	Bohlin Cywinski Jackson
1975	Davis, Brody & Associates	1995	Beyer Blinder Belle
1976	Mitchell/Giurgola Architects	1996	Skidmore, Owings & Merrill
1977	Sert, Jackson and Associates	1997	R. M. Kliment & Frances Halsband Architects
1978	Harry Weese & Associates		
1979	Geddes Brecher Qualls Cunningham	1998	Centerbrook Architects and Planners
1980	Edward Larrabee Barnes Associates	1999	Perkins & Will
1981	Hardy Holzman Pfeiffer Associates	2000	Gensler
1982	Gwathmey Siegel & Associates, Architects	2001	Herbert Lewis Kruse Blunck
1983	Holabird & Root, Architects, Engineers & Planners		

Source: The American Institute of Architects

Sticks, Inc. (Des Moines, IA), a recent project by
Herbert Lewis Kruse Blunck Architecture, is a
rapidly growing artists' studio specializing in the
design and production of contemporary art objects
made from fallen timber and milled wood. A
faceted aluminum framed curtain wall with fifteen
pairs of mahogany doors etched and painted by
the artists (above) provide essential natural light.
Photo: Farshid Assassi.

Arnold W. Brunner Memorial Prize

The American Academy of Arts and Letters annually recognizes an architect who has contributed to architecture as an art with the Arnold W. Brunner Memorial Prize. A prize of $5000 is granted to each recipient. Eligibility is open to architects of any nationality.

For more information, contact the American Academy of Arts and Letters at (212) 368-5900.

1955	Gordon Bunshaft
	Minoru Yamasaki, Honorable Mention
1956	John Yeon
1957	John Carl Warnecke
1958	Paul Rudolph
1959	Edward Larrabee Barnes
1960	Louis I. Kahn
1961	I. M. Pei
1962	Ulrich Franzen
1963	Edward Charles Basset
1964	Harry Weese
1965	Kevin Roche
1966	Romaldo Giurgola
1968	John M. Johansen
1969	Noel Michael McKinnell
1970	Charles Gwathmey and Richard Henderson
1971	John Andrews
1972	Richard Meier
1973	Robert Venturi
1974	Hugh Hardy with Norman Pfeiffer and Malcolm Holzman
1975	Lewis Davis and Samuel Brody
1976	James Stirling
1977	Henry N. Cobb
1978	Cesar Pelli
1979	Charles W. Moore
1980	Michael Graves
1981	Gunnar Birkerts
1982	Helmut Jahn
1983	Frank O. Gehry
1984	Peter K. Eisenman
1985	William Pederson and Arthur May
1986	John Hejduk
1987	James Ingo Freed
1988	Arata Isozaki
1989	Richard Rogers
1990	Steven Holl
1991	Tadao Ando
1992	Sir Norman Foster
1993	Jose Rafael Moneo
1994	Renzo Piano
1995	Daniel Urban Kiley
1996	Tod Williams and Billie Tsien
1997	Henri Ciriani
1998	Alvaro Siza
1999	Fumihiko Maki
2000	Toyo Ito
2001	Henry Smith-Miller and Laurie Hawkinson

Source: American Academy of Arts and Letters

Place is the projection of the image of civilization onto the environment.

Charles W. Moore

The Corning Glass Museum (Corning, NY), a
recent project by Smith-Miller + Hawkinson
Architects. Photo: Eriata Attali.

Henry-Smith Miller and Laurie Hawkinson.
Photo: Dorothy Alexander.

ASLA Medal

Every year the American Society of Landscape Architects (ASLA) awards its highest honor, the ASLA Medal, to an individual who has made a significant contribution to the field of landscape architecture. The following individuals were chosen for their unique and lasting impact through their work in landscape design, planning, writing and/or public service. Eligibility is open to non-members of the ASLA of any nationality.

For more information, contact the ASLA at (202) 898-2444 or visit their Web site at *www.asla.org*.

1971	Hideo Sasaki	1988	Dame Sylvia Crowe
1972	Conrad L. Wirth	1989	Robert N. Royston
1973	John C. Simonds	1990	Ray Freeman
1974	Campbell E. Miller	1991	Meade Palmer
1975	Garrett Eckbo	1992	Robert S. "Doc" Reich
1976	Thomas Church	1993	A. E. "Ed" Bye Jr.
1977	Hubert Owens	1994	Edward D. Stone Jr.
1978	Lawrence Halprin	1995	Dr. Ervin Zube
1979	Norman T. Newton	1996	John Lyle
1980	William G. Swain	1997	Julius Fabos
1981	Sir Geoffrey Jellicoe	1998	Carol R. Johnson
1982	Charles W. Eliot II	1999	Stuart C. Dawson
1983	Theodore O. Osmundson	2000	Carl D. Johnson
1984	Ian McHarg	2001	Robert E. Marvin
1985	Roberto Burle Marx		
1986	William J. Johnson		
1987	Phillip H. Lewis Jr.		

Source: American Society of Landscape Architects

ASLA Professional Awards

The American Society of Landscape Architects' (ASLA) annual Professional Awards program is intended to encourage the profession of landscape architecture by rewarding works of distinction and to generate increased visibility for the winners and the profession in general. Entries are accepted for placement in one of four areas: design, analysis & planning, research, and communication. Eligibility is open to any landscape architect or, in the case of research and communication, any individual or group. Juries for each category are comprised of landscape professionals and appointed by the ASLA's Professional Awards Committee.

For additional information, visit the ASLA's Web site at *www.asla.org* or contact them at (202) 898-2444.

2001 Design Awards Recipients:

Honor Awards:

Zion Canyon, Zion National Park
Springdale, UT
Denver Service Center, National Park Service
   and Zion National Park

McMahon Duell Residence
Edgartown, MA
Horiuchi & Solien Landscape Architects

Silicon Graphics/Charleston Park
Mountain View, CA
SWA Group

Gantry Plaza State Park
Long Island City, NY
Thomas Balsley Associates and Sowinski
   Sullivan Architects with Lee Weintraub

Louisville Waterfront Park
Louisville, KY
Hargreaves Associates

Merit Awards:

Boyhood Farm Restoration - Jimmy Carter
   National Historic Site
Plains, GA
Denver Service Center, National Park Service

White River Gardens
Indianapolis, IN
Rundell Ernstberger Associates, LLC

Battle Road Trail
Concord, Lincoln, and Lexington, MA
Carol R. Johnson Associates, Inc.

Oklahoma City National Memorial
Oklahoma City, OK
Sasaki Associates, Inc.; Butzer Design
   Partnership

Jackson Meadow
Marine on St. Croix, MN
Coen + Stumpf + Associates, Inc.

The Rehabilitation of Washington Plaza
Reston, VA
Stephenson & Good, Inc.

Nikko Kirifuri Resort
Nikko City, Tochigi Prefecture, Japan
Andropogon Associates, Ltd.

The Federal Reserve Bank of Minneapolis
Minneapolis, MN
The HOK Planning Group; McGough
   Construction Co., Inc., and Siebold, Sydow &
   Elfanbaum, Inc.

The landscape for Silicon Graphic's corporate campus is meant to reflect their philosophy of "serious fun."

The McMahon Duell residence is located on former pasture land on Martha's Vineyard and is comprised of a complex of small farm buildings and outdoor spaces that intimately relate to the natural and cultural context. The buildings are clustered at one end of the site to preserve the natural vegetation.

ASLA Professional Awards (Con't)

Anaheim and Disneyland Resort Urban Design
Plans
Anaheim, CA
SWA Group

West Side Light Rail Transit System
Portland, OR
Murase Associates

Kelsey Seybold Clinic Main Campus
Houston, TX
SWA Group

Nike World Headquarters North Expansion
Beaverton, OR
Mayer/Reed

Site Furnishings at Parliament Hill
Ottawa, Ontario, Canada
Phillips Farevaag Smallenberg

Jackson Park Pavilion Fountain Court and
Town Square Court
Chicago, IL
Wolff Clements and Associates, Ltd.

Arizona Canal Demonstration Project Sunny
Slope Community
Phoenix, AZ
M. Paul Friedberg, Landscape Architect; Jackie
Ferrara, Artist

Congressional Medal of Honor Memorial
White River State Park, Indianapolis, IN
NINebark, Inc.

Community Center Park
St. Matthews, KY
Wallace Roberts & Todd, LLC

South Waterfront Park
Portland, OR
Walker Macy

Northside Park
Denver, CO
Wenk Associates, Inc.

2001 Design Jury:
Joseph E. Brown, EDAW, Inc.
Alan Y. Fujimori, Alan Y. Fujimori, Inc.
Patricia O'Donnell, LANDSCAPES

2001 Analysis & Planning Award Recipients:
Honor Awards:
Charles River Basin Master Plan
Boston, Cambridge, and Watertown, MA
Goody, Clancy and Associates, The Halvorson
Company, The Metropolitan District
Commission

San Antonio River Improvements Project -
Concept Design
San Antonio, TX
SWA Group

Yuxi City, Yunnan Province
People's Republic of China
Phillips Farevaag Smallenberg

Merit Awards:
Michigan Department of Transportation
Aesthetic Project Opportunities Inventory
and Scenic Heritage Route Designation
Inventory
Michigan
SmithGroup JJR; Washtenaw Engineering
Company; Woolpert Design, LLP

Los Angeles Civic Center Shared Facilities and
Enhancement Plan
Los Angeles, CA
Meléndrez Design Partners

Euclid Corridor Transportation Project
Cleveland and East Cleveland, OH
URS/BRW

ASLA Professional Awards (Con't)

Investing in the Landscape: University of
Toronto St. George Open Space Master Plan
Toronto, Ontario, Canada
Urban Strategies, Inc.

US Highway 93 Design Discussions
Flathead Indian Reservation, Western Montana
Jones and Jones Architects & Landscape
Architects, Ltd.

Grand Canyon Greenway Master Plan
Grand Canyon National Park, Arizona
Grand Canyon Greenway Collaborative

2001 Analysis & Planning Jury:
Joe A. Porter, Design Workshop, Inc.
Elizabeth E. Fischer, U.S. Department of
Transportation
Ed McMahon, Conservation Fund

2001 Research Award Recipients:
Merit Awards
"Restoring Nature: Perspectives from the Social
Sciences and Humanities"
Paul H. Gobster, North Central Research
Station, USDA Forest Service; Island Press

"Privately Owned Public Space: The New York
City Experience"
Jerold S. Kayden in collaboration with the New
York City Department of City Planning and
the Municipal Art Society of New York

2001 Communications Award Recipients
Honor Awards:
"Ice Age Floods of Alternatives and
Environmental Assessment, Parts of
Montana, Idaho, Washington, and Oregon"
Jones and Jones Architects and Landscape
Architects, Ltd.

Merit Awards:
"Preserving Cultural Landscapes In America"
Arnold R. Alanen, University of Wisconsin and
Robert Z. Melnick, University of Oregon

"Union Square, San Francisco"
April Philips Design Works, Inc. and M.D.
Fotheringham, Landscape Architects, Inc.

"Layers of Rome"
Roger Trancik

"Pioneers of American Landscape Design"
National Park Service Historic Landscape
Initiative, Heritage Preservation Services,
Library of American Landscape History, The
Catalog of Landscape Records in the United
States at Wave Hill, The Cultural Landscape
Foundation

2001 Research & Communications Jury:
Dan W. Donelin, Kansas State University
Daniel Iacofano, Moore Iacofano Goltsman, Inc.
Grady Clay, writer

Source: American Society of Landscape Architects

People, not plants, are the important things in gardens.

Garrett Eckbo

Auguste Perret Prize

The International Union of Architects (UIA) grants the triennial Auguste Perret Prize to an internationally renowned architect or architects for their work in applied technology in architecture.

For more information, visit the UIA's Web site at *www.uia-architectes.org*.

1961
F. Candela (Mexico)
Honorary Mention:
The Architects of the British Ministry for Education Office and the Architects of the Office for the Study of Industrial and Agricultural Buildings of Hungary

1963
K. Mayekawa (Japan)
J. Prouvé (France)

1965
H. Sharoun (GFR)
Honorary Mention:
H. and K. Siren (Finland)

1967
F. Otto and R. Gutbrod (GFR)

1969
Karel Hubacek (Czechoslovakia)

1972
E. Pinez Pinero (Spain)

1975
A.C. Erickson and team (Canada)
Honorary Mention:
J. Cardoso (Brazil)

1978
Kiyonori Kitutake (Japan)
Piano & Rogers (Italy/United Kingdom)

1981
G. Benisch (GFR)
Honorary Mention:
J. Rougerie (France)

1984
Joao Baptista Vilanova Artigas (Brazil)

1987
Santiago Calatrava (Spain)
Honorary Mention:
C. Testa (Argentina)

1990
Adien Fainsilber (France)

1993
KHR AS Arkitekten (Denmark)

1996
Thomas Herzog (Germany)

1999
Ken Yeang (Malaysia)

Source: International Union of Architects

Best of Seniors' Housing Award

The National Council on Seniors' Housing (NCOSH), a council established by the National Association of Home Builders (NAHB) in 1989, each year presents the Best of Seniors' Housing Awards. Winning projects are chosen for their ability to meet the demands and needs of the ever-changing seniors' housing market, including the constraints of seniors' housing in marketability, budget, density and programs. Gold and silver awards are presented in a range of categories based on project type and size.

For photos and full project credits on both gold and silver winners, visit NCOSH online at *www.ncosh.com/awards/*.

2001 Gold Winners:

Renovated Service Enriched Seniors Housing:
The Waterford at All Saints
Sioux Falls, SD
Wattenbarger Architects

On the Boards — Service Enriched Seniors Housing:
Classic Residence by Hyatt at the Glen
Glenview, IL
Solomon Cordwell Buenz & Associates

Service Enriched Seniors Housing — Common Area Interior Design:
University Retirement Community at Davis
Davis, CA
Ankrom Moisan Associated Architects

Small Assisted Living Housing (up to 50 units):
"The Inn" at The Fountains at Millbrook
Millbrook, NY
Woolley/Morris Architects

Large Assisted Living Housing (over 50 units):
Brighton Gardens at Friendship Heights
Chevy Chase, MD
Torti Gallas and Partners—CHK, Inc.

Small and Midsize Continuing Care Retirement Community and Congregate Care Community (up to 200 units):
The Atrium at Cedars
Portland, ME
Tsomides Associates Architects Planners

Large Continuing Care Retirement Community and Congregate Care Community (over 200 units):
University Retirement Community at Davis
Davis, CA
Ankrom Moisan Associated Architects

Special Needs Housing:
The Harbour House
Greendale, WI
KM Development Corp.

Affordable Senior Apartments:
Garden Court at De La Vina
Santa Barbara, CA
Bialosky Peikert Architects

Senior Apartments:
The Terrace at Clear Lake
Webster, TX
Kaufman Meeks + Partners Co.

Mixed Use Project:
Seasons at Ontario Gateway Plaza
Ontario, Canada
Sclater Partners Architects

Best of Seniors' Housing Award (Con't)

"On the Boards" Active Adult Community:
Talega Gallery
San Clemente, CA
JBZ Architectural + Planning; Bassenian
    Lagoni Architects

Aging in Place Design:
Fallsgrove
Murrieta, CA
Bucilla Brooklyn Architecture

Active Adult Home Design (up to 1,500 square feet):
Sun City Lincoln Hills, Pine Hill Model
Lincoln, CA
The Design Collaborative

Active Adult Home Design (1,500 to 2,100 square feet):
Sun City Grand, Coronado Model
Surprise, AZ
JB2 Dorius

Active Adult Home Design (over 2,100 square feet):
Sun City Palm Desert, The Provence Model
Palm Desert, CA
Del Webb Corporation

Small and Midsize Active Adult Community Center Interior Design:
Rancho Resort
Sahuarita, AZ
Arcos Architecture

Small and Midsize Active Adult Community Center:
George M. Gibson Senior Center
Upland, CA
KodamaDiseno

Large Active Adult Community Center:
Sun City Anthem
Henderson, NV
Dahlin Group

Small & Midsize Active Adult Community (up to 1,500 homes):
Heritage Palms
Indio, CA
Lendrum Architecture

Large Active Adult Community (over 1,500 homes):
Heritage Hunt
Gainesville, VA
Architectural Design Group; The Lessard
    Group

Source: National Council on Seniors' Housing

Like music or DNA, design offers an infinite number of solutions based on relatively simple principles.

Scott Simpson

Building Team Project of the Year Awards

Presented annually by *Building Design & Construction* magazine, the Building Team Project of the Year recognizes non-residential buildings whose design and construction reflect the successful integration of expertise from each member of the building team. Winning projects are featured in an issue of *Building Design & Construction.*

For additional information, contact *Building Design & Construction* magazine at (847) 390-2053 or *www.bdcmag.com.*

2001 Grand Award Winners

Chesapeake Bay Foundation Headquarters, Annapolis, MD
Owner/developer: Chesapeake Bay Foundation
Architect, M/E/P engineer: SmithGroup
Structural engineer: Shemro Engineering
General Contractor: The Clark Construction Group, Inc.
M/E/P contractor: L.H. Cranston
Rough carpentry contractor: R.J. Musser
Construction manager: Synthesis Inc.

Experience Music Project, Seattle, WA
Owner: Vulcan Northwest Inc.
Architect: Frank O. Gehry & Associates
Interior architect: LMN Architects
Structural engineer: Skilling Ward Magnusson Barkshire
Mechanical engineer: Notkin Engineers
Electrical engineer: Sparling
General contractor and construction manager: Hoffman Construction Co. of Washington

2001 Merit Award Winners

Ahold Information Services Headquarters, Greenville, S.C.
Owner/developer: Ahold Real Estate Co.
Architect and interior architect: Smallwood, Reynolds, Stewart, Stewart & Associates Inc.
Structural engineer: Walter P. Moore & Associates

Mechanical/electrical engineer: B&A Consulting Engineers
Data center consultants: Kamm & Associates
General contractor: Choate Construction

Block 89, Madison, WI
Owner/developer: Urban Land Interests
Architect/interior architect: Valerio Dewalt Train Associates
Structural engineer: Robert Darvas Associates (buildings); Carl Walker Inc. (parking garage)
Mechanical/electrical engineers: WMA Consulting Engineers Ltd.; Kilgust Mechancial Inc.; Nickles Electric
General contractor: J.H. Findorff & Son

Carmel Clay Public Library, Carmel, IN
Owner/developer: Carmel Clay Public Library
Architect/interior architect: Meyer, Scherer & Rockcastle Ltd.
Executive architect: Browning Day Mullins Dierdorf Inc.
Structural engineer: Congdon Engineering Associates Inc.
Mechanical/electrical engineer: Rotz Engineers Inc.
Construction manager and general contractor: Geupel DeMars Hagerman

Building Team Project of the Year Awards (Con't)

401 Robert, Minneapolis, MN
Owner/developer: Minnesota Life Insurance Co.
Architect/interior architect: Architectural
Alliance
Structural engineer: Meyer, Borgman and
Johnson
Mechanical/electrical engineer: Michaud Cooley
Erickson
General contractor/construction manager:
McGough Construction Inc.

2001 Jury:
Joseph R. Krusinski, Krusinski Construction Co.
T. Gunny Harboe, McClier
Donald A. Shapiro, MB Beitler
Raj P. Gupta, Environmental Systems Design
Inc.
Roger Lang, Turner Construction
Randolph F. Thomas, The Alter Group
Robert C. Sinn, Skidmore, Owings & Merrill

Source: Building Design & Construction *magazine*

Business Week/Architectural Record **Awards**

The *Business Week/Architecture Record* Awards recognize creative design solutions with an emphasis on the achievement of business goals through architecture. Co-sponsored by The American Institute of Architects, the awards are judged by a jury of business leaders, public officials, and designers. Eligible projects must have been completed within the past three years and must be submitted jointly by the architect and the client. Projects may be located anywhere in the world.

For additional information, call (202) 682-3205 or visit the AIA on the Internet at *www.aia.org.*

2000 Award Winners:

Sticks Inc.
Des Moines, IA
Herbert Lewis Kruse Blunck Architecture

Hanjin Container Terminal
Los Angeles, CA
Robert Stewart Architect & Caldwell Architects

Fukuoka Prefectural and International Hall
Fukuoka, Japan
Emilio Ambasz & Associates

Valeo Technical Center
Auburn Hills, MI
Davis Brody Bond

Saint-Hyacinthe School of Trades and
    Technologies
Quebec, Canada
ABCP Architecture

Rose Center for Earth and Space, American
    Museum of Natural History
New York, NY
Polshek Partnership Architects

Mahindra United World College of India
Pune, India
Christopher Charles Benninger & Assoc.

The Children's Place Corp. Headquarters
Secaucus, NJ
Davis Brody Bond

Ground Zero
Marina del Rey, CA
Shubin + Donaldson Architects

Jury:

Carol Ross Barney, Chair
William Agnello
Julie Anixter
Edward Ciffone
Henry N. Cobb
Julie Eizenberg
Robin M. Ellerthorpe
James O. Jonassen
Wilson Pollack
Eric Richert
Yvonne Szeto
Jane Weinzapfel

Source: Architectural Record/Business Week

Carlsberg Architectural Prize

The Carlsberg Architectural Prize is awarded every four years to a living architect or group of architects who has produced works of enduring architectural and social value. As part of Carlsberg's long-standing patronage of the arts, Carlsberg A/S established this prize in 1991 to promote the benefits of quality architecture. Nominations are culled from the international architectural press, and the jury is comprised of architects, scholars, and members of the press. Winners of this international award receive a prize amount equal to $220,000 US.

For more information visit the Carlsberg Web site at *www.carlsberg.com*.

1992 Tadao Ando, Japan
1995 Juha Leiviskä, Finland
1998 Peter Zumthor, Switzerland

Source: Carlsberg A/S

Architecture is the arrangement of space for excitement.

Philip Johnson

Chrysler Design Awards

In order to recognize socially responsible, cutting-edge individuals and companies "reaching beyond the traditional boundaries of the design disciplines," the DaimlerChrysler Corporation presents the annual Chrysler Design Awards. Each year, six designers or design teams in architecture, product design (excluding automotive design), graphic design, landscape architecture, and fashion are nominated by a committee of worldwide design leaders. Judges look toward designers whose work exhibits technological benefits, beauty, accessibility, creativity, and risk-taking. Winners receive a $10,000 prize and a specially designed trophy (usually designed by a previous Chrysler Design Award winner).

For biographies of past winners or photos of the trophies, visit *www.chrysler designawards.com* on the Internet.

1993:
Apple Industrial Design Group
Cross Colours
John Hejduk
Dr. Paul B. MacCready
Ellen Lupton and J. Abbot Miller
Gaetano Pesce

1994:
Muriel Cooper
Todd Katherine and Michael McCoy
Achva Benzinberg Stein
John Todd and Nancy Jack
Rudy Vanderlans and Zuzane Licko
Lebbeus Woods

1995:
Frank O. Gehry
Robert M. Greenberg
Ralf Hotchkiss
ReVerb
SITE
Philip Zimmermann

1996:
Matthew Carter
Niels Diffrient
Craig Hodgetts & Ming Fung
Tibor Kalman
Mack Scogins & Merrill Elam
Richard Saul Wurman

1997:
Elizabeth Diller & Ric Scofidio
Edward Fella
Chuck Hoberman
Lisa Krohn
Burt Rutan
Allan Wexler

1998:
Erik Adegard and Patricia McShane
April Greiman
Steven Holl
Mars Pathfinder Team
Bruce Mau
Tod Williams and Billie Tsien

Chrysler Design Awards (Con't)

1999:
Pablo Ferro
Peter Girardi
John Maeda
Karim Rashid
Jesse Reiser and Nanako Umemoto
Gael Towey

2000:
Will Bruder
James Corner
David M. Kelley
Ted Muehling
Gary Panter
Paula Scher

Source: DaimlerChrysler Corporation

Design for Humanity Award

Every year the American Society of Interior Designers (ASID) grants the Design for Humanity Award to an individual or institution that has made a significant contribution toward improving the quality of the human environment through design related activities that have had a universal and far-reaching effect. A committee appointed by the ASID Board reviews the nominations. The award is presented at ASID's annual national convention.

For additional information about the Design for Humanity Award, contact the ASID at (202) 546-3480 or on the Internet at *www.asid.org*.

1990	The Scavenger Hotline
1991	E.I. Du Pont de Nemours & Company
1992	The Preservation Resource Center
1993	Neighborhood Design Center
1994	Elizabeth Paepcke & The International Design Conference in Aspen
1995	Cranbrook Academy of Art
1996	Wayne Ruga and the Center for Health Design
1997	Barbara J. Campbell, *Accessibility Guidebook For Washington, D.C.*
1998	William L. Wilkoff, District Design
1999	AlliedSignal, Inc.-Polymers Division
2000	Victoria Schomer
2001	ASID Tennessee Chapter, Chattanooga

Source: American Society of Interior Designers

Design for Transportation National Awards

Co-presented by the Department of Transportation (DOT) and the National Endowment for the Arts (NEA), the Design for Transportation National Awards are presented every five years for functional, innovative transportation system projects which solve problems by uniting form and function. Both agencies established criteria for judging, which is carried out by a multi-disciplinary jury of professionals. Entries must achieve one or more of the following DOT goals: tie America together through intermodal and multimodal connections; enhance the environment through compatibility with community life and the physical surroundings; demonstrate sensitivity to the concerns of the traveling public; and provide a secure and safe traveling environment. Innovation, aesthetic sensibility, technical and functional performance, and cost efficiency must all be demonstrated. Awards are presented at two levels, the highest being Honor Awards, followed by Merit Awards. The following projects won an Honor Award in 2000.

Photographs and jury comments for both the Honor and Merit Award recipients can be found on the Internet at *http://ostpxweb. dot.gov.*

2000 Honor Awards:
Admiral Clarey Bridge
Pearl Harbor, Oahu, Hawaii

Grand Central Terminal
New York, New York

Dallas Area Rapid Transit
Dallas, Texas

Historic Columbia River Highway State Trail
Columbia River Gorge, Oregon

Terminal B/C, Ronald Reagan Washington
    National Airport
Washington, D.C.

River Relocation Project
Providence, Rhode Island

Westside Light Rail
Portland, Oregon

United States Port of Entry
Calexico, California

Memorial Tunnel Fire Ventilation Test Program
Charleston, West Virginia

The Bat Dome Culvert
Laredo, Texas

Vessel Traffic Services Project
Lower Mississippi River

2000 Jury:
Alex Krieger, Chair

Architecture, Interior Design, and Historic Preservation:
Alex Krieger, Chair
Kate Diamond
Hanan A. Kivett
Mary Means
Donald Stull

Design for Transportation National Awards (Con't)

Engineering:
   James Poirot, Chair
   Jonathan Esslinger
   Patricia Galloway
   John M. Kulicki
   M. John Vickerman

Landscape Architecture, Urban Design, Planning, Art
and Graphic Design:
   Elizabeth Moule, Chair
   Wendy Feuer
   Roger K. Lewis
   Weiming Lu
   Lynda Schneekloth

Source: U.S. Department of Transportation and National Endowment
*   for the Arts*

Roads are the architecture of our restlessness, of those who wish neither to stay in their built places nor wander in the untouched one, but to keep moving between them... A road is itself a kind of sentence, or story. A real place, it's also a metaphor for time, for future becoming present and then past, for passage.

Rebecca Solnit

Designer of Distinction Award

The Designer of Distinction Award is granted by the American Society of Interior Designers (ASID) to an ASID interior designer whose professional achievements have demonstrated design excellence. Eligibility is open to members in good standing who have practiced within the preceding ten years. Nominations are accepted by ASID's general membership body and reviewed by jury selected by the National President. This is a merit based award and, thus, is not always granted annually.

For more information, visit the ASID on the Internet at *www.asid.org* or contact them at (202) 546-3480.

1979	William Pahlman	1994	Charles D. Gandy
1980	Everett Brown	1995	Andre Staffelbach
1981	Barbara D'Arcy	1996	Joseph Minton
1982	Edward J. Wormley	1997	Phyllis Martin-Vegue
1983	Edward J. Perrault	1998	Janet Schirn
1984	Michael Taylor	1999	Gary E. Wheeler
1985	Norman Dehaan	2000	Paul Vincent Wiseman
1986	Rita St. Clair	2001	William Hodgins
1987	James Merricksmith		
1988	Louis Tregre		

Source: American Society of Interior Designers

Dubai International Award for Best Practices in Improving the Living Environment

The United Nations' Center for Human Settlements (HABITAT), in conjunction with the Municipality of Dubai, United Arab Emirates, biennially awards the Dubai International Award for Best Practices in Improving the Living Environment to initiatives that have made outstanding contributions to improving the quality of life in cities and communities worldwide. The first Best Practices award was presented in 1996 following an international conference on best practices held in Dubai. In 2000, over 700 submissions were received from more than 120 countries. Each project is reviewed for its compliance with the three criteria for a Best Practice: impact, partnership, and sustainability. The award is open to all organizations, including governments and public and private groups. Winners receive a $30,000 prize, trophy and certificate. In addition, all entries are listed in a Best Practices database at *www.bestpractices.org* that contains over 1100 solutions to the common social, economic and environmental problems of an urbanizing world.

For additional information, contact HABITAT at (212) 963-4200, or on the Internet at *www.bestpractices.org*.

2000 Winners:
- Luanda Sul Self-financed Urban Infrastructure, Angola
- Public Security, Human Rights and Citizenship, Brazil
- Creating a Sustainable Community, Hamilton-Wentworth Vision 2020/Air Quality, Canada
- Comprehensive Re-vitalisation of Urban Settlements, Chengdu, China
- Democratisation of Municipal Management, Cotacachi Canton, Ecuador
- Cost Effective and Appropriate Sanitation Systems, India
- Women's Empowerment Programme, Nepal
- Spanish Greenways Programme, Spain
- Shambob Brick Producers Co-operative, Sudan
- Tourism and Coastal Zone Management, Cirali, Turkey

2000 Jury:
- Prof. W. Cecil Steward, USA (Chair)
- Hon. Dato Dr. Siti Zaharah Bt Sulaiman, Malaysia
- Claudia Ximena Balcazar, Colombia
- Hussain Nasser Ahmed Lootah, Dubai Municipality, UAE
- Mayor Josiah K. Magut, Kenya

Source: United Nations' Center for Human Settlements

Architecture means the thoughtful housing of the human spirit in the physical world.

William O. Meyer

Edward C. Kemper Award

Edward C. Kemper served as Executive Director of The American Institute of Architects (AIA) for nearly 35 years, from 1914 to 1948. The Edward C. Kemper Award honors an architect member of the AIA who has similarly served as an outstanding member of the Institute.

For more information, visit the AIA on the Internet at *www.aia.org* or contact the AIA Honors and Awards Department at (202) 626-7586.

1950	William Perkins	1977	Ronald A. Straka
1951	Marshall Shaffer	1978	Carl L. Bradley
1952	William Stanley Parker	1979	Herbert E. Duncan Jr.
1953	Gerrit J. De Gelleke	1980	Herbert Epstein
1954	Henry H. Saylor	1981	Robert L. Durham
1955	Turpin C. Bannister	1982	Leslie N. Boney Jr.
1956	Theodore Irving Coe	1983	Jules Gregory
1957	David C. Baer	1984	Dean F. Hilfinger
1958	Edmund R. Purves	1985	Charles Redmon
1959	Bradley P. Kidder	1986	Harry Harmon
1960	Philip D. Creer	1987	Joseph Monticciolo
1961	Earl H. Reed	1988	David Lewis
1962	Harry D. Payne	1989	Jean P. Carlhian
1963	Samuel E. Lunden	1990	Henry W. Schirmer
1964	Daniel Schwartzman	1991	John F. Hartray Jr.
1965	Joseph Watterson	1992	Betty Lou Custer*
1966	William W. Eshbach	1993	Theodore F. Mariani
1967	Robert H. Levison	1994	Harry C. Hallenbeck
1968	E. James Gambaro	1995	Paul R. Neel
1969	Philip J. Meathe	1996	Sylvester Damianos
1970	Ulysses Floyd Rible	1997	Harold L. Adams
1971	Gerald McCue	1998	Norman L. Koonce
1972	David N. Yerkes	1999	James R. Franklin
1973	Bernard B. Rothschild	2000	James A. Scheeler
1974	Jack D. Train	2001	Charles Harper
1975	F. Carter Williams		
1976	Leo A. Daly		

* Honored posthumously

Source: The American Institute of Architects

Engineering Excellence Awards

The American Consulting Engineers Council's (ACEC) Engineering Excellence Awards are an annual competition that begins at the state level, with finalists moving to the national competition. Each year one project receives the "Grand Conceptor" Award, and up to 23 other projects receive either Grand or Honor Awards. Projects are judged by a panel of 20 – 25 engineers and infrastructure experts on the basis of uniqueness and originality; technical value to the engineering profession; social and economic considerations; complexity; and how successfully the project met the needs of the client. Projects must be entered in one of nine categories: studies, research and consulting engineering services, building support systems; structural systems; surveying and mapping; environmental; water and wastewater; water resources; transportation; and special projects. Any firm engaged in the private practice, consulting engineering, or surveying is eligible to participate. Entries must be submitted to an ACEC Member Organization.

For photographs and descriptions of the winning projects, visit *www.acec.org* on the Internet.

2001 Grand Conceptor Award Winner:
William H. Harsha Bridge
Maysville, Kentucky
American Consulting Engineers, PLC

2001 Grand Award Winners:
Nitrogen Removal - DNA Sequencing Study
Brooklyn, New York
Metcalf & Eddy of New York, Inc.

Experience Music Project
Seattle, Washington
Skilling Ward Magnusson Barkshire, Inc.

Nimitz Highway Reconstructed Sewer
Honolulu, Hawaii
URS Corporation

Santa Monica Urban Runoff Recycling Facility
Santa Monica, California
CH2M HILL

Kapichira Hydroelectric Project
Malawi
TAMS Consultants, Inc.

Whittier Access Project
Whittier, Alaska
HDR Alaska, Inc.

Taiwan National Aquarium
Taiwan, Republic of China
Tetra Tech/KCM International

2001 Honor Award Winners:
Wyoming Valley Inflatable Dam Study
Wilkes-Barre, Pennsylvania
Gannett Fleming, Inc.

Pennsylvania Department of Environmental
    Protection Cambria Office Building
Ebensburg, Pennsylvania
L. Robert Kimball & Associates/Kulp Boecker
    Architects

The structural system of the Experience Music Project employs 240 skeleton-like steel ribs over which a five-inch concrete shell was cast and a skin of 3,000 steel and aluminum panels were wrapped.

Located in the middle of a pedestrian-filled recreational area, the Santa Monica Urban Runoff Facility treats up to 500,000 gallons of dry-weather urban runoff per day. In addition, the facility unfolds in a logical fashion as visitors follow the illuminated water through the purification process, which has educational components about pollution and water treatment integrated throughout.

Engineering Excellence Awards (Con't)

F-22 Robotic Coatings Facility
Marietta, Georgia
Burns & McDonnell

Old Plank Road Trail Bridge
Frankfort, Illinois
Teng & Associates, Inc.

State Route 520 Bridge Rehabilitation
Seattle, Washington
KPFF Consulting Engineers

Enron Field
Houston, Texas
Walter P. Moore and Associates, Inc.

San Juan Submarine Cable Corridor Study
Lopez Island to Anacortes, Washington
David Evans and Associates, Inc.

Backup Power Source/Cogeneration Project
Riverside, California
Montgomery Watson

Dredged Materials Environmental Resources
Houston, Texas
Turner Collie & Braden, Inc./Gahagan & Bryant
    Associates, Inc.

Richmond, Virginia's Double Duty Combined
    Sewer Overflow System
Richmond, Virginia
Greeley and Hansen

Kern Water Bank Expansion Project
Bakersfield, California
Kennedy/Jenks Consultants

Sheffield Junction Flyover Project
Kansas City, Missouri
TranSystems Corporation

Hudson-Bergen Light Rail System - Initial
    Operating Segment
Bergen to Hudson Counties, New Jersey
STV, Incorporated

Philadelphia International Airport Runway 8-26
Philadelphia, Pennsylvania
Turner Collie & Braden, Inc.

Zussman Mounted Urban Training Complex
Fort Knox, Kentucky
Polyengineering, Inc.

Industri-Plex Superfund Site Redevelopment
Woburn, Massachusetts
Vanasse Hangen Brustlin, Inc.

Source: American Consulting Engineers Council

Did you know...

Stretching more than 395,000 square feet and weighing only 68 pounds, the roof on Atlanta's Georgia Dome (Heery International; Rosser Fabrap International; Thompson, Ventulett, Stainback and Associates, 1992) is the largest cable-supported fabric roof in the world.

Excellence on the Waterfront Awards

Awarding projects that convert abandoned or outmoded waterfront spaces into those for constructive use in the public interest, the Excellence on the Waterfront Awards are presented annually by the non-profit Waterfront Center. Any built project on any body of water, new or old, is eligible to win. Categories for project entries include environmental, cultural, historic, commercial, residential, and the working waterfront. A secondary entry category is comprehensive waterfront plans, which are plans that deal with a community's entire waterfront resource, or at least a significant portion, as opposed to efforts that involve a single site. Judging criteria include the design's sensitivity to the water, quality and harmony, civic contribution, environmental impact, and educational components. The group also presents a Clearwater Award that recognizes outstanding grassroots citizen efforts.

Comprehensive information about the awards are available on the Waterfront Center's Web site at *www.waterfrontcenter.org*.

2000 Top Honor Award:
 Woolloomooloo Bay Redevelopment
 Sydney NSW, Australia

2000 Project Honor Awards by Category:
Environmental Enhancement
 Mary Theler Wetlands
 Belfair, Washington

Historic Preservation
 OXO Tower Wharf, South Bank
 London, England

Commercial/Mixed Use
 Marina Bay
 Richmond, California

Parks and Recreation
 Pier A Park and Riverwalk
 Hoboken, New Jersey

 South Waterfront Park
 Portland, Oregon

Comprehensive Waterfront Plans
 Lakes Bhopal Conservation and Management
 Project, Upper and Lower Lakes Bhopal
 Madhya Pradesh, India

 Chicago River Corridor Development Plan and
 Design Guidelines
 Chicago, Illinois

 Above the Falls: A Master Plan for the Upper
 River in Minneapolis, Minnesota
 Minneapolis, Minnesota

Clearwater Awards
 Brooklyn Bridge Park Coalition
 Brooklyn, New York

 Chickasaw Bluffs Conservancy
 Memphis Tennessee

 Richard K. Mills and the Hackensack River
 Stories Project
 Teaneck, New Jersey

Excellence on the Waterfront Awards (Con't)

Northwest Maritime Center
Port Townsend, Washington

2001 Jurors:
Sandy Threlfall, The Waterfront Coalition
(Chair)
Steve Durrant, URS/BRW
Jane Hotz Kay, author
Jorgen, Struever Bros.

Source: Waterfront Center

Exhibition of School Architecture Awards

As part of the juried Exhibition of School Architecture, outstanding school design and educational environments are honored each year with two awards: the Walter Taylor and Shirley Cooper Awards, named in honor of the original organizers of the School Architecture Exhibit. Additional citations may be presented at the discretion of the jury. Sponsored by the American Association of School Administrators (AASA), The American Institute of Architects and the Council of Education Facility Planners International, the Exhibition is open to registered architects and landscape architects. The Exhibition is held during the AASA's National Conference on Education.

For more information, contact the AASA at (703) 528-0070 or visit them on the Internet at *www.aasa.org*.

2001 Walter Taylor Award Winner:
Interdistrict Downtown School
Minneapolis, MN
Cuningham Group

2001 Shirley Cooper Award Winner:
Roy Lee Walker Elementary School
McKinney, TX
SHW Group, Inc.

2001 Citation Honorees:
Arthur D. Healey School
Somerville, MA
HMFH Architects

Center for Advanced Research and Technology
Clovis, CA
TBP/Architecture

Daffodil Valley Elementary School
Sumner, WA
Erickson McGovern Architects

Emerald Ridge High School
Puyallup, WA
Northwest Architectural Co.

Heinavaara Elementary School
Heinavaara, Finland
Cuningham Group

Northwood High School
Irvine, CA
TBP/Architecture

Penncrest High School
Media, PA
L. Robert Kimball & Associates

Walled Lake Central High School
Walled Lake, MI
TMP Associates, Inc.

2001 Jury:
James A. Brady, PageSoutherlandPage
Dr. Donna Cranswick, Creighton Elementary
  School District 14
Jennifer Devlin, Esherick, Homsey, Dodge &
  Davis/EHDD Architecture
Dr. William Maclay, Facility Planning Consultant
Dale Scheideman, Clark County School District
David Soleau, Flansburg & Associates

Source: American Association of School Administrators

The goal of the Roy Lee Walker Elementary School was not only to build the most comprehensive sustainable school in America but to create an environment in which students would directly experience their interdependence with nature. The stone cistern (top), along with five others, is capable of collecting up to 68,000 gallons of rainwater from the roof. The wind energy harvested from the large windmill (bottom) is used to circulate the collected rainwater through the landscape irrigation system and eco-pond. Some of the school's other features include daylighting, solar energy, sundials, a weather station, a water habitat, natural landscaping, community recycling, and sustainable building materials.

Francesco Borromini International Award for Architecture

The City of Rome sponsors the biennial Francesco Borromini International Award for Architecture, named for the 17th Century Italian architect considered to be the father of the Baroque style. The award is presented to architects "whose works, at the time and in the context of their realization, have best interpreted the demands of the contemporary world as well as the needs of our collective life, helping humanity's civil and cultural growth," in two categories: the Borromini Award and the Borromini Award for Young Architects (under age 41). Architects from all over the world are eligible to enter; winners receive prize money and a trophy.

For additional information, visit *www.premioborromini.org* on the Internet.

Borromini Award
2001   Jean Nouvel, France

Borromini Award for Young Architects
2001   Matthias Klontz, Chile

Source: The City of Rome

No matter what things you study, you will always find that those which are good and useful are also graced with beauty.

Baldassare Castiglione, 1528

Gold Key Awards for Excellence in Hospitality Design

For over 20 years the Gold Key Awards for Excellence in Hospitality Design have honored hospitality designers for excellence in six design categories: Restaurants Seating to 110; Restaurants Seating Over 110; Guest Rooms; Suites; Lobby/Reception Area; and Senior Living Facility. The awards are presented by the International Hotel/Motel & Restaurant Show and sponsored by *Hospitality Design* and *Lodging* magazines.

For a description of eligibility requirements and an entry form visit *www.ihmrs.com.*

2000 Grand Prize Winners

Restaurants – Seating to 110
  Katzenberg's Express
  Greenwich, CT
  Haverson Architecture and Design, P.C.

Restaurants – Seating over 110
  Guastavino's Restaurant at Bridgemarket
  New York, NY
  Conran & Partners and Hardy Holzman
    Pfeiffer Associates

Lobby/Reception Area
  The W Hotel
  San Francisco, CA
  Hornberger + Worstell

Guest Rooms
  Westin Plaza Hotel
  Singapore
  Brennan Beer Gorman Monk

Suites
  Royal Suite, Voyager of the Seas
  Royal Caribbean International, Miami, FL
  Howard Snoweiss Design Group

Senior Living Facility
  University Retirement Community at Davis
  Davis, CA
  Ankrom Moisan Associated Architects

Jurors:
  Alexandra Champalimaud, Alexandra
    Champalimaud & Associates, Inc.
  Jeffrey Beers, Jeffrey Beers International
  Mary-Jean Eastman, Perkins Eastman
    Architects, PC
  Didier Picquot, The Pierre, New York

Source: Hospitality Design magazine

Hardy Holzman Pfeiffer Associates recently renovated the
cathedral-like 1909 Bridgemarket space underneath the
Queensboro Bridge in New York City, which originally func-
tioned as a public market and now houses the Guastavino's
restaurant (above), The Terence Conran Shop, and the Food
Emporium. The focal piece of the space is the tiled ceiling
vaults designed by Barcelona immigrant Rafael Guastavino.
Photo: Georgia Glynn Smith.

GSA Design Awards

The U.S. General Services Administration (GSA) presents biennial Design Awards as part of its Design Excellence Program, which seeks the best in design, construction, and restoration for all Federal building projects. The Design Awards were developed to encourage and recognize innovative design in Federal buildings and to honor noteworthy achievements in the preservation and renovation of historic structures.

For additional information about the GSA Design Awards or to view photographs and descriptions of the winners, visit GSA's Web site at *http://designawards.gsa.gov.*

2000 Honor Award Recipients:

Architecture

Sandra Day O'Connor U.S. Courthouse
Phoenix, Arizona
Richard Meier & Partners, Architects

Lloyd D. George U.S. Courthouse
Las Vegas, Nevada
Mehrdad Yazdani, CannonDworsky

U.S. Courthouse and Federal Building
Central Islip, New York
Richard Meier & Partners, Architects

Engineering/Technology/Energy

U. S. Geological Survey Chiller Replacement
Reston, Virginia
J. Vicente Pedraza, JVP Engineers, P.C.

Art

Jurisprudents, at Melvin Price U.S. Courthouse
East St. Louis, Illinois
Ralph Helmick, Stuart Schechter, Helmick & Schechter Sculpture

Construction Excellence

Charles Evans Whittaker U.S. Courthouse
Kansas City, Missouri
Steve Hamline, J.E. Dunn Construction

U.S. Port of Entry
Blaine, Washington
Derek Wright, Intermountain Construction, Inc.

2000 Citation Award Recipients:

Architecture

William J. Nealon Federal Building and U.S. Courthouse
Scranton, Pennsylvania
Bohlin Cywinski Jackson, Architects

Architecture On the Boards

U.S. Courthouse
Hammond, Indiana
Pei Cobb Freed & Partners Architects LLP

U.S. Port of Entry
Sault Sainte Marie, Michigan
Ross Barney + Jankowski, Inc.

U.S. Post Office and Courthouse
Pittsburgh, Pennsylvania
Shalom Baranes Associates, P.C.

Landscape Architecture/Security

Phillip Burton Federal Building and U.S. Courthouse Plaza
San Francisco, California
Della Vale + Bernheimer Design, Inc.

The Lloyd D. George U.S. Courthouse & Federal
Building by Cannon Dworksy features an expansive public plaza elevated above the street and
shaded from the desert sun by an enormous trel-
lis-canopy cantilevered from the roof. Photo: ©
Peter Aaron/Esto. All rights reserved.

GSA Design Awards (Con't)

Engineering/Technology/Energy
David Skaggs Federal Building
Boulder, Colorado
Jerry H. Deal, E. Cube, Inc.

Preservation/Conservation
Restoration of George Segal's sculpture The
    Restaurant
Buffalo, New York
Johnson Atelier

Art
Urns of Justice at U.S. Courthouse
Lafayette, Louisiana
Diana K. Moore, Artist

Graphic Design
Print Materials for Dedication of Tom Otterness
    sculpture
Rockman, Minnesota
Katherine Sechler Stephenson, GSA - PBS
    Business Development

IRS Computing Center Works of Art Brochure
Martinsburg, West Virginia
C.I.A. Creative Intelligence Agency

Construction Excellence
U.S. Courthouse
Fort Myers, Florida
Centex Rooney Construction Company, Inc.

Jury:
Charles Gwathmey (Chair)
David Driskell
Julie Eizenberg
Samuel Y. Harris
Douglas Kelbaugh
Debra Lehman-Smith
Guy Nordenson
Kiku Obata
Michael Rotondi

Source: U.S. General Services Administration

Healthcare Environment Award

Since 1989 the annual Healthcare Environment Awards have recognized innovative, life-enhancing design that contributes to the quality of healthcare. The award is sponsored by The Center for Health Design, *Contract* magazine, and The American Institute of Architecture Students. The competition is open to architects, interior designers, healthcare executives, and students. Winners are presented an award at the annual Symposium on Healthcare. First-place winners also receive two complimentary registrations to the Symposium and their projects are published in *Contract* magazine.

For additional information, contact The Center for Health Design on the Web at *www.healthdesign.org.*

2001 Ambulatory Care Facilities, Winner:

Memorial Breast Care Center at Anaheim Memorial Hospital
Anaheim, CA
Taylor & Associates Architects

2001 Ambulatory Care Facilities, Honorable Mention

University of California San Francisco Pediatric Clinics Remodel
San Francisco, CA
Anshen+Allen Architects

Scripps Polster Breast Care Center
La Jolla, CA
Jain Malkin, Inc.

2001 Acute Care Facilities, Honorable Mention:

St. Lukes Hospital, Helen G. Nassif Center for Women's and Children's Health
Cedar Rapids, IA
Ellerbe Becket

Source: The Center for Health Design

Hugh Ferriss Memorial Prize

The Hugh Ferriss Memorial Prize is awarded annually by the American Society of Architectural Illustrators(ASAI) to recognize excellence in architectural illustration. This international awards program is open to all current members of the Society. A traveling exhibition, Architecture in Perspective, co-sponsored by the Otis Elevator Company, highlights the winners and selected entries and raises awareness of the field.

To see the winning drawings, visit the ASAP's Web site at *www.asai.ws.*

1986
   Lee Dunnette, AIA and James Record
1987
   Richard Lovelace, *One Montvale Avenue*
1988
   Thomas Wells Schaller, AIA, *Proposed Arts and Cultural Center*
1989
   Daniel Willis, AIA, *Edgar Allen Poe Memorial (detail)*
1990
   Gilbert Gorski, AIA, *The Interior of the Basilica Ulpia*
1991
   Luis Blanc, *Affordable Housing Now!*
1992
   Douglas E. Jamieson, *BMC Real Properties Buildings*
1993
   David Sylvester, *Additions and Renovations to Tuckerton Marine Research Field Station*
1994
   Rael D. Slutsky, AIA, *3rd Government Center Competition*

1995
   Lee Dunnette, AIA, *The Pyramid at Le Grand Louvre*
1996
   Paul Stevenson Oles, FAIA, *Hines France Office Tower*
1997
   Advanced Media Design, *World War II Memorial*
1998
   Wei Li, *Baker Library Addition, Dartmouth College*
1999
   Serge Zaleski, *Five Star Deluxe Beach Hotel*
2000
   Thomas W. Schaller, *1000 Wilshire Blvd.*
2001
   Michael McCann, *The Royal Ascot, Finishing Post*

Source: American Society of Architectural Perspectivists

I.D. Annual Design Review

I.D. magazine's Annual Design Review began in 1954 and today is considered America's largest and most prestigious industrial design competition. Entries are placed in one of seven separate categories (consumer products, graphics, packaging, environments, furniture, equipment, concepts and student work) and reviewed by juries of leading practitioners. Within each category, projects are awarded on three levels: Best of Category, Design Distinction, and Honorable Mention. Winning entries are published in a special July/August issue of *I.D.* magazine. The following products received the Best of Category award.

For additional information about the Annual Design Review, contact *I.D.* magazine at (212) 447-1400.

2001 Best of Category Winners:

Consumer Products:
iMac G4 Cube
Apple Industrial Design

Graphics:
Takashimaya Volume 8
Design: M|W

Packaging
Philou
fuseproject

Environments
LAX Gateway
Selbert Perkins Design

Furniture:
Ypsilon Chair
Atelier Bellini

Equipment
Mobile Booster
WeLL Industrial Design BV

Concepts:
Living Memory (LiMe)
Philips International BV

Student Work:
No Winner Chosen

2001 Jury:
Nick Dine, Dinersan, Inc.
Gia Giasullo, Studio eg
Irvin Glassman, Glassman Product Design
Khipra Nichols, Rhode Island School of Design
Gordon Salchow, University of Cincinnati
Sonja Schiefer, frog
Steven Sikora, Design Guys
Susan Yelavich, Cooper-Hewitt National Design Museum

Source: I.D. Magazine

Objects should be de-stressers that bring enjoyment, not encumbrances.

Karim Rashid

Industrial Design Excellence Awards (IDEA)

The Industrial Design Excellence Awards (IDEA), co-sponsored by *Business Week* magazine and the Industrial Designers Society of America (IDSA), are presented annually to honor industrial design worldwide. Any U.S. designer or non-U.S. designer whose product is distributed in North America may enter their designs in one of nine categories. Each year a jury of business executives and design professionals issue as many awards as they deem necessary, evaluating over 1,000 entries on the following criteria: design innovation, benefit to the user, benefit to the client/business, ecological responsibility, and appropriate aesthetics and appeal. Gold, silver, and bronze level citations are granted. The following designs received the Gold award.

For detailed descriptions, photographs, and contact information for all Gold, Silver, and Bronze winners, visit the IDSA on the Internet at *www.idsa.org*.

IDEA2001 Gold Award Winners:

Business & Industrial Products

Compaq MP2800 Microportable Projector
Compaq Computers

Credence Kalos XW Testhead
frog design, inc.

Alcatel 7670 Routing Switch Platform
Alcatel, Canada

SB-200/SB-300 Transport Refrigeration Unit
Thermo King Corp.

Motorola NFL Headset Generation II
Herbst LaZar Bell, Inc. and Motorola Inc.

Consumer Products

BODUM® Santos
BODUM® AG/BODUM Design Group,
Switerland

psa[play 120
Nike, Inc.

Child Safety Night Light
LPK, GE Lighting and Innovata

SmartTrack Kayak Control System
Manatee Design

Spin-Steer TechnologyTM Lawn Tractor
Henry Dreyfuss Associates

Design Exploration

THAAD Mobile Command Shelter Concept
Carlson Technology Inc., Lockheed Martin
Missiles & Space, Raytheon Systems Co.,
Thaad Project Office, Kulick Enterprises Inc.
and PEI Electronics, Inc.

Aura Concept
Herbst LaZar Bell, Inc.

DUO Bi-directional Door Refrigerator
LG Electronics Inc., Korea

2001 Jeep® WILLYS Show Vehicle
DaimlerChrysler Corp.

FedEx Courier Tools & Branding Strategy
Research
ZIBA Design, Inc.

Amtrak Acela Express
IDEO, Nikolaus Frank, Adrian Corry, IDSA,
OH & CO and Amtrak

Digital Media & Interfaces

MoodLogic Magnet Browser
Triplecode

Industrial Design Excellence Awards (IDEA) (Con't)

MF Doom Shockwave.com Music Video
Iguana Studios

Environmental Designs

Amtrak's AcelaTM Station Signage
Calori & Vanden-Eynden/Design Consultants
    and Wallace Roberts & Todd

Rose Center for Earth and Space
Ralph Appelbaum Associates

"50 Years of TV and More"
Ralph Appelbaum Associates

FedEx Center Environment
ZIBA Design, Inc.

Hewlett-Packard COMDEX Trade Show Booth
IDEO, Stone Yamashita Partners, Kaleidoscope,
    Valiant Pictures, Jack Pacheco Creative,
    Contempo Design, Landor Associates, Muse
    Presentation, Scene 2, L.inc design,
    Gamelet.com, Manalagi Group and Flapjack
    Interactive

Furniture

FedEx Furniture System
ZIBA Design, Inc.

Photovoltaic Sunshade
Kawneer Company Inc.

Soft (Lighting) Collection
Karim Rashid Inc.

Medical & Scientific Products
MetriScan
Bridge Design and Alara, Inc

Vistalab Ergonomic Pipette
frog design, inc.

East3 Thoughtcaster
BOLT and Spark

Immersion Medical AccuTouch® Endoscopy
    Simulator
ION Design, LLC and Immersion Medical

Packaging & Graphics

SPOT Endoscopic Marker Packaging
BOLT

Microsoft Office 2001 For Mac
Radius Product Development, Inc. and Ivy Hill
    Corp.

Student Design

SEED
Matthew Boyko, Cranbrook Academy of Art

C*B4
Kelly Kruse, California College of Arts and
    Crafts

ReThinking The Thumbtack
Scott Kochlefl, Michael Vostal, Laura Naughton,
    Matthew Wertz and Teresa Barin of
    University of Illinois at Urbana-Champaign

Transportation

2001 Chrysler PT Cruiser
DaimlerChrysler Corp.

Virgin Atlantic Upper Class Interior and Seat
Virgin Atlantic Airways, United Kingdom,
    Priestman Goode, United Kingdom,
    Pentagram Design, United Kingdom,
    Equation Lighting Design & Productions,
    United Kingdom, and Weave Plan, United
    Kingdom

Karlyn Cleat
Karlyn Group LLC

Islandia
Bombardier Inc., Canada and US

Computer Equipment

Titanium PowerBook G4
Apple Computer, Inc.

IBM TransNote
IBM Corp., US & Japan

WebPad
Whipsaw, Inc.

Left: Karim Rashid's Soft (Lighting) Collection for George Kovacs Lighting offers four different colors and shapes that float inside the clear glass shell, resulting in 64 different configurations.

Below: Scott Kochlefl has updated thumb tack design and expanded its utility. The ReThinking the Thumbtack's horseshoe shape accommodates the stringing of cords, wires, and hooks, and its double pin design increases the tack's strength and stability while reducing the number of tacks needed.

Industrial Design Excellence Awards (IDEA) (Con't)

Microsoft IntelliMouse Optical
Microsoft Corp. and Surface Strategy

M-Systems Flash Key
ZIBA Design, Inc.

IDEA2001 Jury:
Shaun Jackson, Shaun Jackson Design (Chair)
Chris Bangle, BMW
Bill Clem, Strategix I.D.
Heidi Dangelmaier
Clyde Foles, Center for Creative Studies
Martin Gierke, Black & Decker, Inc.
Naomi Gornick, Brunel University
Dallas Grove, Flextronics Design

Gavin Ivester
Nasir Kassamali, Luminaire
Helen Kerr, Kerr and Company
Peter Kuttner, Cambridge Seven Associates
Carl Price, Bose Corp.
Merry Riehm-Constantino, Product Logic
Bryce Rutter, Metaphase Design Group
Jill Shurtleff, The Gillette Company
Tucker Viemeister
Bill Becker, BDI/Becker Designed, Inc.

Source: Industrial Designers Society of America

Did you know...

Since 1996 the following design firms have won the most IDEA awards:

IDEO – 52
ZIBA Design – 32
frog design – 21
Pentagram Design – 20
Fitch – 19
Lunar Design – 16
Herbst LaZar Bell – 15
Altitude – 13
Hauser, Inc. – 12
Smart Design – 12

Interior Design Competition

The Interior Design Competition is presented jointly each year by the International Interior Design Association (IIDA) and *Interior Design* magazine. The Competition was established in 1973 to recognize outstanding interior design and to foster new interior design ideas and techniques. Winning projects appear in Interior Design magazine, and the "Best of Competition" winner receives a $5,000 cash prize.

For more information, contact IIDA at (888) 799-IIDA or visit their Web site at *www.iida.org*.

2001 Best of Competition:
IBM eBusiness Services
Santa Monica, CA
HOK Interiors

2001 Award Winners:
Virgin Atlantic Airline Clubhouse
San Francisco International Airport,
   South San Francisco, CA
Eight Inc.

Madison Dearborn Partners
Chicago, IL
Gary Lee Partners

Rocket Science
Chicago, IL
Interior Space International (ISI)

Allsteel Headquarters
Muscatine, IA
Gensler

Jil Sander Milan Showroom
Milan, Italy
Gabellini Associates

Club Monaco Cafe
Toronto, Ontario, Canada
Burdifilek

2001 Jury:
Bill Arnold, Powell/Kleinschmidt
John Duvivier, Bottom Duvivier
Holly Hunt, Holly Hunt Ltd.
Nestor Santa-Cruz, Skidmore, Owings &
   Merrill

Source: International Interior Design Association and Interior Design *magazine*

Despite its long and narrow dimensions, the Virgin Atlantic Clubhouse offers a variety of spaces for its patrons: a full-service bar, lounges with chairs and sofas for work or relaxation, tables for dining, and a small business center with computers. Arne Jacobsen's Egg chairs line the windows that overlook the runway (top) while oversized armchairs by B&B Italia, a reading light by Artemide, and a digital art installation in the mahogany-paneled wall offer travelers comfort in the lounge (bottom). Photos: William Meppem.

Interiors' Annual Design Awards

Since 1980, *Interiors* magazine has hosted its Annual Design Awards competition to honor and recognize outstanding interior design projects. Entries are judged in one of twelve building types. A jury of design professionals selects winners based on aesthetics, design creativity, function, and achievement of client objectives. Winners are honored at an annual Awards Breakfast in New York.

For more information, contact *Interiors* at (212) 536-5141.

2001 Award Winners:

Best Retail Project
Oscar Bond Salon
New York, New York
Jordon Parnass Digital Architecture & MESH
Architectures

Best Large Office
SHR Perceptual Management Headquarters
Scottsdale, Arizona
Morphosis

Best Small Office
The Firm
Beverly Hills, California
Pugh + Scarpa

Best Restaurant
Rosa Mexicano
New York, New York
Rockwell Group

Best Healthcare Facility
Venture House
Queens, New York
Thanhauser + Esterson Architects

Best Educational Facility
Higgins Hall, Pratt Institute
New York, New York
Rogers Marvel Architects

Best Public Space
Rose Main Reading Room, New York Public
Library
New York, New York
Davis Brody Bond

Best Showroom
Herman Miller National Showroom
Chicago, Illinois
Krueck & Sexton Architects

Best Exhibition
Netherlands Architecture Institute Exhibit
Rotterdam, The Netherlands
Morphosis

Best Residence
Greek Revival Townhouse and Garden
New York, New York
Shelton, Mindel & Assocaites

Best Hotel
The Shoreham Hotel
New York, New York
Pasanella + Klein Stolzman + Berg, Architects

Best Entertainment Venue
Nasdaq MarketSite
New York, New York
Einhorn Yaffee Prescott, Architecture &
Engineering

Interiors' Annual Design Awards (Con't)

Best Restoration
> Radio City Music Hall
> New York, New York
> Hardy Holzman Pfeiffer Associates

Best Environmental Graphic Design
> 225 Varick Street Lobby
> New York, New York
> Studios Architecture

Best Student/Conceptual Work
> "Performance Space"
> Sommerville, Massachusetts
> Brad Koerner, Harvard School of Design

2001 Jury:
> Ralph Appelbaum, Ralph Appelbaum
>   Associates, Inc.
> Shashi Caan, Skidmore, Owings & Merrill,
>   New York
> Michael Graves, Michael Graves & Associates
> David Ling, David Ling Architect
> Carol Ross Barney, Ross Barney+Jankowski
> Lauren Rottet, DMJM Rottet

Source: Interiors

> To me beauty depends on one single person, on the person who looks at something and feels joy in looking at it because it pleases him without second thoughts, irrespective of whether it is useful, whether it is art, or whether it is in good taste.

Eva Zeisel

International Design Award, Osaka

Through its biennial International Design Award, Osaka, the Japan Design Foundation honors organizations and individuals who have made a significant contribution to the promotion of industry culture and the betterment of society through their design work. The award embraces all fields of the design profession. Nominations are solicited from leading figures in design from around the world. Winners are selected by a jury of five Japanese members.

For more information, visit the Japan Design Foundation on the Internet at *www.jidpo.or.jp/jdf/html/en_index.html* or email them at *jdf@silver.ocn.ne.jp*.

1983
   Chermayeff & Geismar Associates (USA)
   Maria Benktzon & Sven-Eric Juhlin (Sweden)
   Paola Navone (Italy)
   Pentagram (United Kingdom)
   *Honorary Award for the Encouragement of Design
      Activities:* Prime Minister, Margaret Thatcher
      (United Kingdom)

1985
   Bang & Olufsen A/S (Denmark)
   Philip Johnson (USA)
   Bruno Munari (Italy)
   Douglas Scott (United Kingdom)
   Honorary Award: Tadashi Tsukasa (Japan)

1987
   Kenji Ekuan (Japan)
   Norman Foster (United Kingdom)
   The Netherlands PTT (Netherlands)

1989
   Otl Aicher (Federal Republic of Germany)
   Jens Nielsen (Denmark)
   Frei Otto (Federal Republic of Germany)
   Yuri Borisovitch Soloviev (U.S.S.R)

1991
   Fritz Hansens Eft. A/S (Denmark)
   Fumihiko Maki (Japan)
   Antti Nurmesniemi and Vuokko Eskolin-
      Nurmesniemi (Finland)

1993
   Department of Architecture and Design of the
      Museum of Modern Art, New York (USA)
   Yusaku Kamekura (Japan)

1995
   Tadao Ando (Japan)
   Lawrence Halprin (USA)
   Arthur J. Pulos (USA)

1997
   Hans J. Wegner (Denmark)

1999
   Pasqual Maragall (Spain)
   Ryohin Keikaku Co., Ltd. (Japan)

2001
   Issey Miyake (Japan)

Source: Japan Design Foundation

International Store Design Competition Award

Visual Merchandising and Store Design (*VM+SD*) magazine and The Institute of Store Planners (ISP) annual present the International Store Design Competition Awards recognizing outstanding design among retail stores worldwide. To be eligible, projects must have been completed within the year and may be entered in only one of the 17 categories. A first place winner and up to two awards of merits are selected in each category, in addition to one Store of the Year winner. The competition is open to any designer or design team involved in retail projects.

For more information or a list of all winners, see *www.visualstore.com* on the Internet.

2000 Store of the Year:
  Rundle Mall
  Adelaide, South Australia
  Robert Young Associates

2000 First Place Winners:
New or Completely Renovated Full-Line Department Store
  Rundle Mall
  Adelaide, South Australia
  Robert Young Associates

New or Completely Renovated Specialty Department Store
  Macy's Home
  South Coast Plaza, Costa Mesa, CA
  Federated Department Stores

New Shop Within an Existing Full-Line or Specialty Department Store
  Bergdorf Goodman Level of Beauty
  Fifth Avenue, New York, NY
  Yabu Pushelberg

Specialty Store, Sales Area 501 to 1500 Sq. Ft.
  Skechers
  Manhattan Beach, CA
  ME Productions Inc.

Specialty Store, Sales Area 1501 to 3000 Sq. Ft.
  Atom & Eve, Promenade Mall
  Thornhill, Ontario, Canada
  II By IV Design Associates Inc.

Specialty Store, Sales Area 3001 to 5000 Sq. Ft.
  Carolina Herrera
  Madison Avenue, New York, NY
  Yabu Pushelberg

Specialty Store, Sales Area 5001 to 10,000 Sq. Ft.
  The Levi's® Store
  Seattle, WA
  Bergmeyer Associates Inc. and Checkland
    Kindleysides

Specialty Store, Sales Area Over 10,000 Sq. Ft.
  The Wiz
  New York, NY
  Retail Planning Associates

Shopping Center Kiosk
  LCBO Millennium Kiosk, Sherway Gardens
  Etobicoke, Ontario, Canada
  The International Design Group

International Store Design Competition Award (Con't)

Specialty Food Court or Counter-Service Restaurant
Fox Sports Skybox
Sky Harbor International Airport, Phoenix, AZ
Fitch/AAD

Sit-Down Restaurant
WB Stage 16
The Venetian Hotel, Las Vegas, NV
Fitch Worldwide

Specialty Food Shop
Cha Tea Bar
Longwood Galleria Food Court, Boston, MA
Connor Architecture

Supermarket
Sentry Foods
Madison, WI
Marco Design Group

Convenience Store
Twin Cities Travel Mart, Minneapolis-St. Paul
  International Airport
St. Paul, MN
The Paradies Shops Inc., and Architectura
  Planning Architecture Interiors Inc.

Entertainment Facility
Illusionz
Issaquah, WA
Callison

Service Retailer (tie)
Lunn Poly, Fosse Park Shopping Centre
Leicester, England
Checkland Kindleysides

Bell World
Eaton Centre
Toronto, Canada
HOK Canada

Manufacturer's Showroom to the Public or Trades
Steelcase at NeoCon 2000
Merchandise Mart, Chicago, IL
Lee Stout Inc.

Special Award: Lighting
Burdines, Florida Mall
Orlando, FL
The Lighting Practice

Special Award: Innovative Retail Concept
The Zone
Glendale Galleria, Glendale, CA
WalkerGroup/CNI

2000 Jury:
Rebecca Van Eman, interior design consultant
Shirley Litman, GD Moore & Co.
Bob Semerau, Visual Accent Inc.
Ed Sierra, WalkerGroup/CNI
Ron Kline, Robinsons May (Moderator)
Carole Winters, VM+SD, (Moderator)

Source: Visual Merchandising and Store Design (VM+SD) *magazine*

James Beard Restaurant Design Award

Since 1995 the James Beard Foundation has awarded the James Beard Restaurant Design Award to that project executed in the United States or Canada that most demonstrates excellence in restaurant design or renovation. Architects and interior designers are eligible to enter restaurant projects that have been completed within the proceeding three years. The award is presented at the annual Beard Birthday Fortnight celebration.

Entry forms and additional information can be found at *www.jamesbeard.org* or by calling the Awards office at (212) 627-2090.

1995
 Fifty Seven Fifty Seven
 New York, NY
 Chhada Siembieda and Partners

1996
 Bar 89
 New York, NY
 Ogawa/Depardon Architects

1997
 Paci Restaurant
 Westport, CT
 Ferris Architects

1998
 Monsoon
 Toronto, Ontario, Canada
 Yabu Pushelberg

1999
 MC Squared
 San Francisco, CA
 Mark Cavagnero Associates

2000
 Brasserie
 New York, NY
 Diller & Scofidio

2001
 Russian Tea Room
 New York, NY
 Leroy Adventures

Source: James Beard Foundation

J.C. Nichols Prize for Visionary Urban Development

The Urban Land Institute (ULI) created the J.C. Nichols Prize for Visionary Urban Development to honor an individual or an institution who has made a commitment to responsible urban community development. As a founding member of the Urban Land Institute and whose work as a visionary developer includes the Country Club Plaza in Kansas City, the award's namesake, J.C. Nichols, embodies the ULI's commitment to fostering responsible land use and reputable development. Nominees can be drawn from a wide range of disciplines, including but not limited to architects, researchers, developers, journalists, public officials, and academics, and must be U.S. or Canadian citizens. A jury of urban experts, each representing diverse backgrounds and experiences, reviews the nominations. Recipients receive a $100,000 honorarium.

For additional information, visit the ULI on the Web at *www.uli.org* or contact them at (202) 624-7000.

2000	Mayor Joseph P. Riley Jr.
2001	Daniel Patrick Moynihan

Source: Urban Land Institute

The way places are arranged can have a profound influence on people at very deep levels.

Tony Hiss

Jean Tschumi Prize

The Jean Tschumi Prize is awarded by the International Union of Architects (UIA) to individuals for their significant contribution to architectural criticism or architectural education.

For more information, visit the UIA's web site at *www.uia-architectes.org.*

1967 J.P. Vouga (Switzerland)
1969 I. Nikolaev (USSR)
       P. Ramirez Vazquez (Mexico)
1972 J.B. Vilanova Artigas (Brazil)
1975 R. Banham (U.K.)
1978 Rectory and Faculty of
       Architecture of the University
       of Lima (Peru)
1981 Neville Quarry (Australia)
       Honorary Mention:
       Jorge Glusberg
       (Argentina) and Tadeusz Barucki (Poland)
1984 Julius Posener (GDR)
1987 C. Norberg-Schulz (Norway)
       A. L. Huxtable (USA)

1990 Eduard Franz Sekler (Austria);
       Honorary Mention:
       Dennis Sharp (U.K.) and
       Claude Parent (France)
1993 Eric Kumchew Lye (Malaysia)
1996 Peter Cook (U.K.); Liangyong Wu (P.R. of
       China)
       Honorary Mention:
       Toshio Nakamura and the
       Mexican editor COMEX
1999 Juhani Pallasmaa (Finland)
       Honorary Mention:
       Jennifer Taylor (Australia)

Source: International Union of Architects

Jot D. Carpenter Medal

On a biennial basis, the American Society of Landscape Architects (ASLA) bestows the Jot D. Carpenter Prize and Medal upon a university educator who has made a sustained and significant teaching contribution to a landscape architecture program at a school with an official ASLA Student Chapter. The award, consisting of a medal and a cash prize, began in 2000 to honor the memory of Ohio State Professor Jot D. Carpenter and his significant contributions to landscape architecture education and the profession. Nominations for the award may be made by an ASLA member or an ASLA student chapter member.

For additional information, call (202) 216-2338 or visit *www. asla.org* on the Web.

2000   Roy H. DeBoer, Rutgers University

Source: American Society of Landscape Architects

Kenneth F. Brown Asia Pacific Culture & Architecture Design Award

Every two years the School of Architecture at the University of Hawai'i at Manoa and the Architects Regional Council of Asia (ARCASIA) sponsor the Kenneth F. Brown Asia Pacific Culture & Architecture Design Award program to recognize outstanding examples of contemporary architecture in Asia and the Pacific Rim that successfully balance spiritual and material aspects and demonstrate a harmony with the natural and cultural settings. Through this award program the sponsors hope to promote the development of humane environments within the multicultural Asia Pacific region as well as inspire a more culturally, socially, and environmentally appropriate approach to architecture. In order to be eligible, projects must have been completed within the previous 10 years and be located in Asia or countries that touch the Pacific Ocean. Winners receive a $US 25,000 cash prize and are invited to speak at the International Symposium on Asia Pacific Architecture.

For additional information or to view photographs and descriptions of winning projects, visit *www2.hawaii.edu/~kbda/* on the Internet.

2000 Award Winner:
Arthur and Yvonne Boyd Education Center
"Riverside"
Nowra, New South Wales, Australia
Glenn Murcutt, Wendy Lewin, Reginald Lark,
Architects Equally in Association (Australia)

2000 Honorable Mentions:
Kim Ok-gill Memorial Hall
Seoul, Korea
Kim In-Cheurl (Korea)

Shanti, A Weekend House
Alibaug, Maharashtra, India
Rahul Mehrotra (India)

LMW Corporate Office
Coimbatore, India
Rahul Mehrotra (India)

26 Everton Road
Singapore
Richard K.F. Ho (Singapore)

2000 Jury:
Kenneth F. Brown, chair (U.S.)
A. I. Abdelhalim (Egypt)
C. Anjalendran (Sri Lanka)
Ricardo Legorreta (Mexico)
Thomas M. Payette (U.S.)

Source: University of Hawai'i at Manoa, School of Architecture

If you get the basics right, a whole lot of by-products you never thought about will flow from them.

Glenn Murcutt

Keystone Award

Created by the American Architectural Foundation (AAF) in 1999, the Keystone Award honors individuals who have furthered the Foundation's vision "of a society that participates in shaping its environment through an understanding of the power of architecture to elevate and enrich the human experience." The award's objective is to recognize and encourage leadership that results in citizen participation in the design process, and advances communication with key decision-makers about how design issues affect a community's quality of life. Nominees may include, but are not limited to, patrons, advocates, critics, activists, clients, government representatives, and educational leaders. The award selection committee is comprised of experts in the fields of community development, communication, design, preservation, and government. Presentation of the award is made at the annual Accent on Architecture Gala in Washington, D.C. in January.

For additional information, contact the AAF at (202) 626-7500 or on the Web at *www.archfoundation.org*.

1999	The Honorable Richard M. Daley
2000	Rick Lowe
2001	*no award granted*

Source: American Architectural Foundation

If ever we are to have a time of architecture again, it must be founded on a love for the city. No planting down of a few costly buildings, ruling some straight streets, provision of fountains or setting up of stone, or bronze dolls is enough without the enthusiasm for corporate life and common ceremonial. Every noble city has a crystallization of the contentment, pride and order of the community.

W.R. Lethaby

Lewis Mumford Prize

Every two years the Society for American City and Regional Planning History (SACRPH) grants the Lewis Mumford Prize to the best book in American city and regional history. Winners are chosen based on originality, depth of research, quality of writing, and the degree to which the book contributes to a greater understanding of the rich history of American city or regional planning. The presentation of a plaque and $500 cash prize is made at the Society's biennial conference.

For additional information, visit the Society on the Internet at *www.urban.uiuc.edu/sacrph/index.html.*

1991-93
The New York Approach: Robert Moses, Urban Liberals, and Redevelopment of the Inner City by Joel Schwartz (Ohio State University Press)

1993-95
The City of Collective Memory: Its Historical Imagery and Architectural Entertainments by M. Christine Boyer (MIT Press)

1995-97
City Center to Regional Mall: Architecture, the Automobile, and Retailing in Los Angeles, 1920-1950 by Richard Longstreth (MIT Press)

1997-99
Boston's Changeful Times: Origins of Preservation and Planning in America by Michael Holleran (Johns Hopkins)

Honorable Mention:
Remaking Chicago: The Political Origins of Urban Industrial Change by Joel Rast (Northern Illinois University Press)

Source: Society for American City and Regional Planning History

A city should be built to give its inhabitants security and happiness.

Aristotle

The façade of the Robertson Branch Library is enlivened by a bisecting preweathered copper "ship's hull" (above). On the inside, the ship's hull houses the stairs (left) that lead to the reading room, circulation, and reference desk while the ground floor contains parking, administrative offices, and a community room. Photos: Tom Bonner.

Library Buildings Awards

The American Institute of Architects (AIA) and the American Library Association (ALA) present the biennial Library Buildings Awards to encourage excellence in the architectural design and planning of libraries. Architects licensed in the United States are eligible to enter any public or private library project from around the world, whether a renovation, addition, conversion, interior project or new construction. Juries consist of three architects and three librarians with extensive library building experience.

Additional information is available on the American Library Association Web site at *www.ala.org/lama/awards/librarybld* or by contacting the AIA Awards Office at (202) 626-7586.

2001 Winners:

Denver Public Library
Denver, CO
Michael Graves & Associates
Klipp Colussy Jenks DuBois Architects, associate architect

Friend Memorial Library
Brooklin, ME
Elliot & Elliot Architecture

Multnomah County Central Library
Portland, OR
Fletcher Farr Ayotte, PC
Hardy Holzman Pfeiffer Associates, associate architect

North Mason Timberland Library
Belfair, WA
Carlson Architects, P.S.

Rhys Carpenter Library, Bryn Mawr College
Bryn Mawr, PA
Helfand Myerberg Guggenheimer

Robertson Branch Library
Los Angeles, CA
Steven Ehrlich Architects

University of New Hampshire Dimond Library
Durham, NH
Graham Gund Architects

Woodstock Branch Library
Portland, OR
Thomas Hacker and Associates

2001 Jury:

Ted Flato (Chair)
Deborah Berke
James C. Childress
Anders Dahlgren
Barbara Norland
Rich Rosenthal

Source: The American Institute of Architects

Did you know...

The Library Tower (Pei Cobb Freed & Partners, 1990) in Los Angeles, CA, is the tallest building ever constructed in a major earthquake zone; it is also the tallest building west of the Mississippi River.

Lighting Design Awards

Presented for lighting installations that couple aesthetic achievement with technical expertise, the Lighting Design Awards are bestowed annually by the International Association of Lighting Designers (IALD) and *Architectural Lighting* magazine. The Awards emphasize design with attention to energy usage, economics, and sustainable design. Projects are judged individually, not in competition with each other. Awards of Excellence and Merit are awarded at the jury's discretion.

For additional information, visit the IALD on the Internet at *www.iald.org.*

2001 Award of Excellence:
American Museum of Natural History Rose
    Center for Earth and Space
New York, NY
Fisher Marantz Stone, Inc

2001 Awards of Merit:
Alexander Graham Bell House British Telecom
    Regional Headquarters
Edinburgh, Scotland, UK
Jonathan Speirs and Associates Ltd.

Fußgängerbrücke (Pedestrian Bridge)
Innenhafen Duisburg, Nordrhein Westfalen,
    Germany
Architektur Licht Bühne

Herz Jesu Kirche (Heart of Jesus Church)
Munich, Germany
George Sexton Associates

Millennium Dome
London, England, UK
Speirs and Major Ltd.

Module VII Chiller Plant, University of
    Pennsylvania
Philadelphia, PA
Lam Partners

Raleigh/Durham Airport Parking Structure
Raleigh, NC
Cline Bettridge Bernstein Lighting Design, Inc.

San Francisco City Hall
San Francisco, CA
Horton Lees Brogden Lighting Design

2001 Special Citation:
The New 42nd Street Studio Building – Façade
    Lighting
New York, NY
Vortex Lighting

2001 Jury:
David Bird, Vision Design Studio
Belmont Freeman, Belmont Freeman
    Architects
Patrick Gallegos, Gallegos Lighting Design in
    Northridge
Stefan Graf, Fantasee Lighting
Scott Himmel, Scott Himmel, Architect
Chinatsu Kaneko, Perkins & Will
Maurizio Rossi, Maurizio Rossi Lighting
    Design
Babu Shankar, Integrated Lighting Design

Source: International Association of Lighting Designers

American Museum of Natural History, Rose
Center for Earth and Space. Photo: Dennis
Finnin/American Museum of Natural History.

Mies van der Rohe Award for European Architecture

Established in 1987 by the European Commission, the European Parliament, and the Mies van der Rohe Foundation, the Mies van der Rohe Award for European Architecture seeks to highlight notable projects within the context of contemporary European architecture. Works by European architects which are constructed in the member states of the European Union and associated European states within the two years following the granting of the previous award are eligible for the program. Winning projects are chosen for their innovative character and excellence in design and execution by an international panel of experts in the field of architecture and architectural criticism. The Award consists of a 50,000 Euro cash prize and a sculpture by Xavier Corberó, a design inspired by the Mies van der Rohe Pavilion.

For more information, visit the Mies van der Rohe Foundation's Web site at *www.miesbcn.com*.

1988
> Borges e Irmão Bank
> Vila do Conde, Portugal
> Alvaro Siza Vieira

1990
> New Terminal Development
> Stansted Airport, London, England
> Norman Foster & Partners

1992
> Municipal Sports Stadium
> Badalona, Barcelona, Spain
> Esteve Bonell and Francesc Rius

1994
> Waterloo International Station
> London, England
> Nicholas Grimshaw & Partners

1996
> Bibliotèque Nationale de France
> Paris, France
> Dominique Perrault

1999
> Art Museum in Bregenz
> Bregenz, Austria
> Peter Zumthor

2001
> Kursaal Congress Centre
> San Sebastian, Spain
> Rafael Moneo

Emerging Architect Special Mention:
> Kaufmann Holz Distribution Centre
> Bobingen, Germany
> Florian Nagler, Florian Nagler Architekt

Source: Mies van der Rohe Foundation

Good design is not about style, but about composing with the right materials for the right function in a conceptually interesting way.

Paola Antonelli

Mies van der Rohe Award for Latin American Architecture

A sister award to the Mies van der Rohe Award for European Architecture, this biennial award recognizes projects in Mexico, Central America, South America, Cuba, and the Dominican Republic. The Foundation created the award in 1987 to bring greater attention to contemporary Latin American architecture by honoring works of considerable conceptual, aesthetic, technical, and construction solutions. In order to be eligible, projects must have been completed within the previous two years prior to the granting of the Award and be located in a member country. The Award itself is identical to that of the European award, a cash prize of 50,000 Euros and a sculpture by Xavier Corberó inspired by the pillars of the Mies van der Rohe Pavilion in Barcelona.

For more information, visit the Mies van der Rohe Foundation's Web site at *www.miesbcn.com.*

1998
    Televisa Headquarters
    Mexico City
    TEN Arquitectos

2000
    São Paulo State Picture Library Building,
        restoration and adaptation
    São Paulo, Brazil
    Paulo A. Mendes da Rocha Arquitetos
        Associados

Source: Mies van der Rohe Foundation

Modernization Awards

Buildings magazine annually honors excellence in building renovation with its Modernization Awards. Winning projects are selected on the basis of aesthetics, functionality, originality, use of materials, sensitivity to site, program and considerations of life safety, among other criteria. *Buildings* publishes winning projects in full color upon their announcement.

An entry form and additional information is available at *www.buildings.com/awards.*

2001 Grand Prize Winner:
  Lafayette Corporate Center
  Boston, MA
  ADD Inc.

2001 Winners:
  Gene Snyder U.S. Courthouse and
    Customhouse
  Louisville, KY
  Luckett and Farley Inc.

  Caxton Block Building
  Moline, IL
  Shive-Hattery Inc.

City Hall Annex Marriott Courtyard Hotel
Philadelphia, PA
Burt Hill Kosar Rittelmann Associates

U.S. Courthouse
Augusta, GA
U.S. General Services Administration

Riverside Center
Newton, MA
Elkus/Manfredi Architects Ltd.

Source: Buildings *magazine*

National Building Museum Honor Award

Since 1986 the National Building Museum has honored individuals and organizations that have made an exceptional contribution to America's built history. The award is presented each year at an elegant gala held in the Museum's Great Hall, which has often been the site of the Presidential Inaugural Ball since 1885.

For more information, contact the National Building Museum at (202) 272-2448 or visit their Web site at *www.nbm.org*.

1986 J. Irwin Miller	1997 Morris Cafritz, Charles E. Smith, Charles A. Horsky and Oliver T. Carr Jr.
1988 James W. Rouse	
1989 Senator Daniel Patrick Moynihan	1998 Riley P. Bechtel and Stephen D. Bechtel Jr. of the Bechtel Group
1990 IBM	
1991 The Rockefeller Family	1999 Harold and Terry McGraw and The McGraw-Hill Companies
1992 The Civic Leadership of Greater Pittsburgh	
1993 J. Carter Brown	2000 Gerald D. Hines
1994 James A. Johnson and Fannie Mae	2001 Michael D. Eisner and The Walt Disney Company
1995 Lady Bird Johnson	
1996 Cindy and Jay Pritzker	

Source: National Building Museum

National Design Awards

Each year the Smithsonian Institution's Cooper-Hewitt, National Design Museum honors American designers with its National Design Awards. Presented in six categories for excellence, innovation, and enhancement of the quality of life, awards are bestowed for a body of work and not a specific project. Award categories are: Lifetime Achievement; Corporate Achievement; Communications Design; Environment Design, and Product Design, plus a special honor for American Originals. Journalists, designers, filmmakers, architects, authors and other professionals are invited by the Smithsonian Institution to make nominations for the awards.

Complete information is available from the Award's Web site, *www.si.edu/ ndm/nda/*.

2000 Winners:
Lifetime Achievement
   Frank Gehry

Corporate Achievement
   Apple Computers

American Originals
   Morris Lapidus
   John Hejduk

Environment Design
   Lawrence Halprin

Product Design
   Paul MacCready

Communications Design
   Ralph Appelbaum

Jury:
   David M. Kelley, IDEO
   Daniel Libeskind, architect
   William Mitchell, MIT
   Martha Stewart, media personality
   Bill Stumpf, Stumpf Webber & Associates, Inc.
   Lorraine Wild, designer and educator

Source: Smithsonian Institution, Cooper-Hewitt, National Design Museum

My whole concept of life is to make it more unusual, more interesting, more warm.

Morris Lapidus

National Design-Build Awards

Every year the Design-Build Institute of America (DBIA) honors exemplary design-build projects through its National Design-Build Awards. Through this award program, the DBIA's goal is to promote the design-build process as an effective project delivery method and recognize outstanding design-build projects. Submitted entries in each category are evaluated on their overall success in fulfilling the owner/user's project goals. The projects' achievement within the design-build approach of efficiency, performance, architecture, risk management, and problem solving and the design team's use of innovation to add value are also considerations. Projects completed within the last five years that met the criteria of a qualified design-build contract are eligible. When merited, the jury may choose to grant the Design-Build Excellence Award to those projects which were outstanding but fell short of the National Design-Build Award.

For additional information, visit DBIA's Web site at *www.dbia.org* or contact them at (202)682-0110.

2000 Recipients:

Best Private Project Over $15 million

Old Navy Pacific Distribution Center, Fresno, CA
James N. Gray Company (design-builder/designer/eng./const.)

Honor Award:

Radisson Hotel, Brisbane, CA
Webcor Builders (design-builder/const.)
Pahl, Pahl, Pahl Architects (designer)
Culp & Tanner (eng.)

Best Private Project Under $15 million

Sauer-Danfoss Manufacturing Facility, Lawrence, KS
Story Design Ltd. (design-builder/ designer/ const.)
Rietz Consultants Ltd. (structural eng.)
KJWW Engineering Consultants, PC (mechanical/electrical eng.)

Raytheon Missile Systems Conference Center, Tucson, AZ
Sundt Construction, Inc. (design-builder/ const.)
SmithGroup (designer)

Honor Award:

Indiana Automotive Fasteners Manufacturing Plant/Office Headquarters, Greenfield, IN
Kajima Construction Services, Inc. (design-builder/designer/const.)
Heapy Engineering (eng.)

Northwest Airlines DC10 Maintenance Hanger, Detroit Metropolitan Wayne County Airport, Romulus, MI
Walbridge Aldinger Company (design-builder/const.)
Farrand & Associates Inc. Architects (designer)
Ruby & Associates PC (eng.)

National Design-Build Awards (Con't)

Best Public Project Over $15 million

St. Charles County Family Arena, St. Charles, MO
J.S. Alberici Construction Company, Inc. (design-builder/const.)
Hastings & Chivetta Architects, Inc. (architect)
Acoustical Design Group (acoustical eng.)
Bay Engineering (civil eng.)
Alper Ladd, Inc. (structural eng.)
McGrath, Inc. (mechanical eng.)
Shannon & Wilson (geotechnical eng.)
Wiegmann & Associates (HVAC D/B eng.)
Murphy Company (plumbing eng.)
Sachs Electric (electrical eng.)

San Francisco Civic Center Complex, San Francisco, CA
HSH Design/Build Inc. (design-builder)
Skidmore, Owings & Merrill (designer)
Clark Construction Group, Inc. (const.)
Hines (development manager)

Honor Award:

Linwood and Howard Avenue Ozonation Facilities, Milwaukee, WI
Black & Veatch Construction Inc./J.S. Alberici Construction Company Joint Venture (design-builder)
HNTB Corporation (designer)
Black & Veatch LLP (eng.)
J.S. Alberici Construction Co. Inc. (const.)

Special Recognition for Sustainable Design-Build:

BEQ-MCPON Plackett Manor and Naval Hospital-Great Lakes Naval Station, Great Lakes, IL
James McHugh Construction Co. (design-builder/const.)
Wight & Co. (designer)
SmithGroup, Inc. (eng.)

Best Public Project Under $15 million

McCoy Baseball Stadium Renovation/Expansion, Pawtucket, RI
O. Ahlborg & Sons/Heery International Joint Venture (design-builder/const.)
Heery International (designer/structural eng.)
Robinson Green Beretta (civil eng.)
Maguire Group (mechanical/electrical/plumbing eng.)
C.A. Pretzer Associates (structural forensics/berm structures)

New Heights Elementary School, East Grand Forks, MN
M.A. Mortenson Company (design-builder/const.)
DLR Group (designer/eng.)

Honor Award:

Aircraft Paint Facility - Tinker Air Force Base, Oklahoma City, OK
The Austin Company (design-builder/designer/eng./const.)

Alameda County Recorder's Building, Oakland, CA
Hensel Phelps Construction Company (design-builder/const.)
Kaplan McLaughlin Diaz (designer)
Gayle Manufacturing Co. (structural eng.)
Critchfield Mechanical (mechanical eng.)
Sasco Electrical (electrical eng.)

Rehabilitation/Renovation/Restoration:

Jackson Hall Remodel - University of Minnesota, Minneapolis, MN
M.A. Mortenson Company (design-builder/const.)
Architectural Alliance (designer)
Ericksen Roed & Associates (structural eng.)
Metropolitan Mechanical Contractors, Inc./Dunham & Associates (mech. eng.)
Elliott Contracting Corporation/Dunham & Associates (electrical eng.)

National Design-Build Awards (Con't)

Excellence Award:
Outrigger Waikoloa Beach Resort Renovation,
Waikoloa, HI
Charles Pankow Builders Ltd. (design-
builder/const.)
Architects Hawaii, Ltd. (designer)
Robert Englekirk Consulting Structural
Engineers (structural eng.)
Lincolne Scott & Kohloss (mechanical eng.)
Moss Engineering (electrical eng.)

Honor Award:
Tolson Youth Activities Ctr., Fort Bragg, NC
Beers/Davidson and Jones Group (design-
builder/const.)
Williams-Russell & Johnson Inc. (arch./eng.)

Best Civil Project Over $15 million
Route 133, Section 1A-Highstown Bypass, East
Windsor Township, NJ
Schiavone Construction Company, Inc. (design-
builder/const.)
Goodkind & O'Dea Inc. (designer/eng.)

B&O Capacity Improvement Project, East Gary,
IN to Greenwich, OH
Sverdrup Civil, Inc. (design-builder/
designer/eng./const.)

Best Civil Project Under $15 million
Aqueduct Improvement Proj., Cranston, RI
CDM Engineers and Constructors, Inc.
(design-builder)
Camp Dresser & McKee Inc. (design/eng.)
RD Installations Inc./Fyfe Inc./Structural
Preservations Systems, Inc. (const.)

Best Industrial/Process Project Over $25 million
Amtrak Acela Maintenance Facilities, Ivy City
Yard, Washington, DC; Southhampton Yard,
Boston, MA; Sunnyside Yard, Queens, NY
STV Construction Services (design-
builder/designer/eng.)
Slattery Skanska (const.)

Honor Award:
Oxford Automotriz de Mexico
Stamping/Assembly Facility, Ramos Arizpe,
Coahuila, Mexico
Kitchell S.A. de C.V./Kitchell Constructors Inc.
of Arizona (design-builder)
SmithGroup, Inc. (designer/eng.)
Kitchell S.A. de C.V. (const.)

Best Industrial/Process Project Under $25 million
Power and Desalinization Plant, Ascension
Island, UK
Caddell Construction Company, Inc. (design-
builder/const.)
Southern Division, Naval Facilities Engineering
Command, U.S. Navy (designer)
Robert and Company (eng.)

Excellence Award:
Knapheide Mfg. Facility, Quincy, IL
The Korte Company (design-builder/ const.)
Korte Design/Christner, Inc. (designer)
Ibrahim Engineering (eng.)

Best Project Under $5 million
Peoria Production Shop
Manufacturing/Assembly Facility, Peoria, IL
River City Construction, LLC (design-
builder/const.)
River City Design Group, LLC (designer)
Brown Engineers, Inc. (structural eng.)
Austin Engineering (civil eng.)

Honor Award:
Superior Consultant's Microsoft Solutions
Center, Alpharetta, GA
Heery International, Inc. (design-
builder/designer/eng./const.)
The Lauck Group (design consultant)

Source: Design-Build Institute of America

National Historic Planning Landmarks

Every year the American Institute of Certified Planners (AICP), the American Planning Association's (APA) professional and educational arm, grants National Historic Planning Landmark status to up to three historically significant projects to the planning profession that are at least 25 years old. In addition, projects must have initiated a new direction in planning, made a significant contribution to the community, and be available for public use and viewing.

For additional information about National Historic Planning Landmarks, contact the AICP at (202) 872-0611 or visit them on the Web at *www.planning.org.*

Arizona
  The Salt River Project (1911)

California
  Bay Conservation and Development
    Commission and Creation of the San
    Francisco Bay Plan (1965-69)
  East Bay Regional Park District, San Francisco
    (1934)
  Los Angeles Co. "Master Plan of Highways"
    (1940) and "Freeways for the Region" (1943)
  Napa County Agricultural Preserve (1968)
  Petaluma Plan (1971-72)
  San Francisco Zoning Ordinance (1867)

Colonial America
  The Laws of the Indies (1573; 1681)

Colorado
  Speer Boulevard, Denver

Connecticut
  The Nine Square Plan of New Haven (1638)

District of Columbia
  Euclid v. Ambler, US Supreme Court (1926)
  First National Conference on City Planning (1909)
  The Improvement of the Park System of the
    District of Columbia (The McMillian Plan)
    (1902)

  National Resources Planning Board (1933-43)
  Plan of Washington, DC (1791)

Georgia
  Plan of Savannah (1733)
Hawaii
  Hawaii's State Land Use Law (1961)

Illinois
  "Local Planning Administration" (1941)
  Merriam Center, Chicago (1930+)
  Plan of Chicago (1909)
  Plan of Park Forest (1948)
  Plan of Riverside (1869)

Indiana
  New Harmony (1814-27)

Kentucky
  Lexington Urban Service Area (1958)

Louisiana
  Plan of the Vieux Carre, New Orleans (1721)

Maryland
  Columbia (1967+)
  Greenbelt (A Greenbelt Town, 1935+)
  Plan of Annapolis (1695)

National Historic Planning Landmarks (Con't)

Massachusetts
"Emerald Necklace" Parks, Boston (1875+)
Founding of the Harvard University Graduate
Planning Program (1929)

Michigan
Kalamazoo Mall (1956)

Missouri
Country Club Plaza, Kansas City (1922)
Founding of the American City Planning
Institute (ACPI, 1917)
Kansas City Parks Plan (1893)

Montana
Yellowstone National Park (1872)

New Jersey
"Radburn" at Fair Lawn (1928-29)
Society for the Establishment of Useful
Manufactures Plan for Paterson (1791-92)
Southern Burlington County (NJ) NAACP v
Township of Mount Laurel (1975)
Yorkship Village, Camden (1918)

New York
Bronx River Parkway and the Westchester
County Parkway System (1907+)
Central Park, New York City (1857)
First Houses, New York City (1935-36)
Forest Hills Gardens (1911+)
Founding of the American City Planning
Institute (ACPI, 1917)
Grand Central Terminal, New York City (1903-
13)
Long Island Parkways (1885) and Parks (1920s)
New York City Zoning Code (1916)
New York State Adirondack Preserve & Park
New York State Commission of Housing and
Regional Planning (1923-26)
Regional Plan of New York & Environs (1929)
Second Regional Plan of the Regional Plan
Association of New York (1968)
Sunnyside Gardens (1924+)

University Settlement House and the
Settlement House Movement (1886)

North Carolina
Blue Ridge Parkway (1935+)

Ohio
Cincinnati Plan of 1925
Cleveland Group Plan (1903)
Founding of Ohio Planning Conference (1919)
Greenhills (A Greenbelt Town, 1935+)
The Plan of Mariemont (1922)
The Miami Valley Region's Fair Share Housing
Plan of 1970

Oregon
Oregon's Statewide Program for Land Use
(1973)

Pennsylvania
Plan of Philadelphia (1683)

Rhode Island
College Hill Demonstration of Historic
Renewal, Providence (1959)

South Carolina
First American Historic District, Charleston
(1931)

Tennessee
Plan of Metro Government, Nashville/Davidson
County (1956)
Tennessee Valley Authority (1933+)
Town of Norris (1933)

Texas
"A Greater Fort Worth Tomorrow" (1956)
Paseo del Rio, San Antonio (1939-41)

Utah
Plat of the City of Zion (1833)

National Historic Planning Landmarks (Con't)

Virginia
   Blue Ridge Parkway (1935+)
   Jeffersonian Precinct, University of Virginia
      (1817)
   Monument Avenue Historic District, Richmond
      (1888)
   Roanoke Plans (1907; 1928)

West Virginia
   Appalachian Trail (1921+)

Wisconsin
   Greendale (A Greenbelt Town, 1935+)
   Wisconsin Planning Enabling Act (1909)

Wyoming
   Yellowstone National Park (1872)

Source: American Institute of Certified Planners

Did you know...

The Cincinnati Plan of 1925 was the first comprehensive plan in American to incorporate public and private land uses, transportation, and public facilities in a long-term strategy for community development.

National Historic Planning Pioneers

Every year the American Institute of Certified Planners (AICP), the American Planning Association's (APA) professional and educational arm, designates up to three National Historic Planning Pioneers for their significant contributions and innovations to American planning. Recipients have impacted planning practice, education, and/or theory on a national scale with long-term beneficial results. Their contributions must have occurred no less than 25 years ago.

For additional information about National Planning Pioneers, contact the American Institute of Certified Planners at (202) 872-0611 or visit them on the Web at *www.planning.org*.

Charles Abrams
Frederick J. Adams
Thomas Adams
Edmund N. Bacon
Harland Bartholomew
Edward M. Bassett
Catherine (Wurster) Bauer
Edward H. Bennett
Alfred Bettman
Walter H. Blucher
Ernest John Bohn
Daniel Hudson Burnham
F. Stuart Chapin Jr.
Charles H. Cheney
Paul Davidoff
Frederic Adrian Delano
Earle S. Draper
Simon Eisner
Carl Feiss
George Burdett Ford
Paul Goodman
Percival Goodman
Aelred Joseph Gray
Frederick Gutheim
S. Herbert Hare
Sid J. Hare
Elisabeth Herlihy
John Tasker Howard
Henry Vincent Hubbard

Theodora Kimball Hubbard
Harlean James
T.J. Kent Jr.
George Edward Kessler
Pierre Charles L'Enfant
Kevin Lynch
Benton MacKaye
Ian Lennox McHarg
Albert Mayer
Harold V. Miller
Corwin R. Mocine
Arthur Ernest Morgan
Robert Moses
Lewis Mumford
Jesse Clyde Nichols
John Nolen Sr.
Charles Dyer Norton
Charles McKim Norton
Frederick Law Olmsted Sr.
Frederick Law Olmsted Jr.
"Outdoor Circle, The"
Harvey S. Perloff
Clarence Arthur Perry
Planners for Equal Opportunity, 1964-1974
John Reps
Jacob August Riis
Charles Mulford Robinson
James W. Rouse
Charlotte Rumbold

National Historic Planning Pioneers (Con't)

Mel Scott
Ladislas Segoe
Flavel Shurtleff
Mary K. Simkhovitch
William E. Spangle
Clarence S. Stein
Telesis, 1939-1953
Rexford Guy Tugwell
Lawrence T. Veiller
Francis Violich
Charles Henry Wacker
Lillian Wald
Gordon Whitnall
Donald Wolbrink
Edith Elmer Wood
Henry Wright

Source: American Institute of Certified Planners

National Medal of Arts

The National Medal of Arts was established by Congress in 1984 to honor individuals and organizations "who in the President's judgement are deserving of special recognition by reason of their outstanding contributions to the excellence, growth, support and availability of the arts in the United States." All categories of the arts are represented; although awards are not always granted in each category every year. No more than 12 medals may be awarded per year. Individuals and organizations nationwide may make nominations to the National Endowment for the Arts (NEA). The National Council on the Arts reviews these nominations and makes recommendations to the President of the United States for final selection of the annual medal. The following individuals received this honor for their work in the design profession.

Visit the NEA's Web site at *www.arts.endow.gov* for additional information or nomination forms.

1988 I.M. Pei - Architect
1989 Leopold Adler - Preservationist
1990 Ian McHarg - Landscape Architect
1991 Pietro Belluschi - Architect
1992 Robert Venturi and Denise Scott Brown - Architects
1995 James Ingo Freed - Architect
1997 Daniel Urban Kiley - Landscape Architect
1998 Frank Gehry - Architect
1999 Michael Graves - Architect

Source: National Endowment for the Arts

P/A Awards

The P/A Awards were first handed out in 1954 by *Progressive Architecture* magazine and are now presented annually by *Architecture* magazine. The awards are designed to "recognize design excellence in unbuilt projects." A jury of designers and architects selects the winners.

For more information, call (212) 536-6221 or visit the magazine on the Internet at *www.architecturemag.com*.

2001 P/A Award Winners:

Changi International Airport Terminal 3
Singapore
Skidmore, Owings & Merrill

Detroit Community Pavilion
Detroit, Michigan
Mark Anderson and Andrew Zago

Kentucky Heritage Center
Park City, Kentucky
Gil Rampy Architect

Casa Familiar: Living Rooms at the Border
San Ysidro, California
Estudio Teddy Cruz

Raybould House and Garden
Fairfield County, Connecticut
Kolatan MacDonald Studio

Winter Gardens
Charlevoix, Quebec, Canada
Pierre Thibault, Architect

Glass House @ 2°
Houston, Texas
Michael Bell Architecture

Crosby Hall Accessible Route
State University of New York at Buffalo, New York
Eric Sutherland and Kent Kleinman

Cable Natural History Museum
Cable, Wisconsin
Vincent James Associates with Salmela Architect

2001 P/A Award Jury:
Deborah Berke, Deborah Berke, Architect PC
Brad Cloepfil, Allied Works Architects
Nathalie de Vries, MVRDV
Hani Rashid, Asymptote
Mark Robbins, National Endowment for the Arts

Source: Architecture *magazine*

Philip Johnson Award

With its Philip Johnson Award, the Society of Architectural Historians (SAH) annually recognizes an outstanding architectural exhibition catalogue. In order to be eligible for this annual recognition, the catalogue must have been published within the preceding two years.

For more information contact the SAH at (312) 573-1365 or visit their Web site at *www.sah.org*.

1990
Los Angeles Blueprints for Modern Living: History and Legacy of the Case Study Houses by Elizabeth A.T. Smith (The Museum of Contemporary Art and MIT Press)

1991
Architecture and Its Image: Four Centuries of Architectural Representation, Works from the Collection of the Canadian Centre for Architecture by Eve Blau and Edward Kaufman, eds. (The Canadian Centre for Architecture and MIT Press)

1992
no award granted

1993
The Making of Virginia Architecture by Charles Brownell (Virginia Museum of Fine Arts and the University Press of Virginia)

Louis Kahn: In the Realm of Architecture by David Brownlee (The Museum of Contemporary Art and Rizzoli International)

1994
Chicago Architecture and Design 1923-1993: Reconfiguration of an American Metropolis by John Zukowsky (Prestel and Art Institute of Chicago)

1995
The Palladian Revival: Lord Burlington, His Villa and Garden in Chiswick by John Harris (Yale University Press)

1996
The Perspective of Anglo-American Architecture by James F. O'Gorman (The Athenaeum of Philadelphia)

An Everyday Modernism: The Houses of William Wurster by Marc Treib (San Francisco Museum of Modern Art and the University of California Press)

1997
Sacred Realm: The Emergence of the Synagogue in the Ancient World by Steven Fine (Yeshiva University Museum and Oxford University Press)

1998
Building for Air Travel: Architecture and Design for Commercial Aviation by John Zukowsky (Art Institute of Chicago and Prestel)

1999
The Work of Charles and Ray Eames: a Legacy of Invention by Donald Albrecht (The Library of Congress, Vitra Design Museum, and Abrams Publishing)

2000
E.W. Godwin: Aesthetic Movement Architect and Designer by Susan Weber Soros (Yale University Press)

2001
Mapping Boston by Alex Krieger and David Cobb, editors (MIT Press)

Source: Society of Architectural Historians

Praemium Imperiale

The Praemium Imperiale is awarded by the Japan Art Association, Japan's premier cultural institution, for lifetime achievement in the fields of painting, sculpture, music, architecture, and theater/film. The following individuals received this honor for architecture which includes a commemorative medal and a 15,000,000 yen ($125,000 approx.) honorarium.

For more information visit the Japan Art Association's Web site at *www.praemiumimperiale.org.*

1989 I. M. Pei (United States)
1990 James Stirling (U.K.)
1991 Gae Aulenti (Italy)
1992 Frank Gehry (United States)
1993 Kenzo Tange (Japan)
1994 Charles Correa (India)
1995 Renzo Piano (Italy)
1996 Tadao Ando (Japan)
1997 Richard Meier (United States)
1998 Alvaro Siza (Portugal)
1999 Fumihiko Maki (Japan)
2000 Richard Rogers (U.K.)
2001 Jean Nouvel (France)

Source: Japan Art Association

Did you know...

In 2001, Renzo Piano was the first architect to win the $50,000 Wexner Prize, given annually by the Wexner Center at Ohio State University to a contemporary artist "who has been consistently original, influential, and challenging to convention."

Presidential Design Awards

Established by President Ronald Reagan in 1983, the Presidential Design Awards recognize outstanding contributions to federal design by government agencies and employees and private designers in the categories of architecture, engineering, graphic design, historic preservation, interior design, landscape architecture, industrial & product design, and urban design & planning. The Presidential Design Awards are administered by the National Endowment for the Arts (NEA) and are presented every four years. Projects are judged based on their purpose, leadership, cost, aesthetics and performance.

For a detailed description of the winners from both award programs and photographs of the projects listed below, visit the NEA's Web site at *www.arts.endow.gov.*

2000 Presidential Awards for Design Excellence Recipients:

U.S. Census Bureau National Data Processing Center
Bowie, Maryland
General Services Administration, National Capital Region; Department of Commerce, U.S. Census Bureau; Davis Brody Bond; Tobey + Davis

U.S. Port of Entry
Calexico, California
General Services Administration, Pacific Rim Region; Dworsky Associates

Grand Central Terminal
New York, New York
Department of Transportation, Federal Transit Administration, Region 2; Metropolitan Transportation Authority; Metro-North Railroad; GCT Venture; Beyer Blinder Belle Architects & Planners LLP; Harry Weese & Associates; STV/Seelye Stevenson, Value & Knecht; Fisher Marantaz Renfro Stone, Inc.; The Rockwell Group

Interstate 70
Glenwood Canyon, Colorado
Department of Transportation, Federal Highway Administration, Colorado Division; Colorado Department of Transportation, Division of Highways; Gruen Associates; Nelson Haley Patterson and Quirk; DMJM Phillips Reister; Joseph Passonneau & Partners; Leigh Whitehead Associates; DeLeuw, Cather & Co.; Citizens Advisory Committee for Glenwood Canyon

Mars Pathfinder Mission
National Aeronautics and Space Administration, Office for Space Science for the Mars Pathfinder Mission and the Jet Propulsion Laboratory

Franklin Delano Roosevelt Memorial
Washington, D.C.
Department of the Interior, National Park Service, Denver Service Center, National Capital Region, and National Capital Parks-Central; Office of Lawrence Halprin; Leonard Baskin; Neil Estern; Robert Graham; Tom Hardy; George Segal; John Benson

Presidential Design Awards (Con't)

National Park Service Park Cultural Landscapes
    Program
Department of the Interior, National Park
    Service, Cultural Resource Stewardship and
    Partnerships

Westside MAX Light Rail
Portland, Oregon
Department of Transportation, Federal Transit
    Administration, Region 10; Tri-County
    Metropolitan Transportation District of
    Oregon; Zimmer, Gunsul, Frasca
    Partnership; Otak, Inc.; Parsons
    Brinckerhoff Quade & Douglas, Inc.; BRW,
    Inc.

The Mayors' Institute on City Design
National Endowment for the Arts, Design
    Program; Joseph P. Riley, Jr.; Jaquelin T.
    Robertson; Adele Chatfield-Taylor; Joan
    Abrahamson

Jury:
Vincent Scully, Yale University (Chair)
James Stewart Polshek, Polshek Partners
    Architects
David P. Billington, Princeton University
April Greiman, Greimanski Labs
George Hargreaves, Hargreaves Associates
David DeLong, University of Pennsylvania
Karal Ann Marling, University of Minnesota
Noel Mayo, The Ohio State University
Elizabeth Smith, The Museum of
    Contemporary Art
Adele Chatfield-Taylor, American Academy in
    Rome

*Source: U.S. General Services Administration and the National
Endowment for the Arts*

Pritzker Architecture Prize

In 1979 Jay and Cindy Pritzker, through the Hyatt Foundation, established the Pritzker Architecture Prize to inspire greater creativity among the architectural profession and to generate a heightened public awareness about architecture. Today it is revered as one of the highest honors in the field of architecture. The Prize is awarded each year to a living architect whose body of work represents a longstanding, significant contribution to the built environment. Nominations are accepted every January from any interested party. Architects from all nations are eligible. Laureates of the Pritzker Prize receive a $100,000 grant, citation certificate, and a bronze medallion.

For additional information, visit their Web site at *www.pritzkerprize.com*.

1979	Philip Johnson (United States)	1992	Alvaro Siza (Portugal)
1980	Luis Barragan (Mexico)	1993	Fumihiko Maki (Japan)
1981	James Stirling (U.K.)	1994	Christian de Portzamparc (France)
1982	Kevin Roche (United States)		
1983	Ieoh Ming Pei (United States)	1995	Tadao Ando (Japan)
1984	Richard Meier (United States)	1996	Rafael Moneo (Spain)
1985	Hans Hollein (Austria)	1997	Sverre Fehn (Norway)
1986	Gottfried Boehm (Germany)	1998	Renzo Piano (Italy)
1987	Kenzo Tange (Japan)	1999	Sir Norman Foster (U.K.)
1988	Gordon Bunshaft (United States)	2000	Rem Koolhaas (The Netherlands)
	Oscar Niemeyer (Brazil)	2001	Jacques Herzog and Pierre de Meuron (Switzerland)
1989	Frank O. Gehry (United States)		
1990	Aldo Rossi (Italy)		
1991	Robert Venturi (United States)		

Source: The Pritzker Architecture Prize

Küppersmühle Museum, Grothe Collection,
Duisburg, Germany, by Herzog & de
Meuron. Photo © Margherita Spiluttini.

Pulitzer Prize for Architectural Criticism

As one of the many lasting contributions he made to the field of journalism, Joseph Pulitzer established the Pulitzer Prize as an incentive to excellence in journalism, music, and letters. Over the years the scope of the awards has been expanded from its original 1917 configuration. Since 1970, the Pulitzer Prize Board has awarded a prize for distinguished journalistic criticism. In the past this category has included winners in the arts, culture, and literary fields. The following individuals received this honor for their work in architectural criticism.

Visit the Pulitzer Prize's Web site at *www.pulitzer.org* for a detailed history, chronology, and archive of past winners.

1970 Ada Louise Huxtable
     The New York Times
1979 Paul Gapp
     Chicago Tribune
1984 Paul Goldberger
     The New York Times

1990 Allan Temko
     San Francisco Chronicle
1996 Robert Campbell
     The Boston Globe
1999 Blair Kamin
     Chicago Tribune

Since 1980 the Pulitzer Prize Board has also acknowledged the two finalists in each category. The following individuals were finalists for their work in architectural criticism.

1981 Allan Temko
     San Francisco Chronicle
1983 Beth Dunlop
     The Miami Herald
1988 Allan Temko
     San Francisco Chronicle
1997 Herbert Muschamp
     The New York Times

Source: The Pulitzer Prize Board

Did you know...

Of the approximately 140 U.S. newspapers with a daily circulation of more than 75,000, only 13 have full-time architecture critics. The nation's largest newspaper, *USA Today*, has no architecture critic at all; nor does Houston, Detroit, Sacramento, or Kansas City.

Source: The Architecture Critic, *National Arts Journalism Program, Columbia University*

RAIA Gold Medal

The Gold Medal is the highest honor bestowed by the Royal Australian Institute of Architects (RAIA). It is presented annually to an architect to recognize a career of distinguished service achieved through a body of designs of high merit, advancement of the architecture profession, or an endowment of the profession in a distinguished manner. Gold medallists are nominated by their peers in confidence, and a jury comprised of past medallists and the national president make the final selection. Since 1970, the Gold Medallist traditionally delivers the AS Hook Address, named in memory of the early RAIA promoter Alfred Samuel Hook, that provides insight into the life, work, and principles of the Gold Medallist and the state of the profession at the time.

For additional information about the Gold Medal or to read past AS Hook Addresses, visit the RAIA on the Internet at *www.raia.com.au.*

1960	Emeritus Prof. Leslie Wilkinson	1983	Gilbert Ridgway Nicol and Ross Kingsley
1961	Louis Layborne-Smith		Chisholm
1962	Joseph Charles Fowell	1984	Philip Sutton Cox
1963	Sir Arthur Stephenson	1985	Prof. Richard Norman Johnson
1964	Cobden Parkes	1986	Richard Butterworth
1965	Sir Osborn McCutcheon	1987	Daryl Sanders Jackson
1966	William Rae Laurie	1988	Romaldo Giurgola
1967	William Purves Race Godfrey	1989	Robin Findlay Gibson
1968	Sir Roy Grounds	1990	Prof. Peter McIntyre
1969	Robin Boyd	1991	Donald Campbell Rupert Bailey
1970	Jack Hobbs McConnell	1992	Glenn Marcus Murcutt
1971	Frederick Bruce Lucas	1993	Kenneth Frank Woolley
1972	Edward Herbert Farmer	1994	Neville Quarry
1973	Jørn Utzon	1995	no award granted
1974	Raymond Berg	1996	Denton Corker Marshall
1975	Sydney Edward Ancher	1997	Roy Simpson
1976	Harry Seidler	1998	Gabriel Poole
1977	Ronald Andrew Gilling	1999	Richard Leplastrier
1978	Mervyn Henry Parry	2000	John Morphett
1979	Harold Bryce Mortlock	2001	Keith Cottier
1980	John Hamilton Andrews		
1981	Colin Frederick Madigan		*Source: Royal Australian Institute of Architects*
1982	Sir John Wallace Overall		

RAIC Gold Medal

The Royal Architectural Institute of Canada (RAIC) began its Gold Medal program in 1967 to recognize the achievements of architects or individuals related to the field and their contributions to Canada's built environment. As the RAIC Gold Medal is merit based, awards are not always granted yearly.

For more information, contact the RAIC at (613) 241-3600 or visit their Web site at *www.raic.org*.

1967	Mayor Jean Drapeau	1989	Raymond T. Affleck
1968	The Right Honorable Vincent Massey	1991	Phyllis Lambert
1970	Dr. Eric R. Arthur	1992	Doug Shadbolt
1970	The Late John A. Russell	1994	Barton Myers
1973	Professor Serge Chermayeff	1995	Moshe Safdie
1976	Dr. Constantinos Doxiadis	1997	Raymond Moriyama
1979	John C. Parkin	1998	Frank O. Gehry
1981	Jane Jacobs	1999	Douglas Cardinal
1982	Ralph Erskine	2001	Jack Diamond
1984	Arthur Erickson		
1985	John Bland		
1986	Ed Zeidler		

Source: The Royal Architectural Institute of Canada

Did you know...

On June 8, 2001, the 134th anniversary of Frank Lloyd Wright's birth, Arthur Erickson, along with Aaron Green, was awarded the first Honorary Master of Architecture from the Frank Lloyd Wright School of Architecture.

Reconstruction Project of the Year Awards

Each year *Building Design & Construction* magazine honors exceptional reno-vation, preservation and adaptive-reuse projects with its Reconstruction Project of the Year Awards. Stressing innovation and technical aspects of a project's design, construction, and development, the competition is open to any architectural, engineering, contracting or development firm. All com-mercial, industrial and institutional buildings are eligible. Feature articles on winning projects are published in the sponsoring magazine.

For additional information, contact *Building Design & Construction* magazine at (847) 390-2053 or *www.bdcmag.com.*

2001 Winners:

Allegheny County Jail
Pittsburgh, PA
A/E IKM Inc.

Coronado Theater
Rockford, IL
van Dijk Pace Westlake Architects

Fulton Building (Renaissance Pittsburgh Hotel)
Pittsburgh, PA
JG Johnson Architecture

Ritz-Carlton Hotel
Philadelphia, PA
The Hillier Group

Landmark Center
Boston, MA
Bruner/Cott & Associates

Blair & Buyers Residence Hall, Princeton
University
Princeton, NJ
Einhorn Yaffee Prescott

Source: Building Design & Construction *magazine*

Did you know...

The recent conversion of Pittsburgh's Fulton Building (Grosvenor Atterbury, 1906) into the lavish Renaissance Pittsburgh Hotel required 40 thousand tons of baking soda to restore the building's copper details, includ-ing the exterior of the rotunda dome, the rooftop, and the seven-story copper clad lightwell.

residential architect **Design Awards**

Established by *residential architect* magazine in 2000 to honor the best in American housing, the annual Residential Architect Design Awards recognize projects in eight categories, though judges may eliminate, add or combine categories—bestowing as many awards or none—as they see fit. Entries may be submitted in the following housing categories: Custom Home, 3,500 square feet or less; Custom Home, more than 3,500 square feet; Renovation; Multifamily Housing; Single Family Production Housing, detached; Single-Family Production Housing, attached; Affordable Housing; and On the Boards. In addition, a Best Residential Project of the Year is selected from among the winning built projects. The jury is comprised of top residential architects and the winning projects are published in *residential architect* magazine.

For photographs and descriptions of all the winning projects, visit *www. residentialarchitect.com* on the Internet.

2001 Best Residential Project of the Year:
  Poulsbo Place
  Poulsbo, WA
  Mithun

2001 Grand Prize Winners:
Custom Home, 3,500 Square Feet or Less
  Deppmeier Residence
  Laurel, MT
  A & E Architects, P.C.

Custom Home, More than 3,500 Square Feet
  Lakeside Residence
  Horseshoe Bay, TX
  Overland Partners

Renovation
  Fitch O'Rourke Residence
  Washington, D.C.
  Robert M. Gurney, Architect

Multifamily Housing
  Johnson Street Townhomes
  Portland, OR
  Mithun

Single-Family Production, Detached
  Poulsbo Place
  Poulsbo, WA
  Mithun

Single-Family Production, Attached
  No award given

Affordable Housing
  Eleventh Avenue Townhomes
  Escondido, CA
  Studio E Architects

2001 Merit Winners:
Custom/3,500 Square Feet or Less
  Tatum Residence
  Scientists Cliffs, MD
  Good Architecture

  Zachary House
  Zachary, LA
  Studio Atkinson

residential architect Design Awards (Con't)

Freeman Residence
Bristol, RI
Estes/Twombly Architects

Custom/More than 3,500 Square Feet
Palm Beach Residence
Palm Beach, FL
Ferguson Shamamian & Rattner Architects

Hoff Residence
Ann Arbor, MI
Damian Farrell Design Group

Renovation
Private Residence
Rural Minnesota
Meyer, Scherer & Rockcastle, Ltd.

Windyridge
Keyser, WV
Robert M. Gurney, Architect

Multifamily
Jake's Run Condominiums
Portland, OR
Fletcher Farr Ayotte

Swan's Marketplace
Oakland, CA
Pyatok Associates

Single-Family Production/Detached
Villa Alta
Fort Worth, TX
RPGA Design Group

Brenthaven
Brentwood, TN
Looney Ricks Kiss

Affordable
Gateway Commons
Emeryville/Oakland, CA
Pyatok Associates

On the Boards
Belle Creek
Commerce City, CO
Arlo Braun & Associates

Bethesda Theatre Residential
Bethesda, MD
Weihe Design Group

Casa Rizo
Miami, FL
Matue Carreno Rizo & Partners

2001 Judge's Award:
216 Alabama
Lawrence, KS
Graduate studio in architecture, University of
Kansas, Lawrence, KS

2001 Jury:
Stephen Muse, Muse Architects
Dennis Wedlick, Dennis Wedlick Architect LLC
Don Jacobs, JBZ Architecture + Planning
Ann Capron, McIntyre Batchelor & Capron
Architects
Sara O'Neil Manion, O'Neil & Manion
Architects

Source: residential architect *magazine*

Through efficient land use and innovative parking solutions, Mithun's site plan for Poulsbo Place, a single-family development outside of Seattle, allows for up to 14 detached units per acre. The homes are grouped around six parks that give residents access to common green space in lieu of large yards. Photo: www.dougscott.com.

Fletcher Farr Ayotte designed the five-unit Jake's Run Condominiums to be reminiscent of a 1910s Arts & Crafts home with a carriage house. With their use of traditional details and materials, the buildings blend seamlessly into the character of their surrounding historic neighborhood. Photo: John Dimaio.

RIBA Royal Gold Medal

Presented annually for distinction in architecture, the Royal Gold Medal is presented by Her Majesty the Queen on the advice of the Royal Institute of British Architects (RIBA). Since it was first granted by Queen Victoria in 1848, the RIBA confers the Royal Gold Medal annually.

For additional information, visit the RIBA on the Internet at *www.architecture.com*.

1848	Charles Robert Cockerell	1883	Fras. Cranmer Penrose
1849	Luigi Canine	1884	William Butterfield
1850	Sir Charles Barry	1885	H. Schliemann
1851	Thomas L. Donaldson	1886	Charles Garnier
1852	Leo von Klenze	1887	Ewan Christian
1853	Sir Robert Smirke	1888	Baron von Hansen
1854	Philip Hardwick	1889	Sir Charles T. Newton
1855	J. I. Hittorff	1890	John Gibson
1856	Sir William Tite	1891	Sir Arthur Blomfield
1857	Owen Jones	1892	Cesar Daly
1858	August Stuler	1893	Richard Morris Hunt
1859	Sir George Gilbert Scott	1894	Lord Leighton
1860	Sydney Smirke	1895	James Brooks
1861	J. B. Lesueur	1896	Sir Ernest George
1862	Rev. Robert Willis	1897	Dr. P.J.H.Cuypers
1863	Anthony Salvin	1898	George Aitchison
1864	E. Violett-le-Duc	1899	George Frederick Badley
1865	Sir James Pennethorne	1900	Rodolfo Amadeo Lancani
1866	Sir M. Digby Wyatt	1901	*(Not awarded due to the death of Queen Victoria)*
1867	Charles Texier		
1868	Sir Henery Layard	1902	Thomas Edward Collcutt
1869	C.R. Lepsius	1903	Charles F. McKim
1870	Benjamin Ferrey	1904	Auguste Choisy
1871	James Fergusson	1905	Sir Aston Webb
1872	Baron von Schmidt	1906	Sir L. Alma-Taderna
1873	Thomas Henry Wyatt	1907	John Belcher
1874	George Edmund Street	1908	Honore Daumet
1875	Edmund Sharpe	1909	Sir Arthur John Evans
1876	Joseph Louis Duc	1910	Sir Thomas Graham Jackson Bart
1877	Charles Barry	1911	Wilhelm Dorpfeld
1878	Alfred Waterhouse	1912	Basil Champneys
1879	Marquis de Vogue	1913	Sir Reginald Blomfield RA
1880	John L. Peerson	1914	Jean Louis Pascal
1881	George Godwin	1915	Frank Darling
1882	Baron von Ferstel	1916	Sir Robert Rowand Anderson

RIBA Royal Gold Medal (Con't)

1917	Henri Paul Nenot	1961	Lewis Mumford
1918	Ernest Newton RA	1962	Sven Gottfrid Markeluis
1919	Leonard Stokes	1963	The Lord Holford
1920	Charles Louis Girault	1964	E. Maxwell Fry
1921	Sir Edwin Landseer Lutyens	1965	Kenzo Tange
1922	Thomas Hastings	1966	Ove Arup
1923	Sir John James Burnet	1967	Sir Nikolaus Pevsner
1924	(Not awarded)	1968	Dr. Richard Buckminster Fuller
1925	Sir Giles Gilbert Scott	1969	Jack Antonio Coia
1926	Ragnar Östberg	1970	Sir Robert Mathew
1927	Sir Herbert Baker	1971	Hubert de Cronin Hastings
1928	Sir Guy Dawber	1972	Louis I. Kahn
1929	Victor Alexandre Frederic Laloux	1973	Sir Leslie Martin
1930	Sir Percy Scott Worthington	1974	Powell & Moya
1931	Sir Edwin Cooper	1975	Michael Scott
1932	Dr. Hendrik Petrus Berlage	1976	Sir John Summerson
1933	Sir Charles Reed Peers	1977	Sir Denys Lasdun
1934	Henry Vaughan Lanchester	1978	Jorn Utzon
1935	Willem Marinus Dudok	1979	The Office of Charles and Ray Eames
1936	Charles Henry Holden	1980	James Stirling
1937	Sir Raymond Unwin	1981	Sir Philip Dowson
1938	Ivar Tengborn	1982	Berthold Lubetkin
1939	Sir Percy Thomas	1983	Sir Norman Foster
1940	Charles Francis Annesley Voysey	1984	Charles Correa
1941	Frank Lloyd Wright	1985	Sir Richard Rogers
1942	William Curtis Green	1986	Arata Isozaki
1943	Sir Charles Herbert Reilly	1987	Ralph Erskine
1944	Sir Edward Maufe	1988	Richard Meier
1945	Victor Vesnin	1989	Renzo Piano
1946	Sir Patrick Abercrombie	1990	Aldo van Eyck
1947	Sir Albert Edward Richardson	1991	Coin Stansfield Smith
1948	Auguste Perret	1992	Peter Rice
1949	Sir Howard Robertson	1993	Giancarlo de Carlo
1950	Eliel Saarinen	1994	Michael and Patty Hopkins
1951	Emanuel Vincent Harris	1995	Colin Rowe
1952	George Grey Wornum	1996	Harry Seidler
1953	Le Corbusier (C.E. Jeanneret)	1997	Tadao Ando
1954	Sir Arthur George Staphenson	1998	Oscar Niemeyer
1955	John Murray Easton	1999	Barcelona, Spain
1956	Dr. Walter Adolf Georg Gropius	2000	Frank Gehry
1957	Hugo Alvar Henrik Aalto	2001	Jean Nouvel
1958	Robert Schofield Morris		
1959	Ludwig Mies van der Rohe		
1960	Pier Luigi Nervi		

Source: Royal Institute of British Architects

Rudy Bruner Award for Urban Excellence

The biennial Rudy Bruner Award for Urban Excellence is awarded to projects which approach urban problems with creative inclusion of often competing political, community, environmental, and formal considerations. Established in 1987, the Award recognizes one Gold Medal Winner and four Silver Medal winners. Any project which fosters urban excellence is eligible to apply. A multi-disciplinary Selection Committee performs an on-site evaluation of each finalist before final selections are made.

For photographs and project descriptions, visit the Bruner Foundation on the Internet at *www.brunerfoundation.org* or contact them at (617) 876-8404.

2001 Gold Medal Winner:
Village of Arts and Humanities
Philadelphia, Pennsylvania

2001 Silver Medal Winners:
Lower East Side Tenement Museum
New York, New York

New Jersey Performing Arts Center
Newark, New Jersey

South Platte River Greenway
Denver, Colorado

Swan's Marketplace
Oakland, California

2001 Selection Committee:
Craig Barton, RBGC Associates and University of Virginia
John Bok, Floey, Hoag, and Eliot, LLP
Rosanne Haggerty, Common Ground, HDFC Inc.
Allan B. Jacobs, University of California at Berkeley
Gail R. Shibley, U.S. Department of Labor
Wellington Webb, Mayor, Denver, CO

Source: The Bruner Foundation

Russel Wright Award

Established by Manitoga, The Russel Wright Center in Garrison, New York, the Russel Wright Award honors individuals who are working in the tradition of the mid-twentieth century design pioneer Russel Wright (1904-1976) to provide outstanding design to the general public. Russel Wright was a well-known home furnishings designer in the 1930s through the 1950s who throughout his career maintained the importance of making well-designed objects accessible to the public. The 75-acre wooded landscape he sculpted, Manitoga, is on the National Register of Historic Places and includes Dragon Rock, the home he designed that exemplifies his philosophy that architecture should enhance rather than dominate its surroundings.

For additional information about the Russel Wright Award, contact the Russel Wright Center, Manitoga, at (914) 424-3812 or *www.manitoga.org*.

2000   Michael Graves
2001   Lella and Massimo Vignelli
       William T. Golden
       Copper-Hewitt National Design Museum,
           Smithsonian Institution

Source: Manitoga, The Russel Wright Center

There is much more public awareness of design these days. Combined with the globalization of the market, this has created an increasing consciousness and awareness. Design is a by-product of education, and we are going to get better design and better products, along with better methods of distribution. Through the Internet and demand of the consumer, design will flow to the market freely and beautifully.

Massimo Vignelli

Lella and Massimo Vignelli.

SCUP/AIA-CAE Excellence in Planning Awards

The Society for College and University Planning (SCUP) and the American Institute of Architects' Committee on Architecture for Education (AIA-CAE) jointly present the annual Excellence in Planning Awards to honor planning and design that recognizes excellence in higher education environments. Not only the quality of the physical environment is considered, but also the comprehensiveness of the planning process. The award is open to any professional who has prepared plans for higher education institutions and the institutions themselves and is presented to all members of the project team.

Additional information can be found at the SCUP Web site, *www.scup.org*, or by calling (734) 998-6595.

2001 Winners:

Award of Excellence
Long Island University
Brooklyn, NY
Mitchell/Giurgola Architects

University of California
Irvine, CA
AC Martin Partners

University System of Georgia
Athens, GA
Sasaki Associates, Inc.

Honorable Mention
University of Utah
Salt Lake City, UT
Hanbury Evans Newill Vlattas & Company

Agnes Scott College
Decatur, GA
Wallace Roberts & Todd

Special Citation
Emmanuel College
Boston, MA
Good Clancy & Associates

Heritage Award
The Air Force Academy
Colorado Springs, CO
Skidmore Owings Merrill

2001 Jury:
Jeff Floyd, Sizemore Floyd Architects (Chair)
John Castellana, TMP Associates
Fred Mayer, University of Michigan
Bob Simha, Cambridge, MA
Pam Loeffelman, Hardy Holzman Pfeiffer
    Associates
Joe Szutz, Georgia Board of Regents
Cal Audrain, Art Institute of Chicago

Source: Society for College and University Planning and the American Institute of Architects' Committee on Architecture for Education

Architecture is in a sense a microcosm of the city.

Dennis Lasdun

SEGD Design Awards

The Society for Environmental Graphic Design's (SEGD) Design Awards recognize the best in environmental design – the planning, design, and specifying of graphic elements in the built and natural environment. Eligible projects include signage, wayfinding systems, mapping, exhibit design, themed environments, retail spaces, sports facilities and campus design. A jury of professionals reviews the entries to determine which projects best help to identify, direct, inform, interpret, and visually enhance our surroundings. Three levels of awards are granted – Honor Awards, Merit Awards, and the Juror Award. Winners are announced at SEGD's annual conference each spring and are honored in an annual exhibition and bi-annual publication.

For photographs and project description of all the winning entries, visit SEGD's Web site at *www.segd.org*.

2001 Honor Awards:

Miami Project Lobby Art Glass & Dedication Signage, University of Miami Lois Pope Neuroscience Research Institute
Miami, Florida
Christina Wallach + the Wallach Glass Studio Inc., Inc.

Brooklyn Academy of Music Signage
Brooklyn, New York
Pentagram Design

New Steuben Flagship Store
New York, New York
Ralph Appelbaum Associates

50 Years of TV and More
Sao Paulo, Brazil
Ralph Appelbaum Associates

LAX Gateway
Los Angeles, California
Selbert Perkins Design

Prince of Wales Hospital Memorial Garden
Sydney, Australia
Minale, Tattersfield, Bryce & Partners

The Point at Cal-Expo
Sacramento, California
Scenic Designs

Microsoft Museum
Redmond, Washington
Girvin, Inc.

Museum of Fine Arts, Houston, Audrey Jones Beck Building
Houston, Texas
Vignelli Associates

VEAG Media Façade
Berlin, Germany
PLEX GmbH

2001 Merit Awards:

Anaheim Resort Signage Program
Anaheim, California
CommArts, Inc.

Desert Lives Trail, Phoenix Zoo
Phoenix, Arizona
Thinking Caps

SEGD Design Awards (Con't)

Teknion Atlanta Showroom
Atlanta, Georgia
Vanderbyl Design

AmericaOne Identity
Vanderbyl Design

Good Grief!, Children's Museum of Manhattan
New York, New York
Children's Museum of Manhattan Exhibitions
    Department

Monsanto Incubator
St. Louis, Missouri
Hellmuth, Obata + Kassabaum

Plazas Las Americas
San Juan, Puerto Rico
RTKL Associates Inc.

Northgate North
Seattle, Washington
WPa, Inc.

McSquared Restaurant + Zeroo
San Francisco, California
Propp + Guerin

Clerc Trade Show Exhibit
Basel, Switzerland
Pentagram Design

Rose Center for Earth and Space
New York, New York
Ralph Appelbaum Associates

"Rockstyle" at the Rock & Roll Hall of Fame &
    Museum
Cleveland, Ohio
Pentagram Design

Streetscape Elements & Tenant Designs at
    Universal Citywalk
Orlando, Florida
Sussman/Prejza & Company, Inc.

POD Restaurant
Philadelphia, Pennsylvania
Rockwell Group

Restaurant Design
Alexey Ikonomou

Jack Daniels Visitor Experience-Visitors Center
    & Tour Path Enhancements
Lynchburg, Tennessee
HOK Studio E

Strands of History, California State University
    Chancellor's Administration Building
Long Beach, California
BJ Krivanek Art + Design

Forum Signage
Sydney, Australia
Emery Vincent Design

Metrius Trade Show Booth
ReVerb

General Motors Technical Center - Wayfinding
    Analysis & Master Plan
Warren Center, Michigan
Two Twelve Associates

More or Less Exhibition, Potter Museum
Melbourne, Australia
Emery Vincent Design

San Mateo Transit Center
San Mateo, California
Gensler - Studio 585

2001 Juror Awards:
Indivisible: Stories of American Community
    Traveling Exhibit, University of Arizona
Tucson, Arizona
Pentagram Design

SEGD Design Awards (Con't)

Aluminum by Design: Jewelry to Jets, Carnegie
  Museum of Art
Pittsburgh, Pennsylvania
Bally Design

Pacific Bell Park
San Francisco, California
Debra Nichols Design

Dodge Detroit Auto Show, NAIAS
Palmtop Publishing

2001 Jurors:
  Jan Lorenc, Lorenc+Yoo Design (Chair)
  David Harvey, American Museum of Natural
    History
  Takenobu Igarashi, sculptor
  Robert A. Ivy, *Architectural Record*

Source: Society for Environmental Graphic Design

Ralph Appelbaum Associates' design for the New Steuben Flagship Store is reminiscent of a museum-like setting, highlighting the beauty and craftsmanship of the Steuben glass. Photo: © Peter Mauss/Esto.

Sir Patrick Abercrombie Prize

The International Union of Architects (UIA) grants this triennial award to an internationally renowned architect or architects for significant work in town planning and territorial development.

For more information, visit the UIA's Web site at *www.uia-architectes.org.*

1961 Town Planning Service of the City of Stockholm (S. Markelius and G. Onblahd, Sweden)

1963 G. Dioxiadis (Greece)

1965 C. Buchanan and team (United Kingdom)
T. Farkas and team (Hungary)

1967 G. De Carlo (Italy)

1969 H. Bennet and team (United Kingdom)
Honorary Mention:
Belaunde Terry (Peru)

1972 Centre for Experimentation, Research and Training (Morocco)

1975 Iosif Bronislavovitch Orlov and Nilolai Ivanovitch Simonov (USSR)

1978 The City of Louvain la Neuve (Belgium)

1981 Warsaw architects (Poland) for the reconstruction of their capital
Honorary Mention:
M. Balderiotte and team (Argentina)

1984 Hans Blumenfeld (Canada)
Lucio Costa (Brazil)

1987 AIA Regional/Urban Design Assistance Team (R/UDAT) (USA)
Honorary Mention:
Eduardo Leira (Spain)
L. Bortenreuter, K. Griebel and H.G. Tiedt for the remodeling of the city center of Gera (Germany)

1990 Edmund N. Bacon (USA)

1993 Jan Gehl (Denmark)

1996 Juan Gil Elizondo (Mexico)

1999 Karl Ganser (Germany)
Honorary Mention:
Master plan of the city of Shenzhen (People's Republic of China)

Source: International Union of Architects

The purpose of Architecture is to improve human life; create timeless, free, joyous spaces for all activities in life. The infinite variety of these spaces can be as varied as life itself and they must be as sensible as nature in deriving from a main idea and flowering into a beautiful entity.

John Lautner

Sir Robert Matthew Prize

The International Union of Architects (UIA) awards the Sir Robert Matthew Prize triennially to an internationally renowned architect or architects whose work has improved the quality of human settlements.

For more information, visit the UIA's web site at *www.uia-architectes.org.*

1978 John F.C. Turner (U.K.)

1981 Hassan Fathy (Egypt);
Honorary Mention:
Rod Hackney (U.K.) and Hardt Walther Hamer (GFR)

1984 Charles Correa (India)

1987 Housing Reconstruction Programme for the City of Mexico (Mexico)

1990 Department of Architecture of the Singapore Housing & Development Board (Singapore)

1993 Laurie Baker (U.K.)

1996 Professor Giancarlo De Carlo (Italy)
Jury citation:
Oberste Baubehörde (the German team under the guidance of architect Benno Brugger and led by Hans Jörg Nussberger)

1999 Martin Treberspurg (Austria)
Honorary Mention:
Development & Construction Branch of the Hong Kong Housing Department

Source: International Union of Architects (UIA)

If architecture is to be of service, it must respond to more than need. The architect must also serve desire; the desire of the building to be what it wants to be and the desire of the human being for self-expression. In serving desire, architecture contributes to the spiritual enrichment of the world.

John Lobell

MAX PAGE

THE CREATIVE DESTRUCTION OF
MANHATTAN
1900-1940

Max Page investigates why New York City became
a place of continuous rebuilding by exploring "the
cultural meanings attached to the fundamental
process of urbanization," which he calls "creative
destruction."

Spiro Kostof Book Award

The Society of Architectural Historians (SAH) grants the annual Spiro Kostof Award to a work that has made the greatest contribution to understanding the historical development of the change in urbanism and architecture.

For more information, contact the SAH at (312) 573-1365 or visit their Web site at *www.sah.org*.

1994
Architecture Power and National Identity by Lawrence J. Vale (Yale University Press)

1995
In the Theatre of Criminal Justice: The Palais de Justice in Second Empire Paris by Katherine Fischer Taylor (Princeton University Press)

1996
The Topkapi Scroll: Geometry and Ornament in Islamic Architecture by Gülru Necipoglu (Getty Center for the History of Art and Humanities)

1997
The Projective Cast: Architecture and Its Three Geometries by Robin Evans (MIT Press)

Auschwitz: 1270 to the Present by Debórah Dwork and Robert Jan van Pelt (Norton)

1998
The Architects and the City by Robert Bruegmann (University of Chicago Press)

Magnetic Los Angeles by Gregory Hise (Johns Hopkins Press)

1999
City Center to Regional Mall: Architecture, the Automobile and Retailing in Los Angeles, 1920-1950 by Richard Longstreth (MIT Press)

Housing Design and Society in Amsterdam: Reconfiguring Urban Order and Identity, 1900-1920 by Nancy Stieber (University of Chicago Press)

2000
The Architecture of Red Vienna 1919-1934 by Eve Blau (MIT Press)

2001
The Creative Destruction of Manhattan, 1900-1940 by Max Page (The University of Chicago Press)

Source: Society of Architectural Historians

Star Award

Through its Star Award the International Interior Design Association (IIDA) recognizes individuals who have made an outstanding contribution to the interior design profession. No more than one award is granted each year. However, as this is merit based, awards are not always given each year. Although non-members are eligible for the Star Award, the IIDA Board of Directors, the selection body, only accepts nominations from IIDA Fellows, chapter presidents, and directors.

For more information about the Star Award, visit IIDA's Web site at *www.iida.org* or contact them at (888) 799-4432.

1985	Lester Dundes	1994	Michael Kroelinger
1986	William Sullivan	1995	Douglas R. Parker
1987	Orlando Diaz-Azcuy	1997	Michael Wirtz
1988	Paul Brayton	1998	Charles and Ray Eames
1989	Florence Knoll Bassett	1999	Michael Brill
1990	Beverly Russell	2000	Eva L. Maddox
1991	Stanley Abercrombie	2001	Andrée Putman
1992	M. Arthur Gensler Jr.		
1993	Sivon C. Reznikoff		

Source: International Interior Designers Association

Andrée Putnam.

Sustainable Design Leadership Awards

The annual Sustainable Design Leadership Awards are presented jointly by the International Interior Design Association (IIDA) and Collins & Aikman Floorcoverings in two categories. The first category honors an individual who has demonstrated a commitment to environmental issues in the design profession; the second category recognizes a U.S.-based company who is working toward becoming environmentally sustainable through design. Companies servicing the interior design and furnishings industry are not eligible.

Additional information is available on the IIDA's Web site at *www.iida.org*.

2001
   Sandra F. Mendler, HOK
   Ford Motor Company

Source: International Interior Design Association

In addition to receiving the 2001 Sustainable
Leadership Award, Sandra Mendler, AIA, is
a vice president and sustainable design principal in HOK's San Francisico's office as well
as the co-author of the *HOK Guidebook to
Sustainable Design*.

Tau Sigma Delta Gold Medal

Presented annually by Tau Sigma Delta, the honor society of architecture and the allied arts, the Gold Medal honors an individual who has made outstanding contributions in the fields of architecture, landscape architecture or an allied profession.

More information on the Medal can be found online at *www.ttu.edu/~tsd*.

1970 Norman Fletcher, Boston, MA	1988 Kenneth Frampton, New York, NY
1971 Gunnar Birkerts, Detroit, MI	1989 Richard Meier, New York, NY
1972 O'Neil Ford, San Antonio, TX	1990 Joseph Escherick, San Francisco, CA
1973 Arthur Erickson, Vancouver, B.C.	1991 Denise Scott-Brown, Philadelphia, PA
1974 Ian McHarg, Philadelphia, PA	1992 Charles Moore, Austin, TX (repeat)
1975 Hugh Stubbins, Cambridge, MA	1993 Harold F. Adams, Baltimore, MD
1976 Vincent G. Kling, Philadelphia, PA	1994 Harvey B. Gantt, Charlotte, NC
1977 Harry Weese, Chicago, IL	1995 Peter Eisenman, New York, NY
1978 William Caudill, Houston, TX	1996 Vincent Scully, NY
1979 Edmond Bacon, Philadelphia, PA	1997 Cesar Pelli, New Haven, CT
1980 Alexander Girard, Santa Fe, NM	1998 William Pedersen,New York, NY
1981 Charles Moore, Los Angeles, CA	1999 William Curtis, NY
1982 Moshe Safdie, Israel	2000 Pierre Koenig, Los Angeles, CA
1983 Ricardo Legoretta, Mexico	2001 Malcolm Holzman, New York, NY
1984 E. Fay Jones, Fayetteville, AR	
1985 Pietro Belluschi, Portland, OR	*Source: Tau Sigma Delta*
1986 Walter A. Netsch, Chicago, IL	
1987 Lawrence Halprin, San Francisco, CA	

When you have all the answers about a building before you start building it, your answers are not true. The building gives you answers as it grows and becomes itself.

Louis Kahn

Malcolm Holzman.

Thomas Jefferson Award for Public Architecture

The Thomas Jefferson Award for Public Architecture is presented annually by The American Institute of Architects (AIA) to recognize and foster the importance of design excellence in government and infrastructure projects. Awards are presented in three categories:

- Category One – Private sector architects who have amassed a portfolio of accomplished and distinguished public facilities (C1)
- Category Two – Public sector architects who produce quality projects within their agencies (C2)
- Category Three – Public officials or others who have been strong advocates for design excellence (C3)

For more information, visit the AIA on the Internet at *www.aia.org* or contact the AIA Honors and Awards Department at (202) 626-7586.

1992 James Ingo Freed (C1)
George M. White (C2)
The Honorable Patrick J. Moynihan (C3)

1993 The Honorable Jack Brooks (C3)

1994 Richard Dattner (C1)
M.J. "Jay" Brodie (C2)
The Honorable Joseph P. Riley Jr. (C3)

1995 Herbert S. Newman (C1)
Edward A. Feiner (C2)
Henry G. Cisneros (C3)

1996 Thomas R. Aidala (C2)
The Honorable Douglas P. Woodlock (C3)

1997 John Tarantino (C2)
Richard A. Kahan (C3)
Hunter Morrison (C3)

1998 Arthur Rosenblatt (C2)

1999 Lewis Davis (C1)
Robert Kroin (C2)

2000 Charles Emil Peterson (C2)
Jay Chatterjee (C3)

2001 Terrel M. Emmons (C2)
Stoud Watson (C3)

Source: The American Institute of Architects

Twenty-Five Year Award

Awarded annually by The American Institute of Architects (AIA), the Twenty-Five Year Award is presented to projects which excel under the test of time. Projects must have been completed 25 to 35 years ago by an architect licensed in the United States, though the nominated facility may be located anywhere in the world. To be eligible submissions must still be carrying out their original program and demonstrate a continued viability in their function and form.

For more information, visit the AIA on the Internet at *www.aia.org* or contact the AIA Honors and Awards Department at (202) 626-7586.

1969
  Rockefeller Center
  New York City, NY
  Reinhard & Hofmeister; Corbett, Harrison &
     MacMurray
1971
  The Crow Island School
  Winnetka, IL
  Perkins, Wheeler & Will; Eliel & Eero Saarinen
1972
  Baldwin Hills Village
  Los Angeles, CA
  Reginald D. Johnson; Wilson, Merrill &
     Alexander; Clarence S. Stein
1973
  Taliesin West
  Paradise Valley, AZ
  Frank Lloyd Wright
1974
  S.C. Johnson & Son Administration Building
  Racine, WI
  Frank Lloyd Wright
1975
  Philip Johnson's Residence ("The Glass House")
  New Caanan, CT
  Philip Johnson
1976
  860-880 North Lakeshore Drive Apartments
  Chicago, IL
  Ludwig Mies van der Rohe

1977
  Christ Lutheran Church
  Minneapolis, MN
  Saarinen, Saarinen & Associates; Hills,
     Gilbertson & Hays
1978
  The Eames House
  Pacific Palisades, CA
  Charles and Ray Eames
1979
  Yale University Art Gallery
  New Haven, CT
  Louis I. Kahn, FAIA
1980
  Lever House
  New York City, NY
  Skidmore, Owings & Merrill
1981
  Farnsworth House
  Plano, IL
  Ludwig Mies van der Rohe
1982
  Equitable Savings and Loan Building
  Portland, OR
  Pietro Belluschi, FAIA
1983
  Price Tower
  Bartlesville, OK
  Frank Lloyd Wright

The corporate headquarters of Weyerhaeuser, one of the world's largest wood products manufacturers, by Skidmore, Ownings & Merrill, is completely integrated within the landscape. The building's five discrete horizontal stories gently nestle into the site's rolling hills. When it was completed in 1971, it was also one of the few pioneering corporate buildings at the time to embrace the concept of the open office plan, which also offered employees an expansive vista of the campus' 230 acres. Photo: © Bob Hollingsworth (top).

Twenty-Five Year Award (Con't)

1984
 Seagram Building
 New York City, NY
 Ludwig Mies van der Rohe
1985
 General Motors Technical Center
 Warren, MI
 Eero Saarinen and Associates with Smith,
   Hinchman & Grylls
1986
 Solomon R. Guggenheim Museum
 New York City, NY
 Frank Lloyd Wright
1987
 Bavinger House
 Norman, OK
 Bruce Goff
1988
 Dulles International Airport Terminal Building
 Chantilly, VA
 Eero Saarinen and Associates
1989
 Vanna Venturi House
 Chestnut Hill, PA
 Robert Venturi, FAIA
1990
 The Gateway Arch
 St. Louis, MO
 Eero Saarinen and Associates
1991
 Sea Ranch Condominium I
 The Sea Ranch, CA
 Moore Lyndon Turnbull Whitaker
1992
 The Salk Institute for Biological Studies
 La Jolla, CA
 Louis I. Kahn, FAIA
1993
 Deere & Company Administrative Center
 Moline, IL
 Eero Saarinen and Associates

1994
 The Haystack Mountain School of Crafts
 Deer Isle, ME
 Edward Larrabee Barnes
1995
 The Ford Foundation Headquarters
 New York City, NY
 Kevin Roche John Dinkeloo and Associates
1996
 The Air Force Academy Cadet Chapel
 Colorado Springs, CO
 Skidmore, Owings & Merrill
1997
 Phillips Exeter Academy Library
 Exeter, NH
 Louis I. Kahn, FAIA
1998
 Kimbell Art Museum
 Fort Worth, TX
 Louis I. Kahn, FAIA
1999
 The John Hancock Center
 Chicago, IL
 Skidmore, Owings & Merrill
2000
 The Smith House
 Darien, CT
 Richard Meier & Partners
2001
 Weyerhaeuser Headquarters
 Tacoma, WA
 Skidmore, Owings & Merrill

Source: The American Institute of Architects

UIA Gold Medal

Every three years at the World Congress of the International Union of Architects (UIA), the UIA awards its Gold Medal to a living architect who has made an outstanding achievement to the field of architecture. This honor recognizes the recipient's lifetime of distinguished practice, contribution to the enrichment of mankind, and the promotion of the art of architecture.

For more information, visit the UIA's Web site at *www.uia-architectes.org.*

1984   Hassan Fathy (Egypt)
1987   Reima Pietila (Finland)
1990   Charles Correa (India)
1993   Fumihiko Maki (Japan)
1996   Rafael Moneo (Spain)
1999   Ricardo Legorreta (Mexico)

Source: International Union of Architects

In the gardens and homes designed by me I have always endeavored to allow for the interior placid murmur of silence and in my fountains, silence sings.

Luis Barragán

Urban Land Institute Awards for Excellence

The Urban Land Institute Awards for Excellence follow the organization's mission "to provide responsible leadership in the use of land in order to enhance the environment." Considered by many the most prestigious award within the development community, the Urban Land Institute has recognized outstanding land development projects throughout the world since 1979. Submissions are accepted from developers in the United States and Canada (except for the International Award which is worldwide in scope) and judged by a panel of experts. Winning entries represent superior design, improve the quality of the built environment, exhibit a sensitivity to the community, display financial viability, and demonstrate relevance to contemporary issues.

For more information about the awards, contact the Urban Land Institute at (800) 321-5011 or visit their Web site at *www.uli.org*.

2000 Awards for Excellence recipients:
Residential Small-Scale Prize
   The Colony, Newport Beach, CA
   Irvine Apartment Communities (owner/dev.)
   McLarand, Vasquez and Partners, Inc. (arch.)
   Sares-Regis Group (builder)
   Bill Burton and Associates (landscape architect)
   Saddleback Interiors (interior designer)

Recreational Large-Scale Prize
   Blackcomb/Whistler, Whistler, British
      Columbia, Canada
   INTRAWEST Corporation (owner/developer)
   Gomberoff Policzer Bell Architects (architect)
   Ray Letkeman Architect Ltd. (architect)
   Amaco Construction Ltd. (builder)

Mixed Use Small-Scale Prize
   DePaul Center, Chicago, IL
   DePaul University (owner/developer)
   Daniel P. Coffey and Associates (architect)
   Globetrotters Engineering Inc. (engineer)
   Don Belford Associates (engineer)
   WMA Consulting Engineers, Inc. (engineer)
   Teng and Associates Inc. (engineer)

W.E. O'Neil Construction Company (general contractor)

New Community Prize
   Coto de Caza, Orange County, CA
   Coto de Caza Ltd./Lennar Communities (owner/developer)
   Clark and Green (landscape architect)
   Archeology Resource Management
   Hunsaker and Associates (planning and civil engineers)
   Forma (planning)
   Harmsworth Associates (environmental)

Rehabilitation Large-Scale Prize
   The Power Plant, Baltimore, MD
   The Cordish Company (owner/developer)
   Design Collective (architect)
   Struever Brothers (contractor)
   First National Bank of Maryland (lender)

Design Collective's $30 million renovation of the 150,000 square foot Power Plant added a vital component to Baltimore's Inner Harbor, with retail, entertainment, and corporate tenants. Bottom photo: Ron Solomon.

Urban Land Institute Awards for Excellence (Con't)

Rehabilitation Small-Scale Prize
Amazon.com Building, Seattle, WA
Wright Runstad and Company (owner/dev.)
Zimmer Gunsul Frasca Partnership (architect)
spAce (architect)
Sellen Construction Company (gen. contractor)
Turner Construction (general contractor)
McKinstry and Company (mechanical engineer)
Sparling (electrical engineer)
ABKJ Engineering (structural engineer)
KeyBank (construction lender)
Washington Partners (broker)

Public Prize
NorthLake Park Community School, Orlando, FL
Lake Nona Land Company (owner/developer)
City of Orlando (public partner)
Orange County Public Schools (public partner)
Central Florida YMCA (non-profit partner)
Orlando Regional Healthcare System
(non-profit partner)
SchenkleSchultz (architect)
Clatting, Jackson, Kercher, Anglin, Lopez (landscape architect)
Donald W. McIntosh Associates, Inc. (civil eng.)
Centex-Rooney Construction Company (general contractor)

The Townhomes on Capitol Hill, Wash., D.C.
Ellen Wilson Community Development
Company and Telesis Corporation (owner/dev.)
Weinstein and Associates (architect)
CorJen Construction, LLC (general contractor)
TCM Corporation (construction manager)
Oehme van Sweden and Associates, Inc. (landscape design)
Corcoran Jennison Management Company
(managing agent)

International Prize
Sony Center am Potsdamer Platz, Berlin,
Germany
Tishman Speyer Properties (owner/developer)
BE-ST Bellevuestrae Development GmbH and
Company First Real Estate KG (owner/dev.)
Murphy/Jahn Inc. (architect)
Dresdner Bank AG (lender)
Westdeutsche Immobilienbank (lender)

Heritage Prize
Burnham Plan of Chicago, Chicago, IL (1909)
The Commercial Club of Chicago (sponsor)

Special Prize
Spring Island, Beaufort County, SC
Chaffin/Light Associates (owner/developer)
Robert Marvin and Associates (land planner)
Edward Pinckney and Associates (land planner)
Thomas and Denzinger Architects and
Historical Concepts (architects)

Jury:
Robert N. Ruth, Trammell Crow Company,
(Chair)
A. Eugene Kohn, Kohn Pederson Fox Assoc. PC
Toni Alexander, InterCommunicationsInc
Karen B. Alschuler, Simon Martin-Vegue
Winkelstein Morris
Daniel A. Biederman, 34th Street
Partnership/Bryant Park Restoration Corp.
Joseph E. Brown, EDAW, Incorporated
James H. Callard, American Apartment
Communities
A. Larry Chapman, Wells Fargo Bank
Lewis M. Goodkin, Goodkin Consulting
Richard L. Michaux, AvalonBay Communities,
Inc.
Diana B. Permar, Permar & Ravenel, Inc.
James A. Ratner, Forest City Commercial Group
Edward D. Stone, Jr., Edward D. Stone & Assoc.

Source: Urban Land Institute

Veronica Rudge Green Prize in Urban Design

Established by Harvard University in 1986, the Veronica Rudge Green Prize in Urban Design awards excellence in urban design with an emphasis on projects that contribute to the public spaces in cities and improve the quality of urban life. The Prize is awarded biennially by a jury of experts in the field of architecture and urban design. Nominations are made to the Harvard Design School by a panel of critics, academics, and practitioners in the field of architecture, landscape architecture, and urban design. Eligible projects must be larger in scope than a single building and must have been constructed within the last 10 years. Winners receive a monetary award and certificate.

Additional information about the award can be found on the Internet at *www.gsd.harvard.edu.*

1988
  Ralph Erskine, Byker Redevelopment in Newcastle upon Tyne, U.K.

  Alvaro Siza Vieira, Malagueira Quarter Housing Project in Evora, Portugal

1990
  The City of Barcelona, Urban Public Spaces of Barcelona

1993
  Fumihiko Maki, Hillside Terrace Complex, Tokyo, Japan

  Luigi Snozzi, Master Plan and Public Buildings of Monte Carasso, Switzerland

1996
  Mexico City, Restoration of the Historic Center of Mexico City and Ecological Restoration of the District of Xochimilco

1998
  Sir Norman Foster and Foster and Partners, subway system in Bilbao, Spain and the development of Carré d'Art Plaza in Nîmes, France

2000
  Jorge Mario Jáuregui and his Rio de Janeiro-based firm, Jorge Mario Jáuregui Architects, for the Favela-Bairro Project in Rio de Janeiro, Brazil

Source: Harvard Graduate School of Design/School of Architecture

What is the city but the people?

Shakespeare (Coriolanus, Act III)

Vincent J. Scully Prize

The National Building Museum founded the Vincent J. Scully Prize to recognize practice, scholarship, and criticism in the design professions – architecture, landscape architecture, historic preservation, city planning, and urban design. By naming the prize after Vincent J. Scully, America's renowned architectural scholar, mentor, and critic whose lifetime of work made a tremendous impact on the profession, the Museum hopes to celebrate others who have yielded a significant contribution to the betterment of our world. The award carries a $25,000 honorarium, and the recipient is invited to present a lecture at the Museum.

For more information about the Vincent J. Scully Prize, contact the National Building Museum at (202) 272-2448 or visit them on the Internet at *www.nbm.org.*

1999 Vincent J. Scully
2000 Jane Jacobs

Source: National Building Museum

...history is essential for architecture, because the architect, who must now deal with everything urban, will therefore always be dealing with historical problems – with the past and, a function of the past, with the future. So the architect should be regarded as a kind of physical historian, because he constructs relationships across time: civilization in fact. And since civilization is based largely upon the capacity of human beings to remember, the architect builds visible history...

Vincent Scully

Whitney M. Young, Jr. Award

The American Institute of Architects (AIA) bestows the Whitney M. Young Jr. Award annually upon an architect or architecturally oriented organization that makes a significant contribution toward meeting the challenge set forth by Mr. Young to architects: to assume a professional responsibility toward current social issues. These issues are ever present and flexible and include such things as housing the homeless, affordable housing, minority and women participation in the profession, disability issues, and literacy.

For more information, visit the AIA on the Internet at *www.aia.org* or contact the AIA Honors and Awards Department at (202) 626-7586.

1972	Robert J. Nash
1973	Architects Workshop of Philadelphia
1974	Stephen Cram*
1975	Van B. Bruner Jr.
1976	Wendell J. Campbell
1980	Leroy M. Campbell*
1981	Robert T. Coles
1982	John S. Chase
1983	Howard Hamilton Mackey Sr.
1984	John Louis Wilson
1985	Milton V. Bergstedt
1986	The Rev. Richard McClure Prosse*
1987	J. Max Bond Jr.
1988	Habitat for Humanity
1989	John H. Spencer
1990	Harry G. Robinson III
1991	Robert Kennard
1992	Curtis J. Moody
1993	David Castro-Blanco
1994	Ki Suh Park
1995	William J. Stanley III
1996	John L. Wilson
1997	Alan Y. Taniguchi
1998	Leon Bridges
1999	Charles McAfee
2000	Louis L. Weller
2001	Cecil A. Alexander Jr.

* *Honored posthumously*

Source: The American Institute of Architects

Wolf Prize for Architecture

Dr. Ricardo Wolf established the Wolf Foundation in 1976 in order to "promote science and arts for the benefit of mankind." In this vein, the Wolf prize is awarded annually to outstanding living scientists and artists in the fields of agriculture, chemistry, mathematics, medicine, physics, and the arts. The awards, an honorarium of US$100,000 and a diploma, are presented each year in Jerusalem's Chagall Hall. In the arts category, the Wolf Prize rotates annually between architecture, music, painting, and sculpture. The following individuals received this honor for their contribution to the field of architecture.

For more information about the Wolf Prize, contact the Wolf Foundation at +972 (9) 955 7120 or visit their Web site at *www.aquanet.co.il/wolf.*

1983   Ralph Erskine (Sweden)

1988   Fumihiko Maki (Japan)
       Giancarlo de Carlo (Italy)

1992   Frank O. Gehry (US)
       Jorn Utzon (Denmark)
       Sir Denys Lasdun (U.K.)

1996   Frei Otto (Germany)
       Aldo van Eyck (Holland)

2001   Alvaro Siza (Portugal)

Source: Wolf Foundation

I do not believe architecture should speak too much. It should remain silent and let nature in the guise of sunlight and wind speak.

Tadao Ando

Muskoka Boathouse. Photos: Shim-Sutcliffe Architects.

Wood Design Awards

The Wood Design Awards annually recognize excellence in wood architecture in the United States and Canada. Judging criteria includes the creative, distinctive and appropriate use of wood materials, though buildings do not need to be constructed entirely of wood. Entries may include residential and non-residential buildings, new construction, or renovation. A category for Architectural Interior Design is also included. Honor, Merit and Citation awards may be given in each category, at the discretion of the jury. Special awards issues of *Wood Design & Building* [U.S.] and *Wood Le Bois* [Canada] magazines feature winning projects.

For project descriptions and photos, visit *www.wood.ca/awards* on the Internet.

2001 Honor Awards
Wood Studio
Durham, NC
Frank Harmon Architect

Conference Barn
Middleburg, VA
Sant Architects, Inc.

Muskoka Boathouse
Lake Muskoka, Ontario, Canada
Shim-Sutcliffe Architects, Inc.

Maple Valley Library
Maple Valley, WA
Johnston Architects & James Cutler Architects

Misha/ Twaddell Residence
Los Gatos, CA
Burks Toma Architects [with Jeffrey L. Day]

2001 Merit Awards
Caretaker's Complex
Litchfield County, CT
Gray Organschi Architecture

Vehicular Bridge
Litchfield County, CT
Gray Organschi Architecture

East Hampton Recreation Center
East Hampton, NY
Davis Brody Bond LLP

Pilchuck Glass School Studio Annex
Stanwood, WA
Weinstein Copeland Architects

Pine Forest Cabin
Winthrop, WA
James Cutler Architects

2001 Citation Awards
Moorelands Camp Dining Hall
Lake Kawagama, Dorset, ON, Canada
Shim-Sutcliffe Architects

Robertson House Crisis Centre
Toronto, ON, Canada
Hariri Pontarini Architects

Private Residence
Napa, CA
Turnbull Griffin Haesloop

T.E.S.T. House,
Portland, Oregon
Brent Hinrichs Architect

Wood Design Awards (Con't)

La Petite Maison de Weekend (unbuilt)
Patkau Architects Inc.

Storybook Farm
Bedford County, TN
Shofner Evans Architects/Interiors

2001 Jury:
Robert E. Hull, The Miller/Hull Partnership
Jane Weinzapfel, Leers, Weinzapfel Associates
    Architects, Inc.
Peter Busby, Busby + Associates Architects

Source: Wood Design & Building & Wood Le Bois *magazines*

The whole difference between construction and creation is exactly this: that a thing constructed can only be loved after it is constructed; but a thing created is loved before it exists.

G. K. Chesterton

World Architecture **Awards**

Providing annual global recognition of architectural excellence, *World Architecture* magazine presents the *World Architecture* Awards. Buildings are honored for excellence within their global region and by building type, which includes Office/Commercial, Housing/Residential, Health, Public/Cultural, Retail/Leisure, Transport/Infrastructure, Education, Industrial/Research & Development and Green/Environmentally Conscious Building of the Year. A $30,000 (U.S.) prize is also given for the overall best building.

For complete competition information, visit *www.worldarchitectureawards.co.uk* on the Internet.

2001 Winner of the Arup World Architecture Award for the World's Best Building:
  Finnish Embassy
  Berlin, Germany
  Viivi Arkkitehtuuri (Rauno Lehtinen, Pekka Mäki, Toni Peltola)

2001 Category Winners:
Housing/Residential
  Wohnen am Lohbach housing
  Innsbruck, Austria
  Baumschlager & Eberle

Public/Cultural
  Japan Pavilion Hanover Expo 2000
  Hanover, Germany
  Shigeru Ban Architects

Sport/Leisure
  NatWest Media Centre at Lord's Cricket Ground
  London, UK
  Future Systems

Office/Retail
  Finnish Embassy
  Berlin, Germany
  Viiva Arkkitehtuuri

Education
  Ahmedabad Management Association
  Ahmedabad, India
  HCP Design and Project Management

Industrial/Research and Development
  Aplix factory
  Nantes, France
  Dominique Perrault

Transport/Infrastructure
  Canary Wharf Station
  London, UK
  Foster & Partners

Green/Environmentally Conscious Building of the Year
  Wohnen am Lohbach housing
  Innsbruck, Austria
  Baumschlager & Eberle

2001 Regional Winners:
Europe
  Finnish Embassy
  Berlin, Germany
  Viiva Arkkitehtuuri

  Japan Pavilion Hanover Expo 2000
  Hanover, Germany
  Shigeru Ban Architects

World Architecture Awards (Con't)

Central and South America
  Puritama Hot Springs
  San Pedro de Atacama, Chile
  Germán del Sol

Australia, Oceania and Pacific Rim
  Carter Tucker House
  Victoria, Australia
  Sean Godsell

North America
  Federal Building and US Courthouse
  Central Islip, New York, United States
  Richard Meier & Partners

Asia
  University of Hong Kong-Kadoorie Biological
    Sciences Laboratory Building
  Hong Kong, People's Republic of China
  Leigh & Orange

East Asia
  Saitama Super Arena
  Saitama, Japan
  Nikken Sekkei in association with Ellerbe
    Becket and Flack + Kurtz Consulting
    Engineers

Africa and Middle East
  Tree House
  Cape Town, South Africa
  Van der Merwe Miszewski Architects

2001 Jury:
  Guy Battle, Battle McCarthy Consulting
    Engineers
  Dominique Boudet, *AMC* magazine
  John Denton, Denton Corker Marshall
  Marco Goldschmied, president, Royal Institute
    of British Architects
  Nicola Jackson, *World Architecture*
  David Jenkins, architectural critic and author
  Roger Kallman, Skidmore, Owings & Merrill
  Martin Pawley, critic
  Ken Yeang, TR Hammzah & Yeang

Source: World Architecture *magazine*

Did you know...

Using a movable architectural block that can shift 9,200 seats along with restrooms, concessions and circulation elements 231 feet, the Saitı85ama Super Arena in Japan (2000, Nikken Sekkei Ltd. with Ellerbe Becket) can convert from a 36,400-seat sports venue to an intimate concert venue for 5,000 in less than 30 minutes.

Saitama Super Arena.
Photos: © Kokyu
Miwa.

Young Architects Award

The Young Architects Award is presented annually by The American Institute of Architects (AIA) to an architect in the early stages of his or her career who has made "significant contributions" to the profession. The competition is open to AIA members who have been licensed to practice for less than 10 years; the term "young architect" has no reference to the age of nominees.

For additional information about the Young Architects Award visit the AIA online at *www.aia.org* or contact the AIA Honors and Awards Department at (202) 626-7586.

1993
  Joan M. Soranno
  Vicki L. Hooper
  Thomas Somerville Howorth
  Brett Keith Laurila

1995
  William A. Blanski
  Anne Tate

1996
  Christopher W. Coe
  George Thrush
  Keith Moskow

1997
  Robert S. Rothman
  William J. Carpenter
  Michael A. Fischer
  Brad Simmons

1998
  J. Windom Kimsey
  Jose Luis Palacious
  Karin M. Pitman
  Charles Rose
  Karl W. Stumpf
  David Louis Swartz
  Maryann Thompson
  Randall C. Vaughn

1999
  Father Terrence Curry
  Victoria Tatna Jacobson
  Michael Thomas Maltzan
  David T. Nagahiro
  Peter Steinbrueck

2000
  Mary Katherine Lanzillotta
  Andrew Travis Smith

2001
  J. Scott Busby
  P. Thomas M. Harboe
  Jeffry Lee Kagermeier
  Elizabeth Chu Richter
  George A. Takoudes

Source: The American Institute of Architects

Organizations

The history, purpose, and membership benefits of the major design associations can be
found in this chapter, with a summary listing
of design and building-related organizations
and government agencies available on page
226. Historic preservation-specific organizations can be found in the Design & Historic
Preservation chapter beginning on page 411.

American Architectural Foundation (AAF)

Headquartered in America's oldest museum devoted to architecture, Washington D.C.'s Octagon, the American Architectural Foundation (AAF) is dedicated to furthering the public's understanding of architecture and the human experience. The non-profit AAF sponsors education and outreach programs which foster public participation in the design process, encourages public stewardship of America's architectural heritage, and promotes alliances between architects and their communities. It is also a repository for a growing architectural archive of over 60,000 drawings, 30,000 photographs, and more.

Address:
1735 New York, Avenue NW
Washington, D.C. 20006
Telephone: (202) 626-7500
Internet: www.archfoundation.com

American Consulting Engineers Council (ACEC)

The American Consulting Engineers Council (ACEC) represents private engineering firms in the U.S. by promoting their interests and providing educational opportunities to members. Specifically, the goals of the group are to help members achieve higher business standards, ensure ethical standards are maintained, act as an information clearinghouse, advise on legislation, and to support the advancement of engineering. The ACEC was formed by the union of the American Institute of Consulting Engineers and the Consulting Engineers Council in 1973. Today it is the largest national organization of consulting engineers. Fifty-two state and regional Member Organizations represent more than 5,700 engineering firms. These firms employ more than 250,000 engineers, architects, land surveyors, scientists, technicians and other professionals who design approximately $100 billion of private and public works annually.

Address:
1015 15th St, NW, #802
Washington, DC 20005
Telephone: (202) 347-7474
Internet: www.acec.org

Did you know...

The steel used in William LeBaron Jenney's 10-story Home Insurance Building (Chicago, 1885), the first tall building to be supported by a metal skeleton, weighed only one-third as much as a 10-story building constructed of heavy masonry.

American Institute of Architects (AIA)

Representing the professional interests of America's architects and seeking to increase national design literacy among the public, The American Institute of Architects (AIA) provides education, government advocacy, community redevelopment and public outreach activities with and for its 62,000 members. With 305 local and state AIA organizations, the Institute monitors closely legislative and regulatory actions at all levels of government. It provides professional development opportunities, industry standard contract documents, information services, and a comprehensive awards program.

Address:
1735 New York Ave., NW
Washington, DC 20006
Telephone: (202) 626-7300 or (800) AIA-3837
Internet: www.aia.org

Design is instilling structure and soul into our naturally chaotic and unintelligible environment.

Laurinda Spear

American Planning Association (APA)

The American Planning Association (APA) represents 30,000 planners, officials and citizens involved with urban and rural planning issues. Sixty-five percent of APA's members are employed by state and local government agencies. The mission of the organization is to encourage planning that will contribute to public well-being by developing communities and environments that meet the needs of people and society more effectively. APA is headquartered in Washington, D.C. and has 46 regional chapters. The American Institute of Certified Planners (AICP) is APA's professional and educational arm, certifying planners who have met specific criteria and passed the certification. The group also has research, publications, conference, and education components.

Address:
1776 Massachusetts Ave., NW
Washington, D.C. 20036
Telephone: (202) 872-0611
Internet: www.planning.org

The materials of city planning are sky, space, trees, steel and cement in that order and in that hierarchy.

Le Corbusier

American Society of Interior Designers (ASID)

The American Society of Interior Designers (ASID) was formed in 1975 with the consolidation of the American Institute of Designers (AID) and the National Society of Interior Designers (NSID). It serves over 30,000 members with continuing education, government affairs, conferences, publications, online services, and more. Members include residential and commercial designers, 3,500 manufacturers of design-related products and services, also known as Industry Partners, and 7,500 students of interior design. ASID has 49 chapters throughout the United States.

Address:
608 Massachusetts Avenue, NE
Washington, DC 20002-6006
Telephone: (202) 546-3480
Internet: www.asid.org

American Society of Landscape Architects (ASLA)

Representing the landscape architecture profession in the United States since 1899, the American Society of Landscape Architects (ASLA) currently serves over 13,000 members through 47 chapters across the country. The ASLA's goal is to advance knowledge, education, and skill in the art and science of landscape architecture. The benefits of membership include a national annual meeting, *Landscape Architecture* magazine, continuing education credits, seminars and workshops, professional interest groups, government advocacy, and award programs. In addition, the U.S. Department of Education has authorized the Landscape Architectural Accreditation Board (LAAB) of the ASLA as the accrediting agency for landscape architecture programs at U.S. colleges and universities.

Address:
636 Eye Street, NW
Washington, DC 20001-3736
Telephone: (202) 898-2444
Internet: www.asla.org

Did you know...

The average public sector landscape architect in the United States impacts nearly 4 million acres and 5 million people each year.

Architects' Council of Europe (ACE)

Membership of the Architects' Council of Europe (ACE) is comprised of most European representative bodies of the architecture profession. Their constitution states: "The Association of member organizations shall be a non-profit association...as the Liaison Committee of the Representative Bodies of the profession of Architecture, be dedicated to the better understanding of cultural values and the promotion of the highest standards of education and practice in architecture, and shall seek to ensure and shall promote the independence and integrity of the Architectural Profession within the European Community and shall, in these matters, act as its Liaison Committee in seeking, insofar as possible, consensus among the Member Organizations; and shall, without prejudice to the right of Derogation set out at Article 11.5 of this Constitution, promote and represent the common interests of the Profession of Architect in the European Community." Currently the ACE is focusing on deregulation, sustainability issues, and continued work on opening up avenues of communication throughout Europe among politicians, developers, and members of the construction industry.

Address:
Avenue Louise 207 b. 10 1050
Brussels, Belgium
Telephone: (32-2) 645-0905
Internet: www.ace-cae.org

Architectural Institute of Japan (AIJ)

The Architectural Institute of Japan (AIJ) is an academic association with nearly 40,000 members. The organization, dedicated to cultivating the talents of its members and promoting architectural quality in Japan, celebrated its 100th anniversary in 1986. AIJ activities include publications, research, prizes, lectures, exhibitions, and library services. The Board of Directors consists of the President, five Vice Presidents, 18 General Directors, and nine Directors representing the nine local chapters.

Address:
26-20, Shiba 5-chome, Minato-ku
Tokyo 108-8414 Japan
Telephone: +81-3-3456-2051
Internet: www.aij.or.jp

Construction Specifications Institute (CSI)

Headquartered in Alexandria, Virginia, the Construction Specifications Institute (CSI) represents nearly 18,000 members, including architects, engineers, specifiers, contractors, building owners, facility managers, and product manufacturers. As a professional association, CSI provides technical information, continuing education, conferences, and product shows for members. It strives to meet the industry's need for a common system of organizing and presenting construction documents, as demonstrated by its MasterFormat™ system and the new Uniform Drawing System™, which are quickly becoming an industry standard. CSI also publishes The *Construction Specifier*, a monthly magazine featuring articles on technologies, applications, legal issues, trends, and new products.

Address:
601 Madison Street
Alexandria, Virginia 22314-1791
Telephone: (800) 689-2900 or (703) 684-0300
Internet: www.csinet.org

Did you know...

The Inland Steel Building (1958, Skidmore, Owings & Merrill) in Chicago was the first major structure to be built on steel pilings instead of concrete.

Council on Tall Buildings and Urban Habitat (CTBUH)

The Council on Tall Buildings and Urban Habitat (CTBUH) was established to study and report on all aspects of the planning, design, construction, and operation of tall buildings. The group is sponsored by architecture, engineering, and planning professionals. One of the Council's major focuses is the publication of monographs on tall buildings, as well as studying not only the technological factors related to tall buildings, but the social and cultural aspects of the structures. They maintain an extensive database of tall buildings and produce the definitive list of the world's tallest buildings. The Council Headquarters is located at Lehigh University in Bethlehem, Pennsylvania.

Address:
CTBUH – Lehigh University
11 East Packer Avenue
Bethlehem, PA
Telephone: (610) 758-3515
Internet: www.ctbuh.org

Did you know...

At 462 feet, the Glasgow Tower at the Glasgow Science Centre, designed by Building Design Partnership (BDP), is the tallest structure in Scotland and the only tower in the world to rotate 360 degrees from its base.

Design-Build Institute of America (DBIA)

The Design-Build Institute of America (DBIA) is a voice supporting the integrated design-build project delivery method. Founded in 1993, DBIA membership includes design-builders, contractors, design professionals, subcontractors, representatives of government agencies, and other professionals. The DBIA strives to improve the level of design-build practice, to disseminate educational information, and to furnish advice and support to facility owners and users. Toward this end, the Institute's programs include dissemination and development of standard procedures and formats, promotion of design-build in public forums and with private corporations and government agencies, educational programs, and providing information support and assistance to members.

Address:
1010 Massachusetts Avenue, N.W.
Suite 350
Washington, D.C. 20001
Telephone: (202) 682-0110
Internet: www.dbia.org

**Design
Futures
Council
(DFC)**

The Design Futures Council (DFC) is a Washington D.C.-based think-tank with the mission to explore trends, changes, and new opportunities in design, architecture, engineering, and building technology for the purpose of fostering innovation and improving the performance of member organizations. Participants represent a full spectrum of design, manufacturing, and service professionals. Council activities include proprietary surveys, industry focus groups, futures invention workshops, and conference facilitation. Members receive a host of benefits, including the monthly newsletter *Design Intelligence*.

Address:
11921 Freedom Drive, Suite 550
Reston, VA 20190
Telephone: (800) 726-8603
internet: www.di.net

Design Management Institute (DMI)

The Design Management Institute (DMI) is a professional organization that primarily serves senior design executives and other executives involved in the development of products, communications, and environments, as well as educators. Through its conferences, publications, and research, DMI strives to be the international authority and advocate on design management. Their quarterly *Design Management Journal*, the industry's only scholarly journal, emphasizes contemporary design management thinking with features from the world's leading experts in design management.

Address:
29 Temple Place
Boston, MA 02111-1350
Telephone: (617) 338-6380
Internet: www.dmi.org

Industrial Designers Society of America (IDSA)

Since 1965, the Industrial Designers Society of America (IDSA) has been dedicated to communicating the value of industrial design to society, business, government, and the general public. IDSA serves its constituency through its professional journal *Innovation*, award programs, annual conference, research, networking opportunities, and promotion of the practice at all levels of government.

Address:
1142 Walker Rd
Great Falls, VA 22066
Telephone: (703) 759-0100
Internet: www.idsa.org

Design depends largely on constraints.

Charles Eames

Initiative for Architectural Research (IAR)

The Initiative for Architectural Research (IAR) was formed by the Association of Collegiate Schools of Architecture (ACSA), American Institute of Architects (AIA) and Architectural Research Centers Consortium (ARCC) primarily to serve as an advocate for architectural research, to serve as a clearinghouse for information about architectural research, and to facilitate research efforts that address specific needs of the architectural profession. The IAR produces *A/R: Architecture/ Research*, the directory of architectural research abstracts from universities, architecture firms, national laboratories, and research centers throughout the US and Canada, as well as co-producing the annual Research Awards with *Architecture* magazine.

Address:
IAR c/o ACSA
1735 New York Avenue, NW
Washington, DC 20006
Telephone: (202) 785-2324
Internet: www.architectureresearch.org

International Council of Societies of Industrial Design (ICSID)

The International Council of Societies of Industrial Design (ICSID) strives to advance the discipline of industrial design worldwide. This non-profit, non-governmental organization was formed in 1957 and is supported by 152 organizations and societies in 53 countries. Through these groups, ICSID represents approximately 150,000 professionals. Member groups work with an Advisory Senate and Executive Board in the areas of practice, education, promotion, and development to enhance the profession.

Address:
Yrjönkatu 11 E
00120 Helsinki
Finland
Telephone: +358 9 696 22 90
Internet: www.icsid.org

Design demands observation.

Achille Castiglioni

International Federation of Interior Architects/ Designers (IFI)

The goals of the International Federation of Interior Architects/Designers (IFI) are to promote the interior architecture and design profession, to represent its practitioners, to act as a clearinghouse for professional and cultural information, to encourage international cooperation, and to assist and serve the industry. The IFI engages in a number of activities to further these ends, such as maintaining a public relations program, lobbying for policies benefiting the practice, organizing conferences and supporting minimum standards of education and a Code of Ethics and Practice. Its membership is composed of professional interior design organizations in countries throughout the world.

Address:
P.O. Box 91640
Auckland Park
Johannesburg, 2006
South Africa
Telephone: +27 11 4772279
Internet: www.ifi.co.za

Interior design is a social art, practiced on an intimate scale.

Marco Pasanella

International Federation of Landscape Architects (IFLA)

The International Federation of Landscape Architects (IFLA) represents various national associations of landscape architects. The non-profit, non-governmental organization was formed in 1948 to promote the practice of landscape architecture and to establish standards of professional practice throughout the world. The IFLA is governed by a World Council with jurisdiction over regional councils. Members join IFLA through their national membership associations; although, individuals from countries which do not have a national representative group may also join. The IFLA publishes a newsletter twice a year and sponsors a biennial World Conference. Other regional meetings are held on a regular basis.

Address:
4 rue Hardy, RP no 914
78009 Versailles
Cedex, France
Internet: www.ifla.net

International Interior Design Association (IIDA)

With a mission of promoting excellence in interior design and advancing the practice through knowledge, the International Interior Design Association (IIDA) provides a variety of services and benefits for its 11,000 members. It advocates for design excellence, nurtures the interior design community worldwide, maintains educational standards, responds to trends in business and design, and provides a wealth of information about interior design and related issues. The organization maintains 9 international regions with more than 30 chapters and 64 U.S. city centers.

Address:
341 Merchandise Mart
Chicago, IL 60654
Telephone: (312) 467-1950
Internet: www.iida.org

International Union of Architects (UIA)

Founded in 1948, the International Union of Architects (UIA) is an international, non-governmental organization dedicated to uniting the architects of the world. Through its 92 UIA Member Sections, the group represents over a million architects. The UIA's mission is to represent architects and promote the practice with other professional organizations worldwide, other non-governmental organizations, and intergovernmental institutions. The UIA General Secretariat is the Union's executive body and the administrative center for the coordination of relations between the UIA Member Sections and their activities. A personal information service is available from the General Secretariat, allowing architects to keep up with UIA activities, its partners, and Member Sections.

Address:
51, rue Raynouard
75 016 Paris, France
Telephone: 33 (1) 45 24 36 88
Internet: www.uia-architectes.org

Japan Institute of Architects (JIA)

The Japan Institute of Architects (JIA) serves to define and promote the social and legal status of professional architects in Japan and to promote their interests abroad. Currently, JIA represents over 6,300 members through 10 chapters. A member of the Architects Regional Council Asia (ARCASIA) as well as the International Union of Architects (IUA), the Japan Institute of Architects was formed in 1987 when the Japan Architects Association (JAA) and the Japan Federation of Professional Architects Association (JFPAA) united.

Address:
2-3-18, Jingumae
Shibuya-ku, Tokyo
150-0001 Japan
Telephone: +81-3-3408-7125
Internet: www.jia.or.jp

Joslyn Castle Institute for Sustainable Communities

Housed in Omaha, Nebraska's historic 1902 Joslyn Castle, the Joslyn Castle Institute for Sustainable Communities is a partnership among Nebraska state government, the Joslyn Art Museum, the University of Nebraska College of Architecture, and other public and private organizations. The Institute focuses on promoting sustainable development through outreach and education programs, as well as research. Its goal is to encourage communities to develop by balancing economic, social and environmental needs. The institute is one of 18 centers worldwide partnering with the United Nations Centre for Human Settlement (UNCHS) in its Best Practices in Local Leadership Program (BLP).

Address:
3902 Davenport Street
Omaha, Nebraska 68131
Telephone: (402) 595-1902
Internet: www.libfind.unl.edu/JCI/

Did you know...

In early 2001, Barcelona's city hall became the first building to comply with the city's new regulation requiring all major new construction and renovation projects to incorporate solar panels for hot water and electricity.

National Institute of Building Sciences (NIBS)

The National Institute of Building Sciences (NIBS) serves the public interest by promoting a rational regulatory environment for the building community, facilitating the introduction of new technology, and disseminating technical information. NIBS was established by Congress as an authoritative national source on building science and technology issues. It is a non-governmental, non-profit organization. Of its 21-member Board of Directors, 15 are elected and six are appointed by the President of the United States with the approval of the U.S. Senate. NIBS committees are integral in establishing industry-wide standards for the construction industry. They also publish many books on specific building technologies and techniques.

Address:
1090 Vermont Avenue, NW, Suite 700
Washington, DC 20005-4905
Telephone: (202) 289-7800
Internet: www.nibs.org

National Organization of Minority Architects (NOMA)

The National Organization of Minority Architects (NOMA) was formed in 1971 for the purpose of enhancing diversity in architecture. Today there are 12 NOMA chapters and 19 student chapters across the country, increasing recognition on university campuses and providing access to government policy makers. The organization works to advance minority architects, from job placement for college students to aiding member firms in securing contracts. NOMA annually holds a conference, organizes a design award program, and produces a newsletter.

Address:
5530 Wisonsin Ave., Ste. 1210
Chevy Chase, MD 20815
Telephone: (301) 941-1065
Internet: www.noma.net

Did you know...

Approximately 1 percent of U.S. architects are African-American.

Royal Architectural Institute of Canada (RAIC)

The Royal Architectural Institute of Canada (RAIC) "works towards a future in which Canadians will view our total environment, both natural and built, as our most important asset and the Institute's members as essential to its creation and maintenance." Established in 1907, the Institute represents more than 3,000 architects, educators, and graduates of accredited Canadian schools of architecture. The organization focuses its activities in five areas: publications, symposia and exhibitions, research, awards, and practice committees.

Address:
55 Murray Street, Suite 330
Ottawa, Ontario, K1N 5M3
Canada
Telephone: (613) 241-3600
Internet: www.raic.org

Royal Australian Institute of Architects (RAIA)

The Royal Australian Institute of Architects (RAIA) represents over 8,000 members in Australia and overseas, largely through eight state and territorial chapters. Established in 1929, the RAIA seeks to raise awareness among the public about the value of architecture and the importance of good design and to promote creativity and continuous training among its members. Their mission is to "unite architects to advance architecture." Each year the RAIA sponsors the Architecture Awards in the states and territories, culminating in national prizes. The group also publishes Australia's premier architecture magazine, *Architecture Australia*, and the highly regarded and regularly updated *Environment Design Guide*.

Address:
2a Mugga Way
Red Hill ACT 2603
Australia
Telephone: (02) 6273 1548
Internet: www.raia.com.au

In architecture, there is such an obsession with the future – an attempt to break all the boundaries of the past and create something new – but then we forget to live in the present. I don't like to think so much about the future, because I'm having such a good time now.

Julie Eizenberg

Royal Institute of British Architects (RIBA)

Founded in 1834, the Royal Institute of British Architects (RIBA) was one of the world's first architectural associations. Representing more than 32,000 members in over 100 countries, the RIBA is a worldwide organization committed to the improvement and enjoyment of the physical environment. Its mission is "the advancement of architecture and the promotion of the acquirement of the knowledge of the arts and sciences connected therewith." The organization sponsors several prestigious award programs including the Stirling Prize and the Royal Gold Medal. Their RIBA Architecture Gallery features many exhibits on architecture and design each year. Members also have access to Ribanet Conference, a global communication system connecting architects through their computers, allowing them to use electronic conferencing to exchange ideas, share files, participate in one-to-one online chats, and send and receive emails. RIBA membership is open to anyone, whether an architect or a patron of the practice. Established in 1934, RIBA's British Architectural Library is the largest and most comprehensive resource in the United Kingdom for research and information on all aspects of architecture.

Address:
66 Portland Place
London W1N 4AD UK
Telephone: 44 171 580 5533
Internet: www.architecture.com

Did you know...

The Queen of England recently knighted architect Terry Farrell, who joins the distinguished fellowship of knighted architects Norman Foster, Richard Rogers, and the late James Stirling.

Society of Architectural Historians (SAH)

Since its founding in 1940, the Society of Architectural Historians (SAH) has sought to promote the history of architecture. The membership of SAH ranges from professionals such as architects, planners, preservationists, and academics to those simply interested in architecture. The Society produces a quarterly journal and monthly newsletter and organizes study tours and an annual conference. There are also a number of associated, although independent, local chapters. The SAH's national headquarters is located in the architecturally significant Charnley-Persky House which was designed in 1891 by the firm of Dankmar Adler and Louis Sullivan. Guided tours of the house are offered.

Address:
1365 North Astor Street
Chicago, Illinois 60610-2144
Telephone: (312) 573-1365
Internet: www.sah.org

Did you know...

Financier LeGrand Lockwood's 1868 Second Empire Style country house (Lockwood-Mathews Mansion, by New York architect Detlef Lienau) in Norwalk, CT, heralded a new era as one of the earliest lavish summer mansions built by a railroad tycoon and had the distinction, at 62 rooms, of being the largest private home in the U.S. at the time it was built.

Society for Environmental Graphic Design (SEGD)

The Society for Environmental Graphic Design (SEGD) is a non-profit organization formed in 1973 to promote public awareness of and professional development in environmental graphic design. This interdisciplinary field encompasses the talents of many design professionals, including graphic designers, architects, landscape architects, product designers, planners, interior designers, and exhibition designers, in the planning and design of graphic elements that shape our built and natural environments. Practitioners in this field design graphic elements to help identify, direct, inform, interpret, and visually enhance our surroundings. From wayfinding systems and mapping to exhibit design and themed environments, environmental graphic design impacts our experiences everywhere. SEGD offers its members an interdisciplinary network to support and enhance their efforts in this growing discipline, a bimonthly newsletter, annual conference, design award program, technical bulletins, job bank listings, and many other formal and informal resources.

Address:
401 F Street NW, Suite 333
Washington, DC 20001
Telephone: (202) 638-5555
Internet: www. segd.org

Society for Marketing Professional Services (SMPS)

The Society for Marketing Professional Services was established in 1973 specifically to serve marketing professionals in the A/E/C industry. The SMPS offers a host of membership benefits and programs to keep its over 4,700 members abreast of changes and initiatives that may impact them. These benefits include the Marketing Communications Awards, the Certified Professional Services Marketer Program, the National Marketing Conference, *Marketer*, a bimonthly journal, as well as electronic services and a bookstore.

Address:
99 Canal Center Plaza, Suite 250
Alexandria, VA 22314
Telephone: (800) 292-7677
Internet: www.smps.org

Did you know...

A recent e-technology survey found that 33% of SMPS members and 38% of A/E/C clients cited keeping up with technology as the single greatest challenge facing their company.

United Nations Centre for Human Settlements (Habitat)

The United Nations Centre for Human Settlements (Habitat) was established in 1978 as the lead agency for coordinating human settlements and development activities within the United Nations family, focusing on the following priority areas: shelter and social services; urban management; environment and infrastructure; and assessment, monitoring, and information. Habitat supports and works in partnership with governments, local authorities, non-governmental organizations, and the private sector. Currently, Habitat has over 200 operational programs and projects underway in 80 countries, focusing on urban management, housing, basic services, and infrastructure development. Habitat promotes sustainable human settlement development through policy formulation, capacity-building, knowledge creation, and the strengthening of partnerships between governments and civil society. In 1996, the United Nations General Assembly designated Habitat as a focal point for the implementation of the Habitat Agenda, the global plan of action adopted at the second United Nations Conference on Human Settlements.

Address:
P. O. Box 30030
Nairobi, Kenya
Tel: (254-2) 623153
Internet: www.unchs.org

Urban Land Institute (ULI)

Formed in 1936 as a research arm of the National Association of Real Estate Boards (now the National Association of Realtors), the Urban Land Institute (ULI) is an independent institution dedicated to promoting the responsible use of land to enhance the total environment. The group represents 15,000 professionals in 50 states and 52 countries. ULI activities include research, forums and task forces, awards, education, and publishing.

Address:
1025 Thomas Jefferson Street, NW
Suite 500 West
Washington, DC 20007
Telephone: (202) 624-7000
Internet: www.uli.org

U.S. Green Building Council

The U.S. Green Building Council was formed in 1993 to integrate, educate, and provide leadership for building industry leaders, environmental groups, designers, retailers, and building owners as they strive to develop and market products and services which are environmentally progressive and responsible. The Council includes more than 250 organizations worldwide with a common interest in green building practices, technologies, policies, and standards. Their most visible program, the LEED™ Green Building Rating System is a voluntary, consensus-based rating system for commercial buildings to provide a national consensus on what constitutes a green building and market incentives to build "green."

Address:
110 Sutter Street, Suite 140
San Francisco, CA 94104
Telephone: (415) 445-9500
Internet: www.usgbc.org

Did you know...

The Philip Merrill Environmental Center, designed for the Chesapeake Bay Foundation by the SmithGroup (2000), received the first platinum rating from the U.S. Green Building Council as part of their LEED Green Building Rating System, marking it the greenest building in the U.S.

Design & Building Related Organizations

The following list of associations, organizations, and government agencies offer a variety of information and support about the design and construction arena.

ASSOCIATIONS & ORGANIZATIONS

Acoustical Society of America
2 Huntington Quadrangle, Suite 1N01
Melville, New York 11747-4052
Tel: (516) 576-2360
Fax: (516) 576-2377
Internet: Internet: www.asa.aip.org

Air-Conditioning & Refrigeration Institute
4301 North Fairfax Dr. #425
Arlington, VA 22203
Tel: (703) 524-8800
Fax: (703) 528-3816
Internet: www.ari.org

Air Conditioning Contractors of America, Inc.
2800 Shirlington Road #300
Arlington, VA 22206
Tel: (703) 575-4477
Fax: (703) 575-4449
Internet: www.acca.org

Alliance to Save Energy
1200 18th St. NW #900
Washington, DC 20036
Tel: (202) 857-0666
Fax: (202) 331-9588
Internet: www.ase.org

American Arbitration Association
335 Madison Ave. 10th Floor
New York, NY 10017-4605
Tel: (212) 716-5800
Fax: (212) 716-5905
Internet: www.adr.org

American Architectural Manufacturers Association
1827 Walden Office Square #104
Schaumburg, IL 60173-4628
Tel: (847) 303-5664
Fax: (847) 303-5774
Internet: www.aamanet.org

American Association of Nurserymen
1250 I Street NW, Suite 500
Washington, DC 20005
Tel: (202) 789-2900
Fax: (202) 789-1893
Internet: www.anla.org

American Center for Design
325 West Huron, Suite 711
Chicago, IL 60610
Tel: (312) 787-2018
Fax: (312) 649-9518
Internet: www.ac4d.org

American Concrete Institute
PO Box 9094
38800 Country Club Drive
Farmington Hills, MI 48331
Tel: (248) 848-3700
Fax: (248) 848-3701
Internet: www.aci-int.org

American Gas Association
400 North Capitol St. NW
Washington, DC 20001
Tel: (202) 824-7000
Fax: (202) 824-7115
Internet: www.aga.org

American Horticultural Society
7931 East Boulevard Drive
Alexandria VA 22308
Tel: (703) 768-5700
Fax: (703) 768-8700
Internet: www.ahs.org

American Institute of Building Design
2505 Main Street #209-B
Stratford, CT 06615
Tel: (800) 366-2423
Fax: (203) 378-3568
Internet: www.aibd.org

American Institute of Steel Construction
One East Wacker Dr. #3100
Chicago, IL 60601-2001
Tel: (312) 670-2400
Fax: (312) 670-5403
Internet: www.aisc.org

Design & Building Related Organizations (Con't)

American National Standards Institute
1819 L Street NW #600
Washington, DC 20036
Tel: (202) 293-8020
Fax: (202) 293-9287
Internet: www.ansi.org

American Resort Development Association
1220 L Street N.W. o Suite 500
Washington, D.C. 20005
Tel: (202) 371-6700
Fax: (202) 289-8544
Internet: www.arda.org

American Society for Horticulture Science
113 South West Street, Suite 200
Alexandria, VA 22314-2851
Tel: (703) 836-4606
Fax: (703) 836-2024
Internet: www.ashs.org

American Society for Testing & Materials
100 Barr Harbor Dr.
West Conshohocken, PA 19428-2959
Tel: (610) 832-9585
Fax: (610) 832-9555
Internet: www.astm.org

American Society of Civil Engineers
1801 Alexander Bell Dr.
Reston, VA 20191-4400
Tel: (703) 295-6300
Fax: (703) 295-6222
Internet: www.asce.org

American Society of Consulting Arborists
15245 Shady Grove Road, Suite 130
Rockville, MD 20850
Tel: (301) 947-0483
Fax: (301) 990-9771
Internet: www. asca-consultants.org

American Society of Golf Course Architects
221 N. LaSalle St.
Chicago, IL 60601
Tel: (312) 372-7090
Fax: (312) 372-6160
Internet: www.golfdesign.org

American Society of Heating, Refrigerating & Air-Conditioning Engineers
1791 Tullie Circle NE
Atlanta, GA 30329
Tel: (404) 636-8400
Fax: (404) 321-5478
Internet: www.ashrae.org

American Society of Mechanical Engineers
Three Park Ave.
New York, NY 10016-5990
Tel: (212) 591-7722
Fax: (212) 591-7674
Internet: www.asme.org

American Society of Plumbing Engineers
8614 W. Catalpa Avenue #1007-1009
Chicago, IL 60656-1116
Tel: (773) 693-2773
Fax: (773) 695-9007
Internet: www.aspe.org

American Society of Professional Estimators
11141 Georgia Ave. #412
Wheaton, Maryland 20902
Tel: (301) 929-8848
Fax: (301) 929-0231
Internet: www.aspenational.com

American Textile Manufacturers Institute
1130 Connecticut Ave., NW, Suite 1200
Washington, DC 20036-3954
Tel: 202-862-0500
Fax: 202-862-0570
Internet: www.atmi.org

APA - The Engineered Wood Association
P.O. Box 11700
Tacoma, Washington 98411-0700
Tel: (253) 565-6600
Fax: (253) 565-7265
Internet: www.apawood.org

Architectural Woodwork Institute
1952 Isaac Newton Square
Reston, VA 20190
Tel: (703) 733-0600
Fax: (703) 733-0584
Internet: www.awinet.org

Design & Building Related Organizations (Con't)

ASFE
8811 Colesville Rd. #G106
Silver Spring, MD 20910
Tel: (301) 565-2733
Fax: (301) 589-2017
Internet: www.asfe.org

Associated Builders & Contractors
1300 North 17th St. 8th Floor
Rosslyn, VA 22209
Tel: (703) 812-2000
Fax: (703) 812-8200
Internet: www.abc.org

Associated General Contractors of America
333 John Carlyle St. #200
Alexandria, VA 22314
Tel: (703) 548-3118
Fax: (703) 548-3119
Internet: www.agc.org

Associated Owners & Developers
PO Box 4163
McLean, VA 22103-4163
Tel: (703) 734-2397
Fax: (703) 734-2908
Internet: www.constructionsite.net

Associated Landscape Contractors of America
150 Elden Street, Suite 270
Herndon, Virginia 20170
Tel: (703) 736-9666
Fax: (703) 736-9668
Internet: www.alca.org

Association for Contract Textiles
P.O. Box 101981
Fort Worth, TX 76185
Tel: (817) 924-8048
Internet: www.contract-textiles.com

Association for Facilities Engineering
8180 Corporate Park Dr. #305
Cincinnati, OH 45242
Tel: (513) 489-2473
Fax: (513) 247-7422
Internet: www.afe.org

Association for the Advancement of Cost Engineering
209 Prairie Ave. #100
Morgantown, WV 26501
Tel: (304) 296-8444
Fax: (304) 291-5728
Internet: www.aacei.org

Association of Energy Engineers
4025 Pleasantdale Rd. #420
Atlanta, GA 30340
Tel: (770) 447-5083
Fax: (770) 446-3969
Internet: www.aeecenter.org

Association of Higher Education Facilities Officers
1643 Prince St.
Alexandria, VA 22314-2818
Tel: (703) 684-1446
Fax: (703) 549-2772
Internet: www.appa.org

Association of the Wall & Ceiling Industries
803 West Broad St. #600
Falls Church, VA 22046
Tel: (703) 534-8300
Fax: (703) 534-8307
Internet: www.awci.org

Building Codes Assistance Project
1200 18th St. NW #900
Washington, DC 20036
Tel: (202) 530-2200
Fax: (202) 331-9588
Internet: www.ase.org

Building Futures Council
PO Box 146
Georgetown, MD 21930
Tel: (410) 648-5362
Fax: (410) 648-5911
Internet: www.arch.gatech.edu/bfc

Building Officials & Code Administrators International
4051 West Flossmoor Rd.
Country Club Hills, IL 60478
Tel: (708) 799-2300
Fax: (708) 799-4981
Internet: www.bocai.org

Building Owners & Managers Association International
1201 New York Ave. NW #300
Washington, DC 20005
Tel: (202) 408-2662
Fax: (202) 371-0181
Internet: www.boma.org

**Design &
Building
Related
Organizations
(Con't)**

Carpet and Rug Institute
P.O. Box 2048
Dalton, GA 30722
Tel: (800) 882-8846
Internet: www.carpet-rug.com

**Center for Environmental Education
and Information**
P.O. Box 1778
Sun Valley, Idaho 83353
Tel: (208) 727-9679
Fax: (208) 727-1713
Internet: www.wcei.org

Center for Health Design
3470 Mt. Diablo Boulevard
Lafayette, CA 94549
Tel: (925) 299-3631
Fax: (925) 299-3642
Internet: www.healthdesign.org

Code Compliance Council
PO Box 656
Saratoga Springs, NY 12866
Tel: (336) 327-8732
Fax: (800) 638-3161
Internet: www.codecomply.com

Color Association of the United States
315 West 39th Street, Studio 507
New York, NY 10018
Tel: (212) 947-7774
Fax: (212) 594-6987
Internet: www.colorassociation.com

**Construction Management
Association of America**
7918 Jones Branch Dr. #540
McLean, VA 22102-3307
Tel: (703) 356-2622
Fax: (703) 356-6388
Internet: www.cmaanet.org

Council of Professional Surveyors
1015 15th St. NW
Washington, DC 20005
Tel: (202) 347-7474
Fax: (202) 898-0068
Internet:
www.acec.org/memship/councilprof-
survey.htm

Deep Foundations Institute
120 Charlotte Pl. 3rd Floor
Englewood Cliffs, NJ 07632
Tel: (201) 567-4232
Fax: (201) 567-4436
Internet: www.dfi.org

Door & Hardware Institute
14150 Newbrook Dr. #200
Chantilly, VA 20151-2223
Tel: (703) 222-2010
Fax: (703) 222-2410
Internet: www.dhi.org

Edison Electric Institute
701 Pennsylvania Ave. NW
Washington, DC 20004-2696
Tel: (202) 508-5000
Fax: (202) 508-5360
Internet: www.eei.org

EIFS Industry Members Association
3000 Corporate Center Dr. #270
Morrow, GA 30260
Tel: (770) 968-7945
Fax: (770) 968-5818
Internet: www.eifsfacts.com

Electrical Power Research Institute
3412 Hillview Ave.
Palo Alto, CA 94304
Tel: (800) 313-3774
Internet: www.epri.com

Gas Technology Institute
1700 S. Mount Prospect
Des Plaines, IL 60018
Tel: (773) 399-8100
Fax: (773) 399-8170
Internet: www.gri.org

Glass Association of North America
2945 SW Wanamaker Dr. #A
Topeka, KS 66614-5321
Tel: (785) 271-0208
Fax: (785) 271-0166
Internet: www.glasswebsite.org

**Hardwood Plywood & Veneer
Association**
P.O. Box 2789
Reston, VA 20195
Tel: (703) 435-2900
Fax: (703) 435-2537
Internet: www.hpva.org

Hearth Products Association
1601 North Kent St. #1001
Arlington, VA 22209
Tel: (703) 522-0086
Fax: (703) 522-0548
Internet: www.hearthassoc.org

Design & Building Related Organizations (Con't)

Human Factors and Ergonomics Society
P.O. Box 1369
Santa Monica. CA 90406
Tel: (310) 394-1811
Fax: (310) 394-2410
Internet: www.hfes.org

Illuminating Engineering Society of North America
120 Wall St. 17th Floor
New York, NY 10005
Tel: (212) 248-5000
Fax: (212) 248-5017
Internet: www.iesna.org

Institute of Electrical & Electronics Engineers Inc.
3 Park Ave. 17th Floor
New York, NY 10016-5997
Tel: (212) 419-7900
Fax: (212) 752-4929
Internet: www.ieee.org

Institute of Store Planners
25 North Broadway
Tarrytown, NY 10591
Tel: (800) 379-9912
Fax: (914) 332-1541
Internet: www.ispo.org

International Association of Lighting Designers
The Merchandise Mart
Suite 9-104
Chicago, IL 60654
Tel: (312) 527-3677
Fax: (312) 527-3680
Internet: www.iald.org

International Code Council
5203 Leesburg Pike, Suite 600
Falls Church, VA 22041
Tel: (703) 931-4533
Fax: (703) 379-1546
Internet: www.intlcode.org

International Conference of Building Code Officials
5360 Workman Mill Rd.
Whittier, CA 90601-2298
Tel: (800) 423-6587
Fax: (562) 692-3853
Internet: www.icbo.org

International Facility Management Association
1 East Greenway Plaza #1100
Houston, TX 77046-0194
Tel: (713) 623-4362
Fax: (713) 623-6124
Internet: www.ifma.org

International Furnishings and Design Association
191 Clarksville Road
Princeton, NJ 08550
Tel: (609) 799-3423
Fax: (609) 799-7032
Internet: www.ifda.com

International Society of Arboriculture
P.O. Box 3129
Champaign, IL 61826-3129
Tel: (217) 355-9411
Fax: (217) 355-9516
www2.champaign.isa-arbor.com

ISA International Society for Measurement & Control
67 Alexander Dr.
Research Triangle Park, NC, 27709
Tel: (919) 549-8411
Fax: (919) 549-8288
Internet: www.isa.org

Irrigation Association
6540 Arlington Boulevard
Falls Church, Virginia, 22042-6638
Tel: (703) 536-7080
Fax: (703) 536-7019
Internet: www.irrigation.org

Light Gauge Steel Engineers Association
1726 M Street NW #601
Washington, DC 20036
Tel: (202) 263-4488
Fax: (202) 785-3856
Internet: www.lgsea.com

Marble Institute of America
30 Eden Alley, Suite 301
Columbus, Ohio 43215
Tel: (614) 228-6194
Fax: (614) 461-1497
Internet: www.marble-institute.com

**Design &
Building
Related
Organizations
(Con't)**

**Metal Building Manufacturers
Association**
1300 Sumner Ave.
Cleveland, OH 44115-2851
Tel: (216) 241-7333
Fax: (216) 241-0105
Internet: www.mbma.com

National Arborist Association, Inc.
3 Perimeter Road, Unit 1
Manchester, NH 03103
Tel: 800-733-2622
Fax: 603-314-5386
Internet: www.natlarb.com

**National Association of
Environmental Professionals**
P.O. Box 2086
Bowie, MD 20718
Tel: (888) 251-9902
Fax: (301) 860-1141
Internet: www.naep.org

**National Association of Home
Builders**
1201 15th street, NW
Washington, DC 20005
Tel: (800) 368-5242
Internet: www.nahb.com

**National Clearinghouse for
Educational Facilities**
1090 Vermont Ave. NW #700
Washington, DC 20005-4905
Tel: (202) 289-7800
Fax: (202) 289-1092
Internet: www.edfacilities.org

**National Concrete Masonry
Association**
2302 Horse Pen Rd.
Herndon, VA 20171-3499
Tel: (703) 713-1900
Fax: (703) 713-1910
Internet: www.ncma.org

**National Conference of States on
Building Codes & Standards, Inc.**
505 Huntmar Park Dr. #210
Herndon, VA 20170
Tel: (703) 437-0100
Fax: (703) 481-3596
Internet: www.ncsbcs.org

**National Council of Acoustical
Consultants**
66 Morris Ave. #1A
Springfield, NJ 07081-1409
Tel: (973) 564-5859
Fax: (973) 564-7480
Internet: www.ncac.com

**National Electrical Contractors
Association**
3 Bethesda Metro Center #1100
Bethesda, MD 20814
Tel: (301) 657-3110
Fax: (301) 215-4500
Internet: www.necanet.org

**National Electrical Manufacturers
Association**
1300 North 17th St. #1847
Rosslyn, VA 22209
Tel: (703) 841-3200
Fax: (703) 841-5900
Internet: www.nema.org

National Fire Protection Association
1 Batterymarch Park
PO Box 9101
Quincy, MA 02269-9101
Tel: (617) 770-3000
Fax: (617) 770-0700
Internet: www.nfpa.org

National Fire Sprinkler Association
40 Jon Barrett Rd.
PO Box 1000
Patterson, NY 12563
Tel: (845) 878-4200
Fax: (845) 878-4215
Internet: www.nfsa.org

National Lighting Bureau
8811 Colesville Road, Suite G106
Silver Spring, MD
Tel: (301) 587-9572
Fax: (301) 589-2017
Internet: www.nlb.org

National Kitchen & Bath Association
687 Willow Grove Street
Hackettstown, NJ 07840
Tel: (877) NKBA-PRO
Fax: (908) 852-1695
Internet: www.nkba.org

Design & Building Related Organizations (Con't)

National Paint & Coatings Association
1500 Rhode Island Ave., NW
Washington, DC 20005
Tel: (202) 462-6272
Fax: (202) 462-8549
Internet: www.paint.org

National Society of Professional Engineers
1420 King St.
Alexandria, VA 22314-2794
Tel: (703) 684-2800
Fax: (703) 836-4875
Internet: www.nspe.org

National Sunroom Association
2945 SW Wanamaker Dr. #A
Topeka, KS 66614-5321
Tel: (785) 271-0208
Fax: (785) 261-0166
Internet:
www.glasswebsite.com/NSA/

National Wood Flooring Association
16388 Westwoods Business Park
Ellisville, MO 63021
Tel: (800) 422-4556
Fax: (636) 391-6137
Internet: www.woodfloors.org

New Buildings Institute
Codes & Standards Office
142 E. Jewett Blvd.
White Salmon, WA 98672
Tel: (509) 493-4468
Fax: (509) 493-4078
Internet: www.newbuildings.org

North American Insulation Manufacturers Association
44 Canal Center Plaza #310
Alexandria, VA 22314
Tel: (703) 684-0084
Fax: (703) 684-0427
Internet: www.naima.org

North American Steel Framing Alliance
1726 M St. NW #601
Washington, DC 20036-4523
Tel: (202) 785-2022
Fax: (202) 785-3856
Internet:
www.steelframingalliance.com

NSSN: A National Resource for Global Standards
American National Standards Institute
11 West 42nd St.
New York, NY 10036
Tel: (212) 642-8908
Fax: (212) 398-0023
Internet: www.nssn.org

Plumbing Manufacturers Institute
1340 Remington Rd. #A
Schaumburg, IL 60173
Tel: (847) 884-9764
Fax: (847) 884-9775
Internet: www.pmihome.org

Precast/Prestressed Concrete Institute
209 W. Jackson Blvd.
Chicago, IL 60606-6938
Tel: (312) 786-0300
Fax: (312) 786-0353
Internet: www.pci.org

Preservation Trades Network, Inc.
731 Hebron Avenue
Glastonbury, CT 06033-2457
Tel: (860) 633-2854
Fax: (860) 657-8241
Internet: www.ptn.org

Professional Construction Estimators Association of America
PO Box 680336
Charlotte, NC 28216
Tel: (704) 987-9978
Fax: (704) 987-9979
Internet: www.pcea.org

Society of Fire Protection Engineers
7315 Wisconsin Ave. #1225 W
Bethesda, MD 20814
Tel: (301) 718-2910
Fax: (301) 718-2242
Internet: www.sfpe.org

Southern Building Code Congress International
900 Montclair Rd.
Birmingham, AL 35213-1206
Tel: (205) 591-1853
Fax: (205) 591-0775
Internet: www.sbcci.org

Design & Building Related Organizations (Con't)

StoneInfo.com
PMB196-8711 East Pinnacle Peak Rd.
Scottsdale, AZ 85255
Tel: (480) 502-5345
Fax: (480) 502-5358
Internet: www.stoneinfo.com

Underwriters Laboratories Inc.
333 Pfingsten Rd.
Northbrook, IL 60062-2096
Tel: (847) 272-8800
Fax: (847) 272-8129
Internet: www.ul.com

Waterfront Center
1622 Wisconsin Avenue, N.W.
Washington, D.C. 20007
Tel: (202) 337-0356
Fax: (202) 625-1654
Internet: www.waterfrontcenter.org

Window & Door Manufacturers Association
1400 East Touhy Ave. #470
Des Plaines, IL 60018
Tel: (800) 223-2301
Fax: (847) 299-1286
Internet: www.nwwda.org

GOVERNMENT AGENCIES
Architectural & Transportation Barriers Compliance Board Access Board
1331 F St. NW #1000
Washington, DC 20004-1111
Tel: (800) 872-2253
Internet: www.accessboard.gov

Army Corps of Engineers
20 Massachusetts Ave. NW
Washington, DC 20314
Tel: (202) 761-0660
Internet: www.usace.army.mil

Bureau of Land Management
1849 C Street, Room 406-LS
Washington, DC 20240
Tel: (202) 452-5125
Fax: (202) 452-5124
Internet: www.blm.gov

Census Bureau Construction Statistics
Manufacturing & Construction Div.
Washington DC 20233-6900
Tel: (301) 457-4100
Fax: (301) 457-4714
Internet:
www.census.gov/const/www

Department of Agriculture
14th & Independence Ave., SW
Washington, DC 20250
Tel: (202) 720-2791
Fax: (202) 720-2166
Internet: www.usda.gov

Department of Energy
Forrestal Bldg.
1000 Independence Ave. SW
Washington, DC 20585
Tel: (800) 342-5363
Fax: (202) 586-4403
Internet: www.energy.gov

Department of Labor
Occupational Safety & Health
Administration
200 Constitution Ave. NW
Washington, DC 20210
Tel: (202) 693-1999
Internet: www.dol.gov

Department of the Interior
1849 C St. NW
Washington, DC 20240
Tel: (202) 208-3100
Internet: www.doi.gov

Department of Transportation
400 7th Street SW
Washington, DC 20590
Tel: (202) 366-4000
Internet: www.dot.gov

Environmental Protection Agency
1200 Pennsylvania Avenue, NW
Washington, DC 20460
Tel: (202) 260-2090
Internet: www.epa.gov

Federal Emergency Management Agency
500 C Street, SW
Washington, DC 20472
Tel: (202) 646-4600
Internet: www.fema.gov

**Design &
Building
Related
Organizations
(Con't)**

General Services Administration
1800 F Street
Washington, DC 20405
Tel: (202) 208-3100
Internet: www.gsa.gov

**National Institute of Standards &
Technology**
100 Bureau Dr. Stop 3460
Gaithersburg, MD 20899-3460
Tel: (301) 975-8295
Internet: www.nist.gov

Museums

Numerous museums around the world are devoted solely to architecture and design, and many major museums maintain strong design collections and regularly host architecture and design related exhibits. This chapter contains a listing of those museums, along with the names and dates of their 2002 exhibitions.

Alvar Aalto Museum

Founded in 1966, Finland's Alvar Aalto Museum houses a permanent collection of the designer/architect's work, produces publications related to his career, and oversees conservation of his buildings. Additionally, the Museum arranges Aalto exhibits worldwide. Its architectural collection contains almost 1,500 original models and artifacts designed by Aino and Alvar Aalto, as well as a photo archive and reproductions of Aalto's original drawings. A library featuring architecture and literature centered around Alvar Aalto is open to researchers and students by appointment.

Address:
Alvar Aallon katu 7
40600 Jyvaskyla, Finland
Telephone: +358 (0)14 624 809
Internet: www.alvaraalto.fi

Exhibition Schedule:
Alvar Aalto. Architect
Permanent exhibit

Please visit the Web site for information about the museum's changing exhibition schedule and traveling exhibitions abroad.

For information about the Alvar Aalto Academy and Alvar Aalto Archives please visit the Web site at www.alvaraalto.fi/academy/index.htm and www.alvaraalto.fi/archive/index.htm.

Architektur Zentrum Wien

The Architektur Zentrum Wien was founded in 1993 by the Austrian Federal Government and the City of Vienna as a forum to promote Austrian architecture. Through its national and international exhibitions, publications, workshops, and panel discussions, the museum is Austria's premier venue for contemporary architecture and urban design. In addition, they host the annual Viennese Seminar on Architecture and the Vienna Architecture Congress. A database on contemporary Austrian architecture is maintained by the museum and available on a limited basis on the Internet. The library, which will be open to the public once the planned library expansion is complete, contains 700 international architecture and art periodicals and a growing collection of books and exhibition catalogues.

Address:
Museumsplatz 1
1070 Vienna
Austria
Telephone: +43 522 31 15 23
Internet: www.azw.at

Exhibition Schedule:
Emerging Architecture: 10 More Austrians
December 6, 2001 - February 4, 2002

Walter Pichler: The House
Spring 2002

Traveling Exhibitions:
TransModernity
May 2002, Austrian Cultural Institute, New York, NY

Art Institute of Chicago, Department of Architecture

The Art Institute of Chicago encompasses The School of the Art Institute of Chicago and a museum with ten curatorial departments. Collections at the Art Institute include: African and Amerindian Art, American Art, Architecture, Asian Art, Ancient Art, European Painting, Photography, European Decorative Arts and Sculpture, Prints and Drawings, Textiles, Arms and Armor and Twentieth-Century Painting and Sculpture. The Department of Architecture at the Art Institute was established in 1981 from the architectural drawings collection within the Burnham Library of Architecture (founded in 1912) and the architectural fragments collection of the Department of American Arts. The Ernest R. Graham Study Center for Architectural Drawings houses a collection of more than 130,000 architectural sketches and drawings, largely of designs by Chicago architects, including Walter Burley Griffin, Louis Sullivan, Ludwig Mies van der Rohe and Frank Lloyd Wright. The collection also features architectural models and fragments, including a reconstruction of the Adler and Sullivan trading room from the Chicago Stock Exchange (1893-94). The Burnham Library of Architecture, one of the first organizations in the United States to collect architectural drawings, architects' papers, and primary documentary materials, is open to researchers and scholars.

Address:
111 South Michigan Avenue
Chicago, Illinois 60603
Telephone: (312) 443-3949
Internet: www.artic.edu/aic

Exhibition Schedule:
Modern Trains and Splendid Stations: Architecture and Design for the 21st Century
December 8, 2001 - July 28, 2002

Art Institute of Chicago, Department of Architecture (Con't)

Exhibition Schedule (Con't):

Helmut Jacoby: Architectural Renderings
August 31 - October 27, 2002

David Adler, Architect: Elements of Style
December 7, 2002 - May 18, 2003

Athenaeum of Philadelphia

The Athenaeum of Philadelphia was founded in 1814 to collect and disseminate information related to American history and the "useable arts." The not-for-profit, member-supported library contains a vast architecture and interior design collection with an emphasis on the period 1800 to 1945. The library is open to qualified readers without charge. The Athenaeum's National Historic Landmark building, designed by John Nott in 1845 near Independence Hall, is also open to the public as a museum furnished with American fine and decorative arts from the first half of the nineteenth century. They offer public programs, lectures and changing exhibitions, as well as administering trusts that provide awards and grants.

Address:
219 S. Sixth Street
Philadelphia, PA 19106-3794
Telephone: (215) 925-2688
Internet: www.PhilaAthenaeum.org

Exhibition Schedule:
(check with the museum for an updated schedule)

Bauhaus Archive/ Museum of Design

With a focus on preservation and research, Berlin's Bauhaus Archive/Museum of Design features a permanent collection, temporary exhibits, and a Bauhaus Shop, dedicated to the Bauhaus (1919-1933) school of architecture, design, and art. Many artifacts comprise the permanent collection, including preliminary course studies, class work, architectural drawings and maquettes, painting, furniture, pottery, metal objects, textiles, and photography. The collection is housed in a 1979 building designed by Walter Gropius, the founder of the Bauhaus.

Address:
Bauhaus-Archiv / Museum für Gestaltung
Klingelhöferstraße 14
D - 10785 Berlin
Telephone: +030 - 25 40 02 0
Internet: www.bauhaus.de

Exhibition Schedule:
The Bauhaus: Weimar-Dessau-Berlin 1919-1933
Permanent exhibition

Ludwig Mies van der Rohe: Architect-Professor, Bauhaus 1930 – 1933
October 25, 2001 – March 10, 2002

A modern harmonic and lively architecture is the visible sign of an authentic democracy.

Walter Gropius

Canadian Centre for Architecture (CCA)

Montréal's Canadian Centre for Architecture (CCA) is a museum and study center devoted to local, national and international architecture, landscape design, and urban planning disciplines. Its exhibits are intended to reveal the richness of architectural culture and to heighten the public's awareness of contemporary issues in architecture. The CCA occupies an award-winning building designed by Peter Rose in 1989 and the adjacent 1874 Shaughnessy House. Its garden, designed by Melvin Charney, serves as both an urban garden and outdoor museum of architecture.

Address:
1920 Baile Street
Montréal, Québec
Canada H3H 2S6
Telephone: (514) 939-7026
Internet: www.cca.qc.ca

Exhibition Schedule:
Souvenir Buildings
May 2, 2001 - January 20, 2002

Floor play: An installation By MEDIUM
September 26, 2001 - March 3, 2002

Mies in America Main Galleries
October 17, 2001 -January 20, 2002

Hal Ingberg
March - July 2002

Herzog & de Meuron: Natural History
April 17 -October 13, 2002

Nicholas Reeves
September 2002 - January 2003

Tangente
October 2002 - February 2003

Asplund/Terragni
November 2002 - March 2003

Cooper-Hewitt, National Design Museum, Smithsonian Institution

The Cooper-Hewitt, National Design Museum, Smithsonian Institution is the only museum in the U.S. devoted exclusively to the study of historical and contemporary design. Reflecting the belief that design links individuals, societies and the natural environment, the museum's program addresses five key issues: function, innovation & creativity, communication, history & criticism, and context. Four curatorial departments care for and evaluate the Museum's collections: applied arts and industrial design, drawings and prints, textiles, and wallcoverings. The Museum's interests also encompass graphic design, architecture, urban planning, and environmental design.

Address:
2 East 91st Street
New York, New York 10128
Telephone: (212) 849-8400
Internet: www.si.edu/ndm/

Exhibition Schedule:
Glass of the Avant-Garde: From Vienna Secession to Bauhaus
The Torsten Bröhan Collection from the Museo Nacional de Artes Decorativas, Madrid
August 21, 2001 - February 24, 2002

Russel Wright: Creating American Lifestyle
November 20, 2001 - March 10, 2002

Skin: Surface and Substance in Contemporary Design
April 22 - September 8, 2002

Did you know...

8000 yards of concrete and 800 tons of reinforcing steel were used in the construction of New York City's Guggenheim Museum (Frank Lloyd Wright, 1959).

Danish Center for Architecture, Gammel Dok

The Danish Center for Architecture, located in the historic 1882 harbor-front warehouse Gammel Dok, is devoted to the advancement of architecture and urban design and to raising awareness of the importance of quality design among professionals, institutions, government, and the public. It serves as a platform for debate and a forum for the display of projects and ideas that strive to improve the physical environment. In addition, they host exhibits on Danish and international architecture, maintain a database of contemporary Danish architecture, define architecture policies, and promote knowledge of architecture in the Danish public schools.

Address:
Strandgade 27B
1401 Copenhagen K
Denmark
Telephone: +45 32 57 19 30
Internet: www.gammeldok.dk

Exhibition Schedule:
(check with the museum for an updated schedule)

Danish Design Center

The Danish Design Center was founded in 1977 to promote Danish design within Denmark and abroad. Through its exhibits, lectures, design competitions, publications, library, and design management consultation services, the Danish Design Center stands at the forefront of the promotion of good design within the industrial design profession and for the benefit of society as a whole. In January 2000 they opened their new building, which was designed by one of Denmark's premier architects, Henning Larsen, across from Tivoli Gardens.

Address:
H C Andersens Boulevard 27
1553 Copenhagen V, Denmark
Telephone: +45 33 69 33 69
Internet: www.ddc.dk

Exhibition Schedule:
The Danish Design Prize 2001
Oct 27, 2001 - January 13, 2002

Made to Move
November 7, 2001 - January 29, 2002

King & Miranda
January 19 - April 14, 2002

Evergreens & Nevergreens: Arne Jacobsen 100 Years
February 11 - June 2, 2002

The Danish Identity
September 26, 2002 - January 5, 2003

The Danish Design Prize 2002
October 26 - January 26, 2003

The ID Prize 1965-1999
Mid - Late 2002

Design Museum

Located in London's South Bank area in a converted 1950s warehouse, the Design Museum is the only museum devoted exclusively to 20th century industrial design. Since its founding in 1989 by the Conran Foundation, the Museum's many changing exhibits and educational programs have offered an insight into the role of design and mass production in our everyday lives. Its exhibits include the Collection gallery, which highlights historical trends and design of the past 100 years; the Review gallery, featuring new, innovative designs and prototypes; and many special exhibitions. The Museum's reach is further extended through its extensive educational program of contract teaching, outreach activities, teacher training courses, and resources for classroom use.

Address:
Shad Thames
London
SE1 2YD
United Kingdom
Telephone: 0171 378 6055
Internet: www.designmuseum.org

Exhibition Schedule:
Memphis Remembered
September 7, 2001 - January 27, 2002

John Galliano at Dior
November 30, 2001 - April 21, 2002

Gio Ponti
May 10 - September 25, 2002

Heinz Architectural Center, Carnegie Museum of Art

Opened by the Carnegie Museum of Art in 1993, the Heinz Architectural Center is dedicated to the collection, study, and exhibition of architectural drawings and models. Though its scope is international, it does foster a principle interest in the architecture of western Pennsylvania. The museum also maintains one of only three architectural cast collections in the world, and the only one in North America.

Address:
4400 Forbes Avenue
Pittsburgh, PA 15213-4080
Telephone: (412) 622-3131
Internet: www.cmoa.org

Exhibition Schedule:
Architecture + Water
February 9-May 12, 2002

Out of the Ordinary: The Architecture and Design of Robert Venturi, Denise Scott Brown and Associates
November 9, 2002-January 12, 2003

The Lighthouse: Scotland's Centre for Architecture, Design & the City

The Lighthouse is one of Europe's largest temporary exhibition venues devoted to promoting access, involvement and participation in architecture and design. The themes of their exhibits range from architecture and design to the city, including monograph shows of architectural and design practices, object led exhibitions of the best products, and experimental explorations of issues related to urban living. The Lighthouse is located in the former 1895 Glasgow Herald building designed by Charles Rennie Mackintosh, Glasgow's celebrated architect, designer and artist. It also houses the Mackintosh Interpretation Centre, a facility for the study of the work and legacy of Charles Rennie Mackintosh.

Address:
11 Mitchell Lane
Glasgow, G1 3NU
U.K.
Telephone: +44 (0) 141 221 6362
Internet: www.thelighthouse.co.uk

Exhibition Schedule:
Re-Design: Daily Objects for the 21st Century
November 9, 2001 - February 3, 2002

BBC Pacific Quay
January - February 2002

House
February - May 2002 (tentative dates)

Loch Lomond National Park
April - May 2002

Unbuilt Mackintosh
July - September 2002

Dollhouses by Architects
November - December 2002

Game On
December 2002 - February 2003

Museum of Contemporary Art, Los Angeles (MOCA)

The Museum of Contemporary Art, Los Angeles (MOCA), is dedicated solely to the collection, presentation and interpretation of contemporary art produced since 1940 in all media. Founded in 1979, MOCA's collection now stands at over 5,000 works. In addition, MOCA maintains a unique programmatic commitment to architecture and design. Past exhibits include *The Architecture of Frank Gehry; Blueprints for Modern Living: History* and *Legacy of the Case Study Houses* featuring 30 scale models of the houses, two walk-through full-scale reconstructions, and a design competition for affordable multi-family housing; *Arata Isozaki 1960/1990 Architecture; Louis I. Kahn: In the Realm of Architecture; Urban Revisions: Current Projects for the Public Realm; Out of Order: Franklin D. Israel*, and *At the End of the Century: One Hundred Years of Architecture*.

The museum is housed in three facilities: MOCA at California Plaza, MOCA at The Geffen Contemporary (formerly the Temporary Contemporary) in Little Tokyo, and The MOCA Gallery at the Pacific Design Center in West Hollywood. MOCA's programs include exhibitions, collection, education and publication designed to serve diverse audiences.

Main Address:
MOCA at California Plaza
250 South Grand Avenue
Los Angeles, CA 90012
Telephone: (213) 626-6222
Internet: www.moca-la.org

Exhibition Schedule:
What's Shakin': New Architecture in LA
September 16, 2001 – January 20, 2002; Pacific Design Center and Geffen Contemporary locations

Museum of Finnish Architecture

The Museum of Finnish Architecture maintains a large collection of drawings and photographs related to Finnish architecture as well as an extensive architectural library. The Museum organizes exhibits about Finnish architecture and 20th century design issues, which they host in Helsinki, as well as throughout Finland and abroad. In addition, they publish books and host lectures to generate support and promote interest in Finnish design.

Address:
Kasarmikatu 24, 00130
Helsinki, Finland
Telephone: +35 8-9-85675100
Internet: www.mfa.fi

Exhibition Schedule:
Finnish Pavilion, Paris 1900
November 14, 2001 - February 2, 2002

Finnish Art Nouveau Villas from 1900
November 14, 2001 - February 2, 2002

Drawings for the Suur-Merijoki Manor by
Gesellius–Lindgren–Saarinen
November 14, 2001 - February 2, 2002

Alvar Aalto, Unrealized Projects (Tentative Title)
Summer 2002

Did you know...

Finnish architect Osmo Lappo, from the newly formed Museum of Finnish Architecture, curated Europe's first exhibition of contemporary Finnish architecture in London in 1957, which generated much interest and curiosity.

Museum of Modern Art (MoMA)

New York City's Museum of Modern Art (MoMA) encompasses six curatorial areas, including the world's first department devoted to architecture and design. Established in 1932, the Department of Architecture and Design's collection contains architectural documents, drawings, and photographs, including the Ludwig Mies van der Rohe Archive and collections from other leading architects. They also maintain over 3,000 design objects, from furniture to tools, automobiles, and textiles and a 4,000 piece graphic design collection. The Lily Auchincloss Study Center for Architecture and Design is open by appointment to researchers who are interested in accessing reference materials related to the Museum's collection of design objects, posters, architectural drawings, models and periodicals.

Address:
11 West 53 Street
New York, NY 10019
Telephone: (212) 708-9400
Internet: www.moma.org

Exhibition Schedule:
Alberto Giacometti
October 11, 2001-January 8, 2002

The Russian Avant-Garde Book, 1910-1934
March 21-May 21, 2002

MoMA Builds
Through April 2002

Traveling Exhibitions:
Mies in Berlin
Altes Museum, Berlin, Germany,
December 14, 2001-March 10, 2002
Fundacion La Caixa, Barcelona, Spain,
July 30, 2002-September 29, 2002

Note: Beginning in the summer 2002 and lasting through 2004, MoMA will be temporary relocating its exhibition space to MoMA QNS—a multi-use arts facility in Long Island City, Queens—during their $650 million renovation and expansion project. Please call the museum or consult their Web site prior to visiting.

National Building Museum

Established by an act of Congress in 1980, the National Building Museum, a private, nonprofit institution, is dedicated to exploring all facets and disciplines of the built environment. From architecture, urban planning, and construction to engineering and design, the Museum reveals the connections between the way we build and the way we live. The Museum is located in Washington D.C.'s historic 1887 Pension Bureau Building designed by U.S. Army General Montgomery C. Meigs. The Museum's impressive Great Hall with its colossal Corinthian columns is often the site of the President's Inaugural Ball among many other gala events. Through its exhibitions and education programs, the Museum serves as a forum for exchanging information about topical issues such as managing suburban growth, preserving landmarks, and revitalizing urban centers.

Address:
401 F Street NW
Washington, DC 20001
Telephone: (202) 272-2448
Internet: www.nbm.org

Exhibition Schedule:
National Building Museum
Tools As Art: The Hechinger Collection – Instruments of Change
Permanent Exhibit

City of Washington (tentative title)
Permanent Exhibit opening Fall 2002

From Arts and Crafts to Modern Design: The Architecture of William Price
August 18, 2001 – March 24, 2002

Cesar Pelli: Connections
September 12, 2001 – April 28, 2002

National Building Museum (Con't)

Exhibition Schedule (Con't):

Monuments and Memory: Washington, D.C., Architects Explore the Language of Monuments
September 29, 2001 – January 13, 2002

A Genius for Place: American Landscapes of the Country Place Era
October 6, 2001 – February 18, 2002

In Transit: Transportation and the American City (working title)
January 26, 2002 – August 11, 2002

Buildings appeal to us in different ways, our eyes may be delighted by the colour, texture and form; our intellect may be stimulated by the skilful use of materials or the brilliance of building technique; or our sense of fitness may be impressed by the excellence of the building for its purpose. In each case, however, we see revealed to us something of the living man, for no architect can give his building a finer quality than exists in his own mind.

Ralph Tubbs

Netherlands Architecture Institute

Located at the edge of Museumpark in the center of Rotterdam and housed in a building designed by Jo Coenen in 1993, the Netherlands Architecture Institute (NAI) is a museum and cultural institution concerned with architecture, urban design and space planning. Through its exhibitions and other programs, the NAI strives to inform, inspire and stimulate architects and laymen alike about the value of design. The NAI possesses one of the largest architectural collections in the world with over 15 kilometers of shelving containing drawings, sketches, models, photographs, books and periodicals, including work by virtually every important Dutch architect since 1800. This collection, as well as its 40,000 volume library, is open to researchers. Lectures, study tours, and a variety of publications are also offered by the NAI.

Address:
Mueumpark 25
3015 CB Rotterdam
Netherlands
Telephone: 31 (0) 10-4401200
Internet: www.nai.nl/nai_eng.html

Exhibition schedule:
(check with the museum for an updated schedule)

Norwegian Museum of Architecture

Founded by the National Association of Norwegian Architects in 1975, the Norwegian Museum of Architecture (NAM) collects, processes, and disseminates information and material concerned with architecture, with a focus towards the 20th century. The Museum is housed in one of Oslo's oldest buildings, Kongens gate 4, part of which dates to 1640. The Museum boasts an archive of over 200,000 drawings and photographs and is available to researchers by appointment. In the past, the Museum's exhibits have been concerned with various aspects of Norwegian architecture, from the work of individuals to overviews of contemporary architecture. The Museum also hosts traveling exhibitions which are typically in English.

Address:
Kongens gate 4, N-0153
Oslo, Norway
Telephone: +47-22 42 40 80
http://www.mnal.no/nam/NAM-eng.html

Exhibition Schedule:
A history of buildings, 1000 years of Norwegian architecture
Permanent exhibit

(check with the museum for an updated exhibition schedule)

The Octagon

Located one block west of the White House, The Octagon was one of Washington, D.C.'s first residences. It was designed by Dr. William Thornton, the first architect of the U.S. Capitol and was completed in 1801. John Tayloe III and his descendants owned the home until it was purchased by The American Institute of Architects (AIA) in 1902 to serve as its headquarters. The American Architectural Foundation (AAF), the foundation established by the AIA in 1942, purchased the building in 1968 and opened it to the public as a museum in 1970. A National Historic Landmark, the Octagon is the oldest architecture and design museum in the United States.

Address:
1799 New York Ave. NW
Washington, D.C., 20006
Telephone: (202) 638-3105
Internet: www.theoctagon.org

Exhibition Schedule:
Skyscrapers: The New Millennium
through April 30, 2002

Inside the Temple of Liberty: Interiors of the United States Capitol.
Paintings by Peter Waddell
Mid-May - October 15, 2002

TBA: Selections from the Octagon's Prints and Drawing Collection
November 2002- April 2003

RIBA Architecture Gallery

The Royal Institute of British Architects' (RIBA) RIBA Architecture Gallery (formerly known as the RIBA Architecture Centre) features both historical and contemporary architecture and design exhibitions. Through exhibitions, talks, publications, events for children and the family, the Internet and collaborations, it provides a cultural focus for the communication and presentation of architecture and a forum for debate and the exchange of ideas.

Address:
66 Portland Square
London W1H 4AD UK
Telephone: +44 (0)171 580 5533
Internet: www.architecture.com

Exhibition Schedule:
(check with the museum for an updated schedule)

I came to think that art must be based on science and that, in everything having to do with artistic composition, the aim should be the unity which is that of nature itself – because the logic of nature is impeccable.

Hector Guimard

San Francisco Museum of Modern Art

Originally named the San Francisco Museum of Art when it opened in 1935, the "modern" in San Francisco Museum of Modern Art (SFMOMA) was added in 1975 to more accurately describe its mission. SFMOMA's international permanent collection consists of over 18,000 works, including 5,600 paintings, sculptures and works on paper; approximately 9,800 photographs; 3,200 architectural drawings, models and design objects, and a growing collection of works related to the media arts. In 1983, the Museum established its Department of Architecture and Design, the first museum on the West Coast to do so. The department focuses on architecture and design projects pertaining to the Bay Area, California, the American West, and Pacific Rim. Its growing collection focuses on architecture, furniture design, product design, and graphic design from both historic and contemporary periods. The department's Architecture and Design Forum also organizes lectures, symposia, and competitions.

Address:
151 Third Street
San Francisco, CA 94103-3159
Telephone: (415) 357-4000
Internet: www.sfmoma.org

Exhibition Schedule:
SFMOMA Experimental Design Award
November 9, 2001 - February 5, 2002

Perfect Acts of Architecture
March 2 - May 26, 2002

Sir John Soane's Museum

Sir John Soane's Museum in London has been open to the public since the mid-19th century. Originally the home of Sir John Soane, R.A., architect (1753 – 1837), in 1833 Soane negotiated an Act of Parliament to settle and preserve the house and his collections of art and antiques for the benefit of amateurs and students in architecture, painting, and sculpture. As a Professor of Architecture at the Royal Academy, Soane arranged his books, casts, and models so that the students might have easy access to them. He opened his house for the use of the Royal Academy students the day before and the day after each of his lectures. Today, as Soane requested, the house has, as much as possible, been left as it was over 150 years ago. The Museum's extensive research library is open to researchers by appointment. Staff is available to help with queries relating to many fields including: the restoration of authentic historic interiors, architectural history from the 17th century to the early 19th century, the conservation of drawings and works of art and methods of display, archives, and architectural models.

Address:
13 Lincoln's Inn Fields
London, WC2A 3BP
United Kingdom
Telephone: +44 (0) 171-405 2107
Internet: www.soane.org

Exhibition Schedule:
Ongoing exhibition of Sir John Soane's Home

[Architecture] is an art purely of invention – and invention is the most painful and most difficult exercise of the human mind.

Sir John Soane

Skyscraper Museum

The Skyscraper Museum is devoted to the study of historical, contemporary and future high-rise buildings. Located in Lower Manhattan, the birthplace of the skyscraper, the Museum was founded in 1996 as a private, not-for-profit, educational corporation and has presented many exhibits in temporary spaces throughout Manhattan. Its mission expands the traditional view of skyscrapers as objects of design and products of technology, viewing them also as investments in real estate, sites of construction, and places of work and residence. In late 2002, the Museum will open in its permanent home in New York's Battery Park City with expanded facilities for permanent and temporary exhibits, as well as a bookstore and study area.

Address (beginning late 2002):
39 Battery Place
New York, NY, 10281
Telephone: (212) 968-1961
Internet: www.skyscraper.org

Exhibition Schedule:
Skyscraper/City
Debuts 2002

Please visit the museum's Web site for information about their current location, gallery hours, and program schedule.

Skyscrapers – mountains for people to climb.

Bruce Graham

Swedish Museum of Architecture

Stockholm's Swedish Museum of Architecture serves as a repository of information about Swedish architecture, maintains a collection of architectural artifacts, and, through its exhibitions, educates people about the architectural heritage of Sweden. Its archives contain over 2,000,000 architectural drawings and nearly 600,000 photographs. The Museum's permanent exhibition, the History of Swedish Building, covers a period of 1,000 years of Swedish design.

Address:
Skeppsholmen, SE-111 49
Stockholm, Sweden
Telephone: 08-587 270 00
Internet: www.arkitekturmuseet.se

Exhibition Schedule:
The History of Swedish Building
Permanent Exhibit

(check with the museum for an updated exhibition schedule)

Vitra Design Museum

Germany's Vitra Design Museum is dedicated to documenting the history and current trends in industrial furniture design. Changing exhibitions are housed in a building Frank O. Gehry designed for the Vitra Design Museum in 1989. Items from the Vitra's permanent collection are housed in the Vitra Fire Station, designed by Zaha Hadid in 1993, and may be viewed by the public on special guided tours only. In addition to its changing exhibits and expansive permanent collection, the Vitra sponsors international travelling exhibitions around the world. The Museum also conducts student workshops, publishes books on design, and manufactures special editions of objects.

Address:
Charles-Eames-Str. 1
D-79576 Weil am Rhein
Germany
Telephone: + 49 7621 702 35 78
Internet: www.design-museum.com

Exhibition Schedule:
Isamu Noguchi - Sculptural Design
December 8, 2001 - April 21, 2002

Living in Motion
May 2 - September 8, 2002

Marcel Breuer - Furniture Design & Architecture
September 21, 2002 - March 9, 2003

Mies Van Der Rohe (left) and his 1928-29 design for the Barcelona Pavilion (bottom).

Vitra Design Museum, Berlin

On July 1, 2000 the Vitra Design Museum opened a branch in Berlin, the first of many planned branches throughout Europe and the U.S. This location will continue the tradition of the museum's patronage of architecture; it will occupy a 1924-26 former transformer plant, "Humboldt," originally designed by Hans Heinrich Müller, an impressive monument of industrial architecture in the Prenzlauer Berg district of Berlin. The large converted transformer halls will house exhibits intended to raise popular awareness of design and architecture.

Address:
Kopenhagener Straße 58
D-10437 Berlin
Germany
Telephone: +49 30 473 777 0
Internet: www.design-museum.com/berlin.asp

Exhibition Schedule:
Mies van der Rohe – Architecture and Design in Stuttgart, Barcelona, Brno
October 27, 2001 - February 24, 2002

The Work of Charles and Ray Eames: A Legacy of Invention
March 9 - June 2, 2002

Living in Motion
September 21, 2002 - May 3, 2003

Zurich Museum of Design

The Zurich Museum of Design (Museum für Gestaltung) is the only Swiss institution to concentrate on the collection of 20th century manufactured products from famous designers to anonymous, everyday objects. They also house a collection of over 250,000 art posters as well as a library and archives. Regular exhibits focus on the question of what constitutes effective design. Special attention is paid to subjects in the fields of design, architecture, visual communication, everyday culture, photography, art and the media. The museum is housed in a building designed by Zurich architects Karl Egender and Adolf Steger in 1933.

Address:
Ausstellungsstr. 60
CH-8005, Zürich
Switzerland
Tel: +411 446 22 11
Internet: www.museum-gestaltung.ch

Exhibition Schedule:
Early Russian Avant Garde Posters
Beginning March 2002

(check with the museum for additional exhibitions)

Noted Individuals

Many recognitions are available to design professionals, most notably induction as a fellow in one of the design associations. In addition, many professionals serve as industry leaders within the design associations. Listings of fellows, honorary members, and presidents of the major design organizations can be found in this chapter. Names in bold indicate new inductees in 2001.

Chancellors of The American Institute of Architects' College of Fellows

Since the founding of The American Institute of Architects' College of Fellows in 1952, the Chancellor is elected, now annually, by the Fellows to preside over the College's investiture ceremonies and business affairs.

1952-53	Ralph Thomas Walker	1984	Bernard B. Rothschild
1954-55	Alexander C. Robinson III	1985	Donald L. Hardison
1956	Edgar I. Williams	1986	Vladimir Ossipoff
1957-60	Roy F. Larson	1987	S. Scott Ferebee Jr.
1961-62	Morris Ketchum	1988	C. William Brubaker
1963-64	Paul Thiry	1989	Preston Morgan Bolton
1965-66	George Holmes Perkins	1990	William A. Rose Jr.
1967-68	Norman J. Schlossman	1991	Robert B. Marquis
1969-70	John Noble Richards	1992	L. Jane Hastings
1971-72	Jefferson Roy Carroll Jr.	1993	John A. Busby Jr.
1973	Ulysses Floyd Rible	1994	Thomas H. Teasdale
1974	Albert S. Golemon	1995	Robert T. Coles
1975	Robert S. Hutchins	1996	Ellis W. Bullock Jr.
1976	William Bachman	1997	Jack DeBartolo Jr.
1977	Phillip J. Meathe	1998	Harold L. Adams
1978	George Edward Kassabaum	1999	Jimmy D. Tittle
1979	David Arthur Pugh	2000	Robert A. Odermatt
1980	Robert L. Durham	2001	Harold Roth
1981	Leslie N. Boney Jr.	2002	C. James Lawler
1982	William Robert Jarratt		
1983	William C. Muchow		

Source: The American Institute of Architects

Fellows of the American Academy in Rome

Every year the American Academy in Rome grants fellowships to study and work in Rome at the Academy's center for independent study, advanced research, and creative work. Also known as the Rome Prize, the fellowships are granted in a broad range of fields including design, music, literature, and archaeology. The following individuals have been the recipients of the Rome Prize for design related disciplines.

Architecture:

Stanley Abercrombie, FAAR'83
Kimberly A. Ackert, FAAR'97
Anthony Ames, FAAR'84
Joseph Amisano, FAAR'52
Amy Anderson, FAAR'81
Ross S. Anderson, FAAR'90
Richard W. Ayers, FAAR'38
Clarence Dale Badgeley, FAAR'29
Gregory S. Baldwin, FAAR'71
Marc Balet, FAAR'75
Richard Bartholomew, FAAR'72
Frederick Blehle, FAAR'87
James L. Bodnar, FAAR'80
Thomas L. Bosworth, FAAR'81
Charles G. Brickbauer, FAAR'57
Cecil C. Briggs, FAAR'31
Turner Brooks, FAAR'84
Andrea Clark Brown, FAAR'80, AIA
Theodore L. Brown, FAAR'88
William Bruder, FAAR'87
Marvin Buchanan, FAAR'76
Walker O. Cain, FAAR'48
Peter Carl, FAAR'76
Daniel Castor, FAAR'98
Judith Chafee, FAAR'77
Coleman Coker, FAAR'96
Caroline B. Constant, FAAR'79
Frederic S. Coolidge, FAAR'48
Roger Crowley, FAAR'85
Teddy Edwin Cruz, FAAR'92
Thomas V. Czarnowski, FAAR'68
Royston T. Daley, FAAR'62
Spero Daltas, FAAR'51
Douglas Darden, FAAR'89

Thomas L. Dawson, FAAR'52
Joseph De Pace, FAAR'85
Andrea O. Dean, FAAR'80
Kathryn Dean, FAAR'87
Judith Di Maio, FAAR'78
Ronald L. Dirsmith, FAAR'60
Robert Ward Evans, FAAR'73
James Favaro, FAAR'86
Ronald C. Filson, FAAR'70, FAIA
Garrett S. Finney, FAAR'95
Mark M. Foster, FAAR'84
Robert M. Golder, FAAR'63
Michael L. Goorevich, FAAR'01
Alexander C. Gorlin, FAAR'84
Michael Graves, FAAR'62, RAAR'78
James A. Gresham, FAAR'56
Brand Norman Griffin, FAAR'74
Olindo Grossi, FAAR'36
Michael Gruber, FAAR'96
Michael Guran, FAAR'71
Steven Harby, FAAR'00
George E. Hartman, FAAR'78, RAAR'96
John D. Heimbaugh, Jr., FAAR'70
George A. Hinds, FAAR'84
Peter Hopprier, FAAR'77
Elizabeth Humstone, FAAR'86
Sanda D. Iliescu, FAAR'95
Franklin D. Israel, FAAR'75
Erling F. Iversen
David J. Jacob, FAAR'58, RAAR'71
Allan B. Jacobs, FAAR'86, RAAR'96
James R. Jarrett, FAAR'59
E. Fay Jones, FAAR'81
Wesley Jones, FAAR'86
Wendy Evans Joseph, FAAR'84

Fellows of the American Academy in Rome (Con't)

Henri V. Jova, FAAR'51

Robert Kahn, FAAR'82

Spence Kass, FAAR'81

Stephen J. Kieran, FAAR'S 1

Alexander Kitchin, FAAR'02

Grace R. Kobayaski, FAAR'90

Johannes M.P. Knoops, FAAR'00

Peter Kommers, FAAR'76

Eugene Kupper, FAAR'83

James R. Lamantia, FAAR'49

James L. Lambeth, FAAR'79

Gary Larson, FAAR'83

Thomas N. Larson, FAAR'64

John Q. Lawson, FAAR'81

David L. Leavitt, FAAR'50

Celia Ledbetter, FAAR'83

Diane Lewis, FAAR'77

Paul Lewis, FAAR'99

Roy W. Lewis, FAAR'86

George T. Licht, FAAR'37

Theodore Liebman, FAAR'66

Robert S. Livesey, FAAR'75

John H. MacFadyen, FAAR'54

Robert Mangurian, FAAR'77

Tallie B. Maule, FAAR'52

Arthur May, FAAR'76

David Mayernik, FAAR'89

John J. McDonald, FAAR'83

William G. McMinn, FAAR'82

Cameron McNall, FAAR'92

D. Blake Middleton, FAAR'82

Henry D. Mirick, FAAR'33

Robert Mittelstadt, FAAR'66

Grover E. Mouton III, FAAR'73

Vincent Mulcahy, FAAR'77

Anne Munly, FAAR'96

Theodore J. Musho, FAAR'61

Robert Myers, FAAR'54

John Naughton, FAAR'85

Stanley H. Pansky, FAAR'53

William Pedersen, FAAR'66

Charles O. Perry, FAAR'66

Warren A. Peterson, FAAR'55

Thomas M. Phifer, FAAR'96

Warren Platner, FAAR'56

Kelly D. Powell, FAAR'02

Antoine S. Predock, FAAR'85, FAIA

George L. Queral, FAAR'88

Patrick J. Quinn, FAAR'80

Jason H. Ramos, FAAR'91

William Reed, FAAR'68

Walter L. Reichardt, FAAR'33

Jesse Reiser, FAAR'85

Richard Rosa, FAAR'99

Peter Miller Schmitt, FAAR'72

Thomas L. Schumacher, FAAR'69, RAAR'91

J. Michael Schwarting, FAAR'70

Frederic D. Schwartz, FAAR'85

Daniel V. Scully, FAAR'70

Catherine Seavitt, FAAR'98

Werner Seligmann, FAAR'81

Thomas Silva, FAAR'89

Jorge Silvetti, FAAR'86

Thomas G. Smith, FAAR'80

Barbara Stauffacher Solomon, FAAR'83

Friedrich St. Florian, FAAR'85

Charles Stifter, FAAR'63

James S. Stokoe, FAAR'79

John J. Stonehill, FAAR'60

Richard Taransky, FAAR'01

Wayne Taylor, FAAR'62

Milo H. Thompson, FAAR'65

Duane Thorbeck, FAAR'64, FAIA

Evelyn Tickle, FAAR'02

James Timberlake, FAAR'83

Robert H. Timme, FAAR'86

Fred Travisano, FAAR'82

William Turnbull, Jr., FAAR'80

James Velleco, FAAR'77

Robert Venturi, FAAR'56

Austris J. Vitols, FAAR'67

Peter D. Waldman, FAAR'00

Craig H. Walton, FAAR'82

Robert A. Weppner, Jr., FAAR'36

Nichole Wiedemann, FAAR'97

Charles D. Wiley, FAAR'48

Fellows of the American Academy in Rome (Con't)

Tod Williams, FAAR'83
Christian Zapatka, FAAR'91
Astra Zarina, FAAR'63

Landscape Architecture
Eric Armstrong, FAAR'61
E. Bruce Baetjer, FAAR'54
Julie Bargmann, FAAR'90
Richard C. Bell, FAAR'53, RAAR'75
Stephen F. Bochkor, FAAR'57
Elise Brewster, FAAR'98
Robert T. Buchanan, FAAR'59
Richard Burck, FAAR'82
Vincent C. Cerasi, FAAR'50
Henri E. Chabanne, FAAR'34
Linda J. Cook, FAAR'89
Joanna Dougherty, FAAR'86
F. W. Edmondson, FAAR'48 (1)
Jon S. Emerson, FAAR'67
Eric Reid Fulford, FAAR'92
Ralph E. Griswold, FAAR'23
Edgar C. Haag, FAAR'79
Robert Mitchell Hanna, FAAR'76
Stephen C. Haus, FAAR'79
Dale H. Hawkins, FAAR'52
Elizabeth Dean Hermann, FAAR'87
Gary R. Hilderbrand, FAAR'95
Walter Hood, FAAR'97
Alden Hopkins, FAAR'35
Dr. Frank D. James, FAAR'68
Dean A. Johnson, FAAR'66
Mary Margaret Jones, FAAR'98
John F. Kirkpatrick, FAAR'39
Robert S. Kitchen, FAAR'38
Mark Klopfer, FAAR'01
Albert R. Lamb, III, FAAR'70
Edward Lawson, FAAR'21
Tom Leader, FAAR'99
James M. Lister, FAAR'37
Roger B. Martin, FAAR'64
Laurel McSherry, FAAR'00
Stuart M. Mertz, FAAR'40
David Meyer, FAAR'01
Stacy T. Moriarty, FAAR'84

Richard C. Murdock, FAAR'33
Norman T. Newton, FAAR'26, RAAR-67
Peter O'Shea, FAAR'96
Laurie D. Olin, FAAR'74, RAAR'90
Don H. Olson, FAAR'62
Peter Osler, FAAR'02
Thomas R. Oslund, FAAR'92
Nell H. Park, FAAR'33
George E. Patton, FAAR'51
Paul R. V. Pawlowski, FAAR'69
Peter M. Pollack, FAAR'71
Thomas D. Price, FAAR'32
Charles A. Rapp, FAAR'72
Michael Rapuano, FAAR'30
Peter G. Rolland, FAAR'78, FASLA
Leslie A. Ryan, FAAR'95
Peter Lindsay Schaudt, FAAR'91, ASLA
Terry Schnadelbach, FAAR'66
Seth H. Seablom, FAAR'68
Stephen Sears, FAAR'00
Charles Sullivan, FAAR'85
Jack Sullivan, FAAR'83
Charles R. Sutton, FAAR'32
Erik A. Svenson, FAAR'58
Andrew Thanh-Son Cao, FAAR'02
L. Azeo Torre, FAAR'76
Morris E. Trotter, FAAR'35
James R. Turner, FAAR'76
Daniel Tuttle, FAAR'88
Michael R. Van Valkenburgh, FAAR'88
E. Michael Vergason, FAAR'80
Craig P. Verzone, FAAR'99
Richard K. Webel, FAAR'29, RAAR'63
Professor James L. Wescoat, FAAR'97
Brooks E. Wigginton, FAAR'50
Gall Wittwer, FAAR'96
John L. Wong, FAAR'81
Prof. Ervin H. Zube, FAAR'61

Historic Preservation and Conservation
Elmo Baca, FAAR'00
Prof. Margaret Holben Ellis, FAAR'94
Shelley Fletcher, FAAR'98
Eric Gordon, FAAR'97

Fellows of the American Academy in Rome (Con't)

Anne Frances Maheux, FAAR'96
Pablo Ojeda-O'Neill, FAAR'96
Alice Boccia Paterakis, FAAR'00
Leslie Rainer, FAAR'99
Bettina A. Raphael, FAAR'94
Elizabeth Riorden, FAAR'02
Thomas C. Roby, FAAR'95
Catherine Sease, FAAR'95
Ellen Phillips Soroka, FAAR'02
Prof. Frederick Steiner, FAAR'98
Jonathan Thorton, FAAR'99
Elizabeth Walmsley, FAAR'01
Dr. George Wheeler, FAAR'97
Deirdre Windsor, FAAR'01

Design Arts

William Adair, FAAR'92
Gerald D. Adams, FAAR'68
Thomas Angotti, FAAR'90
Donald Appleyard, FAAR'75
Joseph H. Aronson, FAAR'74
Morley Baer, FAAR'80
Gordon C. Baldwin, FAAR'78
Phillip R. Baldwin, FAAR'94
Karen Bausman, FAAR'95
Ellen Beasley, FAAR'89
Anna Campbell Bliss, FAAR'84
Robert W. Braunschweiger, FAAR'74
Paul M. Bray, FAAR'97
Steven Brooke, FAAR'91
Michael B. Cadwell, FAAR'99
Heather Carson, FAAR'99
John J. Casbarian, FAAR'86, FAIA
Adele Chatfield-Taylor, FAAR'84
Walter Chatham, FAAR'89
Morison S. Cousins, FAAR'85
Russell Rowe Culp, FAAR'80
Phoebe Cutler, FAAR'89
Joseph Paul D'Urso, FAAR'88
Paul Davis, FAAR'98
Robert S. Davis, FAAR'91
Robert De Fuccio, FAAR'76
Robert Regis Dvorak, FAAR'72

William H. Fain Jr., FAAR'02
Hsin-ming Fung, FAAR'92
Jeanne Giordano, FAAR'87
Miller Horns, FAAR'90
Robert Jensen, FAAR'76
June Meyer Jordan, FAAR'71
Wendy Kaplan, FAAR'00
J. Michael Kirkland, FAAR'70
Robert Kramer, FAAR'72
George Krause, FAAR'77, RAAR'80
Lisa Krohn, FAAR'01
Norman Krumholz, FAAR'87
Michael Lax, FAAR'78
Debra McCall, FAAR'89
R. Alan Melting, FAAR'70
Donald Oenslager
Michael Palladino, FAAR'01
Donald Peting, FAAR'78
William L. Plumb, FAAR'86
William Reed, FAAR'68
Julie Riefler, FAAR'87
Mark Robbins, FAAR'97
Michael Rock, FAAR'00
Danny M. Samuels, FAAR'86
Mark Schimmenti, FAAR'98
Paul D. Schwartzman, FAAR'77
Paul Shaw, FAAR'02
William V. Shaw, FAAR'68
Alison Sky, FAAR'78
Paul L. Steinberg, FAAR'82
Joel Sternfeld, FAAR'91
Michelle Stone, FAAR'78
Edward Marc Treib, FAAR'85
Kevin Walz, FAAR'95
Emily M. Whiteside, FAAR'82
Janet Zweig, FAAR'92

FAAR = Fellow of the American Academy in Rome
RAAR = Resident of the American Academy in Rome

Source: American Academy in Rome

Fellows of the American Academy of Arts and Sciences

Since its founding in 1780, the American Academy of Arts and Sciences has pursued its goal "To cultivate every art and science which may tend to advance the interest, honor, dignity, and happiness of a free, independent, and virtuous people." Throughout its history, the Academy's diverse membership has included the best from the arts, science, business, scholarship, and public affairs. Nominations for new members are taken from existing fellows and evaluated by panels from each discipline and the membership at large.

Design Professionals, Academics, and Writers:

Christopher Alexander '96
U. of Calif., Berkeley

Edward Larrabee Barnes '78
Edward Larrabee Barnes/
John M. Y. Lee Architects, New York

Herbert Lawrence Block '59
Washington, D.C.

Robert Campbell '93
Cambridge, MA

Henry Nichols Cobb '84
Pei, Cobb, Freed & Partners, New York, NY

Peter D. Eisenman '00
Eisenman Architects, New York, NY

Kenneth Frampton '93
Columbia University

James Ingo Freed '94
Pei, Cobb, Freed & Partners, New York, NY

Frank Owen Gehry '91
Frank O. Gehry and Assoc., Santa Monica, CA

Lawrence Halprin '78
San Francisco, CA

Robert S.F. Hughes '93
Time Magazine

Ada Louise Huxtable '74
New York, NY

Philip Johnson '77
Philip Johnson Architects, New York, NY

Gerhard Michael Kallmann '85
Kallmann, McKinnell and Wood, Architects, Inc., Boston, MA

(Noel) Michael McKinnell '85
Kallmann, McKinnell and Wood, Architects, Inc., Boston, MA

Richard Alan Meier '95
New York, NY

Henry Armand Millon '75
National Gallery of Art, Washington, D.C.

William Mitchell '97
Massachusetts Institute of Technology

I(eoh) M(ing) Pei '67
Pei, Cobb, Freed & Partners, New York, NY

Kevin Roche '94
Hamden, CT

Robert Rosenblum '84
New York University

Moshe Safdie '96
Moshe Safdie & Assoc., Sommerville, MA

Denise Scott Brown '93
Venturi Scott Brown & Assoc., Inc., Philadelphia

Vincent J. Scully '86
Yale University

Fellows of the American Academy of Arts and Sciences (Con't)

Hugh Asher-Stubbins '57
Ocean Ridge, FL

Robert Venturi '84
Venturi Scott Brown & Assoc., Inc., Philadelphia

Foreign Honorary Members:

Charles Correa '93
Bombay, India

Carl Theodor Dreyer '65
Copenhagen, Denmark

Norman Robert Foster '96
Foster and Associates, London

Phyllis Lambert '95
Center Canadien d'Architecture, Montreal,
Quebec

Ricardo Legorreta '94
Mexico City, Mexico

Fumihiko Maki '96
Maki and Associates, Tokyo, Japan

J. Rafael Moneo '93
Harvard University

Oscar Niemeyer '49
Rio de Janeiro, Brazil

Renzo Piano '93
London, England

Alvaro Siza '92
Porto, Portugal

Kenzo Tange '67
Tokyo, Japan

Source: American Academy of Arts and Sciences

Fellows of the American Consulting Engineers Council

Fellowship in the American Consulting Engineers Council (ACEC) is open to any individual who has been a principal in a member firm for five or more years; has served ACEC as an officer, director or active committee member or has served a Member Organization as an officer or director; and has notably contributed to the advancement of consulting engineering in administrative leadership, design, science, by literature, in education, or by service to the profession.

Allen M. Acheson	Erwin R. Breihan
A. George Adamson	Arthur N. Brooks
William H. Addington	Joseph L. Brown
Frank E. Alderman	Wayne H. Brown
Harl P. Aldrich	Robert O. Bruton
Norman G. Almquist	Ross Bryan
Raymond G. Alvine	Paul C. Bucknam
Harry G. Anderson	Edmund Burke
Stephen C. Anderson	Robert G. Burkhardt
Al Anderson, CO	Ion Caloger
Al Anderson, WI	R. Neal Campbell
Peter N. Andrews	Aubrey Caplan
C. Adrian Arnold	James W. Carpenter
Frederick G. Aufiero	Charles D. Carr
Quent Augspurger	Dominic B. Carrino
Don Austin	Daniel M. Carson
Charles L. Ballou	Hugh C. Carter
George Barnes	T. Z. Chastain
Michael Barrett	Fu Hua Chen
Robert T. Bates	John H. Clark
Richard T. Baum	James D. Cobb
Clifton R. Baxter	Edward Cohen
Ralph W. Becker	William J. Collins
James G. Bell	Paul E. Conrad
Theodore T. Bell	William H. Cooke
William I. Bigger	Philip M. Corlew
Wilson V. Binger	J. Richard Cottingham
David K. Blake	Paul E. Cox
John A. Blume	L. LeRoy Crandall
Robert C. Bogart	Ralph Crosby
Samuel A. Bogen	John C. Crowser
Ronald L. Bonar	Jeffrey M. Daggett
Lewis A. Bosworth	Henry Eugene Damon
Gary R. Bourne	David L. Davidson
Carl H. Bowen	Edward W. Davidson
Dwight A. Boyd	G. Robert Davidson

Fellows of the American Consulting Engineers Council (Con't)

Ansel L. Davis
Edward T. Davis
Ray H. Davis
Edwin K. Dedeaux
Kenneth L. Delap
Chris Demopulos
Daniel J. DeYoung
H. Boyd Dickenson
Harold Dombeck
Emery Domingue
Wallace L. Donley
Stephen E. Dore
Albert A. Dorman
J. Edward Doyle
Ronald J. Drnevich
James R. Duncan
Lamar Dunn
Howard C. Dutzi
Arthur A. Edwards
Carl Eiden
Stanley D. Elkerton
Clifford E. Evanson
Gilbert L. Faison
H. Ben Faulkner
John R. Fee
Harry R. Feldman
Dean R. Felton
James F. Finn
David E. Fleming
Eric L. Flicker
Harold E. Flight
Robert C. Flory
John H. Foster
Ronald D. Foster
William C. Freeman
E. M. Fucik
Lester Fukuda
David R. Fuller
Thomas D. Furman
Elliot H. Gage
E. B. 'Bas' Gaither
F. Vreeland George
Frank B. Gianotti
Ralph W. Gilbert
Bruce L. Gilmore
Albert B. Gipe
William J. Glover

Stephen G. Goddard
E. Jackson Going
Donald T. Goldberg
Luther Graef
Anthony J. Grasso
Brian L. Gray
David H. Grieves
Robert F. Grimes
Paul D. Guertin
John J. Guth
Wilton N. Hammond
Philip M. Hampton
Richard E. Hangen
Walter E. Hanson
Thomas B. Harrell
Michael J. Hartigan
Arthur F. Hartung
Eugene C. Harvey
James M. Hastings
Donald Hattery
Amy J. Haugerud
Steve M. Hays
George Heck
Alfred Hedefine
Paul L. Heineman
Joseph E. Heney
John F. Hennessy
Marble J. Hensley
Michael A. Hertzberg
Richard J. Hesse
Robert E. Hickman
Lyle F. Hird
Robert E. Hogan
A. W. Holland
Darrel V. Holmquist
Stephen A. Holt
W. N. Holway
Donald E. Houser
Linda L. Huff
Harold E. Hughes
Roger L. Jacobson
J. Edward Jenkins
Clifford W. Johnson
Derrell E. Johnson
Edmund G. Johnson
Melvin E. Jones
Ralph W. Junius

Fellows of the American Consulting Engineers Council (Con't)

C. Hayden Kaiser
Dennis Kamber
John J. Kassner
Stan Kawaguchi
Theodore S. Kawahigashi
Charles W. Keller
Chester C. Kelsey
David D. Kennedy
Todd J. Kenner
Frederick D. A. King
Jack Kinstlinger
George Kirgis
Gordon L. Kirjassoff
Robert C. Kirkpatrick
Donald F. Klebe
Donald H. Kline
Dag I. Knudsen
Kenneth J. Koch
James H. Konkel
Charles W. Kopplin
Emil Kordish
Michael E. Krannitz
Paul B. Krebs
Donald R. LaRochelle
Calvin E. Levis
Raoul L. Levy
Brian J. Lewis
William D. Lewis
David H. Lillard
Frank L. Lincoln
Leon J. Lindbloom
Howard D. Linders
Joseph Lipscomb
Bruce Livingstone
C. Richard Lortz
LeRoy D. Loy
Ray Lundgren
A. J. Macchi
J. L. MacFarlane
Cline L. Mansur
Christopher Marx
Richard E. Masters
Michael P. Matsumoto
David R. Matthews
Aubrey D. May
William (Skip) H. McCombs
Kenneth A. McCord

H. Clay McEldowney
Robert McEldowney
James D. McFall
John C. McGlenn
Larry A. McKee
Robert W. McKenzie
Herbert P. McKim
Arthur W. McKinney
Raymond F. Messer
Charles A. Meyer
Vernon F. Meyer
Henry L. Michel
William J. Mielke
Albert H. Miller
Raymond T. Miller
Robert D. Mitchell
Thomas E. Mohler
Dayton Molzen
R. Duane Monical
Robert C. Moore
Frederick K. Mosher
W. A. Mossbarger
James (Bud) E. Moulder
Edward J. Mulcahy
Salim Najjar
Albert L. Nelson
Kenneth E. Nelson
James R. Nichols
Frank Nicoladis
E. N. Nicolaides
George K. Nishimura
Lennox K. Nishimura
Judith Nitsch
Jack Noblitt
David Novick
Satoshi Oishi
Stephen M. Olko
Pedro J. Ortiz-Santiago
Paul Ostergaard
R. Stanton Over
J. Hambleton Palmer
Ralph J. Palmer
Stewart R. Palmer
Joseph P. Paoluccio
S. G. Papadopoulos
Andrew J. Parker
Charles A. Parthum

Fellows of the American Consulting Engineers Council (Con't)

J. L. Patton
Donald D. Paxton
E. J. Peltier
C. R. Pennoni
Leo F. Peters
Boyd W. Phelps
Emanuel Pisetzner
Richard Piske
Joe H. Pitts
William H. Plautz
Rex T. Pless
James M. Poche'
Lester H. Poggemeyer
James W. Poirot
H. A. Pontier
Allen Poppino
Michael A. Postiglione
Richard Q. Praeger
Paul W. Prendiville
David G. Presnell
Hal Puckett
Richard E. Ragold
Stan L. Rankin
William R. Ratliff
Frederick Reusswig
Robert B. Richards
Theodore J. Richards
Elmo A. Richardson
Louis W. Riggs
G. Michael Ritchie
Cathy S. Ritter
William J. Rizzo
Robert F. Robertson
T.B. Robinson
Elmer O. Rodes
Lawrence P. Rogoway
Sigmund Roos
Robert W. Rosene
Donald E. Ross
Donald K. Ross
David T. Rowe
Robert D. Rowland
George O. Sadler
Leo A. Santowasso
Charles E. Schaffner
Harold A. Schlenger
Paul G. Scott

James F. Shivler
William E. Short
Wayne F. Shuler
Devindar S. Sidhu
Donald J. Smally
Herman E. Smith
Lester H. Smith
Russell L. Smith
E. Per Sorenson
William A. Sowers
James A. Speedie
Gerald E. Speitel
A J. Spiess
Gary J. Spinkelink
Paul F. Sprehe
Richard H. Stanley
Henry A. Stikes
Roger G. Stroud
Billy T. Sumner
Anne C. Symonds
A. J. Szabo
John P. Talerico
Russell C. Taylor
Thomas J. Terrell
James R. Thomas
Gregs G. Thomopulos
Donald E. Thompson
Everett S. Thompson
T. Curtiss Torrance
William A. Clevenger Torrance
Donald R. Trim
Taylor F. Turner
Jack K. Tuttle
J. Howard Van Boerum
J. E. Van Dell
Charles O. Velzy
Donald D. Vick
Carlos C. Villarrceal
Robert C. Wade
Sam H. Wainwright
Robert A. Waitkus
Richard O. Walker
F. Spencer Weber
William W. Webster
Vernon M. Wegerer
Victor Weidmann
Richard Weingardt

Fellows of the American Consulting Engineers Council (Con't)

John P. Weir
Robert G. Werden
Robert D. Wesselink
Lewis H. West
Richard B. Wetzel
Brian R. Whiston
H. Kenneth White
Ronald R. White
Charles K. Whitescarver
C. Leslie Wierson
Eugene R. Wilkinson
Jerald A. Williams
Richard L. Williams
Harry M. Wilson

Arnold L. Windman
Douglas G. Wolfangle
Rudolph A. Wolfson
Riley D. Woodsen
Thomas D. Wosser
Kenneth R. Wright
Robert G. Wright
Theodore E. Wynne
L. Carl Yates
Alfred C. Zuck

Source: American Consulting Engineers Council

Did you know...

Only four airports in the world exceed 2 million square feet: Denver International Airport (United States, Fentress Bradburn Architects, 1995), Inchon Airport (South Korea, Fentress Bradburn Architects, 2001), Kansai Airport (Japan, Renzo Piano, 1994), and Chek Lap Kok Airport (Hong Kong, Norman Foster, 1998).

Fellows of The American Institute of Architects

The College of Fellows of The American Institute of Architects (AIA) is composed of AIA members who have been elected to Fellowship by a jury of their peers. Fellowship is granted for significant contributions to architecture and society and for achieving a high standard of professional excellence. Architect members who have been in good standing for at least 10 years may be nominated for Fellowship. The following individuals are current active members of The American Institute of Architects' College of Fellows.

A

Carlton S. Abbott, Williamsburg, VA
J. C. Abbott Jr., Sarasota, FL
James Abell, Tempe, AZ
Jan M. Abell, Tampa, FL
Stephen N. Abend, Kansas City, MO
Bruce A. Abrahamson, Minneapolis, MN
Max Abramovitz, Pound Ridge, NY
Raymond C. Abst, Modesto, CA
Harold L. Adams, Baltimore, MD
William M. Adams, Venice, CA
William T. Adams, Dallas, TX
Michael Adlerstein, New York, NY
Antonin Aeck, Atlanta, GA
P. Aguirre Jr., Dallas, TX
Loren P. Ahles, Minneapolis, MN
Thomas R. Aidala, San Francisco, CA
Roula Alakiotou, Chicago, IL
Charles A Albanese, Tucson, AZ
Richard K. Albyn, Pisgah Forest, NC
N. Sue Alden, Seattle, WA
Iris S. Alex, New York, NY
Cecil A. Alexander Jr., Atlanta, GA
Earle S. Alexander Jr., Houston, TX
Henry C. Alexander Jr., Coral Gables, FL
James G. Alexander, Boston, MA
A. Notley Alford, Englewood, FL
Stanley N. Allan, Chicago, IL
Maurice B. Allen Jr., Bloomfield Hills, MI
Ralph G. Allen, Chicago, IL
Rex W. Allen, Sonoma, CA
Robert E. Allen, San Francisco, CA
Robert E. Allen, Longview, TX
Susan Allen, Morgantown, IN
Gerald L. Allison, Newport Beach, CA
James V. Allred, Reston, VA
Killis P. Almond Jr., San Antonio, TX
Alfred S. Alschuler, Highland Park, IL
Ronald A. Altoon, Los Angeles, CA
Jesus E. Amaral, San Juan, Puerto Rico
Joseph Amisano, Atlanta, GA
Gregg D. Ander, Irwindale, CA
Dorman D. Anderson, Seattle, WA

Harry F. Anderson, Oakbrook, IL
J. Timothy Anderson, Cambridge, MA
John D. Anderson, Denver, CO
Richard Anderson, Tucson, AZ
Samuel A. Anderson, Charlottesville, VA
William L. Anderson, Des Moines, IA
J. Philip Andrews, Pittsburgh, PA
Lavone D. Andrews, Houston, TX
Martha P. Andrews, Portland, OR
George Anselevicius, Albuquerque, NM
James H. Anstis, West Palm Beach, FL
Natalye Appel, Houston, TX
Richard M. Archer, San Antonio, TX
Peter F. Arfaa, Philadelphia, PA
Bruce P. Arneill, Glastonbury, CT
Chris Arnold, Palo Alto, CA
Christopher C. Arnold, Commerce Twp., MI
Robert V. Arrigoni, San Francisco, CA
Yvonne W. Asken, Portage, MI
Laurin B. Askew, Columbia, MD
Lee Hewlett Askew III, Memphis, TN
Neil L. Astle, Salt Lake City, UT
Louis D. Astorino, Pittsburgh, PA
Charles H. Atherton, Washington, DC
Tony Atkin, Philadelphia, PA
John L. Atkins, Research Triangle Park, NC
Eugene E. Aubry, Holmes Beach, FL
Seymour Auerbach, Chevy Chase, MD
Douglas H. Austin, San Diego, CA
Daniel Avchen, Minneapolis, MN
Donald C. Axon, Laguna Beach, CA
Alfred L. Aydelott, Carmel, CA

B

Howard J. Backen, Sausalito, CA
Edmund N. Bacon, Philadelphia, PA
David C. Baer, Houston, TX
Stuart Baesel, La Jolla, CA
Deon F. Bahr, Lincoln, NE
Ray B. Bailey, Houston, TX
William J. Bain Jr., Seattle, WA
Royden Stanley Bair, Houston, TX
Louis J. Bakanowsky, Cambridge, MA

Fellows of The American Institute of Architects (Con't)

David Baker, San Francisco, CA
Isham O. Baker, Washington, DC
Jack Sherman Baker, Champaign, IL
James Barnes Baker, London, England
Gregory S. Baldwin, Portland, OR
Samuel T. Balen, Waldport, OR
Rex M. Ball, Tulsa, OK
Richard S. Banwell, Walnut Creek, CA
Shalom S. Baranes, Washington, DC
Robert A. Barclay, Cleveland, OH
Paul H. Barkley, Falls Church, VA
John M. Barley, II, Jacksonville, FL
Charles C. Barlow, Jackson, MS
Edward L. Barnes, Cambridge, MA
Linda Barnes, Portland, OR
Rebecca Barnes, Boston, MA
Jay William Barnes Jr., Austin, TX
Jonathan Barnett, Washington, DC
Carol R. Barney, Chicago, IL
Howard R. Barr, Austin, TX
Raj Barr-Kumar, Washington, DC
Nolan E. Barrick, Lubbock, TX
Errol Barron, New Orleans, LA
Richard E. Barrow, Birmingham, AL
Richard W. Bartholomew, Philadelphia, PA
Armand Bartos, New York, NY
Edward C. Bassett, Mill Valley, CA
Fred Bassetti, Seattle, WA
Peter Batchelor, Raleigh, NC
Ronald J. Battaglia, Buffalo, NY
Jay S. Bauer, Newport Beach, CA
Edward Baum, Dallas, TX
Joseph D. Bavaro, Punta Gorda, FL
John Craig Beale, Dallas, TX
Burtch W. Beall Jr., Salt Lake City, UT
Leroy E. Bean, Petaluma, CA
Alan J. Beard, Portland, OR
Lee P. Bearsch, Binghamton, NY
William H. Beaty, Memphis, TN
William B. Bechhoefer, Bethesda, MD
Lee Becker, Washington, DC
Rex L. Becker, St. Louis, MO
Herbert Beckhard, New York, NY
Robert M. Beckley, Ann Arbor, MI
Michael Bednar, Charlottesville, VA
Carmi Bee, New York, NY
David W. Beer, New York, NY
Edgar C. Beery, Springfield, VA
Ann M. Beha, Boston, MA
Byron Bell, New York, NY
Frederic Bell, Long Island City, NY
M. Wayne Bell, Austin, TX
John Belle, New York, NY
Ralph C. Bender, San Antonio, TX
Barry Benepe, New York, NY
Daniel D. Bennett, Fayetteville, AR
David J. Bennett, Minneapolis, MN

Frederick R. Bentel, Locust Valley, NY
Maria A. Bentel, Locust Valley, NY
Kenneth E. Bentsen, Houston, TX
Frederick J. Bentz, Minneapolis, MN
Karl A. Berg, Denver, CO
Richard R. Bergmann, New Canaan, CT
Lloyd F. Bergquist, Bloomington, MN
Robert J. Berkebile, Kansas City, MO
Marlene J. Berkoff, San Rafael, CA
Anthony N. Bernheim, San Francisco, CA
Phillip Bernstein, New Haven, CT
K. Norman Berry, Louisville, KY
Richard J. Bertman, Boston, MA
Ronald P. Bertone, Middletown, NJ
Frederic A. Bertram, Clearwater, FL
Hobart Betts, Sag Harbor, NY
John H. Beyer, New York, NY
William Beyer, Minneapolis, MN
John H. Bickel, Louisville, KY
Frederick C. Biebesheimer, III, Old Lyme, CT
T. J. Biggs, Jackson, MS
Rebecca L. Binder, Playa Del Rey, CA
James Binkley, Arlington, VA
Lance L. Bird, Pasadena, CA
John R. Birge, Omaha, NE
Gunnar Birkerts, Bloomfield Hills, MI
James A. Bishop, Bellville, TX
George Bissell, Newport Beach, CA
Georgia Bizios, Chapel Hill, NC
J. Sinclair Black, Austin, TX
Walter S. Blackburn, Indianapolis, IN
Leonard D. Blackford, Sacramento, CA
Jan Gaede Blackmon, Dallas, TX
Boyd A. Blackner, Salt Lake City, UT
Peter Blake, Riverdale, NY
Frederick A. Bland, New York, NY
Wilfred E. Blessing, Oak Harbor, WA
Richard L. Blinder, New York, NY
Richard L. Bliss, Kirkwood, MO
Robert L. Bliss, Salt Lake City, UT
Ronald B. Blitch, New Orleans, LA
John D. Bloodgood, Des Moines, IA
Martin Bloomenthal, Princeton, NJ
Sigmund F. Blum, Naples, FL
Susan Blumentals, Brooklyn Center, MN
H. M. Blumer, Paradise Valley, AZ
Kirk V. Blunck, Des Moines, IA
William A. Blunden, Cleveland, OH
William E. Blurock, Newport Beach, CA
William Bobenhausen, Norwalk, CT
L. Kirkpatrick Bobo, Memphis, TN
Michael L. Bobrow, Los Angeles, CA
Bruce T. Bockstael, Hartford, CT
William N. Bodouva, New York, NY
Joe Boehning, Albuquerque, NM
Robert J. Boerema, Gainesville, FL
Joseph Boggs, Annapolis, MD

Fellows of The American Institute of Architects (Con't)

Walter F. Bogner, Larchmont, NY
Peter Bohlin, Wilkes Barre, PA
Friedrich K.M. Bohm, Columbus, OH
Mario H. Boiardi, Washington, DC
Stanley G. Boles, Portland, OR
Michael E. Bolinger, Baltimore, MD
Robert D. Bolling, Torrance, CA
Antonio R. Bologna, Memphis, TN
Preston M. Bolton, Houston, TX
James R. Bonar, Los Angeles, CA
J. Max Bond Jr., New York, NY
Charles Hussey Boney, Wilmington, NC
Leslie N. Boney Jr., Wilmington, NC
Paul D. Boney, Wilmington, NC
Dwight M. Bonham, Wichita, KS
Daniel Boone, Abilene, TX
David C. Boone, Santa Cruz, CA
Laurence O. Booth, Chicago, IL
Bill C. Booziotis, Dallas, TX
L. G. Borget, Houston, TX
Bernard Bortnick, Dallas, TX
Thomas L. Bosworth, Seattle, WA
Elmer E. Botsai, Honolulu, HI
Elmer Botsai, Honolulu, HI
Gary A. Bowden, Baltimore, MD
David M. Bowen, Fishers, IN
Gary Bowen, Omaha, NE
Ronald Gene Bowen, Middleton, WI
John A. Bower Jr., Philadelphia, PA
Paul D. Bowers Jr., Grand Rapids, MI
William A. Bowersox, Saint Louis, MO
Chester Bowles Jr., San Francisco, CA
J. Donald Bowman, Bellevue, WA
John Harold Box, Austin, TX
Hugh A. Boyd, Montclair, NJ
Robert A. Boynton, Richmond, VA
John Bozalis, Oklahoma City, OK
James H. Bradburn, Denver, CO
David R. Braden, Dallas, TX
Richard H. Bradfield, Clearwater, FL
Thomas G. Bradley, Decatur, IL
Clyde A. Brady, III, Orlando, FL
Scott W. Braley, Atlanta, GA
Ronald M. Brame, Dallas, TX
Joel Brand, Houston, TX
Robert Brannen, Boston, MA
Charles S. Braun, Longwood, FL
Richard M. Brayton, San Francisco, CA
William E. Brazley Jr., Matteson, IL
Melvin Brecher, Broomall, PA
William N. Breger, New York, NY
Simon Breines, Scarsdale, NY
John Michael Brendle, Denver, CO
Daniel R. Brents, Houston, TX
Adrienne G. Bresnan, New York, NY
Joseph Bresnan, New York, NY
Benjamin E. Brewer Jr., Houston, TX

Leon Bridges, Baltimore, MD
Stanford R. Britt, Washington, DC
Joseph M. Brocato Sr., Alexandria, LA
Myra M. Brocchini, Berkeley, CA
Ronald G. Brocchini, Berkeley, CA
Paul Broches, New York, NY
Raymond D. Brochstein, Houston, TX
William R. Brockway, Baton Rouge, LA
M. J. Brodie, Baltimore, MD
H. Gordon Brooks, II, Lafayette, LA
John W. Broome, Tualatin, OR
Robert C. Broshar, Clear Lake, IA
David J. Brotman, Los Angeles, CA
Charles E. Broudy, Philadelphia, PA
George D. Brown Jr., Peekskill, NY
Jennie Sue Brown, Seattle, WA
Kenneth F. Brown, Honolulu, HI
Paul B. Brown, Traverse City, MI
Robert F. Brown Jr., Philadelphia, PA
Robert L. Brown Jr., Lithonia, GA
Terrance Brown, Albuquerque, NM
Woodlief Brown, Abilene, TX
C. William Brubaker, Chicago, IL
Barry B. Bruce, Bellaire, TX
Van B. Bruner Jr., Haddonfield, NJ
Harry A. Bruno, Walnut Creek, CA
Larry S. Bruton, Portland, OR
Harvey Bryan, Belmont, MA
John H. Bryant, Stillwater, OK
Algimantas V. Bublys, Birmingham, MI
Marvin H. Buchanan, Berkeley, CA
James W. Buckley, Greensboro, GA
Michael P. Buckley, New Haven, CT
Huber H. Buehrer, Maumee, OH
John B. Buenz, Chicago, IL
Glenn A. Buff, Miami, FL
Henrik H. Bull, San Francisco, CA
Ellis W. Bullock Jr., Pensacola, FL
Thomas A. Bullock, Sr., Brenham, TX
W. Glenn Bullock, Knoxville, TN
Franklin S. Bunch, Sugar Land, TX
Richard S. Bundy, San Diego, CA
John H. Burgee, Montecito, CA
Charles E. Burgess, Houston, TX
J. Armand Burgun, Kitty Hawk, NC
Edward M. Burke, Austin, TX
James E. Burlage, Sausalito, CA
Robert Burley, Waitsfield, VT
Arthur L. Burns, Winter Haven, FL
John A. Burns, Alexandria, VA
Norma DeCamp Burns, Raleigh, NC
Robert P. Burns, Raleigh, NC
Rodger E. Burson, Wimberley, TX
John A. Busby Jr., Atlanta, GA
C. Joe Buskuhl, Dallas, TX
H. Kennard Bussard, Des Moines, IA
Jerome R. Butler, Chicago, IL

Fellows of The American Institute of Architects (Con't)

Theodore R. Butler, Minneapolis, MN
Fred W. Butner, Winston Salem, NC
Thomas K. Butt, Point Richmond, CA
Harold Buttrick, New York, NY
Paul S. Byard, New York, NY
Brent Byers, Austin, TX
Jeanne Byrne, Pacific Grove, CA
Arne Bystrom, Seattle, WA

C

Burns Cadwalader, Oakland, CA
Timothy G. Cahill, Kansas City, MO
Harold Calhoun, Houston, TX
Robert Campbell, Cambridge, MA
Wendell J. Campbell, Chicago, IL
Jaime Canaves, Miami, FL
H. F. Candela, Coral Gables, FL
Robert H. Canizaro, Jackson, MS
William T. Cannady, Houston, TX
Jamie Cannon, Town & Country, MO
Marvin J. Cantor, Fairfax, VA
Horace S. Cantrell Jr., Indianapolis, IN
Richard Scott Carde, Santa Monica, CA
Kenneth Harvey Cardwell, Berkeley, CA
Jean P. Carlhian, Boston, MA
William A. Carlisle, Columbia, SC
DeVon M. Carlson, Boulder, CO
Donald Edwin Carlson, Seattle, WA
Clyde R. Carpenter, Lexington, KY
Jack A. Carpenter, San Diego, CA
William J. Carpenter, Atlanta, GA
Edwin Winford Carroll, El Paso, TX
M. E. Carroll, Chevy Chase, MD
Marley Carroll, Charlotte, NC
W. T. Carry, Atlanta, GA
Chris Carson, San Antonio, TX
Donald K. Carter, Pittsburgh, PA
Virgil R. Carter, Newtown Square, PA
David R. Cartnal, San Jose, CA
Timothy A. Casai, Bloomfield Hills, MI
John Casbarian, Houston, TX
A. Cascieri, Lexington, MA
Donald W. Caskey, Irvine, CA
Heather W. Cass, Washington, DC
Joseph W. Casserly, Chicago, IL
John J. Castellana, Bloomfield Hills, MI
Stephan Castellanos, Stockton, CA
Samuel J. Caudill, Aspen, CO
Giorgio Cavaglieri, New York, NY
W. Brooks Cavin Jr., Shelburne, VT
Lawrence Chaffin Jr., Koloa, HI
Ann R. Chaintreuil, Rochester, NY
Alfred V. Chaix, South Pasadena, CA
Dean B. Chambliss, Denver, CO
Junius J. Champeaux, II, Lake Charles, LA
Lo-Yi Chan, Ashley Falls, MA

Wing T. Chao, Burbank, CA
L. William Chapin II, Alexandria, VA
Donald D. Chapman, Kula, HI
John S. Chase, Houston, TX
Walter F. Chatham, New York, NY
Peter Chermayeff, Boston, MA
Edith Cherry, Albuquerque, NM
Edward E. Cherry, Hamden, CT
Robert A. Chervenak, Mount Vernon, WA
Lugean L. Chilcote, Little Rock, AR
G. Cabell Childress, Castle Rock, CO
James C. Childress, Centerbrook, CT
David M. Childs, New York, NY
Maurice F. Childs, Boston, MA
Susan Chin, New York, NY
Robert E. Chisholm, Miami, FL
Gordon H. Chong, San Francisco, CA
Frederick L. Christensen, Salinas, CA
George W. Christensen, Scottsdale, AZ
James W. Christopher, Salt Lake City, UT
Daniel Chun, Honolulu, HI
Eric A. Chung, Radnor, PA
William C. Church, Portland, OR
Richard J. Chylinski, Los Angeles, CA
Mario J. Ciampi, Kentfield, CA
Robert L. Cioppa, New York, NY
Eugene D. Cizek, New Orleans, LA
George L. Claflen, Philadelphia, PA
John M. Clancy, Boston, MA
James F. Clapp Jr., Cambridge, MA
Fred W. Clarke III, New Haven, CT
Gerald L. Clark, Havasu City, AZ
Roger H. Clark, Raleigh, NC
John P. Clarke, Trenton, NJ
Marshall F. Clarke, Greenville, SC
Charles Clary, Destin, FL
Thomas R. Clause, Des Moines, IA
Jerry L. Clement, St. Louis, MO
Glen E. Cline, Boise, ID
Elizabeth Close, St. Paul, MN
Robert K. Clough, Chicago, IL
James A Clutts, Dallas, TX
Henry N. Cobb, New York, NY
R. F. Coffee, Austin, TX
Daniel P. Coffey, Chicago, IL
Andrew S. Cohen, Middlebury, CT
Jack C. Cohen, Bethesda, MD
Martin H. Cohen, Armonk, NY
Stuart Cohen, Evanston, IL
Doris Cole, Concord, MA
Robert Traynham Coles, Buffalo, NY
David S. Collins, Cincinnati, OH
Donald Comstock, Sacramento, CA
William T. Conklin, Washington, DC
Richard T. Conrad, Sacramento, CA
W. M. Conrad, Kansas City, MO
John Conron, Santa Fe, NM

Fellows of The American Institute of Architects (Con't)

J. J. Conroy, Chicago, IL
Eugene E. Cook, Roselle, IL
Lawrence D. Cook, Falls Church, VA
Richard B. Cook, Chicago, IL
William H. Cook, Sonoita, AZ
Alexander Cooper, New York, NY
Jerome M. Cooper, Atlanta, GA
W. Kent Cooper, Washington, DC
Christopher Coover, Phoenix, AZ
Gerald M. Cope, Philadelphia, PA
Lee G. Copeland, Seattle, WA
C. Jack Corgan, Dallas, TX
Jack M. Corgan, Dallas, TX
William Corlett, Berkeley, CA
Araldo A. Cossutta, New York, NY
Walter H. Costa, Lafayette, CA
Anthony J. Costello, Muncie, IN
Leland Cott, Cambridge, MA
John O. Cotton, Marina Del Rey, CA
C. H. Cowell, Houston, TX
Page Ayres Cowley, New York City, NY
Dan C. Cowling, Little Rock, AR
David C. Cox, Washington, DC
Frederic H Cox, Richmond, VA
Warren J. Cox, Washington, DC
Whitson W. Cox, Carmichael, CA
Bruce I. Crabtree Jr., Nashville, TN
Kirk R. Craig, Greenville, SC
Steade Craigo, Sacramento, CA
George M. Crandall, Portland, OR
David A. Crane Tampa, FL
Ronald O. Crawford, Roanoke, VA
Martin W. Crennen, Helena, MT
Frank W. Crimp, Milton, MA
James H. Crissman, Watertown, MA
Edwin B. Crittenden, Anchorage, AK
K. C. Crocco, Chicago, IL
Charles B. Croft, Austin, TX
Edwin B. Cromwell, Little Rock, AR
Eason Cross Jr., Alexandria, VA
Samuel Crothers, III, Radnor, PA
R. L. Crowther, Denver, CO
Randolph R. Croxton, New York, NY
Metcalf Crump, Memphis, TN
Evan D. Cruthers, Honolulu, HI
John W. Cuningham, Minneapolis, MN
Ben Cunningham, St. Petersburg, FL
Gary M. Cunningham, Dallas, TX
Warren W. Cunningham, Philadelphia, PA
James L. Cutler, Bainbridge Is, WA
Bernard J. Cywinski, Havertown, PA

D

Charles E. Dagit Jr., Philadelphia, PA
Fernand W. Dahan, Rockville, MD
David A. Daileda, Springfield, VA

Curt Dale, Denver, CO
Todd Dalland, New York, NY
J. E. Dalton, Kent, OH
Leo A. Daly III, Washington, DC
Paul Damaz, East Hampton, NY
Sylvester Damianos, Pittsburgh, PA
Robert Damora, Bedford, NY
George E. Danforth, Chicago, IL
Arthur C. Danielian, Irvine, CA
George N. Daniels, Salt Lake City, UT
Stanley L. Daniels, Atlanta, GA
Doris Andrews Danna, St. Louis, MO
Robert F. Darby, Jacksonville, FL
Samuel N. Darby, Rockford, IL
Edwin S. Darden, Fresno, CA
Ben R. Darmer, Atlanta, GA
Richard Dattner, New York, NY
Theoharis L. David, New York, NY
D. G. Davidson, Washington, DC
David S. Davidson, Great Falls, MT
Robert I. Davidson, New York, NY
Albert J. Davis, Blacksburg, VA
Arthur Q. Davis, New Orleans, LA
Charles M. Davis, San Francisco, CA
Clark Davis, St. Louis, MO
Clark A. Davis, San Francisco, CA
Jerry A Davis, New York, NY
John M. Davis, Austin, TX
Lewis Davis, New York, NY
Nicholas Davis, Auburn, AL
Steven A. Davis, New York, NY
W. T. Davis, Greenville, SC
Clare Henry Day, Redlands, CA
Frederic L. Day Jr., Concord, MA
Natalie De Blois, San Antonio, TX
John Neff De Haas Jr., Bozeman, MT
Rey de la Reza, Houston, TX
Alfredo De Vido, New York, NY
Jack DeBartolo Jr., Phoenix, AZ
Rudolph V. DeChellis, Woodland Hills, CA
Vernon DeMars, Berkeley, CA
Kenneth DeMay, Watertown, MA
Louis DeMoll, Moylan, PA
J. R. DeStefano, Chicago, IL
Panayotis E. DeVaris, South Orange, NJ
E. L. Deam, Highland Park, IL
Robert C. Dean, Boston, MA
C. M. Deasy, San Luis Obispo, CA
Howard S. Decker, Chicago, IL
Ward W. Deems, Solana Beach, CA
Allan J. Dehar, New Haven, CT
Jorge Del Rio, San Juan, Puerto Rico
Homer T. Delawie, San Diego, CA
Eugene A. Delmar, Olney, MD
Pamela J. Delphenich, New Haven, CT
Sidney L. Delson, East Hampton, NY
Olvia Demetriou, Washington, DC

Fellows of The American Institute of Architects (Con't)

William Deno, Boulder, CO
Jos. Robert Deshayes, Caldwell, TX
Gary L. Desmond, Denver, CO
John J. Desmond, Baton Rouge, LA
Gita Dev, Woodside, CA
Suzanne Di Geronimo, Paramus, NJ
Antonio Di Mambro, Boston, MA
A P. DiBenedetto, Portland, OR
Eugene L. DiLaura, Milan, MI
Robert Diamant, Longboat Key, FL
J. J. J. Diamond, Jacksonville, FL
Katherine Diamond, Los Angeles, CA
Horacio Diaz, San Juan, Puerto Rico
James R. Diaz, San Francisco, CA
David R. Dibner, McLean, VA
Bruce Dicker, Portsmouth, NH
Gerald G. Diehl, Dearborn, MI
Paul E. Dietrich, Cambridge, MA
Robert H. Dietz, Apache Junction, AZ
William M. Dikis, Des Moines, IA
Frank Dimster, Los Angeles, CA
Philip Dinsmore, Tucson, AZ
David D. Dixon, Boston, MA
F. Dail Dixon Jr., Chapel Hill, NC
John M. Dixon, Old Greenwich, CT
Michael A. Dixon, St. Charles, IL
Lawrence S. Doane, San Francisco, CA
Jim C. Doche, Amarillo, TX
Peter H. Dodge, San Francisco, CA
George S. Dolim, San Francisco, CA
Peter Hoyt Dominick Jr., Denver, CO
Milford W. Donaldson, San Diego, CA
Janet Donelson, Seattle, WA
Richard C. Donkervoet, Baltimore, MD
Kermit P. Dorius, Newport Bch, CA
Albert A. Dorman, Los Angeles, CA
Richard L. Dorman, Santa Fe, NM
Robert W. Dorsey, Cincinnati, OH
Darwin V. Doss, Salem, OR
Betsey O. Dougherty, Costa Mesa, CA
Brian P. Dougherty, Costa Mesa, CA
Frank F. Douglas, Houston, TX
H. Robert Douglass, Missouri City, TX
C.R. George Dove, Washington, DC
Gerald A. Doyle, Phoenix, AZ
Peter G. Doyle, Houston, TX
Boris Dramov, San Francisco, CA
Helene Dreiling, Warrenton, VA
Roy M. Drew, San Diego, CA
Albert M. Dreyfuss, Sacramento, CA
Robert W. Drummond, Gainesville, FL
Andres Duany, Miami, FL
Martin David Dubin, Highland Park, IL
George A. Dudley, Rensselaerville, NY
J. Paul Duffendack, Leawood, KS
Herbert E. Duncan, Kansas City, MO
Foster W. Dunwiddie, Henderson, NV

Eugene C. Dunwody, Macon, GA
William L. Duquette, Los Gatos, CA
Almon J. Durkee, Traverse City, MI
William R. Dutcher, Berkeley, CA
Donald J. Dwore, Coral Gables, FL
Daniel L. Dworsky, Los Angeles, CA

E

Mary Jean Eastman, New York, NY
John P. Eberhard, Alexandria, VA
Jeremiah Eck, Boston, MA
Stanton Eckstut, New York, NY
Robert N. Eddy, Bakersfield, CA
Judith Edelman, New York, NY
David J. Edwards Jr., Columbia, SC
Jared I. Edwards, Hartford, CT
Albert Efron, Staten Island, NY
David L. Eggers, West Palm Beach, FL
Ezra D. Ehrenkrantz, New York, NY
John P. Ehrig, Merritt Island, FL
Joseph Ehrlich, Menlo Park, CA
Steven D. Ehrlich, Culver City, CA
Thomas N. Eichbaum, Washington, DC
John A. Eifler, Chicago, IL
Steven L. Einhorn, Albany, NY
Peter D. Eisenman, New York, NY
Sidney H. Eisenshtat, Los Angeles, CA
Richard Karl Eisner, Oakland, CA
Barry P. Elbasani, Berkeley, CA
Joseph L. Eldredge, Vineyard Hvn, MA
Charles N. Eley, San Francisco, CA
James H. Eley, Jackson, MS
Howard F. Elkus, Boston, MA
Harry Ellenzweig, Cambridge, MA
Robin M. Ellerthorpe, Chicago, IL
Dale R. Ellickson, Great Falls, VA
Benjamin P. Elliott, Rockville, MD
Rand L. Elliott, Oklahoma City, OK
John M. Ellis, New York, NY
James E. Ellison, Washington, DC
Frank L. Elmer, Columbus, OH
James W. Elmore, Phoenix, AZ
Frederick E. Emmons, Bel Tiburon, CA
Terrel M. Emmons, Springfield, VA
William Eng, Champaign, IL
Douglas K. Engebretson, West Springfield, MA
Mark C. Engelbrecht, Des Moines, IA
William L. Ensign, Annapolis, MD
Lawrence Enyart, Phoenix, AZ
Herbert Epstein, Delray Beach, FL
Elizabeth S. Ericson, Boston, MA
Jerome R. Ernst, Seattle, WA
Philip A. Esocoff, Washington, DC
Harold Lionel Esten, Silver Spring, MD
A. B. Etherington, Honolulu, HI
Deane M. Evans Jr., Arlington, VA

Fellows of The American Institute of Architects (Con't)

J. Handel Evans, Camarillo, CA
Ralph F. Evans, Salt Lake City, UT
Robert J. Evans, Marshall, CA
William S. Evans, Shreveport, LA
C. Richard Everett, Houston, TX
Gary Everton, Nashville, TN
Thomas J. Eyerman, Chicago, IL

F

Otto Reichert Facilides, Philadelphia, PA
William H. Fain Jr., Los Angeles, CA
James Falick, Houston, TX
Kristine K. Fallon, Chicago, IL
Jay David Farbstein, San Luis Obispo, CA
Michael Farewell, Princeton, NJ
Richard T. Faricy, Saint Paul, MN
Richard C. Farley, Denver, CO
Stephen J. Farneth, San Francisco, CA
Avery C. Faulkner, Delaplane, VA
Winthrop W. Faulkner, Chevy Chase, MD
James G. Fausett, Marietta, GA
Robert E. Fehlberg, Pleasanton, CA
Werner L. Feibes, Schenectady, NY
Daniel J. Feil, Washington, DC
Edward A. Feiner, Fairfax, VA
Jose Feito, Miami, FL
Curtis W. Fentress, Denver, CO
S. Scott Ferebee Jr., Charlotte, NC
Franklin T. Ferguson, Salt Lake City, UT
Richard E. Fernau, Berkeley, CA
Stephanie E. Ferrell, Tampa, FL
Miguel Ferrer, Santurce, Puerto Rico
Richard B. Ferrier, Arlington, TX
James D. Ferris, Michigan City, IN
Robert D. Ferris, San Diego, CA
M. L. Ferro, Weare, NH
Donald E. Ferry, Springfield, IL
Michael T. Fickel, Kansas City, MO
H. H. Field, Shirley, MA
John L. Field, San Francisco, CA
Robert A. Fielden, Las Vegas, NV
Michael M. Fieldman, New York, NY
Kenneth J. Filarski, Providence, RI
R. Jerome Filer, Miami, FL
Bob G. Fillpot, Norman, OK
Ronald C. Filson, New Orleans, LA
Curtis Finch, Lake Oswego, OR
James H. Finch, Alpharetta, GA
Robert A. Findlay, Ames, IA
Maurice N. Finegold, Boston, MA
Ira S. Fink, Berkeley, CA
Jerry V. Finrow, Seattle, WA
A. Robert Fisher, Belvedere, CA
James Herschel Fisher, Dallas, TX
John L. Fisher, Marysville, CA
Hollye C. Fisk, Dallas, TX

Michael A. Fitts, Nolensville, TN
Darrell A. Fitzgerald, Atlanta, GA
James T. Fitzgerald, Cincinnati, OH
Joseph F. Fitzgerald, Chicago, IL
Richard A. Fitzgerald, Houston, TX
Joseph H. Flad, Madison, WI
Earl Robert Flansburgh, Boston, MA
Ted Flato, San Antonio, TX
Joseph L. Fleischer, New York, NY
Richard J. Fleischman, Cleveland, OH
Norman C. Fletcher, Lexington, MA
David J. Flood, Santa Monica, CA
Colden R. Florance, Washington, DC
Luis Flores-Dumont, Santurce, Puerto Rico
J. Chadwick P. Floyd, Centerbrook, CT
Richard F. Floyd, Dallas, TX
W. Jeff Floyd Jr., Atlanta, GA
Ligon B. Flynn, Wilmington, NC
Michael Flynn, New York, NY
John W. Focke, Houston, TX
Bernd Foerster, Manhattan, KS
James Follett, Chicago, IL
Fred L. Foote, San Francisco, CA
Stephen M. Foote, Boston, MA
Peter Forbes, Boston, MA
Robert M. Ford, Starkville, MS
Russell Forester, La Jolla, CA
Bernardo Fort-Brescia, Miami, FL
James R. Foster, Fayetteville, AR
Richard Foster, Wilton, CT
Bruce S. Fowle, New York, NY
Bob J. Fowler, PE, CBO, Pasadena, CA
Marion L. Fowlkes, Nashville, TN
Sheldon Fox, Stamford, CT
Harrison Fraker, Berkeley, CA
Edward D. Francis, Detroit, MI
Jay E. Frank, Dallas, TX
Morton Frank, Redwood City, CA
Richard C. Frank, Gregory, MI
Neil P. Frankel, Chicago, IL
James R. Franklin, San Luis Obispo, CA
Gregory Franta, Boulder, CO
John P. Franzen, Southport, CT
Ulrich J. Franzen, New York, NY
Robert J. Frasca, Portland, OR
James I. Freed, New York, NY
Beverly L. Freeman, Charlotte, NC
William W. Freeman, Burlington, VT
Jeffrey S. French, Philadelphia, PA
Thomas K. Fridstein, Chicago, IL
Stephen Friedlaender, Cambridge, MA
Daniel S. Friedman, Cincinnati, OH
Hans A. Friedman, Evanston, IL
Rodney F. Friedman, Belvedere, CA
Edward Friedrichs, Santa Monica, CA
Louis E. Fry Jr., Washington, DC
Louis E. Fry, Washington, DC

Fellows of The American Institute of Architects (Con't)

Richard E. Fry, Ann Arbor, MI
Joseph Y. Fujikawa, Winnetka, IL
Albert B. Fuller Jr., St. Louis, MO
Frank L. Fuller, IV, Oakland, CA
Duncan T. Fulton, Dallas, TX
David F. Furman, Charlotte, NC
James E. Furr, Houston, TX

G

Robert C. Gaede, Cleveland, OH
Herbert K. Gallagher, Boston, MA
Leslie M. Gallery-Dilworth, Philadelphia, PA
Harvey B. Gantt, Charlotte, NC
Theodore Garduque, Honolulu, HI
Robert D. Garland Jr., El Paso, TX
Charles E. Garrison, Diamondhead, MS
Truitt B. Garrison, Granbury, TX
Alan G. Gass, Denver, CO
Fred C. Gast Jr., Portland, OR
Kirk A. Gastinger, Kansas City, MO
Martha M. Gates, Pittsford, NY
Robert F. Gatje, New York, NY
James B. Gatton, Houston, TX
F. E. Gaulden, Greenville, SC
John C. Gaunt, Lawrence, KS
Robert Geddes, Princeton, NJ
Barbara L. Geddis, Stamford, CT
William J. Geddis, Chestnut Hill, MA
Robert J. Geering, San Francisco, CA
Frank O. Gehry, Santa Monica, CA
Carolyn D. Geise, Seattle, WA
Martin B. Gelber, Los Angeles, CA
M. Arthur Gensler Jr., San Francisco, CA
David W. George, Southlake, TX
Frank Dan George, Stamford, CT
Reagan W. George, Willow City, TX
Robert S. George, San Bruno, CA
Stephen A. George, Pittsburgh, PA
Preston M. Geren, Fort Worth, TX
Phillip H. Gerou, Evergreen, CO
Joe P. Giattina Jr., Birmingham, AL
Dale L. Gibbs, Lincoln, NE
Donald H. Gibbs, Long Beach, CA
Randall C. Gideon, Fort Worth, TX
Sidney P. Gilbert, New York, NY
Victor C. Gilbertson, Minnetonka, MN
Wilmot G. Gilland, Eugene, OR
Norman M. Giller, Miami Beach, FL
W. Douglas Gilpin, Charlottesville, VA
James S. Gimpel, Chicago, IL
Raymond L. Gindroz, Pittsburgh, PA
David L. Ginsberg, New York, NY
Raymond Girvigian, South Pasadena, CA
Joseph Carl Giuliani, Washington, DC
Romaldo Giurgola, Australia
Richard E. Glaser, Cincinnati, OH

William R. Glass, Oakland, CA
David Evan Glasser, Fayetteville, AR
E. A. Glendening, Cincinnati, OH
Val Glitsch, Houston, TX
Richard J. Gluckman, New York, NY
Harold D. Glucksman, Union, NJ
James M. Glymph, Santa Monica, CA
Ronald V. Gobbell, Nashville, TN
James Goettsch, Chicago, IL
Alan E. Goldberg, New Canaan, CT
Steven M. Goldberg, New York, NY
M. H. Goldfinger, New York, NY
Ron Goldman, Malibu, CA
Nicholas Goldsmith, New York, NY
Roger Neal Goldstein, Boston, MA
Stanley J. Goldstein, West Orange, NJ
Harmon H. Goldstone, New York, NY
Harry A. Golemon, Houston, TX
Bennie M. Gonzales, Nogales, AZ
Donald W. Y. Goo, Honolulu, HI
R. L. Good, Dallas, TX
D. B. Goodhue, Monterey, CA
Cary C. Goodman, Kansas City, MO
John P. Goodman, Manlius, NY
Michael K. Goodwin, Phoenix, AZ
Warren N. Goodwin, Brentwood, TN
Joan E. Goody, Boston, MA
Ezra Gordon, Chicago, IL
Harry T. Gordon, Washington, DC
Amy L. Gould, Baltimore, MD
Robert E. Gould, Kansas City, MO
Ronald Gourley, Tucson, AZ
Brian Gracey, Knoxville, TN
Bernard J. Grad, Elberon, NJ
Bruce J. Graham, Hobe Sound, FL
Gary L. Graham, Boston, MA
Roy E. Graham, Washington, DC
Robert E. Gramann, Cincinnati, OH
Warren Wolf Gran, New York, NY
Charles P. Graves, Lexington, KY
Dean W. Graves, Kansas City, MO
Michael Graves, Princeton, NJ
David Lawrence Gray, Santa Monica, CA
Thomas A. Gray, Little Rock, AR
Lyn E. Graziani, Miami, FL
Robert E. Greager, Pleasant Ridge, MI
Dennis W. Grebner, St. Paul, MN
Aaron G. Green, San Francisco, CA
Curtis H. Green, Shorewood, MN
Richard J. Green, Cambridge, MA
Thomas G. Green, Boston, MA
Aubrey J. Greenberg, Chicago, IL
James A. Greene, Oviedo, FL
Sanford R. Greenfield, Westfield, NJ
Susan Greenwald, Chicago, IL
John O. Greer, Bryan, TX
Glenn H. Gregg, New Haven, CT

Fellows of The American Institute of Architects (Con't)

Nonya Grenader, Houston, TX
Raymond Grenald, Narberth, PA
James A. Gresham, Tucson, AZ
William C. Gridley, Washington, DC
L. Duane Grieve, Knoxville, TN
James R. Grieves, Baltimore, MD
Donald I. Grinberg, Boston, MA
Edward A. Grochowiak, San Diego, CA
Olindo Grossi, Manhasset, NY
William H. Grover, Centerbrook, CT
J. C. Grube, Portland, OR
Ernest A. Grunsfeld, Chicago, IL
Jordan L. Gruzen, New York, NY
John C. Guenther, St. Louis, MO
Francis A. Guffey II, Charleston, WV
Paul J. Gumbinger, San Mateo, CA
Graham Gund, Cambridge, MA
Brooks R. Gunsul, Portland, OR
Gerald Gurland, West Orange, NJ
William R. Gustafson, Philadelphia, PA
Dean L. Gustavson, Salt Lake City, UT
Cabell Gwathmey, Harwood, MD
Charles Gwathmey, New York, NY
Willard E. Gwilliam, Hayes, VA

H

E. Keith Haag, Cuyahoga Falls, OH
Lester C. Haas, Shreveport, LA
Wallace L. Haas Jr., Redding, CA
Donald J. Hackl, Chicago, IL
John B. Hackler, Charlotte, NC
L.R. Hahnfeld, Fort Worth, TX
Frank S. Haines, Honolulu, HI
William H. Haire, Stillwater, OK
Gaines B. Hall, Downers Grove, IL
Mark W. Hall, Toronto, ON
William A. Hall, New York, NY
Harry C. Hallenbeck, Sacramento, CA
Stanley I. Hallet, Washington, DC
Gerald Hallissy, Port Washington, NY
Anna M. Halpin, New York, NY
Frances Halsband, New York, NY
William Hamby, New York, NY
Robert L. Hamill Jr., Boise, ID
D.K. Hamilton, Bellaire, TX
E.G. Hamilton Jr., Dallas, TX
Theodore S. Hammer, New York, NY
Gerald S. Hammond, Cincinnati, OH
John Hyatt Hammond, Greensboro, NC
W. Easley Hamner, Cambridge, MA
Mark G. Hampton, Coconut Grove, FL
John Paul C. Hanbury, Norfolk, VA
Peter H. Hand, Atlanta, GA
J. Paul Hansen, Savannah, GA
Richard F. Hansen, Sanibel, FL
Robert E. Hansen, Hendersonville, NC

Alan M. Hantman, Washington, D.C.
Ernest H. Hara, Honolulu, HI
John M. Hara, Honolulu, HI
Dellas H. Harder, Columbus, OH
Donald L. Hardison, El Cerrito, CA
Hugh Hardy, New York, NY
John C. Harkness, Arlington, MA
Sarah P. Harkness, Lexington, MA
Frank Harmon, Raleigh, NC
Harry W. Harmon, Lake San Marcos, CA
John C. Haro, Scottsdale, AZ
Charles F. Harper, Wichita Falls, TX
David M. Harper, Coral Gables, FL
Robert L. Harper, Centerbrook, CT
James W. Harrell, Cincinnati, OH
David A. Harris, Washington, DC
Edwin F. Harris Jr., Raleigh, NC
James Martin Harris, Tacoma, WA
Robert S. Harris, Los Angeles, CA
Robert V.M. Harrison, Jackson, MS
Roy P. Harrover, Memphis, TN
Craig W. Hartman, San Francisco, CA
Douglas C. Hartman, Dallas, TX
George E. Hartman, Washington, DC
Morton Hartman, Highland Park, IL
William E. Hartmann, Castine, ME
John F. Hartray Jr., Chicago, IL
Timothy Hartung, New York, NY
Wilbert R. Hasbrouck, Chicago, IL
Dennis E. Haskell, Seattle, WA
Albert L. Haskins Jr., Raleigh North, NC
Peter M. Hasselman, Orinda, CA
Sami Hassid, Pleasant Hill, CA
Herman A. Hassinger, Moorestown, NJ
George J. Hasslein, San Luis Obispo, CA
L. J. Hastings, Seattle, WA
Marvin Hatami, Denver, CO
Harold D. Hauf, Sun City, AZ
Robert O. Hausner, Santa Fe, NM
Daniel J. Havekost, Denver, CO
Perry A. Haviland, Oakland, CA
Velpeau E. Hawes Jr., Dallas, TX
H. Ralph Hawkins, Dallas, TX
Jasper Stillwell Hawkins, Phoenix, AZ
William J. Hawkins III, Portland, OR
William R. Hawley, E Palo Alto, CA
Bruce A. Hawtin, Jackson, WY
Richard S. Hayden, New York, NY
J. F. Hayes, Cambridge, MA
John Freeman Hayes, Radnor, PA
Irving B. Haynes, Lincoln, RI
Edward H. Healey, Cedar Rapids, IA
Michael M. Hearn, San Francisco, CA
George T. Heery, Atlanta, GA
Clovis Heimsath, Austin, TX
Dan Heinfeld, Irvine, CA
John Hejduk, Bronx, NY

Fellows of The American Institute of Architects (Con't)

Margaret Helfand, New York, NY
Barbara Heller, Washington, D.C.
Jeffrey Heller, San Francisco, CA
Maxwell Boone Hellmann, Cardiff by the Sea, CA
George F. Hellmuth, St. Louis, MO
A. C. Helman, Maitland, FL
David P. Helpern, New York, NY
James C. Hemphill Jr., Charlotte, NC
Arn Henderson, Norman, OK
John D. Henderson, San Diego, CA
Philip C. Henderson, Dallas, TX
James L. Hendricks, Rockwall, TX
William R. Henry, Jackson, MS
Donald C. Hensman, Pasadena, CA
Charles Herbert, Des Moines, IA
Robert G. Herman, San Francisco, CA
William W. Herrin, Huntsville, AL
Ricardo C. Herring, Washington, D.C.
Robert G. Hershberger, Tucson, AZ
Paul A. Hesson, San Antonio, TX
Charles R. Heuer, Charlottesville, VA
D. M. Hewitt, Seattle, WA
Warren Cummings Heylman, Spokane, WA
Mason S. Hicks, Fayetteville, NC
Charles C. Hight, Charlotte, NC
Dean F. Hilfinger, Bloomington, IL
Eric Hill, Detroit, MI
John W. Hill, Baltimore, MD
J. Robert Hillier, Princeton, NJ
Mark Hinshaw, Seattle, WA
Kem G. Hinton, Nashville, TN
Don M. Hisaka, Berkeley, CA
Gregory O. Hnedak, Memphis, TN
Paul S. Hoag, Bellevue, WA
Richard W. Hobbs, Washington, DC
Peter S. Hockaday, Seattle, WA
Murlin R. Hodgell, Norman, OK
Thomas H. Hodne, Minneapolis, MN
David C. Hoedemaker, Seattle, WA
August F. Hoenack, Bethesda, MD
David H. Hoffman, Evant, TX
David L. Hoffman, Wichita, KS
John J. Hoffmann, North Haven, CT
J.David Hoglund, Pittsburgh, PA
John A. Holabird, Chicago, IL
L. M. Holder, Austin, TX
Major L. Holland, Tuskegee, AL
Dwight E. Holmes, Tampa, FL
Jess Holmes, Henderson, NV
Nicholas H. Holmes Jr., Mobile, AL
Harry J. Holroyd, Columbus, OH
David A. Holtz, Potomac, MD
Malcolm Holzman, New York, NY
George W. Homsey, San Francisco, CA
Bobbie S. Hood, San Francisco, CA
Van D. Hooker, Albuquerque, NM
G. N. Hoover, Houston, TX

George Hoover, Denver, CO
Ray C. Hoover III, Atlanta, GA
Frank L. Hope Jr., San Diego, CA
Gene C. Hopkins, Detroit, MI
Edward M. Hord, Baltimore, MD
Howard N. Horii, Newark, NJ
Gerald Horn, Chicago, IL
Patrick Horsbrugh, South Bend, IN
T. Horty, Minneapolis, MN
Reginald D. Hough, Larchmont, NY
Marvin C. Housworth, Atlanta, GA
David C. Hovey, Winnetka, IL
J. Murray Howard, Charlottesville, VA
John Howey, Tampa, FL
Thomas S. Howorth, Oxford, MS
Charles K. Hoyt, Old Lyme, CT
Michael M. Hricak Jr., Venice, CA
Robert Y. Hsiung, Boston, MA
Charles A. Hubbard, Cortez, CO
Jeffrey A. Huberman, Charlotte, NC
Daniel Huberty, Seattle, WA
Richard W. Huffman, Philadelphia, PA
Stephan S. Huh, Minneapolis, MN
Robert E. Hull, Seattle, WA
Charles F. Hummel, Boise, ID
Fred E. Hummel, Sacramento, CA
Harry J. Hunderman, Northbrook, IL
Gregory Hunt, Washington, DC
Frances P. Huppert, New York, NY
Sam T. Hurst, Montecito, CA
Syed V. Husain, Kensington, CA
Mary Alice Hutchins, Portland, OR
Remmert W. Huygens, Wayland, MA
Bryden B. Hyde, Jarretsville, MD
Fred J. Hynek, Parker, CO

I

Dean Illingworth, Indianapolis, IN
Elizabeth W. Ingraham, Colorado Springs, CO
William A. Isley, Bainbridge Island, WA
H. Curtis Ittner, St. Louis, MO
Robert A. Ivy Jr., New York, NY

J

Huson Jackson, Lexington, MA
Mike Jackson, Springfield, IL
R. G. Jackson, Houston, TX
Ralph T. Jackson, Boston, MA
Bernard Jacob, Minneapolis, MN
Harry M. Jacobs, Oakland, CA
Stephen B. Jacobs, New York, NY
Hugh N. Jacobsen, Washington, DC
Phillip L. Jacobson, Seattle, WA
J. P. Jacoby, Menomonee Falls, WI
Helmut Jahn, Chicago, IL

Fellows of The American Institute of Architects (Con't)

Timm Jamieson, Roanoke, VA
Henry A. Jandl, Richmond, VA
William R. Jarratt, Ann Arbor, MI
Lloyd Jary, San Antonio, TX
Peter Jefferson, Highlands, NC
Jordan O. Jelks, Macon, GA
J. J. Jennewein, Tampa, FL
Richard W. Jennings, Austin, TX
Bruce H. Jensen, Salt Lake City, UT
David Jepson, Hartford, CT
Jon Adams Jerde, Venice, CA
John W. Jickling, Birmingham, MI
John M. Johansen, New York, NY
Anthony N. Johns Jr., Mt. Irvine, Trinidad & Tobaga
Arthur D. Johnson, Omaha, NE
Danie Johnson, Asheville, NC
Edwin J. Johnson, Dallas, TX
Eric B. Johnson, Savannah, GA
Floyd E. Johnson, Scottsville, VA
James H. Johnson, Denver, CO
Jed V. Johnson, Wappingers Falls, NY
Marvin R. Johnson, Raleigh, NC
Philip C. Johnson, New York, NY
Ralph E. Johnson, Chicago, IL
Scott Johnson, Los Angeles, CA
Walker C. Johnson, Chicago, IL
Yandell Johnson, Little Rock, AR
Norman J. Johnston, Seattle, WA
James O. Jonassen, Seattle, WA
Arthur E. Jones, Houston, TX
Bernard I. Jones, Carbondale, IL
E. Fay Jones, Fayetteville, AR
J. Delaine Jones, Troy, NY
Jack B. Jones, Tamuning, Guam
Johnpaul Jones, Seattle, WA
Paul Duane Jones, Kailua, HI
Renis Jones, Montgomery, AL
Robert Lawton Jones, Tulsa, OK
Rudard Artaban Jones, Urbana, IL
Bendrew G. Jong, Orinda, CA
Joe J. Jordan, Philadelphia, PA
David A. Jordani, Minneapolis, MN
Roberta W. Jorgensen, Irvine, CA
H. V. Jova, Atlanta, GA
Bruce D. Judd, San Francisco, CA
Yu Sing Jung, Boston, MA
Howard H. Juster, San Diego, CA

K

Carl F. Kaelber Jr., Pittsford, NY
Richard E. Kaeyer, Mt. Kisco, NY
Gerald Kagan, New Haven, CT
David T. Kahler, Milwaukee, WI
Charles H. Kahn, Chapel Hill, NC
Eino O. Kainlauri, Ames, IA
Harry Kale, Conshohocken, PA

Mark Kalin, Newton Center, MA
G. M. Kallmann, Boston, MA
Stephen H. Kanner, Los Angeles, CA
Gary Y. Kaplan, Red Bank, NJ
Richard H. Kaplan, Cleveland, OH
Raymond L. Kappe, Pacific Palisades, CA
Raymond John Kaskey, Washington, DC
Kirby M. Keahey, Houston, TX
Gustave R. Keane, Bradenton, FL
Jan Keane, New York, NY
Richard C. Keating, Marina Del Rey, CA
Allan Kehrt, Princeton, NJ
Douglas S. Kelbaugh, Ann Arbor, MI
Duane A. Kell, St. Paul, MN
John H. Kell, San Antonio, TX
Bernard Kellenyi, Red Bank, NJ
Larry J. Keller, Fairfax, VA
Frank S. Kelly, Houston, TX
F. L. Kelsey, Scottsdale, AZ
Diane Legge Kemp, Chicago, IL
William D. Kendall, Houston, TX
Robert N. Kennedy, Indianapolis, IN
Gertrude L. Kerbis, Chicago, IL
Thomas L. Kerns, Arlington, VA
William H. Kessler, Detroit, MI
Herbert A. Ketcham, Minneapolis, MN
Russell V. Keune, Arlington, VA
A.H. Keyes Jr., Washington, DC
Stephen J. Kieran, Philadelphia, PA
Lee F. Kilbourn, Portland, OR
James R. Killebrew, Grapevine, TX
Edward A. Killingsworth, Long Beach, CA
Tai Soo Kim, Hartford, CT
Jong S. Kimm, Apo
David R. H. King, Washington, DC
Dennis M. King, Huntington Woods, MI
Donald King, Seattle, WA
Gordon L. King, Sacramento, CA
J. Bertram King, Asheville, NC
Leland King, Bodega Bay, CA
Sol King, Palm Beach, FL
M. Ray Kingston, Salt Lake City, UT
Paul Kinnison Jr., San Antonio, TX
Ballard H. Kirk, Columbus, OH
D. W. Kirk Jr., Fort Worth, TX
Stephen J. Kirk, Grosse Pointe Pk, MI
John M. Kirksey, Houston, TX
Peyton E. Kirven, Westlake Village, CA
Robert S. Kitchen, Ocean Hills, CA
Henry Klein, Mount Vernon, WA
J. Arvid Klein, New York, NY
Robert M. Kliment, New York, NY
Stephen A. Kliment, New York, NY
Kenneth F. Klindtworth, Duck Key, FL
Lee B. Kline, Los Angeles, CA
Vincent G. Kling, Chester Springs, PA
James F. Knight, Gunnison, CO

Fellows of The American Institute of Architects (Con't)

Roy F. Knight, Tallahassee, FL
William H. Knight, Santa Rosa, CA
Stuart Knoop, Chevy Chase, MD
Charles M. Kober, Long Beach, CA
Carl Koch, Cambridge, MA
Steven Y. Kodama, San Francisco, CA
Edward J. Kodet Jr., Minneapolis, MN
Pierre F. Koenig, Los Angeles, CA
Alfred H. Koetter, Boston, MA
A. Eugene Kohn, New York, NY
Keith R. Kolb, Seattle, WA
Nathaniel K. Kolb Jr., Dallas, TX
Ronald Kolman, Savannah, GA
S. Richard Komatsu, El Cerrito, CA
Hendrik Koning, Santa Monica, CA
Norman L. Koonce, McLean, VA
James F. Kortan, Atlanta, GA
Panos G. Koulermos, La Crescenta, CA
Alexander Kouzmanoff, Rye Brook, NY
Gerhardt Kramer, Webster Groves, MO
Robert Kramer, Brookline, MA
Peter Krasnow, New York City, NY
M. Stanley Krause Jr., Newport News, VA
Eugene Kremer, Manhattan, KS
J. Richard Kremer, Louisville, KY
Jerrily R. Kress, Washington, DC
John L. Kriken, San Francisco, CA
Robert N. Kronewitter, Denver, CO
Kenneth C. Kruger, Santa Barbara, CA
James O. Kruhly, Philadelphia, PA
Rod Kruse, Des Moines, IA
Denis G. Kuhn, New York, NY
Julian E. Kulski, Orlean, VA
Ernest J. Kump, Zurich, Switzerland
Moritz Kundig, Spokane, WA
Theodore E. Kurz, Cleveland, OH
Peter Kuttner, Cambridge, MA
Sylvia P. Kwan, San Francisco, CA
Michael Kwartler, New York, NY

L

David N. LaBau, Bloomfield, CT
Ronald J. Labinski, Kansas City, MO
John W. Lackens Jr., Minneapolis, MN
Bill N. Lacy, Purchase, NY
Thomas Laging, Lincoln, NE
Henry J. Lagorio, Orinda, CA
Jerry Laiserin, Woodbury, NY
David C. Lake, San Antonio, TX
Charles E. Lamb, Annapolis, MD
James Lambeth, Fayetteville, AR
James I. Lammers, Chisago City, MN
Gregory W. Landahl, Chicago, IL
Peter H. Landon, Chicago, IL
D. E. Landry, Dallas, TX
Jane Landry, Dallas, TX

John M. Laping, West Amherst, NY
Arnold Les Larsen, Port Salerno, FL
Robert G. Larsen, New York City, NY
Dayl A. Larson, Denver, CO
William N. Larson, Park Ridge, IL
William L. Larson, Omaha, NE
Carroll J. Lawler, West Hartford, CT
Charles E. Lawrence, Houston, TX
Jerry Lawrence, Tacoma, WA
Robert M. Lawrence, Oklahoma City, OK
David E. Lawson, Madison, WI
Elizabeth Lawson, Charlottesville, VA
William R. Lawson, Reston, VA
Franklin D. Lawyer, Houston, TX
John C. Le Bey, Savannah, GA
Robert LeMond, Fort Worth, TX
Glen S. LeRoy, Kansas City, MO
Benjamin B. Lee, Honolulu, HI
Donald R. Lee, Charlotte, NC
Elizabeth B. Lee, Lumberton, NC
John Lee, New York, NY
M. David Lee, Boston, MA
Gene Leedy, Winter Haven, FL
James M. Leefe, Sausalito, CA
Andrea P. Leers, Boston, MA
Gillet Lefferts, Darien, CT
Spencer A. Leineweber, Honolulu, HI
Lawrence J. Leis, Louisville, KY
Richard Leitch, South Laguna, CA
Herbert Lembcke, San Francisco, CA
James T. Lendrum, Phoenix, AZ
Peter A. Lendrum, Phoenix, AZ
Eason H. Leonard, Carmel, CA
Ralph Lerner, Princeton, NJ
Nicholas Lesko, Cleveland, OH
Francis D. Lethbridge, Nantucket, MA
Conrad Levenson, New York, NY
Brenda A. Levin, Los Angeles, CA
Richard D. Levin, Longboat Key, FL
Alan G. Levy, Philadelphia, PA
Eugene P. Levy, Little Rock, AR
Herbert W. Levy, Spring House, PA
Morton L. Levy, Houston, TX
Toby S. Levy, San Francisco, CA
Anne McCutcheon Lewis, Washington, DC
Calvin F. Lewis, Des Moines, IA
David Lewis, Homestead, PA
George B. Lewis, Oklahoma City, OK
Howarth Lewis, Jr., West Palm Beach, FL
Richard L. Lewis, Pebble Beach, CA
Roger K. Lewis, Washington, DC
Tom Lewis Jr., Kissimmee, FL
Walter H. Lewis, Champaign, IL
Alan C. Liddle, Lakewood, WA
Frederick Liebhardt, La Jolla, CA
Theodore Liebman, New York, NY
Bernard J. Liff, Pittsburgh, PA

Fellows of The American Institute of Architects (Con't)

John H. Lind, Iowa City, IA
David Lindsey, Seattle, WA
Gail A. Lindsey, Wake Forest, NC
H. Mather Lippincott Jr., Moylan, PA
William H. Liskamm, San Rafael, CA
Robert A. Little, Cleveland, OH
Robert S. Livesey, Columbus, OH
Stanley C. Livingston, San Diego, CA
Thomas W. Livingston, Anchorage, AK
Walter R. Livingston Jr., Crum Lynne, PA
Peter Lizon, Knoxville, TN
W. Kirby Lockard, Tucson, AZ
James L. Loftis, Oklahoma City, OK
Donn Logan, Berkeley, CA
Dirk Lohan, Chicago, IL
Thomas E. Lollini, Berkeley, CA
Jerrold E. Lomax, Carmel Valley, CA
J. Carson Looney, Memphis, TN
R. Nicholas Loope, Phoenix, AZ
Gabor Lorant, Phoenix, AZ
Larry Lord, Atlanta, GA
George H. Loschky, Seattle, WA
John C. Loss, Whitehall, MI
Rex Lotery, Montecito, CA
William C. Louie, New York, NY
William Love, Los Angeles, CA
Ivenue Love-Stanley, Atlanta, GA
Wendell H. Lovett, Seattle, WA
Frank E. Lucas, Charleston, SC
Thomas J. Lucas, Southfield, MI
Lenore M. Lucey, Washington, DC
Carl F. Luckenbach, Ann Arbor, MI
Graham B. Luhn, Houston, TX
Anthony J. Lumsden, Los Angeles, CA
Frithjof Lunde, Center Valley, PA
Phillip Lundwall, Grand Rapids, MI
Victor A. Lundy, Bellaire, TX
Donald H. Lutes, Springfield, OR
Frederic P. Lyman, Sebeka, MN
Robert Dale Lynch, Pittsburgh, PA
Robert J. Lynch, Scottsdale, AZ
Donlyn Lyndon, Berkeley, CA
Maynard Lyndon, Kuessaberg, Germany

M

Michael Maas, W. Hampton Bch, NY
R. Doss Mabe, Los Angeles, CA
John E. MacAllister, San Francisco, CA
Donald MacDonald, San Francisco, CA
Virginia B. MacDonald, Kaneohe, HI
H. A. MacEwen, Tampa, FL
Ian MacKinlay, San Francisco, CA
Charles H. MacMahon, Deland, FL
Robert C. Mack, Minneapolis, MN
Eugene J. Mackey III, St. Louis, MO
John Macsai, Chicago, IL

Robert P. Madison, Cleveland, OH
Peter E. Madsen, Boston, MA
Theodore S. Maffitt Jr., Palestine, TX
Henry J. Magaziner, Philadelphia, PA
Gary Mahaffey, Minneapolis, MN
Victor C. Mahler, New York, NY
John E. Mahlum, Seattle, WA
C. R. Maiwald, Wilmington, NC
Marvin J. Malecha, Raleigh, NC
L. Vic Maloof, Atlanta, GA
Arthur E. Mann, Irvine, CA
Carter H. Manny Jr., Chicago, IL
Clark D. Manus, San Francisco, CA
Virginia S. March, Fairhope, AL
Roger W. Margerum, Detroit, MI
Phillip T. Markwood, Columbus, OH
Harvey V. Marmon Jr., San Antonio, TX
Jud R. Marquardt, Seattle, WA
Clinton Marr Jr., Riverside, CA
Mortimer M. Marshall Jr., Reston, VA
Richard C. Marshall, San Francisco, CA
Albert C. Martin, Los Angeles, CA
Christopher C. Martin, Los Angeles, CA
David C. Martin, Los Angeles, CA
Robert E. Martin, Toledo, OH
W. Mike Martin, Berkeley, CA
Walter B. Martinez, Miami, FL
Thomas S. Marvel, San Juan, Puerto Rico
Joseph V. Marzella, Wallingford, PA
Ronald L. Mason, Denver, CO
George Matsumoto, Oakland, CA
Edward H. Matthei, Chicago, IL
Robert F. Mattox, Boston, MA

Did you know...

The States with the most AIA Fellows:

California - 394
New York - 214
Texas - 208
Illinois - 129
Massachusetts -119
Florida - 104
Washington - 89
Pennsylvania - 77
Virginia - 71
Michigan - 66
D.C. - 66
North Carolina - 60

Fellows of The American Institute of Architects (Con't)

Frank J. Matzke, St. Augustine, FL
John M. Maudlin-Jeronimo, Bethesda, MD
Laurie M. Maurer, Brooklyn, NY
Susan A. Maxman, Philadelphia, PA
Murvan M. Maxwell, Metairie, LA
Arthur May, New York, NY
Kenneth D. Maynard, Anchorage, AK
Marsha Maytum, San Francisco, CA
Charles F. McAfee, Wichita, KS
Charles McCafferty, Saint Clair Shores, MI
E. K. McCagg, II, Kirkland, WA
Joe M. McCall, Dallas, TX
Michael A. McCarthy, New York, NY
John McCartney, Washington, DC
Bruce McCarty, Knoxville, TN
Harlan E. McClure, Pendleton, SC
Wesley A. McClure, Raleigh, NC
Richard E. McCommons, Falls Church, VA
Robert E. McConnell, Tucson, AZ
Edward D. McCrary, Hillsborough, CA
M. Allen McCree, Austin, TX
Gerald M. McCue, Cambridge, MA
Grant G. McCullagh, Chicago, IL
James McCullar, New York, NY
Margaret McCurry, Chicago, IL
William A. McDonough, Charlottesville, VA
Connie S. McFarland, Tulsa, OK
A. S. McGaughan, Washington, DC
John M. McGinty, Houston, TX
Milton B. McGinty, Houston, TX
Richard A. McGinty, Hilton Hd Island, SC
John W. McGough, Spokane, WA
James R. McGranahan, Lacey, WA
Mark McInturff, Bethesda, MD
Herbert P. McKim, Wrightsville Beach, NC
David A. McKinley, Seattle, WA
Noel M. McKinnell, Boston, MA
Thomas L. McKittrick, College Station, TX
H. Roll McLaughlin, Carmel, IN
C. Andrew McLean, II, Atlanta, GA
James M. McManus, Glastonbury, CT
George A. McMath, Portland, OR
William G. McMinn, Coconut Grove, FL
E. Eean McNaughton Jr., New Orleans, LA
Carrell S. McNulty Jr., Cincinnati, OH
E. Keith McPheeters, Auburn, AL
John M. McRae, Starkville, MS
Charles B. McReynolds, Newport News, VA
Franklin Mead, Boston, MA
George C. Means Jr., Clemson, SC
Philip J. Meathe, Grosse Pte Farms, MI
David Meckel, San Francisco, CA
Henry G. Meier, Fishers, IN
Richard A. Meier, New York, NY
Carl R. Meinhardt, New York, NY
Lawrence P. Melillo, Louisville, KY
Roger C. Mellem, Port Republic, MD

R. A. Melting, New York, NY
John O. Merrill, Tiburon, CA
William Dickey Merrill, Carmel, CA
David R. Messersmith, Lubbock, TX
Robert C. Metcalf, Ann Arbor, MI
William H. Metcalf, McLean, VA
Andrew Metter, Evanston, IL
David Metzger, Washington, DC
C. Richard Meyer, Seattle, WA
James H. Meyer, Richardson, TX
John T. Meyer, Saginaw, MI
Kurt W. Meyer, Los Angeles, CA
Richard C. Meyer, Philadelphia, PA
Marshall D. Meyers, Pasadena, CA
Nancy A. Miao, New York, NY
Linda H. Michael, Charlottesville, VA
Constantine E. Michaelides, St. Louis, MO
Valerius Leo Michelson, Minneapolis, MN
Robert Miklos, Boston, MA
Arnold Mikon, Detroit, MI
Juanita M. Mildenberg, Bethesda, MD
Don C. Miles, Seattle, WA
Daniel R. Millen Jr., Cherry Hill, NJ
David E. Miller, Seattle, WA
Ewing H. Miller, Port Republic, MD
George H. Miller, New York, NY
Henry F. Miller, Orange, CT
Hugh C. Miller, Richmond, VA
James W. Miller, Madison, WI
John F. Miller, Cambridge, MA
Joseph Miller, Washington, DC
L. Kirk Miller, San Francisco, CA
Leroy B. Miller, Santa Monica, CA
Richard Miller, Nashville, TN
Steven Miller, Prague, Czechoslovakia
William C. Miller, Salt Lake City, UT
Edward I. Mills, New York, NY
Gordon E. Mills, Dubuque, IA
Michael Mills, Glen Ridge, NJ
Willis N. Mills Jr., Ponte Vedra Beach, FL
Lee Mindel, New York, NY
Adolfo E. Miralles, Altadena, CA
Henry D. Mirick, Fairless Hills, PA
Dan S. Mitchell, St. Louis, MO
Ehrman B. Mitchell Jr., Philadelphia, PA
Melvin L. Mitchell, Baltimore, MD
Richard R. Moger, Port Washington, NY
Ronald L. Moline, Bourbonnais, IL
Robert B. Molseed, Annandale, VA
Lynn H. Molzan, Indianapolis, IN
Frank Montana, Dade City, FL
Joseph D. Monticciolo, Woodbury, NY
Curtis J. Moody, Columbus, OH
Thomas B. Moon, Rancho Santa Margarita, CA
Arthur C. Moore, Washington, DC
Barry M. Moore, Houston, TX
Gerald L. Moorhead, Houston, TX

Fellows of The American Institute of Architects (Con't)

Jill K. Morelli, Columbus, OH
Jesse O. Morgan Jr., Shreveport, LA
Robert Lee Morgan, Port Townsend, WA
W. N. Morgan, Jacksonville, FL
Howard H. Morgridge, Newport Beach, CA
Lamberto G. Moris, San Francisco, CA
Seth I. Morris, Houston, TX
Lionel Morrison, Dallas, TX
John Morse, Seattle, WA
James R. Morter, Vail, CO
Allen D. Moses, Kirkland, WA
Robert Mosher, La Jolla, CA
Samuel Z. Moskowitz, Naples, FL
Eric O. Moss, Culver City, CA
G. Michael Mostoller, Princeton, NJ
Kenneth L. Motley, Roanoke, VA
John K. Mott, Alexandria, VA
Edward A. Moulthrop, Atlanta, GA
Jennifer T. Moulton, Denver, CO
Frederic D. Moyer, Northbrook, IL
Frank R. Mudano, Clearwater, FL
Theodore Mularz, Ashland, OR
Paul Muldawer, Atlanta, GA
John W. Mullen III, Dallas, TX
Rosemary F. Muller, Oakland, CA
Harold C. Munger, Toledo, OH
Frank W. Munzer, Clinton Corners, NY
Charles F. Murphy, Mesa, AZ
Frank N. Murphy, Clayton, MO
David G. Murray, Tulsa, OK
Stephen A. Muse, Washington, DC
Robert C. Mutchler, Fargo, ND
John V. Mutlow, Los Angeles, CA
Donald B. Myer, Washington, DC
John R. Myer, Tamworth, NH
Barton Myers, Beverly Hills, CA
Ralph E. Myers, Prairie Village, KS

N

Daniel J. Nacht, Fair Oaks, CA
Barbara Nadel, Forest Hills, NY
Herbert N. Nadel, Los Angeles, CA
Chester Emil Nagel, Colorado Springs, CO
James L. Nagle, Chicago, IL
Louis Naidorf, Burbank, CA
Noboru Nakamura, Orinda, CA
C. S. Nakata, Colorado Springs, CO
Robert J. Nash, Oxon Hill, MD
Thomas M. Nathan, Memphis, TN
Kenneth H. Natkin, Esq., San Francisco, CA
James A. Neal, Greenville, SC
Paul R. Neel, San Luis Obispo, CA
Ibsen Nelsen, Vashon, WA
Edward H. Nelson, Tucson, AZ
James Richard Nelson, Wilmington, DE
John H. Nelson, Chicago, IL

T. C. Nelson, Kansas City, MO
Ede I. Nemeti, Houston, TX
Donald E. Neptune, Newport Beach, CA
John F. Nesholm, Seattle, WA
Barbara Neski, New York, NY
Julian J. Neski, New York, NY
Walter A. Netsch, Chicago, IL
Perry King Neubauer, Cambridge, MA
J. Victor Neuhaus, III, Hunt, TX
William O. Neuhaus, III, Houston, TX
David J. Neuman, Palo Alto, CA
Hans Neumann, Las Vegas, NV
S. Kenneth Neumann, Beverly Hills, MI
Peter Newlin, Chestertown, MD
Herbert S. Newman, New Haven, CT
Michael Newman, Winston-Salem, NC
Robert L. Newsom, Los Angeles, CA
Chartier C. Newton, Austin, TX
Doreve Nicholaeff, Osterville, MA
Michael H. Nicklas, Raleigh, NC
Robert Duncan Nicol, Oakland, CA
George Z. Nikolajevich, St. Louis, MO
Edward R. Niles, Malibu, CA
Christopher G. Nims, Denver, CO
Ivey L. Nix, Atlanta, GA
Robert J. Nixon, Port Angeles, WA
George M. Notter Jr., Washington, DC
John M. Novack, Dallas, TX
Frederick Noyes, Boston, MA
Jimmie R. Nunn, Flagstaff, AZ
John Nyfeler, Austin, TX

O

W. L. O'Brien Jr., Research Triangle Park, NC
Thomas O'Connor, Detroit, MI
L. J. O'Donnell, Chicago, IL
Arthur F. O'Leary, County Louth, Ireland
Paul Murff O'Neal Jr., Shreveport, LA
Charles W. Oakley, Pacific Palisades, CA
Gyo Obata, Saint Louis, MO
Jeffrey K. Ochsner, Seattle, WA
Robert A. Odermatt, Berkeley, CA
Mary L. Oehrlein, Washington, DC
Rolf H. Ohlhausen, New York, NY
Richard M. Olcott, New York, NY
Edward A. Oldziey, Wyckoff, NJ
P. S. Oles, Newton, MA
H. B. Olin, Chicago, IL
Donald E. Olsen, Berkeley, CA
Carole J. Olshavsky, Columbus, OH
James W. Olson, Seattle, WA
Herbert B. Oppenheimer, New York, NY
Edward L. Oremen, San Diego, CA
Robert E. Oringdulph, Portland, OR
Gordon D. Orr Jr., Madison, WI
David William Osler, Ann Arbor, MI

Fellows of The American Institute of Architects (Con't)

G. F. Oudens, Chevy Chase, MD
Raymond C. Ovresat, Wilmette, IL
Kenneth Owens Jr., Birmingham, AL

P

C. J. Paderewski III, San Diego, CA
Elizabeth Seward Padjen, Marblehead, MA
Gregory Palermo, Des Moines, IA
Joshua J. Pan, Taipei, Taiwan
Solomon Pan, Tucson, AZ
Lester C. Pancoast, Miami, FL
John R. Pangrazio, Seattle, WA
Donald H. Panushka, Salt Lake City, UT
Dennis A. Paoletti, San Francisco, CA
Tician Papachristou, New York, NY
Laszlo Papp, New Canaan, CT
George C. Pappageorge, Chicago, IL
Nicholas A. Pappas, Richmond, VA
Ted P. Pappas, Jacksonville, FL
Charles J. Parise, Grosse Pointe Woods, MI
Ki Suh Park, Los Angeles, CA
Sharon C. Park, Arlington, VA
Alfred B. Parker, Gainesville, FL
Derek Parker, San Francisco, CA
Howard C. Parker, Dallas, TX
Leonard S. Parker, Minneapolis, MN
R. C. Parrott, Knoxville, TN
Steven A. Parshall, Houston, TX
Giovanni Pasanella, New York, NY
C. H. Paseur, Houston, TX
Joseph Passonneau, Washington, DC
Piero Patri, San Francisco, CA
Allen L. Patrick, Columbus, OH
S. Glen Paulsen, Ann Arbor, MI
Charles Harrison Pawley, Coral Gables, FL
Thomas M. Payette, Boston, MA
H. Morse Payne, Lincoln, MA
Richard W. Payne, Houston, TX
George Clayton Pearl, Albuquerque, NM
Bryce Pearsall, Phoenix, AZ
Charles Almond Pearson Jr., Arlington, VA
J. Norman Pease Jr., Charlotte, NC
John G. Pecsok, Indianapolis, IN
William Pedersen Jr., New York, NY
Gerard W. Peer, Charlotte, NC
William R. Peery, Clearwater, FL
I. M. Pei, New York, NY
Maris Peika, Toluca Lake, CA
John W. Peirce, Topsfield, MA
Cesar Pelli, New Haven, CT
William M. Pena, Houston, TX
Thompson E. Penney, Charleston, SC
David L. Perkins, Lafayette, LA
G. Holmes Perkins, Philadelphia, PA
L. Bradford Perkins, New York, NY
John Gray Perry, Portland, OR

Norman K. Perttula, Aurora, OH
Stuart K. Pertz, New York, NY
Robert W. Peters, Albuquerque, NM
Carolyn S. Peterson, San Antonio, TX
Charles E. Peterson, Philadelphia, PA
Leonard A. Peterson, Chicago, IL
Edward G. Petrazio, Spanish Fort, AL
Eleanore Pettersen, Saddle River, NJ
Jay S. Pettitt Jr., Beulah, MI
Mark A. Pfaller, Elm Grove, WI
Norman Pfeiffer, Los Angeles, CA
J. D. Pfluger, Austin, TX
Barton Phelps, Los Angeles, CA
Frederick F. Phillips, Chicago, IL
W. Irving Phillips Jr., Houston, TX
J. Almont Pierce, Falls Church, VA
John Allen Pierce, Dallas, TX
Walter S. Pierce, Lexington, WA
Raymond A. Pigozzi, Evanston, IL
George J. Pillorge, Oxford, MD
Robert J. Piper, Winnetka, IL
Carl W. Pirscher, Windsor, Canada
John W. Pitman, Santa Barbara, CA
Peter A. Piven, Philadelphia, PA
Elizabeth Plater-Zyberk, Miami, FL
Charles A. Platt, New York, NY
Kalvin J. Platt, Sausalito, CA
G. Gray Plosser Jr., Birmingham, AL
Jan Hird Pokorny, New York, NY
Lee A. Polisano, London, England
William M. Polk, Seattle, WA
Wilson Pollock, Cambridge, MA
James Stewart Polshek, New York, NY
Ralph Pomerance, New York, NY
Leason F. Pomeroy, III, Santa Ana, CA
Lee H. Pomeroy, New York, NY
Lynn S. Pomeroy, Sacramento, CA
Gerrard S. Pook, Bronx, NY
Samuel D. Popkin, West Bloomfield, MI
William L. Porter, Cambridge, MA
John C. Portman Jr., Atlanta, GA
Penny H. Posedly, Phoenix, AZ
Raymond G. Post Jr., Baton Rouge, LA
Boone Powell, San Antonio, TX
Peter Pran, Seattle, WA
James Pratt, Dallas, TX
Antoine Predock, Albuquerque, NM
William T. Priestley, Lake Forest, IL
Arnold J. Prima Jr., Washington, DC
Harold E. Prinz, Dallas, TX
Donald Prowler, Philadelphia, PA
Homer L. Puderbaugh, Lincoln, NE
David A. Pugh, Portland, OR
William L. Pulgram, Atlanta, GA
James G. Pulliam, Pasadena, CA
Joe T. Pursell, Jackson, MS
Michael Pyatok, Oakland, CA

Fellows of The American Institute of Architects (Con't)

Q

G. William Quatman, Kansas City, MO
Jerry L. Quebe, Chicago, IL
Robert W. Quigley, San Diego, CA
Marcel Quimby, Dallas, TX
Michael L. Quinn, Washington, DC
Richard W. Quinn, Avon, CT

R

Martin D. Raab, New York, NY
Bruce A. Race, Berkeley, CA
John A. Raeber, San Francisco, CA
Craig E. Rafferty, St. Paul, MN
George E. Rafferty, St. Paul, MN
Richard J. Rafferty, St. Paul, MN
Lemuel Ramos, Miami, FL
Peter A. Rand, Minneapolis, MN
Terry Rankine, Cambridge, MA
Raymond R. Rapp, Galveston, TX
Ralph Rapson, Minneapolis, MN
Howard Terry Rasco, Little Rock, AR
Peter T. Rasmussen, Tacoma, WA
John K. Rauch Jr., Philadelphia, PA
John G. Rauma, Minneapolis, MN
William L. Rawn, Boston, MA
James T. Ream, San Francisco, CA
Mark Reddington, Seattle, WA
Charles Redmon, Cambridge, MA
Louis G. Redstone, Southfield, MI
Ronald Reed, Cleveland, OH
Vernon Reed, Liberty, MO
William R. Reed, Tacoma, WA
Henry S. Reeder Jr., Cambridge, MA
Frank Blair Reeves, Gainesville, FL
I. S. K. Reeves, V, Winter Park, FL
Roscoe Reeves Jr., Chevy Chase, MD
Victor A. Regnier, Los Angeles, CA
Patrick C. Rehse, Phoenix, AZ
Pierce K. Reibsamen, Los Angeles, CA
Jerry Reich, Chicago, IL
Johnstone Reid Jr., Orlando, FL
Leonard H. Reinke, Oshkosh, WI
Ilmar Reinvald, Tacoma, WA
John Rex, Carpinteria, CA
M. Garland Reynolds Jr., Gainesville, GA
David A. Rhodes, Memphis, TN
James W. Rhodes, New York, NY
Kenneth Ricci, New York, NY
Paul J. Ricciuti, Youngstown, OH
David E. Rice, San Diego, CA
Richard L. Rice, Raleigh, NC
James W. Rich, Tulsa, OK
Lisle F. Richards, San Jose, CA
Heidi A. Richardson, Sausalito, CA
Walter J. Richardson, Newport Beach, CA

Charles H. Richter Jr., Baltimore, MD
David R. Richter, Corpus Christi, TX
Hans Riecke, Haiku, HI
James V. Righter, Boston, MA
Jorge Rigau, Rio Piedras, Puerto Rico
Jefferson B. Riley, Centerbrook, CT
Ronnette Riley, New York, NY
David N. Rinehart, La Jolla, CA
David Rinehart, Los Angeles, CA
M. Jack Rinehart Jr., Charlottesville, VA
Mark W. Rios, Los Angeles, CA
Darrel D. Rippeteau, Delray Beach, FL
Dahlen K. Ritchey, Bradfordwoods, PA
P. Richard Rittelmann, Butler, PA
James W. Ritter, Alexandria, VA
Richard E. Ritz, Portland, OR
I. L. Roark, Lawrence, KS
Jack Robbins, Berkeley, CA
Darryl Roberson, San Francisco, CA
Jaquelin T. Robertson, New York, NY
C. David Robinson, San Francisco, CA
Harry G. Robinson III, Washington, DC
J. W. Robinson, Atlanta, GA
Kevin Roche, Hamden, CT
Garth Rockcastle, Minneapolis, MN
George T. Rockrise, Glen Ellen, CA
Burton L. Rockwell, San Francisco, CA
Kenneth A. Rodrigues, San Jose, CA
Carl D. Roehling, Detroit, MI
Chester E. Roemer, St. Louis, MO
Ralph J. Roesling II, San Diego, CA
R. G. Roessner, Austin, TX
Archibald C. Rogers, Baltimore, MD
James G. Rogers III, New York, NY
John B. Rogers, Denver, CO
John D. Rogers, Asheville, NC
Craig W. Roland, Santa Rosa, CA
B. F. Romanowitz, Lexington, KY
James G. Rome, Corpus Christi, TX
Benjamin T. Rook, Charlotte, NC
Robert W. Root, Denver, CO
Richard M. Rosan, Washington, DC
William A. Rose Jr., White Plains, NY
Alan Rosen, Palm Desert, CA
Alan R. Rosen, Lake Forest, IL
Manuel M. Rosen, La Jolla, CA
Arthur Rosenblatt, New York, NY
Norman Rosenfeld, New York, NY
Edgar B. Ross, Tiburon, CA
James S. Rossant, New York, NY
Louis A. Rossetti, Birmingham, MI
Bill Rostenberg, San Francisco, CA
Harold Roth, New Haven, CT
Richard Roth Jr., Freeport,
Edward N. Rothe, Edison, NJ
Martha L. Rothman, Boston, MA
Richard Rothman, Rising Fawn, GA
Bernard B. Rothschild, Atlanta, GA

Fellows of The American Institute of Architects (Con't)

Bernard Rothzeid, New York, NY
Maurice Rotival, Paris, France
Michael Rotondi, Los Angeles, CA
Lauren L. Rottet, Los Angeles, CA
Judith L. Rowe, Oakland, CA
Ralph T. Rowland, Cheshire, CT
Albert W. Rubeling Jr., Towson, MD
John Ruble, Santa Monica, CA
J. Ronald Rucker, Tyler, TX
J. W. Rudd, Knoxville, TN
Gordon E. Ruehl, Spokane, WA
Evett J. Ruffcorn, Seattle, WA
John A. Ruffo, San Francisco, CA
Herman O. Ruhnau, Riverside, CA
Peter L. Rumpel, Saint Augustine, FL
William W. Rupe, St. Louis, MO
T. T. Russell, Miami, FL
Walter A. Rutes, Scottsdale, AZ
H. Mark Ruth, Agana, Guam
Harry R. Rutledge, York, PA
Roger N. Ryan, N. Canton, OH
James E. Rydeen, Rio Verde, AZ
Donald P. Ryder, New Rochelle, NY

S

Werner Sabo, Chicago, IL
Harold G. Sadler, San Diego, CA
Moshe Safdie, Somerville, MA
Carol S. Sakata, Honolulu, HI
Raj Saksena, Bristol, RI
F. Cuthbert Salmon, Stillwater, OK
Nathaniel W. Sample, Madison, WI
Peter Samton, New York, NY
Danny Samuels, Houston, TX
Thomas Samuels, Chicago, IL
Gil A. Sanchez, Santa Cruz, CA
James J. Sanders, Seattle, WA
Linda Sanders, Walnut, CA
Donald Sandy Jr., San Francisco, CA
Adele N. Santos, San Francisco, CA
Carlos R. Sanz, Santurce, Puerto Rico
Charles M. Sappenfield, Sanibel, FL
Angel C. Saqui, Coral Gables, FL
Victor Saroki, Birmingham, MI
Louis Sauer, Pittsburgh, PA
Louis R. Saur, Clayton, MO
Robert W. Sawyer, Wilmington, NC
Peter M. Saylor, Philadelphia, PA
Sam Scaccia, Chicago, IL
Joseph J. Scalabrin, Columbus, OH
Mario L. Schack, Baltimore, MD
K. M. Schaefer, Kirkwood, MO
Robert J. Schaefer, Wichita, KS
Walter Schamu, Baltimore, MD
David Scheatzle, Tempe, AZ
James A. Scheeler, Reston, VA

Jeffrey Allen Scherer, Minneapolis, MN
G. G. Schierle, Los Angeles, CA
Arthur A. Schiller, Manhasset, NY
Don P. Schlegel, Albuquerque, NM
Frank Schlesinger, Washington, DC
Jon R. Schleuning, Portland, OR
John I. Schlossman, Hubbard Woods, IL
Roger Schluntz, Albuquerque, NM
Mildred F. Schmertz, New York, NY
Fred C. Schmidt, Oklahoma City, OK
Wayne S. Schmidt, Indianapolis, IN
R. Christian Schmitt, Charleston, SC
Herbert W. Schneider, Scottsdale, AZ
Walter Scholer Jr., Fort Myers, FL
John P. Schooley, Columbus, OH
Barnett P. Schorr, Seattle, WA
Charles F. Schrader, San Rafael, CA
Douglas F. Schroeder, Chicago, IL
Kenneth A. Schroeder, Chicago, IL
John H. Schruben, North Bethesda, MD
George A. D. Schuett, Glendale, WI
Kenneth Schwartz, Charlottesville, VI
Kenneth E. Schwartz, San Luis Obispo, CA
Robert Schwartz, Washington, DC
Alan Schwartzman, Paris, France
Charles E. Schwing, Baton Rouge, LA
Alan D. Sclater, Seattle, WA
David M. Scott, Pullman, WA
William W. Scott, Taylors Falls, MN
Der Scutt, New York, NY
Jim W. Sealy, Dallas, TX
Linda Searl, Chicago, IL
Thomas J. Sedgewick, Clio, MI
Paul Segal, New York, NY
Lawrence P. Segrue, Visalia, CA
E. J. Seibert, Boca Grande, FL
Alexander Seidel, Belvedere, CA
Larry D. Self, St. Louis, MO
Theodore Seligson, Kansas City, MO
Bruce M. Sellery, Marina Del Rey, CA
Dale E. Selzer, Dallas, TX
John C. Senhauser, Cincinnati, OH
Ronald S. Senseman, Silver Spring, MD
Jerome M. Seracuse, Colorado Springs, CO
Diane Serber, Old Chatham, NY
Phillip K. Settecase, Salem, OR
Betty Lee Seydler-Hepworth, Franklin, MI
Richard S. Sharpe, Norwich, CT
John A. Sharratt, Boston, MA
James L. Shay, San Rafael, CA
Leo G. Shea, Leland, MI
John P. Sheehy, Mill Valley, CA
George C. Sheldon, Portland, OR
W. Overton Shelmire, Dallas, TX
Carol Shen, Berkeley, CA
John V. Sheoris, Grosse Pointe, MI
Herschel E. Shepard, Atlantic Beach, FL

Fellows of The American Institute of Architects (Con't)

Hugh Shepley, Manchester, MA
Patricia C. Sherman, Concord, NH
Takashi Shida, Santa Monica, CA
Roger D. Shiels, Portland, OR
Edward H. Shirley, Atlanta, GA
Philip A. Shive, Charlotte, NC
William C. Shopsin, New York City, NY
Evan H. Shu, Melrose, MA
George Whiteside Shupee, Arlington, TX
Jack T. Sidener, Shatin, New Territories, PRC
Paul G. Sieben, Toledo, OH
Lloyd H. Siegel, Washington, DC
Robert H. Siegel, New York, NY
Charles M. Sieger, Miami, FL
Henry N. Silvestri, Corona Del Mar, CA
Brad Simmons, St. Louis, MO
Cathy J. Simon, San Francisco, CA
Mark Simon, Centerbrook, CT
Lawrence L. Simons, Santa Rosa, CA
Donal R. Simpson, Dallas, TX
Robert T. Simpson Jr., Berkeley, CA
Scott Simpson, Cambridge, MA
Howard F. Sims, Detroit, MI
Jerome J. Sincoff, St. Louis, MO
Donald I. Singer, Fort Lauderdale, FL
E. Crichton Singleton, Kansas City, MO
Charles S. Sink, Denver, CO
Lorri D. Sipes, Ann Arbor, MI
William H. Sippel Jr., Allison Park, PA
Michael M. Sizemore, Atlanta, GA
Ronald L. Skaggs, Dallas, TX
Norma M. Sklarek, Pacific Palisades, CA
Gary Skog, Southfield, MI
Murray A. Slama, Walnut Creek, CA
Clifton M. Smart Jr., Fayetteville, AR
Saul C. Smiley, Minnetonka, MN
Adrian D. Smith, Chicago, IL
Arthur Smith, Southfield, MI
Bill D. Smith, Dallas, TX
Bruce H. Smith, Pontiac, MI
Christopher J. Smith, Honolulu, HI
Cole Smith, Dallas, TX
Colin L. M. Smith, Cambridge, MA
Darrell L. Smith, Eugene, OR
Edward Smith, Salt Lake City, UT
Fleming W. Smith Jr., Nashville, TN
Frank Folsom Smith, Sarasota, FL
Hamilton P. Smith, Garden City, NY
Harwood K. Smith, Dallas, TX
Ivan H. Smith, Jacksonville, FL
John R. Smith, Ketchum, ID
Joseph N. Smith III, Atlanta, GA
Kenneth Smith, Jacksonville, FL
Macon S. Smith, Raleigh, NC
Stephen B. Smith, Salt Lake City, UT
T. Clayton Smith, Baton Rouge, LA
Tyler Smith, Hartford, CT

Whitney R. Smith, Sonoma, CA
David I. Smotrich, New York, NY
Neil H. Smull, Boise, ID
Richard Snibbe, New York, NY
Sheila Snider, Indianapolis, IN
Julie V. Snow, Minneapolis, MN
Walter H. Sobel, Chicago, IL
Daniel Solomon, San Francisco, CA
Richard J. Solomon, Chicago, IL
Stuart B. Solomon, Watertown, MA
James Hamilton Somes Jr., Portsmouth, NH
Hak Son, Santa Monica, CA
John R. Sorrenti, Mineola, NY
Charles B. Soule, Montgomery Village, MD
Michael Southworth, Berkeley, CA
Edward A. Sovik, Northfield, MN
George S. Sowden, Fort Worth, TX
Marvin Sparn, Boulder, CO
Laurinda H. Spear, Miami, FL
Lawrence W. Speck, Austin, TX
Michael H. Spector, New Hyde Park, NY
John H. Spencer, Hampton, VA
Tomas H. Spiers Jr., Camp Hill, PA
Pat Y. Spillman, Dallas, TX
Robert A. Spillman, Bethlehem, PA
Donald E. Sporleder, South Bend, IN
Joseph G. Sprague, Dallas, TX
Kent Spreckelmeyer, Lawrence, KS
Paul D. Spreiregen, Washington, DC
Bernard P. Spring, Brookline, MA
Everett G. Spurling Jr., Bethesda, MD
Dennis W. Stacy, Dallas, TX
Alfred M. Staehli, Portland, OR
Richard P. Stahl, Springfield, MO
Raymond F. Stainback Jr., Atlanta, GA
Duffy B. Stanley, El Paso, TX
William J. Stanley, III, Atlanta, GA
Jane M. Stansfeld, Austin, TX
Michael J. Stanton, San Francisco, CA
Earl M. Starnes, Cedar Key, FL
Frank A. Stasiowski, Newton, MA
Donald J. Stastny, Portland, OR
Russell L. Stecker, Montpelier, VT
Mark W. Steele, La Jolla, CA
John E. Stefany, Tampa, FL
Peter Steffian, Boston, MA
Charles W. Steger Jr., Blacksburg, VA
Douglas Steidl, Akron, OH
Carl Stein, New York, NY
Goodwin B. Steinberg, San Jose, CA
Robert T. Steinberg, San Jose, CA
Ralph Steinglass, New York, NY
Henry Steinhardt, Mercer Island, WA
Douglas E. Steinman Jr., Beaumont, TX
James A. Stenhouse, Charlotte, NC
Donald J. Stephens, Berlin, NY
Michael J. Stepner, San Diego, CA

Fellows of The American Institute of Architects (Con't)

Robert A. M. Stern, New York, NY
William F. Stern, Houston, TX
Preston Stevens Jr., Atlanta, GA
James M. Stevenson, Highland Park, IL
W. Cecil Steward, Lincoln, NE
R. K. Stewart, San Francisco, CA
William W. Stewart, Clayton, MO
Sherwood Stockwell, Wolcott, CO
Claude Stoller, Berkeley, CA
Neal P. Stowe Salt Lake City, UT
H. T. Stowell, Western Springs, IL
Neil E. Strack, Champaign, IL
Ronald A. Straka, Denver, CO
Michael J. Stransky, Salt Lake City, UT
Frank Straub, Troy, MI
Carl A. Strauss, Cincinnati, OH
John R. Street Jr., Marietta, GA
Arthur V. Strock, Santa Ana, CA
Hugh Asher Stubbins Jr., Cambridge, MA
Sidney W. Stubbs Jr., Mount Pleasant, SC
Donald L. Stull, Boston, MA
Robert S. Sturgis, Weston, MA
Erik Sueberkrop, San Francisco, CA
Marvin D. Suer, Willow Grove, PA
John W. Sugden, Park City, UT
Douglas R. Suisman, Santa Monica, CA
Edward Sullam, Honolulu, HI
John P. Sullivan, Valhalla, NY
Patrick M. Sullivan, Claremont, CA
Gene R. Summers, Cloverdale, CA
Alan R. Sumner, Saint Louis, MO
Richard P. Sundberg, Seattle, WA
Donald R. Sunshine, Blacksburg, VA
Eugene L. Surber, Atlanta, GA
Charles R. Sutton, Honolulu, HI
Sharon E. Sutton, Seattle, WA
George Suyama, Seattle, WA
Vernon D. Swaback, Scottsdale, AZ
Eugene C. Swager, Peoria, IL
Robert M. Swatt, San Francisco, CA
Earl Swensson, Nashville, TN
Richard Swett, Copenhagen, Denmark
H. H. Swinburne, Philadelphia, PA
John M. Syvertsen, Chicago, IL

T

William B. Tabler, New York, NY
Edgar Tafel, Venice, FL
Marvin Taff, Beverly Hills, CA
Edward K. Takahashi, Santa Monica, CA
Ray Takata, Sacramento, CA
Francis T. Taliaferro, Santa Monica, CA
R. H. Tan, Spokane, WA
Ted Tokio Tanaka, Marina Del Rey, CA
Virginia W. Tanzmann, Pasadena, CA
Charles R. Tapley, Houston, TX

A. Anthony Tappe, Boston, MA
John Tarantino, New York City, NY
H. Harold Tarleton, Greenville, SC
D. Coder Taylor, Glenview, IL
Marilyn J. Taylor, New York, NY
Richard L. Taylor Jr., Atlanta, GA
Walter Q. Taylor, Jacksonville, FL
Thomas H. Teasdale, Kirkwood, MO
Clinton C. Ternstrom, Los Angeles, CA
Roland Terry, Mt. Vernon, WA
Robert L. Tessier, Yarmouth Port, MA
B. C. Tharp, Montgomery, TX
Dorwin A. J. Thomas, Boston, MA
James B. Thomas, Houston, TX
James L. Thomas, Spartanburg, SC
Joseph F. Thomas, Pasadena, CA
Benjamin Thompson, Cambridge, MA
David C. Thompson, San Diego, CA
Milo H. Thompson, Minneapolis, MN
Robert L. Thompson, Portland, OR
Warren D. Thompson, Fresno, CA
Charles B. Thomsen, Houston, TX
Duane Thorbeck, Minneapolis, MN
Karl Thorne, Gainesville, FL
Oswald H. Thorson, Marco, FL
John P. Tice Jr., Pensacola, FL
Stanley Tigerman, Chicago, IL
Patrick Tillett, Portland, OR
James H. Timberlake, Philadelphia, PA
Robert H. Timme, Los Angeles, CA
Leslie D. Tincknell, Saginaw, MI
James D. Tittle, Abilene, TX
Philip E. Tobey, Reston, VA
Calvin J. Tobin, Highland Park, IL
Logic Tobola II, El Campo, TX
Anderson Todd, Houston, TX
David F. M. Todd, New York, NY
Thomas A. Todd, Jamestown, RI
John Tomassi, Chicago, IL
James E. Tomblinson, Flint, MI
Frank Tomsick, San Francisco, CA
John Francis Torti, Silver Spring, MD
Mark Joseph Tortorich, Martinez, CA
Coulson Tough, The Woodlands, TX
Dennis T. Toyomura, Honolulu, HI
Jack Train, Chicago, IL
Karl E. Treffinger Sr., West Linn, OR
Kenneth Treister, Coconut Grove, FL
Michael Tribble, Charlotte, NC
David M. Trigiani, Jackson, MS
William H. Trogdon, Olga, WA
Leroy Troyer, Mishawaka, IN
William H. Truex Jr. , Burlington, VT
Chiu Lin Tse-Chan, San Francisco, CA
Charles N. Tseckares, Boston, MA
Edward T. M. Tsoi, Arlington, MA
Seab A. Tuck, III, Nashville, TN

Fellows of The American Institute of Architects (Con't)

Jack R. Tucker Jr., Memphis, TN
Thomas B. Tucker, San Diego, CA
Richard L. Tully, Columbus, OH
Emanuel N. Turano, Boca Raton, FL
John Gordon Turnbull, San Francisco, CA
Thomas P. Turner Jr., Charlotte, NC
Wilbur H. Tusler Jr., Kentfield, CA
Ilene R. Tyler, Ann Arbor, MI
James L. Tyler, Pacific Palisades, CA
Robert Tyler, Tarzana, CA
Anne G. Tyng, Philadelphia, PA

U

Edward K. Uhlir, Chicago, IL
Kenneth A. Underwood, Philadelphia, PA
Dean F. Unger, Sacramento, CA
Denorval Unthank Jr., Eugene, OR
Robert H. Uyeda, Los Angeles, CA

V

Joseph D. Vaccaro, Los Angeles, CA
Edward Vaivoda Jr., Portland, OR
William E. Valentine, San Francisco, CA
Joseph M. Valerio, Chicago, IL
William L. Van Alen, Wilmington, DE
Robert Van Deusen, Grand Junction, CO
Peter van Dijk, Cleveland, OH
George V. Van Fossen Schwab, Baltimore, MD
Thomas Van Housen, Minneapolis, MN
Harold F. VanDine Jr., Birmingham, MI
Johannes VanTilburg, Santa Monica, CA
Mitchell Vanbourg, Berkeley, CA
Harutun Vaporciyan, Huntington Woods, MI
Harold R. Varner, Berkley, MI
Leonard M. Veitzer, San Diego, CA
Thomas W. Ventulett, Atlanta, GA
Robert Venturi, Philadelphia, PA
Shirley J. Vernon, Philadelphia, PA
William R. Vick, Sacramento, CA
Robert L. Vickery, Charlottesville, VA
Wilmont Vickrey, Chicago, IL
Gregory D. Villanueva, Los Angeles, CA
John Vinci, Chicago, IL
Rafael Vinoly, New York, NY
Stephen Vogel, Detroit, MI
Leonard W. Volk II, Dallas, TX
A. R. Von Brock, Buchanan, VA
Robert J. Von Dohlen, W Hartford, CT
Richard L. Von Luhrte, Denver, CO
Bartholome Voorsanger, New York, NY
R. Randall Vosbeck, Vail, CO
William F. Vosbeck, Alexandria, VA
Thomas R. Vreeland, Century City, CA
R. E. Vrooman, College Station, TX

W

Hobart D. Wagener, Coronado, CA
William J. Wagner, Dallas Center, IA
John G. Waite, Albany, NY
Lawrence G. Waldron, Mercer Island, WA
Bruce M. Walker, Spokane, WA
Kenneth H. Walker, New York, NY
David A. Wallace, Philadelphia, PA
David D. Wallace, Westport, MA
Donald Q. Wallace, Lexington, KY
Les Wallach, Seattle, WA
Charles G. Walsh, Los Angeles, CA
Lloyd G. Walter Jr., Winston Salem, NC
W. G. Wandelmaier, New York, NY
Sheldon D. Wander, New York, NY
R. J. Warburton, Coral Gables, FL
G. T. Ward, Fairfax, VA
Robertson Ward Jr., Boston, MA
C. E. Ware, Rockford, IL
John Carl Warnecke, San Francisco, CA
Charles H. Warner Jr., Nyack, NY
Clyde K. Warner Jr., Louisville, KY
William D. Warner, Exeter, RI
Sharon F. Washburn, Bethesda, MD
Robert E. Washington, Richmond, VA
Barry L. Wasserman, Sacramento, CA
Joseph Wasserman, Southfield, MA
David H. Watkins, Bellaire, TX
Donald R. Watson, Trumbull, CT
Raymond L. Watson, Newport Beach, CA
William J. Watson, LaJolla, CA
John L. Webb, Ponchatoula, LA
P. R. Webber, Rutland, VT
Arthur M. Weber, Aiea, HI
Frederick S. Webster, Cazenovia, NY
C. R. Wedding, St. Petersburg, FL
Benjamin H. Weese, Chicago, IL
Cynthia Weese, Chicago, IL
Gary K. Weeter, Dallas, TX
Bryce Adair Weigand, Dallas, TX
Joe Neal Weilenman, Pago Pago, American Samoa
Nicholas H. Weingarten, Chicago, IL
Amy Weinstein, Washington, DC
Edward Weinstein, Seattle, WA
Jane Weinzapfel, Boston, MA
Gerald G. Weisbach, San Francisco, CA
Sarelle T. Weisberg, New York, NY
Steven F. Weiss, Chicago, IL
Martha L. Welborne, Los Angeles, CA
Frank D. Welch, Dallas, TX
John A. Welch, Tuskegee, AL
Louis L. Weller, Albuquerque, NM
William P. Wenzler, Milwaukee, WI
Helge Westermann, Cambridge, MA
Merle T. Westlake, Lexington, MA
Paul E. Westlake Jr., Cleveland, OH

Fellows of The American Institute of Architects (Con't)

I. Donald Weston, Brooklyn, NY
Charles H. Wheatley, Charlotte, NC
C. Herbert Wheeler, State College, PA
Daniel H. Wheeler, Chicago, IL
James H. Wheeler Jr., Abilene, TX
Kenneth D. Wheeler, Lake Forest, IL
Richard H. Wheeler, Los Angeles, CA
Murray Whisnant, Charlotte, NC
Arthur B. White, Havertown, PA
George M. White, Bethesda, MD
Janet Rothberg White, Bethesda, MD
Norval C. White, Salisbury, CT
Samuel G. White, New York, NY
Stephen Q. Whitney, Detroit, MI
Leonard S. Wicklund, Long Grove, IL
Christopher Widener, Springfield, OH
Chester A. Widom, Santa Monica, CA
William Wiese, II, Shelburne, VT
E. D. Wilcox, Tyler, TX
Jerry Cooper Wilcox, Little Rock, AR
Gordon L. Wildermuth, Greeley, PA
James E. Wiley, Dallas, TX
Charles E. Wilkerson, Richmond, VA
Joseph A. Wilkes, Annapolis, MD
Michael B. Wilkes, San Diego, CA
Barbara E. Wilks, Baltimore, MD
Paul Willen, Yorktown Heights, NY
A. Richard Williams, Saint Ignace, MI
Allison G. Williams, San Francisco, CA
Daniel E. Williams, Coconut Grove, FL
Donald L. Williams, Houston, TX
E. Stewart Williams, Palm Springs, CA
F. Carter Williams, Raleigh, NC
Frank Williams, New York, NY
George Thomas Williams, Kitty Hawk, NC
Harold L. Williams, Los Angeles, CA
Homer L. Williams, Riverside, MO
John G. Williams, Fayetteville, AR
Lorenzo D. Williams, Minneapolis, MN
Mark F. Williams, Ambler, PA
Roger B. Williams, Seattle, WA
Terrance R. Williams, Washington, DC
Tod C. Williams, New York, NY
W. Gene Williams, The Woodlands, TX
Wayne R. Williams, Harmony, CA
Beverly A. Willis, New York, NY
Michael E. Willis, San Francisco, CA
John C. Wilmot, Damascus, MD
Jeffrey Wilson, Anchorage, AK
John E. Wilson, Richmond, VA
John L. Wilson, Boston, MA
William D. Wilson, Bridgehampton, NY
Steven R. Winkel, Berkeley, CA
Jon Peter Winkelstein, San Francisco, CA
John H. Winkler, Verbank, NY
Paul D. Winslow, Phoenix, AZ
Arch R. Winter, Mobile, AL

Steven Winter, Norwalk, CT
Marjorie M. Wintermute, Lake Oswego, OR
Norman E. Wirkler, Denver, CO
Joseph J. Wisnewski, Alexandria, VA
Gayland B. Witherspoon, Pendleton, SC
Charles Witsell Jr., Little Rock, AR
Gordon G. Wittenberg, Little Rock, AR
Fritz Woehle, Birmingham, AL
Robert L. Wold, Hilton Head, SC
Harry C. Wolf, III, Malibu, CA
Martin F. Wolf, Wilmette, IL
Richard Wolf, San Mateo, CA
Gin D. Wong, Los Angeles, CA
Kellogg H. Wong, New York, NY
William Wong Jr., Taikooshing, PRC
Carolina Y. Woo, San Francisco, CA
George C. Woo, Dallas, TX
Kyu S. Woo, Cambridge, MA
H. A. Wood III, Boston, MA
John M. Woodbridge, Sonoma, CA
David Geoffrey Woodcock, College Station, TX
David Woodhouse, Chicago, IL
Robert S. Woodhurst III, Augusta, GA
Stanford Woodhurst Jr., Augusta, GA
Enrique Woodroffe, Tampa, FL
Thomas E. Woodward, Buena Vista, CO
David L. Wooley, Knoxville, TN
Evans Woollen, Indianapolis, IN
J. R. Wooten, Fort Worth, TX
John C. Worsley, Portland, OR
David H. Wright, Seattle, WA
George S. Wright, Fort Worth, TX
Henry L. Wright, Canby, OR
John L. Wright, Redmond, WA
Marcellus Wright Jr., Richmond, VA
Rodney H. Wright, Liberty, KY
Thomas W. D. Wright, Washington, DC
Cynthia Wuellner, Kansas City, MO
Scott W. Wyatt, Seattle, WA

Y

Jack R. Yardley, Dallas, TX
John L. Yaw, Aspen, CO
Zeno Lanier Yeates, Memphis, TN
Raymond W. Yeh, Honolulu, HI
Ronald W. Yeo, Corona Del Mar, CA
David N. Yerkes, Washington, DC
William R. Yost, Portland, OR
Clayton Young, Seattle, WA
Joseph L. Young, Clemson, SC
Norbert Young Jr., New York, NY
Theodore J. Young, Greenwich, CT
Linda Yowell, New York City, NY
Hachiro Yuasa, Orleans, CA
Robert J. Yudell, Santa Monica, CA

Z

James Zahn, Chicago, IL
Saul Zaik, Portland, OR
H. Alan Zeigel, Denver, CO
J. Zemanek, Houston, TX
Golden J. Zenon Jr., Omaha, NE
Robert L. Ziegelman, Birmingham, MI
Raymond Ziegler, Altadena, CA
Frank Zilm, Kansas City, MO
John J. Zils, Chicago, IL
Bernard B. Zimmerman, Los Angeles, CA
Gary V. Zimmerman, Milwaukee, WI
Thomas A. Zimmerman, Rochester, NY
Hugh M. Zimmers, Philadelphia, PA

Peter Jay Zweig, Houston, TX

Source: The American Institute of Architects

Did you know...

The States with the least AIA Fellows:

West Virginia - 1
Wyoming - 1
North Dakota - 1
Maine - 1
Delaware - 2
Montana - 3
Arkansas - 4
Nevada - 4
Idaho - 5
New Hampshire - 5
Rhode Island - 5
Vermont - 7

Fellows of the American Institute of Certified Planners

Election as a Fellow in the American Institute of Certified Planners (AICP) is one of the highest honors that the AICP can bestow upon a member. Fellowship is granted to planners who have been a member of AICP and have achieved excellence in professional practice, teaching and mentoring, research, public/community service and leadership.

David J. Allor
John E. Anderson
Richard T. Anderson
Uri P. Avin
Edmund Bacon
Robert S. Baldwin
Carol D. Barrett
Ernest R. Bartley
Peter Batchelor
Robert W. Becker
James R. Bell
Teree L. Bergman
Paul A. Bergmann
Richard C. Bernhardt
Dale F. Bertsch
Dave E. Bess
Eugenie Ladner Birch
Alan Black
Lachlan F. Blair
William W. Bowdy
Melville C. Branch
Jane S. Brooks
Nancy Benziger Brown
Martin Bruno
Raymond Burby
Bob Burke
Paulette Carolin
Sam Casella
Anthony James Catanese
Robert A. Catlin
F. Stuart Chapin
Jay Chatterjee
Hyung C. Chung
Philip Hart Clark
Arnold Cogan
Fred Collignon

Connie B. Cooper
Bob Cornish
Linda R. Cox
Paul C. Crawford
Betty Croly
Samuel J. Cullers
Patrick J. Cusick, Jr.
Linda Lund Davis
Lillian Frost Dean
F. John Devaney
James B. Duncan
V. Gail Easley
Leon S. Eplan
Ernest Erber
Craig Farmer
Hermann Haviland Field
Frank Fish
Laurence Conway Gerckens
David R. Godschalk
Carl Goldschmidt
Dennis Andrew Gordon
Sigurd Grava
Clifford W. Graves
Sherman Griselle
Albert Guttenburg
Dianne Guzman
Besim S. Hakim
Irving Hand
Angela N. Harper
Britton Harris
William M. Harris, Sr.
Michael S. Harrison
Roger K. Hedrick
Mary Lou Henry
Vernon G. Henry
Albert Herson

Fellows of the American Institute of Certified Planners (Con't)

Jesus H. Hinojosa
Mark L. Hinshaw
John E. Hirten
Allan A. Hodges
Stanley R. Hoffman
Deborah A. Howe
Robert P. Huefner
Robert Hunter
Fred Hurand
Morris. E. Johnson
Robert J. Juster
Vivian Kahn
Edward Kaiser
Jerome L. Kauffman
Barbara Kautz
Lloyd Keefe
John Keller
Eric Damian Kelly
Kenneth M. Kreutziger
Bruce M. Kriviskey
Donald A. Krueckeberg
Glenn Kumekawa
Bruce Laing
Floyd Lapp
Glen S. LeRoy
Richard R. Lillie
Barbara Lukermann
Marjorie Macris
Riad G. Mahayni
Lawrence Mann
George T. Marcou
Richard May, Jr.
Bruce W. McClendon
Alan McClennen, Jr.
Ron McConnell
Mike McCormick
Margarita P. McCoy
Stuart Meck
Joy Mee
Dwight Merriman
John Merrill
Darrell C. Meyer
Martin Meyerson

J. Laurence Mintier
Vijay Mital
Terry Moore
Harvey Moskowitz
Louis Bert Muhly
John R. Mullin
Arthur C. Nelson
Thomas P. Niederkorn
Perry Norton
Ki Suh Park
Robert J. Paternoster
Phillip D. Peters
Robert J. Piper
David J. Portman
Roy Wilson Potter
Steven A. Preston
David L. Pugh
Mary Joan Pugh
Ray Quay
George Raymond
Robert E. Reiman
Thomas H. Roberts
Sergio Rodriguez
Wolfgang G. Roeseler
Joseph Lee Rodgers
Janet M. Ruggiero
Peter D. Salins
Paul H. Sedway
Sumner Sharpe
Ronald N. Short
Marshall D. Slagle
Herbert H. Smith
Frank So
Lester Solin
Jeff Soule
James A. Spencer
Donald J. Stastny
Stuart W. Stein
Michael J. Stepner
Susan Stoddard
Israel Stollman
Robert L. Sturdivant
Kenneth E. Sulzer

Fellows of the American Institute of Certified Planners (Con't)

Robert B. Teska
Carol J. Thomas
Sidney F. Thomas Jr.
Michael P.C. Tillett
Anthony R. Tomazinis
Kenneth C. Topping
Nohad A. Toulan
Frank F. Turner
Stuart Turner
Richard E. Tustian
Francis Violich
Alan M. Voorhees
Fritz Wagner
Robert Wagoner
Larry W. Watts

Robert Wegner Sr.
Frank B. Wein
Louis B. Wetmore
Sara Jane White
Ronald A. Williamson
J.D. Wingfield
Arch R. Winter
Joel C. Wooldridge
Mark A. Wyckoff
Bruce T. Yoder
Paul Zucker

Source: American Institute of Certified Planners

Did you know...

Julia Morgan (1872-1957) was the only woman to graduate from the University of California-Berkeley College of Engineering in 1894, and the first woman to pass the entrance examination at the Ecole des Beaux-Arts in Paris.

Fellows of the American Society of Interior Designers

The American Society of Interior Designers (ASID) grants fellowship to those members who have made notable and substantial contributions to the profession and society. The following individuals are current, active fellows of the ASID.

Stanley Abercrombie
Dan Acito
Stephen W. Ackerman
Gail Adams
Joy E. Adcock
Michael Alin*
Estelle Alpert
Jerry R. Alsobrook
William F. Andrews
Ellen Angell
Robert H. Angle*
Robert A. Arehart
Warren G. Arnett
Anita Baltimore
David Barrett
Nancy Hoff Barsotti
Jeannine Bazer-Schwartz
Tamara A. Bazzle
Roy F. Beal
Marjorie A. Bedell
Frank Lee Berry
Hal F.B. Birchfield
Adriana Bitter
Edwin Bitter*
Joan Blutter
Daisy Houston Bond*
Penny Bonda
Joseph Daniel Bouligny
William D. Bowden
Blair S. Bowen
Susan Bradford
Bruce J. Brigham
C. Dudley Brown
Everett Brown
R. Michael Brown
Walton E. Brown*
Mary A. Bryan

Eleanor Brydone
Joyce A. Burke-Jones
David M. Butler
Rosalyn Cama
Orville V. Carr
Elizabeth M. Castleman
Juliana M. Catlin
Carl E. Clark
Brian Clay Collins
John P. Conron
Loverne C. Cordes
Herbert Cordier
Jini Costello
Virginia W. Courtenay
P.A. Dale
Hortense Davis
Robert John Dean
Ken Deck
Hon C. Doxiadis*
Dede Draper
Hilda M. East
H. Gerard Ebert
Barbara Ebstein
Garrett Eckbo*
Arlis Ede
Martin Elinoff
John Elmo
Joel M. Ergas
Sammye J. Erickson
Adele Faulkner
Jon J. Fields
Lyn Fontenot
John G. Ford
Deborah Lloyd Forrest
Dorothy L. Fowles
Thomas Frank
Charles D. Gandy

Fellows of the American Society of Interior Designers (Con't)

Marion Gardiner
Francis J. Geck*
Alexander Girard*
Judy Girod
Milton Glaser
Diane Gote
Thomas C. Grabowski
Theodora Kim Graham
Stephen Greenberger
Jody Greenwald
Roberta S. Griffin
Olga Gueft*
Rita C. Guest
David W. Hall
Lawrence Halprin*
James M. Halverson
William D. Hamilton*
A. Niolon Hampton
Patricia Harvey
Dennis Haworth
Dorothy G. Helmer
Albert E. Herbert
Fred B. Hershey
Joseph P. Horan
Elizabeth B. Howard
Nina Hughes
Dorian Hunter
H. Cliff Ivester
Barbara L. Jacobs
Sarah B. Jenkins
Charlotte Jensen
Connie Johannes
Wallace R. Jonason
Richard W. Jones
Henry Jordan
Henri V. Jova
Franklin S. Judson*
Janet E. Kane
Mary V. Knackstedt
Binnie Kramer
Gayle Kreutzfeld
Karlyn Kuper
Anita M. Laird*

Hugh L. Latta
Drue Lawlor
Dennis W. Leczinski
Nila Leiserowitz
Robert S. Lindenthal
Boyd L. Loendorf
Michael Love
Joseph LoVecchio*
Odette Lueck
Ruth K. Lynford
William M. Manly
Helen Masoner
Terri Maurer
Sandra McGowen
James E. McIntosh
James Mezrano
John Richard Miller
Thomas H. Miller
Susan I. Mole
Kathy Ford Montgomery
Mark Nelson
Roi C. Nevaril
Linda Newton
W. E. Noffke
Barbara Nugent
Douglas Parker*
Suzanne Patterson
Lawrence Peabody
Edward J. Perrault
BJ Peterson
H. Albert Phibbs
Dianne H. Pilgrim*
Norman Polsky*
Betty J. Purvis
Catharine G. Rawson
William Dunn Ray
Martha Garriott Rayle
John Robinson
Pedro Rodriguez
Agnes H. Rogers
Wayne Ruga*
Jack G. Ruthazer
Chester F. Sagenkahn

Fellows of the American Society of Interior Designers (Con't)

Barbara A. Sauerbrey
Hollie Schick
Janet S. Schirn
Barbara Schlattman
E. Williard Schurz
Irving D. Schwartz
Otho S. Shaw
Alan Siegel*
James L. Simpson
Theodore A. Simpson
Edna A. Smith
Fran Kellog Smith
James Merrick Smith
Linda Elliot Smith
Sandra H. Sober
Jerrold Sonet*
Michael Sorrentino*
Beulah G. Spiers
Paul D. Spreiregen*
Edward H. Springs
Rita St.Clair
Russell M. Stanley
Ed Starr
Karl L. Steinhauser

Deborah Steinmetz
C. Eugene Stephenson
Blanche F. Strater
Ann Sullivan
Caroline Torley
Doris Nash Upshur
Bernard Vinick
G.F. Weber
Maurice Weir
Vicki Wenger
Gary E. Wheeler
Miriam Whelan
Michael Wiener
William L. Wilkoff
Frances E. Wilson
Gail Casey Winkler
Michael Wirtz
John B. Wisner
D. C. Witte
Edmund D. Wood
Julie M. Wyatt

* Honorary Fellow

Source: American Society of Interior Designers

In the consumer society, beauty can also be a smokescreen – a tool for distracting our attention from the bad and the false.

Bruce Mau

Fellows of the American Society of Landscape Architects

Fellows of the American Society of Landscape Architects (ASLA) are land-scape architects of at least ten years standing as Full Members of the ASLA, elected to Fellowship in honor of their outstanding contributions to the profession. Categories of election are: works of landscape architecture, administrative work, knowledge, and service to the profession. There have been a total of 754 Fellows elected since 1899. The list below indicates current, active Fellows of the ASLA.

Howard G. Abel

Wm. Dwayne Adams Jr.

Marvin I. Adleman

Russell A. Adsit

John F. Ahern

J. Robert Anderson

Domenico Annese

Ellis L. Antuñez

David E. Arbegast

David S. Armbruster

Henry F. Arnold

Sadik C. Artunc

Roy O. Ashley

D. Lyle Aten

Donald B. Austin

Kenneth J. Backman

Ted Baker

William H. Baker

Harry J. Baldwin

Edward B. Ballard

Thomas Balsley

Alton A. Barnes Jr.

Milton Baron

Cheryl Barton

James H. Bassett

Kenneth E. Bassett

Anthony M. Bauer

Clarence W. Baughman

Howard R. Baumgarten

Eldon W. Beck

Yoshiro Befu

Arthur G. Beggs

William A. Behnke

James R. Bell

Richard C. Bell

Vincent Bellafiore

Armand Benedek

Claire R. Bennett

Shary Page Berg

Charles A. Birnbaum

Calvin T. Bishop

David H. Blau

Kerry Blind

Lloyd M. Bond

Norman K. Booth

W. Frank Brandt

Michael Wayne Breedlove

Theodore W. Brickman Jr.

Samuel W. Bridgers

Donald Carl Brinkerhoff

Mark K. Brinkley

Robert F. Bristol

Judy Byrd Brittenum

Joseph E. Brown

Jeffrey L. Bruce

Jackie Karl Bubenik

Alexander Budrevics

Robert S. Budz

Dennis R. Buettner

Wayne L. Buggenhagen

Frank Burggraf Jr.

Arthur E. Bye Jr.

Willard C. Byrd

Raymond F. Cain

Robert A. Callans

William B. Callaway

Fellows of the American Society of Landscape Architects (Con't)

Craig S. Campbell
Paschall Campbell
Dean Cardasis
Robert R. Cardoza
Charles Cares
Bryan D. Carlson
Dennis B. Carmichael
Derr A. Carpenter
Jot D. Carpenter
David B. Carruth
Donald R. Carter
Eugene H. Carter
Anthony B. Casendino
Carlos J. Cashio
James E. Christman
Ann Christoph
Alan B. Clarke
Lewis J. Clarke
Roger D. Clemence
Franklin C. Clements
Jon Charles Coe
Beatriz de Winthuysen Coffin
Laurence E. Coffin Jr.
John F. Collins
Dennis C. Colliton
Richard Conant
George Glenn Cook
Fred J. Correale
Kenneth R. Coulter
Van L. Cox
H. Kenneth Crasco
George E. Creed
Samuel G. Crozier
Joseph H. Crystal
George W. Curry
Jack Curtis
John E. Cutler
Jack R. Daft
Peter Dangermond Jr.
Edward L. Daugherty
Stuart O. Dawson
Dennis J. Day
Francis H. Dean

Neil J. Dean
Roy H. DeBoer
Richard K. Dee
Robert B. Deering
Bruce Dees
C. Christopher Degenhardt
Roger DeWeese
P. Woodward Dike
F. Christopher Dimond
Nicholas T. Dines
Carlton T. Dodge
Dan W. Donelin
Thomas R. Dunbar
Robert W. Dyas
Robert P. Ealy
Garrett Eckbo
Allen R. Edmonson
Jon Stidger Emerson
Katherine G. Emery
Donald H. Ensign
Steve Estrada
Morgan Evans
L. Susan Everett
Julius Gy. Fabos
Barbara Faga
Oliver M. Fanning
Damon Farber
David Fasser
Rudy J. Favretti
Barbara V. Fealy
Bruce K. Ferguson
Donald L. Ferlow
John J. Fernholz
Ian J.W. Firth
Phillip E. Flores
William L. Flournoy Jr.
Everett L. Fly
George E. Fogg
Donald Mark Fox
Kathleen M. Fox
Mark Francis
Carol L. Franklin
Daniel B. Franklin

Fellows of the American Society of Landscape Architects (Con't)

Robert L. Frazer
Jere S. French
John W. Frey
M. Paul Friedberg
John F. Furlong
Emily J. Gabel-Luddy
Paul Gardescu
Harry L. Garnham
Benjamin W. Gary Jr.
George G. Gentile
Richard George Gibbons
James E. Glavin
D. Newton Glick
Donald H. Godi
James B. Godwin
Robert E. Goetz
Susan M. Goltsman
Robert Wilson Good
Philip H. Graham Jr.
Leonard Grassli
Bradford M. Greene
Isabelle Clara Greene
E. Robert Gregan
John N. Grissim
Clare A. Gunn
Anthony M. Guzzardo
Richard Haag
Frederick Edward Halback
Lawrence Halprin
Calvin S. Hamilton
Asa Hanamoto
Byron R. Hanke
Becca Hanson
Richard E. Hanson
Nancy M. Hardesty
George Hargreaves
Terence G. Harkness
Charles W. Harris
Robert R. Harvey
Susan M. Hatchell
Richard G. Hautau
William H. Havens
Richard S. Hawks

Robert Graham Heilig
Kenneth I. Helphand
Edith H. Henderson
Glenn O. Hendrix
Gary R. Hilderbrand
Donald F. Hilderbrandt
Arthur W. Hills
Allen W. Hixon Jr.
Leonard J. Hopper
Mark Elison Hoversten
Perry Howard
Donovan E. Hower
Joseph Hudak
Sam L. Huddleston
Mark B. Hunner
Lester Hikoji Inouye
Alice R. Ireys
Wayne D. Iverson
Ronald M. Izumita
H. Rowland Jackson
Bernard Jacobs
Peter D. A. Jacobs
Susan L.B. Jacobson
Dale G.M. Jaeger
Frederick D. Jarvis
Leerie T. Jenkins Jr.
Linda Lee Jewell
Carl D. Johnson
Carol R. Johnson
Dean A. Johnson
Mark W. Johnson
William J. Johnson
Grant R. Jones
Ilze Jones
Robert Trent Jones
Warren D. Jones
Dirk Jongejan
Gary E. Karner
Joseph P. Karr
Jean Stephans Kavanagh
Frank H. Kawasaki
James E. Keeter
Walter H. Kehm

Fellows of the American Society of Landscape Architects (Con't)

J. Timothy Keller

Leslie A. Kerr

Gary B. Kesler

Masao Kinoshita

Charles L. Knight

Harold Kobayashi

Ken R. Krabbenhoft

Brian S. Kubota

William B. Kuhl

Bruce G. Kulik

Ray O. Kusche

Joseph J. Lalli

Joe W. Langran

Lucille Chenery Lanier

Mary Ann Lasch

Warren E. Lauesen

Michael M. Laurie

Dennis L. Law

Richard K. Law

Jack E. Leaman

Donald F. Lederer

Donald W. Leslie

Aaron Levine

Philip H. Lewis Jr.

J. Roland Lieber

Mark S. Lindhult

Karl Linn

J. Mack Little

Susan P. Little

R. Burton Litton Jr.

Thomas A. Lockett

Nimrod W. E. Long III

David O. Lose

Eldridge Lovelace

Paul C. K. Lu

J. Douglas Macy

Michael H. Malyn

Cameron R. J. Man

Lane L. Marshall

Richard K. Marshall

Edward C. Martin Jr.

Roger B. Martin

Steve Martino

Robert E. Marvin

Robert M. Mattson

Lewis T. May

Richard E. Mayer

Carol Mayer-Reed

Earl Byron McCulley

Vincent C. McDermott

Roger B. McErlane

Ian McHarg

Kathryn E. McKnight-Thalden

David A. McNeal

Gary W. Meisner

Robert Melnick

Dee S. Merriam

Vincent N. Merrill

Stuart M. Mertz

Richard J. Meyers

Luciano Miceli

E. Lynn Miller

Patrick A. Miller

Ann Milovsoroff

Debra L. Mitchell

Michael T. Miyabara

Lawrence R. Moline

Donald J. Molnar

Lynn A. Moore

Patrick C. Moore

Richard A. Moore

Paul F. Morris

Darrel G. Morrison

Mark K. Morrison

Baker H. Morrow

Robert H. Mortensen

Robert K. Murase

Thomas A. Musiak

Kenneth S. Nakaba

Kenichi Nakano

Joan I. Nassauer

Darwina L. Neal

John A. Nelson

William R. Nelson Jr.

Joseph N. Nevius

Thomas J. Nieman

Fellows of the American Society of Landscape Architects (Con't)

Satoru Nishita

Robert L. O'Boyle

Patricia M. O'Donnell

William A. O'Leary

Cornelia A. Oberlander

Warren J. Oblinger

Neil Odenwald

Wolfgang W. Oehme

Laurie D. Olin

Peter J. Olin

Edward J. Olinger

Don H. Olson

Brian Orland

Theodore Osmundson

Dennis Y. Otsuji

J. Steve Ownby

Michael Painter

Meade Palmer

Thomas P. Papandrew

Cary M. Parker

John G. Parsons

Tito Patri

Gerald D. Patten

Courtland P. Paul

Merlyn J. Paulson

Robert Perron

Robert C. Perry Jr.

Owen H. Peters

Karen A. Phillips

Robert W. Pierson

J. Edward Pinckney

Marjorie E. Pitz

Kenneth J. Polakowski

Peter M. Pollack

Harry W. Porter

Joe A. Porter

Neil H. Porterfield

Marion Pressley

William Pressley

Rae L. Price

Paul N. Procopio

Edward L. Pryce

Helen M. Quackenbush

Nicholas Quennell

F. Truitt Rabun Jr.

David C. Racker

John Rahenkamp

Robert S. Reich

Robert G. Reimann

John J. Reynolds

Artemas P. Richardson

Donald Richardson

Jane S. Ries

Robert B. Riley

Craig D. Ritland

William H. Roberts

Gary O. Robinette

Richard H. Rogers

Peter G. Rolland

Clarence Roy

Robert N. Royston

Harvey M. Rubenstein

Robert H. Rucker

Virginia Lockett Russell

Terry Warriner Ryan

Paul M. Saito

Charles S. Saladino II

Margaret Sand

William D. Sanders

Hideo Sasaki

George L. Sass

Terry W. Savage

William Scatchard

Herbert R. Schaal

Horst Schach

Janice C. Schach

Sally Schauman

Mario G. Schjetnan

Arno S. Schmid

Helmut Schmitz

Gunter A. Schoch

Ollie Schrickel

Sunny Jung Scully

Bradford G. Sears

Jonathan G. Seymour

Bruce Sharky

Fellows of the American Society of Landscape Architects (Con't)

Juanita D. Shearer-Swink
Ruth P. Shellhorn
Dr. Hamid Shirvani
J. Kipp Shrack
Jeffrey L. Siegel
Kenneth B. Simmons Jr.
John Ormsbee Simonds
John B. Slater
Gerald L. Smith
Herrick H. Smith
Jerrold Soesbe
Stanley V. Specht
Burton S. Sperber
James C. Stansbury
Barry W. Starke
Richard G. Stauffer
Robert Steenhagen
John Goddfrey Stoddart
Edward D. Stone Jr.
Edward H. Stone II
Allen D. Stovall
William G. Swain
Rodney L. Swink
Austin Paul Tao
Leslee A. Temple
Barry R. Thalden
Robert Thayer Jr.
Michael Theilacker
J. William Thompson
William H. Tishler
Donald H. Tompkins
L. Azeo Torre
Shavaun Towers
Roger T. Trancik
Howard E. Troller
Peter J. Trowbridge
Stephen J. Trudnak
James R. Turner
Jerry Mitchell Turner
Ronald W. Tuttle
Anthony Tyznik
Raymond L. Uecker
Takeo Uesugi

James R. Urban
James Van Sweden
Michael R. Van Valkenburgh
Albert R. Veri
John Wacker
Lawrence L. Walker
Peter E. Walker
Theodore D. Walker
Victor J. Walker
Thomas H. Wallis
Ronald M. Walters
Thomas C. Wang
Barry J. Warner
Kent E. Watson
Dwight W. Weatherford
E. Neal Weatherly Jr.
Richard K. Webel
Scott S. Weinberg
V. Michael Weinmayr
Roger Wells
William E. Wenk
Robert A. Weygand
James K. Wheat
Morgan Dix Wheelock
Robert F. White
George W. Wickstead
Sara Katherine Williams
Richard A. Wilson
Theodore J. Wirth
Robert L. Woerner
J. Daniel Wojcik
David G. Wright
Patrick H. Wyss
Joseph Y. Yamada
Mark J. Zarillo
Floyd W. Zimmerman
Robert L. Zion
Robert W. Zolomij
Ervin H. Zube
Laurence W. Zuelke
K. Richard Zweifel

Source: American Society of Landscape Architects

Fellows of the Construction Specifications Institute

Fellowship in the Construction Specifications Institute (CSI) is the highest honor granted to its members. Fellows are chosen by their peers from those who have been members in good standing for at least five years and who have demonstrated extraordinary service to CSI and notably contributed to the advancement of construction technology, the improvement of construction specifications, and education in the construction profession. The following individuals are current, active Fellows of the CSI.

Jerome H. Alciatore
Joel R. Aftland
John C. Anderson
Stephen John Andros
John C. Arant
Robert E. Armitage
Robert L. Ashbrook
Livingston E. Atkins Jr.
R. Stanley Bair
Jane D. Baker
Frank L. Barsotti
Richard P. Bastyr
Gary A. Betts
Walter F. Bishop
S. Steve Blumenthal
H. Maynard Blumer
J. Steven Bonner
J. Gregg Borchelt
James C. Bort
William Calvin Bowne Jr.
Charles Chief Boyd
David F. Brandt
William M. Brenan
William R. Brightbill
Wayne C. Brock
Larry Brooks
A. Larry Brown
Robert G. Burkhardt
Scott Campbell
Charles R. Carroll Jr.
Michael D. Chambers
S. Elmer Chambers
James A. Chaney

Gary D. Church
Donald G. Clark
Thomas L. Clarke Jr.
Melvin G. Cole
Pamela J. Cole
Lynton B. Cooper Jr.
Eugene H. Cortrell
Frank L. Couch
John Milton Creamer
Wrenn M. Creel
Ray E. Cumrine
Walter E. Damuck
James N. Davis
Douglas W. Day
Larry Craig Dean
Christopher G. Delgado
Charles M. Denisac Jr.
James N. De Serio
Wesley J. Dolginoff
Jo Drummond
William P. Dunne
Jerry W. Durham
R. Grant Easterling
Paul Edlund
Joseph H. Edwards
Richard H. Edwards II
Richard C. Ehmann
Donald G. Engelhard
Rodney E. Erickson
Richard A. Eustis
Dell R. Ewing
Larry G. Fisher
John C. Fleck

Fellows of the Construction Specifications Institute (Con't)

Don W. Fowler
Glenn G. Frazier
Elliot H. Gage
Woodward Garber
George S. George
Michael F. Gibbons
Michael A. Glass
William Goudeket Jr.
Jorgen Graugaard
Alana S. Griffith
Benjamin M. Gruzen
Kenneth E. Guthrie
Dennis J. Hall
Diana M. Hamilton
Craig K. Haney
James B. Hardin
Robert W. Harrington
Robert V.M. Harrison
Douglas C. Hartman
Betty C. Hays
Paul Heineman
Raymond H. Helfer
Marshall A. Hildebrand Jr.
Robert C. Hockaday
Robert W. Holstein
Herman R. Hoyer
Gilman K.M. Hu
Thomas D. Hubbard
Clarence Huettenrauch
Mary A. Hutchins
Harry F. Iram
Sheldon B. Israel
James Jackson
R. Graham Jackson
Seth Jackson
W.L. Jacobsen
Martin J. Janka
Edwin J. Johnson
Harry L. Johnson Jr.
Robert W. Johnson
Wilbur L. Johnson
Joseph H. Kasimer
Walter R. Kaye

Lee F. Kilbourn
Clarence H. King Jr.
Michael J. King
Frederick J. Klemeyer Jr.
Norman Kruchkow
John William Kuremsky
Ralph G. Lane
John B. Lape
Grant Alvin Larsen
Curtis H. Lee
Thomas E. Lewis
William T. Lohmann
David E. Lorenzini
Lendall W. Mains
Donald W. Manley
Dr. Oscar E. Marsch
Mortimer M. Marshall Jr.
Marvin Martin
Robert Kipp Mayer
Charles E. McGuire
Joseph J. McGuire
Robert L. McManus
Hans W. Meier
Donald D. Meisel
Arthur J. Miller
Mori Mitsui
Robert B. Moleseed
Thomas D. Montero
Peter J. Monterose
Kenneth J. Moore
Robert J. Morin
Lee C. Murray
Robert William Myers
Kenneth T. Nagie
Weldon W. Nash Jr.
Ronald R. Nattress
James A. Neison
R. James Noone
Robert W. Nordstrom
Arthur A. Nording
Roger A. Nourse
Harold L. Olsen
Jerome I. Orland

Fellows of the Construction Specifications Institute (Con't)

Michael T. Owen Sr.
Edwin T. Pairo
William C. Pegues
Dennis M. Pelletier
Herbert F. Pendleton
Daniel A. Perkins
Richard C. Perrell
Robert L. Petterson
Milton C. Potee
James Owen Power
Manuel Press
Jerry W. Preston
Katherine S. Proctor
Andrew D. Rae
John A. Raeber
Vincent G. Raney
Larry T. Raymond
Raymond R. Rieger
William F. Riesberg
James M. Robertson
Richard C. Robinson
Harold J. Rosen
Bernard B. Rothschild
Kelsey Y. Saint
Louis H. Sams
Maxwell L. Saul
Kenneth M. Schaefer
Carole E. Schafmeister
Richard C. Schroter
Lawrence E. Schwietz
Kenneth L. Searl
Alice Elizabeth Shelly
Paul W. Simonsen
Robert E. Simpson
Edward F. Smith
William A. Skoglund

Roscoe D. Smith
Tom F. Sneary
Edward L. Soenke
Richard B. Solomon
Michael L. Spence
Ross Spiegel
Everett G. Spurling Jr.
Norbert R. Steeber
Joel E. Stegall Jr.
J. Stewart Stein
Howard R. Steinmann
Terry J. Strong
Albert E. Taylor
David E. Thomas
Paul H. Tiffin
David F.M. Todd
Philip J. Todisco
Knox H. Tumlin
Albert R. Vallin
Donald P. Van Court
George A. Van Niel
William P. Vickers
Terry M. Wadsworth
Edith S. Washington
Wayne N. Watson
E. Ernest Waymon
Richard T. Weatherby
Roger T. Welcome
Raymond Whalley
George F. White Jr.
James F. Whitfield
Thomas I. Young
Werner Edwin Zarnikow

Source: Construction Specifications Institute

Fellows of the Industrial Designers Society of America

Membership in the Industrial Designers Society of America's (IDSA) Academy of Fellows is conferred by a two-thirds majority vote of its Board of Directors. Fellows must be Society members in good standing who have earned the special respect and affection of the membership through distinguished service to the Society and to the profession as a whole. The following individuals are the current, active fellows of the IDSA.

James M. Alexander	James G. Hansen
Wallace H. Appel	Jon W. Hauser
Alfons Bach	Stephen G. Hauser
Alexander Bally	Richard Hollerith
George Beck	Robert H. Hose
Nathaniel Becker	James L. Hvale
Arthur N. BecVar	**Charles Jones**
Melvin H. Best	Marnie Jones
Robert I. Blaich	Lorraine Justice
Alfred M. Blumenfeld	Belle Kogan
Eugene Bordinat	George Kosmak
William Bullock	Rowena Reed Kostellow
Peter Bresseler	Rudolph W. Krolopp
Joseph Carriero	David Kusuma
Arthur H. Crapsey	LeRoy LaCelle
Donald E. Dailey	Richard S. Latham
Thomas David	Raymond Loewy
Niels Diffrient	Peter E. Lowe
Jay Doblin	Paul MacAlister
H. Creston Doner	Tucker P. Madawick
Henry Dreyfuss	**Pascal Malassigné**
Mark Dziersk	Joseph R. Mango
Arden Farey	Katherine J. McCoy
Vincent M. Foote	Donald McFarland
James F. Fulton	Leon Gordon Miller
Roger Funk	Dana W. Mox
Walter Furlani	Peter Müller-Munk
Carroll M. Gantz	C. Stowe Myers
Franceco Gianninoto	George Nelson
Henry P. Glass	Joseph M. Parriott
William Goldsmith	Lee Payne
John S. Griswold	Charles Pelly
Robert Gruen	Nancy Perkins
Olle E. Haggstrom	James J. Pirkl

Fellows of the Industrial Designers Society of America (Con't)

William L. Plumb
Arthur J. Pulos
Robert E. Redmann
Jean Otis Reinecke
Harold Reynolds
Deane W. Richardson
James Ryan
Clair A. Samhammer
Kenneth Schory
F. Eugene Smith
Robert G. Smith
Paul B. Specht
Raymond Spilman
Darrell S. Staley
Budd Steinhilber
Brooks Stevens
Philip H. Stevens

Ernest L. Swarts
Sharyn Thompson
David D. Tompkins
Herbert H. Tyrnauer
John Vassos
Read Viemeister
Tucker Viemeister
Noland Vogt
Sandor Weisz
Steve Wilcox
Arnold Wolf
Peter Wooding
Cooper C. Woodring
Edward J. Zagorski

Source: Industrial Designers Society of America

Did you know...

Due to the unanticipated complexity of the manufacturing process, Herman Miller initially produced only 200 of George Nelson and Irving Harper's Marshmallow Sofas (1956), although they have recently revived production of this classic piece.

Fellows of the International Interior Design Association

Professional members of the International Interior Design Association (IIDA) are inducted into the College of Fellows by a two-thirds vote by their Board of Directors. This honor recognizes members who have demonstrated outstanding service to the IIDA, the community, and the interior design profession. The following individuals are current, active fellows of the IIDA.

Robin Klehr Avia
Laura Bailey
Jeanne Baldwin
Claude Berube
Charles Blumberg
Dan Bouligny
Michael Bourque
Rus Calder
Richard Carlson
Particia Gutierrez Castellanos
Amarjeet Chatrath
Susan Coleman
David Cooke
Eleanor Corkle
Christine Dandan
Eugene Daniels
Carol Disrud
Jacqueline Duncan
Cheryl Duvall
Hilda East
Marilyn Farrow
James Ferguson II
Dorothy Fowles
Neil Frankel
Angela Frey
Charles D. Gandy
Gerald Gelsomino
M. Arthur Gensler Jr.
Carol S. Graham
Karen Guenther
Beth Harmon-Vaughan
Judith Hastings
Jo Heinz
Edna Henner
John Herron

Frederick Hutchirs
David Immenschuh
Cary D. Johnson
Christina Johnson
Carol Jones
Margo Jones
Robert Kennedy
Tessa Kennedy
Sooz Klinkhamer
Mary Knackstedt
Lili Kray
Marjorie Kriebel
Michael Kroelinger
Robert Ledingham
Fola Lerner-Miller
Jack Levin
Neville Lewis
Charles Littleton
Ronald Lubben
Hiroko Machida
Candace MacKenzie
Richard Mazzucotelli
Jose Medrano
Ruth Mellergaard
Kenneth Muller
Donald Parker
Janie Petkus
Paul Petrie
Richard N. Pollack
Shirley Pritchard
Carole Price Shanis
Sandra Ragan
Charles Raymond
Patti Richards
Jane Rohde

Fellows of the International Interior Design Association (Con't)

Wayne Ruga
Joyce Saunders
Mitchell E. Sawasy
Allan Shaivitz
Donald Sherman
Rayne Sherman
Gail Shiel
Bernard Soep
Henrietta Spencer-Churchill
Andre Staffelbach
Andrew Stafford
William Stankiewicz
Janice Stevenor-Dale
Donald Thomas
Joann Thompson
Betty Treanor
Marcia Troyan

Robert Valentine
Margaret Velardo
Roen Viscovich
Allison Carll White
Ron Whitney-Whyte
Glenda Wilcox
Frances Wilson
M. Judith Wilson
D. Geary Winstead
Michael Wirtz
Susan Wood
Minoru Yokoyama
Janice Young

Source: International Interior Design Association

Fellows of the Society of Architectural Historians

Fellowship in the Society of Architectural Historians is granted for "exceptional and distinguished service to the Society."

H. Allen Brooks
Marian C. Donnelly
Alan W. Gowans
Carol Herselle Krinsky
Elisabeth Blair MacDougall
Carter H. Manny
Henry A. Millon

Osmund Overby
Seymour H. Persky
Charles E. Peterson
William H. Pierson Jr.
Adolf K. Placzek
George B. Tatum

Source: Society of Architectural Historians

Fellows of the Society for Marketing Professional Services

The Fellows of the Society for Marketing Professional Services (SMPS) represent the highest level of experience and leadership in marketing within the built and natural environments. Members who have been active in the Society for more than 10 years and who hold a current certification designation (Certified Professional Services Marketer) are eligible to apply. A jury of fellows annually reviews the nominations.

Carol A. Adey
Simon Andrews
Lloyd H. Bakan
James R. Bancroft
R. Tim Barrick
Karleen Belmont
George R. Biderman
Lois E. Boemer
Edward A. Bond
Kate M. Brannelly
Joan Capelin
Pam A. Carman
Jane Cohn
Karen O. Courtney
Weld Coxe
Diane C. Creel
Charles C. Crevo
Susan R. Daylor
Marilyn K. Etheridge
Gregory N. Fern
Ellen Flynn-Heapes
Rolf A. Fuessler
Ron W. Garikes
Kay C. Godwin
Janet Goodman Aubry
Harlan E. Hallquist
Betty S. Hearn
Kal R. Hindo
Dale C. Jones
Peter J. Kienle
Angela M. Kimble
Kay Lentz
Mitchel R. Levitt

Dianne Ludman Frank
Julie G. Luers
Peter A. Lyon
Sheryl Maibach
Laurin McCracken
William H. Morton
Julie Olson
Cheryl O. Paoluccio
Craig Park
Randle Pollock
Alfred K. Potter
Gwendolyn L. Powell Todd
Lisbeth Quebe
Michael J. Reilly
Janet S. Sanders
Carol E. Scheafnocker
Bonnie J. Sloan
Thomas E. Smith Jr.
William R. Strong
Carla D. Thompson
Lyle G. Trease
John R. Turner
Nancy J. Usrey
Jean R. Valence
Philip F. Valence
Dena L. Williams
Karen W. Winters
Ronald D. Worth
Nadine R. Yates
Lou Zickler

Source: Society for Marketing Professional Services

Honorary Fellows of The American Institute of Architects

The American Institute of Architects (AIA) grants Honorary Fellowship to non-members, both architects and non-architects, who have made substantial contributions to the field of architecture.

Kurt H.C. Ackermann, Munich, Germany

Gunnel Adlercreutz, Helsinki, Finland

O. J. Aguilar, Lima, Peru

Hisham Albakri, Kuala Lumpur, Malaysia

William A. Allen, London, England

Alfred V. Alvares, Vancouver, Canada

Jose Alvarez, Lima, Peru

Mario R. Alvarez, Buenos Aires, Argentina

Tadao Ando, Osaka, Japan

John H. Andrews, Australia

Carlos D. Arguelles, Manila, Philippines

Gordon R. Arnott, Regina, Canada

Carl Aubock, Austria

Carlo Aymonino, Venice, Italy

George G. Baines, England

Juan Navarro Baldeweg, Madrid, Spain

W. D. Baldwin, Sterling, Canada

W. K. Banadayga, Sterling, Canada

Essy Baniassad, Halifax, Canada

Nikolai B. Baranov, Moscow, Russia

Geoffrey M. Bawa, Columbo, Sri Lanka

Eugene Beaudouin, France

Gerard Benoit, Paris, France

Jai R. Bhalla, New Delhi, India

Jacob Blegvad, Aalborg, Denmark

Ricardo L. Bofill, Barcelona, Spain

Oriol Bohigas, Barcelona, Spain

Irving D. Boigon, Richmond Hill, Canada

Ferenc Callmeyer, Telki, Hungary

Santiago A. Calvo, Lima, Peru

Felix Candela, Raleigh, North Carolina

Rifat Chadirji, Surrey, England

Suk-Woong Chang, Seoul, Korea

Te L. Chang, Taipei, Taiwan

Bill Chomik, Calgary, Canada

Adolf Ciborowski, Warsaw, Poland

E. Gresley Cohen, Dalkeith, Australia

Charles M. Correa, Bombay, India

Philip S. Cox, Sydney, Australia

Charles H. Cullum, Newfoundland, Canada

Carlos E. Da Silva, Rizal, Philippines

John M. Davidson, Richmond, Australia

David Y. Davies, Surrey, England

Sara T. De Grinberg, Mexico

Rafael De La Hoz, Spain

S. D. De La Tour, Durville, France

Eduardo De Mello, Braga, Portugal

Costantin N. Decavalla, Greece

Ignacio M. Delmonte, Mexico City, Mexico

A. J. Diamond, Toronto, Canada

Ignacio Diaz-Morales, Jalisco, Mexico

Balkrishna V. Doshi, Ahmedabad, India

Philip Dowson, London, England

Kiril Doytchev, Sofia, Bulgaria

G. M. Dubois, Toronto, Canada

Allan F. Duffus, Halifax, Canada

Werner Duttman, Lindenalle, Germany

David W. Edwards, Regina, Canada

Yehya M. Eid, Cairo, Egypt

Abdel W. El Wakil, Kent, England

Arthur C. Erickson, Vancouver, Canada

Lord Esher, England

Inger Exner, Denmark

Johannes Exner, Denmark

Tobias Faber, Copenhagen, Denmark

Francisco B. Fajardo, Philippines

Hassan Fathy, Egypt

Sverre Fehn, Oslo, Norway

Honorary Fellows of The American Institute of Architects (Con't)

Bernard M. Feilden, Norfolk, England

Ji Z. Feng, Shanghai, PRC

Angelina Munoz Fernandez de Madrid, Sonora, Mexico

A. I. Ferrier, Red Hill, Australia

Jozsef Finta, Budapest, Hungary

Antonio F. Flores, Mexico

Cesar X. Flores, Mexico D.F., Mexico

Norman Foster, London, England

Charles A. Fowler, Canada

Jorge Gamboa de Buen, Mexico DF, Mexico

Juan Gonzalez, Spain

Roderick P. Hackney, Cheshire, England

Zaha Hadid, London, England

H. H. Hallen, Australia

Shoji Hayashi, Tokyo, Japan

Tao Ho, North Point, Hong Kong

Barry J. Hobin, Ottawa, Canada

Hans Hollein, Vienna, Austria

Wilhelm Holzbauer, Vienna, Austria

Sir Michael Hopkins, London, England

Lady Patricia Hopkins, London, England

Thomas Howarth, Toronto, Canada

Nobuo Hozumi, Tokyo, Japan

Arata Isozaki, Tokyo, Japan

Toyo Ito, Tokyo, Japan

Daryl Jackson, Melbourne, Australia

R. D. Jackson, Sydney, Australia

Alvaro Joaquim de Meio Siza, Porto, Portugal

P. N. Johnson, Australia

Sumet Jumsai, Bangkok, Thailand

Achyut P. Kanvinde, New Dehli, India

Vladimir Karfik, Brno, Czech Republic

Kiyonori Kikutake, Tokyo, Japan

Reiichiro Kitadai, Tokyo, Japan

Azusa Kito, Tokyo, Japan

Josef P. Kleihues, Berlin, Germany

Rob Krier, Berlin, Germany

Dogan Kuban, Istanbul, Turkey

Alexandr P. Kudryavtsev, Moscow, Russia

Kisho Kurokawa, Tokyo, Japan

Colin Laird, Port of Spain, Trinidad and Tobago

Jean L. Lalonde, Canada

Henning Larsen, Denmark

Denys L. Lasdun, London, England

Kwang-Ro Lee, Seoul, Korea

Kyung-Hoi Lee, Seoul, Korea

Juha Ilmari Leiviska, Helsinki, Finland

Sergio Lenci, Rome, Italy

Jaime Lerner, Parana, Brazil

Wu Liang Yong, Beijing, PRC

Kington Loo, Kuala Lumpur, Malaysia

Aldana E. Lorenzo, San Jeronimo, Mexico

Serapio P. Loza, Jalisco, Mexico

Kjell Lund, Oslo, Norway

Brian MacKay-Lyons, Halifax, Nova Scotia, Canada

Olufemi Majekodunmi, Gaborone, Botswana

Fumihiko Maki, Tokyo, Japan

Matti K. Makinen, Finland

Rutilo Malacara, Mexico D. F., Mexico

Motlatsi Peter Malefane, Johannesburg, South Africa

Albert Mangones, Port Au Prince, Haiti

Yendo Masayoshi, New York, New York

Robert Peter McIntyre, Victoria, Australia

Rodrigo Mejia-Andrion, Panama

Hector Mestre, Mexico, D.F., Mexico

Wladimir Mitrofanoff, Paris, France

Jose Raphael Moneo, Madrid, Spain

Raymond Moriyama, Toronto, Canada

Padraig Murray, Dublin, Ireland

Toshio Nakamura, Tokyo, Japan

Nikola I. Nikolov, Sofia, Bulgaria

Juan Bassegoda Nonell, Barcelona, Spain

Rafael Norma, Mexico City, Mexico

Jean Nouvel, Paris, France

Jorge Nu Ex Verdugo, Mexico

Carl J.A. Nyren, Stockholm, Sweden

ShinIchi Okada, Tokyo, Japan

Oluwole O. Olumyiwa, Lagos, Nigeria

Honorary Fellows of The American Institute of Architects (Con't)

Georgui M. Orlov, Moscow, Russia

Juhani Pallasmaa, Helsinki, Finland

Gustav Peichl, Wein, Austria

Raili Pietila, Helsinki, Finland

Methodi A. Pissarski, Sofia, Bulgaria

Ernst A. Plischke, Wien, Austria

Christian de Portzamparc, Paris, France

Ivor C. Prinsloo, Rondebosch, South Africa

Victor M. Prus, Montreal, Canada

Luis M. Quesada, Lima, Peru

Hector M. Restat, Santiago, Chile

Jose F. Reygadas, Mexico City, Mexico

Philippe Robert, Paris, France

Derry Menzies Robertson, Picton, Canada

Juan J. Rocco, Montevideo, Uruguay

Xavier Cortes Rocha, Coyoacan, Mexico

Aldo A. Rossi, Milano, Italy

Witold Rybczynski, Philadelphia, PA

Thomas J. Sanabria, Miami, FL

Alberto Sartoris, Cossonay Ville, Switzerland

Helmut C. Schulitz, Braunschweig, Germany

Michael Scott, Ireland

Harry Seidler, Australia

J. Francisco Serrano, Mexico City, Mexico

Vassilis C. Sgoutas, Athens, Greece

Haigo T.H. Shen, Taipei, Taiwan

Peter F. Shepheard, Philadelphia, PA

Dr. Tsutomu Shigemura, Kobe, Japan

Kazuo Shinohara, Yokohama, Japan

Brian Sim, Vancouver, Canada

Antonio S. Sindiong, Rizal, Philippines

Heikki Siren, Helsinki, Finland

Kaija Siren, Helsinki, Finland

Nils Slaatto, Oslo, Norway

Vladimir Slapeta, Praha, Czech Republic

Inette L. Smith, Cornwall, England

J. M. Smith, Cornwall, England

Gin Su, Bethesda, Maryland

Timo Suomalainen, Espoo, Finland

Minoru Takeyama, Littleton, Colorado

Yoshio Taniguchi, Tokyo, Japan

German Tellez, Bogota, Colombia

Anders Tengbom, Sweden

Paul-Andre Tetreault, Montreal, Canada

Alexandros N. Tombazis, Athens, Greece

Luben N. Tonev, Bulgaria

Marion Tournon-Branly, Paris, France

Shozo Uchii, Tokyo, Japan

Lennart Uhlin, Stockholm, Sweden

Jorn Utzon, Denmark

Pierre Vago, Noisy, France

Gino Valle, Udine, Italy

Marcelo E. Vargas, Lima, Peru

Pedro R. Vasquez, Mexico City, Mexico

Eva Vecsei, Montreal, Canada

Jorge N. Verdugo, Mexico City, Mexico

Tomas R. Vicuna, Santiago, Chile

Jean-Paul Viguier, Paris, France

Ricardo L. Vilchis, Mexico City, Mexico

Eduardo O. Villacortaq, Lima, Peru

William Whitefield, London, England

Terence J. Williams, Victoria, Canada

Roy W. Willwerth, Halifax, Canada

C. A. Wnderlich, Guatemala City, Guatemala

Chung Soo Won, Seoul, Korea

Bernard Wood, Ottawa, Canada

Rutang Ye, Beijing, PRC

Richard Young, Sterling, Canada

Abraham Zabludovsky, Codesa, Mexico

Jose M. Zaragoza, Philippines

Eberhard Heinrich Zeidler, Toronto, Canada

Source: The American Institute of Architects

Did you know...

Despite designing the majority of St. Peter's Basilica, the 71-year-old Michelangelo refused to be paid for his work on the church.

Honorary Members of The American Institute of Architects

The American Institute of Architects (AIA) grants honorary membership to individuals outside the architecture profession who are not otherwise eligible for membership in the Institute. They are chosen for their distinguished service to architecture or the allied arts and sciences. Nominations may be submitted by the national AIA Board of Directors or a component PIA. National and component staff with 10 years or more of service are also eligible for Honorary Membership.

Suzie Adams, Fort Worth, TX
Ava J. Abramowitz, Chevy Chase, MD
Joseph F. Addonizio, New Rochelle, NY
His Highness The Aga Khan
Joseph Ahearn, Littleton, CO
Michael L. Ainslie, New York, NY
R. Mayne Albright, Charlotte, NC
Barbara Allan, Seattle, WA
George A. Allen, CAE, Tallahassee, FL
Trudy Aron, Topeka, KS
Ludd Ashley, Washington, DC
Janice Axon, Laguna Niguel, CA
William M. Babcock, Madison, WI
Mariana Barthold, Oklahoma City, OK
Augustus Baxter, Sr., Philadelphia, PA
Stephen M. Bennett, Columbus, OH
Leo L. Beranek, Cambridge, MA
Elaine Bergman, Tulsa, OK
James Biddle, Andalusia, PA
J. Bidwill, Chicago, IL
Sherry Birk, Washington, DC
The Honorable Sherwood L. Boehlert
Oriol Bohigas, Barcelona, Spain
Sara H. Boutelle, Santa Cruz, CA
A. S. Boyd, Washington, DC
Ann Marie Boyden, Arlington, VA
Eleanor K. Brassel, Bethesda, MD
John W. Braymer, Richmond, VA
David Brinkley, Chevy Chase, MD
Jack Brooks, Washington, DC
A. B. Brown, Providence, RI

Charlotte Vestal Brown, Raleigh, NC
J. N. Brown, Providence, RI
William A. Brown Sr., Washington, DC
William D. Browning, Snowmass, CO
John M. Bryan, Columbia, SC
Muriel Campaglia, Washington, DC
Donald Canty, Seattle, WA
Joan Capelin, New York, NY
Edward Carlough, Washington, DC
Charles M. Cawley, Wilmington, DE
Henry C. Chambers, Beaufort, SC
Mary Chapman-Smith, Mancelona, MI
William W. Chase, Alexandria, VA
Henry Cisneros, San Antonio, TX
F. J. Clark, Washington, DC
Grady Clay Jr., Louisville, KY
Ernest A. Connally, Alexandria, VA
S. B. Conroy, Washington, DC
Rolaine V. Copeland, Seattle, WA
Weld Coxe, Block Island, RI
Lois Craig, Cambridge, MA
James P. Cramer, Norcross, GA
Alfonse M. D'Amato, Washington, DC
Kathleen L. Daileda, Washington, DC
Ann Davidson, North Canton, OH
Joan K. Davidson, New York, NY
Brent L. Davis, Tucson AZ
Mabel S. Day, Alexandria, VA
Fred R. Deluca, Washington, DC
Deborah Dietsch, Washington, DC
John A. DiNardo, Austin, TX

Honorary Members of The American Institute of Architects (Con't)

Carlos Diniz

Rae Dumke, Detroit, MI

M. Durning, Seattle, WA

J. Sprigg Duvall, Washington, DC

Linda J. Ebitz, Oakland, PA

Judy A. Edwards, New Haven, CT

M. D. Egan, Anderson, SC

James R. Ellis, Seattle, WA

John D. Entenza, Santa Monica, CA

Marie L. Farrell, Belvedere, CA

Alan M. Fern, Chevy Chase, MD

Angelina Munoz Fernandez de Madrid, Sonora, Mexico

L. A. Ferre, San Juan, Puerto Rico

David W. Field, CAE, Columbus, OH

Harold B. Finger, Washington, DC

James M. Fitch, New York, NY

J. D. Forbes, Charlottesville, VA

William S. Fort, Eugene, OR

Arthur J. Fox Jr., New York, NY

Doris C. Freedman, New York, NY

Mildred Friedman, New York, NY

Patsy L. Frost, Columbus, OH

Ruth Fuller, Houston, TX

Paul Gapp, Chicago, IL

D. E. Gardner, Delaware, OH

Paul Genecki, Kensington, MD

C. D. Gibson, Ogden, UT

Brendan Gill, New York, NY

Jorge Glusberg, Buenos Aires, Argentina

Alfred Goldberg, Belvedere Tiburo, CA

Howard G. Goldberg, Esq.

Paul Goldberger, New York, NY

Douglas E. Gordon, Washington, DC

H. B. Gores, Alpharetta, GA

D. R. Graham, Tallahassee, FL

Ginny W. Graves, Prairie Village, KS

Barbara Gray, Takoma Park, MD

Roberta Gratz

Cecil H. Green, Dallas, TX

Thomas Griffith, New York, NY

Roberta J. Guffey, Charleston, WV

Robert Gutman, Princeton, NJ

Richard Hagg

Donald J. Hall, Kansas City, MO

William L. Hall, Eden Prairie, MN

Donalee Hallenbeck, Sacramento, CA

P. Hammer, Beverley Beach, MD

Marga Rose Hancock, Seattle, WA

Partrick K. Harrison, London, England

Dr. F. Otto Hass, Philadelphia, PA

Arthur A. Hart, Boise, ID

Dianne Hart, California

Beverly E. Hauschild-Baron, Minneapolis, MN

A. Hecksher, New York, NY

Andrew Heiskell, New York, NY

Amy Hershfang

Gerald D. Hines, Houston, TX

Charles L. Hite

William Houseman, Portland, ME

Thomas P. Hoving, New York, NY

Philip A. Hutchinson, Harwood, MD

Ada L. Huxtable, New York, NY

J. Michael Huey, Esq.

Donald G. Iselin, Santa Barbara, CA

Kathy C. Jackson, CAE, Jackson, MS

J. B. Johnson, Watertown, NY

Dr. Joseph E. Johnson

Lady B. Johnson, Austin, TX

Gerre Jones, Albuquerque, NM

V. Jordan, Jr., New York, NY

H. A. Judd, Beaverton, OR

Lloyd Kaiser, Oakmont, PA

Shelly Kappe

Robert J. Kapsch, Gaithersburg, MD

Suzanne Keller, Princeton, NJ

Dorothy Kender

Roger G. Kennedy, Alexandria, VA

Jonathan King, Houston, TX

R. Lawrence Kirkegaard, Downers Grove, IL

Lee E. Koppelman, Stonybrook, NY

Peter H. Kostmayer, Washington, DC

Honorary Members of The American Institute of Architects (Con't)

Mabel Krank, Oklahoma City, OK

Florence C. Ladd, Cambridge, MA

Anita M. Laird, Cape May, NJ

David P. Lancaster, Austin, TX

George Latimer, St. Paul, MN

Robin Lee, Washington, D.C.

William J. Le Messurier, Cambridge, MA

Aaron Levine, Menlo Park, CA

E. H. Levitas, Washington, DC

Lawrence Lewis Jr.

Weiming Lu, St. Paul, MN

Major General Eugene Lupia

Jane Maas, New York, NY

Diane Maddox, Washington, DC

Randell Lee Makinson

Stanley Marcus, Dallas, TX

Louis L. Marines, Corte Madera, CA

Judy Marks, Washington, DC

Albert R. Marschall, Alexandria, VA

Maureen Marx, Springfield, VA

Mary Tyler Cheek McClenaham

F. M. McConihe, Potomac, MD

Terrence M. McDermott, Chicago, IL

Evelyn B. McGrath, Holiday, FL

Ian L. McHarg, Philadelphia, PA

Cheri C. Melillo, New York, NY

Paul Mellon, Upperville, VA

Betty H. Meyer

E. P. Mickel, Bethesda, MD

J. I. Miller, Columbus, IN

Martha P. Miller, Portland, OR

R. Miller, Sherman Oaks, CA

Richard B. Miller, Elmsford, NY

Roger Milliken, Spartanburg, SC

Hermine Mitchell, Philadelphia, PA

Martha Barber Montgomery, Ph.D.

William B. Moore Jr., Kilmarnock, VA

John W. Morris, Arlington, VA

Philip A. Morris, Birmingham, AL

Terry B. Morton, Chevy Chase, MD

Woolridge Brown Morton III

Jean G. Muntz, Omaha, NE

Martha Murphree, Houston, TX

Maria Murray, Kensington, MD

Betty J. Musselman, Accokeek, MD

Raymond D. Nasher

Doreen Nelson, Los Angeles, CA

Shirley J. Norvell, Springfield, IL

Laurie D. Olin, Philadelphia, PA

Mary E. Osman, Columbia, SC

Ronald J. Panciera, Bradenton, FL

R. B. Pease, Pittsburgh, PA

C. Ford Peatross, Washington, DC

Robert A. Peck, Esq, Washington, DC

Claiborne Pell, Washington, DC

David Perdue, Silver Spring, MD

Michael D. Perry, Virginia Beach, VA

G. E. Pettengill, Arlington, VA

Janet D. Pike, Lexington, KY

Philip W. Pillsbury Jr., Washington, DC

Walter F. Pritchard II, Costa Mesa, CA

Jay A. Pritzker, Chicago, IL

Jody Proppe, Portland, OR

Sidney A. Rand, Minneapolis, MN

David P. Reynolds, Richmond, VA

William G. Reynolds Jr., Richmond, VA

Brenda Richards

Carolyn Richie

Raymond P. Rhinehart, Washington, DC

Joseph P. Riley, Charleston, SC

J. P. Robin, Pittsburgh, PA

Laurance Rockefeller, New York, NY

Barbara J. Rodriguez, Albany, NY

Gini Rountree, Sacramento, CA

Mario G. Salvadori, New York, NY

Carl M. Sapers, Boston, MA

William D. Schaefer, Baltimore, MD

Martin Schaum, Garden City, NY

Paul Schell, Seattle, WA

Vincent C. Schoemehl Jr., Clayton, MO

Philip Schreiner, Washington, DC

Rosemary Schroeder, Dallas, TX

Honorary Members of The American Institute of Architects (Con't)

Susan E. Schur

Frederick D. Schwengel

Suzanne K. Schwengels, Des Moines, IA

Rex Scouten, Washington, DC

B. Sebastian, San Francisco, CA

James H. Semans, Durham, NC

Julian B. Serrill, Des Moines, IA

Elaine K. Sewell Jones, Los Angeles, CA

Polly E. Shackleton, Washington, DC

Julius Shulman, Los Angeles, CA

Betty W. Silver, Raleigh, NC

Alice Sinkevitch, Chicago, IL

John B. Skilling, Seattle, WA

W. L. Slayton, Washington, DC

Eleanor McNamara Smith, Somerset, WI

Nancy Somerville, Washington, DC

S. Spencer, Washington, DC

Ann Stacy, Baltimore, MD

S. Steinborn, Seattle, WA

Saundra Stevens, Portland, OR

P. D. Stitt, Yreka, CA

Deborah Sussman, Culver City, CA

Anne J. Swager, Pittsburg, PA

Pipsan S. Swanson, Bloomfield, MI

G. B. Tatum, Chester, CT

Anne Taylor, Kansas City, MO

Richard Thevenot, Baton Rouge, LA

J. S. Thurmond, Washington, DC

Carolyn H. Toft, St. Louis, MO

Bernard Tomson, Voorheesville, NY

W. F. Traendly, Thetford Center, VT

R. E. Train, Washington, DC

Pierre Vago, Noisy, France

Mariana L. Verga, Edmond, OK

Wolf Von Eckardt, Washington, DC

Connie C. Wallace, CAE, Nashville, TN

Paul Weidlinger, New York, NY

Paul W. Welch, Jr. Sacramento, CA

Emmet L. Wemple, Los Angeles, CA

Katie Westby, Tulsa, OK

Frank J. Whalen Jr., Cheverly, MD

Richard Guy Wilson, Charlottesville, VA

Gloria Wise, Dallas, TX

Honorable Pete Wilson, Washington, DC

Arol Wolford, Norcross, GA

Marilyn Wood, Santa Fe, NM

Tony P. Wrenn, Fredricksburg, VA

Honorable Sidney Yates, Washington, DC

Jill D. Yeomans, Santa Barbara, CA

John Zukowsky, Chicago, IL

Source: The American Institute of Architects

Honorary Members of the American Society of Landscape Architects

Honorary Membership is granted by the American Society of Landscape Architects' (ASLA) Board of Directors, to persons, other than landscape architects, who have performed notable service to the profession of landscape architecture.

Edward H. Able Jr.
Hon. Douglas Bereuter
Randall Biallas
Hon. Dale Bumpers
Pres. James Earl Carter Jr.
Grady Clay
Russell E. Dickenson
Walter L. Doty
Marvin Durning
Carolyn B. Etter
Don D. Etter
Albert Fein
Charles E. Fraser
Marshall M. Fredericks
Gwen Frostic
Donald M. Harris
George B. Hartzog Jr.
Vance R. Hood
Patrick Horsbrugh
Thomas Hylton
Pres. Lyndon B. Johnson
Dr. Harley Jolley
Genevieve Pace Keller
Hon. Edward M. Kennedy
Peter A. Kirsch
Balthazar Korab

Norbert Kraich
Prof. Walter H. Lewis
Dr. Binyi Liu
John A. Love
Lee MacDonald
Prof. E. Bruce MacDougall
Charles C. McLaughlin
Hugh C. Miller
Philip A. Morris
Frederick L. Noland
Gyo Obata
Ross D. Pallay
R. Max Peterson
William Phelps
Richard Pope, Sr.
Gen. Colin Powell
Peter H. Raven
Hon. Joseph P. Riley Jr.
L. S. Rockefeller
Martin J. Rosen
John Seiberling
Ron Taven
Dr. Ralph J. Warburton

Source: American Society of Landscape Architects

Honorary Members of the Industrial Designers Society of America

The Board of Directors of the Industrial Designers Society of America (IDSA) grants honorary membership to individuals whose relationship to, involvement with, or special efforts on behalf of the design profession merit the recognition and gratitude of the Society. Honorary membership is awarded by a three-quarters majority vote by the Board of Directors.

1965 R. Buckminster Fuller
1965 Edgar Kaufmann Jr.
1981 Ray Eames
1982 Florence Knoll Bassett
1983 Ralph Caplan
1988 Brian J. Wynne
1998 Bruce Nussbaum

Source: Industrial Designers Society of America

Honorary Members of the International Interior Design Association

The International Interior Design Association (IIDA) grants honorary membership to individuals who, although they are not interior designers, have made substantial contributions to the interior design profession. The following individuals are current Honorary Members of the IIDA.

Stanley Abercrombie
Clarellen Adams
George Baer
Shirley Black
Charles Blumberg
Chilton Brown
Margaret Buckingham
Len Corlin
Christine Cralle
James P. Cramer
Tom Cramer
Cheryl Durst
Lori Graham
Dianne Jackman
Cynthia Leibrock

Paul Leonard
Viscount David Linley
Chris McKellar
Doug Parker
Norman Polsky
Lois Powers
John Sample
Thomas Sutton Jr.
Dean Thompson
Jan Toft
Jill Vanderfleet-Scott
John West

Source: International Interior Design Association

Interior Design Hall of Fame

In 1985 *Interior Design* magazine established the Interior Design Hall of Fame to recognize individuals who have made significant contributions to the growth and prominence of the Interior Design profession. New inductees are presented every December at an awards ceremony at New York's Waldorf-Astoria Hotel. This event also serves as a fundraising effort for the non-profit Foundation for Interior Design Education Research (FIDER) and other charitable organizations supporting interior design educational initiatives.

Hall of Fame Members:

Marvin. B Affrime
Kalef Alaton
Davis Allen
Pamela Babey
Benjamin Baldwin
Florence Knoll Bassett
Louis M.S. Beal
Ward Bennett
Maria Bergson
Barbara Berry
Bruce Bierman
Laura Bohn
Joseph Braswell
Robert Bray
Don Brinkmann
Tom Britt
R. Scott Bromley
Mario Buatta
Richard Carlson
Francois Catroux
Steve Chase
Clodagh
Celeste Cooper
Robert Currie
Barbara D'Arcy
Joseph D'Urso
Thierry W. Despont
Orlando Diaz-Azcuy
Angelo Donghia
Jack Dunbar
Tony Duquette
Melvin Dwork
David Easton
Henry End

Mica Ertegun
Bernardo Fort-Brescia
Billy W. Francis
Neil Frankel
Michael Gabellini
Frank Gehry
Arthur Gensler
Richard Gluckman
Mariette Himes Gomez
Jacques Grange
Margo Grant
Michael Graves
Bruce Gregga
Charles Gwathmey
Albert Hadley
Anthony Hall
Mel Hamilton
Mark Hampton
Antony Harbour
Hugh Hardy
David Hicks
Edith Mansfield Hills
Richard Himmel
Howard Hirsch
William Hodgins
Malcolm Holzman
Franklin D. Israel
Carolyn Iu
Eva Jiricna
Jed Johnson
Melanie Kahane
Ronette King
Robert Kleinschmidt
Ronald Krueck
Gary Lee

Interior Design Hall of Fame (Con't)

Sarah Tomerlin Lee
Naomi Leff
Debra Lehman-Smith
Joseph Lembo
Lawrence Lerner
Neville Lewis
Sally Sirkin Lewis
Christian Liaigre
Eva Maddox
Stephen Mallory
Peter Marino
Patrick McConnell
Margaret McCurry
Zack McKown
Kevin McNamara
Richard Meier
Robert Metzger
Lee Mindel
Juan Montoya
Frank Nicholson
James Northcurr
Mrs. Henry Parish II
Norman Pfeiffer
Charles Pfister
Warren Platner
Donald D. Powell
William Pulgram
Andrée Putman
Chessy Rayner
Lauren Rottet
Rita St. Clair
John F. Saladino
Michael Schaible
Denise Scott Brown
Peter Shelton
Berry Sherrill
Robert Siegel
Ethel Smith
Laurinda Spear
Jay Spectre
Andre Staffelbach
Philippe Starck
Robert A.M. Stern
Rysia Suchecka
Lou Switzer
Rose Tarlow
Michael Taylor

Stanley Tigerman
Adam Tihany
Calvin Tsao
Billie Tsien
Carleton Varney
Robert Venturi
Lella Vignelli
Massimo Vignelli
Kenneth H. Walker
Sally Walsh
Kevin Walz
Gary Wheeler
Bunny Williams
Tod Williams
Trisha Wilson
Vincente Wolf

Special Honorees:
Robert O. Anderson
Jaime Ardiles-Arce
Stanley Barrows
Howard Brandston
Adele Chatfield-Taylor
John L. Dowling
Lester Dundes
Sherman R. Emery
Karen Fisher
Arnold Friedmann
Alberto Paolo Gavasci
Jeremiah Goodman
Louis Oliver Gropp
Olga Gueft
Jack Hedrich
Benjamin D. Holloway
Philip E. Kelly
Kips Bay Decorator Show House
Jack Lenor Larsen
Santo Loquasto
Ruth K. Lynford
Gene Moore
Diantha Nype
Dianne Pilgrim
Paige Rense
Ian Schrager
Tony Walton
Winterthur Museum and Gardens

Source: Interior Design *magazine*

Presidents of The American Institute of Architects

1857-76	Richard Upjohn	1966	Morris Ketchum Jr.
1877-87	Thomas U. Walter	1967	Charles M. Nes Jr.
1888-91	Richard M. Hunt	1968	Robert L. Durham
1892-93	Edward H. Kendall	1969	George E. Kassabaum
1894-95	Daniel H. Burnham	1970	Rex W. Allen
1896-98	George B. Post	1971	Robert F. Hastings
1899	Henry Van Brunt	1972	Max O. Urbahn
1900-1	Robert S. Peabody	1973	S. Scott Ferebee Jr.
1902-3	Charles F. McKim	1974	Archibald C. Rogers
1904-5	William S. Eames	1975	William "Chick" Marshall Jr.
1906-7	Frank M. Day	1976	Louis DeMoll
1908-9	Cass Gilbert	1977	John M. McGinty
1910-11	Irving K. Pond	1978	Elmer E. Botsai
1912-3	Walter Cook	1979	Ehrman B. Mitchell Jr.
1914-5	R. Clipston Sturgis	1980	Charles E. Schwing
1916-8	John L. Mauran	1981	R. Randall Vosbeck
1919-20	Thomas R. Kimball	1982	Robert M. Lawrence
1921-2	Henry H. Kendall	1983	Robert C. Broshar
1923-4	William B. Faville	1984	George M. Notter Jr.
1925-6	Dan E. Waid	1985	R. Bruce Patty
1927-8	Milton B. Medary	1986	John A Busby Jr.
1929-30	Charles H. Hammond	1987	Donald J. Hackl
1931-2	Robert D. Kohn	1988	Ted P. Pappas
1933-4	Earnest J. Russell	1989	Benjamin E. Brewer Jr.
1935-6	Stephen F. Voorhees	1990	Sylvester Damianos
1937-8	Charles D. Maginnis	1991	C. James Lawler
1939-40	Edwin Bergstrom	1992	W. Cecil Steward
1941-2	Richmond H. Shreve	1993	Susan A. Maxman
1943-4	Raymond J. Ashton	1994	L. William Chapin Jr.
1945-6	James R. Edmunds Jr.	1995	Chester A. Widom
1947-8	Douglas W. Orr	1996	Raymond G. "Skipper" Post Jr.
1949-50	Ralph T. Walker	1997	Raj Barr-Kumar
1951-2	A. Glenn Stanton	1998	Ronald A. Altoon
1953-4	Clair W. Ditchy	1999	Michael J. Stanton
1955-6	George B. Cummings	2000	Ronald Skaggs
1957-8	Leon Chatelain Jr.	2001	John D. Anderson
1959-60	John Noble Richards	2002	Gordon Chong
1961-2	Philip Will Jr.		
1963	Henry L. Wright		
1964	J. Roy Carroll Jr.		
1965	A. Gould Odell Jr.		

Source: The American Institute of Architects

Presidents of the American Society of Interior Designers

1974-75	Norman DeHann	1989-90	Elizabeth Howard
1974-76	Richard Jones	1990-91	Robert John Dean
1977-78	H. Albert Phibbs	1991-92	Raymond Kennedy
1978-79	Irving Schwartz	1992-93	Martha G. Rayle
1979-80	Rita St. Clair	1993-94	BJ Peterson
1980-81	Wallace Jonason	1994-95	Gary Wheeler
1981-82	Jack Lowery	1995-96	Penny Bonda
1982-83	Martin Ellinoff	1996-97	Kathy Ford Montgomery
1984-85	William Richard Waley	1997-98	Joyce Burke Jones
1985-86	Gail Adams	1998-99	Rosalyn Cama
1986-87	Janet Schirn	1999-2000	Juliana M. Catlin
1987-88	Joy Adcock	2000-01	Terri Maurer
1988-89	Charles Gandy	2001-02	Barbara Nugent

Source: American Society of Interior Designers

Style, like the weather, is only discussed when it is extraordinarily good or bad.

Paola Antonelli

Presidents of the American Society of Landscape Architects

1899-1901	John C. Olmsted*	1975-1976	Edward H. Stone II
1902	Samuel Parsons Jr.*	1976-1977	Benjamin W. Gary Jr.
1903	Nathan F. Barrett*	1977-1978	Lane L. Marshall
1904-1905	John C. Olmsted*	1978-1979	Jot Carpenter
1906-1907	Samuel Parsons Jr.*	1979-1980	Robert L. Woerner
1908-1909	Frederick Law Olmsted Jr.*	1980-1981	William A. Behnke
1910-1911	Charles N. Lowrie*	1981-1982	Calvin T. Bishop
1912	Harold A. Caparn	1982-1983	Theodore J. Wirth
1913	Ossian C. Simonds*	1983-1984	Darwina L. Neal
1914	Warren H. Manning*	1984-1985	Robert H. Mortensen
1915-1918	James Sturgis Pray	1985-1986	John Wacker
1919-1922	Frederick Law Olmsted Jr.*	1986-1987	Roger B. Martin
1923-1927	James L. Greenleaf	1987-1988	Cheryl L. Barton
1927-1931	Arthur A. Shurcliff	1988-1989	Brain S. Kubota
1931-1935	Henry Vincent Hubbard	1989-1990	Gerald D. Patten
1935-1941	Albert D. Taylor	1990-1991	Claire R. Bennett
1941-1945	S. Herbert Hare	1991-1992	Cameron R.J. Man
1945-1949	Markley Stevenson	1992-1993	Debra L. Mitchell
1949-1951	Gilmore D. Clarke	1993-1994	Thomas Papandrew
1951-1953	Lawrence G. Linnard	1994-1995	Dennis Y. Otsuji
1953-1957	Leon Zach	1995-1996	Vincent Bellafiore
1957-1961	Norman T. Newton	1996-1997	Donald W. Leslie
1961-1963	John I. Rogers	1997-1998	Thomas R. Dunbar
1963-1965	John Ormsbee Simonds	1998-1999	Barry W. Starke
1965-1967	Hubert B. Owens	1999-2000	Janice Cervelli Schach
1967-1969	Theodore Osmundson	2000-2001	Leonard J. Hopper
1969-1971	Campbell E. Miller	2001-2002	Paul Morris
1971-1973	Raymond L. Freeman		
1973-1974	William G. Swain	*Charter Member	
1974-1975	Owen H. Peters		

Source: American Society of Landscape Architects

Presidents of the Association of Collegiate Schools of Architecture

1912-21	Warren Laird, Univ. of Pennsylvania	1961-63	Olindo Grossi, Pratt Institute
1921-23	Emil Lorch, Univ. of Michigan	1963-65	Henry Kamphoefner, North Carolina St. College
1923-25	William Emerson, Massachusetts Institute of Technology	1965-67	Walter Sanders, Univ. of Michigan
1925-27	Francke Bosworth, Jr., Cornell Univ.	1967-69	Robert Bliss, Univ. of Utah
1927-29	Goldwin Goldsmith, Univ. of Kansas	1969-71	Charles Burchard, Virginia Polytechnic
1929-31	Everett Meeks, Yale Univ.	1971-72	Alan Taniguchi, Rice Univ. & Univ. of Texas, Austin
1931-34	Ellis Lawrence, Univ. of Oregon	1972-73	Robert Harris, Univ. of Oregon
1934-36	Roy Childs Jones, Univ. of Minnesota	1973-74	Sanford Greenfield, Boston Arch. Center
1936-38	Sherely Morgan, Princeton Univ.	1974-75	Don Schlegal, Univ. of New Mexico
1938-40	George Young, Jr., Cornell Univ.	1975-76	Bertram Berenson, Univ. of Illinois at Chicago
1940-42	Leopold Arnaud, Columbia Univ.	1976-77	Donlyn Lyndon, Massachusetts Institute of Technology
1942-45	Wells Bennett, Univ. of Michigan	1977-78	Dwayne Nuzum, Univ. of Colorado, Boulder
1945-47	Loring Provine, Univ. of Illinois	1978-79	William Turner, Tulane Univ.
1947-49	Paul Weigel, Kansas State College	1979-80	Robert Burns, North Carolina State Univ.
1949-51	B. Kenneth Johnstone, Carnegie Institute	1980-81	Richard Peters, Univ. of California, Berkeley
1951-53	Thomas FitzPatrick, Iowa State College	1981-82	Eugene Kremer, Kansas State Univ.
1953-55	Lawrence Anderson, Massachusetts Institute of Technology	1982-83	O. Jack Mitchell, Rice Univ.
1955-57	Elliott Whitaker, Ohio State Univ.	1983-84	Charles Hight, Univ. of North Carolina, Charlotte
1957-59	Buford Pickens, Washington Univ.	1984-85	Wilmot Gilland, Univ. of Oregon
1959-61	Harlan McClure, Clemson College	1985-86	George Anselevicius, Univ. of New Mexico

Presidents of the Association of Collegiate Schools of Architecture (Con't)

1986-87	Blanche Lemco van Ginkel, Univ. of Toronto	1995-96	Robert Greenstreet, Univ. of Wisconsin-Milwaukee
1987-88	J. Thomas Regan, Univ. of Miami	1996-97	Linda W. Sanders, Calif. State Polytechnic Univ.
1988-89	Robert Beckley, Univ. of Michigan	1997-98	John M. McRae, Mississippi State Univ.
1989-90	Marvin Malecha, Cal. State Poly. Univ., Pomona	1998-99	R. Wayne Drummond, Univ. of Florida
1990-91	John Meunier, Arizona State Univ.	1999-00	Jerry Finrow, Univ. of Washington
1991-92	Patrick Quinn, Rensselaer Polytechnic Institute	2000-01	Tony Schuman, New Jersey Institute of Technology
1992-93	James Barker, Clemson Univ.	2001-02	Frances Bronet, Renssalaer Polytechnic Institute
1993-94	Kent Hubbell, Cornell Univ.		
1994-95	Diane Ghirardo, Univ. of Southern California		

Source: Association of Collegiate Schools of Architecture

Did you know...

The Eiffel Tower is repainted every seven years with 50 tons of dark brown paint.

Presidents of the Construction Specifications Institute

1948-49	James B. Moore	1976-77	Philip J. Todisco
1949-50	James B. Moore	1977-78	Louis H. Sams
1950-51	Francis R. Wragg	1978-79	R. Stanley Bair
1951-52	Carl J. Ebert	1979-80	Howard R. Steinmann
1952-53	Carl J. Ebert	1980-81	George S. George
1953-54	Lester T. Burn	1981-82	Robert J. Schmidt
1954-55	Lester T. Burn	1982-83	Terry J. Strong
1955-56	Joseph A. McGinnis	1983-84	Donald D. Meisel
1956-57	J. Norman Hunter	1984-85	Terry M. Wadsworth
1957-58	J. Norman Hunter	1985-86	Richard B. Solomon
1958-59	J. Stewart Stein	1986-87	Charles Chief Boyd
1959-60	J. Stewart Stein	1987-88	Robert L. McManus
1960-61	Glen H. Abplanalp	1988-89	Weldon W. Nash, Jr.
1961-62	James C. Bort	1989-90	S. Steve Blumenthal
1962-63	Edwin T. Pairo	1990-91	Robert W. Johnson
1963-64	Jack R. Lewis	1991-92	Sheldon B. Israel
1964-65	Terrell R. Harper	1992-93	Thomas I. Young
1965-66	Henry B. Baume	1993-94	Jerome H. Alciatore
1966-67	Henry B. Baume	1994-95	William F. Riesberg
1967-68	John C. Anderson	1995-96	Jane D. Baker
1968-69	Kelsey Y. Saint	1996-97	Richard A. Eustis
1969-70	Arthur W. Brown	1997-98	Robert R. Molseed
1970-71	Ben F. Greenwood	1998-99	Kenneth E. Guthrie
1971-72	Arthur J. Miller	1999-00	Alana Griffith
1972-73	John C. Fleck	2000-01	James Chaney
1973-74	Robert E. Vansant	2001-02	Ross Spiegel
1974-75	Larry C. Dean		
1975-76	Larry C. Dean		

Source: Construction Specification Institute

Presidents of the Industrial Designers Society of America

1965	Henry Dreyfuss	1985-86	Cooper C. Woodring
1966	Joseph M. Parriott	1987-88	Peter H. Wooding
1967-68	Robert Hose	1989-90	Peter W. Bressler
1969-70	Tucker Madawick	1991-92	Charles Pelly
1971-72	William Goldsmith	1993-94	David Tompkins
1973-74	Arthur Pulos	1995-96	James Ryan
1975-76	James Fulton	1997-98	Craig Vogel
1977-78	Richard Hollerith	1999-00	Mark Dziersk
1979-80	Carroll M. Gantz	2001-02	Betty Baugh
1981-82	Robert G. Smith		
1983-84	Katherine J. McCoy		

Source: Industrial Designers Society of America

Every object has a story. Design has become so shallow, just about the radius of a corner; but there is so much more. You have to say something.

Ingo Maurer

Presidents of the International Interior Design Association

1994-1995   Marilyn Farrow
1995-1996   Judith Hastings
1996-1997   Beth Harmon-Vaughan
1997-1998   Karen Guenther
1998-1999   Neil Frankel
1999-2000   Carol Jones
2000-2001   Richard Pollack
2001-2002   Cary D. Johnson

Source: International Interior Design Association

Unless we can come to terms
with the global image economy
and the way it permeates the
things we make and see, we are
doomed to a life of decorating
and redecorating.

Bruce Mau

Presidents of the National Council for Architectural Registration Boards

1920-22	Emil Loch	1973	Thomas J. Sedgewick
1923-24	Arthur Peabody	1974	E.G. Hamilton
1925	Miller I. Kast	1975	John (Mel) O'Brien Jr.
1926-27	W.H. Lord	1976	William C. Muchow
1928	George D. Mason	1977	Charles A. Blondheim Jr.
1929-30	Clarence W. Brazer	1978	Paul H. Graven
1931-32	James M. White	1979	Lorenzo D. Williams
1933	A.L. Brockway	1980	John R. Ross
1933	A.M. Edelman	1981	Dwight M. Bonham
1934-35	Joseph W. Holman	1982	Thomas H. Flesher Jr.
1936	Charles Butler	1983	Sid Frier
1938-39	William Perkins	1984	Ballard H.T. Kirk
1940-41	Mellen C. Greeley	1985	Robert E. Oringdulph
1942-44	Louis J. Gill	1986	Theodore L. Mularz
1945-46	Solis Seiferth	1987	Robert L. Tessier
1947-49	Warren D. Miller	1988	Walter T. Carry
1950	Clinton H. Cowgill	1989	George B. Terrien
1951	Roger C. Kirchoff	1990	Herbert P. McKim
1952-52	Charles E. Firestone	1991	Charles E. Garrison
1954-55	Fred L. Markham	1992	Robert H. Burke Jr.
1956-58	Edgar H. Berners	1993	Harry G. Robinson III
1959-60	Walter F. Martens		William Wiese II (Honorary Past
1961	A. Reinhold Melander		President)
1962	Chandler C. Cohagen	1994	Robert A. Fielden
1963	Paul W. Drake	1995	Homer L. Williams
1964	Ralph O. Mott	1996	Richard W. Quinn
1965	C.J. "Pat" Paderewski	1997	Darrell L. Smith
1966	Earl L. Mathes	1998	Ann R. Chaintreuil
1967	George F. Schatz	1999	Susan May Allen
1968-69	Howard T. Blanchard	2000	Joseph P. Giattina Jr.
1970	Dean L. Gustavson	2001	William Bevins
1971	William J. Geddis		
1972	Daniel Boone		

Source: National Council for Architectural Registration Boards

Presidents of the Royal Institute of British Architects

1835-59	Earl de Grey	1935-37	Sir Percy Thomas
1860	Charles Robert Cockerell	1937-39	H.S. Goodhart-Rendel
1861-63	Sir William Tite	1939-40	E. Stanley Hall
1863-65	Thomas L. Donaldson	1940-43	W.H. Ansell
1865-67	A.J.B. Beresford Hope	1943-46	Sir Percy Thomas
1867-70	Sir William Tite	1946-48	Sir Lancelot Keay
1870-73	Thomas Henry Wyatt	1948-50	Michael T. Waterhouse
1873-76	Sir Gilbert G. Scott	1950-52	A. Graham Henderson
1876-79	Charles Barry	1952-54	Sir Howard Robertson
1879-81	John Whichcord	1954-56	C.H. Aslin
1881	George Edmund Street	1956-58	Kenneth M.B. Cross
1882-84	Sir Horace Jones	1958-60	Sir Basil Spence
1884-86	Ewan Christian	1960-62	The Lord Holford
1886-87	Edward l'Anson	1962-64	Sir Robert Matthew
1888-91	Alfred Watershouse	1964-65	Sir Donald Gibson
1891-94	J. Macvicar Anderson	1965-67	The Viscount Esher
1884-96	Francis C. Penrose	1967-69	Sir Hugh Wilson
1896-99	George Aitchison	1969-71	Sir Peter Shepheard
1899-1902	Sir William Emerson	1971-73	Sir Alex Gordon
1902-04	Sir Aston Webb	1973-75	F.B. Pooley
1904-06	John Belcher	1975-77	Eric Lyons
1906-08	Thomas Edward Collcutt	1977-79	Gordon Graham
1908-10	Sir Ernest George	1979-81	Bryan Jefferson
1910-12	Leonard Stokes	1981-83	Owen Luder
1912-14	Sir Reginald Blomfield	1983-85	Michael Manser
1914-17	Ernest Newton	1985-87	Larry Rolland
1917-19	Henry Thomas Hare	1987-89	Rod Hackney
1919-21	Sir John William Simpson	1989-91	Max Hutchinson
1921-23	Paul Waterhouse	1991-93	Richard C. MacCormac
1923-25	J. Alfred Gotch	1993-95	Frank Duffy
1925-27	Sir Guy Dawber	1995-97	Owen Luder
1927-29	Sir Walter Tapper	1997-99	David Rock
1929-31	Sir Banister Fletcher	1999-2001	Marco Goldschmied
1931-33	Sir Raymond Unwin	2001-03	Paul Hyett
1933-35	Sir Giles Gilbert Scott		

Source: Royal Institute of British Architects

Presidents of the Society of Architectural Historians

1941-42	Turpin C. Bannister		1970-71	James F. O'Gorman
1943-44	Rexford Newcomb		1972-74	Alan W. Gowans
1945-47	Kenneth John Conant		1975-76	Spiro Kostof
1948-49	Carroll L.V. Meeks		1976-78	Marian C. Donnelly
1950	Buford L. Pickens		1978-80	Adolph K. Placzek
1951	Charles E. Peterson		1982-84	Damie Stillman
1952-53	Henry-Russell Hitchcock		1984-86	Carol Herselle Krinsky
1954	Agnes Addison Gilchrist		1986-88	Osmund Overby
1955-56	James G. Van Derpool		1988-90	Richard J. Betts
1957-58	Carroll L. V. Meeks		1990-93	Elisabeth Blair MacDougall
1959	Walter L. Creese		1993-94	Franklin Toker
1960-61	Barbara Wriston		1994-96	Keith N. Morgan
1962-63	John D. Forbes		1996-98	Patricia Waddy
1964-65	H. Allen Brooks		1998-00	Richard Longstreth
1966-67	George B. Tatum		2000-02	Christopher Mead
1968-69	Henry A. Millon			

Source: Society of Architectural Historians

Did you know...

The cupola on St. Peter's Basilica in the Vatican stands 435 feet above the ground, almost 150 feet taller than the U.S. Capitol.

Records, Rankings
& Achievements

The world's tallest buildings, sports stadiums, and the leading 20th century women design leaders are just some of the notable accomplishments covered in this chapter. Numerous other rankings and ratings are available for professional reference and diversion. Firm-specific rankings can be found in The Firms chapter beginning on page 477, and a listing of the most visited historic house museums is available on page 436.

Architecture Critics

Below is a listing of the major U.S. newspapers that regulary feature architectural writing and criticism. Some papers have a staff architecture critic while others an art critic or critic-at-large that routinely cover architecture stories for the paper.

Arizona Republic
John Carlos Billian
Art & Architecture Critic
200 East Van Buren Street
Phoenix, AZ 85004
Tel: (602) 448-8000
Internet: www.arizonarepublic.com

Atlanta Journal-Constitution
Cathy Fox
Architecture Critic
PO Box 4689
Atlanta, GA 30302
Tel: (404) 526-5151
Internet: www.ajc.com

Austin American-Statesman
Michael Barnes
Arts Critic
PO Box 670
Austin, TX 78767
Tel: (512) 445-3500
Internet: www.statesman.com

Baltimore Sun
Edward Gunts
Critic-at-Large/Reporter
501 N. Calvert Street
P.O. Box 1377
Baltimore, MD 21278
Tel: (410) 332-6000
Internet: www.baltimoresun.com

Bergen Record
John Zeaman
Art Critic
150 River Street
Hackensack, NJ 07601
Tel: (201) 646-4000
Internet: www.bergen.com

Boston Globe
Robert Campbell
Architecture Critic
320 Congress Street
Boston, MA 02110
Tel: (617) 929-2000
Internet: www.bostonglobe.com

Boston Herald
Robert Campbell
Architecture Critic
One Herald Square
P.O. Box 2056
Boston, MA 02106
Tel: (617) 426-3000
Internet: www.bostonherald.com

Charleston Post and Courier
Robert Behre
Architecture & Preservation Critic
134 Columbus Street
Charleston, SC 29403-4800
Tel: (843) 577-7111
Internet: www.charleston.net

Charlotte Observer
Richard Maschal
Home Editor
600 S. Tryon Street
Charlotte, NC 28202
Tel: (704) 377-5555
Internet: www.charlotte.com

Chicago Tribune
Blair Kamin
Architecture Critic
435 N. Michigan Avenue
Chicago, IL 60611
Tel: (312) 222-3232
Internet: www.chicagotribune.com

Architecture Critics (Con't)

Cleveland Plain Dealer
Steve Lit
Art & Architecture Critic
700 West St. Clair Avenue
Suite 414
Cleveland, OH 44113
Tel: (800) 362-0727
Internet: www.cleveland.com

Dallas Morning News
Janet Kutner
Art Critic
P.O. Box 655237
Dallas, TX 75265
Tel: (214) 977-8222
Internet: www.dallasnews.com

Dayton Daily News
Ron Rollins
Critic-at-Large
45 S. Ludlow Street
Dayton, OH 45402
Tel: (937) 225-2000
Internet: www.daytondailynews.com

Denver Post
Kyle MacMillan
Critic-at-Large
1560 Broadway
Denver, CO 80202
Tel: (800) 366-7678
Internet: www.denverpost.com

Los Angeles Times
Nicolai Ouroussoff
Architecture Critic
202 West 1st Street
Los Angeles, CA 90012
Tel: (213) 237-5000
Internet: www.latimes.com

Louisville Courier-Journal
Diane Heilenman
Art Critic
525 W. Broadway
P.O. Box 740031
Louisville, KY 40201-7431
Tel: (502) 582-4011
Internet: www.courier-journal.com

Milwaukee Journal Sentinel
Whitney Gould
Urban Landscape Writer
P.O. Box 371
Milwaukee, WI 53201
Tel: (414) 224-2358
Internet: www.onwis.com

Minneapolis Star-Tribune
Linda Mack
Architecture Critic
425 Portland Avenue
Minneapolis, MN 55488
Tel: (612) 673-4000
Internet: www.startribune.com

New York Times
Herbert Muschamp
Architecture Critic
229 43rd Street
New York, NY 10036
Tel: (212) 556-1234
Internet: www.nyt.com

New Yorker
Paul Goldberger
Architectire Critic
4 Times Square
New York, NY 10036-6592
Tel: (212) 286-5400
Internet: www.newyorker.com

Newark Star-Ledger
Stan Bischoff
Art Critic
1 Star-Ledger Plaza
Newark, NJ 07102
Tel: (973) 877-4141
Internet: www.nj.com

Newport News Daily Press
Mark Erickson
Critic-at-Large/Reporter
7505 Warwick Boulevard
Newport News, VA 23607
Tel: (757) 247-4800
Internet: www.dailypress.com

Architecture Critics (Con't)

Philadelphia Inquirer
Inga Saffron
Architecture Critic
400 N. Broad Street
P.O. Box 8263
Philadelphia, PA 19101
Tel: (215) 854-2000
Internet: www.phillynews.com

Pittsburgh Post-Gazette
Patricia Lowry
Architecture Critic
34 Blvd. Of the Allies
Pittsburgh, PA 15222
Tel: (412) 263-1100
Internet: www.post-gazette.com

Portland Oregonian
Randy Gragg
Architecture Critic
1320 SW Broadway
Portland, OR 97201
Tel: (503) 221-8327
Internet: www.oregonian.com

Providence Journal
Bill VanSiclen
Art Critic
28 Pelham Street
Providence, RI 02840-3044
Tel: (401) 277-7000
Internet: www.projo.com

Raleigh News & Observer
Christina Dyrness
Critic-at-Large
215 S. McDowell Street
P.O. Box 191
Raleigh, NC 27601
Tel: (919) 829-4500
Internet: www.news-observer.com

Rocky Mountain News
Mary Voelz Chandler
Art Critic
400 West Colfax Avenue
Denver, CO 80204
Tel: (303) 892-5000
Internet: www.rockymountainnews.com

San Antonio Express-News
Mike Greenberg
Arts & Entertainment Critic
400 3rd Street
San Antonia, TX 78287-2171
Tel: (210) 250-3000
Internet: www.mysanantonio.com

San Diego Union-Tribune
Ann Jarmusch
Architecture Critic
P.O. Box 120191
San Diego, CA 92112-0191
Tel: (619) 299-3131
Internet: www.uniontrib.com

San Francisco Chronicle
Allan Temko
Critic-at-Large/Reporter
901 Mission Street
San Francisco, CA 94103
Tel: (415) 777-1111
Internet: www.sfgate.com

San Jose Mercury News
Alan Hess
Architecture Writer
750 Ridder Park Drive
San Jose, CA 95190
Tel: (408) 920-5000
Internet: www.mercurycenter.com

Seattle Times
Linda Parrish
Home & Garden Critic
1120 John Street
Seattle, WA 98109
Tel: (206) 464-2111
Internet: www.seattletimes.nwsource.com

South Florida Sun-Sentinel
Matt Schudell
Art & Architecture Critic
200 E. Las Olas Blvd
Ft. Lauderdale, FL 33301
Tel: (954) 356-4000
Internet: www.sun-sentinel.com

Architecture Critics (Con't)

St. Paul Pioneer Press
Larry Millett
Architecture Critic
345 Cedar Street
St. Paul, MN 55101
Tel: (651) 222-1111
Internet: www.pioneerplanet.com

Toledo Blade
Sally Vallongo
Feature Editor
541 N. Superior Street
Toledo, OH 43660
Tel: (419) 724-6000
Internet: www.toledoblade.com

Washington Post
Ben Forgey
Architecture Critic
1150 15th Street NW
Washington, DC 20071
Tel: (202) 334-6000
Internet: www.washingtonpost.com

Source: Council House Research

Century's Top 10 Construction Achievements

The Top 10 Construction Achievements of the 20th Century were chosen from a list of over a 100 international nominations which included such diverse projects as bridges, dams, highways, roads, tunnels, buildings, stadiums, commercial centers, and transportation facilities. Besides requiring that the projects be entirely developed during the 20th century, the selection criteria also included integrity in construction and design, contribution to improving the quality of life, technological progressiveness, and positive economic impact. This program was established to promote the construction industry's increased contribution to the advancement of our society. The final judging occurred at the triennial CONEXPO-CON/AGG exposition in March 1999 in Las Vegas by a panel of editors and executives from the construction and construction materials industry.

1. The Channel Tunnel between Dover, England and Calais, France

2. The Golden Gate Bridge, San Francisco

3. The U.S. Interstate Highway System

4. The Empire State Building, New York City

5. Hoover Dam, Nevada and Arizona

6. The Panama Canal

7. Sydney Opera House, Sydney, Australia

8. Aswan High Dam, Egypt

9. The World Trade Center, New York City

10. Chek Lap Kok Airport, Hong Kong

Source: Architecture *magazine and CONEXPO-CON/AGG*

Did you know...

The Pantheon dome (142 feet in diameter), completed in 123 A.D., remained the world's largest dome for 1,300 years.

Construction Costs - 25 Least Expensive Cities

The following cities are currently the least expensive locales in the United States and Canada to construct a building according to R.S. Means, the country's leading construction costing company. This ranking is based on 2000 square foot costs for a 2-4 story office building of average construction type. Costs include labor, materials, and professional design fees.

1. Fayetteville, Arkansas
2. Alliance, Nebraska
3. Asheville, North Carolina
    Charlotte, North Carolina
    Winston-Salem, North Carolina
    Charleston, South Carolina
    Columbia, South Carolina
8. Jackson, Mississippi
    Durham, North Carolina
    Greensboro, South Carolina
    Raleigh, North Carolina
    McAllen, Texas
    Martinsburg, West Virginia
14. Tallahassee, Florida
    Laredo, Texas
    Yellowstone Nat. Pk., Wyoming

17. Columbus, Georgia
    Aberdeen, South Dakota
    El Paso, Texas
20. Rapid City, South Dakota
    Abilene, Texas
    Corpus Christi, Texas
23. Montgomery, Alabama
    Biloxi, Mississippi
    Knoxville, Tennessee
    Lubbock, Texas
    Waco, Texas
    Wichita Falls, Texas

Source: R.S. Means

Did you know...

The retrofit of California's Big Tujunga Canyon Road Bridge managed to preserve the structure's historic aesthetics as well as reduce costs by 30-50% by wrapping the bridge in Tyfo Fibrwrap, a .051 inch thick mesh fabric composed of fiberglass, Kevlar, and carbon fiber.

Construction Costs - 25 Most Expensive Cities

The following cities are currently the most expensive locales in the United States and Canada to construct a building according to R.S. Means, the country's leading construction costing company. This ranking is based on 2000 square foot costs for a 2-4 story office building of average construction type. Costs include labor, materials, and professional design fees.

1. New York, New York
2. Brooklyn, New York
3. Anchorage, Alaska
   Fairbanks, Alaska
   San Francisco, California
6. Honolulu, Hawaii
7. Yonkers, New York
8. San Jose, California
9. Oakland, California
10. Berkeley, California
    Palo Alto, California
12. Santa Rosa, California
13. Boston, Massachusetts
14. Vallejo, California

15. Salinas, California
    Chicago, Illinois
    Newark, New Jersey
    Paterson, New Jersey
19. Philadelphia, Pennsylvania
    Toronto, Ontario, Canada
21. Sacramento, California
    Jersey City, New Jersey
    Trenton, New Jersey
24. Modesto, California
    Stockton, California
    North Suburban, Illinois
    South Suburban, Illinois

Source: R.S. Means

Did you know...

The following U.S. cities were the fastest growing in the 1990s in terms of the increase in their housing stock between 1990 and 1998: Las Vegas, NV; Naples, FL; Provo, UT; Boise City, ID; Laredo, TX; Wilmington, NC; Raleigh-Durham, NC; Orlando, FL; Atlanta, GA; Fort Collins, CO.

Leading Women Architects and Designers of the 20th Century

The following women are some of many female leaders in the design professions throughout the 20th Century, selected by the editors of the *Almanac of Architecture & Design* to broaden awareness of and generate interest in the contributions of women to design. There are, however, many outstanding female contributors to the profession, and, as such, this is list is only intended to serve as the beginnings of an understanding of the influential role of women architects and designers during the last century.

Aino Aalto

Finnish. Born Aino Marso (1894-1949). Aino Aalto graduated from the Helsinki University of Technology in 1919. In 1921 she married and formed a professional partnership with Alvar Aalto in Jyväskylä, Finland. Aino designed interiors, furniture, fixtures and glass objects. Her glass designs, which were awarded a prize at the Milan Triennial in 1936, are still being manufactured today. She was the principal in Artek, which manufactured furniture and artifacts, from its founding in 1936 until her death. Aino designed the majority of Artek's furniture, lamps, screens, household objects, mats and other textiles. Up until 1949, all of Alvar Aalto's exhibitions and works were signed 'Aino and Alvar Aalto.'

Suzana Antonakakis

Greek. Born Suzana-Maria Kolokytha in Athens, Greece on June 25, 1935. Suzana Antonakakis studied at the National Technical University, School of Architecture, in Athens, 1954-59, and established a partnership with her husband Dimitris in 1958. She has also worked as an architect/consultant for the Archaeological and Restoration Service of Athens and has lectured internationally. Her firm has been influenced by Modernism and the rich historical environment of Greece. Her architecture demonstrates a creative use of space. Geometry, materials, and socio-cultural values are combined in a rational yet complex structure.

Gae(tana) Aulenti

Italian. Born in Palazolo dello Stella (Udine), Italy on December 4, 1927. Gae Aulenti received her Dip. Arch. from the Milan Polytechnic's School of Architecture in 1954. She has been in private practice in Milan as an exhibition and industrial designer since 1954. She has also taught in Venice, Milan, Barcelona, and Stockholm. Her other professional involvements include serving as a member of the editorial staff of *Casabella-Continuità* from 1955-65 and on the Directional Board of *Lotus International* magazine since 1974. Aulenti's work, which includes exhibition design, interiors as well as architecture, evolved in the Milanese architecture scene of which she has become one of its major exponents. She has won many prestigious industrial design and architectural prizes. Her most famous work to date is her conversion of the Gare d'Orsay in Paris into the highly successful Museum d'Orsay.

Mary Jane Elizabeth Colter

American. Born in Pittsburgh, Pennsylvania (1869-1958). Mary Jane Colter attended the California School of Design in 1886 and then apprenticed at a local architect's office in 1887. In 1901 she began a forty-year career as a designer for the Fred Harvey Company, which operated hotels, restaurants, shops and dining cars for the Santa Fe Railway. She was one of the few female architects working in the United States at that time. Her buildings include Hopi House, Lookout Studio,

Leading Women Architects and Designers of the 20th Century (Con't)

Hermit's Rest, and the Watchtower (all at the Grand Canyon). Colter used local building traditions and materials to create buildings that appropriately fit into the spectacular natural wonder of the South Rim of the Grand Canyon.

Sylvia Crowe

British. Born in Barnbury, Oxfordshire, England (1901-97). Sylvia Crowe studied at Swanley Horticultural College in Kent, 1920-22, and worked in private practice as a landscape architect in London beginning in 1945. Crowe was President of the Institute of Landscape Architects in London from 1957-61. She also won the Woman of the Year Award from London's Architects' Journal in 1970. Sylvia Crowe held Honorary Doctorates from the University of Newcastle, Heriot–Watt University in Edinburgh, University of Sussex, and University of Brighton. She was also made an Honorary Fellow of the Royal Institute of British Architects in 1969. Although Crowe was first recognized for her domestic garden designs, her career was largely served with postwar architects and town planners. Through her professional work and books, Crowe dedicated her career to the interests of landscape as a whole.

Jane Beverly Drew

British. Born in Thornton Heath, Surrey, England (1911-96). Drew received her diploma from London's Architectural Association, School of Architecture in 1934. She worked with her husband, E. Maxwell Fry, from 1945-77 in Fry Drew and Partners, London, and served as the joint editor of the *Architects Yearbook* from 1946-62. Drew also taught at the Massachusetts Institute of Technology and Harvard University. Among her awards are Honorary Doctorates from the University of Ibadan, Nigeria; Open University, Milton Keynes, Buckinghamshire; University of Newcastle; and Witwaterstrand University, Johannesburg. Much of Drew's work was in Africa and on the Indian continent. Her architecture is characterized by a functional adaptation of the modern idiom to tropical buildings. Some of her best earlier work was in conjunction with Le Corbusier, Pierre Jeanneret and Maxwell Fry in Chandigarh, India.

Joan Edelman Goody

American. Born Joan Edelman in New York City, December 1, 1935. Joan Goody studied at the University of Paris from 1954-55, received her B.A from Cornell University in 1956, and earned a M. Arch. degree from the Harvard Graduate School of Design in 1960. She has been a principal at Goody, Clancy and Associates in Boston since 1961. In 1983 she received *Progressive Architecture's* Urban Planing Award and has won numerous awards from The American Institute of Architects, the Boston Society of Architects, and the American Planning Association. Much of Good's work is contextual and demonstrates sensitivity to community, scale, and regional building traditions.

Eileen Gray

Irish. Born in Brownswood, Enniscorthy, County Wexford, Ireland, (1879-1976). Eileen Gray studied at the Slate School of Art in London from 1898-1902 and worked as an architect in France from 1926 until her death in 1976. She was awarded the Honorary Royal Designer for Industry from the Royal Society of Arts, London, in 1972 and was made a Fellow of the Royal Institute of Irish Architects, Dublin, in 1973. Eileen Gray was a furniture designer who also designed a small number of buildings and interiors. Her architecture reflected the close affinity between furniture and building. She also brought humanity to modernism. Although small in number, her architectural work was quite original and skillful, such as her house, E. 1027, which was sometimes attributed to Le Corbusier or to the architect and critic Jean Badovici who assisted Gray on the house.

Leading Women Architects and Designers of the 20th Century (Con't)

Zaha Hadid
Iraqi. Born in Baghdad in 1950. Zaha Hadid studied at the American University in Beirut and under Rem Koolhaas at London's Architectural Association, School of Architecture from which she graduated in 1977. She was a Unit Master at the Architectural Association from 1977-87 and a visiting professor at Harvard and Columbia University in 1986 and 1987. Hadid received the British Architectural Awards' Gold Medal in 1982. Although she won numerous first prizes in international building competitions during the 1980s, Hadid actually built little during that period. Generally known as a Deconstructivist, Hadid has been classified in this group since the 1988 MoMA exhibition entitled "Deconstructive Architecture." Her recent work, such as the Vitra Fire Station and her garden pavilion, both in Weil am Rhein, Germany, displays a mastery of form and technology.

Itsuko Hasegawa
Japanese. Born in Yaizu City, Japan in 1941. Itsuko Hasegawa graduated from the College of Engineering, Kanto Gakuin University in 1964. In 1976 she established the Itsuko Hasegawa Atelier, which was renamed the Architectural Design Studio in 1979. Hasegawa has also served as lecturer at the Women's College of Art in Tokyo since 1972 and has lectured internationally. She won the Prize of Architectural Institute of Japan for Design in 1986 and the Grand Prize of Proposal Design Competition for the Niigata Municipal Cultural Hall in 1993. Hasegawa is one of the most famous female architects practicing in Japan today. Her architecture combines expressive forms inspired by nature with the innovative use of leading edge materials.

Florence Knoll
American. Born Florence Schust in Saginaw, Michigan in 1917. Florence Knoll graduated from the Cranbrook Academy of Art and studied under Le Corbusier at the Architectural Association in London. In 1942 she completed her architectural training under Ludwig Mies van der Rohe at the Armour Institute (now the Illinois Institute of Technology) in Chicago. In 1946 with her husband Hans Knoll, she formed Knoll Associates in which she organized and directed Knoll's Planning Unit to handle its interior-design operations. She was a pioneer for modern design and designed offices, furniture, and the Knoll show rooms which projected the company's image. Hers was the mind, the controlling hand and the animating spirit behind Knoll's success.

Julia Morgan
American. Born in San Francisco (1872-1957). Julia Morgan studied at the University of California at Berkeley where she was one of the first women to graduate with a Degree in Civil Engineering in 1894. With the encouragement of Bernard Maybeck, she went to Paris to study architecture and became the first women architect granted a L'Ecole des Beaux Arts certificate in 1902. She established her own practice in San Francisco in 1904 and over her long career designed over 700 buildings – from the Hearst Castle at San Simeon, to private homes and pubic buildings. Morgan's approach to architecture reflected the classicism of her Beaux-Arts education and the influence of the California Arts and Crafts movement.

Käpy Paavilainen
Finish. Born in Vaasa, Finland in 1944. Käpy Paavilainen studied at the Helsinki University of

Did you know...

In 1888 Louise Blanchard Bethune (1856-1913) became the first woman to be accepted into The American Institute of Architects.

Leading Women Architects and Designers of the 20th Century (Con't)

Technology where she received a Dip. Arch. in 1975. In 1977 she established a partnership with her husband in Helsinki. She has been a visiting lecturer at the Helsinki University of Technology since 1982 and served as a visiting lecturer in Barcelona and Berlin. Paavilainen won the Architectural Prize, Tiili, in 1983 and the State Award for Architecture and Community Planning. Most of her work is in Finland. Her architecture is minimal yet has important classical influences and is characterized by close attention to place with materials that provide a contextual richness.

Patricia Patkau

Canadian. Born in Winnipeg, Manitoba in 1950. Patricia Patkau received a BA in 1973 from the University of Manitoba and a MA from Yale University in 1978. Since 1992 she has been an associate professor at the School of Architecture, University of British Columbia. In 1978 she established a partnership with her husband John in Edmonton, Alberta, which in 1984 moved to Vancouver, British Columbia. The firm has won numerous awards of excellence and many first prizes in competitions. Patricia Patkau describes her work as focusing on the particular in an effort to balance the tendency towards generalization which is increasingly dominant in Western culture.

Charlotte Perriand

French. Born in Paris, France (1903-99). Charlotte Perriand studied design at the Ecole de l'Union Centrale des Arts Décoratifs in Paris from 1920-25. She began working in private practice in Paris in 1927 when she established her own studio in the Place Saint Suplice, 1927-30, and in the Boulevard de Montparnasse, 1930-37. She also served as the associate in charge of furniture and fittings in the studio of Le Corbusier from 1927-37. From 1937-40 she worked with Jean Prouvé, Pierre Jeanneret, and Georges Blanchon in Paris. She also began an office for prefabricated building

research in Paris in 1940. Throughout her career she worked frequently in Tokyo, Rio de Janeiro and other cities in Latin America. She served as a member of the editorial board for *Architecture d'aujourd'hui* in Paris, 1930-74. During her long and highly successful career, Perriand received international recognition for her interior designs as well as their furnishings.

Elizabeth Plater-Zyberk

American. Born in Bryn Mawr, Pennsylvania in 1950. Elizabeth Plater-Zyberk received her B.A. in Architecture and Urban Planning from Princeton University in 1971 and a Master of Architecture from Yale in 1974. Plater-Zyberk is a co-founder and principal in Duany Plater-Zyberk & Company, which was begun in 1980, as well as an Associate Professor and Director of the Masters of Architecture program at the University of Miami. She and her partner, Andres Duany, have developed design principles of urban form based on traditional towns, which they implemented in the now famous town of Seaside, Florida. Since 1980 they have designed over eighty new towns and revitalization projects for existing communities and won many awards and much international recognition.

Madhu Sarin

Indian. Born in India in 1945. Madhu Sarin studied at the Punjab University, Chandigarh, India, where she received a Bachelor of Architecture in 1967. She also earned a post graduate diploma in Tropical Studies from the Architectural Association School of Architecture in London in 1980. She subsequently established her own practice and has worked as an advisor to the Indian Government and international organizations as well as directly with poor communities in the Punjab and Rajasthan. She has received several awards for professional excellence, including India's prestigious Vishwakarma Award in 1989. Madhu has always used her architectural training

Leading Women Architects and Designers of the 20th Century (Con't)

in creative ways to help those who most need her skills. In response to the fuel crisis in the Shiwalik foothills of the Himalayas, she designed a fuel efficient stove known as the Nadu Chula that has improved the lives of thousands of people living in many parts of the world where deforestation has occurred.

Denise Scott Brown

American. Born Denise Lakofskiin Nkana in Zambia, October 3, 1931. Denise Scott Brown emigrated to the United States in 1958 and was naturalized in 1967. Scott Brown studied at the University of the Witwaterstrand, Johannesburg, South Africa from 1948-51 and at the Architectural Association, School of Architecture in London, 1952-55, where she received an AA Diploma and Certificate in Tropical Architecture in 1956. She also studied at the University of Pennsylvania under Louis I. Kahn, 1958-60, and earned a Masters in City Planning in 1960. She has been the principal in charge of urban planning and design at Venturi, Scott Brown and Associates since 1989. Denise Scott Brown has taught at a number of Universities including Yale, University of Pennsylvania, Harvard, and MIT. Her work has received national and international recognition. Along with her husband, Robert Venturi, Scott Brown's built work and books such as *Learning from Las Vegas* ushered in Post-Modernism and influenced an entire generation of architects.

Alison Smithson

British. Born Alison Margaret Gill in Sheffield, England (1928-93). Alison Smithson studied architecture at the University of Durham, 1944-49. In 1950 she formed a partnership with her husband Peter. She was a founding member of Independent Group and was associated with Team 10 throughout her career. She also served as a lecturer at the Architectural Association, School of Architecture in London. Smithson practiced, taught, and also wrote a number of books. With

her husband-partner, she formed a team whose architectural influence extended beyond England. Their work has been described as a "Gentle Cultural Accommodation." Through their teaching at the Architectural Association they influenced generations of students throughout the world, among these Denise Scott-Brown.

Laurinda Spear

American. Born 1951. Laurinda Spear studied Fine Arts at Brown University, receiving her BA in 1972. She also earned a MA from Columbia University in 1975. She won the Rome Prize in Architecture in 1978 and awards from *Progressive Architecture* in 1978 and 1980. Spear is the principal and co-founder of Arquitectonica, which she formed in 1977 with her husband Barnardo Fort-Brescia. Their work is characterized by sculpted intersecting geometric forms and bright colors and is recognized as being stylistically appropriate for Miami.

Helena Syrkus

Polish. Born Helena Niemirowska in Warsaw, Poland, (1900-82). Helena Syrkus studied architecture at Warsaw's Institute of Technology from 1918-23 and humanities and philosophy at the University of Warsaw from 1923-25. Syrkus combined practice with teaching for much of her career, lecturing at the Institute of Architecture and Town Planning in Warsaw. She established a partnership with her husband in 1962 until her death in 1982. She won many national awards for both her architectural work and her writings. The life and work of Helena and her husband Szymon Syrkus are linked to international avant-garde architectural thought. The fundamental principle of their long partnership is that social co-operation is more rewarding than competition and rivalry.

Susana Torre

American. Born in Puan, Buenos Aires, Argentina, November 2, 1944 and later emigrated to the

Leading Women Architects and Designers of the 20th Century (Con't)

United States. Torre studied at the Universidad de La Plata, 1961-63 and received her Dipl. Arch. from the Universidad de Buenos Aires in 1967. Susana Torre also did post-graduate studies at Columbia University. She has been a principal of Susana Torre and Associates in New York since 1988 and has lectured and been a visiting critic at Columbia University, Yale University, Cooper Union, Carnegie Mellon and Syracuse University. She also served as a member of the editorial board for the *Journal of Architectural Education* from 1983-85 and received awards from Architectural Record and the National Endowment for the Arts. Her work is interesting for its recognition of groups who have experienced displacement (i.e. new immigrants) and its critical feminist consciousness. Urban memory also plays an important role in her designs.

Eva Vecsei

Canadian. Born Eva Hollo in Vienna, Austria, August 21, 1930, and emigrated to Canada in 1957 where she was naturalized in 1962. Eva Vecsei studied at the University of Technical Sciences, School of Architecture in Budapest from 1948-52 where she earned a BA in 1952. She has been in partnership with Andrew Vescei at Vescei Architects since 1984. She has received 5 Massey Architecture Awards and an Award of Excellence from *Canadian Architect*. In her 30s, she became the head designer for one of the largest buildings in the world, the Place Bonaventure in Montreal. Her second mammoth project was La Cité, Montreal's first large-scale mixed-use downtown development. No woman architect has ever before had such broad responsibility for the design and construction of projects of this magnitude and excellence.

Source: Pauline Morin

Did you know...

Percentage of women employed in architecture firms:

Overall architecture staff	**20%**
Principals/partners	**12**
Licensed architects	**13**
Interns	**31**
Other staff	**63**

Source: The American Institute of Architects

Most Admired Poll

In the fall 2001, *DesignIntelligence* assembled a jury of architects to rank various aspects of the built world, including cities, colleges & universities, and airports. In their consideration of cities–both in North America and the rest of the world–the jury ranked those most admired for their architecture and urban design merit. Cities of all sizes were considered, no other criteria were used. The jury also deliberated on airports and colleges & universities, which were ranked for their architectural merit, including aesthetics, functionality, and contribution to the built environment.

Most Admired Cities – North America
1. Chicago
2. Vancouver
3. Savannah
4. Toronto
5. San Francisco
6. Boston
7. Denver
8. Columbus (IN)
9. Minneapolis
10. Quebec

Most Admired Cities – Outside North America
1. Paris
2. Barcelona
3. Stockholm
4. Rome
5. Copenhagen
6. London
7. Sydney
8. Vienna
9. Venice
10. Berlin

Most Admired Airports
1. Ronald Reagan National Airport (Washington, D.C.)
2. Denver International Airport
3. Dulles International Airport (Chantilly, VA)
4. Chek Lap Kok International Airport (Hong Kong)
5. Kansai International Airport (Osaka, Japan)
6. Charles de Gaulle Airport (Paris, France)
7. United Terminal, O'Hare International Airport (Chicago)
8. Inchon International Airport (Seoul, Korea)
9. Copenhagen Airport (Denmark)
10. Orlando International Airport

Most Admired College and University Campuses
1. University of Virginia
2. Oxford University
3. Yale University
4. United States Air Force Academy
5. Cranbrook Academy of Art
6. Stanford University
7. Oberlin College
8. University of California, Santa Cruz
9. Harvard University
10. Cornell University

Jury:
James P. Cramer, Greenway (Chair)
Friedl Bohm, NBBJ
Arlo Braun, Arlo Braun & Associates
Fernando Castillo, Pavlik Design Team
Georgio Cavaglieri, Castro–Blanco Piscion
Chuck Davis, Esherick Homsey Dodge and Davis
Robert Deering, IA, Dallas
William Eberhard, Oliver Design Group
Guy Geier, The Hillier Group
James M. Herman, Herman Gibans Fodor, Inc.
Hugh Jacobsen, Hugh Newell Jacobsen Architects
Charles Knight, Perkins & Will
Ryc Loope, Durrant
Alan Roush, HKS Architects
Scott Simpson, The Stubbins Associates
Bernard Smith, Langdon Wilson
David Standard, MSTSD Inc.
Stanley Tigerman, Tigerman McCurry Architects
Ron Van der Veen, Mithun

Source: DesignIntelligence

Most Popular U.S. Buildings

The following rankings provide a glimpse into the minds of architects (and, in one case, architecture critics) as they reflect on the question of what are America's best buildings.

1885 Poll conducted by the *American Architect &* *Building News*:

1. **Trinity Church**, Boston, MA
   H.H. Richardson, 1877
2. **U.S. Capitol**, Washington, D.C.
   William Thornton, Benjamin Henry Latrobe, Charles Bulfinch, 1793-1829
3. **Vanderbilt House**, New York, NY
   Richard Morris Hunt, 1883
4. **Trinity Church**, New York, NY
   Richard Upjohn, 1846
5. **Jefferson Market Courthouse**, New York, NY
   Frederick Withers & Calvert Vaux, 1877
6. **Connecticut State Capitol**, Hartford, CT
   Richard Upjohn, 1879
7. **City Hall**, Albany, NY
   H.H. Richardson, 1883
8. **Sever Hall**, Harvard University, Cambridge, MA
   H.H. Richardson, 1880
9. **New York State Capitol**, Albany, NY
   H.H. Richardson, 1886
10. **Town Hall**, North Easton, MA
    H.H. Richardson, 1881

Source: American Architect & Building News

1986 Poll conducted by The American Institute of Architects:

1. **Fallingwater**, Mill Run, PA
   Frank Lloyd Wright, 1936
2. **Seagram Building**, New York, NY
   Ludwig Mies van der Rohe, 1954-58
3. **Dulles Airport**, Chantilly, VA
   Eero Saarinen, 1962
4. **University of Virginia**, Charlottesville, VA
   Thomas Jefferson, 1826
5. **Robie House**, Chicago, IL
   Frank Lloyd Wright, 1909
6. **Trinity Church**, Boston, MA
   H.H. Richardson, 1877

7. **East Wing**, National Gallery, Washington, D.C.
   I.M. Pei & Partners, 1978
8. **Rockefeller Center**, New York, NY
   Raymond Hood, 1940
9. **S. C. Johnson & Son Admin. Building**, Racine, WI
   Frank Lloyd Wright, 1936
10. **Monticello**, Charlottesville, VA
    Thomas Jefferson, 1769-84; 1796-1809

Source: The American Institute of Architects

2000 Building of the Century Poll conducted at the 2000 AIA Convention in Philadelphia:

1. **Fallingwater**, Mill Run, PA
   Frank Lloyd Wright,1936
2. **Chrysler Building**, New York, NY
   William Van Alen, 1930
3. **Seagram Building**, New York, NY
   Ludwig Mies van der Rohe, 1958
4. **Thorncrown Chapel**, Eureka, AR
   E. Fay Jones, 1980
5. **Dulles Airport**, Chantilly, VA
   Eero Saarinen, 1962
6. **Salk Institute**, La Jolla, CA
   Louis I. Kahn, 1966
7. **Vietnam Veterans Memorial**, Washington, D.C.
   Maya Lin, 1982
8. **Robie House**, Chicago, IL
   Frank Lloyd Wright, 1909
9. **Guggenheim Museum**, New York, NY
   Frank Lloyd Wright, 1959
10. **East Wing, National Gallery**, Washington, D.C.
    I.M. Pei, 1978
11. **S. C. Johnson & Son Admin. Building**, Racine, WI
    Frank Lloyd Wright, 1939

Source: The American Institute of Architects

Most Popular U.S. Buildings (Con't)

2001 Architecture Critics' Poll of the Top Rated Buildings:

1. **Brooklyn Bridge**, New York, NY
   John Augustus Roebling, 1883
2. **Grand Central Station**, New York, NY
   Warren & Wetmore, Reed & Stem, 1913
3. **Chrysler Building**, New York, NY
   William Van Alen, 1930
4. **Monticello**, Charlottesville, VA
   Thomas Jefferson, 1769-84; 1796-1809
5. **University of Virginia**, Charlottesville, VA
   Thomas Jefferson, 1826
6. **Robie House**, Chicago, IL
   Frank Lloyd Wright, 1909
7. **Carson Pirie Scott Building**, Chicago, IL
   Louis Sullivan, 1904
8. **Empire State Building**, New York, NY
   Shreve, Lamb & Harmon, 1931
9. **S. C. Johnson & Son Admin. Building**, Racine, WI
   Frank Lloyd Wright, 1939
10. **Unity Temple**, Oak Park, IL
    Frank Lloyd Wright, 1907

Source: The Architecture Critic, *National Arts Journalism Program,*

Oldest Practicing Architecture Firms in the United States

The following firms were all founded prior to 1900 (their specific founding dates indicated below) and are still operational today.

1827 The Mason & Hanger Group, Inc., Lexington, KY

1832 Lockwood Greene, Spartanburg, SC

1853 Luckett & Farley Architects, Engineers and Construction Managers, Inc., Louisville, KY

1853 SmithGroup, Detroit, MI

1862 Freeman White, Inc., Raleigh, NC

1868 Jensen and Halstead Ltd., Chicago, IL

1868 King & King Architects, Manlius, NY

1870 Harriman Associates, Auburn, ME

1871 Scholtz-Gowey-Gere-Marolf Architects & Interior Designers, PC, Davenport, IA

1872 Brunner & Brunner Architects & Engineers, St. Joseph, MO

1873 Graham Anderson Probst & White, Chicago, IL

1874 Chandler, Palmer & King, Norwich, CT

1874 Shepley Bulfinch Richardson and Abbott Inc., Boston, MA

1878 The Austin Company, Kansas City, MO

1878 Ballinger, Philadelphia, PA

1880 Beatty Harvey & Associates, Architects, New York, NY

1880 Green Nelson Weaver, Inc., Minneapolis, MN

1880 Holabird & Root LLP, Chicago, IL

1880 Zeidler Roberts Partnership, Inc., Toronto, Canada

1881 Keffer/Overton Architects, Des Moines, IA

1883 Ritterbush-Ellig-Hulsing PC, Bismarck, ND

1883 SMRT Architecture Engineering Planning, Portland, ME

1885 Cromwell Architects Engineers, Little Rock, AR

1885 HLW International LLP, New York, NY

1887 Bradley & Bradley, Rockford, IL

1888 Reid & Stuhldreher, Inc., Pittsburgh, PA

1889 Architectural Design West Inc., Salt Lake City, UT

1889 CSHQA Architects/Engineers/ Planners, Boise, ID

1889 MacLachlan, Cornelius & Filoni, Inc., Pittsburgh, PA

1889 Wank Adams Slavin Associates, New York, New York

1890 Kendall, Taylor & Company, Inc., Billerica, MA

1890 The Mathes Group PC, New Orleans, LA

1890 Plunkett Raysich Architects, Milwaukee, WI

1891 Shive/Spinelli/Perantoni & Associates, Somerville, NJ

1891 Wilkins Wood Goforth Mace Associates Ltd., Florence, SC

1892 Bauer Stark + Lashbrook, Inc., Toledo, OH

1893 Foor & Associates, Elmira, NY

1893 Wright, Porteous & Lowe/Bonar, Indianapolis, IN

1894 Colgan Perry Lawler Architects, Nyack, NY

1894 Freese and Nichols, Inc., Fort Worth, TX

1894 Parkinson Field Associates, Austin, TX

1895 Brooks Borg Skiles Architecture Engineering LLP, Des Moines, IA

1895 Albert Kahn Associates, Inc., Detroit, MI

1896 Hummel Architects, PA, Boise, ID

1896 Kessels DiBoll Kessels & Associates, New Orleans, LA

1896 Lehman Architectural Partnership, Roseland, NJ

1897 Baskervill & Son, Richmond, VA

1897 L_H_R_S Architects, Inc., Huntington, IN

1898 Beardsley Design Associates, Auburn, NY

1898 Berners/Schober Associates, Inc., Green Bay, WI

1898 Bottelli Associates, Summit, NJ

1898 Burns & McDonnell, Kansas City, MO

1898 Eckles Architecture, New Castle, PA

1898 Emery Roth Associates, New York, NY

1898 Foss Associates, Fargo, ND & Moorhead, MN

1898 PageSoutherlandPage, Austin, TX

1899 William B. Ittner, Inc., St. Louis, MO

Source: Counsel House Research

Staples Center. Photo: John Edward Linden.

Paul Brown Stadium. Photo: Tim Griffith.

Sports Stadiums

From classic ballparks to cutting edge stadiums, the following charts provide major statistics and architectural information for all major league baseball, basketball, football, and hockey stadiums. All cost and architectural information refers to the parks as they were originally built and does not include any subsequent additions, renovations, or expansions. Capacity figures are the current numbers for their respective sports.

Top: Conseco Fieldhouse. Photo: © Timothy Hursley.
Bottom: Comerica Park. Photo: Justin Maconochie © Hedrich Blessing.

Sports Stadiums: Baseball

BASEBALL	Stadium Name	Location	Opened	Cost (original)
American League				
Anaheim Angels	Edison International Field	Anaheim, CA	1966	$25 M
Baltimore Orioles	Oriole Park @ Camden Yards	Baltimore, MD	1992	$210 M
Boston Red Sox	Fenway Park	Boston, MA	1912	$365,000
Cleveland Indians	Jacobs Field	Cleveland, OH	1994	$173 M
Chicago White Sox	Comiskey Park II	Chicago, IL	1991	$150 M
Detroit Tigers	Comerica Park	Detroit, MI	2000	$300 M
Kansas City Royals	Kauffman Stadium	Kansas City, MO	1973	$50.45 M
Minnesota Twins	Hubert H. Humphrey Metrodome	Minneapolis, MN	1982	$75 M
New York Yankees	Yankee Stadium	Bronx, NY	1923	$3.1 M
Oakland Athletics	Network Associates Coliseum	Oakland, CA	1966	$25 M
Seattle Mariners	Safeco Field	Seattle, WA	1999	$517.6 M
Tampa Bay Devil Rays	Tropicana Field	St. Petersburg, FL	1990	$138 M
Texas Rangers	The Ballpark in Arlington	Arlington, TX	1994	$190 M
Toronto Blue Jays	Skydome	Toronto, Ontario, Canada	1989	$442 M

Capacity (current)	Architect (original)	Surface	Roof Type	Naming Rights
45,050	HOK Sports Facilities Group and Robert A.M. Stern Architects	Bluegrass		$50 M (over 20 yrs)
48,876	HOK with RTKL	Grass		
33,871	Osborn Engineering	Bluegrass		
43,345	HOK Sport	Kentucky Bluegrass		
44,321	HOK Sports	Bluegrass		
40,637	HOK Sports, SHG Inc.	Grass		$ 66M (over 30 yrs)
40,625	HNTB	Grass		
55,883	Skidmore, Owings & Merrill	Astroturf	Air-supported dome	
57,545	Osborne Engineering Company	Merion Bluegrass		
48,219	Skidmore, Owings & Merrill; HNTB	Bluegrass		5.8M (over 5 yrs)
46,621	NBBJ	Grass	Retractable	$1.8 M annually for 20 yrs
45,360	HOK Sport, Lescher & Mahoney Sports, Criswell, Blizzard & Blouin Architects	FieldTurf with dirt infield		
49,115	David M. Schwarz Architectural Services, HKS, Inc.	Bermuda Tifway 419 Grass		
50,516	Rod Robbie and Michael Allen	Astroturf	Retractable	

Sports Stadiums: Baseball (Con't)

BASEBALL	Stadium Name	Location	Opened	Cost (original)
National League				
Arizona Diamondbacks	Bank One Ballpark	Phoenix, AZ	1998	$355 M
Atlanta Braves	Turner Field	Atlanta, GA	1997	$250 M
Chicago Cubs	Wrigley Field	Chicago, IL	1914	$250,000
Cincinnati Reds	Cinergy Field	Cincinnati, OH	1970	$54.4 M
Colorado Rockies	Coors Field	Denver, CO	1995	$215 M
Florida Marlins	Pro Player Stadium	Miami, FL	1987	$145 M
Houston Astros	Enron Field	Houston, TX	2000	$248.1 M
Los Angeles Dodgers	Dodger Stadium	Los Angeles, CA	1962	$24.47 M
Milwaukee Brewers	Miller Park	Milwaukee, WI	2001	$399.4 M
Montreal Expos	Olympic Stadium	Montreal, Quebec, Canada	1977	$770 M
New York Mets	Shea Stadium	Flushing, NY	1964	$24 M
Philadelphia Phillies	Veterans Stadium	Philadelphia, PA	1971	$49.5 M
Pittsburgh Pirates	PNC Park	Pittsburgh, PA	2001	$262 M
San Diego Padres	Qualcomm Stadium	San Diego, CA	1967	$27.75 M
San Francisco Giants	Pacific Bell Park	San Francisco, CA	2000	$345 M
St. Louis Cardinals	Busch Stadium	St. Louis, MO	1966	$24 M

Capacity (current)	Architect (original)	Surface	Roof Type	Naming Rights
49,033	Ellerbe Becket, with Bill Johnson	Kentucky Bluegrass	Convertible	
49,831	Heery International, Inc., Williams-Russell and Johnson, Inc., and Ellerbe Becket, Inc.	GN-1 Bermuda Grass		
38,765	Zachary Taylor Davis	Merion Bluegrass and Clover		
52,952	Heery & Heery	Grass		
50,445	HOK Sport	Grass		
47,662	HOK Sports Facilities	Tifway 419 Bermuda Grass		
40,950	HOK Sport	Grass	Retractable	
56,000	Captain Emil Praeger	Santa Ana Bermuda Grass		
42,500	HKS, NBBJ, Eppstein Uhen Architects	Grass	Convertible	$40 M
46,500	Roger Taillibert	Astroturf	Retractable (inoperable)	
55,601	Praeger-Kavanaugh-Waterbury	Bluegrass		
62,382	Hugh Stubbins & Associates	NeXturf		
38,000	HOK Sports, L.D. Astorino & Associates	Grass		$1.5 M/yr until 2020
56,133	Frank Hope	Santa Ana Bermuda Grass		$18 M
40,800	HOK Sports	Sports Turf (blend of 4 low-growing bluegrass hybrid turf grasses)		$100 M
49,676	Sverdrup & Parcel and Associates, Edward Durell Stone, Schwarz & Van Hoefen, Associated	Grass		

Sports Stadiums: Basketball

BASKETBALL	Stadium Name	Location	Opened
Eastern Conference			
Atlantic			
Boston Celtics	The Fleet Center	Boston, MA	1995
Miami Heat	The American Airlines Arena	Miami, FL	1998
New Jersey Nets	Continental Airlines Arena	East Rutherford, NJ	1981
New York Knickerbockers	Madison Square Garden IV The Theater	New York, NY	1968
Orlando Magic	TD Waterhouse Centre	Orlando, FL	1989
Philadelphia 76ers	The First Union Center	Philadelphia, PA	1996
Washington Wizards	MCI Center	Washington, DC	1997
Central			
Atlanta Hawks	Philips Arena	Atlanta, GA	1999
Charlotte Hornets	The Charlotte Coliseum	Charlotte, NC	1988
Chicago Bulls	The United Center	Chicago, IL	1994
Cleveland Cavaliers	The Gund Arena	Cleveland, OH	1994
Detroit Pistons	The Palace of Auburn Hills	Auburn Hills, MI	1988
Indiana Pacers	Conseco Fieldhouse	Indianapolis, IN	1999
Milwaukee Bucks	The Bradley Center	Milwaukee, WI	1988
Toronto Raptors	Air Canada Centre	Toronto, ON, Canada	1999

Cost (original)	Capacity (current)	Architect (original)	Naming Rights
$160 M	18,624	Ellerbe Becket	$30 M (over 15 yrs)
$175 M	19,600	Arquitectonica	$42 M (over 20 yrs)
$85 M	19,040	Grad Partnership/DiLullo, Clauss, Ostroski & Partners	$29 M (over 12 yrs)
$116 M	19,763	Charles Luckman	
$98 M	17,248	Lloyd Jones Philpot; Cambridge Seven	$7.8 M (over 5 yrs)
$206 M	20,444	Ellerbe Becket	$40 M (over 29 yrs)
$260 M	20,674	Ellerbe Becket	undisclosed
$213.5 M	20,300	HOK, Architectonica	
$52 M	24,042	Odell Associates	
$175 M	21,711	HOK Sport, Marmon Mok, W.E. Simpson Company	$1.8 M annually for 20 yrs
$152 M	20,562	Ellerbe Becket	$14 M (over 20 yrs)
$70 M	21,454	Rossetti Associates/Architects Planners	
$183 M	18,345	Ellerbe Becket	
$90 M	18,717	HOK	
C$265 M	19,800	HOK Sport; Brisbin, Brook and Benyon	C$40 M (over 20 yrs)

Sports Stadiums: Basketball (Con't)

BASKETBALL	Stadium Name	Location	Opened
Western Conference			
Midwest			
Dallas Mavericks	American Airlines Center	Dallas, TX	1980
Denver Nuggets	Pepsi Center	Denver, CO	1999
Houston Rockets	The Compaq Center	Houston, TX	1975
Minnesota Timberwolves	The Target Center	Minneapolis, MN	1990
San Antonio Spurs	Alamodome	San Antonio, TX	1993
Utah Jazz	The Delta Center	Salt Lake City, UT	1991
Vancouver Grizzlies	General Motors Place	Vancouver, BC, Canada	1995
Pacific			
Golden State Warriors	The New Arena in Oakland	Oakland, CA	1966
Los Angeles Clippers	The Arrowhead Pond of Anaheim	Anaheim, CA	1993
Los Angeles Lakers	Staples Center	Los Angeles, CA	1999
Phoenix Suns	America West Arena	Phoenix, AZ	1992
Portland Trail Blazers	The Rose Garden	Portland, OR	1995
Sacramento Kings	The Arco Arena	Sacramento, CA	1988
Seattle SuperSonics	The Key Arena	Seattle, WA	1983

Cost (original)	Capacity (current)	Architect (original)	Naming Rights
$27 M	17,502	David Schwarz	
$160 M	19,309	HOK	$68 M
	16,285	Kenneth Bensen & Associates w/ Lloyd & Jones	
$104 M	19,006	KMR Architects	$18.75 M (over 15 yrs)
$186 M	20,662	HOK, Marmon Mok, W.E. Simpson Company	
$94 M	19,911	FFKR Architecture	$25 M (over 20 yrs)
C$160 M	19,193	Brisbin, Brook and Beynon	$18.5 M (over 20 yrs)
	19,200	HNTB	
$120 M	16,021	HOK Sports	$15 M (over 10 yrs)
$330 M	20,000	NBBJ	$100 M (20 yrs)
$90 M	19,023	Ellerbe Becket	$26 M (over 30 yrs)
$262 M	21,538	Ellerbe Becket	
$40 M	17,317	Rann Haight	undisclosed
	17,072	NBBJ	$15.1 M (over 15 yrs)

Sports Stadiums: Football

FOOTBALL	Stadium Name	Location	Opened	Cost (original)
AFC East				
Buffalo Bills	Ralph Wilson Stadium	Orchard Park, NY	1973	$22 M
Indianapolis Colts	RCA Dome - Stadia Net	Indianapolis, IN	1984	$82 M
Miami Dolphins	Pro Player Stadium	Miami, FL	1987	$125 M
New England Patriots	Foxboro Stadium	Foxboro, MA	1971	$61 M
New York Jets	Giants Stadium	Rutherford, NJ	1976	$78 M
AFC Central				
Baltimore Ravens	PSINet Stadium	Baltimore, MD	1998	$220 M
Cincinnati Bengals	Paul Brown Stadium	Cincinnati, OH	2000	$400 M
Cleveland Browns	Cleveland Browns Stadium	Cleveland, OH	1999	$283 M
Jacksonville Jaguars	Alltel Stadium	Jacksonville, FL	1995	$138 M
Pittsburgh Steelers	Three Rivers Stadium	Pittsburgh, PA	1970	$35 M
Tennessee Titans	Adelphia Coliseum	Nashville, TN	1999	$290 M
AFC West				
Denver Broncos	Invesco Field @ Mile High Stadium	Denver, CO	2001	
Kansas City Chiefs	Arrowhead Stadium	Kansas City, MO	1972	$43 M
Oakland Raiders	Network Associates Coliseum	Oakland, CA	1966	
San Diego Chargers	Qualcomm Stadium	San Diego, CA	1967	$27 M
Seattle Seahawks	*	Seattle, WA	2002	

* The new Seattle Seahawks stadium is currently under construction with a scheduled completion date of August 2002. The stadium has yet to be named. In the interim, the Seahawks are playing at Husky Stadium at the University of Washington.

Capacity (current)	Architect (original)	Turf	Roof	Naming Rights
73,800	HNTB	AstroTurf-12	Open-Air	
60,127	HNTB	AstroTurf-12	Dome	$10 M (over 10 yrs.)
74,916	HOK Sports Facilities Group	Natural Grass	Open-Air	$20 M (over 10 yrs.)
60,293	David Berg Inc., Finch/Heery	Natural Grass	Open-Air	
79,670	HOK Sports Facilities Group	Natural Grass	Open-Air	
69,084	HOK Sports Facilities Group	Natural Grass	Open-Air	$100 M (over 20 yrs.)
65,535	NBBJ	Natural Turf	Open-Air	unknown
73,200	HOK Sports Facilities Group	Natural Grass	Open-Air	
73,000	HOK Sports Facilities Group	Natural Grass	Open-Air	$6.2 M (over 10 yrs.)
59,030	HOK Sports Facilities Group	Artificial	Open-Air	
67,000	HOK Sports Facilities Group	Natural Grass	Open-Air	$30 M (over 15 yrs.)
76,125	HNTB w/Fentress Bradburn Architects	Natural Grass	Open-Air	
79,409	Kivett and Meyers	Natural Grass	Open-Air	
62,026	HNTB	Natural Grass	Suspension (fixed)	
71,294	Frank L. Hope and Associates	Natural Grass	Open-Air	$18 M (over 20 yrs.)
67,000	Ellerbe Becket			

Sports Stadiums: Football (Con't)

FOOTBALL	Stadium Name	Location	Opened	Cost (original)
NFC East				
Arizona Cardinals	Sun Devil Stadium	Tempe, AZ	1958	$1 M
Dallas Cowboys	Texas Stadium	Irving, TX	1971	$35 M
New York Jets	Giants Stadium	E. Rutherford, NJ	1976	
Philadelphia Eagles	Veterans Stadium	Philadelphia, PA	1971	$50 M
Washington Redskins	FedEx Field (Jack Kent Cooke Stadium)	Landover, MD	1996	$250.5 M
NFC Central				
Chicago Bears	Soldier Field	Chicago, IL	1924	$10 M
Detroit Lions	Pontiac Silverdome	Pontiac, MI	1975	$55.7 M
Green Bay Packers	Lambeau Field	Green Bay, WI	1957	$960,000
Minnesota Vikings	Hubert H. Humphrey Metrodome	Minneapolis, MN	1982	$55 M
Tampa Bay Buccaneers	Raymond James Stadium	Tampa, FL	1998	$168.5 M
NFC West				
Atlanta Falcons	Georgia Dome	Atlanta, GA	1992	$214 M
Carolina Panthers	Ericsson Stadium	Charlotte, NC	1996	$248 M
New Orleans Saints	Superdome	New Orleans, LA	1975	$134 M
St. Louis Rams	Trans World Dome	St. Louis, MO	1995	$280 M
San Francisco 49ers	3Com Park	San Francisco, CA	1960	$24.6 M

Capacity (current)	Architect (original)	Turf	Roof	Naming Rights
74,186	Edward L. Varney	Natural Grass	Open-Air	
65,846	Warren Morey	Artificial	Partial Roof	
79,670	HOK Sports Facilities Inc.	Natural Grass		
65,352	Hugh Stubbins Associates	Artificial	Open-Air	
80,116	HOK Sports Facilities Inc.	Natural Grass	Open-Air	undisclosed
66,944	Holabird and Roche	Natural Grass	Open-Air	
80,311	O'Dell/Hewlett & Luckenbach	Artificial Turf	Dome	
60,890	John Somerville	Natural Grass	Open-Air	
64,121	SOM	Artificial Turf	Dome	
66,000	HOK Sports Facilities Group	Natural Grass	Open-Air	
71,149	Heery International	Artificial Turf	Dome	
73,258	HOK Sports Facilities Group	Natural Grass	Open-Air	$20 M (over 10 yrs.)
69,065	Curtis & Davis Architects	Artificial Turf	Dome	
66,000	HOK Sports Facilities Group	Astroturf	TVC	$1.3 M annually for 20 yrs.
69,843	John & Bolles	Natural Grass	Open-Air	

Sports Stadiums: Hockey

HOCKEY	Stadium Name	Location	Opened
Eastern Conference			
Atlantic Division			
New Jersey Devils	Continental Airlines Arena	East Rutherford, NJ	1981
New York Islanders	Nassau Veterans Memorial Coliseum	Uniondale, NY	1972
New York Rangers	Madison Square Garden IV The Theater	New York, NY	1968
Philadelphia Flyers	The First Union Center	Philadelphia, PA	1996
Pittsburgh Penguins	Mellon Arena	Pittsburgh, PA	1961
Northeast Division			
Boston Bruins	The Fleet Center	Boston, MA	1995
Buffalo Sabres	HSBC Arena/Marine Midland	Buffalo, NY	1996
Montreal Canadiens	Le Centre Molson	Montreal, QC, Canada	1996
Ottawa Senators	The Corel Centre	Kanata, ON, Canada	1996
Toronto Maple Leafs	Air Canada Centre	Toronto, ON, Canada	1999
Southeast Division			
Atlanta Thrashers	Philips Arena	Atlanta, GA	1999
Carolina Hurricanes	Raleigh Entertainment and Sports Arena	Raleigh, NC	1999
Florida Panthers	National Car Rental Center	Sunrise, FL	1998
Tampa Bay Lightning	Ice Palace	Tampa, FL	1996
Washington Capitals	MCI Center	Washington, DC	1997

Cost (original)	Capacity (current)	Architect (original)	Naming Rights
$85 M	19,040	Grad Partnership/DiLullo, Clauss, Ostroski & Partners	$29 M (over 12 years)
$31 M	16,297	Welton Becket	
$116 M	18,200	Charles Luckman	
$206 M	18,168	Ellerbe Becket	$40M (over 29 years)
$22 M	17,323	Mitchell and Ritchie	
$160 M	17,565	Ellerbe Becket	$30 M (over 15 years)
$127.5 M	18,595	Ellerbe Becket	$15 M (over 20 years)
C$280 M	21,273	Consortium of Quebec Architects	
C$200M	18,500	Rossetti Associates Architects	C$26 M (over 20 years)
C$265 M	18,800	HOK Sport; Brisbin, Brook and Benyon	C$40 M (over 20 years)
$213.5 M	18,750	HOK, Architectonica	
$158 M	18,176	Odell & Associates	
$212 M	19,452	Ellerbe Becket	$42 M (over 20 years)
$139 M	19,500	Ellerbe Becket	
$260 M	19,700	Ellerbe Becket	undisclosed

Sports Stadiums: Hockey (Con't)

HOCKEY	Stadium Name	Location	Opened
Western Conference			
Central Division			
Chicago Blackhawks	The United Center	Chicago, IL	1994
Columbus Blue Jackets	Nationwide Arena	Columbus, OH	2000
Detroit Red Wings	Joe Louis Arena	Detroit, MI	1979
Nashville Predators	Gaylord Entertainment Center	Nashville, TN	1997
St. Louis Blues	Savvis Center	St. Louis, MO	1994
Northwest Division			
Calgary Flames	Pengrowth Saddledome	Calgary, AB, Canada	1983
Colorado Avalanche	Pepsi Center	Denver, CO	1999
Edmonton Oilers	Skyreach Centre	Edmonton, AB, Canada	1974
Minnesota Wild	Xcel Energy Center	Saint Paul, MN	2000
Vancouver Canucks	General Motors Place	Vancouver, BC, Canada	1995
Pacific Division			
Anaheim Mighty Ducks	The Arrowhead Pond of Anaheim	Anaheim, CA	1993
Dallas Stars	American Airlines Center	Dallas, TX	1980
Los Angeles Kings	Staples Center	Los Angeles, CA	1999
Phoenix Coyotes	America West Arena	Phoenix, AZ	1992
San Jose Sharks	Compac Center at San Jose	San Jose, CA	1993

Cost (original)	Capacity (current)	Architect (original)	Naming Rights
$175 M	20,500	HOK Sport; Marmon Mok; W.E. Simpson Company	$1.8 M annually for 20 years
$150 M	18,500	Heinlein & Schrock, Inc., NBBJ	
$57 M	18,785	Smith, Hinchmen and Grylls Associates	
$144 M	17,500	HOK	$80 M (over 20 years)
$170 M	19,260	Ellerbe Becket	$70 M (over 20 years)
C$176 M	20,140	Graham Edmunds/Graham McCourt	
$160 M	18,129	HOK	$68 M
C$22.5 M	16,900	Phillips, Barrett, Hillier, Jones & Partners w/ Wynn, Forbes, Lord, Feldberg & Schmidt	
$130 M	18,064	HOK Sport	$3 M annually for 25 years
C$160 M	18,422	Brisbin, Brook and Beynon	$18.5 M (over 20 years)
$120 M	17,174	HOK Sports	$15 M (over 10 years)
$27 M	16,924	David Schwarz	
$330 M	18,500	NBBJ	$100 M (over 20 years)
$90 M	16,210	Ellerbe Becket	$26 M (over 30 years)
$162.5 M	17,483	Sink Combs Dethlefs	$3.13 M annually until 2015

State Capitols and their Architects

The architect(s) of each U.S. state capitol and the national Capitol is listed below. When available, the contractor(s) is also listed immediately below the architect in italics.

Alabama
Montgomery, 1851
George Nichols

Alaska
Juneau, 1931
Treasury Department architects with James A.
    Wetmore, supervising architect
N.P. Severin Company

Arizona
Phoenix, 1900
James Riley Gordon
Tom Lovell

Arkansas
Little Rock, 1911-1915
George R. Mann; Cass Gilbert
Caldwell and Drake; William Miller & Sons

California
Sacramento, 1874
Miner F. Butler; Ruben Clark and G. Parker
    Cummings

Colorado
Denver, 1894-1908
Elijah E. Myers, Frank E. Edbrooke

Connecticut
Hartford, 1779
Richard M. Upjohn
James G. Batterson

Delaware
Dover, 1933
William Martin

Florida
Tallahassee, 1977
Edward Durell Stone with Reynolds, Smith and
    Hills

Georgia
Atlanta, 1889
Edbrooke & Burnham
Miles and Horne

Hawaii
Honolulu, 1969
John Carl Warnecke with Belt, Lemman and Lo
Reed and Martin

Idaho
Boise, 1912-1920
John E. Tourtellotte
Stewart and Company with Herbert Quigley, construction supervisor

Illinois
Springfield, 1877-87
J. C. Cochrane with Alfred H. Piquenard; W. W.
    Boyington

Indiana
Indianapolis, 1888
Edwin May; Adolf Scherrer
*Kanmacher and Dengi; Elias F. Gobel and Columbus
    Cummings*

Iowa
Des Moines, 1884-86
J. C. Cochrane and Alfred H. Piquenard; M.E. Bell
    and W. F. Hackney

Kansas
Topeka, 1873-1906
John G. Haskell; E.T. Carr and George Ropes
*D. J. Silver & Son; Bogart and Babcock; William
    Tweeddale and Company*

Kentucky
Frankfort, 1910
Frank Mills Andrews

Iowa State Capitol.

State Capitols and their Architects (Con't)

Louisiana
Baton Rouge, 1931
Weiss, Dryfous and Seiferth
Kenneth McDonald

Maine
Augusta, 1832
Charles Bulfinch; John C. Spofford, 1891 rear wing
   addition; G. Henri Desmond, 1911 expansion

Maryland
Annapolis, 1779
Joseph Horatio Anderson and Joseph Clark, interi-
   or architect; Baldwin and Pennington, 1905 rear
   annex
Charles Wallace; Thomas Wallace

Massachusetts
Boston, 1798
Charles Bulfinch; Charles Brigham, 1895 rear
   addition; R. Clipson, William Chapman, and
   Robert Agnew, 1917 side wing additions

Michigan
Lansing, 1878-79
Elijah E. Myers
N. Osborne & Co.

Minnesota
St. Paul, 1905
Cass Gilbert

Mississippi
Jackson, 1903
Theodore C. Link; George R. Mann, dome
Wells Brothers Company

Missouri
Jefferson City, 1917
Tracy and Swartwout
*T.H. Johnson; A. Anderson & Company; John Gill &
   Sons*

Montana
Helena, 1902
Bell and Kent; Frank Mills Andrews and Link &
   Hare, 1912 east and west wing addition

Nebraska
Lincoln, 1932
Bertram Grosvenor Goodhue
*W.J. Assenmacher Company; J.H. Wiese Company;
   Peter Kewittand Sons; Metz Construction Co.*

Nevada
Carson City, 1871
Joseph Gosling; Frederic J. Delongchamps and
   C.G. Sellman, 1913 addition
Peter Cavanough and Son

New Hampshire
Concord, 1819
Stuart James Park; Gridley J. F. Bryant and David
   Bryce, 1866 addition; Peabody and Stearns,
   1909 addition

New Jersey
Trenton, 1792
Jonathan Doane; John Notman, 1845 expansion
   and renovation; Samuel Sloan, 1872 expansion;
   Lewis Broome and James Moylan, c.1885 reno-
   vations; Karr Poole and Lum, 1900 expansion;
   Arnold Moses, 1903 Senate wing renovations

New Mexico
Santa Fe, 1966
W. C. Kruger & Associates with John Gaw Meem,
   design consultant
Robert E. McKee General Contractor, Inc.

New York
Albany, 1879-99
Thomas Fuller; Leopold Eidlitz, Frederick Law
   Olmsted, Henry Hobson Richardson; Isaac G.
   Perry

North Carolina
Raleigh, 1840
Town and Davis, David Paton

North Dakota
Bismarck, 1934
Holabird & Root with Joseph B. DeRemer and
   William F. Kirke
Lundoff and Bicknell

392 *Almanac of Architecture & Design*

State Capitols and their Architects (Con't)

Ohio
Columbus, 1857-1861
Henry Walter; William R. West; Nathan B. Kelly

Oklahoma
Oklahoma City, 1917
Layton and Smith

Oregon
Salem, 1938
Francis Keally of Trowbridge and Livingston

Pennsylvania
Harrisburg, 1906
Joseph M. Huston
George F. Payne Company

Rhode Island
Providence, 1904
McKim, Mead and White
Norcross Brothers Construction

South Carolina
Columbia, 1854-1907
John Rudolph Niernsee, 1854-85; J. Crawford
    Neilson, 1885-88; Frank Niernsee, 1888-91;
    Frank P. Milburn, 1900-04; Charles Coker
    Wilson, 1904-07

South Dakota
Pierre, 1911
C.E. Bell and M.S. Detwiler
*O.H. Olsen with Samuel H. Lea, state engineer and
    construction supervisor*

Tennessee
Nashville, 1859
William Strickland
A.G. Payne

Texas
Austin, 1888
Elijah E. Myers
*Mattheas Schnell; Taylor, Babcock & Co. with Abner
    Taylore*

Utah
Salt Lake City, 1915-16
Richard K. A. Kletting
James Stewart & Company

Vermont
Montpelier, 1859
Thomas W. Silloway; Joseph R. Richards

Virginia
Richmond, 1789
Thomas Jefferson with Charles-Louis Clérisseau; J.
    Kevin Peebles, Frye & Chesterman,1906 wings

Washington
Olympia, 1928
Walter R. Wilder and Harry K. White

West Virginia
Charleston, 1932
Cass Gilbert
George H. Fuller Company; James Baird Company

Wisconsin
Madison, 1909-1915
George B. Post & Sons

Wyoming
Cheyenne, 1890
David W. Gibbs; William Dubois, 1915 extension
*Adam Feick & Brother; Moses P. Keefe, 1890 wings;
    John W. Howard, 1915 extension*

U.S. Capitol
Washington, DC, 1800-1829
William Thornton, 1793; Benjamin Henry Latrobe,
    1803-11, 1815-17; Charles Bulfinch, 1818-29;
    Thomas Ustick Walter, 1851-65; Edward Clark,
    1865-1902; Elliot Woods, 1902-23; David Lynn,
    1923-54; J. George Stewart, 1954-70; George
    Malcolm White, FAIA, 1971-95; Alan M.
    Hantman, AIA, 1997-present

Source: Counsel House Research

Tallest Buildings in the World

The following list ranks the world's 100 tallest buildings. Each building's architect, number of stories, height, location, and completion year are also provided. (Buildings which have reached their full height but are still under construction are deemed eligible and are indicated below with a 'UC' in the year category.)

For additional resources about tall buildings, visit the Council on Tall Buildings and Urban Habitat on the Internet at *www.ctbuh.org* and *www.skyscrapers.com*.

Rank	Building	Year	City/Country	Feet/ Meters	Stories	Architect
1	Petronas Tower 1	1998	Kuala Lumpur, Malaysia	1483/452	88	Cesar Pelli & Associates
2	Petronas Tower 2	1998	Kuala Lumpur, Malaysia	1483/452	88	Cesar Pelli & Associates
3	Sears Tower	1974	Chicago, USA	1450/442	110	Skidmore, Owings & Merrill
4	Jin Mao Building	1999	Shanghai, China	1381/421	88	Skidmore, Owings & Merrill
5	World Trade Center One	1972	New York, USA	1368/417	110	M. Yamasaki, Emery Roth & Sons
6	World Trade Center Two	1973	New York, USA	1362/415	110	M. Yamasaki, Emery Roth & Sons
5	CITIC Plaza	1996	Guangzhou, China	1283/391	80	Dennis Lau & Ng Chun Man & Associates
6	Shun Hing Square	1996	Shenzhen, China	1260/384	69	K.Y. Cheung Design Associates
7	Empire State Building	1931	New York, USA	1250/381	102	Shreve, Lamb & Harmon
8	Central Plaza	1992	Hong Kong, China	1227/374	78	Ng Chun Man & Associates
9	Bank of China	1989	Hong Kong, China	1209/369	70	I.M. Pei & Partners
10	Emirates Tower One	2000	Dubai, U.A.E	1165/355	55	NORR Group Consultants
11	The Center	1998	Hong Kong, China	1148/350	79	Dennis Lau & Ng Chun Man & Associates
12	T & C Tower	1997	Kaohsiung, Taiwan	1140/348	85	C.Y. Lee/Hellmuth, Obata & Kassabaum
13	Aon Centre (Amoco Building)	1973	Chicago, USA	1136/346	80	Edward D. Stone
14	John Hancock Center	1969	Chicago, USA	1127/344	100	Skidmore, Owings & Merrill

Tallest Buildings in the World (Con't)

Rank	Building	Year	City/Country	Feet/ Meters	Stories	Architect
15	Burj al Arab Hotel	2000	Dubai, U.A.E.	1053/321	60	W. S. Atkins & Partners
16	Baiyoke Tower II	1997	Bangkok, Thailand	1050/320	90	Plan Architects Co.
17	Chrysler Building	1930	New York, USA	1046/319	77	William van Alen
18	Bank of America Plaza	1993	Atlanta, USA	1023/312	55	Kevin Roche, John Dinkeloo & Associates
19	Library Tower	1990	Los Angeles, USA	1018/310	75	Pei Cobb Freed & Partners
20	Telekom Malaysia Headquarters	1999	Kuala Lumpur, Malaysia	1017/310	55	Daewoo & Partners
21	Emirates Tower Two	UC00	Dubai, U.A.E	1014/309	54	NORR Group Consultants
22	AT&T Corporate Center	1989	Chicago, USA	1007/307	60	Skidmore, Owings & Merrill
23	Chase Tower	1982	Houston, USA	1000/305	75	I. M. Pei & Partners
24	Two Prudential Plaza	1990	Chicago, USA	995/303	64	Leobl Schlossman Dart & Hackl
25	Ryugyong Hotel	1995	Pyongyang, N. Korea	984/300	105	Baikdoosan Architects & Engineers
26	Commerzbank Tower	1997	Frankfurt, Germany	981/299	63	Sir Norman Foster & Partners
27	Kingdom Centre	UC02	Riyadh, Saudi Arabia	979/298	30	Ellerbe Becket and Omrania
28	Wells Fargo Plaza	1983	Houston, USA	972/296	71	Skidmore, Owings & Merrill
29	Landmark Tower	1993	Yokohama, Japan	971/296	70	Stubbins Associates
30	311 S. Wacker Drive	1990	Chicago, USA	961/293	65	Kohn Pedersen Fox Associates
31	SEG Plaza	2000	Shenzen, China	957/292	72	Hua Yi Design
32	Bank of America Center	1984	Seattle, USA	954/291	76	Chester Lindsey Architects
33	American International Building	1932	New York, USA	952/290	67	Clinton & Russell
34	Cheung Kong Centre	1999	Hong Kong, China	951/290	70	Cesar Pelli & Associates, Leo A. Daly
35	First Canadian Place	1975	Toronto, Canada	951/290	72	Bregman + Hamann Architects
36	Key Tower	1991	Cleveland, USA	950/290	57	Cesar Pelli & Associates
37	One Liberty Place	1987	Philadelphia, USA	945/288	61	Murphy/Jahn

Tallest Buildings in the World (Con't)

Rank	Building	Year	City/Country	Feet/ Meters	Stories	Architect
38	Plaza 66	UC01	Shanghai, China	945/288	66	Kohn Pedersen Fox Associates
39	Sunjoy Tomorrow Square	1999	Shanghai, China	934/285	59	John Portman and Associates
40	The Trump Building	1930	New York, USA	927/283	72	H. Craig Severance
41	Bank of America Plaza	1985	Dallas, USA	921/281	72	JPJ Architects
42	Overseas Union Bank Centre	1986	Singapore, Singapore	919/280	66	Kenzo Tange Associates
43	United Overseas Bank Plaza	1992	Singapore, Singapore	919/280	66	Kenzo Tange Associates
44	Republic Plaza	1995	Singapore, Singapore	919/280	66	Kisho Kurokawa
45	Citicorp Center	1977	New York, USA	915/279	59	Stubbins Associates
46	Scotia Plaza	1989	Toronto, Canada	902/275	68	The Webb Zerafa Menkes Housden Partnership
47	Williams Tower	1983	Houston, USA	901/275	64	Johnson/Burgee Architects
48	Trump World Tower	2001	New York, USA	900/274	72	Costas Kondylis & Associates
49	Faisaliah Complex	UC00	Riyadh, Saudi Arabia	899/274	30	Sir Norman Foster & Partners
50	Renaissance Tower	1975	Dallas, USA	886/270	56	Skidmore, Owings & Merrill
51	900 N. Michigan Ave.	1989	Chicago, USA	871/265	66	Kohn Pedersen Fox Associates
52	NationsBank Corporate Center	1992	Charlotte, USA	871/265	60	Cesar Pelli & Associates
53	Sun Trust Plaza	1992	Atlanta, USA	871/265	60	John Portman & Associates
54	Hong Kong New World Building	2001	Shanghai, China	871/265	58	
55	BCE Place-Canada Trust Tower	1990	Toronto, Canada	863/263	51	Skidmore, Owings & Merrill, Bregman + Hamann
56	Water Tower Place	1976	Chicago, USA	859/262	74	Loebl Schlossman Dart & Hackl
57	First Interstate Tower	1974	Los Angeles, USA	858/262	62	Charles Luckman & Associates
68	Transamerica Pyramid	1972	San Francisco, USA	853/260	48	William Pereira
59	G. E. Building/ Rockefeller Center	1933	New York, USA	850/259	70	Raymond Hood
60	First National Plaza	1969	Chicago, USA	850/259	60	C.F. Murphy

Tallest Buildings in the World (Con't)

Rank	Building	Year	City/Country	Feet/ Meters	Stories	Architect
61	Two Liberty Place	1990	Philadelphia, USA	848/258	58	Murphy/Jahn
62	Park Tower	2000	Chicago, USA	844/257	67	Lucien Lagrange
63	Messeturm	1990	Frankfurt, Germany	843/257	70	Murphy/Jahn
64	USX Tower	1970	Pittsburgh, USA	841/256	64	Harrison & Abramovitz
65	Rinku Gate Tower	1996	Osaka, Japan	840/256	56	Nikken Sekkei
66	Osaka World Trade Center	1995	Osaka, Japan	827/252	55	Nikken Sekkei
67	One Atlantic Center	1987	Atlanta, USA	820/250	50	Johnson/Burgee Architects
68	BNI City Tower	1995	Jakarta, Indonesia	820/250	46	Zeidler Roberts Partnership with DP Architects
69	Korea Life Insurance Company	1985	Seoul, South Korea	817/249	60	C.M. Park with SOM
70	CitySpire	1989	New York, USA	814/248	75	Murphy/Jahn
71	Rialto Tower	1985	Melbourne, Australia	814/248	63	Gerard de Preu & Partners
72	One Chase Manhattan Plaza	1961	New York, USA	813/248	60	Skidmore, Owings & Merrill
73	Bank One Tower	1989	Indianapolis, USA	811/247	48	The Stubbins Associates
74	Conde Nast Building	1999	New York, USA	809/247	48	Fox & Fowle Architects
75	MetLife	1963	New York, USA	808/246	59	Emery Roth & Sons, Pietro Belluschi
76	JR Central Towers	UC00	Nagoya, Japan	804/245	51	Kohn Pedersen Fox Associates
77	Shin Kong Life Tower	1993	Taipei, Taiwan	801/244	51	K.M.G. Architects & Engineers
78	Malayan Bank	1988	Kuala Lumpur, Malaysia	799/244	50	Hijjas Kasturi Associates
79	Tokyo Metropolitan Government	1991	Tokyo, Japan	797/243	48	Kenzo Tange Associates
80	Woolworth Building	1913	New York, USA	792/241	57	Cass Gilbert
81	Mellon Bank Center	1991	Philadelphia, USA	792/241	54	Kohn Pedersen Fox Associates
82	Philippine Bank of Communications	2000	Makati	791/241	52	Skidmore,Owings & Merrill , G.F. & Partners
83	John Hancock Tower	1976	Boston, USA	788/240	60	I. M. Pei & Partners

Tallest Buildings in the World (Con't)

Rank	Building	Year	City/Country	Feet/Meters	Stories	Architect
84	Bank One Center	1987	Dallas, USA	787/240	60	Johnson/Burgee Architects
85	Canadian Imperial Bank of Commerce	1973	Toronto, Canada	784/239	57	Page & Steele, I. M. Pei & Partners
86	Moscow State University	1953	Moscow, Russia	784/239	26	L. Roudnev, P. Abrossimov, A. Khariakov
87	Empire Tower	1994	Kuala Lumpur, Malaysia	781/238	62	ADC AKITEK
88	NationsBank Center	1984	Houston, USA	780/238	56	Johnson/Burgee Architects
89	Bank of America Center	1969	San Francisco, USA	779/237	52	Skidmore, Owings & Merrill
90	Office Towers	1985	Caracas, Venezuela	778/237	60	
91	Worldwide Plaza	1989	New York, USA	778/237	47	Skidmore, Owings & Merrill
92	First Bank Place	1992	Minneapolis, USA	775/236	58	Pei Cobb Freed & Partners
93	IDS Center	1973	Minneapolis, USA	775/236	57	Johnson/Burgee Architects
94	One Canada Square	1991	London, UK	774/236	50	Cesar Pelli & Associates
95	Norwest Center	1988	Minneapolis, USA	773/235	57	Cesar Pelli & Associates
96	Treasury Building	1986	Singapore	771/235	52	Stubbins Associates
97	191 Peachtree Tower	1992	Atlanta, USA	770/235	50	Johnson/Burgee Architects
98	Opera City Tower	1997	Tokyo, Japan	768/234	54	NTT, Urban Planning & Design, TAK
99	First Union Financial Center	1983	Dallas, USA	764/233	55	Skidmore, Owings & Merrill
100	Shinjuku Park Tower	1994	Tokyo, Japan	764/233	52	Kenzo Tange Associates

Source: Council on Tall Buildings and Urban Habitat, Lehigh University

Tallest Free-Standing Towers

Because of their primarily utilitarian function as platforms for transmission equipment, the following structures are considered free-standing towers, not skyscrapers. According to internationally-recognized standards, in order to be deemed a skyscraper a structure must be intended for human occupancy with the great majority of its height divided into habitable floors. The following free-standing towers are the tallest in the world; only structures over 200 meters are eligible for the list. Structures currently under construction are indicated with a 'UC' in the year category.

For more information about tall towers and buildings, visit *www.skyscrapers. com* on the Internet.

Rank	Name	City	Country	Height (m)	Height (ft.)	Completion Year
1	Indosat Telkom Tower	Jakarta	Indonesia	558	1831	UC
2	CN Tower	Toronto	Canada	553	1815	1976
3	Ostankino Tower	Moscow	Russia	540	1772	1967
4	Xi'an Broadcasting, Telephone and Television Tower	Xi'an	China	470	1542	UC
5	Oriental Pearl Television Tower	Shanghai	China	468	1535	1995
6	Tehran Telecommunications Tower	Tehran	Iran	435	1427	UC
7	Manara Kuala Lumpur	Kuala Lumpur	Malaysia	420	1379	1996
8	Beijing Radio & T.V. Tower	Beijing	China	417	1369	1992
9	Tianjin Radio & T.V. Tower	Tianjin	China	415	1362	1991
10	Tashkent Tower	Tashkent	Uzbekistan	375	1230	1985
11	Alma-Ata Tower	Alma-Ata	Kazakhstan	370	1214	1982
12	Liberation Tower	Kuwait City	Kuwait	370	1214	1996
13	T.V. Tower	Riga	Latvia	368	1208	1987
14	Fernsehturm Tower	Berlin	Germany	365	1198	1969
15	Stratosphere Tower	Las Vegas	United States	350	1149	1996

Toronto's CN Tower celebrated its 25th
anniversary on June 26, 2001.

Tallest Free-Standing Towers (Con't)

Rank	Name	City	Country	Height (m)	Height (ft.)	Completion Year
16	Heifei Feicui T.V. Tower	Heifei	China	339	1112	UC
17	Macau Tower	Macau	China	338	1109	UC
18	Dragon Tower	Harbin	China	336	1102	
19	Tokyo Tower	Tokyo	Japan	333	1092	1958
20	T.V. Tower	Frankfurt	Germany	331	1086	1979
21	National Telecommunications Transmitter	Emely Moor	United Kingdom	329	1080	
22	Sky Tower	Auckland	New Zealand	328	1075	1997
23	Vilnius T.V. Tower	Vilnius	Lithuania	327	1072	1980
24	WTVR Tower	Richmond	United States	319	1045	
25	KCTV Tower	Kansas City	United States	318	1042	1956
26	T.V. Tower	Tallinn	Estonia	314	1030	1975
27	Nanjing T.V. Tower	Nanjing	China	310	1017	
28	Nuremberger Fernmeldeturm	Nuremburg	Germany	308	1011	1977
29	T.V. Tower	Shenyang	China	307	1006	
30	AMP Tower	Sydney	Australia	305	1000	1981
31	Eiffel Tower	Paris	France	300	986	1889
32	T.V. Tower	Bombay	India	300	984	1974
33	Sutro Tower	San Francisco	United States	298	977	1972
34	Zhuzhou T.V. Tower	Zhuzhou	China	293	961	1998
35	Olympic Tower	Munich	Germany	290	951	1968
36	Torre de Collserola	Barcelona	Spain	288	945	1992
37	Heinrich Hertz Tower	Hamburg	Germany	285	933	1967

Tallest Free-Standing Towers (Con't)

Rank	Name	City	Country	Height (m)	Height (ft.)	Completion Year
38	Shijiazhuang T.V. Tower	Shijiazhuang	China	280	919	1998
39	Telemaxx Tower	Hannover	Germany	277	908	1992
40	T.V. Tower	Tbilisi	Georgia	270	886	1970
41	J.G. Strijdom Tower	Johannesburg	South Africa	269	882	1970
42	Colonius Tower	Cologne	Germany	266	872	1981
43	Menara Mahsuri	Langkawi	Malaysia	250	853	UC
44	Koblenz Tower	Koblenz	Germany	255	837	1976
45	T.V. Tower	Brussels	Belgium	253	830	
46	Donauturm	Vienna	Austria	252	827	1964
47	Dresden Tower	Dresden	Germany	252	826	1966
48	Jested T.V. Tower	Prague	Czech Republic	250	819	1968
49	Saint Chrischona Telecommunications Tower	Basel	Switzerland	249	817	1976
50	Seoul Tower	Seoul	South Korea	237	777	1980
51	Pitampura TV Tower	New Dehli	India	235	771	1988
52	Rheinturm	Dusseldorf	Germany	234	768	1982
53	Fukuoka Tower	Fukuoka	Japan	234	768	1996
54	Johannesburg Tower	Johannesburg	South Africa	232	761	1958
55	T.V. Tower	Qingdao	China	232	761	
56	Endem Broadcasting Center	Istanbul	Turkey	230	755	UC
57	Fernmeldeturm Kiel	Kiel	Germany	230	753	1972
58	Fernmeldeturm	Bremen	Germany	228	748	
59	Hebi T.V. Tower	Hebi	China	228	748	1996

Tallest Free-Standing Towers (Con't)

Rank	Name	City	Country	Height (m)	Height (ft.)	Completion Year
60	Puyang T.V. Tower	Puyang	China	227	745	1996
61	Torre de Espana	Madrid	Spain	220	721	1982
62	Dortmund Tower	Dortmund	Germany	219	720	
63	Deyang T.V. Tower	Deyang	China	218	715	1995
64	Guangzhou T.V. Tower	Guangzhou	China	218	715	1991
65	Jilin T.V. Tower	Jilin	China	218	715	1996
66	Shaoxing T.V. Tower	Shaoxing	China	218	715	1995
67	Taizhou T.V. Tower	Taizhou	China	218	715	1994
68	Fernmeldeturm	Stuttgart	Germany	217	711	1956
69	Zizkov T.V. Tower	Prague	Czech Republic	216	709	1992
70	Torre T.V. Bandeirantes	Sao Paulo	Brazil	212	696	1997
71	West Berlin Tower	Berlin	Germany	212	695	
72	Donnersburg Tower	Donnersberg	Germany	207	678	
73	Saddam Tower	Bagdad	Iraq	205	674	
74	Fernmeldeturm	Mannheim	Germany	204	669	1975
75	Helpterberg Tower	Helpterberg	Germany	203	666	
76	Hwaseong Observation Tower	Suwan City	South Korea	200	657	UC
77	Cancun Tower	Cancun	Mexico	200	656	
78	Belgrade Tower	Belgrade	Yugoslavia	200	656	

Source: Marshall Gerometta & Jeff Hertzer

10 Greenest Designs

The 10 Greenest Designs were selected by The American Institute of Architects' (AIA) Committee on the Environment (COTE) to highlight viable architectural design solutions that protect and enhance the environment. COTE represents architects who are committed to making environmental considerations and sustainable design integral to their practice. The following projects address one or more significant environmental challenges such as energy and water conservation, use of recycled construction materials, and designs which improve indoor air quality. Responsible use of building materials, use of daylight over artificial lighting, designs that produce efficiency in heating or cooling, and overall sensitivity to local environmental issues were some of the reasons COTE selected these projects.

To view photographs and descriptions, visit *www.aia.org/pia/vote/topten* on the Internet.

2001 Greenest Designs:
ABN-AMRO Bank World Headquarters
Amsterdam, The Netherlands
Pei Cobb Freed & Partners Architects LLP

Adeline Street Urban Salvage Project
Berkeley, CA
Leger Wanaselja Architecture

BigHorn Home Improvement Center
Silverthorne, CO
Marketplace Architects

Chesapeake Bay Foundation Headquarters
Annapolis, MD
SmithGroup

Denver REI Flagship
Denver, CO
Mithun Architects + Partners

Montgomery Campus, California College of Arts & Crafts
San Francisco, CA
Leddy-Maytum Stacy Architects

Nidus Center for Scientific Enterprise
Creve Coeur, MO
Hellmuth, Obata + Kassabaum

PNC Firstside Center
Pittsburgh, PA
LDA-L.D. Astorino Companies

Sleeping Lady Conference and Retreat Center
Leavenworth, WA
Jones & Jones Architects and Landscape Architects

Zion National Park Visitor Center
Springdale, UT
National Park Service-Denver Service Center

Source: The American Institute of Architects

Did you know...

According to the U.S. Dept. of Energy (DOE), 32 percent of electricity generated in the United States is used to heat, light, and cool commercial buildings.

30 Best Buildings of the 20th Century

The following 30 buildings were judged by a panel of industry experts to be the Best Buildings of the 20th Century. Buildings designed and constructed during the 20th century, regardless of location, were deemed eligible. Buildings were judged based on the following: their influence on the course of 20th century architecture, significant aesthetic contribution, promotion of design principles which have had a positive impact on the built environment, and/or a lasting impact on the history of the 20th century. The buildings below are listed alphabetically and are not ranked in any order.

Air Force Academy Chapel
Colorado Springs, CO
SOM, 1962

Chrysler Building
New York, NY
William Van Alen, 1930

Dulles Airport
Chantilly, VA
Eero Saarinen, 1962

East Wing, National Gallery
Washington, D.C.
I.M. Pei, 1978

Empire State Building
New York, NY
Shreve, Lamb and Harmon, 1931

Fallingwater
Mill Run, PA
Frank Lloyd Wright, 1936

Flatiron Building
New York, NY
Daniel Burnham, 1902

Gamble House
Pasadena, CA
Greene and Greene, 1909

Getty Center
Los Angeles, CA
Richard Meier, 1997

Glass House
New Canaan, CT
Philip Johnson, 1949

Guggenheim Museum
Bilbao, Spain
Frank Gehry, 1997

Hearst Castle
San Simeon, CA
Julia Morgan, 1927-47

Hong Kong and Shanghai Bank
Hong Kong, China
Norman Foster, 1986

Il Palazzo Hotel
Fukuota, Japan
Aldo Rossi, 1987

John Deere Headquarters
Moline, IL
Eero Saarinen, 1963

John Hancock Building
Chicago, IL
SOM, 1970

30 Best Buildings of the 20th Century (Con't)

S.C. Johnson & Son Administration Building
Racine, WI
Frank Lloyd Wright, 1939

Kimbell Art Musuem
Fort Worth, TX
Louis Kahn, 1972

La Sagrada Familia
Barcelona, Spain
Antonio Gaudi, 1882-1926

National Farmers' Bank
Owatonna, MN
Louis Sullivan, 1908

Nebraska State Capitol
Lincoln, NE
Bertram Goodhue, 1924

Notre Dame-du-Haut
Ronchamp, France
Le Corbusier, 1955

Salk Institute
La Jolla, CA
Louis Kahn, 1966

Seagram Building
New York, NY
Mies van der Rohe, 1956

Stockholm City Hall
Stockholm, Sweden
Ragnar Östberg, 1923

Sydney Opera House
Sydney, Australia
Jørn Utzon, 1973

Thorncrown Chapel
Eureka Springs, AR
E. Fay Jones, 1980

Tokyo City Hall
Tokyo, Japan
Kenzo Tange, 1991

Villa Savoye
Poissy, France
Le Corbusier, 1929

Woolworth Building
New York, NY
Cass Gilbert, 1913

Source: Council House Research

World's Best Skylines

This list ranks the impressiveness of the world's skylines by measuring the density and height of the skyscrapers in each city. Each building over 295 feet (90 meters) tall contributes points to its home city's score equal to the number of feet it exceeds this benchmark height. This list also provides the name of the tallest buildings in each city along with its height and world ranking.

For more information about skyscrapers worldwide, a ranking of over 100 skylines, and an explanation of how the ranking is calculated, visit *www.skycrapers.com*, the compiler of this list.

Rank	Points	City	Country	# Buildings >295 feet (90m)	Tallest Bldg./World Ranking
1*	25,620	New York	USA	461	One World Trade Center (1,368 ft, #5)
2	15,887	Hong Kong	China	231	Central Plaza (1,227ft, #10)
3	11,956	Chicago	USA	219	Sears Tower (1,450 ft, #3)
4	6,769	Shanghai	China	114	Jin Mao Building (1,381 ft, #4)
5	5,608	Tokyo	Japan	91	Tokyo Metropolitan Government (797 ft, #81)
6	4,224	Houston	USA	85	Chase Tower (1,000 ft, #25)
7	3,695	Dallas	USA	84	Bank of America Plaza (921 ft, #43)
8	3,570	Kuala Lumpur	Malaysia	49	Petronas Tower I (1,483 ft, #1)
9	3,377	Toronto	Canada	64	First Canadian Place (951 ft, #37)
10	3,371	Sydney	Australia	72	MLC Center (751 ft. #108)
11	3,289	Los Angeles	USA	58	Library Tower (1,018 ft, #21)
12	3,288	San Francisco	USA	101	Transamerica Pyramid (853 ft, #60)
13	3,132	Shenzhen	China	45	Shun Hing Square (1,260 ft, #8)
14	2,630	Atlanta	USA	53	Bank of America Plaza (1,023 ft, #20)
15	2,609	Melbourne	Australia	60	Rialto Tower (814 ft, #73)

World's Best Skylines (Con't)

Rank	Points	City	Country	# Buildings >295 feet (90m)	Tallest Bldg./World Ranking
16	2,448	Paris	France	102	Tour Maine Montparnasse (686 ft., #187)
17	2,161	Philadelphia	USA	57	One Liberty Place (945 ft, #39)
18	2,159	Boston	USA	45	John Hancock Tower (788 ft, #85)
19	2,120	Seoul	South Korea	34	Korea Life Insurance Company (817 ft, #71)
20	1,951	Seattle	USA	44	Bank of America Tower (954 ft, #34)
21	1,948	Calgary	Canada	45	Petro-Canada I (689 ft., #181)
22	1,763	Minneapolis	USA	46	First Bank Place (775 ft, #94)
23	1,725	Frankfurt	Germany	32	Commerzbank Tower (981 ft, #28)
24	1,714	Makati	Philippines	23	Philippine Bank of Communications (791 ft, #84)
25	1,666	Bangkok	Thailand	18	Baiyoke Tower II (1,050 ft, #18)

* At press time, the World's Best Skylines ranking had not been recalculated pursuant to events on September 11, 2001. Despite the loss of the World Trade Center Towers and surrounding buildings, New York City is expected to still rank number one.

Source: SKYSCRAPERS.COM

The city's skyline is a physical representation of its facts of life. But a skyline is also a potential work of art.

Paul Spreiregen

Design & Historic Preservation

Over the last decades, awareness of historic
preservation has grown throughout the
United States. This chapter highlights many
of the organizations that assist individuals,
professionals, and communities with preservation efforts, and the numerous advocacy
programs that alert the public to historic
resources, both in the U.S. and worldwide, in
danger of being lost. Preservation programs
and awards are also included.

Abbott Lowell Cummings Award

The Abbott Lowell Cummings Award is presented annually by the Vernacular Architecture Forum (VAF), honoring outstanding books published about North American vernacular architecture and landscape. A review committee prioritizes submissions on new information, the role of fieldwork in research, critical approach and the model provided in writing and research methods. A founder of the VAF, Abbott Lowell Cummings was a prolific researcher and writer. He is best known for his magnum opus, *The Framed Houses of Massachusetts Bay, 1625-1725* (1979).

For additional information, visit the VAF's Web site at *www.vernacular architecture.org*.

1983
"'In a Manner and Fashion Suitable to Their Degree': An Investigation of the Material Culture of Early Rural Pennsylvania," in *Working Papers from the Regional Economic History Research Center vol. 5 no. 1*, by Jack Michel

1984
no award granted

1985
Big House, Little House, Back House, Barn: The Connected Farm Buildings of New England by Thomas Hubka (University Press of New England)

1986
Hollybush by Charles Martin (University of Tennessee Press)

1987
Holy Things and Profane: Anglican Parish Churches in Colonial Virginia by Dell Upton (Architectural History Foundation)

1988
Architecture and Rural Life in Central Delaware, 1700-1900 by Bernard L. Herman (University of Tennessee Press)

1989
Study Report for Slave Quarters Reconstruction at Carter's Grove by the Colonial Williamsburg Foundation

Study Report for the Bixby House Restoration by Old Sturbridge Village

1990
Manhattan for Rent, 1785-1850 by Elizabeth Blackmar (Cornell University Press)

Building the Octagon by Orlando Rideout (American Institute of Architects)

1991
Architects and Builders in North Carolina by Catherine Bishir, Charlotte Brown, Carl Lounsbury, and Ernest Wood, III (University of North Carolina Press)

1992
Alone Together: A History of New York's Early Apartments by Elizabeth Cromley (Cornell University Press)

A Place to Belong, Community, Order and Everyday Space in Calvert, Newfoundland by Gerald Pocius (University of Georgia Press)

Vernacular Architecture

Henry Glassie

Henry Glassie's most recent work deals with the way common buildings can contribute to a more democratic history, using examples from the United States, Ireland, England, Sweden, Turkey, and Bangladesh.

Abbott Lowell Cummings Award (Con't)

1993
> Homeplace: The Social Use and Meaning of the Folk Dwelling in Southwestern North Carolina by Michael Ann Williams (University of Georgia Press)

> The Park and the People: A History of Central Park by Roy Rosenzweig and Elizabeth Blackmar (Cornell University Press)

1994
> The Stolen House by Bernard L. Herman (University Press of Virginia)

1995
> Living Downtown: The History of Residential Hotels in the United States by Paul Groth (University of California Press)

1996
> An Illustrated Glossary of Early Southern Architecture and Landscape by Carl Lounsbury (Oxford University Press)

1997
> Unplanned Suburbs: Toronto's American Tragedy, 1900-1950 by Richard Harris (Johns Hopkins University Press)

1998
> City Center to Regional Mall: Architecture, the Automobile, and Retailing in Los Angeles, 1920-1950 by Richard Longstreth (MIT Press)

1999
> The Myth of Santa Fe: Creating a Modern Regional Tradition by Chris Wilson (University of New Mexico Press)

> Architecture of the United States by Dell Upton (Oxford University Press)

2000
> Delta Sugar: Louisiana's Vanishing Plantation Landscape by John B. Rehder (Johns Hopkins University Press)

Honorable Mentions
> Cheap, Quick & Easy: Imitative Architectural Materials, 1870-1930 by Pamela H. Simpson (University of Tennessee Press)

> Building Community, Keeping the Faith: German Catholic Vernacular Architecture in a Rural Minnesota Parish by Fred W. Peterson (Minnesota Historical Society Press)

2001
> Vernacular Architecture by Henry Glassie (Indiana University Press)

Source: Vernacular Architecture Forum

America's 11 Most Endangered Historic Places

Every June the National Trust for Historic Preservation, in conjunction with the History Channel, compiles a list of the 11 most threatened historic sites in the United States. Since 1988, the 11 Most Endangered list has highlighted more than 100 historic places threatened by neglect, deterioration, insufficient funds, inappropriate development, or insensitive public policy. While being listed does not guarantee protection or financial support, in the past the attention generated by the Endangered Historic Places has brought a broader awareness to the country's diminishing historic resources and generated local support for the threatened sites.

For photos and a history about each site, visit the National Trust's Web site at *www.nthp.org/11most/*.

2001 America's 11 Most Endangered Historic Places:

Historic American Movie Theaters, *Nationwide*
Independent theaters nationwide can't compete with studio-owned multiplexes that monopolize first-run movies; fewer than 300 still operate.

Bok Kai Temple, *Marysville, California*
This 1880 Taoist temple's exquisite murals, gilt statues and intricate wood carvings have fallen victim to weather and deterioration.

Telluride Valley Floor, *Telluride, Colorado*
A massive resort development threatens to destroy this lush glacial valley and Telluride's historic context, forever altering one of the Rockies' last intact mining towns.

CIGNA Campus, *Bloomfield, Connecticut*
One of the country's first suburban office campuses and milestones in modern architecture, these International Style buildings may be demolished.

Carter G. Woodson Home, *Washington, D.C.*
Home to the founder of the Black History movement and long a center of African-American culture, this rowhouse has deteriorated and needs immediate stabilization.

Ford Island at Pearl Harbor, *Honolulu, Hawaii*
The original airfield, air tower and World War II-era bungalows still remain after the 1941 attack; a major development initiative begun by the Navy could forever alter this National Historic Landmark.

Miller-Purdue Barn, *Grant County, Indiana*
Like hundreds of historic barns nationwide that are burned down or allowed to deteriorate, this 1850s American icon could disappear unless an adaptive reuse is found.

Stevens Creek Settlements, *Lincoln, Nebraska*
Pastoral landscapes and immigrant farms, some in the same families for seven generations, are threatened by a proposed expansion of the Lincoln beltway.

Prairie Churches of North Dakota
These centers of community, heritage and hope, founded by settlers from all walks of life, are threatened by deterioration as state population declines.

Source: National Trust for Historic Preservation

One of North Dakota's many vacant prairie churches, the Ukrainian Orthodox Church in Wilton, North Dakota. Photo: Jim Lindberg.

A view down Second Street in the Historic Jackson Ward, Richmond, Virginia. Photo: Historic Jackson Ward Association, Inc.

America's 11 Most Endangered Historic Places (Con't)

Los Caminos del Rio, *Lower Rio Grande Valley,*
Texas
The diverse culture and architecture of this region
is threatened by development pressures and
neglect.

Historic Jackson Ward, *Richmond, Virginia*
The "Harlem of the South," this Richmond neighborhood needs investment, protection from demolition and a master plan.

Source: National Trust for Historic Preservation

Did you know...

In its 13-year history, the Most
Endangered Historic Places program has managed to save every
listed property from demolition
except the Mapes Hotel in Reno,
NV, which was destroyed on
January 30, 2000.

America's Most Historic Small Towns

The Internet site ePodunk.com, a repository of in-depth information about more than 20,000 communities around the United States, maintains a list of the most historic small towns in the country. This Historic Small Towns Index was prepared by assigning a value to each of the following conditions: the number of buildings listed on the National Register of Historic Places, the size of National Register Historic Districts, the age of its housing, and the number of projects awarded federal preservation tax credits. Numbers were analyzed for counties with fewer than 100,000 residents.

For more information about this list, profiles of each of the ranked towns, or for other statistical information about small towns, visit *www.epodunk.com* on the Internet.

Top 10 Most Historic Small Towns in America

1. Shirley, Massachusetts
2. Woonsocket, Rhode Island
3. Wheeling, West Virginia
4. Bristol, Connecticut
5. Montpelier, Vermont
6. Natchez, Mississippi
7. Deadwood, South Dakota
8. Hudson, New York
9. Newport, Kentucky
10. Quincy, Illinois

Top-Ranked Towns By State

ALABAMA
  Greenville
  Florence
  Marion

ARIZONA
  Prescott
  Douglas
  Flagstaff

ARKANSAS
  Hot Springs
  Eureka Springs
  Searcy

CALIFORNIA
  El Portal & Yosemite National Park
  Mendocino
  Sonora

COLORADO
  Dolores
  Trinidad
  Durango

CONNECTICUT
  Bristol
  Westport
  Branford

DELAWARE
  New Castle
  Dover
  Laurel

FLORIDA
  Key West
  Apalachicola
  Palatka

GEORGIA
  Rome
  Thomasville
  Greensboro

America's Most Historic Small Towns (Con't)

IDAHO
- Wallace
- Lewiston
- Pocatello

ILLINOIS
- Quincy
- Galena
- Chautauqua

INDIANA
- Cambridge City
- Vincennes
- Rockville

IOWA
- Guttenberg
- Dubuque
- Maquoketa

KANSAS
- Leavenworth
- White Cloud

KENTUCKY
- Newport
- Versailles
- Danville

LOUISIANA
- Natchitoches
- Donaldsonville
- Franklin

MAINE
- Kennebunkport
- Castine
- Rockland

MARYLAND
- Frostburg
- Easton
- Princess Anne

MASSACHUSETTS
- Shirley
- Newburyport
- Easton

MICHIGAN
- Hancock
- Petoskey
- Crystal Falls

MINNESOTA
- Red Wing
- Winona
- Faribault

MISSISSIPPI
- Natchez
- Meridian
- Columbus

MISSOURI
- Saint Joseph
- Boonville
- Hannibal

MONTANA
- Missoula
- Kalispell
- Bozeman

NEBRASKA
- Nebraska City
- Fremont
- Red Cloud

NEVADA
- Virginia City
- Ely

NEW HAMPSHIRE
- Harrisville
- Lyme
- Concord

NEW JERSEY
- Glen Ridge
- Trenton
- Bordentown

NEW MEXICO
- Las Vegas
- Los Ojos
- Gallup

America's Most Historic Small Towns (Con't)

NEW YORK
  Hudson
  Essex
  Cooperstown

NORTH CAROLINA
  Roanoke Rapids
  Wilson
  New Bern

OHIO
  Kelleys Island
  Casstown
  Zanesville

OKLAHOMA
  Ardmore
  Okmulgee

OREGON
  Astoria
  McMinnville
  The Dalles

PENNSYLVANIA
  Gettysburg
  Mount Union
  Paint

RHODE ISLAND
  Woonsocket
  Westerly
  Newport

SOUTH CAROLINA
  Bennettsville
  Chester
  Union

SOUTH DAKOTA
  Deadwood
  Rapid City
  Yankton

TENNESSEE
  Columbia
  Oak Ridge

  Shelbyville

TEXAS
  Bastrop
  Brenham
  Cuero

UTAH
  Spring City
  Logan
  Park City

VIRGINIA
  Charlottesville
  Onancock
  Staunton

VERMONT
  Montpelier
  Hartford
  Arlington

WASHINGTON
  Port Townsend
  Roslyn
  Chehalis

WISCONSIN
  Mineral Point
  Sturgeon Bay
  Watertown

WEST VIRGINIA
  Wheeling
  Martinsburg
  Parkersburg

WYOMING
  Cheyenne
  Moose
  Rawlins

Source: ePodunk.com

Antoinette Forrester Downing Award

The Society of Architectural Historians annually grants the Antoinette Forrester Downing Award to an author for an outstanding publication in the field of historic preservation. Works published in the two years prior to the award are eligible.

For more information contact the SAH at 312-573-1365 or visit their Web site at *www.sah.org*.

1987
Providence, A Citywide Survey of Historic Resources by William McKenzie Woodward and Edward F. Sanderson (Rhode Island Historic Preservation Commission)

1990
East Cambridge: A Survey of Architectural History in Cambridge by Susan E. Maycock (MIT Press)

1991
Somerset: An Architectural History by Paul Baker Touart (Maryland Historical Trust and Somerset County Historical Trust)

1994
The Buried Past: An Archaeological History of Philadelphia by John L. Cotter (University of Pennsylvania Press)

1995
Along the Seaboard Side: the Architectural History of Worcester County, Maryland by Paul Baker Touart (Worcester County)

1996
The Historic Architecture of Wake County, North Carolina by Kelly A. Lally (Wake County Government)

1997
A Guide to the National Road and The National Road by Karl B. Raitz (Johns Hopkins University Press)

1998
A Guide to the Historic Architecture of Eastern North Carolina by Catherine W. Bishir & Michael T. Southern (Chapel Hill University of N.C. Press)

1999
no award granted

2000
Boston's Changeful Times by Michael Holleran (Johns Hopkins University Press)

2001
Preserving Cultural Landscapes in America, by Arnold R. Alanen and Robert Z. Melnick, editors (John Hopkins University Press)

Source: Society for Architectural Historians

Did you know...

Washington, D.C.'s True Reformer Building (John Anderson Lankford, 1903), one of the first buildings designed, financed and built by African-Americans after Reconstruction, was recently renovated by the Public Welfare Foundation, a philanthropic group.

Preserving Cultural Landscapes in America

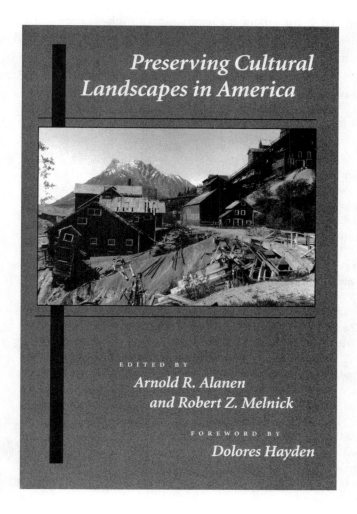

EDITED BY

Arnold R. Alanen
and Robert Z. Melnick

FOREWORD BY

Dolores Hayden

Landscape and Urban Planning has described this book as a "thorough examination . . . [that] has initiated discussions that will be critical to the future practice of general preservation for years to come."

Crowninshield Award

The National Trust for Historic Preservation's highest honor, the Louise DuPont Crowninshield Award, each year recognizes an individual or organization who has demonstrated extraordinary lifetime achievement in the preservation of America's heritage. Winners are selected by the Preservation Committee of the National Trust's Board of Trustees.

For more information contact the National Trust at (800) 944-6847 or visit their Web site at *www.nthp.org*.

1960 The Mount Vernon Ladies Association	1984 Leopold Adler II
1961 Henry Francis DuPont	1985 James Marston Fitch
1962 Katherine Prentis Murphy	1986 Antoinette Downing
1963 Martha Gilmore Robinson	1987 Blair Reeves
1964 Mr. and Mrs. Bertram R. Little	1988 Robert Stipe
1965 Charles E. Peterson	1989 Fred Rath
1966 Ima Hogg	Association of Junior Leagues
Mary Gordon Latham Kellenberger	1990 Frederick Gutheim
1967 no award granted	1991 Robert Garvey
1968 St. Clair Wright	1992 Joan Bacchus Maynard
1969 Mr. and Mrs. Henry N. Flynt	1993 Carl B. Westmoreland
1970 Frank L. Horton	Arthur P. Ziegler Jr.
1971 Frances R. Edmunds	1994 Walter Beinecke Jr.
1972 Alice Winchester	1995 Dana Crawford
1973 Dr. Ricardo E. Alegria	1996 Richard H. Jenrette
1974 Mr. and Mrs. Jacob H. Morrison	1997 Marguerite Neel Williams
1975 no award granted	1998 Frederick Williamson
1976 Katherine U. Warren	Anice Barber Read
1977 San Antonio Conservation Society	1999 Senator Daniel Patrick Moynihan
1978 Helen Duprey Bullock	2000 National Park Service
1979 Old Post Office Landmark Committee	2001 George and Cynthia Mitchell
1980 William J. Murtagh	
Ernest Allen Connally	
1981 Gordon C. Gray	*Source: National Trust for Historic Preservation*
1982 Helen Abell	
1983 Historic American Buildings Survey (HABS) of the National Park Service, U.S. Department of the Interior, in cooperation with The American Institute of Architects and the Library of Congress, Washington, D.C.	

DOCOMOMO International

DOCOMOMO (Documentation and Conservation of Buildings, Sites and Neighborhoods of the Modern Movement) International is headquartered in Eindhoven, Holland, with working parties in 33 countries. Membership consists of architects, engineers, historians, and others dedicated to preserving the architectural heritage of the Modern Movement through documentation and conservation. Founded in 1990, the group has six specialist committees concentrating on registers, technology, education, urbanism, landscapes and gardens, and publications. They also produce the *DOCOMOMO Journal*, published twice a year, with thematic articles and news from the individual chapters. Their technical publications focus on conservation issues related to modern structures.

Address:
DOCOMOMO International Secretariat
DOCOMOMO International
Delft University of Technology, Faculty of
Architecture
Berlageweg 1
2628 CR Delft
The Netherlands
Telephone: +31-15-2788755
Fax: +31-15-2788750
Internet: www.docomomo.com

DOCOMOMO US
Theodore H.M. Prudon, president
P.O. Box 250532
New York, New York 10025
Telephone: 718-624-4304
Fax: 212-8742843
E-mail: docomomo@aol.com

Did you know...

Architectural publisher Bernard Tachsen recently renovated John Lautner's long-neglected, space-age Chemosphere (1960, Los Angeles).

Dozen Distinctive Destinations

The Dozen Distinctive Destinations list is compiled each year by the National Trust for Historic Preservation (NTHP), recognizing the best pre-served and unique communities in the United States. Selected communities are judged on the following criteria: well-managed growth, a dynamic down-town, a commitment to historic preservation with a protected historic core and meaningful context, interesting and attractive architecture, cultural diversity, an economic base of locally owned small businesses, and walkabili-ty for residents and visitors.

For more information on the Dozen Distinctive Destinations, visit the National Trust's Web site at *www.nthp.org*.

2000 Destinations:
San Luis Obispo, CA
Boulder, CO
Thomasville, GA
Lawrence, KS
Lowell, MA
Petoskey, MI
Cooperstown, NY
Pittman Center, TN
Fredricksburg, TX
Lexington, KY
Port Townsend, WA
Chippewa Falls, WI

2001 Destinations:
Eureka Springs, AR
Calistoga, CA
Silverton, CO
Madison, IN
Bonaparte, IA
Northampton, MA
Red Lodge, MT
Las Vegas, NM
Jacksonville, OR
Doylestown, PA
Beaufort, SC
Staunton, VA

Source: National Trust for Historic Preservation

Great American Main Street Awards

Each year the National Trust for Historic Preservation's National Main Street Center selects five communities that have demonstrated considerable success with preservation based revitalization. These towns have all generated broad based support from its residents and business leaders, drawn financial assistance from both public and private sources, and created innovative solutions for their unique situations. Winners each receive $5000 to be used towards further revitalization efforts, a bronze plaque, road signs, and a certificate. Since its inception, the Main Street Center has helped over 1400 communities, which has resulted in an average of $35 in new downtown investments for every dollar spent on the revitalization effort.

For more information, visit the Main Street Center's Web site at *www.mainst.org* or contact them at (202) 588-6219.

1995
- Clarksville, MO
- Dubuque, IA
- Franklin, TN
- Sheboygan Falls, WI
- Old Pasadena, CA

1996
- Bonaparte, IA
- Chippewa Falls, WI
- East Carson Street Business District, Pittsburgh, PA
- Saratoga Springs, NY
- Wooster, OH

1997
- Burlington, VT
- DeLand, FL
- Georgetown, TX
- Holland, MI
- Libertyville, IL

1998
- Corning, IA
- Lanesboro, MN
- Morgantown, WV
- Thomasville, GA
- York, PA

1999
- Bay City, MI
- Cordell, OK
- Denton, TX
- Lafayette, IN
- San Luis Obispo, CA

2000
- Coronado, CA
- Keokuk, IA
- Newkirk, OK
- Port Townsend, WA
- St. Charles, IL

2001
- Danville, KY
- Elkader, IA
- Enid, OK
- Mansfield, OH
- Walla Walla, WA

Source: The National Trust Main Street Center

Guidelines for the Treatment of Cultural Landscapes

The Secretary of the Interior is responsible for establishing professional standards and providing advice on the preservation of cultural resources listed or eligible for listing on the National Register of Historic Places. As the definition and scope of preservation has continued to broaden, the Secretary of the Interior developed the Guidelines for the Treatment of Cultural Landscapes to provide expert guidance when planning and implementing work involving cultural landscapes. A cultural landscape is defined as "a geographic area, including both cultural and natural resources and the wildlife or domestic animals therein, associated with a historic event, activity, or person or exhibiting other cultural or aesthetic values."

For more information about cultural landscapes and their preservation, visit the National Park Service's Web site at *www2.cr.nps.gov/hli/ introguid.htm.*

1. Before undertaking project work, research of a cultural landscape is essential. Research findings help to identify a landscape's historic period(s) of ownership, occupancy and development, and bring greater understanding of the associations that make them significant. Research findings also provide a foundation to make educated decisions for project treatment, and can guide management, maintenance, and interpretation. In addition, research findings may be useful in satisfying compliance reviews (e.g. Section 106 of the National Historic Preservation Act as amended).

2. Although there is no single way to inventory a landscape, the goal of documentation is to provide a record of the landscape as it exists at the present time, thus providing a baseline from which to operate. All component landscapes and features (see definitions below) that contribute to the landscape's historic character should be recorded. The level of documentation needed depends on the nature and the significance of the resource. For example, plant material documentation may ideally include botanical name or species, common name and size. To ensure full representation of existing herba-

ceous plants, care should be taken to document the landscape in different seasons. This level of research may most often be the ideal goal for smaller properties, but may prove impractical for large, vernacular landscapes.

3. Assessing a landscape as a continuum through history is critical in assessing cultural and historic value. By analyzing the landscape, change over time -the chronological and physical "layers" of the landscape –can be understood. Based on analysis, individual features may be attributed to a discrete period of introduction, their presence or absence substantiated to a given date and, therefore the landscape's significance and integrity evaluated. In addition, analysis allows the property to be viewed within the context of other cultural landscapes.

4. In order for the landscape to be considered significant, character-defining features that convey its significance in history must not only be present, but they also must possess historic integrity. Location, setting, design, materials, workmanship, feeling and association should be considered in determining whether a landscape and its character-defining features possess historic integrity.

Guidelines for the Treatment of Cultural Landscapes (Con't)

5. Preservation planning for cultural landscapes involves a broad array of dynamic variables. Adopting comprehensive treatment and management plans, in concert with a preservation maintenance strategy, acknowledges a cultural landscape's ever-changing nature and the inter-relationship of treatment, management and maintenance.

Source: Department of the Interior, National Park Service

Integration of the site's history and culture into design considerations results in buildings that reflect or enhance their environment.

Curtis Worth Fentress

Historic American Buildings Survey (HABS)

The Historic American Buildings Survey (HABS) operates as part of the National Park Service and is dedicated to recording America's historic buildings through measured drawings, written histories, and large-format photographs. The program was started in 1933 as a Civil Works Administration project using unemployed architects to make permanent records of historic American architecture. Following a drop-off in activity after World War II, the program was restored in the early 1950's with student architects providing the research, a practice that continues to the present day. In 1969, the Historic American Engineering Record (HAER) was established as a companion program focusing on America's technological heritage. Records of the over 32,000 recorded historic structures and sites are available to the public through the Prints and Photographs Division of the Library of Congress.

Address:
National Park Service
HABS/HAER Division
1849 "C" Street, NW, Room NC300
Washington, D.C. 20240
Telephone: (202) 343-9625
Internet: www.cr.nps.gov/habshaer/

For information on HABS and HAER archives, contact:

Prints and Photographs Reading Room
Library of Congress
James Madison Building, Room LM-337
Washington, DC 20540-4730
Telephone: (202) 707-6394
Internet: www.loc.gov/rr/print

Some of a city's diversity, historic continuity and character is destroyed when old buildings are razed. The historic significance of architectural styles is as indisputable as the historic events surrounding them. After all, we do not throw out the wedding pictures of our parents because their dress now looks funny, or because the pictures are not quite so wonderful as we once thought they were.

Wolf Von Eckardt

Historic Landscape Initiative

The Historic Landscape Initiative promotes responsible preservation practices to protect America's irreplaceable cultural landscapes, the result of which can lead to an improved quality of life, a sense of place, and identity for future generations, as well as scenic, economic, ecological, recreational, social and educational opportunities. As with historic properties, America's historic landscapes are threatened by loss and change through inappropriate uses, insensitive development, vandalism, and natural forces. The Initiative provides guidance on sound preservation practices for a variety of landscapes, including parks, gardens, rural villages, industrial sites, and agricultural landscapes. Through their workshops, publications, technical assistance, and national policy advisement, the Initiative serves as a clearinghouse for information related to cultural landscapes and their preservation.

Address:
Heritage Preservation Services
National Park Service
1849 C Street NW NC330
Washington, D.C. 20240
Telephone: (202) 343-9597
Internet: www2.cr.nps.gov/hli/

Landscape implies far more than high-style aesthetics; it is a document of the shared aspirations, ingenuity, memories, and culture of its builders.

J.B. Jackson

International Centre for the Study of the Preservation and Restoration of Cultural Property (ICCROM)

Founded by the United Nations' Educational, Scientific and Cultural Organization (UNESCO) in 1956, the International Centre for the Study of the Preservation and Restoration of Cultural Property (ICCROM) is an intergovernmental organization dedicated to the conservation of heritage of all types. It is funded by contributions from its 95 Member States, plus donors and sponsors. ICCROM provides members with information, publications and training; offers technical assistance and sponsors workshops; performs ongoing research and archives findings; and serves as an advocate for preservation. The group maintains one of the largest conservation libraries in the world.

Address:
13, Via di San Michele
I-00153 Rome, Italy
Telephone: +39 06 585 531
Internet: www.iccrom.org

International Council on Monuments and Sites (ICOMOS)

Dedicated to the conservation of the world's historic monuments and sites, the International Council on Monuments and Sites (ICOMOS) is an international, non-governmental organization with National Committees in over 90 countries. The group is the United Nations' Educational, Scientific and Cultural Organization's (UNESCO) principal advisor in matters concerning the conservation of monuments and sites. With the World Conservation Union (IUCN), ICOMOS advises the World Heritage Committee and UNESCO on the nomination of new sites to the World Heritage List. The group also works to establish international standards for the preservation, restoration and management of the cultural environment. ICOMOS members are professional architects, archaeologists, urban planners, engineers, heritage administrators, art historians, and archivists. All members join ICOMOS through the National Committee of their respective countries.

Address:
49-51 rue de la Fédération
75015 Paris, France
Telephone: +33 (0) 1 45 67 67 70
Internet: www.icomos.org

Longest Covered Bridges in the World

Covered bridges still survive throughout the world from many periods of history and are also being restored and rebuilt by covered bridge enthusiasts. The following list contains the 30 longest covered bridges in the world.

For additional information about covered bridges, contact the National Society for the Preservation of Covered Bridges at *dickroycb1@juno.com* or visit *www.atawalk.com* on the Web for covered bridge listings, photographs, and events from around the world.

Rank	Bridge	Feet	Location	Truss Type	# spans	Year built
1	Hartland Bridge	1282	Carleton County, New Brunswick, Canada	Howe	7	1921
2	Reinbrücke	673	Between Stein, Switzerland and Sackingen, Germany	Multiple Queen (overlapping)	7	1803
3	Kapellbrücke	656	Luzern, Switzerland	1 multiple King span, 25 stringers	26	1333
4	Marchand Bridge	499	Pontiac County, Quebec, Canada	Town lattice & Queen	6	1898
5	Perrault Bridge	495	Beauce County, Quebec, Canada	Town lattice variation	4	1928
6	Sevelen/Vaduz Bridge	480	Liechtenstein-Canton of St. Gallen, Switzerland	Howe (double X)	6	1901
7	Cornish-Windsor Bridge	460	Sullivan County, New Hampshire & Windsor County, Vermont	Timber Notch Lattice	2	1866
8	Rosenstein Park Footbridge	449	Baden-Wurrtemberg State, Germany	Ext. Queen & Ext. Steel Queen	2	1977
9	Medora Bridge	434	Jackson County, Indiana	Burr Arch	3	1875
10	unknown	410	Heilbronn-Kochendorf, Germany	Stringer	6	1976
11	Ashnola River Road Bridge	400	Similkameen Division, British-Columbia, Canada	Howe	3	1923
12	Williams Bridge	376	Lawrence County, Indiana	Howe	2	1884
12	Bath Bridge	376	Grafton County, New-Hampshire	Multiple King Post	4	1832

Longest Covered Bridges in the World (Con't)

Rank	Bridge	Feet	Location	Truss Type	# spans	Year built
14	Degussa Footbridge	369	Baden-Wurtemberg State, Germany	Stringer	7	1979
15	Schwäbisch-Hall's Stadtwerke Footbridge	362	Schwabisch-Hall, Germany	Inverted Multiple King	6	1981
16	Cesky Krumlov Footbridge	361	Southern Bohemia, Czech Republic	unknown	unknown	
16	Betlemska-Kaple Bridge	361	Central Bohemia, Czech Republic	unknown	unknown	
18	Medno Footbridge	348	Mendo, Slovenia	Suspension	1	1934
19	Moscow Bridge	334	Rush County, Indiana	Burr Arch	2	1886
20	Shieldstown Bridge	331	Jackson County, Indiana	Burr Arch	2	1876
21	Bell's Ford Bridge	330	Jackson County, Indiana	Post	2	1869
21	Kasernenbrücke	330	Bern Canton, Switzerland	Ext. King	5	1549
21	Knights Ferry Bridge	330	Stanislaus County, California	Pratt	4	1864
24	Swann or Joy Bridge	320	Blount County, Alabama	Town lattice	3	1933
25	West Union Bridge	315	Parke County, Indiana	Burr Arch	2	1876
26	Academia/Pomeroy	305	Juniata County, Pennsylvania	Burr Arch	2	1901
26	Eschikofen-Bonau Bridge	305	Thurgau Canton, Switzerland	Multiple Queen	5	1837
28	Philippi Bridge	304	Barbour County, West Virginia	Burr Arch variation	2	1852
29	St-Edgar Bridge	293	Bonaventure County, Quebec, Canada	Town lattice variation	2	1938
30	Hall Footbridge	290	Tirol Province, Austria	Stringer (above deck)	3	1979

Source: National Society for the Preservation of Covered Bridges, Inc.

Most Visited Historic House Museums in the United States

Every year Counsel House Research, in conjunction with the *Almanac of Architecture & Design*, polls America's historic house museums to determine which are the most popular destinations. For the purposes of this study, "house museum" is defined as a historic house that is currently exhibited and interpreted as a dwelling place. The following houses are this year's most visited historic house museums.

1. Mount Vernon, Mount Vernon, VA
   George Washington, 1785-86

2. Biltmore Estate, Asheville, NC
   Richard Morris Hunt, 1895

3. Hearst Castle, San Simeon, CA
   Julia Morgan, 1927-1947

4. Graceland, Memphis, TN
   Furbringer & Ehrman, 1939

5. Monticello, Home of Thomas Jefferson, Charlottesville, VA
   Thomas Jefferson, 1768-79, 1793-1809

6. Vanderbilt Mansion, Hyde Park, NY
   McKim, Mead, and White, 1898

7. The Breakers, Newport, RI
   Richard Morris Hunt, 1895

8. Arlington House, The Robert E. Lee Memorial, Arlington, VA
   George Hadfield, 1817

9. The Edison and Ford Winter Estates, Fort Myers, FL
   Thomas Edison, 1886 (Edison home)
   Architect unknown, 1911 (Ford home)

10. Betsy Ross House, Philadelphia, PA
    Architect unknown, 1740

11. Paul Revere House, Boston, MA
    Architect unknown, c.1680

12. Boldt Castle, Alexandria Bay, NY
    Hewitt, Stevens & Paist, 1900-04

13. Marble House, Newport, RI
    Richard Morris Hunt, 1892

14. The Hermitage: Home of President Andrew Jackson, Hermitage, TN
    Architect unknown, 1819

15. Lincoln Home, Springfield, IL
    Architect unknown, 1839

16. Carter's Grove, Williamsburg, VA
    John Wheatley, c. 1750-55

17. Viscaya, Miami, FL
    Burrall Hoffman, 1916

18. House of the Seven Gables, Salem, MA
    Architect unknown, 1668

19. Franklin D. Roosevelt Cottage, Lubec, ME
    William T. Sears, 1897

20. Fallingwater, Mill Run, PA
    Frank Lloyd Wright, 1939

21. Franklin D. Roosevelt Home, Hyde Park, NY
    Architect unknown, 1826

22. Laura: A Creole Plantation, Vacherie, LA
    Architect unknown, 1805

23. Beehive House, Salt Lake City, Utah
    Truman Angel, 1854

24. Taliesen West, Scottsdale, AZ
    Frank Lloyd Wright, 1937

25. Rosecliff, Newport, RI
    Stanford White, 1902

Source: Counsel House Research

Biltmore Estate. Photo: © The Biltmore Company.

National Center for Preservation Technology and Training (NCPTT)

The National Center for Preservation Technology and Training (NCPTT) promotes and enhances the preservation and conservation of prehistoric and historic resources in the United States through the advancement and dissemination of preservation technology and training. Created by Congress, the NCPTT is an interdisciplinary program of the National Park Service intended to advance the art, craft and science of historic preservation in the fields of archeology, historic architecture, historic landscapes, objects, materials conservation, and interpretation through research, education and information management. The Center also administers the Preservation Technology and Training Grants Program, one of the few preservation and conservation grants programs devoted to training, technology and basic research issues.

Address:
Northwestern State University
Box 5682
Natchitoches, LA 71497
Telephone: (318) 357-6464
Internet: www. ncptt.nps.gov

Did you know...

Since 1994, more than $4 million in grants have been awarded by the National Center for Preservation Technology and Training (NCPTT).

National Heritage Areas

Since 1984, the United States Congress has designated 18 National Heritage Areas, which are managed by partnerships among federal, state and local governments and the private sector. This distinction is awarded in an effort to preserve areas where "natural, cultural, historic, and scenic resources combine to form a cohesive, nationally distinctive landscape arising from patterns of human activity shaped by geography." The National Park Service provides technical as well as financial assistance for a limited number of years following initial designation. Though Heritage Areas often remain in private hands, activities such as tours, museums and festivals take place through voluntary efforts.

For additional information, including maps, visit ParkNet, the Web site of the National Park Service, at *www.ncrc.nps.gov/heritage.*

National Heritage Areas:
Illinois & Michigan National Heritage Corridor, IL
John H. Chafee Blackstone River Valley National Heritage Corridor, MA
Delaware & Lehigh National Heritage Corridor, PA
Southwestern Pennsylvania Industrial Heritage Route (Path of Progress), PA
Cane River National Heritage Area, LA
Quinebaug & Shetucket Rivers Valley National Heritage Corridor, CT & MA
Cache La Poudre River Corridor, CO
America's Agricultural Heritage Partnership (Silos & Smokestacks), IA

Augusta Canal National Heritage Area, GA
Essex National Heritage Area, MA
Hudson River Valley National Heritage Area, NY
National Coal Heritage Area, WV
Ohio & Erie Canal National Heritage Corridor, OH
Rivers of Steel National Heritage Area, PA
Shenandoah Valley Battlefields National Historic District Commission , VA
South Carolina National Heritage Corridor, SC
Tennessee Civil War Heritage Area, TN
Automobile National Heritage Area, MI

Source: National Park Service

Right: Central Park
Conservancy.

Below: Portland Observatory.

National Preservation Honor Awards

The National Preservation Honor Awards are the National Trust for Historic Preservation's (NTHP) annual program to recognize projects that demonstrate a high level of dedication and support of the ideals and benefits of historic preservation. A jury of preservation professionals and representatives selects winning projects based on their positive effect on the community, pioneering nature, quality, and degree of difficulty. Special interest is placed on those undertakings which utilize historic preservation as a method of revitalization.

For more information, contact the National Trust at (800) 944-6847 or visit their Web site at *www.nthp.org*.

2001 Award Winners:

Parker Westbrook, *Nashville, AR*
Westbrook has spent a lifetime pioneering local, state and national preservation programs and policies.

Tramway Building, *Denver, CO* (1901)
REI chose to put its Denver flagship store in a former power plant, a stirring and successful example to other corporations.

Theresa Brown, *Washington, D.C.*
For more than 35 years, Brown has inspired others by fighting to bring her neighborhood back to life.

Delta Air Lines DC-3, *Atlanta, GA*
Delta and thousands of volunteers partnered to restore one of its first DC-3 airplanes to mint flying condition.

Reliance Building, *Chicago, IL* (1895)
A complex restoration and a public-private partnership transformed one of the nation's first skyscrapers into a high-end boutique hotel.

Portland Observatory, *Portland, ME* (1807)
The nation's last maritime signal station, dark since 1923, is again a community mainstay thanks to community support.

Trustees of Reservations, *Beverly, MA*
With 25,000 members, the Trustees care for 87 historic properties and 12,000 acres of protected land.

Redeemer Missionary Baptist Church, *Minneapolis, MN* (1910)
After urban flight and highway intrusion, this congregation rallied to save its unique Prairie-style church.

KiMo Theatre, *Albuquerque, NM* (1927)
This unique Pueblo Deco theater recovered from time and neglect and inspired a neighborhood rebirth.

Central Park Conservancy, *New York, NY*
The Conservancy restored New York's centerpiece landscape in a massive 15-year undertaking and partnership with the city.

Severance Hall, *Cleveland, OH* (1930)
Home to one of the world's most famous orchestras, this Neoclassical and Art Deco concert hall is ready for the 21st century.

McClain High School, *Greenfield, OH* (1915)
Rather than demolish, the community chose to save this landmark, bringing education and preservation into the 21st century.

National Preservation Honor Awards (Con't)

Providence Preservation Society Revolving Fund,
Providence, RI
For 21 years, the Fund has helped bring the city's
inner neighborhoods back to life.

Heritage Commons at Fort Douglas, *Salt Lake City,
UT* (1863)
The University of Utah integrated this historic fort
into its plans for the Olympics and student housing.

Steam Plant Square, *Spokane, WA* (1916)
After heating downtown Spokane for 70 years, the
Steam Plant now hosts offices, shops and restau-
rant.

Source: National Trust for Historic Preservation

Left: Steam Plant Square.

Bottom (L-R): Parker Westbrook, Theresa Brown.

National Preservation Institute (NPI)

The National Preservation Institute (NPI) is a non-profit organization dedicated to the management, development, and preservation of historic, cultural, and environmental resources. Toward this end, NPI offers specialized information, continuing education, and, upon request, professional training tailored to the sponsor's needs. Many preservation-related services are available from NPI, including authentication of historic reproductions and historic real estate. NPI is also registered with The American Institute of Architects Continuing Education System.

Address:
P.O. Box 1702
Alexandria, VA 22313
Telephone: (703) 765-0100
Internet: www.npi.org

Did you know...

The Robie House (Frank Lloyd Wright, 1909) was originally built for $35,000, the equivalent of approx. $600,000 today; its planned restoration will cost at least $7 million.

National Trust for Historic Preservation

Since its founding in 1949, the National Trust for Historic Preservation (NTHP) has worked to preserve historic buildings and neighborhoods. Through educational programs, publications, financial assistance and government advocacy, the National Trust has been successful in revitalizing communities across the country. This private, non-profit organization operates six regional offices, 20 historic sites, publishes the award winning *Preservation* magazine, hosts the nation's largest preservation conference every year, and works with thousands of local community groups nationwide, through such programs as Main Street, to preserve their history and buildings.

Address:
1785 Massachusetts Avenue, NW
Washington, DC 20036
Telephone: (202) 588-6000
www.nthp.org

Did you know...

The NTHP now owns and operates 20 U.S. historic sites, which received nearly 803,000 visitors in 2000.

National Trust Historic Hotels of America

The properties listed on the National Trust for Historic Preservation's Historic Hotels of America are a compilation of some of the country's most noteworthy historic hotels, resorts, and inns. Each of the properties are fifty years or older. In addition, they are either eligible for or listed on the National Register of Historic Places or of locally recognized historic significance.

For more information, contact the National Trust for Historic Preservation at (800) 944-6847 or visit the Historic Hotels of America on the Web at *www.historichotels.org.*

ALABAMA
Radisson Admiral Semmes, Mobile

ARIZONA
Royal Palms Hotel and Casitas, Phoenix
Arizona Inn, Tucson

ARKANSAS
Crescent Hotel & Spa, Eureka Springs

CALIFORNIA
La Playa, Carmel
Hotel Del Coronado, Coronado
Furnace Creek Inn, Death Valley
Eureka Inn, Eureka
Grande Colonial, La Jolla
La Valencia, La Jolla
Regal Biltmore, Los Angeles
Mendocino Hotel & Garden Suites, Mendocino
Ojai Valley Inn & Spa, Ojai
Paso Robles Inn, Paso Robles
Mission Inn, Riverside
Delta King Hotel, Sacramento
Fairmont Hotel San Francisco, San Francisco
Sir Francis Drake, San Francisco
Hyatt Sainte Claire, San Jose
El Encanto Hotel & Garden Villas, Santa Barbara
The Georgian Hotel, Santa Monica
Hotel La Rose, Santa Rosa

COLORADO
Hotel Jerome, Aspen
Hotel Boulderado, Boulder
The Brown Palace Hotel, Denver
The Oxford Hotel, Denver
Historic Strater Hotel, Durango
The Cliff House Inn, Manitou Springs
The Redstone Inn, Redstone

CONNECTICUT
The Lighthouse Inn, New London

DELAWARE
The Inn at Montchanin Village, Montchanin
Hotel du Pont, Wilmington

DISTRICT OF COLUMBIA
The Hay-Adams Hotel
Henley Park Hotel
The Jefferson Hotel
Morrison-Clark Inn
Renaissance Mayflower

FLORIDA
The Biltmore, Coral Gables
The Colony Hotel & Cabaña Club, Delray Beach
Greyfield Inn, Fernandina Beach
Gulf Stream Hotel, Lake Worth
The Hotel, Miami Beach
Lakeside Inn, Mt. Dora
Park Central Hotel, South Beach
Casa Monica Hotel, St. Augustine

National Trust Historic Hotels of America (Con't)

Don CeSar Beach Resort and Spa, St. Pete Beach
Renaissance Vinoy Resort, St. Petersburg

GEORGIA
The Windsor Hotel, Americus
The Georgian Terrace, Atlanta
The Partridge Inn, Augusta
Jekyll Island Club, Jekyll Island
Marshall House, Savannah
River Street Inn, Savannah
The King and Prince Beach & Golf Resort, St.
   Simons Island
Melhana Plantation, Thomasville

ILLINOIS
Omni Ambassador East, Chicago
Regal Knickerbocker, Chicago
Deer Path Inn, Lake Forest
Hotel Baker, St. Charles

INDIANA
French Lick Springs Resort, French Lick

IOWA
Hotel Winneshiek, Decorah
Hotel Savery, Des Moines
Hotel Pattee, Perry

KANSAS
The Eldridge, Lawrence

KENTUCKY
Boone Tavern Hotel, Berea
The Brown Hotel, Louisville

LOUISIANA
Delta Queen Steamboat, New Orleans
Fairmont New Orleans, New Orleans
Le Pavillon Hotel, New Orleans
Hotel Maison de Ville, New Orleans
Hotel Monteleone, New Orleans

MAINE
The Colony Hotel, Kennebunkport
Asticou Inn, Northeast Harbor
Portland Regency Inn, Portland

MARYLAND
Historic Inns of Annapolis, Annapolis
Admiral Fell Inn, Baltimore
Kent Manor Inn, Stevensville

MASSACHUSETTS
Boston Park Plaza Hotel, Boston
The Fairmont Copley Plaza, Boston
The Lenox, Boston
Chatham Bars Inn, Chatham
Harbor View Hotel, Edgartown
Cranwell Resort & Golf Club, Lenox
Hotel Northampton, Northampton
Hawthorne Hotel, Salem
The Red Lion Inn, Stockbridge

MICHIGAN
Grand Hotel, Mackinac Island
The Landmark Inn, Marquette

MINNESOTA
St. James Hotel, Red Wing
The Saint Paul Hotel, St. Paul

MISSISSIPPI
Monmouth Plantation, Natchez

MISSOURI
Raphael Hotel, Kansas City
Hyatt Regency St. Louis at Union Station

MONTANA
The Pollard, Red Lodge

NEW HAMPSHIRE
Mount Washington Hotel & Resort, Bretton
   Woods
The Balsams, Dixville Notch
Eagle Mountain House, Jackson

NEW JERSEY
Seaview Marriott Resort, Absecon

NEW MEXICO
Hotel St. Francis, Santa Fe
La Fonda, Santa Fe
Bishop's Lodge, Sante Fe

National Trust Historic Hotels of America (Con't)

NEW YORK
The Sagamore, Bolton Landing, Lake George
Otesaga Hotel, Cooperstown
Mohonk Mountain House, New Paltz
The Algonquin, A Camberley Hotel, New York City
The Plaza, New York City
The Sherry Netherland, New York City
The Waldorf-Astoria, New York City
The Warwick, New York City
American Hotel, Sag Harbor
Hotel Saranac of Paul Smith's College, Saranac Lake
Dolce Tarrytown House, Tarrytown

NORTH CAROLINA
Grove Park Inn, Asheville
The Carolina Inn, Chapel Hill
The Dunhill, Charlotte
Lords Proprietors' Inn, Edenton

OHIO
The Cincinnatian, Cincinnati
Omni Netherland Plaza, Cincinnati
Renaissance Cleveland Hotel, Cleveland
The Lafayette, Marietta
Vernon Manor, Cincinnati

OKLAHOMA
Hotel Ambassador, Tulsa

OREGON
The Governor Hotel, Portland
The Heathman, Portland

PENNSYLVANIA
The Hotel Hershey, Hershey
Leola Village Inn & Suites, Leola
Park Hyatt Philadelphia at the Bellevue, Philadelphia
Skytop Lodge, Skytop
Nittany Lion Inn, State College
Yorktowne Hotel, York

PUERTO RICO
Hotel El Convento, Old San Juan

RHODE ISLAND
Inn at Newport Beach, Middletown
Hotel Viking, Newport

SOUTH CAROLINA
John Rutledge House Inn, Charleston
Kings Courtyard Inn, Charleston
Westin Francis Marion Hotel, Charleston

TENNESSEE
The Peabody, Memphis
The Hermitage Hotel, Nashville

TEXAS
The Driskill, Austin
Stoneleigh Hotel, Dallas
Camino Real Hotel, El Paso
Stockyards Hotel, Ft. Worth
Renaissance Casa de Palmas, McAllen
The Menger, San Antonio

UTAH
Ben Lomond Historic Suite Hotel, Ogden

VERMONT
The Old Tavern at Grafton, Grafton
The Equinox, Manchester Village
Middlebury Inn, Middlebury
Green Mountain Inn, Stowe
Basin Harbor Club, Vergennes

VIRGINIA
Abingdon's Martha Washington Inn, Abingdon
Boar's Head Inn, Charlottesville
Bailiwick Inn, Fairfax
The Homestead, Hot Springs
Wayside Inn, Middletown
The Jefferson, Richmond
Linden Row Inn, Richmond
Williamsburg Inn, Williamsburg
Williamsburg Colonial Houses, Williamsburg
The Hotel Roanoke, Roanoke

National Trust Historic Hotels of America (Con't)

WASHINGTON
    Rosario Resort, Eastsound, Orcas Island
    The Paradise Inn, Mt. Rainier National Park
    Mayflower Park Hotel, Seattle

WEST VIRGINIA
    The Greenbrier, White Sulphur Springs

WISCONSIN
    The American Club, Kohler
    Hotel Metro, Milwaukee
    The Pfister Hotel, Milwaukee

Hotel names in bold are new members.

Source: National Trust for Historic Preservation

NTHP/HUD Secretary's Award for Excellence in Historic Preservation

Each year, as part of its Preservation Conference, the National Trust for Historic Places (NTHP) confers several awards for preservation, including the HUD Secretary's Award for Excellence in Historic Preservation. This award specifically honors preservation projects which also provide affordable housing and/or expanded economic opportunities for low- and moderate-income families and individuals. The criteria for the award includes the project's impact on the community, quality and degree of difficulty, unusual or pioneering nature, affordable housing/economic development opportunities, and ability to fit into an overall community redevelopment plan.

For additional information and to request an application, call HUD USER at (800) 245-2691 and select "Secretary's Awards" when prompted, or visit the HUD Web site at *www.huduser.org/research/secaward.html*.

1998
  A.T. Lewis and Rio Grande Lofts, Denver, CO
1999
  Belle Shore Apartments, Chicago, IL
2000
  The city of Covington, KY
2001
  Notre Dame Academy, Cleveland, OH

Source: National Trust for Historic Places/HUD

Did you know...

Since the early 1980s, the city of Covington, KY, through their Urban Reclamation Program, has restored 134 historic buildings, reselling many of them to low- and moderate-income homeowners.

Rural Heritage Program

The Rural Heritage Program (RHP), a part of the National Trust for Historic Preservation, is dedicated to the recognition and preservation of rural historic and cultural resources. Through their educational programs, publications, and technical assistance, the RHP supports the efforts of rural communities across the United States to both preserve and live with their heritage. The program works with communities on such topics as farmland preservation, scenic byways, heritage areas and parks, historic roads, and sprawl.

Address:
1785 Massachusetts Avenue, NW
Washington, DC 20036
Telephone: (202) 588-6279
Internet: www.ruralheritage.org

Using the things we know or sense about places but seldom put into words, we can bring all of our minds to bear on the problems of how our communities, regions, and landscapes should change. We each have a contribution to make.

Tony Hiss

Save America's Treasures

Launched in May 1998, Save America's Treasures is a public-private initiative between the White House Millennium Council and the National Trust for Historic Preservation dedicated to identifying and rescuing the enduring symbols of America and to raising public awareness and support for their preservation. This national effort to protect America's threatened cultural treasures includes significant documents, works of art, maps, journals, and historic structures that document and illuminate the history and culture of the United States. Applications to be designated an Official Project are accepted on an ongoing basis from non-profit organizations and federal, state, and local agencies that are involved in the preservation, restoration, or conservation of historic buildings, sites, documents, artifacts, objects, or related educational activities. Becoming an Official Project is the first step towards eligibility for Save America's Treasures grants and, in and of itself, often generates local support. In the two years since its founding, Save America's Treasures has designated 523 Official Projects, a list of which is available on their Web site, and raised over $100 million in public-private funds to support preservation efforts.

Address:
1785 Massachusetts Avenue, N.W.
Washington, D.C. 20036
Telephone: (202) 588-6202
Internet: www.saveamericastreasures.org

Did you know...

By the end of 2000, Save America's Treasures had designated more than 700 official projects in all 50 states and generated more than $150 million in preservation funding.

Secretary of the Interior's Standards for Rehabilitation

The Secretary of the Interior's Standards for Rehabilitation were developed to help protect our nation's irreplaceable cultural resources by promoting consistent preservation practices. The Standards recognize the need to alter or add to a historic property in order to meet continuing or changing uses. Following the Standards helps to preserve the distinctive character of a historic building and its site while accommodating new uses. The Standards (36 CFR Part 67) apply to historic buildings of all periods, styles, types, materials, and sizes, as well as to both the exterior and the interior of historic buildings. The Standards also encompass related landscape features and the building's site and environment as well as attached, adjacent, or related new construction. In addition, in order for a rehabilitation project to be eligible for the 20% rehabilitation tax credit, the Standards must be followed.

For more information about how to apply these Standards to restoration projects and tax credits, visit the National Park Service's Web site at *www2.cr.nps.gov/tps/tax/rehabstandards.htm*.

1. A property shall be used for its historic purpose or be placed in a new use that requires minimal change to the defining characteristics of the building and its site and environment.

2. The historic character of a property shall be retained and preserved. The removal of historic materials or alteration of features and spaces that characterize a property shall be avoided.

3. Each property shall be recognized as a physical record of its time, place, and use. Changes that create a false sense of historical development, such as adding conjectural features or architectural elements from other buildings, shall not be undertaken.

4. Most properties change over time; those changes that have acquired historic significance in their own right shall be retained and preserved.

5. Distinctive features, finishes, and construction techniques or examples of craftsmanship that characterize a historic property shall be preserved.

6. Deteriorated historic features shall be repaired rather than replaced. Where the severity of deterioration requires replacement of a distinctive feature, the new feature shall match the old in design, color, texture, and other visual qualities and, where possible, materials. Replacement of missing features shall be substantiated by documentary, physical, or pictorial evidence.

7. Chemical or physical treatments, such as sandblasting, that cause damage to historic materials shall not be used. The surface cleaning of structures, if appropriate, shall be undertaken using the gentlest means possible.

Secretary of the Interior's Standards for Rehabilitation (Con't)

8. Significant archeological resources affected by a project shall be protected and preserved. If such resources must be disturbed, mitigation measures shall be undertaken.

9. New additions, exterior alterations, or related new construction shall not destroy historic materials that characterize the property. The new work shall be differentiated from the old and shall be compatible with the massing, size, scale, and architectural features to protect the historic integrity of the property and its environment.

10. New additions and adjacent or related new construction shall be undertaken in such a manner that if removed in the future, the essential form and integrity of the historic property and its environment would be unimpaired.

Source: Department of the Interior, National Park Service

Did you know...

Recent legislation passed in Maryland grants tax credits to new and rehabilitated buildings – commercial and residential – that save 35 percent more energy than required under the most stringent codes.

Threatened National Historic Landmarks

National Historic Landmarks are buildings, sites, districts, structures, and objects determined by the Secretary of the Interior to possess national significance to American history and culture and are deemed worthy of preservation. Every two years, out of the almost 2,500 National Historic Landmarks, the National Park Service compiles a list of those that are in eminent danger of destruction due to deterioration, incompatible new construction, demolition, erosion, vandalism, and looting. The purpose of this list is to alert the Federal government and the American people of this potential loss of their heritage.

For additional information about the National Historic Landmarks program or the Threatened List, visit the National Park's web site at *www.nps.gov/nhl/* or contact Heritage Preservation Services at (202) 343-9583.

2001 Threatened National Historic Landmarks – Buildings and Historic Districts

Alaska
Adak Army Base and Adak Naval Operating Base, Adak Station
Cape Field at Fort Glenn, Fort Glenn
Holy Assumption Orthodox Church, Kenai
Kake Cannery, Kake

Arizona
Fort Huachuca
Old Oraibi, Oraibi

Arkansas
Bathhouse Row, Hot Springs

California
Aquatic Park Historic District, San Francisco
Locke Historic District, Locke
Mare Island Naval Shipyard, Vallejo
Presidio of San Francisco
Warner's Ranch, Warner Springs

Colorado
Central City/Black Hawk Historic District, Central City
Cripple Creek Historic District, Cripple Creek

District of Columbia
Terrell (Mary Church) House

Hawaii
Kalaupapa Leprosy Settlement
United States Naval Base, Pearl Harbor, Pearl City

Illinois
Adler Planetarium, Chicago
Grant Park Stadium. Chicago
Orchestra Hall, Chicago
Pullman Historic District, Chicago
Sears, Roebuck, and Company 1905-6 Complex, Chicago
Unity Temple, Oak Park

Indiana
Bailly (Joseph) Homestead, Porter County
Cannelton Cotton Mills, Cannelton
Debs (Eugene V.) Home, Terre Haute
Eleutherian College Classroom and Chapel Building, Lancaster

Iowa
Fort Des Moines Provisional Army Officer Training School, Des Moines

Threatened National Historic Landmarks (Con't)

Kansas
Fort Leavenworth, Leavenworth

Louisiana
Courthouse (The) and Lawyer's Row, Clinton

Maryland
Chestertown Historic District, Chestertown
Resurrection Manor, Hollywood

Massachusetts
Boston Naval Shipyard
Fenway Studio, Boston
Nantucket Historic District, Nantucket
Old Deerfield Historic District, Deerfield
Springfield Armory, Springfield

Michigan
Fair Lane, Dearborn
Pewabic Pottery, Detroit

Minnesota
Fort Snelling, Minneapolis-St. Paul
Volstead (Andrew J.) House, Granite Falls

Mississippi
Champion Hill Battlefield, Bolton
Montgomery (I.T.) House, Mount Bayou
Siege and Battle of Corinth Sites, Corinth

Missouri
Arrow Rock, Arrow Rock
Tower Grove Park, St. Louis

Montana
Butte Historic District, Butte
Fort Benton, Fort Benton
Great Northern Railway Buildings, Glacier
National Park

Nevada
Virginia City Historic District, Virginia City

New Jersey
Cape May Historic District, Cape May
Fort Hancock and Sandy Hook Proving Ground
Historic District, Sandy Hook
Great Falls of the Passaic Society for Universal
Manufacturing Historic District, Patterson
Monmouth Battlefield, Freehold

New Mexico
Anderson Basin, Clovis
Lincoln Historic District, Lincoln
National Park Service Region III Headquarters
Building, Santa Fe
Seton Village, Santa Fe
San Estevan del Ray Mission Church, Acoma
Village of Columbus and Camp Furlong,
Columbus
Watrous (La Junta), Watrous
Zuni-Cibola Complex, Zuni

New York
Mount Lebanon Shaker Village, Mount Lebanon

Ohio
Ohio and Erie Canal, Valley View Village
Rocket Engine Test Facility, Cleveland

Oklahoma
101 Ranch Historic District, Ponca City
Cherokee National Capitol, Tahlequah
Fort Gibson
Wheelock Academy, Durant

Oregon
Jacksonville Historic District, Jacksonville

Pennsylvania
Bedford Springs Hotel Historic District,
Bedford
Brandywine Battlefield, Chadds Ford
Cambria Iron Company, Johnstown
East Broad Top Railroad, Rockhill Furnace
Eastern State Penitentiary, Philadelphia
Gallatin (Albert) House, Point Marion
Harrisburg Station and Train Shed, Harrisburg
Honey Hollow Watershed, New Hope
Meason (Isaac) House, Dunbar Township
United States Naval Asylum, Philadelphia
Woodlands, Philadelphia

Rhode Island
Fort Adams, Newport

South Carolina
Chapelle Administration Building, Columbia
Fort Hill (John C. Calhoun House), Clemson

Threatened National Historic Landmarks (Con't)

South Dakota

Frawley Ranch Historic District, Spearfish

Texas

Fort Brown, Brownsville

Garner (John Nance) House, Uvalde

Vermont

Robbins and Lawrence Armory and Machine
Shop, Windsor

Virginia

Bacon's Castle, Surry County

Jackson Ward Historic District, Richmond

Washington

Pioneer Building, Pergola, and Totem Pole,
Seattle

Seattle Electric Company Georgetown Steam
Plant, Seattle

West Virginia

Elkins Coal and Coke, Bretz

Weston Hospital Main Building, Weston

Wyoming

Sun (Tom) Ranch, Casper vicinity

Swan Land and Cattle Company Headquarters,
Chugwater

Source: National Park Service

Did you know...

Since its establishment in 1966, the National Register of Historic Places has designated nearly 73,000 districts, sites, buildings, structures, and objects as significant in American history, architecture, archeology, engineering, and culture; fewer than 2,500 listings bear the designation of National Historic Landmark, reserved for those sites which are most significant to our nation's history.

Top: Bushell's Tea
House, Sydney,
Australia.

Middle: National
Archives Building,
Jakarta, Indonesia.

Bottom: Krishan
Temple, Village
Kishankot, Punjab,
India.

UNESCO Asia-Pacific Heritage Awards for Culture Heritage Conservation

As a part of the United Nations' Educational, Scientific and Cultural Organization's (UNESCO) culture heritage program in Asia and the Pacific, the Awards for Culture Heritage Conservation are presented each year to individuals and organizations within the private sector for superior conservation and restoration of structures over 50 years old. The projects must have been restored within the past 10 years and must also be privately leased or owned. One entry will be selected for an Award of Excellence, while two projects will be honored with an Award of Distinction. Awards of Merit and Honorable Mentions will be awarded to a number of praiseworthy projects.

Regulations and entry forms can be found online at *www.unescobkk.org/ culture/heritageawards.*

2001 Award of Excellence:
National Archives Building
Jakarta, Indonesia

2001 Award of Distinction:
Bushell's Tea House
Sydney, Australia

Krishan Temple
Village Kishankot, Punjab, India

2001 Award of Merit:
DBS House
Mumbai, India

King Law Ka Shuk Temple
Hong Kong SAR, China

Tea Factory Hotel
Kandapola, Sri Lanka

Xijin Ferry Project: Zhaoguan Stone Pagoda,
   Buddha Hole, Building of Lifesaving Union
Zhenjiang, China

Zhongshan Road
Quanshou City, Fujian Province, China

2001 Honorable Mention:
Jin Lan Tea House
Kunming, China

Library Building at Fort Campus, University of
   Mumbai
Mumbai, India

Nielson Tower, The Filipinas Heritage Library
Manila, Philippines

St. Joseph Church
Macau SAR, China

Thian Hock Keng Temple
Singapore

Source: Office of the Regional Advisor for Culture in Asia and the Pacific, United Nations Educational, Scientific and Cultural Organization, Bangkok Office

Vernacular Architecture Forum (VAF)

Devoted to the "ordinary" architecture of North America, the Vernacular Architecture Forum (VAF) was formed in 1980 to encourage the study and preservation of traditional structures and landscapes. These include agricultural buildings, industrial and commercial structures, twentieth-century suburban houses, settlement patterns and cultural landscapes, and areas historically overlooked by scholars. The VAF embraces multidisciplinary interaction. Historians, designers, archaeologists, folklorists, architectural historians, geographers, museum curators and historic preservationists contribute to the organization. The VAF holds its conference every spring with part of the agenda focusing on the vernacular architecture of that region. Every few years papers are selected from past conferences and published in the series *Perspectives in Vernacular Architecture*. The VAF presents two annual awards: the Abbott Lowell Cummings Award for the best book published on North American vernacular architecture and cultural landscapes, and the Paul E. Buchanan Award for the best non-published work on North American vernacular architecture.

Address:
P.O. Box 1511
Harrisonburg, VA 22803-1511
Internet: www.vernaculararchitecture.org

> The architect who combines in his being the powers of vision, of imagination, of intellect, of sympathy with human need and the power to interpret them in a language vernacular and time – is he who shall create poems in stone.

Louis Sullivan

World Heritage List

Since 1972 the World Heritage Committee has inscribed 582 properties on the World Heritage List (445 cultural, 117 natural and 20 mixed properties in 114 States Parties). The World Heritage List was established under terms of The Convention Concerning the Protection of the World Cultural and Natural Heritage, adopted in November 1972 at the 17th General Conference of the United Nations Educational, Scientific, and Cultural Organization (UNESCO). The Convention states that a World Heritage Committee "will establish, keep up-to-date and publish" a World Heritage List of cultural and natural properties, submitted by the States Parties and considered to be of outstanding universal value. One of the main responsibilities of this Committee is to provide technical cooperation under the World Heritage Fund for the safeguarding of World Heritage properties to States Parties whose resources are insufficient. Assistance with the nomination process, training, grants, and loans is also available.

For a complete listing of all the World Heritage properties with detailed descriptions and photographs, visit their Web site at *www.unesco.org/whc*.

Algeria:
  M'Zab Valley
  Djémila
  Tipasa
  Timgad
  Kasbah of Algiers

Argentina and Brazil:
  Jesuit Missions of the Guaranis: San Ignacio Mini, Santa Ana, Nuestra Señora de Loreto and Santa Maria Mayor (Argentina), Ruins of Sao Miguel das Missoes (Brazil)

Argentina:
  The Jesuit Block and the Jesuit Estancias of Córdoba

Armenia:
  Monastery of Haghpat
  Archaeological Site of Zvartnots
  The Cathedral and Churches of Echmiatsin
  The Monastery of Geghard and the Upper Azat Valley

Austria:
  City of Graz - Historic Centre
  Historic Centre of the City of Salzburg
  Palace and Gardens of Schönbrunn
  Hallstatt-Dachstein Salzkammergut Cultural Landscape
  Semmering Railway
  The Wachau Cultural Landscape

Azerbaijan:
  Walled City of Baku

Bangladesh:
  Historic Mosque City of Bagerhat
  Ruins of the Buddhist Vihara at Paharpur

Belarus
  The Mir Castle Complex

Belgium:
  Belfries of Flanders and Wallonia
  Flemish Béguinages
  The Four Lifts on the Canal du Centre and their Environs, La Louvière and Le Roeulx (Hainault)

World Heritage List (Con't)

Grand-Place, Brussels

Historic Centre of Brugge

Notre-Dame Cathedral in Tournai

The Major Town Houses of the architect Victor
Horta (Brussels):Hôtel Tassel, Hôtel Solvay,
Hôtel van Eetvelde, and Maison & Atelier
Horta

Benin:
Royal Palaces of Abomey*

Bolivia:
City of Potosi

Jesuit Missions of the Chiquitos

Historic City of Sucre

El Fuerte de Samaipata

Tiwanaku: Spiritual and Political Centre of the
Tiwanaku Culture

Brazil:
Historic Centre of the Town of Diamantina

Historic Town of Ouro Preto

Historic Centre of the Town of Olinda

Historic Centre of Salvador de Bahia

Sanctuary of Bom Jesus do Congonhas Brasilia

Historic Centre of São Luis

Bulgaria:
Boyana Church

Rock-hewn Churches of Ivanovo

Thracian Tomb of Kazanlak

Ancient City of Nessebar

Rila Monastery

Thracian Tomb of Sveshtari

Cambodia:
Angkor*

Canada:
Quebec (Historic Area)

Lunenburg Old Town

Chile
The Churches of Chiloé

China:
The Great Wall

Mount Taishan

Imperial Palace of the Ming and Qing Dynasties

Mausoleum of the First Qin Emperor

The Mountain Resort and its Outlying Temples,
Chengde

Temple and Cemetery of Confucius, and the
Kong Family Mansion in Qufu

Ancient Building Complex in the Wudang
Mountains

Potala Palace, Lhasa

Lushan National Park

Mount Emei and Leshan Giant Buddha

Old Town of Lijiang

Ancient City of Ping Yao

Classical Gardens of Suzhou

Summer Palace, an Imperial Garden in Beijing

Temple of Heaven -- an Imperial Sacrificial
Altar in Beijing

Ancient Villages in Southern Anhui - Xidi and
Hongcun

Imperial Tombs of the Ming and Qing Dynasties

Longmen Grottoes

Colombia:
Port, Fortresses and Group of Monuments,
Cartagena

Historic Centre of Santa Cruz de Mompox

Croatia:
Old City of Dubrovnik

Historic Complex of Split with the Palace of
Diocletian

Episcopal Complex of the Euphrasian Basilica
in the Historic Centre of Porec

Historic City of Trogir

Cathedral of St. James in Sibenik

Cuba:
Old Havana and its Fortifications

Trinidad and the Valley de los Ingenios

San Pedro de la Roca Castle, Santiago de Cuba

World Heritage List (Con't)

Cyprus:
Paphos
Painted Churches in the Troodos Region
Choirokoitia

Czech Republic:
Historic Centre of Prague
Historic Centre of Cesky Krumlov
Historic Centre of Telc
Pilgrimage Church of St. John of Nepomuk at
 Zelena Hora
Kutná Hora: Historical Town Centre with the
 Church of Saint Barbara and the Cathedral
 of Our Lady at Sedlec
Lednice-Valtice Cultural Landscape
Holasovice Historical Village Reservation
Gardens and Castle at Kromeríz
Litomysl Castle
Holy Trinity Column in Olomouc

Denmark:
Roskilde Cathedral
Kronborg Castle

Dominican Republic:
Colonial City of Santo Domingo

Ecuador:
City of Quito
Historic Center of Santa Ana de los Rios de
 Cuenca

Egypt:
Memphis and its Necropolis - the Pyramid
 Fields from Giza to Dahshur
Ancient Thebes with its Necropolis
Nubian Monuments from Abu Simbel to Philae
Islamic Cairo
Abu Mena

Estonia:
The Historic Centre (Old Town) of Tallinn

Ethiopia:
Rock-hewn Churches, Lalibela
Fasil Ghebbi, Gondar Region
Aksum

Finland:
Old Rauma
Fortress of Suomenlinna
Petäjävesi Old Church
Verla Groundwood and Board Mill

Former Yugoslav Rep. of Macedonia
Ohrid Region, including its cultural and historic aspects, and its natural environment

France:
Mont-Saint-Michel and its Bay
Chartres Cathedral
Palace and Park of Versailles
Vézelay, Church and Hill
Palace and Park of Fontainebleau
Chateau and Estate of Chambord
Amiens Cathedral
Roman Theatre and its Surroundings and the
 "Triumphal Arch" of Orange
Roman and Romanesque Monuments of Arles
Cistercian Abbey of Fontenay
Royal Saltworks of Arc-et-Senans
Place Stanislas, Place de la Carrière, and Place
 d'Alliance in Nancy
Church of Saint-Savin sur Gartempe
Pont du Gard (Roman Aqueduct)
Strasbourg-Grande îsle
Paris, Banks of the Seine
Cathedral of Notre-Dame, Former Abbey of
 Saint-Remi and Palace of Tau, Reims
Bourges Cathedral
Historic Centre of Avignon
Canal du Midi
Historic Fortified City of Carcassonne
Routes of Santiago de Compostela in France
Historic Site of Lyons
The Jurisdiction of Saint-Emilion
The Loire Valley between Chalonnes and Sully-
 sur-Loire

Georgia:
City-Museum Reserve of Mtskheta
Bagrati Cathedral and Gelati Monastery
Upper Svaneti

World Heritage List (Con't)

Germany:
Aachen Cathedral
Speyer Cathedral
Würzburg Residence, with the Court Gardens
and Residence Square
Pilgrimage Church of Wies
The Castles of Augustusburg and Falkenlust at
Brühl
St. Mary's Cathedral and St. Michael's Church
at Hildesheim
Roman Monuments, Cathedral and Liebfrauen-
Church in Trier
Hanseatic City of Lübeck
Palaces and Parks of Potsdam and Berlin
Abbey and Altenmünster of Lorsch
Mines of Rammelsberg and Historic Town of
Goslar
Town of Bamberg
Maulbronn Monastery Complex
Collegiate Church, Castle, and old Town of
Quedlinburg
Völklingen Ironworks
Cologne Cathedral
Bauhaus and its sites in Weimar and Dessau
Luther Memorials in Eisleben and Wittenberg
Classical Weimar
Museumsinsel (Museum Island)
Wartburg Castle
The Garden Kingdom of Dessau-Wörlitz
Monastic Island of Reichenau

Ghana:
Forts and Castles, Volta Greater Accra, Central
and Western Regions
Ashanti Traditional Buildings

Greece:
Temple of Apollo Epicurius at Bassae
Archaeological Site of Delphi
Acropolis, Athens
Mount Athos
Meteora
Paleochristian and Byzantine Monuments of
Thessalonika

Archaeological Site of Epidaurus
Medieval City of Rhodes
Mystras
Archaeological Site of Olympia
Delos
Monasteries of Daphni, Hossios Luckas and
Nea Moni of Chios
Pythagoreion and Heraion of Samos
The Historic Centre (Chorá) on the Island of
Pátmos

Guatemala:
Antigua Guatemala

Haiti:
National History Park – Citadel, Sans-Souci,
Ramiers

Holy See:
Vatican City

Honduras:
Mayan Site of Copan

Hungary:
Budapest, the Banks of the Danube and the
Buda Castle Quarter
Hollokö
Millenary Benedictine Monastery of
Pannonhalma and its Natural Environment
The Pécs (Sopianae) Early Christian Cemetery

India:
Ajanta Caves
Ellora Caves
Agra Fort
Taj Mahal
Sun Temple, Konarak
Group of Monuments at Mahabalipuram
Churches and Convents of Goa
Khajuraho Group of Monuments
Group of Monuments at Hampi
Fatehpur Sikri
Group of Monuments at Pattadakal
Brihadisvara Temple, Thanjavur
Buddhist Monuments at Sanchi

World Heritage List (Con't)

Humayun's Tomb, Delhi
Qutb Minar and its Monuments, Delhi

Indonesia:
Borobudur Temple Compounds
Prambanan Temple Compounds

Iran:
Tchogha Zanbil
Persepolis
Meidan Emam, Esfahan

Iraq:
Hatra

Ireland:
Skellig Michael

Italy:
The Church and Dominican Convent of Santa
   Maria delle Grazie with "The Last Supper"
   by Leonardo da Vinci
Historic Centre of Florence
Venice and its Lagoon
Piazza del Duomo, Pisa
Historic Centre of San Gimignano
I Sassi di Matera
City of Vicenza and the Palladian Villas of the
   Veneto
Historic Centre of Siena
Historic Centre of Naples
Crespi d'Adda
Ferrara: City of the Renaissance
Castel del Monte
The Trulli of Alberobello
Early Christian Monuments of Ravenna
Historic Centre of the City of Pienza
18th-Century Royal Palace at Caserta with the
   Park, the Aqueduct of Vanvitelli and the San
   Leucio Complex
Residences of the Royal House of Savoy
Botanical Garden (Orto Botanico), Padua
Portovenere, Cinque Terre, and the Islands
   (Palmaria, Tino and Tinetto)
Cathedral, Torre Civica and Piazza Grande,
   Modena

Archaeological Areas of Pompei, Herculaneum,
   and Torre Annuziata
Costiera Amalfitana
Villa Romana del Casale
Archaeological Areas of Agrigento
Su Nuraxi di Barumini
Archaeological Area and the Patriarchal Basilica
   of Aquileia
Cilento and Vallo di Diano National Park with
   the Archeological Sites of Paestum and
   Velia, and the Certosa di Padula
Historic Centre of Urbino
Villa Adriana
Assisi, the Basilica of San Francesco and Other
   Franciscan Sites
City of Verona

Italy/Holy See:
Historic Centre of Rome, the Properties of the
   Holy See in that City Enjoying
   Extraterritorial Rights, and San Paolo Fuori
   le Mura

Japan:
Buddhist Monuments in the Horyu-ji Area
Himeji-jo
Historic Monuments of Ancient Kyoto (Kyoto,
   Uji and Otsu Cities)
Historic Villages of Shirakawa-go and
   Gokayama
Itsukushima Shinto Shrine
Historic Monuments of Ancient Nara
Shrines and Temples of Nikko
Gusuku Sites and Related Properties of the
   Kingdom of Ryukyu

Jerusalem:
Old City of Jerusalem and its Walls*

Jordan:
Petra
Quseir Amra

Lao People's Democratic Republic:
Town of Luang Prabang

World Heritage List (Con't)

Latvia:
Historic Centre of Riga

Lebanon:
Anjar
Baalbek
Byblos
Tyre
Ouadi Qadisha (the Holy Valley) and the Forest
of the Cedars of God (Horsh Arz el-Rab)

Libyan Arab Jamahiriya:
Archaeological Site of Leptis Magna
Archaeological Site of Sabratha
Archaeological Site of Cyrene
Old Town of Ghadames

Lithuania:
Vilnius Historic Centre

Lithuania/Russian Federation
Curonian Spit

Luxembourg:
City of Luxemburg: its Old Quarters and
Fortifications

Mali:
Old Towns of Djenné
Timbuktu*

Malta:
City of Valetta
Megalithic Temples of Malta

Mauritania:
Ancient Ksour of Ouadane, Chinguetti, Tichitt
and Oualata

Mexico:
Pre-Hispanic City and National Park of
Palenque
Historic Centre of Mexico City and Xochimilco
Pre-Hispanic City of Teotihuacan
Historic Centre of Oaxaca and Archaeological
Site of Monte Alban
Historic Centre of Puebla

Historic Town of Guanajuato and Adjacent
Mines
Pre-Hispanic City of Chichen-Itza
Historic Centre of Morelia
El Tajin, Pre-Hispanic City
Historic Centre of Zacatecas
Earliest 16th-Century Monasteries on the
Slopes of Popocatepetl
Pre-Hispanic Town of Uxmal
Historic Monuments Zone of Querétaro
Hospicio Cabañas, Guadalajara
Archaeological Zone of Paquimé, Casas
Grandes
Historic Monuments Zone of Tlacotalpan
Historic Fortified Town of Campeche

Morocco:
Medina of Fez
Medina of Marrakesh
Ksar of Aït-Ben-Haddou
Historic City of Meknes
The Medina of Tétouan (formerly known as
Titawin)

Mozambique:
Island of Mozambique

Nepal:
Kathmandu Valley
Lumbini, the Birthplace of the Lord Buddha

Netherlands:
Schokland and Surroundings
Defense Line of Amsterdam
Mill Network at Kinderdijk-Elshout
Historic Area of Willemstad, Inner City, and
Harbour, the Netherlands Antilles
Ir.D.F. Woudagemaal (D.F. Wouda Steam
Pumping Station)
Droogmakerij de Beemster (The Beemster
Polder)
Rietveld Schröderhuis (Rietveld Schröder
House)

World Heritage List (Con't)

Nigeria:
Sukur Cultural Landscape

Norway:
Urnes Stave Church
Bryggen
Røros

Oman:
Bahla Fort*

Pakistan:
Archaeological Ruins at Moenjodaro
Taxila
Buddhist Ruins of Takht-i-Bahi and
Neighbouring City Remains at Sahi-i-Bahlol
Historic Monuments of Thatta
Fort and Shalamar Gardens in Lahore
Rohtas Fort

Panama:
Fortifications on the Caribbean side of Panama:
Portobelo-San Lorenzo
The Historic District of Panamá, with the Salón
Bolivar

Paraguay:
Jesuit Missions of La Santisima Trinidad de
Parana and Jesus de Tavarangue

Peru:
City of Cuzco
Historic Sanctuary of Machu Picchu
Chavin
Chan Chan Archaeological Zone*
Historic Centre of Lima
Historical Centre of the City of Arequipa

Philippines:
Baroque Churches of the Philippines
Historic Town of Vigan

Poland:
Cracow's Historic Centre
Wieliczka Salt Mine
Historic Centre of Warsaw
Old City of Zamosc

The Medieval Town of Torun
Castle of the Teutonic Order in Malbork
Kalwaria Zebrzydowska

Portugal:
Central Zone of the Town of Angra do
Heroismo in the Azores
Monastery of the Hieronymites and Tower of
Belem in Lisbon
Monastery of Batalha
Convent of Christ in Tomar
Historic Centre of Evora
Monastery of Alcobaça
Cultural Landscape of Sintra
Historic Centre of Oporto

Republic of Korea:
Sokkuram Buddhist Grotto
Haiensa Temple Changgyong P'ango, the
Depositories for the Tripitaka Koreana
Woodblocks
Chongmyo Shrine
Ch'angdokkung Palace Complex
Hwasong Fortress
Kyongju Historic Areas

Romania:
Biertan and its Fortified Church
Monastery of Horezu
Churches of Moldavia
Historic Centre of Sighisoara
The Wooden Churches of Maramures
The Dacian Fortresses of the Orastie Mountains

Russian Federation:
Historic Centre of St. Petersburg and Related
Groups of Monuments
Kizhi Pogost
Kremlin and Red Square, Moscow
Historic Monuments of Novgorod and
Surroundings
Cultural and Historic Ensemble of the
Solovetsky Islands
White Monuments of Vladimir and Suzdal

World Heritage List (Con't)

Architectural Ensemble of the Trinity Sergius
  Lavra in Sergiev Posad
Church of the Ascension, Kolomenskoye
Historic and Architectural Complex of the
  Kazan Kremlin
The Ensemble of Ferapontov Monastery

Saint Christopher & Nevis
Brimstone Hill Fortress National Park

Senegal:
Island of Gorée
Island of Saint-Louis

Slovakia:
Vlkolinec
Banska Stiavnica
Spissky Hrad and its Associated Cultural
  Monuments
Bardejov Town Conservation Reserve

South Africa:
Robben Island

Spain:
Historic Centre of Cordoba
Alhambra, Generalife and Albayzin, Granada
Burgos Cathedral
Monastery and Site of the Escurial, Madrid
Parque Güell, Palacio Güell and Casa Mila in
  Barcelona
Old Town of Segovia and its Aqueduct
Monuments of Oviedo and the Kingdom of the
  Asturias
Santiago de Compostela (Old town)
Old Town of Avila, with its Extra-Muros
  Churches
Mudejar Architecture of Teruel
Historic City of Toledo
Old Town of Caceres
Cathedral, Alcazar and Archivo de Indias in
  Seville
Old City of Salamanca
Poblet Monastery
Archaeological Ensemble of Mérida
Royal Monastery of Santa Maria de Guadalupe
Route of Santiago de Compostela

Historic Walled Town of Cuenca
La Lonja de la Seda de Valencia
Las Médulas
The Palau de la Música Catalana and the
  Hospital de Sant Pau, Barcelona
San Millán Yuso and Suso Monasteries
University and Historic Precinct of Alcalá de
  Henares
San Critóbal de la Laguna
Catalan Romanesque Churches of the Vall de
  Boí
The Roman Walls of Lugo

Sri Lanka:
Sacred City of Anuradhapura
Ancient City of Polonnaruva
Ancient City of Sigiriya
Sacred City of Kandy
Old Town of Galle and its Fortifications
Golden Temple of Dambulla

Sweden:
Royal Domain of Drottningholm
Birka and Hovgården
Engelsberg Ironworks
Skogskyrkogården
Hanseatic Town of Visby
Church Village of Gammelstad, Luleå
Naval Port of Karlskrona

Switzerland:
Convent of St. Gall
Benedictine Convent of St. John at Müstair
Old City of Berne
Three Castles, Defensive Wall and Ramparts of
  the Market Town of Bellinzone

Syrian Arab Republic:
Ancient City of Damascus
Ancient City of Bosra
Site of Palmyra
Ancient City of Aleppo

Thailand:
Historic Town of Sukhothai and Associated
  Historic Towns

World Heritage List (Con't)

Historic City of Ayutthaya and Associated
Historic Towns

Tunisia:
Medina of Tunis
Site of Carthage
Amphitheatre of El Jem
Punic Town of Kerkuane and its Necropolis
Medina of Sousse
Kairouan
Dougga/Thugga

Turkey:
Historic Areas of Istanbul
Göreme National Park and the Rock Sites of
Cappadocia
Great Mosque and Hospital of Divrigi
Hattusha
Nemrut Dag
Xanthos-Letoon
Hierapolis-Pamukkale
City of Safranbolu
Archaeological Site of Troy

Turkmenistan:
State Historical and Cultural Park 'Ancient
Merv'

Ukraine:
Kiev: Saint-Sophia Cathedral and Related
Monastic Buildings, Kiev-Pechersk Lavra
L'viv - the Ensemble of the Historic Centre

United Kingdom:
Durham Castle and Cathedral
Ironbridge Gorge
Studley Royal Park, including the Ruins of
Fountains Abbey
Stonehenge, Avebury and Associated Sites
Castles and Town Walls of King Edward in
Gwynedd
St. Kilda
Blenheim Palace
City of Bath
Hadrian's Wall

Westminster Palace, Westminster Abbey, and
Saint Margaret's Church
Tower of London
Canterbury Cathedral, St. Augustine's Abbey
and St. Martin's Church
Old and New Towns of Edinburgh
Maritime Greenwich
The Historic Town of St. George and Related
Fortifications, Bermuda

United Republic of Tanzania:
Ruins of Kilwa Kisiwani and Ruins of Songo
Mnara
The Stone Town of Zanzibar

United States of America:
Independence Hall
La Fortaleza and San Juan Historic Site in
Puerto Rico
The Statue of Liberty
Monticello, and University of Virginia in
Charlottesville
Pueblos de Taos

Uruguay:
Historic Quarter of the City of Colonia del
Sacramento

Uzbekistan:
Itchan Kala
Historic Centre of Bukhara
Historic Centre of Shakhrisyabz

Venezuela:
Coro and its Port
Ciudad Universitaria de Caracas

Viet Nam:
Complex of Hué Monuments
Hoi An Ancient Town
My Son Sanctuary

Yemen:
Old Walled City of Shibam
Old City of Sana'a
Historic Town of Zabid

World Heritage List (Con't)

Yugoslavia:
Stari Ras and Sopocani
Natural and Culturo-Historical Region of
    Kotor*
Studenica Monastery

Zimbabwe:
Khami Ruins National Monument

* Indicates the site is also on the List of World
  Heritage in Danger as determined by the World
  Heritage Committee.

Source: World Heritage Committee, UNESCO

Did you know...

Caral, the newly excavated site in Peru which dates to 2627 B.C., is the oldest human settlement found in the Americas.

World's 100 Most Endangered Sites

The World Monuments Fund's biennial List of 100 Most Endangered Sites designates those cultural sites most in danger of destruction, either by natural or man-made causes. For many sites, inclusion on the List is their only hope for survival. Initial nominations for the list are solicited from governments, heritage conservation organizations, and concerned individuals, and each site must have the support of a sponsoring institution, substantial cultural significance, an urgent need for intervention, and a viable intervention plan. The final selection committee is comprised of a panel of international experts. Limited financial support is also available from the World Monuments Watch Fund and is awarded on a competitive basis to selected sites. The World Monuments Fund is a private, non-profit organization created in 1965 with the purpose of fostering a greater awareness of the world's cultural, artistic, and historic resources; facilitating preservation and conservation efforts; and generating private financial assistance.

For information and photos on each site, visit the World Monuments Fund's Web site at *www.worldmonuments.org* or contact them at (646) 424 9594.

2002 List of 100 Most Endangered Sites:

Albania
Voskopojë Churches, Korcë

Bahamas
Whylly Plantation at Clifton Point, New Providence

Belarus
Pervomaisk Church, Uzdensky

Bosnia & Herzegovina
Mostar Historic Center, Mostar

Brazil
Vila de Paranapiacaba, Santo André

Cambodia
Banteay Chhmar Temple of Jayavarman VII, Thmar Puok

Chile
Ruedas de Agua, Pichidegua, Larmahue

China
Da Qin Christian Pagoda and Monastery, Shannxi

Great Wall of China Cultural Landscape, Beijing
Ohel Rachel Synagogue, Shanghai
Shaxi Market Area, Shaxi Valley

Croatia
Maritime Quarantine—Lazareti, Dubrovnik
Vukovar City Center, Vukovar

Cuba
National Art Schools, Havana

Czech Republic
Terezin Fortress, Terezin

Egypt
Sultan Al-Muayyad Hospital, Cairo
Temple of Khasekhemwy at Hierakonpolis, Edfu, Kom el Ahmar
Valley of the Kings, Luxor (Ancient Thebes)
White and Red Monasteries, Sohag

France
Château de Chantilly, Oise
St. Pierre Cathedral, Beauvais

Right: Art Nouveau Buildings, Tbilisi, Georgia.
Below: Larabanga Mosque, Larabanga, Ghana.
Bottom: St. Pierre Cathedral, Beauvais, France.

World's 100 Most Endangered Sites (Con't)

Georgia
Art Nouveau Buildings, Tbilisi
Bodbe Cathedral, Qedeli Village, Signakhi
   Region
Tbilisi Historical District, Tbilisi

Germany
Carl-Theodor Bridge, Heidelberg

Ghana
Larabanga Mosque, Larabanga

Greece
Palaikastro Archaeological Site, Crete

Guatemala
Piedras Negras Archaeological Site, Piedras
   Negras

India
Anagundi Historic Settlement, Karnataka
Maitreya Temples of Basgo Gompa, Leh, Ladakh
Dwarka Dheesh Mandir Temple, Ahmedabad
Lutyens Bungalow Zone, Delhi
Nako Temples, Himachal
Osmania Women's College, Hyderabad

Indonesia
Omo Hada, Nias, North Sumatra

Iraq
Erbil Citadel, Kurdish Autonomous Region
Nineveh and Nimrud Palaces, near Mosul

Israel
Bet She'arim Archaeological Site, Kiryat Tiv'on

Italy
Bridge of Chains, Bagni di Lucca
Cinque Terre, Liguria
Port of Trajan Archaeological Park, Fiumicino

Jamaica
Falmouth Historic Town, Parish of Trelawny

Japan
Tomo Port Town, Fukuyama

Jordan
Petra Archaeological Site, Wadi Mousa

Kenya
Thimlich Ohinga Cultural Landscape, Migori

Lebanon
Enfeh Archaeological Site, near Tripoli

Malaysia
George Town Historic Enclave, Penang State
Kampung Cina River Frontage, Kuala
   Terengganu

Mali
Médine Fort, Médine

Malta
Mnajdra Prehistoric Temples

Mexico
Immaculada Concepción Chapel, Nurio,
   Michoacán
San Juan de Ulúa Fort, Veracruz
Yaxchilán Archaeological Site, Cuenca del
   Usumacinta, Chiapas

Moldova
Barbary-Bosia Monastery Complex, Butuceni,
   Judet Orhei

Myanmar
Sri-Ksetra Temples, Hmawa

Nepal
Teku Thapatali Monument Zone, Kathmandu
Itum Baha Monastery, Kathmandu

Nigeria
Benin City Earthworks, Edo State

Pakistan
Uch Monument Complex, Bahawalpur District,
   Punjab Province

Panama
San Lorenzo Castle and San Gerónimo Fort,
   Colón and Portobelo

Peru
Caral Archaeological Site, Supe Pueblo,
   Barranca Province
Historic Center of Cuzco, Cuzco

World's 100 Most Endangered Sites (Con't)

Peru (Con't)

Los Pinchudos Archaeological Site, Rio Abiseo
  National Park
Oyón Valley Missionary Chapels, near Lima
San Pedro de Morropé Chapel, Morropé
Santuario de Nuestra Señora de Cocharcas,
  Chincheros

Poland

Wislica Archaeological Site, Wislica

Russia

Archangelskoye State Museum, Moscow
Assumption Church, Kondopoga, Karelia
Church of Our Savior on the Marketplace and
  Rostov Veliky Historic Center, Rostov Veliky
Karelian Petroglyphs, Belomorsky and
  Pudozhsky Districts
Narcomfin Building, Moscow
Oranienbaum State Museum Reserve,
  Lomonosov
Resurrection New Jerusalem Monastery, Istra
Viipuri Library, Vyborg

Syria

The Citadel of Aleppo, Aleppo
Damascus Old City and Saddle Souk, Damascus

Tanzania

Bagamoyo Historic Town, Bagamoyo

Turkey

Ani Archaeological Site, Ocarli Köyü, Kars
Küçük Ayasofya Camii (Little Hagia Sophia
  Mosque), Istanbul
Temple of Augustus, Ankara
Tepebasi District, Gaziantep

Turkmenistan

Merv Archaeological Site, Bairam Ali

Ukraine

Ancient Chersonesos, Sevastopol
Church of Our Savior of Berestove, Kiev

United Kingdom

Brading Roman Villa, Isle of Wight, England
Greenock Sugar Warehouses, Renfrewshire,
  Scotland
St. George's Church, London, England
Selby Abbey, North Yorkshire, England
Sinclair and Girnigoe Castles, Caithness,
  Scotland
Stowe House, Buckingham, Buckinghamshire,
  England

United States

A. Conger Goodyear House, Old Westbury, New
  York
Historic Lower Manhattan, New York, New
  York*
San Esteban del Rey Mission at Acoma Pueblo,
  New Mexico
St. Ann and the Holy Trinity Church, Brooklyn,
  New York
San Juan Capistrano Mission Church, San Juan
  Capistrano, California
Schindler Kings Road House and Studio, Los
  Angeles, California

Yemen

Tarim, Tarim and Wadi Hadramaut

Yugoslavia

Pec and Decani Monasteries, Kosovo and
  Metohiha
Prizren Historic Center, Kosovo
Subotica Synagogue, Subotica

* 101st site added after September 11, 2001

Source: World Monuments Fund

The Firms

This chapter contains rankings and achievements specific to individual firms as well as a breakdown of firm statistics by state and an updated salary and compensation guide for design professionals. Rankings of buildings can be found in the Records, Rankings & Achievements chapter beginning on page 353.

Architecture Firm Profiles by State: 1997

	Number of Establishments	Receipts ($1,000)	Annual Payroll ($1,000)	Paid Employees [1]
U.S Total	20,602	16,988,338	6,468,524	146,702
Alabama	229	154,208	55,838	1,352
Alaska	47	45,369	16,417	337
Arizona	474	323,750	116,499	2,910
Arkansas	147	80,119	29,606	811
California	2,789	2,482,256	909,074	18,911
Colorado	596	382,471	143,569	3,389
Connecticut	324	238,061	85,065	1,727
Delaware	38	30,790	9,918	227
District of Columbia	122	243,985	91,375	1,901
Florida	1,472	937,583	307,179	7,826
Georgia	538	506,929	200,887	4,222
Hawaii	165	141,688	45,767	1,013
Idaho	119	66,761	25,544	678
Illinois	1,023	772,167	326,319	7,015
Indiana	287	206,895	86,331	2,114
Iowa	130	86,271	33,124	840
Kansas	160	122,655	48,643	1,282
Kentucky	161	115,140	42,390	1,098
Louisiana	262	143,042	52,856	1,428
Maine	83	49,569	21,270	529
Maryland	378	281,833	109,403	2,372
Massachusetts	699	1,147,248	393,708	8,005
Michigan	559	416,101	184,418	4,137
Minnesota	378	377,127	165,869	3,701
Mississippi	112	68,175	27,343	679
Missouri	400	427,846	177,863	3,767

States with Most Architecture Firms

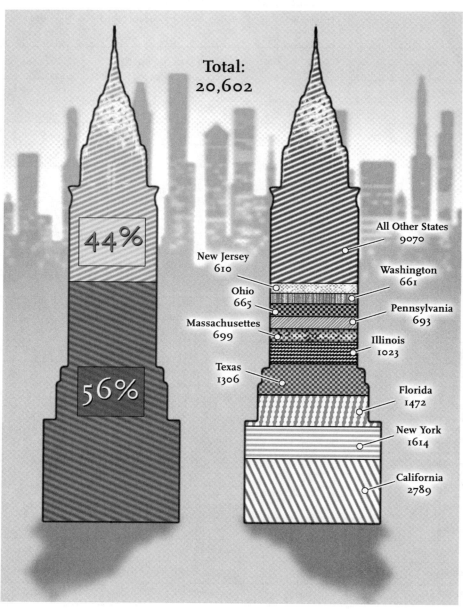

Total:
20,602

44%

56%

All Other States
9070

New Jersey
610

Washington
661

Ohio
665

Pennsylvania
693

Massachusettes
699

Illinois
1023

Texas
1306

Florida
1472

New York
1614

California
2789

Source: Counsel House Research

Fifty-six percent of all architecture firms are located in only ten states.

States with the Highest per Employee Revenue, Architecture Firms

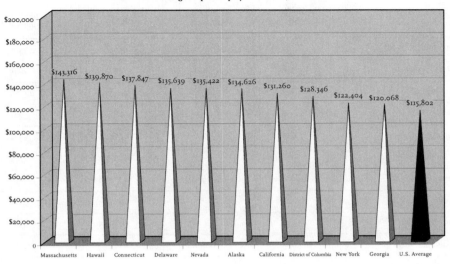

	Massachusetts	Hawaii	Connecticut	Delaware	Nevada	Alaska	California	District of Columbia	New York	Georgia	U.S. Average
	$143,316	$139,870	$137,847	$135,639	$135,422	$134,626	$131,260	$128,346	$122,404	$120,068	$115,802

States with the Lowest per Employee Revenue, Architecture Firms

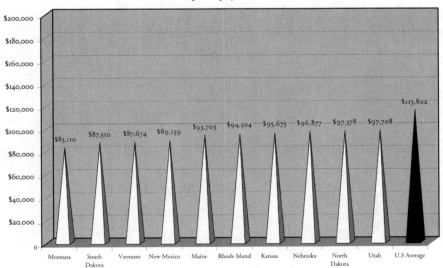

	Montana	South Dakota	Vermont	New Mexico	Maine	Rhode Island	Kansas	Nebraska	North Dakota	Utah	U.S Average
	$83,110	$87,510	$87,674	$89,159	$93,703	$94,504	$95,675	$96,877	$97,378	$97,708	$115,802

Source: Counsel House Research

Architecture Firm Profiles by State: 1997 (Con't)

	Number of Establishments	Receipts ($1,000)	Annual Payroll ($1,000)	Paid Employees [1]
Montana	82	43,134	16,486	519
Nebraska	116	108,018	45,516	1,115
Nevada	131	144,766	49,791	1,069
New Hampshire	66	32,192	12,718	313
New Jersey	610	387,938	143,028	3,381
New Mexico	161	85,771	30,154	962
New York	1,614	1,455,388	548,028	11,890
North Carolina	513	355,173	148,493	3,375
North Dakota	36	24,442	8,465	251
Ohio	665	520,814	216,760	5,212
Oklahoma	168	170,195	63,231	1,685
Oregon	308	247,565	91,205	2,215
Pennsylvania	693	655,071	263,098	6,284
Rhode Island	75	32,226	12,588	341
South Carolina	229	141,394	61,209	1,337
South Dakota	40	20,915	8,417	239
Tennessee	296	292,064	116,769	2,623
Texas	1,306	1,160,271	444,352	9,746
Utah	168	110,703	41,372	1,133
Vermont	84	28,757	10,291	328
Virginia	514	369,194	147,818	3,521
Washington	661	494,026	181,146	4,363
West Virginia	45	22,702	9,428	222
Wisconsin	286	217,008	86,594	2,125
Wyoming	43	20,572	5,292	182

1 Paid employees for the pay period including March 12

Source: U.S. Census Bureau, 1997 Economic Census

Firm Anniversaries

The following currently practicing architecture firms were founded in 1902, 1927, 1952, and 1977 respectively.

Firms Celebrating their 100th Anniversary
WBRC Architects/Engineers, Bangor, ME

Firms Celebrating their 75th Anniversary
Flad & Associates, Inc., Madison, WI
Gaudreau Inc., Baltimore, MD
Lorenz + Williams Incorporated, Dayton, OH
MCG Architecture, Pasadena, CA
Munger Munger + Associates Architects Inc., Toledo, OH
Short Elliott Hendrickson, Inc., St. Paul, MN

Firms Celebrating their 50th Anniversary
ACI / Frangkiser Hutchens, Leawood, KS
John Badgley, AIA, Architect, San Rafael, CA
Bialosky + Partners, Architects, Cleveland, OH
John S. Chase, FAIA, Architects Inc., Houston, TX
Corlett, Skaer DeVoto Architects, Inc., San Francisco, CA
Davis Brody Bond, LLP, New York, NY
Day and Associates Architects, Redlands, CA
Downing Architects, PC, Bettendorf, IA
Evan Terry Associates, PC, Birmingham, AL
Gowland and Johanson, Architects, Payette, ID
Hayes-Howell, PA, Southern Pines, NC
Hayes, Seay, Mattern & Mattern, Inc. Virginia Beach, VA
Heery International, Inc., Atlanta, GA
HGM Architecture Inc., Oshkosh, WI
A. Calvin Hoiland Architect, Great Falls, MT
The JH Group Architects, Baltimore, MD
David J. Katz & Associates, Inc., Schererville, IN
Pierre Koenig, FAIA, Los Angeles, CA
Lew & Patnaude Inc., Fresno, CA
Marshall Erdman & Associates, Inc., Plano, TX
MTA Architects-Planners, Inc., Houston, TX
Prigmore Krievins Haines Limon Architects, PA, El Dorado, KS

RBB Architects Inc., Los Angeles, CA
Ross & Associates Architects, Cleveland, OH
Edward K. Schroeder - Architect/Specifications Consulting, Gurnee IL
tBP/Architecture, Newport Beach, CA
Waterleaf Architecture & Interiors, Portland, OR
Theo J. Wofford Architect, St. Louis, MO
Woods & Starr Associates, Inc., Hays, KS

Firms Celebrating their 25th Anniversary
3D/International/Southeast Group, Orlando, FL
Acorn Associates, Architecture, Ltd., Tucson, AZ
The Addington Partnership, Bakersfield, CA
ADEP Architects, PA, Charlotte, NC
Albanese-Brooks Associates, PC, Architecture and Planning, Tucson, AZ
Anton and Associates, Architects, Lompoc, CA
Architects & Company, Omaha, NE
Architectural Design Works, Ashland, OR
Architecture, Building Codes & Inspection by Dysart, Carbondale, CO
Arcturis, St. Louis, MO
Arquitectonica, Miami, FL
ASC Architects, Inc., Chicago, IL
Atkinson/Dyer/Watson Architects, Charlotte, NC
Austin Veum Robbins Parshalle, San Diego, CA
Pat Bales, Architect & Associates, Inc., Chattanooga, TN
Balsamo, Olson & Lewis, Ltd., Villa Park, IL
Barger + Dean Architects Inc., Sarasota, FL
Barker Architects, Kirkland, WA
The Architects Barnes / Associates Inc., Fort Worth, TX
Barrett Studio Architects, Boulder, CO
Bauform Architecture & Interiors, White Plains, NY
Ann Beha Associates, Inc., Boston, MA
Berggren & Woll, Architects, Lincoln, NE
Black River Architects, Inc., Cambridge, MA

Firm Anniversaries (Con't)

James L. Blair Architect, Charlotte, NC

David A. Block, AIA, Architect, Ames, IA

Brackett-Krennerich and Associates, PA, Jonesboro, AR

Brooks Coronado Associates, Houston, TX

Brown Associates Architects, Montgomery, AL

Architects Richard Bundy & David Thompson, San Diego, CA

Burleson Associates Architects, Dallas, TX

Burlini/Silberschlag, Ltd., Tucson, AZ

Robert David Burow Architects Inc., Mendota Heights, MN

Alan Paul Cajacob, AIA, Architecture/Planning, Deland, FL

Caldwell Architects, Marina del Rey, CA

Michael E. Caldwell Architect, Thibodaux, LA

Dean Robert Camlin & Associates, Inc., Westminster, MD

Charles L. Campbell - Architect, Colorado Springs, CO

Mauro J. Cappitella, AIA, Saddle River, NJ

Carrier Johnson, San Diego, CA

CDH Partners Inc., Marietta, GA

Center Ridge Design Services Inc., Westlake, OH

Edith Cherry/D. James See Architects, Albuquerque, NM

Chesney Morales & Associates, Inc., San Antonio, TX

C J Architecture & Design, Mercer Island, WA

FJ Clark Incorporated, Anderson, SC

Clark & Post Architects, Inc., Lorain, OH

Clarke Caton Hintz, Trenton, NJ

Cohen Freedman Encinosa & Associates - Architects, PA, Hialeah, FL

Charles J. Collins, Jr. / Architect, Medford, NJ

Jerry A. Cook, AIA, Architect, Raleigh, NC

Corkill Cush Reeves, PA, Bowie, MD

Corporate Design of America, PC, Brooklyn, NY

Corporate Facility Planning Inc., Dallas, TX

Patrick J. Crowley, Architect/Urban Planner, San Diego, CA

John Cruet Jr., AIA, Guilford, CT

DaSilva Black Calcagni Chesser Architects PC, New York, NY

Davis-Kane, Architects, PA, Raleigh, NC

Clive Dawson, AIA, Architect & Planner, Malibu, CA

DeMattia & Associates, Plymouth, MI

The Design Alliance Architects, Pittsburgh, PA

Dettmer Architecture, San Luis Obispo, CA

Dewberry & Davis, Danville, VA

Di Donno Associates Architects, Brooklyn, NY

D/I + A, Fort Thomas, KY

Diekema/Hamann/Architects, Inc., Portage, MI

Dimensions Inc., Kokomo, IN

Dimery Associates Architects, Oxford, GA

DLR Group, Farmington, NM

Don Dommer Associates, Oakland, CA

Dove, Knight and Whitehurst Architects, Rocky Mount, NC

Al Drap Architect and Landscape Architect, Fort Smith, AR

Elliott Dudnik + Associates, Evanston, IL

Robert T. Eckels, AIA, Architect, Martinsburg, WV

Steven Ehrlich Architects, Culver City, CA

Ellinwood Design Associates Ltd., Raleigh, NC

Emick Howard & Seibert, Inc., Seattle, WA

Environment Associates, Architects & Consultants, Houston, TX

Robert E. Euans Architects Inc., Columbus, OH

Michael Fancher & Associates, Seattle, WA

Feitlowitz & Kosten Architects, PA, Livingston, NJ

Foit-Albert Associates, Architecture, Engineering & Surveying, PC, Buffalo, NY

Alfred French and Associates Inc., Naples, FL

Alex Friehauf, AIA, & Associates Inc., Solana Beach, CA

John L. Frullo, AIA, Architect, Rock Springs, WY

Gabert/Abuzalaf & Associates, Inc., Houston, TX

John F. Gamache, AIA, Hingham, MA

Ganos Associates Architects, PC, Phoenix, AZ

Gobbell Hays Partners, Inc., Nashville, TN

Steven Goldstein Architect, Sacramento, CA

Firm Anniversaries (Con't)

Gordon & Associates Architects, Mount Dora, FL

GPR Planners Collaborative, Inc., A Jacobs Facilities Inc. Company, Purchase, NY

Grainger/Park, Inc., Flint, MI

Gunn Levine Associates, Detroit, MI

Haag Muller, Inc., Grafton, WI

Syd Harrison, AIA, Architect, Denver, CO

Hawkins Development Company, Nashville, TN

HDN Architects PC, Portland, OR

John Philip Hesslein AIA Architect, New York, NY

Ron Hobbs Architects, Garland, TX

Hoffmann Architects, North Haven, CT

Holster & Associates, Inc., College Station, TX

Hood Miller Associates, San Francisco, CA

Hord Coplan Macht, Inc., Baltimore, MD

Hoskins Scott & Partners Inc., Boston, MA

House Reh Burwell Architects, Inc., Houston, TX

Cynthia Howard, AIA, Architect & Preservation Planner, Biddeford Pool, ME

Hughes/Beattie/Johnson/Law & Associates, PC Architects/Planners, Aiken, SC

Hughes Group Architects, Sterling, VA

Michael W. Hyland Associates, PA, Ocean City, NJ

The Jenkins Group, Inc., Itasca, IL

The Jerde Partnership International, Venice, CA

JMP Architects Inc., Avon, CO

Johnson Braund Design Group, Inc., Seattle, WA

Johnson McAdams Firm, PA, Greenwood, MS

J. B. Jones Architects Inc., Tamuning, Guam

Joy, McCoola & Zilch Architects and Planners, PC, Glens Falls, NY

Jon R. Jurgens & Associates, Inc., Beaverton, OR

Kaeyer, Garment & Davidson, Architects, PC, Mount Kisco, NY

Kallmann McKinnell & Wood, Boston, MA

Keefe Associates Inc., Boston, MA

Keniston Architects, San Diego, CA

Kleier Associates, Louisville, KY

Klein McCarthy & Company, Ltd. Architects Inc., Minneapolis, MN

Carl R. Klimek & Associates, Chicago, IL

Knight Associates Inc., Blue Hill, ME

Knudson Gloss Architects Planners, Boulder, CO

John D. Kohler, Architect, PC, Monroe, MI

D. Edward Kontz Jr., Architect, Gleneden Beach, OR

Kostak Associates Architects, Mount Prospect, IL

Kramer/Marks Architects, Fort Washington, PA

James Oleg Kruhly + Associates, Philadelphia, PA

Kumin Associates Inc., Anchorage, AK

Laleyan Architects, San Francisco, CA

Lambert Architects, Lewisville, TX

Edwin W. Laurinat, North Platte, NE

Richard A. Lefcourt, Architect PA Corporation, Longmont, CO

Lindemon Winckelmann Deupree Martin and Associates PC, Jersey City, NJ

Lindquist & Associates, Hawthorn Woods, IL

Lisec & Biederman Ltd., Chicago, IL

LeRoy Lowe, Bellevue, WA

James Lynch & Associates Architects & Planners, Portland, OR

MacDonald & Mack Architects, Ltd., Minneapolis, MN

Maloney Associates, Manitowoc, WI

Marcus Associates, Hastings-on-Hudson, NY

Roger Marshall AIA, Architect, Springfield, VT

John Martin Associates, Torrington, CT

MBA Architects, Inc., Fort Worth, TX

J. Nelson McKellin III Architect, Stillwater, MN

McLeod Associates Architect, Matthews, NC

McMillan Associates Architects & Consultants, Inc., Greenville, SC

Mill Creek Studios, Ltd., Furlong, PA

Mitzel & Scroggs Architects, Inc., Columbia, MO

Molten / Lamar Architects Inc., Columbia, SC

Moore Ruble Yudell Architects & Planners, Santa Monica, CA

Moyer Associates Inc., Northbrook, IL

MWM Architects Inc., Lubbock, TX

Dennis W. Neifert, AIA, Architect, Sun Valley, ID

Neumann Monson PC, Iowa City, IA

Newberry Roadcap Architects, Abilene, TX

NJRA Architects, Salt Lake City, UT

Firm Anniversaries (Con't)

Northwest Associates Architecture, Lenoir, NC
Odell Associates Inc., Richmond, VA
Olsen & Associates Architects, Champaign, IL
Omura Casey Morel, Inc., North Palm Beach, FL
Peter Orleans, Architect, Denver, CO
Peel/Langenwalter Architects, LLC, Vail, CO
Pellham-Phillips-Hagerman Architects &
 Engineers, Inc., Springfield, MO
Cesar Pelli & Associates Inc., New Haven, CT
Perkins & Will, Atlanta, GA
Preston Phillips Architect, Bridgehampton, NY
Pointe Design Architects P.C., Norman, OK
Lincoln A. Poley, AIA, Architect, Ann Arbor, MI
Polk Stanley Yeary Architects, Ltd., Little Rock, AR
Popham Walter Burford Architects, Houston, TX
Potter & Cox Architects, Louisville, KY
Preiss/Breismeister PC Architects, Stamford, CT
Professional Management Services, Inc., Eau
 Claire, WI
George Ranalli, New York, NY
Raphael Architects, Hartford, CT
Russell Rex, AIA, Architect, San Diego, CA
RMO Architects, Grover Beach, CA
Rounds Vanduzer Architects PC, Falls Church,
 VA
Michael Rubenstein, Architect, New York, NY
Russell Scott Steedle & Capone Architects Inc.,
 Cambridge, MA
Salazar Associates Architects, Ltd., Phoenix, AZ
Saunders, Roberts, & Johnson, Architects, Inc.,
 Albany, GA
Schroeder & Holt Architects, Ltd., Milwaukee, WI
Seay, Seay & Litchfield Architects/Interior
 Designers, PC, Montgomery, AL
Ward Seymour & Associates/Architecture,
 Atlanta, GA
Shaver Architects, Chicago, IL
The Sheward Partnership, Philadelphia, PA
Peter G. Shutts, AIA, Pleasanton, CA
Richard M. Sibly & Associates Inc, Atlanta, GA
Silling Associates Inc. Architects/Planners,
 Charleston, WV
Simmons & Associates Inc., Indianapolis, IN

William Simpson, AIA, Architect, Orinda, CA
Gregg Sims Architect, Dalton, GA
SKD Architects, Inc., Minneapolis, MN
Slonaker McCall Architects, York, PA
Smith Architecture and Planning, Fuquay
 Varina, NC
Smith Edwards Architects PC, Hartford, CT
Smith Hyatt Architects, Bountiful, UT
SPACEPLAN/Architecture, Interiors &
 Planning, PA, Asheville, NC
Sparkman & Associates Architects, Inc.,
 Knoxville, TN
St. Louis Design Alliance Inc., St. Louis, MO
Stickney Murphy Romine Architects PLLC,
 Seattle, WA
Dennis T. Su, AIA, Architects & Consultants,
 Mercer Island, WA
The Sullivan Company Inc., Edmonds, WA
Robert Edson Swain, AIA, Seattle, WA
Takase Associates, Woodland Hills, CA
Albert Taus & Associates, Philadelphia, PA
Thomas, Miller & Partners LLC, Brentwood, TN
Norman Tilley, AIA, Jackson, CA
TPC Architects, Fair Oaks, CA
The Turkel Collaborative Architects & Planners,
 New York, NY
Tvenge Associates Architects & Planners, PC,
 Bismarck, ND
Washer, Hill & Lipscomb Inc. An Architectural
 Corporation, Baton Rouge, LA
Weese Langley Weese Architects Ltd., Chicago, IL
The Weidt Group, Minnetonka, MN
Whitener-Rohe, Inc., Dallas, TX
Wilkerson Associates Inc., Charlotte, NC
The Wilson Architectural Group, Canton, OH
Withee Malcolm Partnership, Architects,
 Torrance, CA
Joseph Wong Design Associates, Inc., San
 Diego, CA
Alan H. Yeaton, Architect, Manchester, NH
Ziegler Cooper Architects, Houston, TX
Zyscovich, Inc., Miami, FL

Source: Counsel House Research

Interior Design Firm Profiles by State: 1997

	Number of Establishments	Receipts ($1,000)	Annual Payroll ($1,000)	Paid Employees [1]
U.S Total	9,612	4,945,340	1,021,531	33,915
Alabama	126	41,901	5,695	338
Alaska	9	5,249	1,131	40
Arizona	169	88,732	14,273	465
Arkansas	35	D	D	c
California	1,122	791,655	171,073	5,169
Colorado	228	112,807	20,557	729
Connecticut	132	78,739	18,181	479
Delaware	24	D	D	c
District of Columbia	51	62,038	20,540	377
Florida	1,096	566,916	88,792	3,363
Georgia	349	210,603	48,584	1,380
Hawaii	28	D	D	b
Idaho	31	18,860	2,023	118
Illinois	533	266,766	68,911	1,978
Indiana	170	55,904	10,743	520
Iowa	55	15,975	2,301	117
Kansas	66	D	D	c
Kentucky	90	28,226	4,951	259
Louisiana	93	33,153	6,127	325
Maine	24	D	D	b
Maryland	199	82,918	17,592	591
Massachusetts	213	122,184	29,392	812
Michigan	287	107,290	19,969	841
Minnesota	178	82,482	16,618	562
Mississippi	49	12,652	1,415	126
Missouri	183	64,571	14,242	573
Montana	18	D	D	b
Nebraska	43	18,844	3,720	225
Nevada	87	46,674	9,635	326
New Hampshire	27	9,214	1,687	58

States with the Most Interior Design Firms

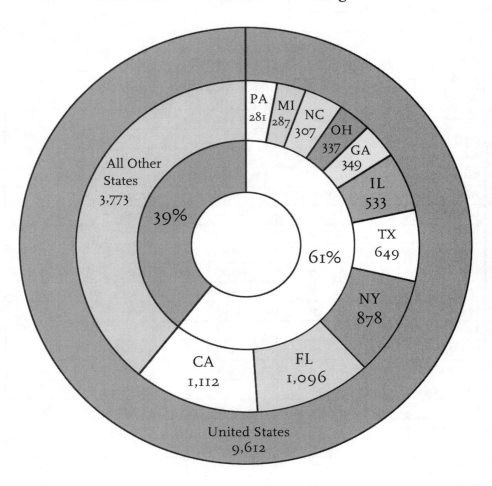

All Other States 3,773

39%

61%

PA 281

MI 287

NC 307

OH 337

GA 349

IL 533

TX 649

NY 878

FL 1,096

CA 1,112

United States 9,612

Source: Counsel House Research

Sixty-one percent of all interior design firms are located in only ten states.

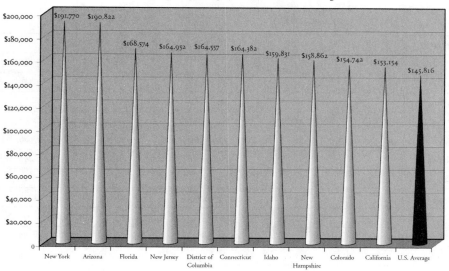

States with the Highest per Employee Revenue, Interior Design Firms

New York	$191,770
Arizona	$190,822
Florida	$168,574
New Jersey	$164,952
District of Columbia	$164,557
Connecticut	$164,382
Idaho	$159,831
New Hampshire	$158,862
Colorado	$154,742
California	$153,154
U.S. Average	$145,816

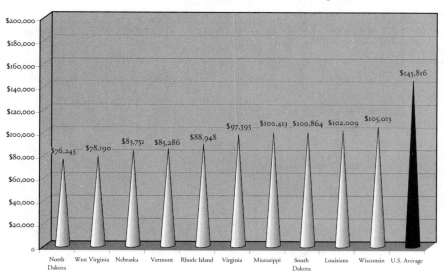

States with the Lowest per Employee Revenue, Interior Design Firms

North Dakota	$76,245
West Virginia	$78,190
Nebraska	$83,751
Vermont	$85,286
Rhode Island	$88,948
Virginia	$97,595
Mississippi	$100,413
South Dakota	$100,864
Louisiana	$102,009
Wisconsin	$105,013
U.S. Average	$145,816

Source: Counsel House Research

Interior Design Firm Profiles by State: 1997

	Number of Establishments	Receipts ($1,000)	Annual Payroll ($1,000)	Paid Employees [1]
New Jersey	276	117,941	21,140	715
New Mexico	31	8,426	1,454	69
New York	878	638,212	144,230	3,328
North Carolina	307	118,018	19,037	807
North Dakota	14	3,736	580	49
Ohio	337	162,636	34,824	1,306
Oklahoma	94	28,930	5,286	240
Oregon	107	43,064	7,100	310
Pennsylvania	281	141,426	33,193	1,132
Rhode Island	36	15,388	4,755	173
South Carolina	105	42,192	6,150	317
South Dakota	12	2,219	281	22
Tennessee	136	68,323	12,391	458
Texas	649	323,655	70,325	2,464
Utah	65	30,098	4,435	222
Vermont	18	5,373	1,864	63
Virginia	250	79,247	20,224	812
Washington	151	60,898	12,075	465
West Virginia	21	6,568	1,358	84
Wisconsin	121	48,201	9,203	459
Wyoming	8	1,173	164	10

1   Paid employees for the pay period including March 12
D: Withheld to avoid disclosing data of individual companies
b: 20 to 99 employees
c: 100 to 249 employees

Source: U.S. Census Bureau, 1997 Economic Census

Largest Architecture Firms by City

The following architecture firms are the largest in their respective cities (based on total 2000 U.S. design billings, as provided by the individual firms). If 2000 billings were unavailable, 1999 billings were substituted. For New York City, 1999 world wide construction volume was used. Only firms headquartered in each city were considered.

Atlanta	**Heery International**	Minneapolis	**Ellerbe Becket**
Baltimore	**RTKL**	New Orleans	**Sizeler Architects**
Boston	**Sasaki Associates**	New York City	**HLW International**
Chicago	**Skidmore, Owings & Merrill**	Philadelphia	**Kling Lindquist**
Dallas	**HKS Inc**	Phoenix	**DLR Group**
Denver	**RNL Design**	San Francisco	**URS**
Detroit	**SmithGroup**	Seattle	**NBBJ**
Houston	**3D/International**	St. Louis	**Hellmuth Obata & Kassabaum**
Kansas City	**HNTB**	Washington, D.C.	**Leo A. Daly**
Los Angeles	**Daniel, Mann, Johnson & Mendenhall**		

Source: Counsel House Research

Largest Architecture Firms By Project Type

The following architecture firms are the top ten in the respective building types. The rankings are primarily based on architectural staff size and firm specialization. Gross billings in each focus area were used as secondary criteria.

Airports/Airline Facilities
1. HNTB
2. Skidmore, Owings & Merrill
3. HOK
4. Gensler
5. NBBJ
6. Zimmer Gunsel Frasca Partnership
7. HKS
8. Corgan Associates
9. CH2M Hill
10. Heery International

Banking/Financial
1. Gensler
2. HOK
3. Skidmore, Owings & Merrill
4. Callison Architects
5. Carlson
6. IA, Interior Architects
7. O'Donnell Wicklund Pigozzi & Peterson
8. Perkins & Will
9. ADD Inc.
10. Little & Associates
    Brennan Beer Gorman

Convention Centers
1. Thompson Ventulett Stainback & Associates
2. LMN Architects
3. Gensler
4. HOK
5. RTKL
6. The Hillier Group
7. HNTB
8. Heery International
9. The Durrant Group
10. Kohn Pederson Fox Associates

Corporate Office:
1. Gensler
2. HOK
3. Mancini-Duffy
4. Phillips Group
5. Perkins & Will
6. RTKL
7. Environments Group
8. The Hillier Group
9. ASD
10. SpAce

Correctional/Detention Facilities:
1. NBBJ
2. HOK
3. URS
4. Heery International
5. HDR Architects
6. Kaplan McLaughlin Diaz
7. The Durrant Group
8. DLR Group
9. HLM
10. RNL Design

Entertainment: Theatres
1. Gensler
2. RTKL
3. Morris Architects
4. Wimberly Allison Tong & Goo
5. TMP Associates
6. Kohn Pederson Fox Associates
7. Shalom Baranes Associates
8. Centerbrook Architects
9. Jung/Brannen
10. Gould Evans Goodman

Largest Architecture Firms By Project Type (Con't)

Entertainment: Theme Parks
1. HKS
2. Cuningham Group
3. Holmes & Narver
4. RTKL
5. The Jerde Partnership
6. TAMS Consultants
7. Gensler
8. Morris Architects
9. Wimberly Allison Tong & Goo
10. Peckham Guyton Albers & Viets

Government: Courthouses/Civic Service Centers
1. HOK
2. HNTB Corporation
3. Ellerbe Becket
4. RTKL
5. Heery International
6. NBBJ
7. Skidmore, Owings & Merrill
8. Zimmer Gunsul Frasca Partnership
9. Leo A. Daly
10. A. Epstein and Sons Inernational

Government: General
1. HOK
2. Skidmore, Owings & Merrill
3. Ellerbe Becket
4. U.S. Army Corp of Engineers
5. Zimmer Gunsul Frasca Partnership
6. RTKL
   Heery International
8. Ewing Cole Cherry Brott
9. SmithGroup
10. HNTB Corporation

Health Care: Hospitals
1. NBBJ
2. HKS
3. RTKL
4. Perkins & Will
5. Gresham, Smith and Partners
6. HDR

7. Hammel, Green & Abrahamson
8. Ellerbe Becket
9. TRO/The Richie Organization
10. Kaplan McLaughlin Diaz
    HLM Design
    O'Donnell Wicklund Pigozzi & Peterson

Health Care: Medical Centers
1. NBBJ
2. HKS
3. Perkins and Will
4. HOK
5. SmithGroup
6. Hammel Green and Abrahamson
7. TRO/The Richie Organization
8. Shepley Bullfinch Richardson & Abbott
9. HDR Architecture
10. Kaplan McLaughlin Diaz

Hospitality: Hotels
1. RTKL
2. Wimberly Allison Tong & Goo
3. Callison Architecture
4. Smallwood, Reynolds, Stewart, Stewart, and Associates
5. The Hillier Group
6. Gensler
7. Arrowsmith
8. Kohn Pederson & Fox Associates
9. DLR Group
10. Brennan Beer Gorman

Hospitality: Resort Hotels
1. Hirsch Bednar
2. Wilson and Associates
3. RTKL
4. Wimberly Allison Tong & Goo
5. DiLeonardo
6. Brennan Beer Gorman Monk
7. The Hillier Group
8. Callison Architects
9. Cooper Carry
10. H. Chambers Company

Largest Architecture Firms By Project Type (Con't)

Libraries

1. HOK
2. The Hillier Group
3. Perkins Eastman Architects
4. Gould Evans Goodman Associates
5. Shepley, Bullfinch, Richardson and Abbott
6. Perkins & Will
7. Holmes & Narver
8. Little & Associates
9. Pierce Goodwin Alexander & Linville
10. The Durrant Group
    Meyer Scherer & Rockcastle

Performing Arts Centers

1. Gensler
2. NBBJ
3. Skidmore, Owings & Merrill
4. Zimmer Gunsul Frasca Partnership
5. LMN Architects
6. Smallwood, Reynolds, Stewart, Stewart
7. Hammel, Green & Abrahamson
8. RMW Architecture
9. Sasaki Associates
10. Hardy Holtzman Pfeiffer

Religious Facilities

1. Hammel, Green, & Abrahamson
2. HarleyEllis
3. Perkins Eastman Architects
4. RMW Architecture & Interiors
5. The Durrant Group
6. The Stichler Design Group
7. RNL Design
8. Grimm and Parker
9. CTA Architects
10. Tsoi/Kobus Associates
    Centerbrook Architects & Planners

Schools/Educational Facilities

1. Einhorn Yaffee Prescott
2. Perkins & Will
3. Leo A. Daly
4. Cannon Design

5. DLR Group
6. Zimmer Gunsul Frasca Partnership
7. The Hillier Group
8. HOK
9. Thompson, Ventulett, Stainback & Associates
10. Hammel, Green & Abrahamson

Sports: General

1. HOK Sport
2. NBBJ
3. Ellerbe Becket
4. HNTB
5. HKS Architects
6. LMN Architects
7. Ewing Cole Cherry Brott
8. Smallwood, Reynolds, Stewart, Stewart & Associates
9. Sasaki Associates
10. Heery International

Sports: Golf

1. HNTB
2. Shalom Baranes Associates
3. Hornberger + Worstell
4. LS3P Associates
5. Wimberly Allison Tong & Goo
6. KBJ Architects
7. MCG Architecture
8. Urban Design Group
9. Niles Bolton Associates
10. Sandy & Babcock

Retail: Individual Stores

1. Pavlik Design Team
2. FRCH Worldwide
3. Callison Architects
4. Gensler
5. The Tricarico Group
6. Communication Arts
7. RTKL
8. Retail Planning Associates
9. Mithun, Carter & Burgess
10. WD Partners

Largest Architecture Firms By Project Type (Con't)

Retail: Shopping Centers
1. Callison Architects
2. RTKL
3. URS
4. HOK
5. Thompson Ventulett Stainback & Associates
6. O'Donnell Wicklund Pigozzi & Peterson
7. Smallwood Reynolds Stewart Stewart & Associates
8. ADD Inc.
9. Carter & Burgess
10. The Nadel Partnership

Zoos/Aquariums:
1. HOK
2. Cuningham Group
3. RNL Design
4. Cambridge Seven
5. Morris Architects
6. Peckham Guyton Albers & Viets
7. Lohan Associates
8. GBBN Architects
9. Ankrom Moisan Associates
10. Gartner, Burdick, Bauer-Nilsen

Source: Counsel House Research

$100,000,000 Architecture Firms

The following architecture firms generated over $100,000,000 in billings (based on total 2000 U.S. billings). In order to qualify, firms must be known for their design work, with such work comprising a significant portion of their business. Construction and engineering firms are not eligible.

Einhorn Yaffe Prescott, Albany, NY
Heery International, Atlanta
RTKL, Baltimore
Skidmore, Owings & Merrill, Chicago
HKS Inc, Dallas
SmithGroup, Detroit
3D/International, Houston
Ellerbe Becket, Minneapolis
Gensler, San Francisco
URS, San Francisco
NBBJ, Seattle
Hellmuth Obata & Kassabaum, St. Louis

Source: Counsel House Research

Salary and Compensation Guide

Each year Greenway Consulting's Counsel House Research division tracks the hiring of design professionals and reviews compensation packages for marketplace comparisons. Figures below reflect actual positions and include bonus and profit sharing target amounts. In recent surveys, 75% of leaders/owners in the design professions have incentive programs that significantly expand their annual earnings. Trends indicate that principals in small and medium size firms can earn at compensation levels at or above those of larger firms. This varies depending on the percentage of ownership in the firm (equity position), corporate legal status of the firm, and the business and compensation philosophy of the firm relative to the management of its balance sheet.

The study also tracks salary ranges and national averages for a select category of positions. (Again, specific salaries reflect actual filled positions, not necessarily the average in each city.) Please use caution in drawing any quick or precise conclusions from this broad survey, as there can be significant fluctuations depending on geographic location and micro-economic fluctuations within certain building types. While cash compensation increased neared an average of 4.75% in 2001, firms report flat to only modest increases expected for 2002 with a trend to downsizing fixed expenses such as number of employees. Information from the U.S. Department of Labor, Bureau of Labor Statistics' Occupational Outlook Handbook is also included.

ARCHITECTURE
U.S. Department of Labor, Bureau of Labor Statistics:
 Median: $47,710
 Median range: $37,380 – $68,920
 3 to 5 years experience, median: $41,100
 8 to 10 years experience, non-managers: $54,700
 Principals/partners: $132,500

Intern Architect:
 National Average: $45,400
 Range: $39,000 – $52,000

Architect – 5 years Experience:
 National Average: $45,400
 Range: 39,000 – $52,000

Architect – 10 years Experience:
 National Average: $53,500
 Range: $44,000 – $68,250

Architect – 15 Years Experience:
 National Average: $60,000
 Range: $50,500 – $92,000

Architect/Engineer – Project Manager with at least 10 years experience:
 National Average: $75,800
 Range: $48,000 – $92,500
 Austin: $71,000
 Houston: $68,000
 Kansas City: $63,000
 Phoenix: $58,500

Salary and Compensation Guide (Con't)

Architect/Engineer – Project Manager with at least 10 years experience (Con't):
Portland: $64,000
Sioux Falls: $59,000
Washington DC: $80,000

Design Technology Supervisors – responsibility for all hardware and software systems:
National Average: $65,000
Range: $44,000 – $82,000

Executive Architect – private sector work in corporate settings, significant span of responsibility:
National Average: N/A
Range: $85,000 – $350,000+

Architect/Principal/Owner – small sole proprietorship/owner transitions (under 10 employees):
National Average: $86,400
Range: $47,500 – $175,000+
Boston: $98,000
Cape Cod: $145,000+
Denver: $84,000+
Florida: $88,000+
New York City: $310,000
San Francisco: $145,000
South Carolina: $123,000

Managing Principal/President – medium size firm (10 to 50 employees):
National Average: $120,250
Range: $88,000 – $250,000+
Atlanta: $90,000+
Dallas: $225,000+
Los Angeles: $125,000+
Omaha: $185,000
Philadelphia: $210,000+
St. Paul: $110,000
Washington DC: $135,000

Owner/Principal – large full service firm, may include A/E and design-build services (50 to 225 employees):
National Average: $145,500
Range: $138,000 – $335,000+

CEO/President – large multi-national firm (over 225 employees):
National Average: $228,000
Range: $175,000 – $450,000+
Chicago: $250,000+
Detroit: $145,000+
Houston: $210,000
Kansas City $145,000+
Minneapolis: $225,000+
New York City: $400,000+
Seattle: $225,000+

Marketing Director (Architecture, Interior Design, Engineering):
National Average: $69,000
Range: $50,000 – $105,000

University Architecture and Design Faculty and Administration:
Dean, Architecture: $133,000
Dean, Engineering: $150,300
Chief Facilities Architect: $102,000
Professor: $78,500
Associate Professor: $55,800
Assistant Professor: $47,000
Average Salaries in Architecture and Related
    Programs: $60,400

INDUSTRIAL DESIGN
U.S. Department of Labor, Bureau of Labor Statistics:
1 to 2 years experience: $31,000
5 years experience: $39,000
8 years experience: $51,000
Managers/Executives: $75,000 – $100,000

Salary and Compensation Guide (Con't)

Industrial Designer/Product Designer in Private Practice:
National Average: N/A
Range: $ $52,000 – $86,000

Industrial Designer/Product Designer with Ownership and Principal/President of Firm:
National Average: N/A
Range: $90,000 – $300,000+

INTERIOR DESIGN
U.S. Department of Labor, Bureau of Labor Statistics:
Median: $31,760
Median range: $23,580 – $42,570

Interior Designer – 10-15 years experience:
National Average: $63,000
Range: $35,000 – $93,000

Interior Designer Owner/Principal of Small Firm (under 10 employees):
National Average: N/A
Range: $45,000 - $225,000+

Interior Designer Owner/Principal of Firm in size above 10 employees, which may also include architectural services:
National Average: $83,500
Range: $46,500 – $300,000

Marketing Director (Architecture, Interior Design, Engineering):
National Average: $69,000
Range: $50,000 – $105,000

LANDSCAPE ARCHITECTURE
U.S. Department of Labor, Bureau of Labor Statistics:
Median: $37,930
Median range: $28,820 – $50,550
Federal employees (all levels), median: $57,500

Landscape Architect Principal/Owner of Firm 10-50 employees:
National Average $88,000
Range: $63,000 – $165,000

URBAN AND REGIONAL PLANNING
U.S. Department of Labor, Bureau of Labor Statistics:
Median: $42,860
Median range: $32,920 – $56,150
Local government employees, median: $40,700
State government employees, median: $38,900

Sources: Greenway Consulting, DesignIntelligence, The American Institute of Architects, International Interior Design Association, Industrial Designers Society of America, Chronicle of Higher Education, American Society of Interior Designers, Occupational Outlook Handbook (U.S. Department of Labor, Bureau of Labor Statistics)

Top Architecture Firms by City

The following architecture firms are the top ten in ten of America's largest cities. Rankings are based on size and revenue (in millions), as indicated in the individual listings, not necessarily the quality of work. All information was supplied by the individual firms and gathered by local business publications. For more detailed information, consult the individual sources listed below.

Boston (based on 1999 total billings)

1. **TAMS Consultants Inc. ($72)**
    38 Chauncey Street
    Boston, MA 02111
    (617) 482-4835
    www.tamsconsultants.com

2. **Cannon Design ($47.24)**
    One Center Plaza
    Boston, MA 02108
    (617) 742-5440
    www.cannondesign.com

3. **Sasaki Associates Inc. ($44)**
    64 Pleasant Street
    Watertown, MA 02472
    (617) 926-3300
    www.sasaki.com

4. **Shepley Bullfinch Richardson & Abbott ($25.7)**
    40 Broad Street
    Boston, MA 02109
    (617) 423-1700
    www.sbra.com

5. **Elkus/Manfredi Architects ($23)**
    530 Atlantic Avenue
    Boston, MA 02210
    (617) 426-1300
    www.elkus-manfredi.com

6. **Payette Associates ($20.7)**
    285 Summer Street
    Boston, MA 02210
    (617) 895-1000
    www.payette.com

7. **TRO/The Richie Organization ($20.51)**
    80 Bridge Street
    Newton, MA 02458
    www.troarch.com

8. **CBT/Childs Bertman Tseckares Inc. ($16.9)**
    306 Dartmouth Street
    Boston, MA 02116
    (617) 262-4354
    www.cbtarchitects.com

9. **Arrowstreet Inc. ($16.6)**
    212 Elm Street
    Somerville, MA 02144
    (617) 623-5555
    www.arrowstreet.com

10. **Tsoi/Kobus & Associates ($16)**
    One Brattle Square
    Cambridge, MA 02238
    www.tka-architects.com

Source: Adapted from the Boston Business Journal *[bizjournals. bcentral.com/boston/, (617) 330-1000]*

Chicago (based on 2000 local registered architects)

1. **OWP&P Architects (103)**
    111 W. Washington Street
    Chicago, IL 60602
    (312) 332-9600
    www.owpp.com

2. **Skidmore Owings & Merrill (80)**
    224 S. Michigan Avenue
    Chicago, IL 60604
    (312) 554-9090
    www.som.com

Top Architecture Firms by City (Con't)

3. **VOA Associates (62)**
   224 S. Michigan Avenue
   Chicago, IL 60604
   (312) 554-1400
   www.voa.com

4. **McClier (60)**
   401 E. Illinois Street
   Chicago, IL 60611
   (312) 836-7700
   www.mcclier.com

5. **Solomon Cordwell Buenz & Associates (45)**
   625 N. Michigan Avenue, Suite 800
   Chicago, IL 60611
   (312) 896-1100
   www.scbdesign.com

6. **Loebl Schlossman & Hackl (42)**
   130 E. Randolph Drive, Suite 3400
   Chicago, IL 60601
   (312) 565-1800
   www.lshdesign.com

7. **Teng & Associates (41)**
   205 N. Michigan Avenue
   Chicago, IL (312) 616-0000
   www.teng.com

8. **DeStefano & Partners (40)**
   445 E. Illinois Street, Suite 250
   Chicago, IL 60611
   (312) 836-4321
   www.destefanoandpartners.com

9. **Lohan Associates (38)**
   225 N. Michigan Avenue, Suite 800
   Chicago, IL 60601
   (312) 938-4455
   www.lohan.com

10. **Perkins & Will (37)**
    330 N. Wabash Avenue, Suite 300
    Chicago, IL 60611
    (312) 755-0770
    www.perkinswill.com

Source: Adapted from Crain's Chicago Business. *[www.crainschicago business.com, (312) 649-5411]*

Los Angeles (based on 1999 LA country billings)

1. **Daniel, Mann, Johnson & Mendenhall ($62.5M)**
   320 Wilshire Blvd.
   Los Angeles, CA 90010
   www.dmjm.com

2. **Gensler ($27M)**
   2500 Broadway, Suite 300
   Santa Monica, CA 90404
   www.gensler.com

3. **MCG Architecture ($25.4M)**
   200 S. Los Robles Avenue, Suite 300
   Pasadena, CA 91101
   www.mcgarchitecture.com

4. **Jerde Partnership International ($20M)**
   913 Ocean Front Walk
   Venice, CA 90291
   www.jerde.com

5. **HNTB Corp ($20M)**
   611 W. Sixth Street, Suite 1800
   Los Angeles, CA 90017
   www.hntb.com

6. **Perkins & Will ($19.9M)**
   2700 Colorado Blvd, Suite 400
   Santa Monica, CA 90404
   www.perkinswill.com

7. **Hellmuth, Obata + Kassabaum ($19.1M)**
   1655 26th Street, Suite 200
   Santa Monica, CA 90404
   www.hok.com

8. **Perkowitz + Ruth Architects ($18M)**
   111 West Ocean Blvd, 21st Floor
   Long Beach, CA 90802
   www.prarchitects.com

Did you know...

Skidmore Owings & Merrill, second in number of registered architects, led all Chicago firms with $96 million in billings, 50% of which came directly from its architecture division.

Top Architecture Firms by City (Con't)

9. **RTKL Associates ($16.7M)**
   333 S. Hope Street, Suite C-200
   Los Angeles, CA 90017
   www.rtkl.com
10. **Langdon-Wilson ($16.5M)**
   1055 Wilshire Blvd, Suite 1500
   Los Angeles, CA 90017
   www.langsonwilson.com

Source: Adapted from the Los Angeles Business Journal. *[www.labusinessjournal.com, (323) 549-5225]*

Minneapolis/St. Paul (based on 2000 metro-area architectural billings)
1. **Ellerbe Becket ($53M)**
   800 LaSalle Avenue
   Minneapolis, MN 55402
   (612) 376-2000
   www.ellerbebecket.com
2. **Hammel Green and Abrahamson Inc. ($21M)**
   701 Washington Avenue North
   Minneapolis, MN 55401
   (612) 758-4000
   www.hga.com
3. **KKE Architects ($17.7M)**
   300 First Avenue N.
   Minneapolis, MN 55401
   (612) 339-4200
   www.kke.com
4. **RSP Architects ($15.67M)**
   120 First Avenue N.
   Minneapolis, MN 55401
   (612) 339-0313
   www.rsparch.com
5. **BWBR Architects ($12.5M)**
   400 Sibley Street, Suite 500
   St. Paul, MN 55102
   (651) 222-3701
   www.bwbr.com
6. **DLR Group ($8.3M)**
   9521 W. 78th Street
   Eden Prairie, MN 55344
   (952) 941-8950
   www.dlrgroup.com

7. **Setter Leach & Lindstrom ($8.2M)**
   1100 Peavey Bldg.
   Minneapolis, MN 55402
   (612) 338-8741
   www.setterleach.com
8. **Wold Architects and Engineers ($8.163M)**
   305 St. Peter Street
   St. Paul, MN 55102
   (651) 227-7773
   www.woldae.com
9. **Opus Architects/Engineers ($7M)**
   P.O. Box 59110
   Minnetonka, MN 55459
   (952) 656-4444
   www.opuscorp.com
10. **Cuningham Group ($6.9M)**
   201 Main Street S.E., Suite 325
   Minneapolis, MN 55414
   (612) 379-3400
   www.cuningham.com

Source: Reprinted with permission of CityBusiness. *[www.amcity.com/twincities/, (612) 288-2100]*

New York City (based on 2000 area architects)
1. **Perkins Eastman Architects (102)**
   115 Fifth Ave.
   New York, NY 10003
   (212) 353-7200
   www.peapc.com

Did you know...

Only 4 of the top 25 architecture firms in the Minneapolis/St. Paul metropolitan area are headquartered in St. Paul compared to 17 that are headquartered in Minneapolis.

Top Architecture Firms by City (Con't)

2. **Kohn Pedersen Fox Associates (90)**
   111 W. 57th Street
   New York, NY 10019
   (212) 977-6500
   www.kpf.com

3. **Gensler (74)**
   1 Rockefeller Plaza
   New York, NY 10020
   (212) 492-1400
   www.gensler.com

3. **HLW International (74)**
   115 Fifth Avenue
   New York, NY 10003
   (212) 353-4600
   www.hlw.com

5. **Skidmore, Owings & Merrill (68)**
   14 Wall Street
   New York, NY 10005
   (212) 298-9300
   www.som.com

6. **Perkins & Will (59)**
   1 Park Avenue
   New York, NY 10016
   (212) 251-7000
   www.perkinswill.com

7. **Wank Adams Slavin Associates (57)**
   740 Broadway
   New York, NY 10003
   (212) 420-1160
   www.go2wasa.com

8. **Fox & Fowle (55)**
   22 W. 19th Street
   New York, NY 10011
   (212) 627-1700
   www.foxfowle.com

9. **Pei Cobb Freed & Partners Associates (51)**
   600 Madison Avenue
   New York, NY 10022
   (212) 751-3122
   www.pcf-p.com

10. **Gruzen Samton Architects, Planners & Interior Designers (45)**
    304 Park Avenue South
    New York, NY 10010
    (212) 477-0900
    www.gruzensamton.com

Source: Reprinted with permission of Crain's New York Business. [www.crainsny.com, (212) 210-0270]

Philadelphia (based on 1999 local architectural billings)

1. **Kling Lindquist ($50M)**
   2301 Chestnut Street
   Philadelphia, PA 19103
   (215) 569-2900
   www.tklp.com

2. **Ewing Cherry Cole Brott ($30.2M)**
   100 N. 6th Street
   Philadelphia, PA 19106
   (215) 923-2020
   www.ewingcole.com

3. **Vitetta Group ($25.4M)**
   4747 S. Broad Street
   Philadelphia, PA 19112
   (215) 218-4747
   www.vitetta.com

Did you know...

Venturi, Scott Brown and Associates, Inc., the groundbreaking Philadelphia architecture firm that was recently honored with a retrospective exhibit at the Philadelphia Art Museum, ranked 12th with $7.4 million in local billings.

Top Architecture Firms by City (Con't)

4. **Ballinger ($20.2M)**
   2005 Market Street, Suite 1500
   Philadelphia, PA 19103
   (215) 665-0900
   www.ballinger-ae.com

5. **Granary Associates ($18.6M)**
   411 N. 20th Street
   Philadelphia, PA 19130
   (215) 665-7000
   www.granaryassoc.com

6. **Wallace Roberts & Todd LLC ($12M)**
   260 S. Broad Street, 8th Floor
   Philadelphia, PA 19102
   (215) 732-5215
   www.wrtdesign.com

7. **Francis, Cauffman, Foley, Hoffman ($9.5M)**
   2120 Arch Street
   Philadelphia, PA 1910
   (215) 568-8250
   www.fcfh-did.com

8. **Daroff Design Inc and DDI Architects ($9.2M)**
   2300 Ionic Street
   Philadelphia, PA 19103
   (215) 636-9900
   www.daroffdesign.com

9. **The Hillier Group ($9M)**
   One South Penn Square
   The Widener Building
   Philadelphia, PA 19107
   (215) 636-9999
   www.hillier.com

10. **BLM Group ($8.6)**
    161 Rock Hill Road
    Bala Cynwyd, PA 19004
    (610) 667-8877
    www.theblmgroup.com

Phoenix (based on 2000 local registered architects)

1. **SmithGroup (37)**
   2800 N. Central Avenue
   Phoenix, AZ 85004
   (602) 265-2200
   www.smithgroup.com

2. **The Orcutt/Winslow Partnership (28)**
   1130 N. Second Street
   Phoenix, AZ 85004
   (602) 257-1764
   www.owp.com

3. **DLR Group (25)**
   2141 E. Camelback Road
   Phoenix, AZ 85016
   (602) 381-8580
   www.dlrgroup.com

4. **Cornoyer-Hedrick (20)**
   2425 Camelback Road
   Phoenix, AZ 85016
   (602) 381-4848
   www.cornoyerhedrick.com

5. **Durrant (20)**
   426 N. 44th Street
   Phoenix, AZ 85008
   (602) 275-6830
   www.durrant.com

6. **Leo A. Daly (19)**
   3344 E. Camelback Road
   Phoenix, AZ 85018
   (602) 954-0818
   www.leoadaly.com

Source: Reprinted with permission of the Philadelphia Business Journal. *[www.bizjournals.bcentral.com/philadelphia/, (215) 238-5100]*

Did you know...

The Phoenix office of the SmithGroup, the largest architectural office in Phoenix, would only rank 15 in New York City.

Top Architecture Firms by City (Con't)

7. **Todd & Associates (17)**
   4019 N. 44th Street
   Phoenix, AZ 85018
   (602) 952-8280
   www.toddassoc.com

8. **Archicon LC (16)**
   3707 N. Seventh Street
   Phoenix, AZ 85014
   (602) 222-4266
   www.archicon.com

9. **CCBG Architects (15)**
   818 N. First Street
   Phoenix, AZ 85004
   (602) 258-2211
   www.ccbg-arch.com

9. **Langdon Wilson (15)**
   455 N. Third Street
   Phoenix, AZ 85004
   (602) 252-2555
   www.langdonwilson.com

Source: Reprinted with permission of the Phoenix Business Journal.
[www.amcity.com/phoenix/, (602) 230-8400]

Seattle/Puget Sound (based on total 1999 local
office billings)

1. **NBBJ ($71.9M)**
   111 S. Jackson Street
   Seattle, WA 98101
   (206) 223-5000
   www.nbbj.com

2. **Callison Architects Inc. ($62M)**
   1420 Fifth Ave, Suite 2400
   Seattle, WA 98101
   (206) 623-4646
   www.callison.com

3. **Mulvanny.G2 Architects ($21.6M)**
   11820 Northup Way, Suite E300
   Bellevue, WA 98005
   (425) 822-0444
   www.mulvanny.com

4. **Zimmer Gunsul Frasca Partnership ($20.5M)**
   1191 Second Ave, Suite 800
   Seattle, WA 98101
   (206) 623-9414
   www.zgf.com

5. **Mithun ($16.2M)**
   1201 Alaskan Way, Suite 200
   Seattle, WA 98101
   (206) 623-3344
   www.mithun.com

6. **LMN Architects ($12.6M)**
   801 Second Ave, Suite 501
   Seattle, WA 98104
   (206) 682-3460
   www.lmnarchitects.com

7. **DLR Group ($11.1M)**
   Fourth Avenue, Suite 400
   Seattle, WA 98164
   (206) 461-6000
   www.dlrgroup.com

8. **Mahlum ($10.8M)**
   71 Columbia Street, Suite 400
   Seattle, WA 98104
   (206) 441-4151
   www.mahlum.com

9. **JPC Architects PLLC ($9.3M)**
   13201 Bel-Red Road
   Bellevue, WA 08005
   (425) 641-9200
   www.jpcarchitects.com

10. **BJSS Duarte Bryant ($7.5M)**
    724 Columbia Street NW, Suite 400
    Olympia, WA 98501
    (360) 943-4650
    www.djssdb.com

10. **GGLO Architecture and Design ($7.5M)**
    1301 First Ave, Suite 300
    Seattle, WA 98101
    (206) 467-5828
    www.gglo.com

Source: Reprinted with permission of Puget Sound Business Journal.
[www.amcity.com/seattle/, (206) 583-0701]

Top Architecture Firms by City (Con't)

St Louis (based on 2000 local registered architects)

1. **Hospital Designers Inc. (100)**
   11330 Olive Street,
   St. Louis, MO 63141
   (314) 567-9000
   www.hbecorp.com

2. **Hellmuth, Obata + Kasabaum Inc. (52)**
   211 N. Broadway
   St. Louis, MO 63102
   (314) 421-2000
   www.hok.com

3. **Jacobs Facilities Inc. [formerly Sverdrup CRSS] (43)**
   400 S. Fourth Street
   St. Louis, MO 63102
   (314) 436-7600
   www.jacobsfacilities.com

4. **CASCO Corp. (37)**
   10877 Watson Road
   St. Louis, MO 63127
   (314) 821-1100
   www.cascocorp.com

5. **Christner Inc. (30)**
   7711 Bonhomme Avenue
   St. Louis, MO 63105
   www.christnerinc.com

6. **Cannon Design (29)**
   One City Center, Suite 2500
   St. Louis, MO 63101
   (314) 241-6250
   www.cannondesign.com

7. **Hastings & Chivetta Architects, Inc. (28)**
   700 Corporate Park Drive
   St. Louis, MO 63105
   (314) 863-5717
   www.hastingschivetta.com

8. **The Lawrence Group (19)**
   319 N. 4th Street, Suite 1000
   St. Louis, MO 63102
   (314) 231-5700
   www.thelawrencegroup.com

9. **Mackay Mitchell Associates (17)**
   800 St. Louis Union Station
   St. Louis, MO 63103
   (314) 421-1815
   www.mackaymitchell.com

10. **Wischmeyer Architects (16)**
    1221 Locust Street, Suite 1200
    St. Louis, MO 63103
    (314) 231-4704
    www.f-w.com

Source: Reprinted with permission of the St. Louis Business Journal. *[www. stlouis.bcentral.com/, (314) 421-6200]*

Washington, D.C. (based on 1999 metro-area architectural billings)

1. **SmithGroup ($30M)**
   1825 Eye Street, Suite 250
   Washington, DC 20006
   (202) 842-2100
   www.smithgroup.com

2. **Sverdrup, CRSS ($26M)**
   1300 Wilson Blvd.
   Arlington, VA 22209
   (703) 351-4200
   www.sverdrup.com

3. **Daniel, Mann, Johnson & Mendenhall ($24.5M)**
   1525 Wilson Blvd, Suite 100
   Arlington, VA 22209
   (703) 807-2500
   www.dmjm.com

4. **Leo A. Daly ($22M)**
   1201 Connecticut Avenue NW
   Washington, DC 20036
   (202) 861-4600
   www.leoadaly.com

5. **Hellmuth Obata & Kassabaum ($17.2M)**
   3223 Grace Street NW
   Washington, DC 20007
   (202) 339-8700
   www.hok.com

Top Architecture Firms by City (Con't)

6. **RTKL Associates ($16M)**
   1250 Connecticut Avenue NW
   Washington, DC 20036
   (202) 833-4400
   www.rtkl.com

7. **URS ($13.8M)**
   2020 K Street NW
   Washington, DC 20006
   (202) 872-0277
   www.urscorp.com

8. **HNTB Corporation ($13.5M)**
   99 Canal Center Plaza
   Alexandria, VA 22314
   (703) 684-2700
   www.hntb.com

9. **Case Design/Remodeling ($13.4M)**
   4701 Sangmore Road, Suite 40
   Bethesda, MD 20816
   (301) 229-4600
   www.casedesign.com

10. **Einhorn Yaffee Prescott ($13.1M)**
    1000 Potomac Street NW
    Washington, DC 20007
    (202) 471-5000
    www.eypae.com

Source: Reprinted with permission of the Washington Business Journal. *[www.amcity.com/washington/, (703) 875-2200]*

Did you know...

Only 1 of the top 10 firms in the Washington, D.C. metro-area is headquartered in the city.

Design Education

Current and future design students will find valuable information in this chapter from student award programs and associations to a comprehensive listing of design degree programs, a ranking of the top schools for architecture and interior design, and a salary and recruiting guide for recent graduates. Of related interest are the annual student essays on pages 21 and 25 in the Speeches & Essays chapter.

ACSA Distinguished Professor Award

The Association of Collegiate Schools of Architecture's (ACSA) Distinguished Professor Award is presented annually for "sustained creative achievement" in the field of architectural education, whether through teaching, design, scholarship, research, or service. Eligible candidates must be living faculty of an ACSA member school for a minimum of 10 years or be otherwise allied with architectural education at an ACSA member school. Students or faculty of an ACSA member school may make nominations. Each year, an Honors and Awards Committee recommends a maximum of five candidates to the ACSA Board. Winners are entitled to use the title 'ACSA Distinguished Professor' for life.

For additional information about the ACSA Distinguished Professor Award, contact the Association at (202) 785-2324, or visit their Web site at *www.acsa-arch.org*.

1984-85
Alfred Caldwell, Illinois Institute of Technology
Robert S. Harris, Univ. of Southern Calif.
Fay Jones, Univ. of Arkansas
Charles Moore, Univ. of Texas at Austin
Ralph Rapson, Univ. of Minnesota

1985-86
James Marston Fitch, Columbia Univ.
Leslie J. Laskey, Washington Univ.
Harlan McClure, Clemson Univ.
Edward Romieniec, Texas A & M Univ.
Richard Williams, U. of Illinois, Champaign-Urbana

1986-87
Christopher Alexander, Univ. of California, Berkeley
Harwell Hamilton Harris, North Carolina State Univ.
Stanislawa Nowicki, Univ. of Pennsylvania
Douglas Shadbolt, Univ. of British Columbia
Jerzy Soltan, Harvard Univ.

1987-88
Harold Cooledge, Jr., Clemson Univ.
Bernd Foerster, Kansas State Univ.
Romaldo Giurgola, Columbia Univ.
Joseph Passonneau, Washington Univ.
John G. Willams, Univ. of Arkansas

1988-89
Peter R. Lee, Jr., Clemson Univ.
E. Keith McPheeters, Auburn Univ.
Stanley Salzman, Pratt Institute
Calvin C. Straub, Arizona State Univ.
Blanche Lemco van Ginkel, Univ. of Toronto

1989-90
Gunnar Birkerts, Univ. of Michigan
Olivio C. Ferrari, Virginia Polytechnic Institute
George C. Means, Jr., Clemson Univ.
Malcolm Quantrill, Texas A & M Univ.

1990-91
Denise Scott Brown, Univ. of Pennsylvania
Panos Koulermos, Univ. of Southern Calif.
William McMinn, Cornell Univ.
Forrest Wilson, The Catholic Univ. of America
David Woodcock, Texas A & M Univ.

ACSA Distinguished Professor Award (Con't)

1991-92

M. David Egan, Clemson Univ.
Robert D. Dripps, Univ. of Virginia
Richard C. Peters, Univ. of California, Berkeley
David L. Niland, Univ. of Cincinnati

1992-93

Stanley W. Crawley, Univ. of Utah
Don P. Schlegel, Univ. of New Mexico
Thomas L. Schumacher, Univ. of Maryland

1993-94

George Anselevicius, Univ. of New Mexico
Hal Box, Univ. of Texas at Austin
Peter McCleary, Univ. of Pennsylvania
Douglas Rhyn, Univ. of Wisconsin-Milwaukee
Alan Stacell, Texas A & M Univ.

1994-95

Blake Alexander, Univ. of Texas at Austin
Robert Burns, North Carolina State Univ.
Robert Heck, Louisiana State Univ.
Ralph Knowles, Univ. of Southern California

1995-96

James Barker, Clemson Univ.
Mui Ho, Univ. of California, Berkley
Patricia O'Leary, Univ. of Colorado
Sharon Sutton, Univ. of Minnesota
Peter Waldman, Univ. of Virginia

1996-97

Colin H. Davidson, Universite de Montreal
Michael Fazio, Mississippi State Univ.
Ben J. Refuerzo, Univ. of Calif., Los Angeles
Max Underwood, Arizona State Univ.
J. Stroud Watson, Univ. of Tennessee

1997-98

Roger H. Clark, North Carolina State Univ.
Bob E. Heatly, Oklahoma State Univ.
John S. Reynolds, Univ. of Oregon
Marvin E. Rosenman, Ball State Univ.
Anne Taylor, Univ. of New Mexico

1998-99

Ralph Bennett, Univ. of Maryland
Diane Ghirardo, Univ. of Southern California
Robert Greenstreet, Univ. of Wisconsin-
    Milwaukee
Thomas Kass, Univ. of Utah
Norbert Schoenauer, McGill Univ.
Jan Wampler, Massachusetts Inst. of Tech.

1999-2000

Maelee Thomson Foster, Univ. of Florida
Louis Inserra, Pennsylvania State Univ.
Henry Sanoff, North Carolina State Univ.

2000-01

Ikhlas Sabouni, Prairie View A&M University
Raymond J. Cole, University of British
    Columbia

Source: Association of Collegiate Schools of Architecture

ACSP Distinguished Educator Award

The ACSP Distinguished Educator Award is presented annually by the Association of Collegiate Schools of Planning (ACSP) in appreciation of distinguished service to planning education and practice. Nominations are welcomed from chairs and faculty members of ACSP member schools and are reviewed by the award committee. Recipients are chosen for their scholarly contributions, teaching excellence, service to the profession, and significant contributions to planning education and/or practice.

For additional information about the Distinguished Educator Award, visit ACSP's Web site at *www.uwm.edu/Org/acsp/*.

1983	Harvey Perloff, University of California, Los Angeles	1995	Alan Feldt, University of Michigan
1984	John Reps, Cornell University	1996	Martin Meyerson, University of Pennsylvania
1986	F. Stuart Chapin, University of North Carolina at Chapel Hill	1997	Lloyd Rodwin, Massachusetts Institute of Technology
1987	John Friedmann, University of California, Los Angeles	1998	Michael Teitz, University of California, Berkeley
1989	John Dyckman, Johns Hopkins University	1999	Lisa Redfield Peattie, Massachusetts Institute of Technology
1990	Barclay Gibbs Jones, Cornell University	2000	Melvin M. Webber University of Calfornia, Berkeley
1991	Britton Harris, University of Pennsylvania		
1992	Melville Branch, University of Southern California		
1993	Ann Strong, University of Pennsylvania		*Source: Association of Collegiate Schools of Planning*
1994	John A. Parker, University of North Carolina at Chapel Hill		

AICP Outstanding Student Award

The American Institute of Certified Planners (AICP) each year presents its Outstanding Student Awards to recognize outstanding graduating students in accredited university planning programs, both at the undergraduate and graduate levels. Awarded students have been selected for the honor by their schools' department head and colleagues who establish criteria with an emphasis on quality of work in the student's courses in planning and likelihood of success as a professional planner.

Additional information can be found on the American Planning Association Web site at *www.planning.org* or by calling the Washington, D.C. office of the American Planning Association at (202) 872-0611.

2001 Winners:

Bachelor's Degree

Brad Beaubien, Ball State University
Cheung Wong, California Polytechnic State University, San Luis Obispo
Nicholas Liguori, California State Polytechnic University, Pomona
David Eli White, University of Cincinnati
Bradley Deets, Iowa State University
David Paradis, University of Montreal
Joseph Simpson Farland, University of Virginia

Master's Degree

Jitin Kain, Ball State University
Scott Duiven, California Polytechnic State University, San Luis Obispo
Nathan de Boom, California State Polytechnic University, Pomona
Della Gott Rucker, University of Cincinnati
Jason M. Peek, Clemson University
Alice Bojanowski, University of Florida
Marci Monchek, Florida Atlantic University
Robert Mosriem, Florida State University
Claudia Martin, Georgia Institute of Technology
Tamara Greenfield, Hunter College, City University of New York
Carmen Carruthers, University of Iowa
Michael Clay, Iowa State University
Molly Katherine Whalen, University of Kansas

Erik Pollom, Kansas State University
Heather Whitlow, University of Maryland
Jennifer L. James, Massachusetts Institute of Technology
Emily Trenholm, University of Memphis
Leah Goldstein, University of Minnesota
Dominic Duford, University of Montreal
Michael C. Latsu, Morgan State University
Jeffrey Vincent, University of Nebraska
Kelly Thompson Cochran, University of North Carolina
Kelly Dufour, The Ohio State University
Kathy Lynn, University of Oregon
Bonnie R. Nickerson, University of Rhode Island
Diana Marie Downton, Rutgers University
Thanicha Niyomwan, San Jose State University
Katherine Louise Campbell, University of Virginia
Elizabeth Reynolds, Virginia Commonwealth University
Sarah Rice, University of Washington
Danielle Alisa Salus, University of Wisconsin, Madison
Greg Summers, University of Wisconsin, Milwaukee

Source: American Institute of Certified Planners

AICP Outstanding Student Project Award

Recognizing outstanding achievements that contribute to advances in the field of planning, the American Institute of Certified Planners (AICP) presents the Outstanding Student Project Award each year at the National Planning Conference. Students or groups of students in an accredited planning curriculum may enter a paper or class project; no more than three awards will be given. Award categories include the project that best demonstrates the contribution of planning to contemporary issues and the project best applying the planning process.

Student Project Award nomination packets are available by calling (202) 872-0611.

2001 Winners:

Applied Research
 "The Growth Management Toolbox: A Better
 Way to Live"
 University of Virginia, Charlottesville, VA
 Carrie Beach, Laura Everitt, Chris Galanty,
 Shannon Garvey, DJ Gerken, Brian Haluska,
 Porter Ingrum, Jim Lamey, Tianjin Luo,
 Rose-Anne McGrail, Jyothsna Ramesh,
 Jaymie Sheffield, Sean Suder, Melissa C.
 Tronquet, Suzanne Usak

*Demonstrating the Contribution of Planning to
Contemporary Issues*
 "The Economic Development Plan for the Hopi
 Winslow Trust Property"
 University of Arizona, Tucson, AZ
 Tripti Agarwal, Hilary Anderson, Peter A.
 Cherberg, Donovan Durband, Jennifer Greig,
 Matthew Keough, Susan I. Morrison, Tiffany
 C. Rich, Adam B. Smith, Lisa A. Verts, Jeffrey
 Wegener

Applying the Planning Process
 "Future Land Use in the Town of Dryden:
 Alternatives & Recommendations"
 Cornell University, Ithaca, NY
 Julie Amato, Lawrence Bice, Karen Edelstein,
 Jessica Feldman, Tika Gurung, Ryan Harris,
 Danielle Hauntaniemi, Bethany Johnson,
 Tim Logue, Juan Carlos Londono, Jonathan
 Martin, Mark Rodman, Megan Rupnik, David
 Whitley, Martha Wittosch, Yizhao Yang

2001 Jurors:
 Dean Palos
 Alfred Raby
 Sam Parker, Jr.

Source: American Institute of Certified Planners

Did you know...

The 1909 Wisconsin Planning Enabling Act was the first state act to grant a clear right to municipalities to engage in city planning activities. It subsequently served as a national model.

Alpha Rho Chi

Alpha Rho Chi is a national coeducational professional fraternity for students and professionals of architecture and the allied arts, which was founded in 1914 when the Arcus Society of the University of Illinois and Sigma Upsilon of the University of Michigan united. The organization remains dedicated to "promoting the artistic, scientific and practical proficiency of its membership and the profession." For membership information, contact your local Alpha Rho Chi chapter.

Contact:
Additional information about Alpha Rho Chi, including a list of chapters and their contacts, can be found online at *www.alpharhochi.org*.

Did you know...

Actor Anthony Quinn, who died on June 3, 2001, at age 86, studied architecture under Frank Lloyd Wright at Taliesin; and it was Wright who suggested Quinn take acting lessons to improve his communication skills.

Alpha Rho Chi Bronze Medal

Alpha Rho Chi, a national professional coeducational fraternity for students in architecture and the allied arts, selects its annual Bronze Medal recipients from over 100 schools of architecture. The award was established in 1931 by the Grand Council of Alpha Rho Chi to "encourage professional leadership by regarding student accomplishment; promote the ideals of professional service by acknowledging distinctive individual contributions to social life; and stimulate professional merit by commending qualities in the student not necessarily pertaining to scholarship." Nominees are graduating seniors selected by faculty who best exemplify the aforementioned qualities.

Additional information may be found on the fraternity's Web site: *www.alpharhochi.org.*

2001 Winners:

David A. Edwards, Andrews University
Michelle Watanabi, Arizona State University
Matthew T. Leavell, Auburn University
Antonio Pina, Boston Architectural Center
Robert Lee Ettenger, V, California Polytechnic State University
Kevin Joshua Martin, Carleton University
Lori M. Hashimoto, Carnegie Mellon
Michele Adrianse, Carnegie Mellon
Donna A. Ellis, Catholic Univ. of America
Patricia M. McDermott, City College of New York
Jane Kim, Columbia University
Alexander Gil, The Cooper Union
Kevin Andrew Oliver, Cornell University
Kelly C. W. Chow, Dalhousie University
Jennifer Summers, Drexel University
Theresa M. English, Drury University
Kelly Browning, Florida A & M University
Jason Snyder, Georgia Institute of Technology
Derek A. Ham, Hampton University
Matthew L. Stewart, Iowa State University
Addie M. Johnson, Kansas State University
Laura Gill, Kent State University
William Cross Duncan, Louisiana Tech University
Daniel Velazquez, Louisiana State University

Rolando J. Mendoza, Massachusetts Institute of Technology
Melissa Dalton, Miami University
Casey Newman, Mississippi State University
Andrew Weyrauch, Montana State University
Eric Preston Miller, New Jersey Institute of Technology
Sharon Gehl, Newschool of Architecture
Thomas Haynes, New York Institute of Technology
Jesse S. Turck, North Dakota State University
William Allen Brothers, Norwich University
Francis X. Weaver, The Ohio State University
Adam Michael St. Cyr, Oklahoma State University
Nicole Themis Pappas, Parsons School of Design
Carl J. Heyne, Pennsylvania State University
Jeremy Curtis, Prairie View A&M University
David Lyle Hays, Princeton University
Daniel Jaconetti, Jr., Rensselaer Polytechnic Institute
Delia Wendel, Rice University
Bradly T. Lunz, Savannah College of Art and Design
Kristina Nöel Alg, Southern California Institute of Architecture

Alpha Rho Chi Bronze Medal (Con't)

Charles T. Smith, III, Southern Polytechnic State University

Carrie Lynn Galuski, State University of New York at Buffalo

Jeffrey D. Sipprell, Syracuse University

Julie R. Goldberg, Temple University

Wayne R. Baker, Texas A & M University

Mackenzie Miller Jeans, Tulane University

Mylene Hamel, Universite Laval

Richard K. Begay, Jr., University of Arizona

James W. Nutt, University of Arkansas

Sandra Eng, University of British Columbia

Nicole Howard, University of Calgary

Monica Guilbault, University of California, Berkeley

Humberto Herrero, University of California, Los Angeles

James T. Casanova, University of Colorado at Denver

Adrianna M. Melchior, University of Detroit, Mercy

Donovan J. Bumanglag, University of Hawaii

Neal M. Kido, University of Hawaii

Kari E. Rose, University of Idaho

Taylor James Pierce, University of Illinois

Deborah J. Chiu, University of Illinois-Champaign

Katie E. Griffiths, University of Kansas

Rebecca A. Sayles, University of Kentucky

Bayardo Selva, University of Louisiana, Lafayette

Christian Bret Calleri, University of Maryland

Talisha L. Sainvil, University of Miami

Daniel Morgen West, University of Michigan

Timothy Politis, University of Nebraska-Lincoln

Sarah Lindenfeld, University of New Mexico

Zacharias Karl Alsentzer, University of North Carolina-Charlotte

Geno P. Knowles, Jr., University of South Florida

Flavia Augusta Almeida, University of Tennessee

Sara Cecilia Galvan, University of Texas

Jay J. Lems, University of Utah

Ian Harry Douglas, University of Toronto

Halldor Eiriksson, University of Virginia

David Colussi, University of Waterloo

Korrine Haeffel, University of Wisconsin-Milwaukee

Michael Kolejka, Virginia Tech

Brie Gargano, Washington State University

Steven Rosenstein, Woodbury University

AnnMarie Brennan, Yale University

Source: Alpha Rho Chi

American Institute of Architecture Students (AIAS)

The American Institute of Architecture Students (AIAS) is a non-profit, independent, student-run organization that seeks to promote excellence in architecture education, training and practice, as well as to organize architecture students and promote the practice of architecture. The AIAS was formed in 1956 and today serves over 7,500 undergraduate and graduate architecture students. More than 150 chapters at U.S. and Canadian colleges and universities support members with professional development seminars, community projects, curriculum advisory committees, guest speakers and many other programs.

Address:
1735 New York Avenue, NW
Washington, DC 20006
Telephone: (202) 626-7472
Internet: www.aiasnatl.org

We know that the good building is not the one that hurts the landscape, but is one that makes the landscape more beautiful than it was before the building was built.

Frank Lloyd Wright

Architecture Student Demographics

Based on a study conducted by the National Architectural Accrediting Board (NAAB), the following information outlines demographic information about NAAB accredited architecture degree programs at U.S. colleges and universities.

	1993/94	1994/95	1995/96	1996/97	1997/98	1998/99	1999/00
Pre-professional Undergrad. Programs							
Full-time students	10,420	10,790	9,655	12,130	11,789	12,062	13,391
Part-time students	1,504	1,577	1,494	1,602	1,524	1386	1,782
Women students	3,419	3,895	3,432	4,317	4,419	4495	5,314
African-American students	635	723	496	660	682	641	789
American Indian students	59	59	80	62	67	78	77
Asian/Pacific Isle students	929	1,010	807	1,112	1,065	1042	1,106
Hispanic students	1,144	967	750	991	955	929	1,368
Total Graduates	2,260	2,369	2,154	2,324	2,199	2397	2,716
Women graduates	662	708	603	746	807	774	1,044
African-American graduates	105	75	74	83	81	85	96
American Indian graduates	7	7	6	10	9	12	11
Asian/Pacific Isle graduates	238	219	198	225	233	226	244
Hispanic graduates	149	147	101	157	162	157	229
Accredited B. Arch Programs							
Full-time students	16,899	16,500	16,424	16,025	16,423	15312	14,792
Part-time students	1,924	1,500	1,364	1,178	1,377	1606	1,568
Women students	5,007	5,107	5,155	5,046	5,413	5201	5,789
African-American students	1,252	1,174	1,247	1,122	1,165	1243	1,342
American Indian students	101	143	195	163	138	151	129
Asian/Pacific Isle students	1,699	1,735	1,665	1,591	1,497	1425	1,552
Hispanic students	1,473	1,466	1,436	1,340	1,249	1184	1,400
Total Graduates	3,206	2,837	2,948	3,028	2,710	2617	2,825
Women graduates	832	775	742	849	762	754	749
African-American graduates	152	144	148	131	111	131	137

B. Arch. Demographics, 1999-2000

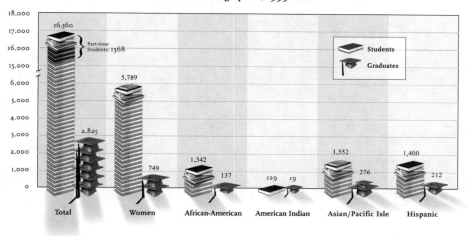

Part-time Students: 1568

	Students	Graduates
Total	16,360	2,825
Women	5,789	749
African-American	1,342	137
American Indian	129	19
Asian/Pacific Isle	1,552	276
Hispanic	1,400	212

M. Arch. Demographics, 1999-2000

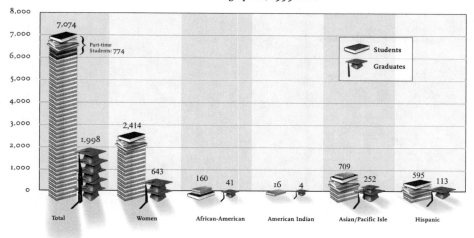

Part-time Students: 774

	Students	Graduates
Total	7,074	1,998
Women	2,414	643
African-American	160	41
American Indian	16	4
Asian/Pacific Isle	709	252
Hispanic	595	113

Source: Counsel House Research

Architecture Student Demographics (Con't)

	1993/94	1994/95	1995/96	1996/97	1997/98	1998/99	1999/00
American Indian graduates	20	16	14	14	8	13	19
Asian/Pacific Isle graduates	282	277	276	307	294	239	276
Hispanic graduates	188	185	215	223	222	198	212
Accredited M. Arch Programs							
Full-time students	4,812	4,664	5,196	5,252	5,461	5769	6,302
Part-time students	537	491	724	533	677	689	772
Women students	1,855	1,883	2,164	2,143	2,273	2210	2,414
African-American students	117	121	142	133	133	119	160
American Indian students	18	11	21	17	20	42	16
Asian/Pacific Isle students	521	508	540	522	550	607	709
Hispanic students	260	235	267	302	301	427	595
Total Graduates	1,654	1,629	1,676	1,645	1,799	2002	1,998
Women graduates	541	580	558	580	747	744	643
African-American graduates	28	28	26	45	32	40	41
American Indian graduates	1	3	5	3	9	10	4
Asian/Pacific Isle graduates	158	169	140	156	164	197	252
Hispanic graduates	75	87	83	82	92	104	113

Source: National Architectural Accrediting Board

ASLA National Student Design Competition

The American Society of Landscape Architects annually conducts a competition to identify and recognize outstanding works of design and research from landscape architecture students. Any landscape architecture student, undergraduate or graduate, in the U.S. or Canada is eligible to enter. Awards are granted by the jury at their discretion. All winning entries are displayed at the ASLA's annual conference. Winners receive a certificate, and first place winners receive a complimentary conference registration.

For additional information about the Competition, contact the ASLA at (202) 898-2444 or *www.asla.org*.

2001 Research Category Winners:

Undergraduate First Place
   "Telling Stories, Provoking Change"
   Susan B. Jones
   University of Nevada, Las Vegas

Undergraduate Commendation
   "The Trees of Lawrenceville"
   Elaine A. Mills
   Rutgers University

Graduate Commendation
   "Evaluation Paradigms and the Value of
      Landscape in Commercial Real Estate"
   John B. St. Clair
   University of Texas at Arlington

Graduate, Second Professional Degree First Place
   "Perceptual Differences in Computer Rendering
      Depicting Landscapes"
   Roberta Kunz
   Louisiana State University

2001 Design Category Winners:

Undergraduate First Place
   "Hydro Corridor - Linkage Between Suburban
      and Urban Infrastructure"
   Chak Lam Cheng
   University of Toronto

"Old Solider Creek"
David Werner
Kansas State University

"Experiential Equality"
Raymon Yim
University of Guelph

Undergraduate Commendation
   "Adrenalscapes: Designing Thrill"
   Jack Vanstone
   University of Guelph,, ON, Canada

   "alt'wal(s)":www.altwals.com
   Michele A. Shelor
   Arizona State University

"Ventura Promenade Revitalization"
Tana Berry
California Polytechnic State University, San Luis
   Obispo

Undergraduate Team Commendation
   "Poly Arts Complex...Collaboration Movements"
   Shawna Harrison and Isreal Pena
   California Polytechnic State Universit, San Luis
      Obispo

ASLA National Student Design Competition (Con't)

2001 Jury:
- Daniel Ashworth Jr.
- David Barnes
- Terry Clements
- Paula Horrigan
- Steven Rogers
- Erica Simon

Source: American Society of Landscape Architects

Did you know...

In 1900, Frederick Law Olmsted Jr. and Arthur A. Shurcliff began the first professional program for landscape architecture at Harvard University.

Association Student Chapters

The following national design associations offer student memberships, often at reduced rates, as well as operate student chapters at many U.S. colleges and universities. Student newsletters, leadership opportunities, networking, job postings, discounts, and many other member benefits are typically available to students. More information about specific benefits and a current listing of the active student chapters are available from the organizations and their Web sites. Profiles of the associations are also available in the Organizations chapter.

American Planning Association (APA)
www.planning.org/abtapa/student.htm

American Society of Interior Designers (ASID)
www.asid.org/students/schools.asp

American Society of Landscape Architects (ASLA)
www.asla.org/nonmembers/STCH2000.htm

International Interior Design Association (IIDA)
www.iida.org/membership/student.html

Industrial Designers Society of America (IDSA)
www.idsa.org/studentedu/studentedu.htm

Degree Programs

The following chart provides a list of schools in the United States offering design and design related degrees. The degrees offered include associates (A), certificate (C), professional (P), bachelors (B), masters (M). All the architecture, interior design, landscape architecture, and planning programs indicated below are accredited by the disciplines' respective accrediting bodies: National Architectural Accrediting Board, Foundation for Interior Design Education Research, Landscape Architectural Accrediting Board, and Planning Accreditation Board. For degree programs not listed and accredited by other bodies and students seeking Ph.D. programs, the individual schools should be consulted.

School	City	Web Address	Architecture	Architecture History	Historic Preservation	Industrial Design	Interior Design	Landscape Architecture	Planning
ALABAMA									
Alabama A&M University	Normal	aamu.edu							B M
Auburn University	Auburn	auburn.edu	B			B M *	B	M	
Samford University	Birmingham	samford.edu					B		
Tuskegee University	Tuskegee	tusk.edu	B						
University of Alabama	Tuscaloosa	ua.edu					B		
ARIZONA									
Arizona State University	Tempe	asu.edu	M			B M	B	B	M
Frank Lloyd Wright School of Architecture	Scottsdale	taliesin.edu	M						
University of Arizona	Tucson	arizona.edu	B					M	M
ARKANSAS									
University of Arkansas	Fayetteville	uark.edu	B				B	B	
CALIFORNIA									
Academy of Art College	San Francisco	academyart. edu				B M *	B		
American Inter-Continental University	Los Angeles	aiuniv.edu					B		

Degree Programs (Con't)

School	City	Web Address	Architecture	Architecture History	Historic Preservation	Industrial Design	Interior Design	Landscape Architecture	Planning
Art Center College of Design	Pasadena	artcenter.edu				B M *			
Brooks College	Long Beach	brookscollege.edu					A		
California College of Arts and Crafts	San Francisco	ccac-art.edu	B			B *	B		
California Polytechnic State University	San Luis Obispo	calpoly.edu	B					B	B M
California State Polytechnic University	Pomona	csupomona.edu	B M	.				B M	B M
California State University, Fresno	Fresno	csufresno.edu					B		
California State University, Long Beach	Long Beach	csulb.edu				B M *			
California State University, Northridge	Northridge	csun.edu				B*	B		
California State University, Sacramento	Sacramento	csus.edu					B		
College of the Redwoods	Eureka	redwoods.cc.ca.us			C				
Design Institute of San Diego	San Diego	disd.edu					B		
Fashion Inst. of Design and Merchandising	Los Angeles	fidm.edu					A		
Interior Designers Institute	Newport Beach	idi.edu					B		
ITT Technical Institute	San Bernardino	itt-tech.edu				B			
Newschool of Architecture	San Diego	newschoolarch.edu	B M						
San Diego Mesa College	San Diego	Sdmesa.sdccd.cc.ca.us					A		
San Francisco State University	San Francisco	sfsu.edu				B M			
San Jose State University	San Jose	sjsu.edu				B *			M
Southern California Institute of Architecture	Los Angeles	sciarc.edu	B M						
Stanford University	Stanford	stanford.edu				B M			
University of California, Berkeley	Berkeley	berkeley.edu	M	M				M	M
University of California, Berkeley Extension	Berkeley	unex.berkeley.edu					C		

Degree Programs (Con't)

School	City	Web Address	Architecture	Architecture History	Historic Preservation	Industrial Design	Interior Design	Landscape Architecture	Planning
University of California at Davis	Davis	ucdavis.edu						B	
University of California at Irvine	Irvine	uci.edu							M
University of California at Los Angeles	Los Angeles	ucla.edu	M	M					M
University of California at Los Angeles Extension	Los Angeles	online learning.net					P		
University of California at Santa Barbara	Santa Barbara	ucsb.edu		M					
University of Southern California	Los Angeles	usc.edu	B						M
West Valley College	Saratoga	westvalley.edu					C		
Woodbury University	Burbank	woodbury.edu	B				B		
COLORADO									
Art Institute of Colorado	Denver	cia.aii.edu				B			
Colorado State University	Fort Collins	colostate.edu					B	B	
Metropolitan State College of Denver	Denver	mscd.edu				B			
University of Colorado at Denver/Boulder	Denver	cudenver.edu	M	M				M	M
CONNECTICUT									
University of Bridgeport	Bridgeport	bridgeport.edu				B *			
University of Connecticut	Storrs	uconn.edu						B	
Yale University	New Haven	yale.edu	M						
DELAWARE									
University of Delaware	Newark	s.art.udel.edu		M					
DISTRICT OF COLUMBIA									
Catholic University of America	Washington	cua.edu	B M						
George Washington University	Washington	www.gwu.edu		M					

Degree Programs (Con't)

School	City	Web Address	Architecture	Architecture History	Historic Preservation	Industrial Design	Interior Design	Landscape Architecture	Planning
George Washington Univ. at Mount Vernon College	Washington	www.mvc.gwu.edu					B		
Howard University	Washington	howard.edu	B						
FLORIDA									
Art Institute of Fort Lauderdale	Fort Lauderdale	aifl.edu				B			
Florida A&M University	Tallahassee	famu.edu	B M						
Florida Atlantic University	Fort Lauderdale	fau.edu	B						M
Florida International University	Miami	fiu.edu	M					M	
Florida State University	Tallahassee	fsu.edu		M			B		M
International Academy of Design, Tampa	Tampa	academy.edu					B		
International Fine Arts College	Miami	ifac.edu					A		
Ringling School of Art and Design	Sarasota	rsad.edu					B		
Seminole Community College	Sanford	seminole.cc.fl.us					A		
University of Florida	Gainesville	ufl.edu	M				B	B M	M
University of Miami	Miami	miami.edu	B M						
University of South Florida	Tampa	usf.edu	M						
GEORGIA									
American Inter-continental University	Atlanta	aiuniv.edu					B		
Art Institute of Atlanta	Dunwoody	aia.aii.edu					B		
Atlanta College of Art	Atlanta	aca.edu					B		
Bauder College	Atlanta	bauder.edu					A		
Brenau University	Gainesville	brenau.edu					B		
Georgia Institute of Technology	Atlanta	gatech.edu	M	M		B M			M

Degree Programs (Con't)

School	City	Web Address	Architecture	Architecture History	Historic Preservation	Industrial Design	Interior Design	Landscape Architecture	Planning
Georgia Southern University	Statesboro	gasou.edu					B		
Georgia State University	Atlanta	gsu.edu			M				
Savannah College of Art and Design	Savannah	scad.edu	B M	M	B M	B M			
Southern Polytechnic State University	Marietta	spsu.edu	B						
University of Georgia	Athens	uga.edu			C M		B	B M	
HAWAII									
University of Hawaii at Manoa	Honolulu	hawaii.edu	B M						M
IDAHO									
Ricks College	Rexburg	ricks.edu					P/3yr.		
University of Idaho	Moscow	uidaho.edu	B M					B	
ILLINOIS									
Art Institute of Chicago	Chicago	artic.edu			M				
Illinois Institute of Art at Schaumburg	Schaumburg	ilia.aii.edu					B		
Illinois Institute of Technology	Chicago	iit.edu	B M			M			
Int'l Academy of Merch. and Design, Chicago	Chicago	iamd.edu					B		
Judson College	Elgin	judson-il.edu/depts/dada	M²						
Southern Illinois University at Carbondale	Carbondale	siu.edu				B *	B		
University of Chicago	Chicago	uchicago.edu		M					
University of Illinois at Chicago	Chicago	uic.edu	B M	M		B M*			M
University of Illinois at Urbana-Champaign	Urbana-Champaign	uiuc.edu	M	M		B M *		B M	B M
INDIANA									
Ball State University	Muncie	bsu.edu	B		M			B M	

Degree Programs (Con't)

School	City	Web Address	Architecture	Architecture History	Historic Preservation	Industrial Design	Interior Design	Landscape Architecture	Planning
Indiana University	Bloomington	indiana.edu					B		
ITT Technical Institute	Fort Wayne	itt-tech.edu				B			
Purdue University	Lafayette	purdue.edu				B M	B	B	
University of Notre Dame	South Bend	nd.edu	B M			B M			
IOWA									
Iowa State University	Ames	iastate.edu	B M				B	B	B M
University of Iowa	Iowa City	uiowa.edu		M					M
KANSAS									
Kansas State University	Manhattan	ksu.edu	B				B	B M	M
University of Kansas	Lawrence	ukans.edu	B M			B M *			M
KENTUCKY									
University of Kentucky	Lexington	uky.edu	B		M		B	B	
University of Louisville	Louisville	louisville.edu		M			B		
LOUISIANA									
Louisiana State University	Baton Rouge	lsu.edu	B				B	B M	
Louisiana Tech University	Ruston	latech.edu	B				B		
Southern University A&M College	Baton Rouge	subr.edu	B						
Tulane University	New Orleans	tulane.edu	B M		M				
University of Louisiana at Lafayette	Lafayette	louisiana.edu	B			B	B		
University of New Orleans	New Orleans	uno.edu							M
MARYLAND									
Goucher College	Baltimore	goucher.edu			B M				

Degree Programs (Con't)

School	City	Web Address	Architecture	Architecture History	Historic Preservation	Industrial Design	Interior Design	Landscape Architecture	Planning
Morgan State University	Baltimore	morgan.edu	M					M	M
University of Maryland	College Park	umd.edu	M	M	M C			B	M
MASSACHUSETTS									
Boston Architectural Center	Boston	the-bac.edu	B M²						
Boston University	Boston	bu.edu		M	M				
Endicott College	Beverly	endicott.edu					B		
Harvard University	Cambridge	harvard.edu	M					M	M
Massachusetts College of Art	Boston	massart.edu				B M *			
Massachusetts Institute of Technology	Cambridge	mit.edu	M	M					M
Mount Ida College	Newton	mountida.edu					B		
Newbury College	Brookline	newbury.edu					A		
New England School of Art & Des. at Suffolk U.	Boston	suffolk.edu					B		
Northeastern University	Boston	architecture.neu.edu	M²						
University of Massachusetts/Amherst	Amherst	umass.edu					B	B M	M
Wentworth Institute of Technology	Boston	wit.edu	B			B	B		
MICHIGAN									
Andrews University	Berrien Springs	andrews.edu	B						
Center for Creative Studies	Detriot	ccscad.edu				B *			
Cranbrook Academy of Art	Bloomfield Hills	cranbrookart.edu				M *			
Eastern Michigan University	Ypsilanti	emich.edu			M		B		B
Kendall College of Art and Design	Grand Rapids	kcad.edu				B *	B		
Lawrence Technological University	Southfield	ltu.edu	B M				B		

Degree Programs (Con't)

School	City	Web Address	Architecture	Architecture History	Historic Preservation	Industrial Design	Interior Design	Landscape Architecture	Planning
Michigan State University	East Lansing	msu.edu					B	B	B M
University of Detroit Mercy	Detroit	udmercy.edu	B						
University of Michigan	Ann Arbor	umich.edu	M			B M *		M	M
Wayne State University	Detriot	wayne.edu							M
Western Michigan University	Kalamazoo	wmich.edu				B *	B		
MINNESOTA									
University of Minnesota	St. Paul/Mpls.	umn.edu	B M				B	M	M
MISSISSIPPI									
Mississippi State University	Mississippi State	msstate.edu	B				B	B	
University of Southern Mississippi	Hattiesburg	usm.edu					B		
MISSOURI									
Drury University	Springfield	drury.edu	B						
Kansas City Art Institute	Kansas City	kcai.edu				B*			
Maryville University of St. Louis	St. Louis	Maryville.edu					B		
Southeast Missouri State University	Cape Girardeau	semo.edu			B M				
University of Missouri, Columbia	Columbia	missouri.edu		M			B		
Washington University	St. Louis	Wustl.edu	M						
MONTANA									
Montana State University	Bozeman	Montana.edu	B M						
NEBRASKA									
University of Nebraska	Lincoln	unl.edu	M				B		M
NEVADA									
University of Nevada, Las Vegas	Las Vegas	unlv.edu	M				B	B	

Degree Programs (Con't)

School	City	Web Address	Architecture	Architecture History	Historic Preservation	Industrial Design	Interior Design	Landscape Architecture	Planning
NEW JERSEY									
Kean University	Union	kean.edu					B		
New Jersey Institute of Technology	Newark	njit.edu	B M						
Princeton University	Princeton	princeton.edu	M						
Rutgers, The State University of New Jersey	New Brunswick	rutgers.edu		M				B	M
NEW MEXICO									
University of New Mexico	Albuquerque	unm.edu	M	M					M
NEW YORK									
Buffalo State	Buffalo	buffalostate. edu				B			
City College of the City University of New York	New York	ccny.cuny.edu	B					B	
Columbia University	New York	columbia.edu	M	M	M				M
Cooper Union	New York	cooper.edu	B						
Cornell University	Ithaca	cornell.edu	B	M	M		B	B M	M
Fashion Inst. of Tech. State Univ. of New York	New York	Fitnyc.suny. edu					B		
Hunter College, City University of New York	New York	hunter.cuny. edu							M
New York Inst. of Tech. - Old Westbury	Old Westbury	nyit.edu	B?				B		
New York School of Interior Design	New York	nysid.edu					B		
New York University	New York	nyu.edu		M					M
Parsons School of Design	New York	parsons.edu	M			B *			
Pratt Institute	Brooklyn	pratt.edu	B			B M *	B		M
Rensselaer Polytechnic Institute	Troy	rpi.edu	B M						
Rochester Institute of Technology	Rochester	rit.edu				B M *	B		
School of Visual Arts	New York	schoolof visualarts.edu			B				

Degree Programs (Con't)

School	City	Web Address	Architecture	Architecture History	Historic Preservation	Industrial Design	Interior Design	Landscape Architecture	Planning
State University of New York at Binghamton	Binghamton	binghamton.edu		M					
State University of New York at Buffalo	Buffalo	buffalo.edu	M						M^I
State University of New York at Syracuse	Syracuse	esf.edu						B M	
Suffolk County Community College	Riverhead	sunysuffolk.edu					A		
Syracuse University	Syracuse	syr.edu	B M	M		B M *	B		
University at Albany, Suny	Albany	albany.edu							B M
Villa Maria College of Buffalo	Buffalo	villa.edu					A		
NORTH CAROLINA									
East Carolina University	Greenville	ecu.edu					B		
Meredith College	Raleigh	meredith.edu					B		
North Carolina A & T State University	Greensboro	ncat.edu					B	B	
North Carolina State University	Raleigh	ncsu.edu	B M			B M		B M	
University of North Carolina at Chapel Hill	Chapel Hill	unc.edu							M
University of North Carolina at Charlotte	Charlotte	uncc.edu	B M^2						
University of North Carolina at Greensboro	Greensboro	uncg.edu					B		
Western Carolina University	Cullowhee	wcu.edu					B		
NORTH DAKOTA									
North Dakota State University	Fargo	ndsu.nodak.edu	B				B	B	
OHIO									
Belmont Technical College	St. Clairsville	belmont.cc.oh.us			A				
Cleveland Institute of Art	Cleveland	cia.edu				B *			
Cleveland State University	Cleveland	csuohio.edu							M
Columbus College of Art & Design	Columbus	ccad.edu				B *	B		

Degree Programs (Con't)

School	City	Web Address	Architecture	Architecture History	Historic Preservation	Industrial Design	Interior Design	Landscape Architecture	Planning
Kent State University	Kent	kent.edu	B				B		
Miami University	Oxford	Muohio.edu	M						
Ohio State University	Columbus	ohio-state.edu	M	M		B M *	B	B M	M
Ohio University	Athens	ohiou.edu					B		
University of Akron	Akron	uakron.edu					B		
University of Cincinnati	Cincinnati	uc.edu	B			B M *	B		B M
OKLAHOMA									
Oklahoma State University	Stillwater	okstate.edu	B				B	B	
University of Oklahoma	Norman	ou.edu	B M				B	M	M
OREGON									
Portland State University	Portland	pdx.edu							M
University of Oregon	Eugene	Uoregon.edu	B M	M	M		B M	B	M
PENNSYLVANIA									
Bucks County Community College	Newtown	bucks.edu			C				
Carnegie Mellon University	Pittsburgh	cmu.edu	B			B M *			
Drexel University	Philadelphia	drexel.edu	B				B		
La Roche College	Pittsburgh	laroche.edu					B		
Moore College of Art and Design	Philadelphia	moore.edu					B		
Pennsylvania State University	State College	psu.edu	B	M				B	
Philadelphia University	Philadelphia	philau.edu	B			B	B		
Temple University	Philadelphia	temple.edu	B					B	
University of Pennsylvania	Philadelphia	upenn.edu	M	M	M			M	M

Degree Programs (Con't)

School	City	Web Address	Architecture	Architecture History	Historic Preservation	Industrial Design	Interior Design	Landscape Architecture	Planning
University of Pittsburgh	Pittsburgh	pitt.edu		M					
University of the Arts	Philadelphia	uarts.edu				B M *			
RHODE ISLAND									
Brown University	Providence	brown.edu		M					
Rhode Island School of Design	Providence	risd.edu	B M			B M *		B M	
Roger Williams University	Bristol	rwu.edu	B M^2		B				
University of Rhode Island	Kingston	uri.edu						B	M
SOUTH CAROLINA									
Clemson University	Clemson	Clemson.edu	M					B	M
College of Charleston	Charleston	cofc.edu			B				
Winthrop University	Rock Hill	winthrop.edu					B		
TENNESSEE									
Middle Tennessee State University	Murfreesboro	mtsu.edu				M	B		
O'More College of Design	Franklin	omorecollege.edu					B		
University of Memphis	Memphis	memphis.edu							M
University of Tennessee, Knoxville	Knoxville	utk.edu	B M				B		M
Watkins College of Art & Design	Nashville	watkins.edu					A		
TEXAS									
El Centro College	Dallas	ecc.dcccd.edu					C		
Houston Comm. College System/Central College	Houston	hccs.cc.tx.us/					A		
Prairie View A&M University	Prairie View	pvamu.edu	B						
Rice University	Houston	rice.edu	B M						
Southwest Texas State University	San Marcos	swt.edu					B		

Degree Programs (Con't)

School	City	Web Address	Architecture	Architecture History	Historic Preservation	Industrial Design	Interior Design	Landscape Architecture	Planning
Stephen F. Austin State University	Nacogdoches	sfasu.edu					B		
Texas A&M University	College Station	tamu.edu	M					B M	M
Texas Christian University	Fort Worth	tcu.edu					B		
Texas Tech University	Lubbock	ttu.edu	B M				B	B	
University of Houston	Houston	uh.edu	B M						
University of North Texas	Denton	unt.edu					B		
University of Texas at Arlington	Arlington	uta.edu	M				B	M	M
University of Texas at Austin	Austin	utexas.edu	B M	M	C M		B		M
University of Texas at San Antonio	San Antonio	utsa.edu	M^2				B		
UTAH									
ITT Technical Institute	Murray	itt-tech.edu				B			
University of Utah	Salt Lake City	utah.edu	M		M				
Utah State University	Logan	usu.edu					B	B M	
VERMONT									
Norwich University	Northfield	norwich.edu	B M						
University of Vermont	Burlington	uvm.edu			M				
VIRGINIA									
Hampton University	Hampton	hamptonu.edu	B						
James Madison University	Harrisonburg	jmu.edu					B		
Marymount University	Arlington	marymount.edu					B		
Mary Washington College	Fredericksburg	mwc.edu			B				
University of Virginia	Charlottesville	virginia.edu	M	M				M	B M
Virginia Commonwealth University	Richmond	vcu.edu		M			B		M

Degree Programs (Con't)

School	City	Web Address	Architecture	Architecture History	Historic Preservation	Industrial Design	Interior Design	Landscape Architecture	Planning
Virginia Polytechnic Inst. and State University	Blacksburg	vt.edu	B M			B M	B	B M	M
WASHINGTON									
Eastern Washington University	Spokane	ewu.edu							B M
Washington State University	Pullman	wsu.edu	B				B	B	
Western Washington University	Bellingham	wwu.edu				B			
University of Washington	Seattle	washington.edu	M	M		B M		B M	M
WEST VIRGINIA									
West Virginia University	Morgantown	wvu.edu					B	B	
WISCONSIN									
Milwaukee Institute of Art & Design	Milwaukee	miad.edu				B *			
Mount Mary College	Milwaukee	mtmary.edu					B		
University of Wisconsin, Madison	Madison	wisc.edu		M			B	B	M
University of Wisconsin, Milwaukee	Milwaukee	uwm.edu	M						M
University of Wisconsin, Stevens Point	Stevens Point	uwsp.edu					B		
University of Wisconsin, Stout	Menomonie	uwstout.edu				B *	B		

1 This program is currently in probationary status with the Planning Accreditation Board (PAB).
2 This program is currently in candidate status for National Architectural Accreditation Board (NAAB) accreditation.
* This Program is accredited by the National Association of Schools of Art & Design.

Source: Foundation for Interior Design Education Research (FIDER),Industrial Designers Society of America (IDSA), Landscape Architectural Accreditation Board (LAAB), National Architectural Accrediting Board (NAAB), National Council for Preservation Education (NCPE), Planning Accreditation Board (PAB), Society of Architectural Historians (SAH)

Doctorate Programs in Architecture and Design

The following schools offer Doctorate and Ph.D. degrees in architecture and design. Detailed information about entrance requirements and the programs' field of study is available from the individual schools.

ARCHITECTURE

Arizona State University (Tempe)
Carnegie Mellon University (Pittsburgh, PA)
Columbia University (New York, NY)
Georgia Institute of Technology (Atlanta)
Harvard University (Cambridge, MA)
Illinois Institute of Technology (Chicago)
Massachusetts Institute of Technology (Cambridge)
Princeton University (Princeton, NJ)
Rice University (Houston, TX)
Texas A&M University (College Station)
Texas Tech University (Lubbock)
University of California, Berkeley
University of California, Los Angeles
University of Colorado (Denver)
University of Florida (Gainesville)
University of Hawaii (Honolulu)
University of Michigan (Ann Arbor)
University of Nebraska-Lincoln
University of Pennsylvania (Philadelphia)
University of Texas at Austin
University of Wisconsin, Milwaukee
Virginia Polytechnic Institute (Blacksburg)

ARCHITECTURAL HISTORY

The Society of Architectural Historians' web site, www.sah.org, in addition to the individual schools, offers detailed information about each program, including their areas of focus, faculty data, and statistics.

Brown University (Providence, RI)
City University of New York (New York)
Columbia University (New York, NY)
Cornell University (Ithaca, NY)
Florida State University (Tallahassee)
George Washington University (Washington, DC)
Georgia Institute of Technology (Atlanta)
Harvard University (Cambridge, MA)

Massachusetts Institute of Technology (Cambridge)
New York University (New York)
Northwestern University (Evanston, IL)
Ohio State University (Columbus)
Pennsylvania State University (State College)
Princeton University (Princeton, NJ)
Rutgers University (New Brunswick, NJ)
Stanford University (Stanford, CA)
State University of New York at Binghamton
University of California at Berkeley
University of California at Los Angeles
University of California at Santa Barbara
University of Chicago (IL)
University of Delaware (Newark)
University of Colorado at Denver
University of Illinois at Chicago
University of Illinois at Urbana-Champaign
University of Iowa (Iowa City)
University of Louisville (KY)
University of Maryland (College Park)
University of Missouri-Columbia
University of New Mexico (Albuquerque)
University of Oregon (Eugene)
University of Pennsylvania (Philadelphia)
University of Pittsburgh (PA)
University of Texas at Austin
University of Virginia (Charlottesville)
University of Washington (Seattle)
University of Wisconsin-Madison
Virginia Commonwealth University (Richmond)
Yale University (New Haven, CT)

HISTORIC PRESERVATION

Cornell University (Ithaca, NY)
University of Texas at Austin

INDUSTRIAL DESIGN

Carnegie Mellon University (Pittsburgh, PA)

Doctorate Programs in Architecture and Design (Con't)

INTERIOR DESIGN
Arizona State University (Tempe)
Bard Graduate Center for Studies in the
    Decorative Arts, Design and Culture (New
    York, NY)
Michigan State University (East Lansing)
Oregon State University (Eugene)
Texas Tech University (Lubbock)
Virginia Polytechnic Institute and State
    University (Blacksburg)
University of Minnesota (St. Paul/Minneapolis)
University of Missouri-Columbia

LANDSCAPE ARCHITECTURE
*In addition to landscape architecture, other schools
offer related Ph.D. degrees that may be of interest with
such titles as environmental design and land use planning.*

Harvard University (Cambridge, MA)
University of Illinois at Urbana-Champaign
University of Michigan (Ann Arbor)

PLANNING
Arizona State University (Tempe)
Cleveland State University (OH)
Columbia University (New York, NY)
Cornell University (Ithaca, NY)
Florida State University (Tallahassee)
Georgia Institute of Technology (Atlanta)
Harvard University (Cambridge, MA)
Massachusetts Institute of Technology
    (Cambridge)
Ohio State University (Columbus)
Portland State University (OR)
Princeton University (Princeton, NJ)
Rutgers, The State University of New Jersey
    (New Brunswick)
Texas A&M University (College Station)
University of Akron (OH)
University of California, Berkeley
University of California, Irvine
University of California, Los Angeles
University of Colorado (Boulder)
University of Illinois at Chicago
University of Illinois at Urbana-Champaign

University of Massachusetts (Amherst)
University of Michigan (Ann Arbor)
University of New Orleans (LA)
University of North Carolina at Chapel Hill
University of Pennsylvania (Philadelphia)
University of Southern California (Los Angeles)
University of Texas at Austin
University of Washington (Seattle)
University of Wisconsin-Madison
Virginia Polytechnic Institute and State
    University (Blacksburg)
Washington State University (Pullman)

*Source: Association of Collegiate Schools of Architecture (ACSA);
Society of Architectural Historians (SAH); National Council for
Preservation Education (NCPE); Industrial Designers Society of
America (IDSA); Interior Design Educators Council (IDEC);
Association of Collegiate Schools of Planning (ACSP); American Society
of Landscape Architects (ASLA)*

Educational Resources

In addition to the individuals schools, the following organizations can provide information about design education.

ARCHITECTURE

Association of Collegiate Schools of
Architecture (ACSA)
1735 New York Avenue, NW
Washington, DC 20006
Tel: (202) 785-2324
Fax: (202) 628-0448
Internet: www.acsa-arch.org

National Architectural Accrediting
Board (NAAB)
1735 New York Avenue, NW
Washington, DC 20006
Telephone: (202) 783-2007
Fax: (202) 783-2822
Internet: www.naab.org

ARCHITECTURE HISTORY

Society of Architectural Historians (SAH)
1365 North Astor Street
Chicago, Illinois 60610
Telephone: (312) 573-1365
Fax: (312) 573-1141
Internet: www.sah.org

HISTORIC PRESERVATION

National Council for Preservation
Education (NCPE)
Internet: www.uvm.edu/histpres/ncpe/

INDUSTRIAL DESIGN

Industrial Designers Society of America (IDSA)
1142 Walker Road
Great Falls, VA 22066
Telephone: 703-759-0100
Fax: (703) 759-7679
Internet: www.idsa.org

INTERIOR DESIGN

Foundation for Interior Design Education
Research (FIDER)
146 Monroe Center NW, Suite 1318
Grand Rapids, MI 49503-2822
Telephone: (616) 458-0400
Fax: (616) 458-0460
Internet: www.fider.org

Interior Design Educators Council (IDEC)
9202 North Meridian Street, Ste. 200
Indianapolis, IN 46260-1810
Telephone: (317) 816-6261
Fax: (317) 571-5603
Internet: www.idec.org

LANDSCAPE ARCHITECTURE

Council of Educators in Landscape
Architecture (CELA)
Internet: www.ssc.msu.edu/~la/cela/

Landscape Architectural Accreditation
Board (LAAB)
Internet: www.asla.org/nonmembers/
accredited_programs.cfm

PLANNING

Association of Collegiate Schools of
Planning (ACSP)
Internet: www.uwm.edu/Org/acsp/

Planning Accreditation Board (PAB)
Internet: http://showcase.netins.net/web/
pab_fi66/

Henry Adams Medal

Each year The American Institute of Architects and The American Architectural Foundation award an engraved medal and certificate of merit to the top-ranking graduating student from each architecture program accredited by the National Architectural Accrediting Board (NAAB). A certificate of merit is also awarded to the second-ranking graduating student. The recipients are chosen by the architecture faculty at each school and are determined by the highest scholastic standings. Formerly called "The School Medal," the program began in 1914 and, to date, has honored approximately 8,800 students. The top-ranking student(s) is listed below first followed by the second-ranked student(s). In some cases, only the first-rank student was honored. Not all schools participate each year.

For more information about the Medal, contact the individual schools' architecture department or Mary Felber at The American Architectural Foundation at (202) 626-7511.

2001 Undergraduate Recipients:

Andrews University
Aaron Valentin
Rose Chow-Hibler

Arizona State University
Kristopher R. Stenger
Jeffrey T. Kershaw

Auburn University
Andrew S. Olds
Justin T. Donovan

Ball State University
Steven C. Zabel
Daniel S. Brueggert

Boston Architectural Center
Berton B. Bremer
James Daniel MacPhee
Carol J. Fisher

California Polytechnic State University, San Luis Obispo
John Hyunku Son
Jeffrey Kin Wai Hong

Carleton University
Kevin Stuart Thomas
Winga Lam

Carnegie Mellon University
Wai-Ki Tracy Yu
Sacha H. Leong

Catholic University of America
Ismini Naos
Angel Rama

City College of the City University of New York
Jonathan Cohen-Litant
Nnadozie Okeke

Clemson University
Anna Starr Kellett
Amy Palmer Clement
Shae Suzanne Hensley
Andrew Matthew Clark

Cooper Union
Anca Vasiliu
Hayley Eber

Henry Adams Medal (Con't)

Cornell University
Jason Frantzen
Brian Fanning

Drexel University
Kirsti M. Kuhns
David M. Ade
Edward S. Althouse Jr.

Drury University
Jody Corynne Boulware-Miller
Gregory Joseph Hoffman

Ecole D'Architecture De L'Universite Laval
Cedeanne Simard
Hughes Desbiens

Florida A&M University
Michael Ruiz
Scott Gann

Florida Atlantic University
Juliette Schiff
Maureen Kussler

Georgia Institute of Technology
Justin Park
Richard Vanzeyl

Hampton University
Amanda L. Pillo
Janeen A. Harrell

Harvard University
Jonathan Ramsey
Tinchuck Agnes Ng

Howard University
Ahkilah Johnson
Victoria Taylor

Illinois Institute of Technology
Juliane Wolf
Timothy Jacobson

Iowa State University
Terrence J. Schroeder
Andrew J. Weyenberg

Kent State University
Jeremy Hall
Sean Burns

Louisiana State University
Lauren E. Broussard
Naim Jabbour

Louisiana Tech University
Mandi Renee Austin
Kristopher Paul Linzay
Jessica Ruth

Mississippi State University
Matt Sze Mun Lam
Carolyn L. Hudson

Montana State University
Douglas Minarik
Brian Ho

New Jersey Institute of Technology
Anna Maria Peterson
Donna M. Dempsey

New York Institute of Technology
Christopher Pelella
Zi Mai

Norwich University
Candace J. Pratt
James P. Weikert

Parsons School of Design/New School University
Francisco Simmons
Rise Endo

Pennsylvania State University
Andrew Lefkowitz
Carmen Gerdes

Henry Adams Medal (Con't)

Philadelphia University
Sara Harrison
Dave Myers

Polytechnic University of Puerto Rico
Jose Lorenzo-Torres

Prairie View A&M University
Roujanou Shojaardalan
Jeremy Curtis

Rensselaer Polytechnic Institute
Paul Joseph Lipchak
Daniel Jaconetti Jr.

Rhode Island School of Design
Dutch Osborne
Peter Lefkovits

Roger Williams University
Jennifer L. Roy
Robert Pavlik

Savannah College of Art and Design
Carolina Lloveras
Matthew Deierlein

Southern California Institute of Architecture
Sing-Sing Lee
Jeffrey Chan

Southern Polytechnic State University
Brandy M. Herlinger
Kevin L. Byrd

Syracuse University
John W. Erskine
Creighton H. Willis

Temple University
Artiss L. Powell III
Tiffany C. Strother

Texas Tech University
Stuart Ray Brummett
Taylor Brian Callaway

Tulane University
Guru Dev Kaur Khalsa
Christian Glauser Benz

University of Arizona
Thomas Robert Reiner
Allison Rachel Park

University of Arkansas
Todd Furgason
Marina Skiles
Marcy Conrad

University of British Columbia
Robert Harold Dare

University of Calgary
Shelley Joyce Nycz
Chad Allan Zyla

University of California at Berkeley
Ken Ishiguro
Alice Roche

University of California at Los Angeles
Kevin Gotsch
Susan Wong

University of Colorado at Denver/Boulder
Erik Alan Sommerfeld
Jeffrey Neil Montague

University of Detroit Mercy
Nicholas D. Juhasz
Adrianna M. Melchior

University of Florida
Carolee Eyles
Rhoda Kennedy

University of Hawaii at Manoa
Neal Kido
Bonnie Choy

Henry Adams Medal (Con't)

University of Illinois at Chicago
Thomas Kennedy Daky
Jeffrey L. Morgan

University of Illinois at Urbana-Champaign
Tristen Marie Zednik
Alyssa M. Fee

University of Kansas
Andrew J. Gilles
Ricardo Muniz Moreira

University of Kentucky
Thomas V. Fulda
Rebecca A. Sayles

University of Louisiana at Lafayette
Aaron Hinkston
Corey Callegan

University of Miami
Georgy John
Maria del Pilar Ruiz-Fernandez

University of Montreal
Marco Carlone
Philippe St. Germain

University of New Mexico
Douglas Patterson
Luciana Lins de Mello

University of North Carolina at Charlotte
Todd A. Meckley
Sara K. Melanson

University of South Florida
Peeti Sastrawaha

University of Tennessee, Knoxville
Ashley Elizabeth Beals
Kirsten Michelle Heilig

University of Texas at Austin
Ezra Ingvald Wheeler
William Lawrence Hodge
Gerald Lawrence Colombo

University of Toronto
Stephen Thomas Bauer
Kirsten Larissa Adam

University of Waterloo
Omer Arbel
Tho Quan Ha

University of Wisconsin-Milwaukee
Martin Lechner
Samuel Edwards

Virginia Polytechnic Institute and State University
Kristin Carole Adsit
Lam H. Vuong

Washington State University
Robert Aaron Smith
Junkun Shi

Yale University
Mathew M. Combrink
Adam Joseph Ruedig

2001 Graduate Recipients:
Catholic University of America
Yari Robles (one and one-half year program)
Viet Tran (two year program)
Nina Cochran (three year program)
Todd E. Burns (one and one-half year program)
Ninh Nguyen (two year program)
Carol J. Smith (three year program)

Columbia University
Audra Tuskes
Allen Chan

Dalhousie University
Melanie Hayne
Cameron Gillies

Henry Adams Medal (Con't)

Florida A&M University
Dwayne Daniels
Patrick Vaughan

Illinois Institute of Technology
Yufang Zhou
James Edward Miller

Iowa State University
Tony J. Hogge
Sarah K. Mannes

McGill University
Lily Lau
Andre Kirchboff

Miami University
Mark H. Thurnauer
Vickie L. Anderson

Morgan State University
Daniel Simon
Anne Fullenkamp

New Jersey Institute of Technology
Kevin M. Edwards
Amy Patel

Ohio State University
Ping Cai
Bharat P. Baste

Princeton University
Monte Antrim
Janette Kim

Rensselaer Polytechnic Institute
Kevin Baker

Southern California Institute of Architecture
Britton Lee Hefner
Ho Yuen Grace Lau

Syracuse University
John J. Barbera
Nelson Carvalho

Texas A&M University
Thane M. Eddington
Troy A. Frazee

Tulane University
Ian Alexander Dreyer
Tamara Dawn Say

University at Buffalo
Carrie Lynn Galuski
Korydon Howard Smith

University of Hawaii at Manoa
Domingo Fornoles
Yung-Ning Yen

University of Kansas
Brenda LeAnne Brosa
Michael A. Miller

University of Manitoba
Brian Paul Gasmena
Michael Thomas Farion

University of Maryland
Robert Coles McClennan
Scot Alan Welch

University of Miami
Daniel Sloan
Ana Paola Sacasa

University of Michigan
David Christopher Sass
Judy B. Myers

University of Minnesota
Sarah Birtles
Michael Kumpula

University of Pennsylvania
Rashida Z. Ng
Maria-Paz Gutierrez

Henry Adams Medal (Con't)

University of Tennessee, Knoxville
Sumaya El-Attar
John Blythe Bailey

University of Utah
Aaron Lynn Arbuckle
Robert Beishline

University of Virginia
Derek Todd West
Sutana Mokkhavesa

University of Washington
Brendan Connolly
Matthew Somerton

Virginia Polytechnic Institute and State University
Andrew Queen
Carlton Bolton; Timothy Hart

Source: The American Architectural Foundation

What is architecture anyway? Is it the vast collection of the various buildings which have been built to please the varying taste of the various lords of mankind? I think not. No, I know that architecture is life; or at least it is life itself taking form and therefore it is the truest record of life as it was lived in the world yesterday, as it is lived today or ever will be lived. So architecture I know to be a Great Spirit...Architecture is that great living creative spirit which from generation to generation, from age to age, proceeds, persists, creates, according to the nature of man, and his circumstances as they change. That is really architecture.

Frank Lloyd Wright

IDSA Education Award

The Industrial Designers Society of America (IDSA) grants the Education Award to recognize excellence in industrial design education. Educators are presented this award in honor of their significant and distinguished contributions.

For additional information, visit IDSA on the Internet at *www.idsa.org*.

1988   Arthur J. Pulos
Syracuse University

1989   Robert Lepper
Carnegie Mellon University

1990   Edward Zagorski
University of Illinois, Champaign-Urbana

1991   James Alexander
Art Center College of Design

1992   Strother MacMinn
Art Center College of Design

Robert Redmann
University of Bridgeport

1993   Vincent Foote
North Carolina State University

Herbert Tyrnauer
California State University at Long Beach

1994   Hin Bredendieck
Georgia Institute of Technology

Joseph Koncelik
Ohio State University

1996   Toby Thompson
Rochester Institute of Technology

1997   Marc Harrison
Rhode Island School of Design

1998   Bruce Hannah
Pratt Institute

1999   Michael Nielsen
Arizona State University

2000   Katherine McCoy
Illinois Institute of Technology

Michael McCoy
Illinois Institute of Technology

2001   Jim Pirkl
Syracuse University

Source: Industrial Designers Society of America

Michael Tatum Excellence in Education Award

The Michael Tatum Excellence in Education Award was created by the International Interior Design Association (IIDA) and sponsored by Tecknion to honor outstanding interior design educators. The Award also celebrates the life and career of Michael Tatum, an outstanding educator and IIDA member who passed away in 1998. When reviewing the nominations, the awards committee considers excellence in teaching, innovative teaching techniques, student mentoring, contributions to the profession, creative scholarship, including the publication of scholarly research, and leadership in interior design education within the community. Nominees must be full-time faculty at FIDER-accredited schools. Recipients are awarded a $5,500 cash prize and are invited to present a scholarly paper to the IIDA membership.

For more information about the Tatum Award, contact IIDA at (312) 467-1950 or visit them on the Internet at *www.iida.org*.

1999   Joy Dohr
       University of Wisconsin at Madison

2000   Henry P. Hildebrandt
       University of Cincinnati

2001   Stephen Marc Klein
       Pratt Institute

Source: International Interior Design Association

Polsky Academic Achievement Award

In order to recognize outstanding design research or a thesis project by an undergraduate or graduate student, the American Society of Interior Designers (ASID) presents the ASID Educational Foundation/Joel Polsky Academic Achievement Award. The winner receives a $1,000 prize. Winning entries should address the needs of the public, designers and students on topics related to design business, education, process, research, behavioral science, theory or other technical subjects.

More information is available on ASID's Web site, *www.asid.org*, or by calling the ASID Educational Foundation at (202) 546-3480.

1988   *Open Office Programming: Assessment of the Workstation Game*, Nancy C. Canestaro, Ph.D.

1989   *Restroom Usage in Selected Public Buildings and Facilities: A Comparison of Males and Females*, Sandra K. Rawls, Ph.D.

1990   *Preference, Mystery and Visual Attributes of Interiors: A Study of Relationships*, Suzanne Benedict Scott, Ph.D.

1991   *The History of the Railroad of New Jersey Maritime Terminal in Jersey City, New Jersey, Commemorating its Centennial 1889-1989*, Sharon K. Sommerlad Keenan

1992   *Design for a Residential Facility for the Elderly in Combination with a Child Care Facility*, Marida A. Stearns

1993   *View to Nature: Effects on Attentional Capacity*, Carolyn Marie Gilker

1994   *WAYFINDING - You are Here/You are There*, Jacqueline Gommel

1995   *Home Builders' and Remodelers' Role in the Adoption and Diffusion of Universally Designed Housing*, Beatriz E. Blanco

   Honorable Mention: Impact on the Campus Physical Environment on Older Adult Learners, Maurine Moore

1996   *Impact of Interior Design on the Dining Disabilities of the Elderly Residents in Assisted Living and Nursing Homes*, Elizabeth Rylan

   Honorable Mention: Computers in the Design Process: Comparing Creativity Ratings of Interior Design Solutions Using Pencil Based Design Methods in Schematic Development, Lynn Brandon

1997   *A Comparison of Spatial Interpretations of NASA's Payload Operations Control Center, Marshall Space Flight Center, Using Real World and Virtual Reality Observations*, Patricia F. Lindsey

   La Bottega D'Artigianato Regionale in the Palazzo Massimo alle Colonne, Rome, Italy: A Story of Adaptive Reuse, Cigdem T. Bulut

1998   *Residential Interior Environments of Retired Government Employees in Thailand*, Benjamas Kutintara

   Physical and Social Attributes Influencing Mobile Workers' Sense of Place, Jacquelyn Purintan

1999   *Interior Design for Alzheimer Care Facilities: Investigating Established Design Recommendations*, Kathleen L. Cackowski

Polsky Academic Achievement Award (Con't)

Graduate Education Research and the Interior Design Profession, Patti Lawlor

2000 *A Comparison of Career Preparation and Development Between Two-year and Four-Year Interior Design Graduates*, Barbara Marini

2001 *Universal Design Standards for Single-Family Housing*, Nancy L. Wolford

Source: American Society of Interior Designers

Design is one of the most typical art forms of our time (as well as fashion, photography, music, cinema). The Italian philosopher Gianni Vattimo has called them "commercial arts," meaning that, opposite from the classic arts, they need the consent of the public.

Alberto Alessi

Presidents of the American Institute of Architecture Students

1956-57	James R. Barry, Rice Univ.		1977-78	Charles Guerin, Univ. of Houston
1957-58	Robert Harris, Princeton Univ.		1978-79	John Maudlin-Jeronimo, Univ. of Miami
1958-59	Paul Ricciutti, Case Western Reserve Univ.		1979-80	Richard Martini, Boston Architectural Center
1959-60	Charles Jones, Univ. of Arizona		1980-81	Alejandro Barbarena, Univ. of Houston
1960-61	Ray Gaio, Univ. of Notre Dame		1981-82	Bill Plimpton, Univ. of California at Berkeley
1961-62	Donald Williams, Univ. of Illinois at Urbana-Champaign		1982-83	Robert Klancher, Univ. of Cincinnati
1962-63	Carl Schubert, California State Polytechnic Univ.		1983-84	Robert Fox, Temple Univ.
1964-65	Joseph Morse, Howard Univ.		1984-85	Thomas Fowler IV, NYIT–Old Westbury
1965-66	Kenneth Alexander, Pratt Institute		1985-86	Scott Norberg, Univ. of Nebraska
1966-67	Jack Worth III, Georgia Institute of Technology		1986-87	Scott Norberg, Univ. of Nebraska
1967-68	Morten Awes, Univ. of Idaho		1987-88	Kent Davidson, Univ. of Nebraska
1968-69	Edward Mathes, Univ. of Southwestern Louisiana		1988-89	Matthew W. Gilbertson, Univ. of Minnesota
1969-70	Taylor Culver, Howard Univ.		1989-90	Douglas A. Bailey, Montana State Univ.
1970-71	Michael Interbartolo, Boston Architectural Center		1990-91	Alan D.S. Paradis, Roger Williams College
1971-72	Joseph Siff, Rice Univ.		1991-92	Lynn N. Simon, Univ. of Washington
1972-73	Fay D'Avignon, Boston Architectural Center		1992-93	Courtney E. Miller, Univ. of Maryland
1973-74	Fay D'Avignon, Boston Architectural Center		1993-94	Garen D. Miller, Drury College
1974-75	Patric Davis, Boston Architectural Center		1994-95	Dee Christy Briggs, City College of New York
1975-76	Ella Hall, North Carolina State Univ.		1995-96	Robert J. Rowan, Washington State Univ.
1976-77	Jerry Compton, Southern California Inst. of Arch.		1996-97	Raymond H. Dehn, Univ. of Minnesota

Presidents of the American Institute of Architecture Students (Con't)

1997-98 Robert L. Morgan,
         Clemson Univ.
1998-99 Jay M. Palu,
         Univ. of Nebraska
1999-00 Melissa Mileff,
         Univ. of Oklahoma
2000-01 Scott Baldermann,
         Univ. of Nebraska
2001-02 Matt Herb,
         University of Maryland

Source: American Institute of Architects Students

In fact all art loving people love nature first then the rest must follow.

Charles Sumner Greene

Salary and Recruiting Guide for Architecture and Design Students

As part of this year's Top Interior Design and Architecture Schools survey (pages 558 and 559), firms were polled about their recruiting activity, salary practices and the preparedness of graduates for professional practice. Principals, design directors, and human resource directors in over 800 architecture firms and 150 interior design firms were contacted about their experience with recent graduates. For landscape architecture, salary and benefit information from the American Society of Landscape Architects was used.

ARCHITECTURE

Recruiting Activity

76% of responding firms reported that they actively recruit on school campuses

Single most successful recruiting activity for young architects utilized within the past two years:

- 34% On-campus recruiting
- 14% Relationships with college departments
- 13% Internships, co-ops
- 13% Newspaper & internet advertisement, including company Web site
- 11% Employee referrals
- 6% Firm open house
- 5% Staff teaching at universities
- 2% Salary and benefits
- 2% Outside recruiter/headhunter
- 2% Published work

2001 Salary Information

Average starting salary for 2001 graduate hires:

- 16% $25-29,999
- 49% $30-34,999
- 27% $35-39,999
- 8% $40-44,999

Skills Assessment

Within the past three years, firms have noted a number of skill deficiencies in their new graduate hires (respondents were asked to name up to three):

- 90% Building/structural knowledge
- 78% Oral and written communication skills
- 28% Practical business and practice knowledge
- 19% Work ethic, self motivation
- 16% Computer skills, including CAD
- 14% Sketching skills
- 7% Detailing knowledge
- 6% Design theory, knowledge and history
- 5% Teamwork skills & discipline
- 5% Analytical thinking/problem solving
- 3% Project management
- 2% Knowledge of interiors
- 2% Research skills
- 2% Design skills
- 2% Relationship between design & technology

Salary and Recruiting Guide for Recent Graduates (Con't)

INTERIOR DESIGN

Recruiting Activity

57% of responding firms reported that they actively recruit on school campuses

Single most successful recruiting activity for young architects utilized within the past two years:
- 28% Internet job postings, including firm Web site
- 25% Hiring interns
- 15% Active participation in university programs
- 14% Campus job fairs
- 6% Employee referrals
- 3% Head hunters/recruiting agencies
- 3% Networking with fellow design firms
- 3% Networking with representatives of manufacturers
- 3% Mission/culture statement
- 3% ASID Conference

2001 Salary Information

Average starting salary for 2001 graduate hires:
- 8% $20-24,999
- 32% $25-29,999
- 44% $30-34,999
- 16% $35-39,999

Skills Assessment

Within the past three years, firms have noted a number of skill deficiencies in their new graduate hires (respondents were asked to name up to three):
- 51% Technical knowledge
- 32% Oral and written communication skills
- 24% Conceptual design philosophy and theory
- 22% Computer skills, including CAD
- 16% Practical business and practice knowledge
- 16% Sketching skills, illustration techniques
- 14% Understanding the design process
- 5% Real world project application skills, practical experience

- 3% Holistic design
- 3% Lighting design
- 3% Product knowledge
- 3% Knowledge of commercial design
- 3% Time management
- 3% Level of taste
- 3% Professional expectations

LANDSCAPE ARCHITECTURE

The following information was complied by the American Society of Landscape Architects from a survey of the 2001 landscape architecture graduates.

Average Starting Salary for 2001 Undergraduate Hires:
- 77% $21 - 25,000
- 15% $26 - 30,000
- 8% $31 - 40,000
- 2% $41 - 50,000
- 1% $51 - 64,000

Average Starting Salary for 2001 Graduate Hires:
- 15% $21 - 25,000
- 46% $26 - 30,000
- 27% $31 - 40,000
- 10% $41 - 50,000
- 2% $51 - 64,000

Source: Counsel House Research

Tau Sigma Delta

Formed in 1913 at the University of Michigan, Tau Sigma Delta is an honor society for Architecture and the Allied Arts. University juniors and seniors who are majoring in architecture, architectural engineering, architectural design, landscape architecture, painting, sculpting, planning, decorative design, interior design and all allied arts are eligible for membership. To date, over 65 chapters have been organized at schools across the U.S., each administered by the universities' Schools of Architecture. The honor society presents both a Gold Medal to honor a professional and a Bronze medal to honor an outstanding student, each year.

Additional information about Tau Sigma Delta, including a list of chapters and their contacts, can be found online at *www.ttu.edu/~tsd/*.

Did you know...

The Grand Hyatt Shanghai, located in the Jin Mao Tower (Skidmore, Owings & Merrill, 1999), holds many records: the highest hotel in the world, the tallest atrium and the longest laundry chute ever built.

Top 15 Colleges and Universities of Interior Design

Each year *DesignIntelligence* and the Design Futures Council conducts a study in conjunction with the *Almanac of Architecture & Design* to determine the best colleges and universities for interior design in the United States. Principals of over 300 leading U.S. interior design and A/ID firms were asked the question "From which schools have you had the best experience hiring employees?" – relative to their experience during the past ten years. Respondents chose from FIDER (Foundation for Interior Design Education Research) accredited programs.

This research is the only 'customer-satisfaction' -oriented study of leading firms, including industry giants, top sector leaders, and award winning firms. Firms in each market sector and throughout all regions of the country were contacted. The results of the third annual study are presented below, with the schools ranked in the order of the most highly acclaimed (with last year's ranking given in parenthesis). Firms were also asked to comment on their recruiting practices and compensation of recent graduates, the results of which can be found on page 555.

1. University of Cincinnati (1)
2. Kansas State University* (3)
3. Pratt Institute (2)
4. Cornell University (4)
5. Auburn University (6)
6. Syracuse University* (5)
7. Arizona State University (6)
8. Rhode Island School of Design
9. University of Oregon (9)
10. Iowa State University
11. Virginia Polytechnic Institute and State University (13)
12. Drexel University (9)
13. University of Florida (11)
14. Harrington Institute of Design
    University of Nebraska
    University of Wisconsin-Madison

* This survey combined Kansas State University's Interior Architecture and Interior Design programs and Syracuse University's Environmental Design/Interior and Interior Design programs.

Source: DesignIntelligence and Counsel House Research

Top 15 Schools and Colleges of Architecture

Each year *DesignIntelligence* and the Design Futures Council conducts a study in conjunction with the *Almanac of Architecture & Design* to determine the best schools and colleges for architecture in the United States. Principals of over 800 leading U.S. architecture firms were asked the question "From which schools have you had the best experience hiring employees?" – relative to their experience during the past ten years. Respondents chose from NAAB (National Architectural Accrediting Board) accredited programs.

This research is the only 'customer-satisfaction' -oriented study of leading firms, including industry giants, top sector leaders, and award winning firms. Firms in each market sector – including commercial, health care, education, hospitality, residential, institutional, laboratory, sports facilities, and office buildings – and throughout all regions of the country were contacted. The results of the third annual study are presented below, with the schools ranked in the order of the most highly acclaimed (with last year's ranking given in parenthesis). Firms were also asked to comment on their recruiting practices and compensation of recent graduates, the results of which can be found on page 555.

1. Cornell University (1)
2. Harvard University (2)
3. University of Cincinnati (6)
4. Syracuse University
5. Georgia Institute of Technology
    University of Michigan (5)
7. Iowa State University
8. University of Illinois at Urbana-Champaign
    University of Virginia (14)
10. Texas A&M University (15)
    Yale University (3)
12. Massachusetts Institute of Technology (8)
13. Columbia University (7)
14. University of Notre Dame
15. University of Pennsylvania (11)

Source: DesignIntelligence and Counsel House Research

TOPAZ Medallion

The TOPAZ Medallion is jointly awarded by The American Institute of Architects (AIA) and the American Collegiate Schools of Architecture (ACSA) to honor individuals who have made an outstanding contribution to the field of architectural education. Candidates are nominated by colleagues, students and former students. Recipients have made a significant impact on the field of architecture, expanded into fields beyond their specialty, and affected a lasting impact on their students.

For additional information about this award program, visit the AIA's Web site at *www.aia.org.*

1976	Jean Labatut Princeton University	1990	Raymond L. Kappe Southern California Institute of Architecture
1977	Henry Kamphoefner North Carolina State University	1991	Kenneth B. Frampton Columbia University
1978	Lawrence Anderson Massachusetts Inst. of Technology	1992	Spiro Kostof University of California, Berkeley*
1979	G. Holmes Perkins University of Pennsylvania	1993	Mario Salvadori Columbia University
1980	Serge Chermayeff Yale University	1994	Harlan E. McClure Clemson University
1981	Marcel Breuer Harvard University	1995	Henry N. Cobb Harvard University
1982	Joseph Esherick University of California, Berkeley	1996	Denise Scott Brown University of Pennsylvania
1983	Charles E. Burchard Virginia Polytechnic University	1997	Donlyn Lyndon University of California, Berkeley
1984	Robert Geddes Princeton University	1998	Werner Seligmann Syracuse University
1985	Colin Rowe Cornell University	1999	W. Cecil Steward University of Nebraska
1986	Vincent Scully Jr. Yale University	2000	Alan H. Balfour Rensselaer Polytechnic Institute
1987	Ralph Rapson University of Minnesota	2001	Lee G. Copeland Washington College and University of Pennsylvania
1988	John Hejduk Cooper Union		
1989	Charles Moore, University of California, Berkeley		

* honored posthumously

Source: The American Institute of Architects

Design Econometrics

Construction and design-related statistics are available in this chapter. Firm-specific statistics can be found in The Firms chapter beginning on page 475.

Average Number of Months From Start to Completion of New One-Family Houses

Year	United States	Region				Construction Purpose		
		Northeast	Midwest	South	West	Built for Sale	Contractor Built	Owner Built
1989	6.4	9.3	5.8	5.6	6.5	5.9	5.3	10.2
1990	6.4	9.3	5.6	5.7	6.9	5.9	5.3	10.3
1991	6.3	8.9	5.6	5.5	6.9	5.6	5.1	10.2
1992	5.8	7.6	5.6	5.1	6.1	5.0	5.0	9.5
1993	5.6	7.2	5.5	5.2	6.0	4.9	5.4	9.0
1994	5.6	7.1	5.7	5.3	5.6	4.9	5.3	9.1
1995	5.9	7.4	6.0	5.4	6.0	5.2	5.8	9.5
1996	6.0	8.2	6.1	5.6	5.6	5.2	5.8	9.9
1997	6.0	7.3	6.2	5.6	5.8	5.2	5.9	9.8
1998	6.0	7.1	6.2	5.5	6.1	5.4	6.0	9.5
1999	6.2	7.1	7.0	5.7	6.3	5.6	6.4	9.6
2000	6.3	7.6	6.5	5.9	6.1	5.6	6.6	9.9

Source: US Census Bureau

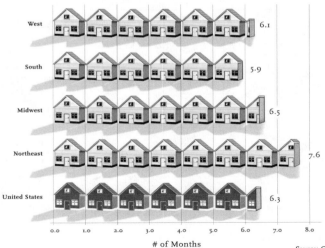

Average Time from Start to Completion of New Single-Family Houses

West 6.1
South 5.9
Midwest 6.5
Northeast 7.6
United States 6.3

# of Months

Source: Counsel House Research

Commercial Building Characteristics: 1995 (in thousands)

Building Characteristics	All Buildings	Buildings by Size			
		1,001 to 5,000 Square Feet	5,001 to 10,000 Square Feet	10,001 to 25,000 Square Feet	25,001 to 50,000 Square Feet
All Buildings	4,579	2,399	1,035	745	213
Principal Building Activity					
Education	309	100	60	62	49
Food Sales	137	108	Q	Q	Q
Food Service	285	210	52	Q	Q
Health Care	105	57	Q	16	5
Lodging	158	46	40	43	14
Mercantile and Service	1,289	736	295	195	33
Office	705	405	131	94	35
Public Assembly	326	128	110	64	13
Public Order and Safety	87	Q	Q	23	Q
Religious Worship	269	92	84	78	11
Warehouse and Storage	580	2B6	135	95	34
Other	67	Q	Q	Q	Q
Vacant	261	149	68	34	4
Year Constructed					
1919 or Before	353	175	92	65	11
1920 to 1945	562	309	145	70	17
1946 to 1959	867	461	222	123	34
1960 to 1969	718	343	159	135	45
1970 to 1979	813	428	174	137	38
1980 to 1989	846	422	151	186	46
1990 to 1992	218	132	50	16	11
1993 to 1995	202	129	43	13	9
Floors					
One	3,018	1,894	618	358	90
Two	1,002	378	283	236	62
Three	399	123	97	115	37
Four to Nine	148	Q	37	35	24
Ten or More	12	Q	Q	Q	Q

Buildings by Size				Building Characteristics
50,001 to 100,000 Square Feet	100,001 to 200,000 Square Feet	200,001 to 500,000 Square Feet	Over 500,000 Square Feet	
115	48	19	6	**All Buildings**
				Principal Building Activity
26	9	3	Q	Education
Q	Q	Q	Q	Food Sales
Q	Q	0	Q	Food Service
2	Q	2	1	Health Care
9	4	2	Q	Lodging
18	8	2	2	Mercantile and Service
22	10	5	1	Office
7	2	1	Q	Public Assembly
Q	Q	Q	Q	Public Order and Safety
Q	Q	Q	Q	Religious Worship
17	9	3	1	Warehouse and Storage
Q	Q	Q	Q	Other
3	Q	Q	Q	Vacant
				Year Constructed
6	2	Q	Q	1919 or Before
11	6	2	1	1920 to 1945
19	5	3	*	1946 to 1959
21	12	3	1	1960 to 1969
20	9	4	1	1970 to 1979
26	9	4	1	1980 to 1989
6	3	1	*	1990 to 1992
6	Q	*	*	1993 to 1995
				Floors
37	16	4	1	One
32	8	2	1	Two
18	7	2	*	Three
26	14	7	1	Four to Nine
Q	3	4	2	Ten or More

Commercial Building Characteristics: 1995 - 2000 (Con't)

Building Characteristics	All Buildings	Buildings by Size			
		1,001 to 5,000 Square Feet	5,001 to 10,000 Square Feet	10,001 to 25,000 Square Feet	25,001 to 50,000 Square Feet
Census Region					
Northeast	725	351	162	139	38
Midwest	1,139	638	224	181	48
South	1,750	953	380	276	74
West	964	457	269	149	53
Ownership and Occupancy					
Nongovernment Owned	4,025	2,176	909	646	158
Owner Occupied	3,158	1,746	704	503	109
Nonowner Occupied	698	325	163	126	47
Unoccupied	170	105	Q	Q	Q
Government Owned	553	223	125	98	55
Predominant Ext. Wall Material					
Masonry	3,061	1,454	749	545	170
Siding or Shingles	639	465	116	50	5
Metal Panels	662	390	146	97	18
Concrete Panels	106	Q	10	30	14
Window Glass	46	Q	Q	Q	4
Other	50	Q	Q	Q	Q
No One Major Type	15	Q	Q	Q	Q
Predominant Roof Material					
Built-up	1,369	591	331	258	97
Shingles (Not Wood)	1,486	915	331	191	29
Metal Surfacing	908	512	192	158	29
Synthetic or Rubber	351	133	62	71	40
Slate or Tile	202	105	60	21	10
Wooden Materials	152	72	50	Q	Q
Concrete	58	Q	Q	Q	Q
Other	36	Q	Q	Q	Q
No One Major Type	Q	Q	Q	Q	Q

Q: Data withheld because the Relative Standard Error (RSE) was greater than 50 percent, or fewer than 20 buildings were sampled.

* = Value rounds to zero in the units displayed.

Buildings by Size				Building Characteristics
50,001 to 100,000 Square Feet	100,001 to 200,000 Square Feet	200,001 to 500,000 Square Feet	Over 500,000 Square Feet	
				Census Region
20	10	5	2	Northeast
28	14	5	1	Midwest
42	17	6	1	South
24	8	3	1	West
				Ownership and Occupancy
83	35	13	4	Nongovernment Owned
58	24	10	4	Owner Occupied
24	10	3	*	Nonowner Occupied
Q	Q	Q	Q	Unoccupied
32	13	6	1	Government Owned
				Predominant Ext. Wall Material
91	35	14	4	Masonry
Q	Q	Q	Q	Siding or Shingles
7	2	Q	*	Metal Panels
12	6	2	*	Concrete Panels
3	2	1	1	Window Glass
Q	Q	*	Q	Other
Q	Q	Q	Q	No One Major Type
				Predominant Roof Material
54	25	10	3	Built-up
14	4	1	*	Shingles (Not Wood)
13	3	1	Q	Metal Surfacing
25	13	5	2	Synthetic or Rubber
4	Q	Q	Q	Slate or Tile
Q	Q	Q	Q	Wooden Materials
Q	Q	Q	*	Concrete
Q	0	Q	Q	Other
Q	Q	Q	Q	No One Major Type

Source: Energy Information Administration, Office of Energy Markets and End Use,1995 Commercial Buildings Energy Consumption Survey

Construction Costs by City (in dollars per square foot)

Location	CCI	Apartment 1-3 Story	Church	College Classroom 2-3 Story	College Laboratory	Factory 1 Story	Fire Station 1 Story	Hospital 4-8 Story	Hotel 4-7 Story
National Average		105.05	118.65	113.25	119.85	72.00	106.80	123.70	103.15
ALABAMA									
Birmingham	0.86	90.34	102.04	97.40	103.07	61.92	91.85	106.38	88.71
Huntsville	0.82	86.14	97.29	92.87	98.28	59.04	87.58	101.43	84.58
Montgomery	0.80	84.04	94.92	90.60	95.88	57.60	85.44	98.96	82.52
Mobile	0.82	86.14	97.29	92.87	98.28	59.04	87.58	101.43	84.58
ALASKA									
Anchorage	1.24	130.26	147.13	140.43	148.61	89.28	132.43	153.39	127.91
Fairbanks	1.24	130.26	147.13	140.43	148.61	89.28	132.43	153.39	127.91
ARIZONA									
Mesa/Tempe	0.84	88.24	99.67	95.13	100.67	60.48	89.71	103.91	86.65
Phoenix	0.89	93.49	105.60	100.79	106.67	64.08	95.05	110.09	91.80
Tucson	0.87	91.39	103.23	98.53	104.27	62.64	92.92	107.62	89.74
ARKANSAS									
Fayetteville	0.66	69.33	78.31	74.75	79.10	47.52	70.49	81.64	68.08
Little Rock	0.81	85.09	96.11	91.73	97.08	58.32	86.51	100.20	83.55
CALIFORNIA									
Anaheim	1.08	113.45	128.14	122.31	129.44	77.76	115.34	133.60	111.40
Bakersfield	1.06	111.35	125.77	120.05	127.04	76.32	113.21	131.12	109.34
Berkeley	1.18	123.96	140.01	133.64	141.42	84.96	126.02	145.97	121.72
Fresno	1.08	113.45	128.14	122.31	129.44	77.76	115.34	133.60	111.40
Inglewood	1.06	111.35	125.77	120.05	127.04	76.32	113.21	131.12	109.34
Long Beach	1.07	112.40	126.96	121.18	128.24	77.04	114.28	132.36	110.37
Los Angeles	1.08	113.45	128.14	122.31	129.44	77.76	115.34	133.60	111.40
Modesto	1.09	114.50	129.33	123.44	130.64	78.48	116.41	134.83	112.43
Oakland	1.19	125.01	141.19	134.77	142.62	85.68	127.09	147.20	122.75
Oxnard	1.08	113.45	128.14	122.31	129.44	77.76	115.34	133.60	111.40
Palo Alto	1.18	123.96	140.01	133.64	141.42	84.96	126.02	145.97	121.72
Pasadena	1.07	112.40	126.96	121.18	128.24	77.04	114.28	132.36	110.37
Riverside	1.07	112.40	126.96	121.18	128.24	77.04	114.28	132.36	110.37
Sacramento	1.10	115.56	130.52	124.58	131.84	79.20	117.48	136.07	113.47
Salinas	1.12	117.66	132.89	126.84	134.23	80.64	119.62	138.54	115.53
San Bernardino	1.04	109.25	123.40	117.78	124.64	74.88	111.07	128.65	107.28
San Diego	1.06	111.35	125.77	120.05	127.04	76.32	113.21	131.12	109.34

Jail	Library	Nursing Home	Office 2-4 Story	Post Office	School Elementary	School High, 2-3 Story	Store Retail	Warehouse	Location
180.75	104.8	103.35	106.65	86.5	89.6	94.45	78.2	56.55	**National Average**
									ALABAMA
155.45	90.13	88.88	91.72	74.39	77.06	81.23	67.25	48.63	Birmingham
148.22	85.94	84.75	87.45	70.93	73.47	77.45	64.12	46.37	Huntsville
144.6	83.84	82.68	85.32	69.2	71.68	75.56	62.56	45.24	Montgomery
148.22	85.94	84.75	87.45	70.93	73.47	77.45	64.12	46.37	Mobile
									ALASKA
224.13	129.95	128.15	132.25	107.26	111.1	117.12	96.97	70.12	Anchorage
224.13	129.95	128.15	132.25	107.26	111.1	117.12	96.97	70.12	Fairbanks
									ARIZONA
151.83	88.03	86.81	89.59	72.66	75.26	79.34	65.69	47.5	Mesa/Tempe
160.87	93.27	91.98	94.92	76.99	79.74	84.06	69.6	50.33	Phoenix
157.25	91.18	89.91	92.79	75.26	77.95	82.17	68.03	49.2	Tucson
									ARKANSAS
119.3	69.17	68.21	70.39	57.09	59.14	62.34	51.61	37.32	Fayetteville
146.41	84.89	83.71	86.39	70.07	72.58	76.5	63.34	45.81	Little Rock
									CALIFORNIA
195.21	113.18	111.62	115.18	93.42	96.77	102.01	84.46	61.07	Anaheim
191.6	111.09	109.55	113.05	91.69	94.98	100.12	82.89	59.94	Bakersfield
213.29	123.66	121.95	125.85	102.07	105.73	111.45	92.28	66.73	Berkeley
195.21	113.18	111.62	115.18	93.42	96.77	102.01	84.46	61.07	Fresno
191.6	111.09	109.55	113.05	91.69	94.98	100.12	82.89	59.94	Inglewood
193.4	112.14	110.58	114.12	92.56	95.87	101.06	83.67	60.51	Long Beach
195.21	113.18	111.62	115.18	93.42	96.77	102.01	84.46	61.07	Los Angeles
197.02	114.23	112.65	116.25	94.29	97.66	102.95	85.24	61.64	Modesto
215.09	124.71	122.99	126.91	102.94	106.62	112.4	93.06	67.29	Oakland
195.21	113.18	111.62	115.18	93.42	96.77	102.01	84.46	61.07	Oxnard
213.29	123.66	121.95	125.85	102.07	105.73	111.45	92.28	66.73	Palo Alto
193.4	112.14	110.58	114.12	92.56	95.87	101.06	83.67	60.51	Pasadena
193.4	112.14	110.58	114.12	92.56	95.87	101.06	83.67	60.51	Riverside
198.83	115.28	113.69	117.32	95.15	98.56	103.9	86.02	62.21	Sacramento
202.44	117.38	115.75	119.45	96.88	100.35	105.78	87.58	63.34	Salinas
187.98	108.99	107.48	110.92	89.96	93.18	98.23	81.33	58.81	San Bernardino
191.6	111.09	109.55	113.05	91.69	94.98	100.12	82.89	59.94	San Diego

Construction Costs by City (Con't)

Location	CCI	Apartment 1-3 Story	Church	College Classroom 2-3 Story	College Laboratory	Factory 1 Story	Fire Station 1 Story	Hospital 4-8 Story	Hotel 4-7 Story
San Francisco	1.24	130.26	147.13	140.43	148.61	89.28	132.43	153.39	127.91
San Jose	1.20	126.06	142.38	135.90	143.82	86.40	128.16	148.44	123.78
Santa Ana	1.06	111.35	125.77	120.05	127.04	76.32	113.21	131.12	109.34
Santa Barbara	1.08	113.45	128.14	122.31	129.44	77.76	115.34	133.60	111.40
Santa Rosa	1.17	122.91	138.82	132.50	140.22	84.24	124.96	144.73	120.69
Stockton	1.09	114.50	129.33	123.44	130.64	78.48	116.41	134.83	112.43
Vallejo	1.14	119.76	135.26	129.11	136.63	82.08	121.75	141.02	117.59
COLORADO									
Colorado Springs	0.92	96.65	109.16	104.19	110.26	66.24	98.26	113.80	94.90
Denver	0.95	99.80	112.72	107.59	113.86	68.40	101.46	117.52	97.99
Fort Collins	0.92	96.65	109.16	104.19	110.26	66.24	98.26	113.80	94.90
CONNECTICUT									
Bridgeport	1.05	110.30	124.58	118.91	125.84	75.60	112.14	129.89	108.31
Hartford	1.05	110.30	124.58	118.91	125.84	75.60	112.14	129.89	108.31
New Haven	1.05	110.30	124.58	118.91	125.84	75.60	112.14	129.89	108.31
Stamford	1.08	113.45	128.14	122.31	129.44	77.76	115.34	133.60	111.40
Waterbury	1.05	110.30	124.58	118.91	125.84	75.60	112.14	129.89	108.31
D.C.									
Washington	0.95	99.80	112.72	107.59	113.86	68.40	101.46	117.52	97.99
DELAWARE									
Wilmington	1.01	106.10	119.84	114.38	121.05	72.72	107.87	124.94	104.18
FLORIDA									
Fort Lauderdale	0.85	89.29	100.85	96.26	101.87	61.20	90.78	105.15	87.68
Jacksonville	0.82	86.14	97.29	92.87	98.28	59.04	87.58	101.43	84.58
Miami	0.85	89.29	100.85	96.26	101.87	61.20	90.78	105.15	87.68
Orlando	0.84	88.24	99.67	95.13	100.67	60.48	89.71	103.91	86.65
St. Petersburg	0.83	87.19	98.48	94.00	99.48	59.76	88.64	102.67	85.61
Tallahassee	0.77	80.89	91.36	87.20	92.28	55.44	82.24	95.25	79.43
Tampa	0.82	86.14	97.29	92.87	98.28	59.04	87.58	101.43	84.58
GEORGIA									
Atlanta	0.90	94.55	106.79	101.93	107.87	64.80	96.12	111.33	92.84
Columbus	0.78	81.94	92.55	88.34	93.48	56.16	83.30	96.49	80.46
Macon	0.81	85.09	96.11	91.73	97.08	58.32	86.51	100.20	83.55
Savannah	0.81	85.09	96.11	91.73	97.08	58.32	86.51	100.20	83.55
HAWAII									
Honolulu	1.23	129.21	145.94	139.30	147.42	88.56	131.36	152.15	126.87

Jail	Library	Nursing Home	Office 2-4 Story	Post Office	School Elementary	School High, 2-3 Story	Store Retail	Warehouse	Location
224.13	129.95	128.15	132.25	107.26	111.1	117.12	96.97	70.12	San Francisco
216.9	125.76	124.02	127.98	103.8	107.52	113.34	93.84	67.86	San Jose
191.6	111.09	109.55	113.05	91.69	94.98	100.12	82.89	59.94	Santa Ana
195.21	113.18	111.62	115.18	93.42	96.77	102.01	84.46	61.07	Santa Barbara
211.48	122.62	120.92	124.78	101.21	104.83	110.51	91.49	66.16	Santa Rosa
197.02	114.23	112.65	116.25	94.29	97.66	102.95	85.24	61.64	Stockton
206.06	119.47	117.82	121.58	98.61	102.14	107.67	89.15	64.47	Vallejo
									COLORADO
166.29	96.42	95.08	98.12	79.58	82.43	86.89	71.94	52.03	Colorado Springs
171.71	99.56	98.18	101.32	82.18	85.12	89.73	74.29	53.72	Denver
166.29	96.42	95.08	98.12	79.58	82.43	86.89	71.94	52.03	Fort Collins
									CONNECTICUT
189.79	110.04	108.52	111.98	90.83	94.08	99.17	82.11	59.38	Bridgeport
189.79	110.04	108.52	111.98	90.83	94.08	99.17	82.11	59.38	Hartford
189.79	110.04	108.52	111.98	90.83	94.08	99.17	82.11	59.38	New Haven
195.21	113.18	111.62	115.18	93.42	96.77	102.01	84.46	61.07	Stamford
189.79	110.04	108.52	111.98	90.83	94.08	99.17	82.11	59.38	Waterbury
									D.C.
171.71	99.56	98.18	101.32	82.18	85.12	89.73	74.29	53.72	Washington
									DELAWARE
182.56	105.85	104.38	107.72	87.37	90.5	95.39	78.98	57.12	Wilmington
									FLORIDA
153.64	89.08	87.85	90.65	73.53	76.16	80.28	66.47	48.07	Fort Lauderdale
148.22	85.94	84.75	87.45	70.93	73.47	77.45	64.12	46.37	Jacksonville
153.64	89.08	87.85	90.65	73.53	76.16	80.28	66.47	48.07	Miami
151.83	88.03	86.81	89.59	72.66	75.26	79.34	65.69	47.5	Orlando
150.02	86.98	85.78	88.52	71.8	74.37	78.39	64.91	46.94	St. Petersburg
139.18	80.7	79.58	82.12	66.61	68.99	72.73	60.21	43.54	Tallahassee
148.22	85.94	84.75	87.45	70.93	73.47	77.45	64.12	46.37	Tampa
									GEORGIA
162.68	94.32	93.02	95.99	77.85	80.64	85.01	70.38	50.9	Atlanta
140.99	81.74	80.61	83.19	67.47	69.89	73.67	61	44.11	Columbus
146.41	84.89	83.71	86.39	70.07	72.58	76.5	63.34	45.81	Macon
146.41	84.89	83.71	86.39	70.07	72.58	76.5	63.34	45.81	Savannah
									HAWAII
222.32	128.9	127.12	131.18	106.4	110.21	116.17	96.19	69.56	Honolulu

Construction Costs by City (Con't)

Location	CCI	Apartment 1-3 Story	Church	College Classroom 2-3 Story	College Laboratory	Factory 1 Story	Fire Station 1 Story	Hospital 4-8 Story	Hotel 4-7 Story
IDAHO									
Boise	0.93	97.70	110.34	105.32	111.46	66.96	99.32	115.04	95.93
ILLINOIS									
Bloomington	1.00	105.05	118.65	113.25	119.85	72.00	106.80	123.70	103.15
Champaign	1.01	106.10	119.84	114.38	121.05	72.72	107.87	124.94	104.18
Chicago	1.12	117.66	132.89	126.84	134.23	80.64	119.62	138.54	115.53
North Suburban	1.09	114.50	129.33	123.44	130.64	78.48	116.41	134.83	112.43
Peoria	1.02	107.15	121.02	115.52	122.25	73.44	108.94	126.17	105.21
Rockford	1.04	109.25	123.40	117.78	124.64	74.88	111.07	128.65	107.28
South Suburban	1.09	114.50	129.33	123.44	130.64	78.48	116.41	134.83	112.43
Springfield	0.98	102.95	116.28	110.99	117.45	70.56	104.66	121.23	101.09
INDIANA									
Bloomington	0.93	97.70	110.34	105.32	111.46	66.96	99.32	115.04	95.93
Columbus	0.93	97.70	110.34	105.32	111.46	66.96	99.32	115.04	95.93
Evansville	0.95	99.80	112.72	107.59	113.86	68.40	101.46	117.52	97.99
Fort Wayne	0.93	97.70	110.34	105.32	111.46	66.96	99.32	115.04	95.93
Gary	1.02	107.15	121.02	115.52	122.25	73.44	108.94	126.17	105.21
Indianapolis	0.96	100.85	113.90	108.72	115.06	69.12	102.53	118.75	99.02
South Bend	0.92	96.65	109.16	104.19	110.26	66.24	98.26	113.80	94.90
IOWA									
Cedar Rapids	0.92	96.65	109.16	104.19	110.26	66.24	98.26	113.80	94.90
Des Moines	0.93	97.70	110.34	105.32	111.46	66.96	99.32	115.04	95.93
Dubuque	0.88	92.44	104.41	99.66	105.47	63.36	93.98	108.86	90.77
KANSAS									
Kansas City	0.94	98.75	111.53	106.46	112.66	67.68	100.39	116.28	96.96
Topeka	0.85	89.29	100.85	96.26	101.87	61.20	90.78	105.15	87.68
Wichita	0.86	90.34	102.04	97.40	103.07	61.92	91.85	106.38	88.71
KENTUCKY									
Frankfort	0.86	90.34	102.04	97.40	103.07	61.92	91.85	106.38	88.71
Lexington	0.84	88.24	99.67	95.13	100.67	60.48	89.71	103.91	86.65
Louisville	0.92	96.65	109.16	104.19	110.26	66.24	98.26	113.80	94.90
LOUISIANA									
Baton Rouge	0.81	85.09	96.11	91.73	97.08	58.32	86.51	100.20	83.55
Lafayette	0.81	85.09	96.11	91.73	97.08	58.32	86.51	100.20	83.55
New Orleans	0.85	89.29	100.85	96.26	101.87	61.20	90.78	105.15	87.68
Shreveport	0.81	85.09	96.11	91.73	97.08	58.32	86.51	100.20	83.55

Jail	Library	Nursing Home	Office 2-4 Story	Post Office	School Elementary	School High, 2-3 Story	Store Retail	Warehouse	Location
									IDAHO
168.1	97.46	96.12	99.18	80.45	83.33	87.84	72.73	52.59	Boise
									ILLINOIS
180.75	104.8	103.35	106.65	86.5	89.6	94.45	78.2	56.55	Bloomington
182.56	105.85	104.38	107.72	87.37	90.5	95.39	78.98	57.12	Champaign
202.44	117.38	115.75	119.45	96.88	100.35	105.78	87.58	63.34	Chicago
197.02	114.23	112.65	116.25	94.29	97.66	102.95	85.24	61.64	North Suburban
184.37	106.9	105.42	108.78	88.23	91.39	96.34	79.76	57.68	Peoria
187.98	108.99	107.48	110.92	89.96	93.18	98.23	81.33	58.81	Rockford
197.02	114.23	112.65	116.25	94.29	97.66	102.95	85.24	61.64	South Suburban
177.14	102.7	101.28	104.52	84.77	87.81	92.56	76.64	55.42	Springfield
									INDIANA
168.1	97.46	96.12	99.18	80.45	83.33	87.84	72.73	52.59	Bloomington
168.1	97.46	96.12	99.18	80.45	83.33	87.84	72.73	52.59	Columbus
171.71	99.56	98.18	101.32	82.18	85.12	89.73	74.29	53.72	Evansville
168.1	97.46	96.12	99.18	80.45	83.33	87.84	72.73	52.59	Fort Wayne
184.37	106.9	105.42	108.78	88.23	91.39	96.34	79.76	57.68	Gary
173.52	100.61	99.22	102.38	83.04	86.02	90.67	75.07	54.29	Indianapolis
166.29	96.42	95.08	98.12	79.58	82.43	86.89	71.94	52.03	South Bend
									IOWA
166.29	96.42	95.08	98.12	79.58	82.43	86.89	71.94	52.03	Cedar Rapids
168.1	97.46	96.12	99.18	80.45	83.33	87.84	72.73	52.59	Des Moines
159.06	92.22	90.95	93.85	76.12	78.85	83.12	68.82	49.76	Dubuque
									KANSAS
169.91	98.51	97.15	100.25	81.31	84.22	88.78	73.51	53.16	Kansas City
153.64	89.08	87.85	90.65	73.53	76.16	80.28	66.47	48.07	Topeka
155.45	90.13	88.88	91.72	74.39	77.06	81.23	67.25	48.63	Wichita
									KENTUCKY
155.45	90.13	88.88	91.72	74.39	77.06	81.23	67.25	48.63	Frankfort
151.83	88.03	86.81	89.59	72.66	75.26	79.34	65.69	47.5	Lexington
166.29	96.42	95.08	98.12	79.58	82.43	86.89	71.94	52.03	Louisville
									LOUISIANA
146.41	84.89	83.71	86.39	70.07	72.58	76.5	63.34	45.81	Baton Rouge
146.41	84.89	83.71	86.39	70.07	72.58	76.5	63.34	45.81	Lafayette
153.64	89.08	87.85	90.65	73.53	76.16	80.28	66.47	48.07	New Orleans
146.41	84.89	83.71	86.39	70.07	72.58	76.5	63.34	45.81	Shreveport

Construction Costs by City (Con't)

Location	CCI	Apartment 1-3 Story	Church	College Classroom 2-3 Story	College Laboratory	Factory 1 Story	Fire Station 1 Story	Hospital 4-8 Story	Hotel 4-7 Story
MAINE									
Bangor	0.93	97.70	110.34	105.32	111.46	66.96	99.32	115.04	95.93
Portland	0.93	97.70	110.34	105.32	111.46	66.96	99.32	115.04	95.93
MARYLAND									
Annapolis	0.90	94.55	106.79	101.93	107.87	64.80	96.12	111.33	92.84
Baltimore	0.91	95.60	107.97	103.06	109.06	65.52	97.19	112.57	93.87
MASSACHUSETTS									
Boston	1.15	120.81	136.45	130.24	137.83	82.80	122.82	142.26	118.62
Lowell	1.08	113.45	128.14	122.31	129.44	77.76	115.34	133.60	111.40
Springfield	1.02	107.15	121.02	115.52	122.25	73.44	108.94	126.17	105.21
Worcester	1.06	111.35	125.77	120.05	127.04	76.32	113.21	131.12	109.34
MICHIGAN									
Ann Arbor	1.03	108.20	122.21	116.65	123.45	74.16	110.00	127.41	106.24
Detroit	1.06	111.35	125.77	120.05	127.04	76.32	113.21	131.12	109.34
Flint	1.00	105.05	118.65	113.25	119.85	72.00	106.80	123.70	103.15
Grand Rapids	0.85	89.29	100.85	96.26	101.87	61.20	90.78	105.15	87.68
Lansing	0.98	102.95	116.28	110.99	117.45	70.56	104.66	121.23	101.09
MINNESOTA									
Bemidji	0.98	102.95	116.28	110.99	117.45	70.56	104.66	121.23	101.09
Duluth	1.05	110.30	124.58	118.91	125.84	75.60	112.14	129.89	108.31
Minneapolis	1.08	113.45	128.14	122.31	129.44	77.76	115.34	133.60	111.40
Rochester	0.99	104.00	117.46	112.12	118.65	71.28	105.73	122.46	102.12
Saint Paul	1.07	112.40	126.96	121.18	128.24	77.04	114.28	132.36	110.37
MISSISSIPPI									
Biloxi	0.80	84.04	94.92	90.60	95.88	57.60	85.44	98.96	82.52
Jackson	0.76	79.84	90.17	86.07	91.09	54.72	81.17	94.01	78.39
MISSOURI									
Kansas City	1.01	106.10	119.84	114.38	121.05	72.72	107.87	124.94	104.18
St. Louis	1.03	108.20	122.21	116.65	123.45	74.16	110.00	127.41	106.24
MONTANA									
Billings	0.91	95.60	107.97	103.06	109.06	65.52	97.19	112.57	93.87
Great Falls	0.91	95.60	107.97	103.06	109.06	65.52	97.19	112.57	93.87
NEBRASKA									
Alliance	0.71	74.59	84.24	80.41	85.09	51.12	75.83	87.83	73.24
Lincoln	0.83	87.19	98.48	94.00	99.48	59.76	88.64	102.67	85.61
Omaha	0.91	95.60	107.97	103.06	109.06	65.52	97.19	112.57	93.87

Jail	Library	Nursing Home	Office 2-4 Story	Post Office	School Elementary	School High, 2-3 Story	Store Retail	Warehouse	Location
									MAINE
168.1	97.46	96.12	99.18	80.45	83.33	87.84	72.73	52.59	Bangor
168.1	97.46	96.12	99.18	80.45	83.33	87.84	72.73	52.59	Portland
									MARYLAND
162.68	94.32	93.02	95.99	77.85	80.64	85.01	70.38	50.9	Annapolis
164.48	95.37	94.05	97.05	78.72	81.54	85.95	71.16	51.46	Baltimore
									MASSACHUSETTS
207.86	120.52	118.85	122.65	99.48	103.04	108.62	89.93	65.03	Boston
195.21	113.18	111.62	115.18	93.42	96.77	102.01	84.46	61.07	Lowell
184.37	106.9	105.42	108.78	88.23	91.39	96.34	79.76	57.68	Springfield
191.6	111.09	109.55	113.05	91.69	94.98	100.12	82.89	59.94	Worcester
									MICHIGAN
186.17	107.94	106.45	109.85	89.1	92.29	97.28	80.55	58.25	Ann Arbor
191.6	111.09	109.55	113.05	91.69	94.98	100.12	82.89	59.94	Detroit
180.75	104.8	103.35	106.65	86.5	89.6	94.45	78.2	56.55	Flint
153.64	89.08	87.85	90.65	73.53	76.16	80.28	66.47	48.07	Grand Rapids
177.14	102.7	101.28	104.52	84.77	87.81	92.56	76.64	55.42	Lansing
									MINNESOTA
177.14	102.7	101.28	104.52	84.77	87.81	92.56	76.64	55.42	Bemidji
189.79	110.04	108.52	111.98	90.83	94.08	99.17	82.11	59.38	Duluth
195.21	113.18	111.62	115.18	93.42	96.77	102.01	84.46	61.07	Minneapolis
178.94	103.75	102.32	105.58	85.64	88.7	93.51	77.42	55.98	Rochester
193.4	112.14	110.58	114.12	92.56	95.87	101.06	83.67	60.51	Saint Paul
									MISSISSIPPI
144.6	83.84	82.68	85.32	69.2	71.68	75.56	62.56	45.24	Biloxi
137.37	79.65	78.55	81.05	65.74	68.1	71.78	59.43	42.98	Jackson
									MISSOURI
182.56	105.85	104.38	107.72	87.37	90.5	95.39	78.98	57.12	Kansas City
186.17	107.94	106.45	109.85	89.1	92.29	97.28	80.55	58.25	St. Louis
									MONTANA
164.48	95.37	94.05	97.05	78.72	81.54	85.95	71.16	51.46	Billings
164.48	95.37	94.05	97.05	78.72	81.54	85.95	71.16	51.46	Great Falls
									NEBRASKA
128.33	74.41	73.38	75.72	61.42	63.62	67.06	55.52	40.15	Alliance
150.02	86.98	85.78	88.52	71.8	74.37	78.39	64.91	46.94	Lincoln
164.48	95.37	94.05	97.05	78.72	81.54	85.95	71.16	51.46	Omaha

Construction Costs by City (Con't)

Location	CCI	Apartment 1-3 Story	Church	College Classroom 2-3 Story	College Laboratory	Factory 1 Story	Fire Station 1 Story	Hospital 4-8 Story	Hotel 4-7 Story
NEVADA									
Las Vegas	1.04	109.25	123.40	117.78	124.64	74.88	111.07	128.65	107.28
Reno	1.00	105.05	118.65	113.25	119.85	72.00	106.80	123.70	103.15
NEW HAMPSHIRE									
Nashua	0.95	99.80	112.72	107.59	113.86	68.40	101.46	117.52	97.99
Portsmouth	0.92	96.65	109.16	104.19	110.26	66.24	98.26	113.80	94.90
NEW JERSEY									
Elizabeth	1.08	113.45	128.14	122.31	129.44	77.76	115.34	133.60	111.40
Jersey City	1.10	115.56	130.52	124.58	131.84	79.20	117.48	136.07	113.47
Newark	1.12	117.66	132.89	126.84	134.23	80.64	119.62	138.54	115.53
Paterson	1.12	117.66	132.89	126.84	134.23	80.64	119.62	138.54	115.53
Trenton	1.10	115.56	130.52	124.58	131.84	79.20	117.48	136.07	113.47
NEW MEXICO									
Albuquerque	0.90	94.55	106.79	101.93	107.87	64.80	96.12	111.33	92.84
Santa Fe	0.90	94.55	106.79	101.93	107.87	64.80	96.12	111.33	92.84
NEW YORK									
Albany	0.97	101.90	115.09	109.85	116.25	69.84	103.60	119.99	100.06
Brooklyn	1.31	137.62	155.43	148.36	157.00	94.32	139.91	162.05	135.13
Buffalo	1.02	107.15	121.02	115.52	122.25	73.44	108.94	126.17	105.21
New York	1.35	141.82	160.18	152.89	161.80	97.20	144.18	167.00	139.25
Rochester	1.00	105.05	118.65	113.25	119.85	72.00	106.80	123.70	103.15
Syracuse	0.97	101.90	115.09	109.85	116.25	69.84	103.60	119.99	100.06
Yonkers	1.22	128.16	144.75	138.17	146.22	87.84	130.30	150.91	125.84
NORTH CAROLINA									
Asheville	0.75	78.79	88.99	84.94	89.89	54.00	80.10	92.78	77.36
Charlotte	0.75	78.79	88.99	84.94	89.89	54.00	80.10	92.78	77.36
Durham	0.76	79.84	90.17	86.07	91.09	54.72	81.17	94.01	78.39
Greensboro	0.76	79.84	90.17	86.07	91.09	54.72	81.17	94.01	78.39
Raleigh	0.76	79.84	90.17	86.07	91.09	54.72	81.17	94.01	78.39
Winston-Salem	0.75	78.79	88.99	84.94	89.89	54.00	80.10	92.78	77.36
NORTH DAKOTA									
Bismarck	0.84	88.24	99.67	95.13	100.67	60.48	89.71	103.91	86.65
Fargo	0.84	88.24	99.67	95.13	100.67	60.48	89.71	103.91	86.65
Grand Forks	0.82	86.14	97.29	92.87	98.28	59.04	87.58	101.43	84.58
OHIO									
Akron	1.01	106.10	119.84	114.38	121.05	72.72	107.87	124.94	104.18

Jail	Library	Nursing Home	Office 2-4 Story	Post Office	School Elementary	School High, 2-3 Story	Store Retail	Warehouse	Location
									NEVADA
187.98	108.99	107.48	110.92	89.96	93.18	98.23	81.33	58.81	Las Vegas
180.75	104.8	103.35	106.65	86.5	89.6	94.45	78.2	56.55	Reno
									NEW HAMPSHIRE
171.71	99.56	98.18	101.32	82.18	85.12	89.73	74.29	53.72	Nashua
166.29	96.42	95.08	98.12	79.58	82.43	86.89	71.94	52.03	Portsmouth
									NEW JERSEY
195.21	113.18	111.62	115.18	93.42	96.77	102.01	84.46	61.07	Elizabeth
198.83	115.28	113.69	117.32	95.15	98.56	103.9	86.02	62.21	Jersey City
202.44	117.38	115.75	119.45	96.88	100.35	105.78	87.58	63.34	Newark
202.44	117.38	115.75	119.45	96.88	100.35	105.78	87.58	63.34	Paterson
198.83	115.28	113.69	117.32	95.15	98.56	103.9	86.02	62.21	Trenton
									NEW MEXICO
162.68	94.32	93.02	95.99	77.85	80.64	85.01	70.38	50.9	Albuquerque
162.68	94.32	93.02	95.99	77.85	80.64	85.01	70.38	50.9	Santa Fe
									NEW YORK
175.33	101.66	100.25	103.45	83.91	86.91	91.62	75.85	54.85	Albany
236.78	137.29	135.39	139.71	113.32	117.38	123.73	102.44	74.08	Brooklyn
184.37	106.9	105.42	108.78	88.23	91.39	96.34	79.76	57.68	Buffalo
244.01	141.48	139.52	143.98	116.78	120.96	127.51	105.57	76.34	New York
180.75	104.8	103.35	106.65	86.5	89.6	94.45	78.2	56.55	Rochester
175.33	101.66	100.25	103.45	83.91	86.91	91.62	75.85	54.85	Syracuse
220.52	127.86	126.09	130.11	105.53	109.31	115.23	95.4	68.99	Yonkers
									NORTH CAROLINA
135.56	78.6	77.51	79.99	64.88	67.2	70.84	58.65	42.41	Asheville
135.56	78.6	77.51	79.99	64.88	67.2	70.84	58.65	42.41	Charlotte
137.37	79.65	78.55	81.05	65.74	68.1	71.78	59.43	42.98	Durham
137.37	79.65	78.55	81.05	65.74	68.1	71.78	59.43	42.98	Greensboro
137.37	79.65	78.55	81.05	65.74	68.1	71.78	59.43	42.98	Raleigh
135.56	78.6	77.51	79.99	64.88	67.2	70.84	58.65	42.41	Winston-Salem
									NORTH DAKOTA
151.83	88.03	86.81	89.59	72.66	75.26	79.34	65.69	47.5	Bismarck
151.83	88.03	86.81	89.59	72.66	75.26	79.34	65.69	47.5	Fargo
148.22	85.94	84.75	87.45	70.93	73.47	77.45	64.12	46.37	Grand Forks
									OHIO
182.56	105.85	104.38	107.72	87.37	90.5	95.39	78.98	57.12	Akron

Construction Costs by City (Con't)

Location	CCI	Apartment 1-3 Story	Church	College Classroom 2-3 Story	College Laboratory	Factory 1 Story	Fire Station 1 Story	Hospital 4-8 Story	Hotel 4-7 Story
Cincinnati	0.94	98.75	111.53	106.46	112.66	67.68	100.39	116.28	96.96
Cleveland	1.03	108.20	122.21	116.65	123.45	74.16	110.00	127.41	106.24
Columbus	0.96	100.85	113.90	108.72	115.06	69.12	102.53	118.75	99.02
Dayton	0.93	97.70	110.34	105.32	111.46	66.96	99.32	115.04	95.93
Toledo	1.01	106.10	119.84	114.38	121.05	72.72	107.87	124.94	104.18
Zanesville	0.92	96.65	109.16	104.19	110.26	66.24	98.26	113.80	94.90
OKLAHOMA									
Oklahoma City	0.84	88.24	99.67	95.13	100.67	60.48	89.71	103.91	86.65
Tulsa	0.81	85.09	96.11	91.73	97.08	58.32	86.51	100.20	83.55
OREGON									
Eugene	1.04	109.25	123.40	117.78	124.64	74.88	111.07	128.65	107.28
Portland	1.06	111.35	125.77	120.05	127.04	76.32	113.21	131.12	109.34
Salem	1.05	110.30	124.58	118.91	125.84	75.60	112.14	129.89	108.31
PENNSYLVANIA									
Allentown	1.00	105.05	118.65	113.25	119.85	72.00	106.80	123.70	103.15
Erie	0.97	101.90	115.09	109.85	116.25	69.84	103.60	119.99	100.06
Philadelphia	1.11	116.61	131.70	125.71	133.03	79.92	118.55	137.31	114.50
Pittsburgh	1.02	107.15	121.02	115.52	122.25	73.44	108.94	126.17	105.21
RHODE ISLAND									
Providence	1.04	109.25	123.40	117.78	124.64	74.88	111.07	128.65	107.28
SOUTH CAROLINA									
Charleston	0.75	78.79	88.99	84.94	89.89	54.00	80.10	92.78	77.36
Columbia	0.75	78.79	88.99	84.94	89.89	54.00	80.10	92.78	77.36
SOUTH DAKOTA									
Aberdeen	0.78	81.94	92.55	88.34	93.48	56.16	83.30	96.49	80.46
Rapid City	0.79	82.99	93.73	89.47	94.68	56.88	84.37	97.72	81.49
Sioux Falls	0.81	85.09	96.11	91.73	97.08	58.32	86.51	100.20	83.55
TENNESSEE									
Chattanooga	0.81	85.09	96.11	91.73	97.08	58.32	86.51	100.20	83.55
Knoxville	0.80	84.04	94.92	90.60	95.88	57.60	85.44	98.96	82.52
Memphis	0.84	88.24	99.67	95.13	100.67	60.48	89.71	103.91	86.65
Nashville	0.86	90.34	102.04	97.40	103.07	61.92	91.85	106.38	88.71
TEXAS									
Abilene	0.79	82.99	93.73	89.47	94.68	56.88	84.37	97.72	81.49
Amarillo	0.81	85.09	96.11	91.73	97.08	58.32	86.51	100.20	83.55
Austin	0.81	85.09	96.11	91.73	97.08	58.32	86.51	100.20	83.55

Jail	Library	Nursing Home	Office 2-4 Story	Post Office	School Elementary	School High, 2-3 Story	Store Retail	Warehouse	Location
169.91	98.51	97.15	100.25	81.31	84.22	88.78	73.51	53.16	Cincinnati
186.17	107.94	106.45	109.85	89.1	92.29	97.28	80.55	58.25	Cleveland
173.52	100.61	99.22	102.38	83.04	86.02	90.67	75.07	54.29	Columbus
168.1	97.46	96.12	99.18	80.45	83.33	87.84	72.73	52.59	Dayton
182.56	105.85	104.38	107.72	87.37	90.5	95.39	78.98	57.12	Toledo
166.29	96.42	95.08	98.12	79.58	82.43	86.89	71.94	52.03	Zanesville
									OKLAHOMA
151.83	88.03	86.81	89.59	72.66	75.26	79.34	65.69	47.5	Oklahoma City
146.41	84.89	83.71	86.39	70.07	72.58	76.5	63.34	45.81	Tulsa
									OREGON
187.98	108.99	107.48	110.92	89.96	93.18	98.23	81.33	58.81	Eugene
191.6	111.09	109.55	113.05	91.69	94.98	100.12	82.89	59.94	Portland
189.79	110.04	108.52	111.98	90.83	94.08	99.17	82.11	59.38	Salem
									PENNSYLVANIA
180.75	104.8	103.35	106.65	86.5	89.6	94.45	78.2	56.55	Allentown
175.33	101.66	100.25	103.45	83.91	86.91	91.62	75.85	54.85	Erie
200.63	116.33	114.72	118.38	96.02	99.46	104.84	86.8	62.77	Philadelphia
184.37	106.9	105.42	108.78	88.23	91.39	96.34	79.76	57.68	Pittsburgh
									RHODE ISLAND
187.98	108.99	107.48	110.92	89.96	93.18	98.23	81.33	58.81	Providence
									SOUTH CAROLINA
135.56	78.6	77.51	79.99	64.88	67.2	70.84	58.65	42.41	Charleston
135.56	78.6	77.51	79.99	64.88	67.2	70.84	58.65	42.41	Columbia
									SOUTH DAKOTA
140.99	81.74	80.61	83.19	67.47	69.89	73.67	61	44.11	Aberdeen
142.79	82.79	81.65	84.25	68.34	70.78	74.62	61.78	44.67	Rapid City
146.41	84.89	83.71	86.39	70.07	72.58	76.5	63.34	45.81	Sioux Falls
									TENNESSEE
146.41	84.89	83.71	86.39	70.07	72.58	76.5	63.34	45.81	Chattanooga
144.6	83.84	82.68	85.32	69.2	71.68	75.56	62.56	45.24	Knoxville
151.83	88.03	86.81	89.59	72.66	75.26	79.34	65.69	47.5	Memphis
155.45	90.13	88.88	91.72	74.39	77.06	81.23	67.25	48.63	Nashville
									TEXAS
142.79	82.79	81.65	84.25	68.34	70.78	74.62	61.78	44.67	Abilene
146.41	84.89	83.71	86.39	70.07	72.58	76.5	63.34	45.81	Amarillo
146.41	84.89	83.71	86.39	70.07	72.58	76.5	63.34	45.81	Austin

Construction Costs by City (Con't)

Location	CCI	Apartment 1-3 Story	Church	College Classroom 2-3 Story	College Laboratory	Factory 1 Story	Fire Station 1 Story	Hospital 4-8 Story	Hotel 4-7 Story
Beaumont	0.83	87.19	98.48	94.00	99.48	59.76	88.64	102.67	85.61
Corpus Christi	0.79	82.99	93.73	89.47	94.68	56.88	84.37	97.72	81.49
Dallas	0.85	89.29	100.85	96.26	101.87	61.20	90.78	105.15	87.68
El Paso	0.78	81.94	92.55	88.34	93.48	56.16	83.30	96.49	80.46
Fort Worth	0.82	86.14	97.29	92.87	98.28	59.04	87.58	101.43	84.58
Houston	0.88	92.44	104.41	99.66	105.47	63.36	93.98	108.86	90.77
Laredo	0.77	80.89	91.36	87.20	92.28	55.44	82.24	95.25	79.43
Lubbock	0.80	84.04	94.92	90.60	95.88	57.60	85.44	98.96	82.52
Mc Allen	0.76	79.84	90.17	86.07	91.09	54.72	81.17	94.01	78.39
San Antonio	0.83	87.19	98.48	94.00	99.48	59.76	88.64	102.67	85.61
Waco	0.80	84.04	94.92	90.60	95.88	57.60	85.44	98.96	82.52
Wichita Falls	0.80	84.04	94.92	90.60	95.88	57.60	85.44	98.96	82.52
UTAH									
Provo	0.89	93.49	105.60	100.79	106.67	64.08	95.05	110.09	91.80
Salt Lake City	0.89	93.49	105.60	100.79	106.67	64.08	95.05	110.09	91.80
VERMONT									
Burlington	0.86	90.34	102.04	97.40	103.07	61.92	91.85	106.38	88.71
Montpelier	0.85	89.29	100.85	96.26	101.87	61.20	90.78	105.15	87.68
VIRGINIA									
Alexandria	0.90	94.55	106.79	101.93	107.87	64.80	96.12	111.33	92.84
Arlington	0.90	94.55	106.79	101.93	107.87	64.80	96.12	111.33	92.84
Fairfax	0.90	94.55	106.79	101.93	107.87	64.80	96.12	111.33	92.84
Fredericksburg	0.84	88.24	99.67	95.13	100.67	60.48	89.71	103.91	86.65
Newport News	0.81	85.09	96.11	91.73	97.08	58.32	86.51	100.20	83.55
Portsmouth	0.81	85.09	96.11	91.73	97.08	58.32	86.51	100.20	83.55
Richmond	0.84	88.24	99.67	95.13	100.67	60.48	89.71	103.91	86.65
WASHINGTON									
Seattle	1.05	110.30	124.58	118.91	125.84	75.60	112.14	129.89	108.31
Spokane	0.98	102.95	116.28	110.99	117.45	70.56	104.66	121.23	101.09
Tacoma	1.03	108.20	122.21	116.65	123.45	74.16	110.00	127.41	106.24
WEST VIRGINIA									
Charleston	0.93	97.70	110.34	105.32	111.46	66.96	99.32	115.04	95.93
Martinsburg	0.76	79.84	90.17	86.07	91.09	54.72	81.17	94.01	78.39
Morgantown	0.94	98.75	111.53	106.46	112.66	67.68	100.39	116.28	96.96
WISCONSIN									
Milwaukee	1.01	106.10	119.84	114.38	121.05	72.72	107.87	124.94	104.18

Jail	Library	Nursing Home	Office 2-4 Story	Post Office	School Elementary	School High, 2-3 Story	Store Retail	Warehouse	Location
150.02	86.98	85.78	88.52	71.8	74.37	78.39	64.91	46.94	Beaumont
142.79	82.79	81.65	84.25	68.34	70.78	74.62	61.78	44.67	Corpus Christi
153.64	89.08	87.85	90.65	73.53	76.16	80.28	66.47	48.07	Dallas
140.99	81.74	80.61	83.19	67.47	69.89	73.67	61	44.11	El Paso
148.22	85.94	84.75	87.45	70.93	73.47	77.45	64.12	46.37	Fort Worth
159.06	92.22	90.95	93.85	76.12	78.85	83.12	68.82	49.76	Houston
139.18	80.7	79.58	82.12	66.61	68.99	72.73	60.21	43.54	Laredo
144.6	83.84	82.68	85.32	69.2	71.68	75.56	62.56	45.24	Lubbock
137.37	79.65	78.55	81.05	65.74	68.1	71.78	59.43	42.98	Mc Allen
150.02	86.98	85.78	88.52	71.8	74.37	78.39	64.91	46.94	San Antonio
144.6	83.84	82.68	85.32	69.2	71.68	75.56	62.56	45.24	Waco
144.6	83.84	82.68	85.32	69.2	71.68	75.56	62.56	45.24	Wichita Falls
									UTAH
160.87	93.27	91.98	94.92	76.99	79.74	84.06	69.6	50.33	Provo
160.87	93.27	91.98	94.92	76.99	79.74	84.06	69.6	50.33	Salt Lake City
									VERMONT
155.45	90.13	88.88	91.72	74.39	77.06	81.23	67.25	48.63	Burlington
153.64	89.08	87.85	90.65	73.53	76.16	80.28	66.47	48.07	Montpelier
									VIRGINIA
162.68	94.32	93.02	95.99	77.85	80.64	85.01	70.38	50.9	Alexandria
162.68	94.32	93.02	95.99	77.85	80.64	85.01	70.38	50.9	Arlington
162.68	94.32	93.02	95.99	77.85	80.64	85.01	70.38	50.9	Fairfax
151.83	88.03	86.81	89.59	72.66	75.26	79.34	65.69	47.5	Fredericksburg
146.41	84.89	83.71	86.39	70.07	72.58	76.5	63.34	45.81	Newport News
146.41	84.89	83.71	86.39	70.07	72.58	76.5	63.34	45.81	Portsmouth
151.83	88.03	86.81	89.59	72.66	75.26	79.34	65.69	47.5	Richmond
									WASHINGTON
189.79	110.04	108.52	111.98	90.83	94.08	99.17	82.11	59.38	Seattle
177.14	102.7	101.28	104.52	84.77	87.81	92.56	76.64	55.42	Spokane
186.17	107.94	106.45	109.85	89.1	92.29	97.28	80.55	58.25	Tacoma
									WEST VIRGINIA
168.1	97.46	96.12	99.18	80.45	83.33	87.84	72.73	52.59	Charleston
137.37	79.65	78.55	81.05	65.74	68.1	71.78	59.43	42.98	Martinsburg
169.91	98.51	97.15	100.25	81.31	84.22	88.78	73.51	53.16	Morgantown
									WISCONSIN
182.56	105.85	104.38	107.72	87.37	90.5	95.39	78.98	57.12	Milwaukee

Construction Costs by City (Con't)

Location	CCI	Apartment 1-3 Story	Church	College Classroom 2-3 Story	College Laboratory	Factory 1 Story	Fire Station 1 Story	Hospital 4-8 Story	Hotel 4-7 Story
Green Bay	0.97	101.90	115.09	109.85	116.25	69.84	103.60	119.99	100.06
Madison	0.98	102.95	116.28	110.99	117.45	70.56	104.66	121.23	101.09
WYOMING									
Casper	0.82	86.14	97.29	92.87	98.28	59.04	87.58	101.43	84.58
Cheyenne	0.81	85.09	96.11	91.73	97.08	58.32	86.51	100.20	83.55
Yellowstone Nat. Pk.	0.77	80.89	91.36	87.20	92.28	55.44	82.24	95.25	79.43
CANADA									
Calgary	0.96	100.85	113.90	108.72	115.06	69.12	102.53	118.75	99.02
Charlottetown	0.90	94.55	106.79	101.93	107.87	64.80	96.12	111.33	92.84
Edmonton	0.96	100.85	113.90	108.72	115.06	69.12	102.53	118.75	99.02
Halifax	0.95	99.80	112.72	107.59	113.86	68.40	101.46	117.52	97.99
Moncton	0.90	94.55	106.79	101.93	107.87	64.80	96.12	111.33	92.84
Montreal	1.01	106.10	119.84	114.38	121.05	72.72	107.87	124.94	104.18
Ottawa	1.07	112.40	126.96	121.18	128.24	77.04	114.28	132.36	110.37
Quebec	1.02	107.15	121.02	115.52	122.25	73.44	108.94	126.17	105.21
Regina	0.92	96.65	109.16	104.19	110.26	66.24	98.26	113.80	94.90
Saint John	0.94	98.75	111.53	106.46	112.66	67.68	100.39	116.28	96.96
Saskatoon	0.91	95.60	107.97	103.06	109.06	65.52	97.19	112.57	93.87
St. John's	0.93	97.70	110.34	105.32	111.46	66.96	99.32	115.04	95.93
Thunder Bay	1.03	108.20	122.21	116.65	123.45	74.16	110.00	127.41	106.24
Toronto	1.11	116.61	131.70	125.71	133.03	79.92	118.55	137.31	114.50
Vancouver	1.06	111.35	125.77	120.05	127.04	76.32	113.21	131.12	109.34
Victoria	1.05	110.30	124.58	118.91	125.84	75.60	112.14	129.89	108.31
Winnipeg	0.96	100.85	113.90	108.72	115.06	69.12	102.53	118.75	99.02

Jail	Library	Nursing Home	Office 2-4 Story	Post Office	School Elementary	School High, 2-3 Story	Store Retail	Warehouse	Location
175.33	101.66	100.25	103.45	83.91	86.91	91.62	75.85	54.85	Green Bay
177.14	102.7	101.28	104.52	84.77	87.81	92.56	76.64	55.42	Madison
									WYOMING
148.22	85.94	84.75	87.45	70.93	73.47	77.45	64.12	46.37	Casper
146.41	84.89	83.71	86.39	70.07	72.58	76.5	63.34	45.81	Cheyenne
139.18	80.7	79.58	82.12	66.61	68.99	72.73	60.21	43.54	Yellowstone Nat. Pk.
									CANADA
173.52	100.61	99.22	102.38	83.04	86.02	90.67	75.07	54.29	Calgary
162.68	94.32	93.02	95.99	77.85	80.64	85.01	70.38	50.9	Charlottetown
173.52	100.61	99.22	102.38	83.04	86.02	90.67	75.07	54.29	Edmonton
171.71	99.56	98.18	101.32	82.18	85.12	89.73	74.29	53.72	Halifax
162.68	94.32	93.02	95.99	77.85	80.64	85.01	70.38	50.9	Moncton
182.56	105.85	104.38	107.72	87.37	90.5	95.39	78.98	57.12	Montreal
193.4	112.14	110.58	114.12	92.56	95.87	101.06	83.67	60.51	Ottawa
184.37	106.9	105.42	108.78	88.23	91.39	96.34	79.76	57.68	Quebec
166.29	96.42	95.08	98.12	79.58	82.43	86.89	71.94	52.03	Regina
169.91	98.51	97.15	100.25	81.31	84.22	88.78	73.51	53.16	Saint John
164.48	95.37	94.05	97.05	78.72	81.54	85.95	71.16	51.46	Saskatoon
168.1	97.46	96.12	99.18	80.45	83.33	87.84	72.73	52.59	St. John's
186.17	107.94	106.45	109.85	89.1	92.29	97.28	80.55	58.25	Thunder Bay
200.63	116.33	114.72	118.38	96.02	99.46	104.84	86.8	62.77	Toronto
191.6	111.09	109.55	113.05	91.69	94.98	100.12	82.89	59.94	Vancouver
189.79	110.04	108.52	111.98	90.83	94.08	99.17	82.11	59.38	Victoria
173.52	100.61	99.22	102.38	83.04	86.02	90.67	75.07	54.29	Winnipeg

Source: R.S. Means

Expenditures to Owner-Occupied Residential Properties: 1993 to 1999
(millions of dollars)

Type of job	1993	1994	1995	1996	1997	1998	1999
Total	79,800	90,655	83,911	88,532	93,962	99,400	99,281
Additions	14,909	12,034	9,784	13,964	12,057	10,175	10,773
Decks and porches	1,890	1,651	2,466	2,411	2,911	1,704	2,407
Attached garages	2,332	1,937	2,227	1,441	472	1,775	544
Rooms	10,688	8,446	5,092	10,112	8,674	6,697	7,822
Alterations	20,209	24,343	20,022	23,386	26,566	29,868	33,678
Plumbing	892	671	919	790	1,587	667	1,297
HVAC	972	1,623	1,229	1,986	1,952	1,730	2,127
Electrical	537	812	495	737	556	487	628
Flooring	1,823	2,246	1,970	3,022	2,573	3,303	2,999
Kitchen remodeling	2,769	3,716	2,781	2,738	5,064	7,720	4,823
Bathroom remodeling	1,593	1,407	1,532	2,086	3,281	2,708	2,498
Kitchen and bathroom remodeling	641	1,606	600	898	171	953	180
Finishing space	1,122	723	1,172	1,224	1,216	1,066	1,284
Interior restructuring	1,456	3,651	2,363	3,778	3,639	4,428	3,151
Siding	994	1,270	369	1,398	1,164	692	1,328
Windows and doors	863	718	320	550	620	486	756
Other alterations	6,547	5,900	6,271	4,180	4,741	5,629	12,606
Outside Additions and Alteration	7,402	11,253	8,824	10,215	9,805	10,053	11,351
Detached buildings	587	2,197	1,492	1,912	3,235	2,843	1,464
Patios and terraces	529	790	495	1,006	1,357	687	794
Driveways and walkways	885	477	866	508	1,240	1,350	1,292
Fences	1,475	1,305	1,441	1,453	1,564	1,629	2,079
Other outside additions and alterations	3,925	6,483	4,530	5,336	2,409	3,544	5,723
Major Replacements	14,749	17,013	18,086	18,816	18,206	22,264	19,229
Plumbing	1,684	1,848	2,029	1,343	1,555	1,159	1,334
HVAC	3,684	2,978	5,307	3,807	4,603	4,140	3,120
Siding	1,190	1,083	1,110	1,971	1,105	1,599	1,972
Roofing	3,060	4,203	3,732	5,528	5,450	6,664	5,375
Driveways and walkways	774	893	435	468	551	1,170	990
Windows	1,871	2,537	2,436	3,167	2,959	4,117	3,291

Expenditures to Owner-Occupied Residential Properties: 1993 to 1999 (Con't)

Type of job	1993	1994	1995	1996	1997	1998	1999
Doors	975	1,180	846	1,009	1,008	1,097	1,188
Other major replacements	1,510	2,291	2,189	1,524	975	2,318	1,958
Maintenance and Repairs	22,531	26,012	27,194	22,150	27,328	27,040	24,250
Painting and papering	6,956	6,813	7,379	7,257	7,958	9,094	6,788
Plumbing	2,038	3,004	2,218	2,443	2,687	2,302	2,548
HVAC	1,710	1,719	1,614	2,092	1,411	1,897	1,400
Electrical	492	562	610	428	516	508	524
Siding	595	507	634	247	725	307	1,003
Roofing	2,755	2,487	2,999	1,710	2,735	2,361	2,650
Flooring	788	1,520	1,407	1,127	1,681	849	1,520
Windows and doors	357	872	740	528	875	820	537
Materials to have on hand	2,001	2,316	1,982	2,713	2,796	3,324	362
Other maintenance and repairs	4,838	6,209	7,610	3,606	5,943	5,578	6,918

Note: Components may not add to totals because of rounding.
N/A: Not applicable
1 The expenditures given for each specified type of job consist of those outlays which have been identified as being primarily of the specified type. Thus, expenditures for one type of job done incidental to another type are included under the latter classification. For example,
  the relatively minor cost of painting done in conjunction with a roofing job is included in the roofing category.

Source U.S. Census Bureau

Homeownership Rates (percentage)

	1900	1910	1920	1930	1940
U.S. Total	**46.50**	**45.90**	**45.60**	**47.80**	**43.60**
Alabama	34.40	35.10	35.00	34.20	33.60
Alaska	(N/A)	(N/A)	(N/A)	(N/A)	(N/A)
Arizona	57.50	49.20	42.80	44.80	47.90
Arkansas	47.70	46.60	45.10	40.10	39.70
California	46.30	49.50	43.70	46.10	43.40
Colorado	46.60	51.50	51.60	50.70	46.30
Connecticut	39.00	37.30	37.60	44.50	40.50
Delaware	36.30	40.70	44.70	52.10	47.10
District of Columbia	24.00	25.20	30.30	38.60	29.90
Florida	46.80	44.20	42.50	42.00	43.60
Georgia	30.60	30.50	30.90	30.60	30.80
Hawaii	(N/A)	(N/A)	(N/A)	(N/A)	(N/A)
Idaho	71.60	68.10	60.90	57.00	57.90
Illinois	45.00	44.10	43.80	46.50	40.30
Indiana	56.10	54.80	54.80	57.30	53.10
Iowa	60.50	58.40	58.10	54.70	51.50
Kansas	58.10	59.10	56.90	56.00	51.00
Kentucky	51.50	51.60	51.60	51.30	48.00
Louisiana	31.40	32.20	33.70	35.00	36.90
Maine	64.80	62.50	59.60	61.70	57.30
Maryland	40.00	44.00	49.90	55.20	47.40
Massachusetts	35.00	33.10	34.80	43.50	38.10
Michigan	62.30	61.70	58.90	59.00	55.40
Minnesota	63.50	61.90	60.70	58.90	55.20
Mississippi	34.50	34.00	34.00	32.50	33.30
Missouri	50.90	51.10	49.50	49.90	44.30
Montana	56.60	60.00	60.50	54.50	52.00
Nebraska	56.80	59.10	57.40	54.30	47.10
Nevada	66.20	53.40	47.60	47.10	46.10
New Hampshire	59.30	51.20	49.80	55.00	51.70
New Jersey	34.30	35.00	38.30	48.40	39.40
New Mexico	68.50	70.60	59.40	57.40	57.30
New York	33.20	31.00	30.70	37.10	30.30
North Carolina	46.60	47.30	47.40	44.50	42.40
North Dakota	80.00	75.70	65.30	58.60	49.80

1950	1960	1970	1980	1990	
55.00	61.90	62.90	64.40	64.20	U.S. Total
49.40	59.70	66.70	70.10	70.50	Alabama
54.50	48.30	50.30	58.30	56.10	Alaska
56.40	63.90	65.30	68.30	64.20	Arizona
54.50	61.40	66.70	70.50	69.60	Arkansas
54.50	61.40	54.90	55.90	55.60	California
58.10	63.80	63.40	64.50	62.20	Colorado
51.10	61.90	62.50	63.90	65.60	Connecticut
58.90	66.90	68.00	69.10	70.20	Delaware
32.30	30.00	28.20	35.50	38.90	District of Columbia
57.60	67.50	68.60	68.30	67.20	Florida
46.50	56.20	61.10	65.00	64.90	Georgia
33.00	41.10	46.90	51.70	53.90	Hawaii
65.50	70.50	70.10	72.00	70.10	Idaho
50.10	57.80	59.40	62.60	64.20	Illinois
65.50	71.10	71.70	71.70	70.20	Indiana
63.40	69.10	71.70	71.80	70.00	Iowa
63.90	68.90	69.10	70.20	67.90	Kansas
58.70	64.30	66.90	70.00	69.60	Kentucky
50.30	59.00	63.10	65.50	65.90	Louisiana
62.80	66.50	70.10	70.90	70.50	Maine
56.30	64.50	58.80	62.00	65.00	Maryland
47.90	55.90	57.50	57.50	59.30	Massachusetts
67.50	74.40	74.40	72.70	71.00	Michigan
66.40	72.10	71.50	71.70	71.80	Minnesota
47.80	57.70	66.30	71.00	71.50	Mississippi
57.70	64.30	67.20	69.90	68.80	Missouri
60.30	64.00	65.70	68.60	67.30	Montana
60.60	64.80	66.40	68.40	66.50	Nebraska
48.70	56.30	58.50	59.60	54.80	Nevada
58.10	65.10	68.20	67.60	68.20	New Hampshire
53.10	61.30	60.90	62.00	64.90	New Jersey
58.80	65.30	66.40	68.10	67.40	New Mexico
37.90	44.80	47.30	48.60	52.20	New York
53.30	60.10	65.40	68.40	68.00	North Carolina
66.20	68.40	68.40	68.70	65.60	North Dakota

Homeownership Rates (Con't)

	1900	1910	1920	1930	1940
Ohio	52.50	51.30	51.60	54.40	50.00
Oklahoma	54.20	45.40	45.50	41.30	42.80
Oregon	58.70	60.10	54.80	59.10	55.40
Pennsylvania	41.20	41.60	45.20	54.40	45.90
Rhode Island	28.60	28.30	31.10	41.20	37.40
South Carolina	30.60	30.80	32.20	30.90	30.60
South Dakota	71.20	68.20	61.50	53.10	45.00
Tennessee	46.30	47.00	47.70	46.20	44.10
Texas	46.50	45.10	42.80	41.70	42.80
Utah	67.80	64.80	60.00	60.90	61.10
Vermont	60.40	58.50	57.50	59.80	55.90
Virginia	48.80	51.50	51.10	52.40	48.90
Washington	54.50	57.30	54.70	59.40	57.00
West Virginia	54.60	49.50	46.80	45.90	43.70
Wisconsin	66.40	64.60	63.60	63.20	54.40
Wyoming	55.20	54.50	51.90	48.30	48.60

Note: Alaska and Hawaii are NOT included in the 1950 US total.

Source: U.S. Census Bureau

1950	1960	1970	1980	1990	
61.10	67.40	67.70	68.40	67.50	Ohio
60.00	67.00	69.20	70.70	68.10	Oklahoma
65.30	69.30	66.10	65.10	63.10	Oregon
59.70	68.30	68.80	69.90	70.60	Pennsylvania
45.30	54.50	57.90	58.80	59.50	Rhode Island
45.10	57.30	66.10	70.20	69.80	South Carolina
62.20	67.20	69.60	69.30	66.10	South Dakota
56.50	63.70	66.70	68.60	68.00	Tennessee
56.70	64.80	64.70	64.30	60.90	Texas
65.30	71.70	69.30	70.70	68.10	Utah
61.30	66.00	69.10	68.70	69.00	Vermont
55.10	61.30	62.00	65.60	66.30	Virginia
65.00	68.50	66.80	65.60	62.60	Washington
55.00	64.30	68.90	73.90	74.10	West Virginia
63.50	68.60	69.10	68.20	66.70	Wisconsin
54.00	62.20	66.40	69.20	67.80	Wyoming

Housing Characteristics: 1997 (percentage)

Housing Unit Characteristics	Total	Census Region			
		Northeast	Midwest	South	West
Total	100.0	100.0	100.0	100.0	100.0
Census Region and Division					
Northeast	19.4	100.0	-	-	-
New England	5.2	26.9	-	-	-
Middle Atlantic	14.2	73.1	-	-	-
Midwest	23.7	-	100.0	-	-
East North Central	16.7	-	70.3	-	-
West North Central	7.0	-	29.7	-	-
South	35.4	-	-	100.0	-
South Atlantic	18.4	-	-	52.1	-
East South Central	6.3	-	-	17.7	-
West South Central	10.7	-	-	30.2	-
West	21.5	-	-	-	100.0
Mountain	6.1	-	-	-	28.3
Pacific	15.4	-	-	-	71.7
Urban Status					
Urban	77.5	82.5	73.9	70.6	88.4
Central City	36.2	30.3	36.2	34.0	45.5
Suburban	41.2	52.2	37.7	36.6	42.9
Rural	22.5	17.5	26.1	29.4	11.6
Estimated Floorspace [1] (in square feet)					
Fewer than 600	7.8	9.7	6.9	5.7	10.3
600 to 900	21.2	22.4	21.3	19.0	23.4
1000 to 1,599	29.9	25.8	28.8	32.8	30.0
1,600 to 1,999	15.1	12.2	17.5	15.8	13.7
2,000 to 2,399	7.8	6.9	7.6	8.3	7.9
2,400 to 2,999	5.3	4.9	5.8	5.0	5.3
3,000 or more	4.1	3.4	4.1	5.1	3.0
No estimate provided	9.0	14.8	7.9	8.2	6.3

Housing Characteristics: 1997 (Con't)

Housing Unit Characteristics	Total	Census Region			
		Northeast	Midwest	South	West
Ownership of Unit					
Owned	67.4	64.6	71.8	70.7	59.8
Rented	32.6	35.4	28.2	29.3	40.2
Type and Ownership of Housing Unit					
Single-Family Detached	62.8	54.0	69.1	66.6	57.7
Owned	54.8	49.9	61.7	57.6	46.9
Rented	8.0	4.1	7.4	9.0	10.7
Single-Family Attached	9.8	15.6	7.6	7.7	10.6
Owned	5.4	9.7	3.9	4.8	4.2
Rented	4.4	5.9	3.7	2.8	6.4
Multifamily (2 to 4 units)	5.5	8.6	7.1	3.9	3.7
Owned	0.9	1.7	1.7	Q	Q
Rented	4.6	6.9	5.4	3.6	3.5
Multifamily (5 or more units)	15.6	19.3	11.7	13.4	20.1
Owned	1.1	1.5	Q	1.0	1.7
Rented	14.4	17.8	11.1	12.4	18.3
Mobile Home	6.2	2.5	4.6	8.3	8.0
Owned	5.2	1.8	4.0	6.9	6.7
Rented	1.0	Q	0.5	1.5	1.3
Year of Construction					
1939 or before	18.4	32.2	30.0	8.6	9.5
1940 to 1949	9.1	9.8	8.7	7.9	10.7
1950 to 1959	12.4	13.7	11.3	11.7	13.4
1960 to 1969	14.3	13.2	13.2	14.2	16.5
1970 to 1979	19.3	13.4	16.7	21.8	23.4
1980 to 1989	17.1	11.9	12.0	22.8	17.8
1990 to 1997 [2]	9.6	5.9	8.2	12.9	8.8
Observed Location of Household					
City	47.5	34.8	47.3	45.8	62.1
Town	17.9	26.2	18.8	14.8	14.8

Housing Characteristics: 1997 (Con't)

Housing Unit Characteristics	Total	Census Region			
		Northeast	Midwest	South	West
Suburbs	18.3	21.8	18.7	19.3	13.1
Rural or Open Country	16.2	17.2	15.1	20.1	10.0
Total Number of Rooms (Excluding Bathrooms)					
1 or 2	3.0	3.2	2.3	1.7	5.8
3	9.0	11.3	6.2	7.9	12.0
4	18.0	18.1	17.8	16.2	21.2
5	20.9	17.3	20.1	24.2	19.9
6	19.7	19.8	20.1	20.7	17.8
7	14.0	14.1	15.0	15.0	11.3
8	8.2	8.7	10.7	7.6	6.2
9 or more	6.9	7.4	7.8	6.8	5.8
Bedrooms					
None or 1	13.0	16.6	11.4	9.7	16.9
2	28.4	28.2	27.7	27.4	30.9
3	40.3	36.1	40.6	46.1	34.5
4 or More	18.3	19.1	20.4	16.8	17.7
Other Rooms (Excluding Bathrooms)					
None or 1	5.0	5.0	3.1	3.6	9.3
2	38.1	35.4	34.8	38.1	43.9
3	30.5	31.8	30.5	31.3	28.2
4	17.3	18.5	20.1	18.2	11.7
5 or More	9.1	9.3	11.5	8.1	6.9
Full Bathrooms					
None or 1	58.5	71.9	64.5	50.6	52.8
2	35.4	25.4	30.2	42.4	38.9
3 or More	6.1	2.7	5.4	7.0	8.3
Half Bathrooms					
None	72.0	66.4	68.7	74.0	77.2
1	26.1	30.9	28.9	24.5	21.5
2 or More	Q	Q	Q	Q	Q

Housing Characteristics: 1997 (Con't)

Housing Unit Characteristics	Total	Census Region			
		Northeast	Midwest	South	West
Number of Stories					
Single-Family Homes	72.7	69.7	76.7	74.3	68.2
1 Story	40.5	19.3	33.7	53.0	46.5
2 Stories	26.5	42.8	34.6	17.4	18.1
3 Stories	3.2	5.7	3.6	2.3	1.9
Split-Level	2.4	1.6	4.7	1.6	1.7
Other	Q	Q	Q	Q	Q
Mobile Homes	6.2	2.5	4.6	8.3	8.0
Foundation/Basement of Single-Family Homes (More than one may apply)					
Basement	32.7	57.1	58.6	13.7	13.3
Crawlspace	22.2	7.2	16.1	30.1	29.3
Concrete Slab	22.6	9.8	9.5	34.2	29.7
Not Asked (Mobile Homes and Multi-Family Units)	27.3	30.3	23.3	25.7	31.8
Garage/Carport					
Yes	53.7	47.4	62.1	48.3	58.9
1-Car Garage	16.0	22.9	17.3	13.0	13.3
2-Car Garage	29.2	21.5	38.0	24.2	34.7
3-Car Garage	2.7	1.9	4.6	1.2	3.8
Covered Carport	6.3	1.4	2.3	10.9	7.8
No	25.2	24.7	19.1	34.3	17.3
Not Asked (Apartments)	21.1	27.9	18.8	17.4	23.8
Main Heating Fuel					
Natural Gas	52.4	46.7	73.4	38.4	57.5
Electricity	29.6	12.2	12.4	48.7	33.0
Fuel Oil	9.2	35.0	4.3	3.2	1.0
LPG	4.4	1.2	7.1	5.5	2.6
Wood	2.2	2.2	1.9	1.9	3.1
Kerosene	0.9	1.9	Q	1.2	Q
Solar	Q	Q	Q	Q	Q
Other/None	0.3	0.7	Q	Q	Q

1   Estimated based on heated floorspace area.
2   Does not include all new construction for 1997.
Q: Data withheld either because the Relative Standard Error (RSE) was greater than 50 percent or fewer than 10 households were sampled.

Source: Energy Information Administration, Office of Energy Markets and End Use, 1997 Residential Energy Consumption Survey

Housing Density: 1940 to 1990

	Total Housing Units	Total Land Area (in square miles)	Housing Density (per square mile)	Total Population	Population Density (per square mile)
1990	102,263,678	3,536,338	28.9	248,709,873	70.3
1980	88,410,627	3,539,289	25.0	226,542,199	64.0
1970	68,704,315	3,536,855	19.4	203,302,031	57.5
1960	58,326,357	3,540,911	16.5	179,323,175	50.6
1950	46,137,076	3,550,206	13.0	151,325,798	42.6
1940	37,438,714	3,554,608	10.5	132,164,569	37.2

Source: US Census Bureau

Number of Licensed Landscape Architects by State

The number of licensed landscape architects in a state is comprised of both the number of resident landscape architects and reciprocal, or non-resident, registrants. Based on current population levels, the chart below also provides the number per capita number of resident landscape architects in each state. Note that some states do not maintain a breakdown between resident and non-resident registrants.

State	Resident Land. Arch.	Reciprocal Land. Arch.	Total	Population [1]	Per capita # of Resident L.A. (per 100,000)
Alabama	104	97	201	4,447,100	2.3
Alaska	12	0	12	626,932	1.9
Arizona	253	364	617	5,130,632	4.9
Arkansas	N/A	N/A	138	2,673,400	N/A
California	2,665	314	2,979	33,871,648	7.9
Connecticut	196	202	398	3,405,565	5.8
Delaware	42	50	92	783,600	5.4
Florida	722	184	906	15,982,378	4.5
Georgia	N/A	N/A	4,882	8,186,453	N/A
Hawaii	93	40	133	1,211,537	7.7
Idaho	82	78	160	1,293,953	6.3
Illinois	603	134	737	12,419,293	4.9
Indiana	247	108	355	6,080,485	4.1
Iowa	116	70	186	2,926,324	4
Kansas	143	268	411	2,688,418	5.3
Kentucky	132	102	234	4,041,769	3.3
Louisiana	190	151	341	4,468,976	4.3
Maine	55	68	123	1,274,923	4.3
Maryland	N/A	N/A	625	5,296,486	N/A
Massachusetts	N/A	N/A	783	6,349,097	N/A
Michigan	357	154	511	9,938,444	3.6
Minnesota	251	92	343	4,919,479	5.1
Mississippi	88	83	171	2,844,658	3.1
Missouri	118	92	210	5,595,211	2.1
Montana	33	41	74	902,195	3.7
Nebraska	42	34	76	1,711,263	2.5

Number of Licensed Landscape Architects by State (Con't)

State	Resident Land. Arch.	Reciprocal Land. Arch.	Total	Population [1]	Per capita # of Resident L.A. (per 100,000)
Nevada	62	172	234	1,998,257	3.1
New Jersey	323	153	476	8,414,350	3.8
New Mexico	101	63	164	1,819,046	5.6
New York	571	267	838	18,976,457	3
North Carolina	349	142	491	8,049,313	4.3
Ohio	370	188	558	11,353,140	3.3
Oklahoma	250	0	250	3,450,654	7.2
Oregon	726	110	836	3,421,399	21.2
Pennsylvania	74	0	74	12,281,054	0.6
Rhode Island	159	132	291	1,048,319	15.2
South Carolina	8	278	286	4,012,012	0.2
South Dakota	143	10	153	754,844	18.9
Tennessee	879	121	1,000	5,689,283	15.5
Texas	N/A	N/A	304	20,851,820	N/A
Utah	N/A	N/A	280	2,233,169	N/A
Virginia	N/A	N/A	515	7,078,515	N/A
Washington	385	91	476	5,894,121	6.5
West Virginia	46	12	58	1,808,344	2.5
Wisconsin	310	101	411	5,363,675	5.8
Wyoming	18	54	72	493,782	3.6
Totals	**11,318**	**4,620**	**23,465**	**274,061,773**	

[1] 2000 Population Estimate from the U.S. Census Bureau

Note: Colorado, Washington, D.C., New Hampshire, North Dakota, and Vermont currently do not have a Landscape Architecture licensure program.

Source: Council of Landscape Architectural Registration Boards

Number of New Privately Owned Housing Units Completed
(in thousands of units)

Period	Total	In structures with-			
		I unit	2 units	3 and 4 units	5 units or more
1989	1,422.8	1,026.3	24.1	34.6	337.9
1990	1,308.0	966.0	16.5	28.2	297.3
1991	1,090.8	837.6	16.9	19.7	216.6
1992	1,157.5	963.6	15.1	20.8	158.0
1993	1,192.7	1,039.4	9.5	16.7	127.1
1994	1,346.9	1,160.3	12.1	19.5	154.9
1995	1,312.6	1,065.5	14.8	19.8	212.4
1996	1,412.9	1,128.5	13.6	19.5	251.3
1997	1,400.5	1,116.4	13.6	23.4	247.1
1998	1,474.2	1,159.7	16.2	24.4	273.9
1999	1,636.1	1,307.2	12.0	25.2	291.8
2000	1,609.0	1,282.8	11.0	15.3	300.0

Note: Detail may not add to total because of rounding.
N/A: Not available.
I Metropolitan statistical areas.

Source: U.S. Census Bureau

Period	Inside MSAS [1]	Outside MSAS [1]	Northeast	Midwest	South	West
1989	1,181.2	241.7	218.8	267.1	549.4	387.5
1990	1,060.2	247.7	157.7	263.3	510.7	376.3
1991	862.1	228.7	120.1	240.4	438.9	291.3
1992	909.5	248.0	136.4	268.4	462.4	290.3
1993	943.0	249.8	117.6	273.3	512.0	290.0
1994	1,086.3	260.6	123.4	307.1	580.9	335.5
1995	1,065.0	247.6	126.9	287.9	581.1	316.7
1996	1,163.4	249.4	125.1	304.5	637.1	346.2
1997	1,152.8	247.7	134.0	295.9	634.1	336.4
1998	1,228.5	245.7	137.3	305.1	671.6	360.2
1999	1,378.1	258.0	145.4	337.5	750.4	402.7
2000	1,363.3	245.7	148.1	341.3	749.6	370.0

Number of Registered Architects by State

Registered architects in each state can be divided into two categories: resident and reciprocal, or non-resident, registrants. Based on current population levels, the chart below also calculates the number of resident architects per 100,000 of population in each state.

State	Resident Architects	Reciprocal Registrations	Total	Population1	Per capita # of Resident Architects (per 100,000)
Alabama	718	979	1,697	4,447,100	16
Alaska	300	204	504	626,932	48
Arizona	1,975	3,300	5,275	5,130,632	38
Arkansas	484	778	1,262	2,673,400	18
California	16,415	4,476	20,891	33,871,648	48
Colorado	2,603	3,135	5,738	4,301,261	61
Connecticut	1,391	7,879	9,270	3,405,565	41
Delaware	120	1,009	1,129	783,600	15
D.C.	546	2,632	3,178	572,059	95
Florida	4,477	3,526	8,003	15,982,378	28
Georgia	2,232	2,665	4,897	8,186,453	27
Hawaii	977	814	1,791	1,211,537	81
Idaho	490	1,312	1,802	1,293,953	38
Illinois	5,475	3,686	9,161	12,419,293	44
Indiana	1,095	3,248	4,343	6,080,485	18
Iowa	419	1,018	1,437	2,926,324	14
Kansas	980	1,496	2,476	2,688,418	36
Kentucky	701	1,757	2,458	4,041,769	17
Louisiana	1,123	1,509	2,632	4,468,976	25
Maine	327	796	1,123	1,274,923	26
Maryland	1,658	2,826	4,484	5,296,486	31
Massachusetts	3,290	2,698	5,988	6,349,097	52
Michigan	2,472	2,378	4,850	9,938,444	25
Minnesota	1,762	1,445	3,207	4,919,479	36
Mississippi	271	973	1,244	2,844,658	10
Missouri	1,854	2,374	4,228	5,595,211	33
Montana	349	655	1,004	902,195	39
Nebraska	546	944	1,490	1,711,263	32

States with the Most Registered Architects

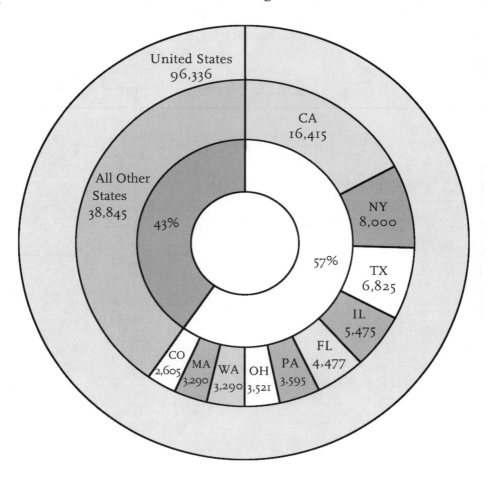

United States
96,336

CA
16,415

All Other
States
38,845

43%

NY
8,000

TX
6,825

IL
5,475

57%

FL
4,477

CO
2,605

MA
3,290

WA
3,290

OH
3,521

PA
3,595

Source: Counsel House Research

Sixty percent of all registered architects are located in only ten states.

Number of Registered Architects by State (Con't)

State	Resident Architects	Reciprocal Registrations	Total	Population[1]	Per capita # of Resident Architects (per 100,000)
Nevada	446	1,928	2,374	1,998,257	22
New Hampshire	252	764	1,016	1,235,786	20
New Jersey	2,400	4,600	7,000	8,414,350	29
New Mexico	725	1,291	2,016	1,819,046	40
New York	8,000	5,000	13,000	18,976,457	42
North Carolina	1,860	2,626	4,486	8,049,313	23
North Dakota	125	375	500	642,200	19
Ohio	3,521	2,881	6,402	11,353,140	31
Oklahoma	749	1,240	1,989	3,450,654	22
Oregon	1,399	1,150	2,549	3,421,399	41
Pennsylvania	3,595	3,536	7,131	12,281,054	29
Rhode Island	257	1,011	1,268	1,048,319	25
South Carolina	950	2,038	2,988	4,012,012	24
South Dakota	111	559	670	754,844	15
Tennessee	1,600	1,590	3,190	5,689,283	28
Texas	6,825	3,187	10,012	20,851,820	33
Utah	837	800	1,637	2,233,169	37
Vermont	294	524	818	608,827	48
Virginia	2,306	3,121	5,427	7,078,515	33
Washington	3,290	1,627	4,917	5,894,121	56
West Virginia	130	920	1,050	1,808,344	7
Wisconsin	1,502	2,815	4,317	5,363,675	28
Wyoming	112	724	836	493,782	23
Totals	**96,336**	**104,819**	**201,155**	**281,421,906**	**34**

[1] 2000 Population Estimate from the U.S. Census Bureau

Source: National Council of Architectural Registration Boards

No. Architects in Each State
(Per 100,000)

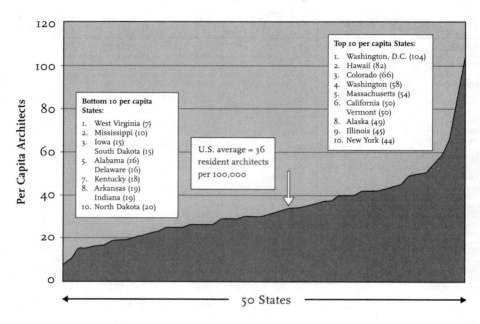

Per Capita Architects

120
100
80
60
40
20
0

Top 10 per capita States:
1. Washington, D.C. (104)
2. Hawaii (82)
3. Colorado (66)
4. Washington (58)
5. Massachusetts (54)
6. California (50)
   Vermont (50)
8. Alaska (49)
9. Illinois (45)
10. New York (44)

Bottom 10 per capita States:
1. West Virginia (7)
2. Mississippi (10)
3. Iowa (15)
   South Dakota (15)
5. Alabama (16)
   Delaware (16)
7. Kentucky (18)
8. Arkansas (19)
   Indiana (19)
10. North Dakota (20)

U.S. average = 36 resident architects per 100,000

50 States

Resident v. Reciprocal (Non-resident) Architects

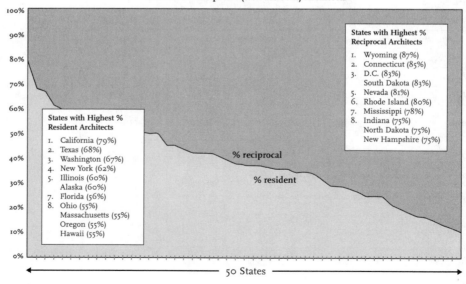

100%
90%
80%
70%
60%
50%
40%
30%
20%
10%
0%

States with Highest % Reciprocal Architects
1. Wyoming (87%)
2. Connecticut (85%)
3. D.C. (83%)
   South Dakota (83%)
5. Nevada (81%)
6. Rhode Island (80%)
7. Mississippi (78%)
8. Indiana (75%)
   North Dakota (75%)
   New Hampshire (75%)

States with Highest % Resident Architects
1. California (79%)
2. Texas (68%)
3. Washington (67%)
4. New York (62%)
5. Illinois (60%)
   Alaska (60%)
7. Florida (56%)
8. Ohio (55%)
   Massachusetts (55%)
   Oregon (55%)
   Hawaii (55%)

% reciprocal

% resident

50 States

Source: Counsel House Research

Office Building Vacancy Rates: 1980 to 1999

	1980	1985	1990	1991	1992	1993
Total [1]	4.6	16.9	20.0	20.2	20.5	19.4
Atlanta, GA	10.0	21.0	19.1	19.5	19.4	16.8
Baltimore, MD	7.2	11.5	20.0	21.0	20.6	17.3
Boston, MA	3.8	13.1	19.6	19.1	17.5	17.7
Charlotte, NC	(N/A)	16.7	16.5	19.4	(N/A)	(N/A)
Chicago, IL	7.0	16.5	18.6	20.0	22.1	21.4
Cincinnati, OH	(N/A)	(N/A)	(N/A)	(N/A)	19.4	(N/A)
Colorado Springs, CI	(N/A)	(N/A)	(N/A)	(N/A)	(N/A)	(N/A)
Dallas, TX	8.6	23.0	25.8	26.0	31.3	29.5
Denver, CO	6.6	24.7	24.8	23.0	21.5	15.9
Detroit, MI	(N/A)	(N/A)	(N/A)	(N/A)	(N/A)	21.4
Emmonton, CN	(N/A)	(N/A)	(N/A)	(N/A)	(N/A)	(N/A)
Fort Lauderdale, FL	(N/A)	(N/A)	23.0	24.9	22.9	(N/A)
Houston, TX	4.0	27.6	24.9	27.3	27.0	25.1
Indianapolis, IN	(N/A)	(N/A)	21.2	21.4	22.4	18.8
Los Angeles, CA	0.9	15.3	16.8	20.2	21.2	21.0
Memphis, TN	(N/A)	(N/A)	(N/A)	(N/A)	(N/A)	(N/A)
Miami, FL	2.4	20.9	23.4	22.6	18.5	19.0
Milwaukee, WI	(N/A)	(N/A)	22.9	(N/A)	18.4	21.0
Minneapolis, MN	(N/A)	(N/A)	(N/A)	18.9	19.9	(N/A)
Montreal, CN	(N/A)	(N/A)	(N/A)	(N/A)	(N/A)	(N/A)
Nashville, TN	(N/A)	(N/A)	25.1	18.4	(N/A)	(N/A)
New Jersey (Central)	(N/A)	(N/A)	(N/A)	(N/A)	(N/A)	(N/A)
New Jersey (North)	(N/A)	(N/A)	(N/A)	(N/A)	(N/A)	(N/A)
New York, NY [2]	3.1	7.9	16.0	18.8	18.3	17.9
Orlando, FL	(N/A)	(N/A)	(N/A)	(N/A)	(N/A)	(N/A)
Ottawa, CN	(N/A)	(N/A)	(N/A)	(N/A)	(N/A)	(N/A)
Philadelphia, PA	6.3	14.5	18.2	17.3	19.0	17.8
Phoenix, AZ	(N/A)	(N/A)	27.6	24.8	24.4	(N/A)
Pittsburgh, PA	1.2	(N/A)	16.3	14.2	(N/A)	17.0
Portland, OR	(N/A)	(N/A)	(N/A)	(N/A)	14.5	(N/A)

1994	1995	1996	1997	1998	1999	
16.2	14.3	12.4	10.4	9.7		Total[1]
13.0	10.4	9.2	10.5	11.2	11.8	Atlanta, GA
15.5	17.0	14.3	11.6	10.0	(N/A)	Baltimore, MD
13.3	10.4	6.2	4.4	7.1	(N/A)	Boston, MA
10.0	8.9	8.2	7.1	7.2	9.5	Charlotte, NC
18.7	15.5	15.5	(N/A)	14.4	14.6	Chicago, IL
15.3	(N/A)	13.1	11.5	9.9	9.9	Cincinnati, OH
(N/A)	(N/A)	(N/A)	(N/A)	8.1	7.9	Colorado Springs, CI
21.7	18.7	16.2	14.7	15.0	18.5	Dallas, TX
12.8	12.1	10.8	9.3	7.6	8.2	Denver, CO
19.7	16.9	11.1	8.5	6.9	(N/A)	Detroit, MI
(N/A)	(N/A)	(N/A)	(N/A)	(N/A)	12.0	Emmonton, CN
10.8	(N/A)	10.5	10.4	10.0	(N/A)	Fort Lauderdale, FL
24.7	21.9	17.5	12.1	10.7	12.7	Houston, TX
18.4	14.3	(N/A)	14.2	11.2	10.8	Indianapolis, IN
19.6	23.2	22.1	13.8	14.2	11.5	Los Angeles, CA
(N/A)	(N/A)	13.6	12.0	12.5	11.2	Memphis, TN
15.4	13.8	12.4	11.2	11.4	10.7	Miami, FL
17.6	16.3	(N/A)	(N/A)	(N/A)	16.9	Milwaukee, WI
8.2	(N/A)	6.5	6.2	7.0	7.6	Minneapolis, MN
21.3	(N/A)	20.5	19.1	17.5	14.4	Montreal, CN
7.5	(N/A)	6.9	6.0	7.5	9.7	Nashville, TN
20.7	(N/A)	16.0	11.2	9.9	10.1	New Jersey (Central)
16.5	(N/A)	14.5	11.9	10.0	9.6	New Jersey (North)
16.3	17.0	16.0	(N/A)	8.6	7.3	New York, NY [2]
12.1	(N/A)	6.5	6.4	7.1	9.5	Orlando, FL
14.5	(N/A)	14.6	10.6	8.0	8.2	Ottawa, CN
16.3	16.2	13.7	10.9	12.4	11.1	Philadelphia, PA
11.8	(N/A)	11.5	9.3	8.9	13.4	Phoenix, AZ
15.8	14.5	(N/A)	15.4	14.0	13	Pittsburgh, PA
9.4	(N/A)	5.8	5.6	(N/A)	(N/A)	Portland, OR

Office Building Vacancy Rates: 1980 to 1999 (Con't)

	1980	1985	1990	1991	1992	1993
Raleigh, NC	(N/A)	(N/A)	(N/A)	(N/A)	(N/A)	(N/A)
Richmond, VA	(N/A)	(N/A)	(N/A)	(N/A)	(N/A)	(N/A)
Sacramento, CA	(N/A)	(N/A)	(N/A)	(N/A)	(N/A)	(N/A)
San Diego, CA	(N/A)	24.7	19.5	23.7	23.8	22.1
San Francisco, CA	0.3	13.7	14.7	13.3	12.5	13 7
Seattle, WA	(N/A)	(N/A)	12.3	12.8	15.9	17.6
Silicon Valley, CA	(N/A)	(N/A)	(N/A)	(N/A)	(N/A)	(N/A)
St. Louis, MO	(N/A)	(N/A)	21.0	20.5	21.8	19.1
St Paul, MN	(N/A)	(N/A)	(N/A)	19.7	18.5	(N/A)
Tampa/St. Petersburg, FL	(N/A)	(N/A)	(N/A)	(N/A)	(N/A)	(N/A)
Toronto, CN	(N/A)	(N/A)	(N/A)	(N/A)	(N/A)	(N/A)
Vancouver, CN	(N/A)	(N/A)	(N/A)	(N/A)	(N/A)	(N/A)
Washington, DC	2.5	9.0	19.0	17.6	15.4	14.1
West Palm Beach, CA	(N/A)	(N/A)	(N/A)	(N/A)	(N/A)	(N/A)
Wilmington, DE	(N/A)	(N/A)	20.3	21.0	19.8	(N/A)
Winston-Salem/Greensboro, NC	(N/A)	(N/A)	(N/A)	(N/A)	(N/A)	(N/A)

[1] Includes other North American markets not shown separately. In 1998, 45 markets were covered.

Source: ONCOR International, Houston, TX, 1980 and 1985, National Office Market Report, semi-annual; 1989-1990, International Office Market

1994	1995	1996	1997	1998	1999	
(N/A)	(N/A)	(N/A)	(N/A)	6.0	8	Raleigh, NC
11.9	(N/A)	9.7	9.7	10.7	9.3	Richmond, VA
14.1	(N/A)	12.4	12.3	11.8	12.4	Sacramento, CA
18.8	17.4	14.1	10.1	9.1	10.1	San Diego, CA
11.7	10.2	5.4	4.0	(N/A)	(N/A)	San Francisco, CA
14.7	7.1	5.3	4.5	(N/A)	(N/A)	Seattle, WA
12.7	(N/A)	8.7	5.8	8.3	(N/A)	Silicon Valley, CA
18.1	12.7	13.4	12.3	9.6	11.2	St. Louis, MO
15.2	(N/A)	12.5	9.9	7.2	9.2	St Paul, MN
(N/A)	(N/A)	13.0	9.1	8.8	10.0	Tampa/St. Petersburg, FL
19.9	(N/A)	19.4	13.2	11.9	11.0	Toronto, CN
8.2	(N/A)	7.6	7.0	6.7	7.6	Vancouver, CN
13.4	10.8	9.3	8.0	5.8	(N/A)	Washington, DC
16.8	(N/A)	12.0	12.3	13.5	13.0	West Palm Beach, CA
16.7	(N/A)	9.5	9.7	8.7	(N/A)	Wilmington, DE
13.2	(N/A)	14.1	12.3	14.5	15.7	Winston-Salem/Greensboro, NC

Value of Construction Put in Place: 1995-2000

Type of construction	Constant (1996) dollars (in millions)					
	1995	1996	1997	1998	1999	2,000
Total construction	567,900	613,454	635,765	670,859	692,477	704,346
Private construction	434,450	474,307	486,273	520,613	535,625	544,382
Residential buildings	251,937	281,229	280,748	297,886	315,757	312,703
New housing units	174,585	191,212	192,386	212,068	225,896	226,416
1 unit	156,363	170,865	170,154	188,785	201,210	202,167
2 units or more	18,222	20,347	22,232	23,283	24,686	24,248
Improvements	77,352	90,018	88,362	85,818	89,860	(NA)
Nonresidential buildings	139,711	153,866	166,754	177,639	175,048	187,045
Industrial	34,814	36,215	35,411	37,715	31,214	34,912
Office	26,218	27,875	33,058	39,333	41,643	46,287
Hotels, motels	7,274	10,909	12,438	13,794	14,262	14,007
Other commercial	43,636	48,170	49,948	49,915	51,067	52,519
Religious	4,426	4,531	5,565	6,139	6,701	6,839
Educational	5,621	6,737	8,375	9,039	8,743	10,191
Hospital and institutional	11,512	11,778	13,066	12,853	12,183	13,306
Miscellaneous [1]	6,209	7,650	8,892	8,850	9,235	8,985
Farm nonresidential	3,084	3,657	3,675	3,989	3,977	(NA)
Public utilities	36,740	33,124	32,884	38,616	38,166	(NA)
Telecommunications	11,556	11,791	12,159	13,036	15,142	(NA)
Other public utilities	25,184	21,333	20,725	25,581	23,024	(NA)
Railroads	3,609	4,391	4,745	5,463	4,540	(NA)
Electric light and power	14,310	11,209	11,122	11,885	13,393	(NA)
Gas	6,329	4,720	3,911	7,020	3,690	(NA)
Petroleum pipelines	936	1,013	947	1,213	1,401	(NA)
All other private [2]	2,979	2,431	2,212	2,482	2,678	2,836

Value of Construction Put in Place: 1995-2000 (Con't)

Type of construction	Constant (1996) dollars (in millions)					
	1995	1996	1997	1998	1999	2,000
Public construction	133,450	139,147	149,493	150,246	156,852	159,964
Buildings	59,074	63,446	69,319	68,334	69,497	74,617
Housing and redevelopment	4,786	5,046	5,084	4,853	5,088	4,715
Industrial	1,544	1,390	965	941	828	928
Educational	26,374	28,577	33,136	33,743	35,497	39,922
Hospital	4,335	4,617	4,970	3,642	3,548	3,591
Other3	22,034	23,815	25,164	25,155	24,537	25,460
Highways and streets	38,952	39,412	42,535	45,877	48,827	44,894
Military facilities	3,102	2,593	2,466	2,377	1,909	1,946
Conservation and development	6,443	6,000	5,541	5,219	5,602	5,404
Sewer systems	8,600	9,778	10,034	9,743	10,438	10,204
Water supply facilities	4,809	5,609	6,275	6,552	7,142	7,023
Miscellaneous public 4	12,468	12,310	13,323	12,145	13,436	15,876

[1] Includes amusement and recreational buildings, bus and airline terminals, animal hospitals and shelters, etc.

[2] Includes privately owned streets and bridges, parking areas, sewer and water facilities, parks and playgrounds, golf courses, airfields, etc.

[3] Includes general administrative buildings, prisons, police and fire stations, courthouses, civic centers, passenger terminals, space facilities, postal facilities, etc.

[4] Includes open amusement and recreational facilities, power generating facilities, transit systems, airfields, open parking facilities, etc.

Source: U.S. Census Bureau

Value of Construction Work by Region: 1997 (in U.S. dollars)

Type of Construction	Value of Construction Work			
	Total	New Construction	Additions, Alterations, or Reconstruction	Maintenance and Repair
UNITED STATES				
Building Construction, Total	667,892,335	441,085,796	160,098,787	66,707,752
Single-family houses, detached and attached	23,830,160	179,325,838	38,743,071	20,232,700
Single-family houses, detached	20,863,659	157,912,589	33,607,561	17,116,443
Single-family houses, attached	29,665,014	21,413,248	5,135,510	3,116,256
Apartment buildings/condos/cooperatives	35,912,059	23,549,029	7,294,218	5,068,813
All other residential building	1,450,935	879,677	409,889	161,370
Manufacturing/light industrial buildings	64,026,464	33,796,938	18,857,654	11,371,872
Manufacturing/light industrial warehouses	20,252,089	13,494,830	4,676,949	2,080,311
Hotels and motels	17,209,304	12,623,672	3,254,698	1,330,934
Office buildings	80,588,781	44,449,862	27,694,812	8,444,108
All other commercial buildings	69,545,794	43,566,415	18,638,395	7,340,984
Commercial warehouses	16,628,141	11,912,121	3,298,378	1,417,642
Religious buildings	9,400,127	5,343,590	2,969,442	1,087,095
Educational buildings	46,826,417	28,102,206	15,751,455	2,972,756
Health care and institutional buildings	33,942,469	19,754,714	11,763,387	2,424,369
Public safety buildings	10,119,930	7,346,218	2,200,704	573,008
Farm buildings, non-residential	3,473,574	2,508,098	530,901	434,575
Amusement/recreational buildings	10,429,599	7,893,895	2,073,509	462,196
Other building construction	9,785,043	6,538,695	1,941,327	1,305,021
NORTHEAST				
Building Construction, Total	114,550,714	61,638,403	38,682,611	14,229,699
Single-family houses, detached and attached	33,390,774	21,353,228	8,110,557	3,926,988
Single-family houses, detached	29,304,397	18,772,133	7,165,276	3,366,988
Single-family houses, attached	4,086,377	2,581,095	945,281	560,000
Apartment buildings/condos/cooperatives	6,792,548	3,020,707	2,338,623	1,433,218
All other residential building	194,851	96,982	61,320	36,550
Manufacturing and light industrial buildings	10,582,581	4,601,673	3,964,725	2,016,184
Manufacturing/light industrial warehouses	3,034,256	1,725,600	918,682	389,974
Hotels and motels	2,905,562	2,118,378	552,064	235,121
Office buildings	18,254,802	7,394,081	8,494,958	2,365,764
All other commercial buildings	12,565,856	6,637,924	4,331,737	1,596,195
Commercial warehouses	2,400,908	1,499,852	648,143	252,913
Religious buildings	1,348,655	530,739	539,552	278,365

Value of Construction Work by Region: 1997 (Con't)

Type of Construction	Value of Construction Work			
	Total	New Construction	Additions, Alterations, or Reconstruction	Maintenance and Repair
Educational buildings	9,726,636	4,946,851	4,114,060	665,725
Health care and institutional buildings	7,175,532	3,598,754	3,033,203	543,575
Public safety buildings	2,134,622	1,386,588	593,033	155,002
Farm buildings, non-residential	297,071	180,313	S	63,762
Amusement/recreational buildings	1,941,746	1,365,768	474,866	101,112
Other building construction	1,804,313	1,180,965	454,095	169,253
MIDWEST				
Building Construction, Total	158,651,020	101,737,168	39,706,572	17,207,280
Single-family houses, detached and attached	53,833,933	38,958,807	9,656,226	5,218,899
Single-family houses, detached	45,147,441	32,478,358	8,219,880	4,449,202
Single-family houses, attached	8,686,491	6,480,448	1,436,346	769,697
Apartment buildings/condos/cooperatives	7,209,912	4,935,375	1,317,092	957,444
All other residential building	244,676	144,642	75,448	24,586
Manufacturing/light industrial buildings	20,345,765	9,903,563	6,734,854	3,707,348
Manufacturing/light industrial warehouses	6,825,379	4,550,954	1,615,813	658,612
Hotels and motels	3,084,878	2,277,278	505,195	302,405
Office buildings	15,997,117	9,507,477	4,824,179	1,665,460
All other commercial buildings	16,070,258	9,829,218	4,397,665	1,843,375
Commercial warehouses	4,078,833	2,878,960	804,428	395,445
Religious buildings	2,571,423	1,357,789	879,028	334,606
Educational buildings	11,876,924	6,844,123	4,204,103	828,697
Health care and institutional buildings	9,171,992	5,303,575	3,162,981	705,437
Public safety buildings	2,189,952	1,519,131	521,041	149,781
Farm buildings, non-residential	1,558,036	1,148,443	224,798	184,796
Amusement/recreational buildings	1,918,469	1,400,700	425,435	92,333
Other building construction	1,673,473	1,177,131	358,286	138,056
SOUTH				
Building Construction, Total	229,801,000	161,014,229	46,788,740	21,998,031
Single-family houses, detached and attached	83,894,701	66,017,870	11,198,818	6,678,013
Single-family houses, detached	74,615,340	59,110,291	9,817,716	5,687,334
Single-family houses, attached	9,279,361	6,907,580	1,381,101	990,679
Apartment buildings/condos/cooperatives	13,425,146	9,679,705	2,136,636	1,608,805
All other residential building	553,268	373,872	123,283	56,113
Manufacturing/light industrial buildings	19,050,234	10,219,135	4,779,694	4,051,405

Value of Construction Work by Region: 1997 (Con't)

Type of Construction	Value of Construction Work			
	Total	New Construction	Additions, Alterations, or Reconstruction	Maintenance and Repair
Manufacturing/light industrial warehouses	6,064,446	4,231,672	1,212,149	620,625
Hotels and motels	5,781,393	4,202,038	1,136,776	442,579
Office buildings	27,062,275	16,141,975	8,233,658	2,686,642
All other commercial buildings	24,678,078	16,771,875	5,509,675	2,396,528
Commercial warehouses	5,627,487	4,150,277	1,027,871	449,339
Religious buildings	4,156,019	2,722,947	1,106,427	326,645
Educational buildings	15,749,219	10,556,575	4,348,666	843,977
Health care and institutional buildings	12,010,633	7,409,749	3,852,706	748,178
Public safety buildings	3,484,524	2,665,738	660,353	158,433
Farm buildings, non-residential	1,084,727	798,042	164,109	122,575
Amusement/recreational buildings	3,567,082	2,777,176	625,841	164,064
Other building construction	3,611,768	2,295,582	672,077	644,109
WEST				
Building Construction, Total	164,889,602	116,695,996	34,920,864	13,272,741
Single-family houses, detached and attached	67,182,200	52,995,932	9,777,470	4,408,799
Single-family houses, detached	59,569,415	47,551,807	8,404,689	3,612,919
Single-family houses, attached	7,612,785	5,444,124	1,372,781	795,880
Apartment buildings/condos/cooperatives	8,484,453	5,913,242	1,501,866	1,069,345
All other residential building	458,140	264,182	149,837	44,121
Manufacturing/light industrial buildings	14,047,884	9,072,567	3,378,382	1,596,935
Manufacturing/light industrial warehouses	4,328,009	2,986,604	930,304	411,100
Hotels and motels	5,437,471	4,025,979	1,060,663	350,829
Office buildings	19,274,587	11,406,329	6,142,017	1,726,242
All other commercial buildings	16,231,602	10,327,398	4,399,318	1,504,887
Commercial warehouses	4,520,913	3,383,032	817,936	319,946
Religious buildings	1,324,029	732,114	444,436	147,479
Educational buildings	9,473,638	5,754,656	3,084,625	634,357
Health care and institutional buildings	5,584,312	3,442,635	1,714,497	427,179
Public safety buildings	2,310,831	1,774,761	426,278	109,792
Farm buildings, non-residential	533,740	381,300	88,999	63,441
Amusement/recreational buildings	3,002,303	2,350,250	547,366	104,687
Other building construction	2,695,489	1,885,017	456,870	353,602

S: Information withheld because estimates did not meet publication standards.

Source: U.S. Census Bureau, 1997 Economic Census

Registration Laws

Currently laws in most states require a registration process for architects, interior designer and landscape architects. At this time, architecture is the only profession with such laws in all 50 states. This chapter provides a brief introduction to state requirements with contact information for additional support.

Architecture Registration Laws

The following information provides a brief overview of the major components of initial licensure requirements for architects including work experience, degree requirements, and the Architectural Registration Exam (ARE). Complete information regarding registration requirements, renewal procedures, interstate registration, and corporate practice guidelines is available from the individual state boards at the phone numbers listed below. Due to the complex and changing nature of the requirements, it is recommended that the state licensing board(s) be contacted to receive the most up-to-date information. The National Council of Architectural Registration Boards (NCARB) also maintains information about registration on their Web site at *www.ncarb.org*.

States and State Boards	Type of Law		Initial Requirements			Ongoing Requir.
	Title Act	Practice Act	College Degree Required	Internship Required	ARE Exam Required	Continuing Education Required
Alabama (334) 242-4179	X	X	X	X	X	X
Alaska (907) 465-1676	X	X	X	X	X	
Arizona (602) 255-4053 x210	X	X			X	
Arkansas (501) 682-3171	X	X	X	X	X	X
California (916) 445-3394	X	X			X	
Colorado (303) 894-7801	X	X		CB	X	
Connecticut (860) 713-6145	X	X	X	X	X	
Delaware (302) 739-4522 x218	X	X	X	X	X	
District of Columbia (202) 442-4461	X	X	X	CB	X	
Florida (850) 487-7992	X	X	X	X	X	X
Georgia (478) 207-1400	X	X		X	X	
Hawaii (808) 586-2702	X	X		P	X	
Idaho (208) 334-3233	X	X		X	X	
Illinois (217) 785-0877	X	X		X	X	

Architecture Registration Laws (Con't)

States and State Boards	Type of Law		Initial Requirements			Ongoing Requir.
	Title Act	Practice Act	College Degree Required	Internship Required	ARE Exam Required	Continuing Education Required
Indiana (317) 233-6223	X	X	X	X	X	
Iowa (515) 281-7362	X	X	X	X	X	X
Kansas (785) 296-3053	X	X	X	X	X	X
Kentucky (859) 246-2069	X	X	CB	X	X	X
Louisiana (225) 925-4802	X	X	X	X	X	X
Maine (207) 624-8522	X	X		X	X	
Maryland (410) 333-6322	X	X		X	X	
Massachusetts (617) 727-3072	X	X	X	X	X	
Michigan (517) 241-9253	X	X	X	X	X	
Minnesota (651) 296-2388	X	X	X	X	X	X
Mississippi (601) 899-9071	X	X	X	X	X	
Missouri (573) 751-0047	X	X			X	
Montana (406) 841-2386	X	X	X	X	X	
Nebraska (402) 471-2021	X	X	X	X	X	X
Nevada (702) 486-7300	X	X	X	X	X	
New Hampshire (603) 271-2219	X	X		X	X	
New Jersey (973) 504-6385	X	X	X	X	X	
New Mexico (505) 827-6375	X	X	X	X	X	X
New York (518) 474-3817 x110	X	X		X	X	X
North Carolina (919) 733-9544	X	X	X	X	X	X
North Dakota (701) 223-3184	X	X	X	X	X	
Ohio (614) 466-2316	X	X	CB	X	X	

Architecture Registration Laws (Con't)

States and State Boards	Type of Law		Initial Requirements			Ongoing Requir.
	Title Act	Practice Act	College Degree Required	Internship Required	ARE Exam Required	Continuing Education Required
Oklahoma (405) 751-6512	X	X	X	X	X	X
Oregon (503) 378-4270	X	X	X	X	X	X
Pennsylvania (717) 783-3397	X	X	X	X	X	
Rhode Island (401) 222-2565	X	X	X	X	X	
South Carolina (803) 896-4408	X	X	X	X	X	
South Dakota (605) 394-2510	X	X	X	X	X	X
Tennessee (615) 741-3221	X	X		X	X	X
Texas (512) 305-8535	X	X	CB	X	X	P
Utah (801) 503-6403	X	X	X	X	X	
Vermont (802) 828-2373	X	X			X	X
Virginia (804) 367-8514	X	X	X	X	X	
Washington (360) 664-1388	X	X			X	
West Virginia (304) 528-5825	X	X	X	X	X	X
Wisconsin (608) 266-5511 x42	X	X		X	X	
Wyoming (307) 777-7788	X	X	X	X	X	P

P = There is current legislation pending regarding this requirement.

Source: National Council of Architectural Registration Boards

Global Architecture Practice Standards

The following guidelines outline the major requirements U.S. architects and architecture firms must fulfill in order to practice in other countries. This information is meant to be an overview and should not be used as a substitute for the complex and changing stipulations. Architects should always contact the appropriate agency in each country (indicated below) prior to the start of any project for the most up-to-date regulations. U.S. Embassies in each country may also be helpful in understanding and fulfilling requirements.

Country	License or Reg. Required for Indigenous Arch.	License or Reg. Required for Foreign Arch.	Local Representative Required	Local Participation Required	English Official Language	Metric System Standard	Official Licensing Body
Australia	X	X			X	X	Architects Registration Boards in each state
Austria	X	3	X	X		X	Federal Ministry of Economic Affairs +43 (1) 71-1000
Belgium	X	X			4	X	Orde Van Architecten, Nationale Raad
Bermuda	X	X	X	X	X	X	Architects Registration Council (809) 297-7705
Brazil	X	X		X	4	X	Regional Council of Engineering, Architecture, and Agronomy in each state
Canada	X	X	X	X	X	X	Professional bodies in each province
China	X	X	X		4	X	National Administrative Board of Architectural Registration +86 (1) 839-4250
Colombia	X	X	X	X		X	Consejo Profesional Nacional de Ingenieria y Arquitectura
Czech Republic	X		X	X		X	Czech Chamber of Architects +42 (2) 2451-0112

Global Architecture Practice Standards (Con't)

Country	License or Reg. Required for Indigenous Arch.	License or Reg. Required for Foreign Arch.	Local Representative Required	Local Participation Required	English Official Language	Metric System Standard	Official Licensing Body
Denmark	X					X	None
Egypt	X	X	X	X	4	X	Egyptian Engineering Syndicate +20 (2) 74-0092
El Salvador	X	X		X		X	Registro Nacional de Arquitectos e Ingenieros
Finland	1	2		X	4	X	None
France	1	X				X	Ministere de l'Equipment, des Transports et du Tourisme
Germany	X	X				X	Chamber of Architects in each state
Greece	X	X	X		4	X	Technical Chamber of Greece +30 (1) 325-4590
Guatemala	X		X	X		X	Colegio de Arquitectos +50 (2) 69-3672
Honduras	X	X	X	U		X	National Autonomous University of Honduras & Colegio de Arquitectos de Honduras +504 38-5385
Hungary	X	X			4	X	Registration Board of Ministry of Environmental Protection & Regional Development
Iceland	X	X			4	X	Ministry of Industry +354 (1) 60-9420
India	X	X			X	X	Council of Architecture +91 (11) 331-5757

Global Architecture Practice Standards (Con't)

Country	License or Reg. Required for Indigenous Arch.	License or Reg. Required for Foreign Arch.	Local Representative Required	Local Participation Required	English Official Language	Metric System Standard	Official Licensing Body
Indonesia	X	X	X	U	X	X	Ministry of Internal Affairs
Ireland					X	X	None
Israel	X	X	X	U	4	X	Architects and Engineers Registrar
Italy	X	X	X		4	X	Consiglio Nazionale Architetti
Jamaica	X	X	X		4	X	Architects Registration Board
Japan	X	X	X			X	Ministry of Construction +81 (3) 3580-4311
Jordon	X	X	X	X	X	X	Jordon Engineers Association +926 (6) 607-616
Kenya	X	X	X	X	X	X	Board of Registration of Architects and Quantity Surveyors +254 (2) 72-0438
Korea	X	X	X	U		X	Ministry of Construction +82 (2) 503-7357
Lebanon	X	X	X		4	X	Order of Engineers +961 (1) 83-0286
Luxembourg	X	X	U	U		X	Ordre des Architectes et des Ingenieurs Conseils +352 42-2406
Malaysia	X	X	X	X	4	X	Lembaga Arkitek Malaysia +60 (3) 298-8733

Global Architecture Practice Standards (Con't)

Country	License or Reg. Required for Indigenous Arch.	License or Reg. Required for Foreign Arch.	Local Representative Required	Local Participation Required	English Official Language	Metric System Standard	Official Licensing Body
Mexico	X	X	X	U		X	Direccion General de Professiones en Mexico +52 (5) 550-9000
Netherlands						X	Stichting Bureau Architectenregister +31 (70) 360-7020
New Zealand					X	X	Architects Education and Registration Board
Nicaragua	X	X	X				Asociacion Nicarguense de Arquitectos Camara de La Construcion + 505 (2) 43-796
Norway						X	None
Panama	X		X	U		X	Junta Tecnica de Ingenieria y Arquitectura +507 23-7851
Peru	1	2	X			X	Colegio de Arquitectos del Peru +51 (41) 71-3778
Philippines	X	3	X	X	X	X	Professional Regulation Commission +63 (2) 741-6076
Poland	X	X		X		X	Government Offices in each province
Portugal	1	2				X	Associaçao dos Arquitectos Portugueses +351 (1) 343-2454
Romania	X	X	X		4	X	Union of Romanian Architects +40 (1) 312-0956
Russia	X	3	X	X		X	Russian License Architectural Centre

Global Architecture Practice Standards (Con't)

Country	License or Reg. Required for Indigenous Arch.	License or Reg. Required for Foreign Arch.	Local Representative Required	Local Participation Required	English Official Language	Metric System Standard	Official Licensing Body
Saudi Arabia	X	X	X	X		X	Ministry of Commerce +966 (1) 401-2222
Singapore	X	X			X	X	Board of Architects +65 222-5295
South Africa	X	X			X	X	South African Council for Architects +27 (11) 486-1683
Spain	X	X	U	U	4	X	Colegios de Arquitectos in each region
Sweden						X	None
Switzerland	X	U			4	X	Schweizerisches Register der Ingenieure, Architekten und Techniker +41 (1) 252-3222
Taiwan	X	X	X	X		X	Construction & Planning Administration , MOI +886 (4) 328-1560
Turkey	X	X			4	X	Turkiye Mimarlar Odasi +90 (4) 417-3727
United Kingdom	U	X			X	X	Architects Registration Council of the United Kingdom +44 (71)580-5861
Venezuela	X	X				X	Colegio de Ingenieros, Arquitectos y Profesiones Afines de Venezuela +58 (2) 241-8007

U Specific requirements are unclear. The local agency should be contacted.
1 A license or registration is not required for indigenous architects; however, there are other stipulations which must be met in order for indigenous persons to practice architecture.
2 A license or registration is not required for foreign architects; however, there are other stipulations which must be met in order for a foreign architect to practice architecture.
3 Generally US architects may not practice in the country independently.
4 Although not the official language, English is commonly used in the commercial arena.

Source: National Council of Architectural Registration Boards

Interior Design Registration Laws

The following information provides a brief overview of the major components of initial registration requirements for interior designers, including work experience, degree requirements and the National Council for Interior Design Qualification (NCIDQ) exam. More specific details about these requirements is available from the individual state boards reachable at the phone numbers listed below. Due to the complex and changing nature of registration laws, it is recommended that the state licensing board(s) be contacted for the most up to date information. The American Society of Interior Designers (ASID) also maintains information about registration on their Web site at *www.asid.org*.

States and State Board Phone Numbers	Type of Law		Initial Requirements			Ongoing Requir.
	Title Act	Practice Act	Post-HS Education Required	Work Experience Required	NCIDQ Exam Required	Continuing Education Required
Alabama (256) 340-9003	X		X		X	
Arkansas (501) 664-3008	X		X	X	X	X
California (760) 761-4734	*			X	X	X
Connecticut (860) 713-6135	X		X	X	X	
Florida (850) 488-6685	X	X	X	X	X	X
Georgia (404) 656-3941	X		X		X	X
Illinois (217) 785-0813	X		X	X	X	
Louisiana (225) 298-1283	X	X	X	X	X	X
Maine (207) 624-8603	X		X	X	X	
Maryland (410) 333-6322	X		X	X	X	X
Minnesota (651) 296-2388	X		X	X	X	X
Missouri (573) 522-4683	X		X	X	X	X
Nevada (702) 486-7300	X	X	X	X	X	
New Mexico (505) 476-7077	X		X	X	X	X
New York (518) 474-3846	X		X	X	X	

Interior Design Registration Laws (Con't)

States and State Board Phone Numbers	Type of Law		Initial Requirements			Ongoing Requir.
	Title Act	Practice Act	Post-HS Education Required	Work Experience Required	NCIDQ Exam Required	Continuing Education Required
Tennessee (615) 741-3221	X		X	X	X	X
Texas (512) 305-8539	X		X	X	X	X
Virginia (804) 367-8514	X		X	X	X	
Washington, D.C. (202) 442-4330	X	X	X	X	X	X
Wisconsin (608) 266-5439	X		X	X	X	X

* Self-Certification Act

Source: American Society of Interior Designers

Landscape Architecture Licensure Laws

The following matrix provides a brief overview of the major components of initial licensure for landscape architects including work experience and degree requirements. Complete information regarding licensing requirements, renewal procedures, and reciprocity is available from the individual state boards, at the phone numbers listed below. Due to the complex and changing nature of the regulations, it is recommended that the state licensing board(s) be contacted for the most up to date information. The Council of Landscape Architectural Registration Boards (CLARB) and the American Society of Landscape Architects (ASLA) also maintain information about licensure on their Web sites at *www.clarb.org* and *www.asla.org*, respectively.

States & State Board Phone Numbers	Type of Law		Initial Requirements			Ongoing Req.
	Title Act	Practice Act	Accredited LA Degree	Work Experience Required	LARE Exam Required	Continuing Education Required [+]
Alabama (334) 262-1351	X	X	2	X	X	X
Alaska (907) 465-2540	X	X	4	X	X	
Arizona (602) 255-4053 x209	X	X	2	X	X	
Arkansas (501) 682-3171	X	X	2, 3	X	X	
California (916) 445-4954	X	X	X	X	X	
Connecticut (860) 713-6145	X	X	2	X	X	X
Delaware (302) 739-4522 x204	X	X	2	X	X	X
Florida (850) 488-1470	X	X	2	X	X	
Georgia (478) 207-1400	X	X	X	X	X	X
Hawaii (808) 586-2874	X	X	2	X	X	
Idaho (208) 334-3233	X	X	2	X	X	
Illinois (217) 782-6742	X		X	X	X	
Indiana (317) 233-6223	X	X	X	X	X	
Iowa (515) 281-5596	X		2,4	X	X	X

Landscape Architecture Licensure Laws (Con't)

States & State Board Phone Numbers	Type of Law		Initial Requirements			Ongoing Req.
	Title Act	Practice Act	Accredited LA Degree	Work Experience Required	LARE Exam Required	Continuing Education Required +
Kansas (785) 296-3053	X	X	X	X	X	X
Kentucky (859) 246-2069	X	X	X	X	X	X
Louisiana (225) 925-7772	X	X	2,3	X	X	
Maine (207) 624-8603	X	X	2,4	*	X	
Maryland (410) 230-6322	X	X	2	X	X	
Massachusetts (617) 727-3072	X		2,3,4	X	X	
Michigan (517) 241-9201	X	X	4	X	X	
Minnesota (651) 296-2388	X	X	2,3,4	X	X	X
Mississippi (601) 899-9071	X	X	3,4	*	X	
Missouri (573) 751-0039	X		2	X	X	
Montana (406) 841-2395	X	X			X	
Nebraska (402) 471-2021	X	X	2	X	X	X
Nevada (775) 626-0604	X	X	2,3,4	X	X	
New Jersey (973) 504-6385		X	X	X	X	X
New Mexico (505) 476-7079	X	X	2,4	X	X	X
New York (518) 474-3817	X	X	2,3,4	X	X	
North Carolina (919) 850-9088	X	X	2,3,4	X	X	X
Ohio (614) 466-2316	X		X	X	X	
Oklahoma (405) 751-6512	X	X	X	X	X	X
Oregon (503) 589-0093		X	2	X	X	X
Pennsylvania (717) 772-8528	X	X	2	X	X	X
Rhode Island (401) 222-2565	X	X	X	X	X	

Landscape Architecture Licensure Laws (Con't)

States & State Board Phone Numbers	Type of Law		Initial Requirements			Ongoing Req.
	Title Act	Practice Act	Accredited LA Degree	Work Experience Required	LARE Exam Required	Continuing Education Required [+]
South Carolina (803) 734-9131	X	X	2,3,4	X	X	
South Dakota (605) 394-2510	X		X	X	X	X
Tennessee (615) 741-3221	X	X	X	X	X	
Texas (512) 305-8519	X	X		X	X	X
Utah (801) 530-6632	X	X	2	X	X	
Virginia (804) 367-8514	X		2		X	
Washington (360) 664-1388	X		X	X	X	
West Virginia (304) 293-2141 x4490	X		2	X	X	
Wisconsin (608) 266-5511	X		4	X	X	
Wyoming (307) 777-7788	X	X	X	X	X	

Note: Colorado, Washington, D.C., New Hampshire, North Dakota, and Vermont currently do not have a Landscape Architecture licensure program.

1   Also referred to as Professional Development Hours (PDH).

2   Work experience may be substitute for the education requirement.

3   A degree from an allied field may be accepted.

4   A non-accredited landscape architecture degree may be accepted will additional work experience.

5   No experience is required with a Landscape Architectural Accreditation Board (LAAB) accredited Landscape Architecture degree; however, other degree types may require experience.

Source: Council of Landscape Architectural Registration Boards and American Society of Landscape Architects

Bookstores

A listing of U.S. bookstores that specialize in design and design-related titles are available in this chapter.

Architecture & Design Bookstores

The following list outlines the specialty bookstores of architecture and design throughout the United States including rare and out-of-print dealers that specialize in design titles.

ARIZONA
Builder's Book Depot
1033 E. Jefferson, Suite 500
Phoenix, AZ 85034
(800) 284-3434
www.buildersbookdepot.com

CALIFORNIA
Builders Booksource
1817 Fourth Street
Berkeley, CA 94710
(510) 845-6874
www.buildersbooksite.com

J.B. Muns Fine Arts Books
1162 Shattuck Avenue
Berkeley, CA 94707
(510) 525-2420

Moe's Art & Antiquarian Books
2476 Telegraph Avenue
Berkeley, CA 94704
(510) 849-2133

Builder's Book
8001 Canoga Avenue
Canoga Park, CA 91304
(818) 887-7828

Form Zero Architectural Books + Gallery
811 Traction Avenue, Suite 1A
Los Angeles, CA 90013
(213) 620-1920
www.formzero.com

Builders Booksource
Ghirardelli Square
900 North Point
San Francisco, CA 94109
(415) 440-5773
www.buildersbooksite.com

William Stout Architectural Books
804 Montgomery Street
San Francisco, CA 94133
(415) 391-6757
www.stoutbooks.com

Sullivan Goss Books and Prints Ltd.
7 E. Anapamu Street
Santa Barbara, CA 93101
(805)730-1460
www.sullivangoss.com

Hennessey & Ingalls Art and Architecture Books
1254 Third Street Promenade
Santa Monica, CA 90401
(310) 458-9074
www.hennesseyingalls.com

COLORADO
Tattered Cover Bookstore
1628 16th Street
Denver, CO 80202
(303) 436-1070
www.tatteredcover.com

Tattered Cover Bookstore
2955 East First Avenue
Denver, CO 80206
(303) 322-7727
www.tatteredcover.com

DISTRICT OF COLUMBIA
AIA Bookstore
The American Institute of Architects
1735 New York Avenue NW
Washington, DC 20006
(202) 626-7475

Franz Bader Bookstore
1911 I Street NW
Washington, DC 20006
(202) 337-5440

National Building Museum Shop
401 F Street NW
Washington, DC 20001
(202) 272-7706

GEORGIA
Architectural Book Center
231 Peachtree Street NE Suite B-4
Atlanta, GA 30303
(404) 222-9920

Architecture & Design Bookstores (Con't)

ILLINOIS
Chicago Architecture Foundation Bookstore
224 S. Michigan Avenue
Chicago, IL 60604
(312) 922-3432
www.architecture.org

Chicago Architecture Foundation Bookstore
John Hancock Center
875 N. Michigan Avenue
Chicago, IL 60611
(312) 751-1380
www.architecture.org

Prairie Avenue Bookshop
418 S. Wabash Avenue
Chicago, IL 60605-1209
(312) 922-8311
www.pabook.com

INDIANA
Architectural Center Bookstore
Indiana Society of Architects
47 S. Pennsylvania Street, Suite 110
Indianapolis, IN 46204
(317) 634-3871

MASSACHUSETTS
Ars Libri
560 Harrison Avenue
Boston, MA 02118
(617) 357-5212
www.arslibri.com

F.A. Bernett
144 Lincoln Street
Boston, MA 02111
(617) 350-7778

Cambridge Architectural Books
12 Bow Street
Cambridge, MA 02138
(617) 354-5300
www.archbook.com

Charles B. Wood III Antiquarian Booksellers
P.O. Box 2369
Cambridge, MA 02238
(617) 868-1711

MARYLAND
Baltimore AIA Bookstore
11 1/2 Chase Street
Baltimore, MD 21201
(410) 625-2585
www.aiabalt.com

NEW YORK
Archivia: The Decorative Arts Bookshop
1063 Madison
New York, NY 10028
(212) 439-9194

Argosy Bookstore
116 E. 59th Street
New York, NY 10022
(212) 753-4455
www.argosybooks.com

Cooper-Hewitt Museum Bookstore
2 East 91st St
New York, NY 10128
(212) 849-8404

Hacker Art Books
45 W. 57th Street
New York, NY 10019
(212) 688-7600
www.hackerartbooks.com

McGraw-Hill Bookstore
1221 Avenue of the Americas
New York, NY 10020
(212) 512-4100
www.bookstore.mcgraw-hill.com

Perimeter Books
21 Cleveland Place
New York, NY 10012
(212) 334-6559
www.perimeterbooks.com

Rizzoli Bookstore
31 W. 57th Street
New York, NY 10019
(212) 759-2424

Royoung Bookseller
564 Ashford Avenue
Ardsley, NY 10502
(914) 693-6116
www.royoung.com

Architecture & Design Bookstores (Con't)

Strand Book Store
828 Broadway
New York, NY 10003
(212) 473-1452
www.strandbooks.com

Urban Center Books
Villard Houses
457 Madison Avenue
New York, NY 10022
(212) 935-3592
http://colophon.com/urbancenterbooks/

Ursus Books
981 Madison Avenue
New York, NY 10021
(212) 772-8787
www.ursusbooks.com

Ursus Books
132 W. 21st Street
New York, NY 10011
(212) 627-5370
www.ursusbooks.com

OHIO
Wexner Center Bookstore
1871 N. High Street
Columbus, OH 43210-1105
(614) 292-1807

OREGON
David Morrison Books
530 NW 12th Street
Portland, OR 97209
(503) 295-6882

PENNSYLVANIA
AIA Bookstore & Design Center
17th and Sansom Streets
Philadelphia, PA 19103
(215) 569-3188
www.aiaphila.org

TEXAS
Brazos Bookstore
2421 Bissonnet Street
Houston, TX 77005
(713) 523-0701
www.brazosbookstore.com

WASHINGTON
Peter Miller Architecture and Design Books
1930 First Avenue
Seattle, WA 98101
(206) 441-4114
www.petermiller.com

Did you know...

By 1867, The American Institute of Architects had established the first U.S. architectural library open to the public as a source of information on architecture and an educational resource for its members.

Journals & Magazines

This chapter contains a listing of major national and international journals and magazines devoted to architecture and design, with their publication information.

Architecture & Design Journals and Magazines

The following is a list of major architecture and design journals and magazines from around the world, ranging from the most popular to the cutting edge. Whether looking for periodicals that take a less traditional approach or for exposure to the most recent projects and design news, it is hoped this list will provide an opportunity to explore new ideas and perspectives about design and expand knowledge about the profession.

U.S. PUBLICATIONS

Archi-Tech
P.O. Box 10915
Portland, ME 04104
(207) 761-2177
Published 5 times a year.

Architectural Digest
6300 Wilshire Boulevard
Los Angeles, CA 90048
(800) 365-8032
www.archdigest.com
Published monthly by Conde Nast Publications, Inc.

Architectural Record
Two Penn Plaza
New York, NY 10121-2298
(212) 904-2594
www.architecturalrecord.com
The official magazine of the AIA, published monthly.

Architecture
770 Broadway
New York, NY 10003
(646) 654-5766
www.architecturemag.com
Published monthly by BPI Communications.

ASID ICON
608 Massachusetts Ave. NW
Washington, D.C. 20002-6006
(202) 546-3480
www.asid.org
The magazine of the American Society of Interior Designers, published quarterly.

Contract Magazine
770 Broadway, 4th Fl.
New York, NY 10003-9595
(646) 654-4500
www.contractmagazine.com
Published monthly by Bill Communications.

Communication Arts
410 Sherman Ave.
P.O. Box 10300
Palo Alto, CA 94303
(650) 326-6040
www.commarts.com
Published 8 times per year.

Design Book Review
California College of Arts and Crafts
1111 Eighth Street
San Francisco, CA 94107
(415) 551-9232
Published quarterly by the California College of Arts and Crafts.

Dwell
99 Osgood Place
San Francisco, CA 94133
(415) 743-9990
www.dwellmag.com
Published bi-monthly by Pixie Communications.

Engineering News Record
2 Penn Plaza
9th Floor
New York, NY 10121
www.enr.com
Published by McGraw-Hill Construction Information Group.

Fine Homebuilding
Taunton Press
63 S. Main St.
P.O. Box 5506
Newtown, CT 06470-5506
(203) 426-8171
www.taunton.com/fh/
Published bi-monthly by Taunton Press.

Architecture & Design Journals & Magazines (Con't)

Harvard Design Magazine
48 Quincy St.
Cambridge, MA 02138
(617) 495-7814
www.harvard.edu/hdm
*Published 3 times a year by Harvard University's
Graduate School of Design.*

I.D.
116 East 27th St. Floor 6
New York, NY 10016
(212) 447-1400
www.idonline.com
Published 8 times per year.

Innovation
1142 Walker Rd.
Great Falls, VA 22066
(703) 759-0100
www.idsa.org
*Quarterly Journal of the Industrial Designers Society
of America.*

Interior Design
345 Hudson St.
New York, NY 10014
(212) 519-7200
Published 15 times a year by Cahners Publishing Co.

Interiors & Sources
666 Dundee Rd., Ste. 807
Northbrook, IL 60062-2769
(847) 498-6495
www.isdesignet.com
Published 8 times per year.

Journal of Architectural Education (JAE)
Association of Collegiate Schools of Architecture
1735 New York Avenue, NW
Washington, DC 20006
(202) 785-2324
www.acsa-arch.org
Published quarterly by MIT Press for the ACSA.

Journal of Interior Design
Interior Design Educators Council, Inc.
9202 North Meridian Street, Suite 200
Indianapolis, IN 46206-1810
(317) 816-6261
www.idec.org
*Published bi-annually by the Interior Design
Educators Council.*

Journal of the American Planning Association
122 S. Michigan Ave.
Suite 1600
Chicago, IL 60603-6107
(312) 431-9100
www.planning.org
Published quarterly.

Journal of the Society of Architectural Historians
1365 N. Astor St.
Chicago, IL 60610
(215) 735-0224
www.sah.org
*Published quarterly by the Society of Architectural
Historians.*

Landscape Architecture
636 Eye St. NW
Washington, DC 20001-3736
(800) 787-5257
www.asla.org
*Published monthly by the American Society of
Landscape Architects.*

Metropolis
61 W. 23rd St.
New York, NY 10010
(212) 627-9977
www.metropolismag.com
Published 10 times a year.

Nest
P.O. Box 2446
Lenox Hill Station
New York, NY 10021
(888) 321-6378
www.nestmagazine.com
Published quarterly.

Old House Journal
2 Main St.
Gloucester, MA 01930
(978) 283-3200
Published bimonthly.

ONE
42 Decatur St.
San Francisco, CA 94103-4517
(800) 456-6051
www.onemedia.com
Published monthly by ONE Media.

Architecture & Design Journals & Magazines (Con't)

Perspective
341 Merchandise Mart
Chicago, IL 60654
(312) 467-1950
www.iida.org
The International Magazine of the International Interior Design Association, published quarterly.

Places
Center for Environmental Design Research
University of California
390 Wurster Hall
Berkeley, CA 94720
(510) 642-1495
www.cedr.berkeley.edu
Published 3 times a year by the Design History Foundation.

Preservation
1785 Massachusetts Ave. NW
Washington, DC 20036
(202) 588-6000
www.nthp.org
Published bimonthly by the National Trust for Historic Preservation.

INTERNATIONAL PUBLICATIONS

Abitare
Editrice Abitare Segesta
15 Corso Monforte
Milano, 20122
Italy
+39 027 60902202
www.abitare.it
Monthly magazine in Italian and English.

AD (Architectural Design)
c/o John Wiley & Sons, Inc.
Journals Administration Department
605 Third Avenue
New York, NY 10158
(212) 850-6645
Bimonthly; Published by John Wiley & Sons, Inc.

AJ (Architects' Journal)
151 Rosebery Avenue
33 39 Bowling Green Lane
London, EC1R 4GB
U.K.
+44 020 8956 3504
www.ajplus.co.uk
Published by EMAP Construct.

l'Arca
Via Valcava 6
Milano, 20155
Italy
+39 02 325246
www.arcadata.it
Published 11 times a year.

Archis
Elsevier Bedrijfsinformatie bv
PO Box 4
BA Doetinchem, 7000
The Netherlands
+31 314-349888
www.archis.org
Monthly bilingual magazine published by the Netherlands Architecture Institute (NAI) in collaboration with Elsevier Business Information BV.

Architectural History: The Journal of the Society of Architectural Historians of Great Britain
Pixham Mill, Pixham Lane
Dorking, Surrey, RH14 1PQ
U.K.
www.sahgb.org.uk
Published annually.

Architectural Review
151 Rosebery Avenue
33 39 Bowling Green Lane
London, EC1R 4GB
U.K.
+44 020 8956 3504
Published by EMAP Construct.

Architecture Australia
4 Princes Street
Level 3
Port Melbourne, Victoria 3207
Australia
+61 (03) 9646 4760
www.archmedia.com.au/aa/aa.htm
Official magazine of the RAIA.

l'architecture d'aujourd'jui
6, rue Lhomond
Paris, F-75005
France
+33 1 44321860
www.architecture-aujourdhui.presse.fr
Published 6 times a year in French and English.

Architecture & Design Journals & Magazines (Con't)

Arkitektur
Norrlandsgatan 18, 2fr
P.O. Box 1742
Stockholm, S-111 87
Sweden
+46 8 679 6105
www.arkitektur-forlag.se
Published eight times yearly, with English summaries.

a+u magazine
30-8, Yushima 2-chome, Bunkyo-ku
Tokyo, 113-0034
Japan
+81 33816-2935
www.japan-architect.co.jp
Published monthly in Japanese and English by A+U Publishing Co., Ltd.

Blueprint
Freepost, LON8209
London NW
U.K.
+ 44 171 706 4596
Published monthly except August, by Aspen Publishing.

Canadian Architect
1450 Don Mills Road
Don Mills, Ontario, M3B 2X7
Canada
(416) 510-6854
www.cdnarchitect.com
Published monthly by Southam Magazine Group Limited.

Casabella
Via Manzoni 12
Rozzano
Milan, 20089
Italy
+39 2 57512575
Published monthly in Italian with an English summary.

El Croquis
Av. De los Reyes Catolicos 9
Madrid, E-28280 El Escorial
Spain
+34 918969414
www.elcroquis.es
Published bimonthly in Spanish and English.

Daidalos
Redaktion Daidalos
Littenstra Be 106/107
Berlin, D-10179
Germany
+49 30246575
www.gbhap.com/magazine
Published quarterly in English by The Gordon and Breach Publishing Group.

Domus
Via Achille Grandi 5-7
Rozzano
Milan, 20089
Italy
+39 0282472265
http://domus.edidomus.it
Published 11 times a year in Italian and English.

Hinge
17/F, Queen's centre. Queen's Road east
Wanchai,
Hong Kong
+852 2520 2468
www.hingenet.com/hinge/hinge.htm
Published monthly.

Japan Architect
31-2 Yshima 2-chome
Bunkyo-ku
Tokyo, 113-8501
Japan
+81 33811-7101
www.japan-architect.co.jp
Published quarterly in Japanese and English.

Journal of Architecture
11 New Fetter Lane
London, EC4P 4EE
U.K.
+44 171 583 9855
http://journals.routledge.com/
Published four times a year by Routledge for the RIBA.

Journal of Urban Design
Institute of Urban Planning
University of Nottingham
University Park
Nottingham, NG7 2RD
U.K.
+44 115 951 4873
www.carfax.co.uk
Published 3 times a year by Carfax Publishing Limited for the Institute of Urban Planning.

Architecture & Design Journals & Magazines (Con't)

Ottagono
Via Stalingrado, 97/2
Bologna, 40128
Italy
+39 051 4199711
www.ottagono.com
Published bimonthly in Italian and English.

Rassegna
Via Stalingrado 97-2
Bologna, 40128
Italy
+39 51 4199211
www.compositori.it
Published quarterly in Italian and English by Editrice Compositori.

Wallpaper
Brettenham House
Lancaster Place
London, WC2E7TL
U.K.
+44 2073221177
www.wallpaper.com
Published ten times a year.

World Architecture
Exchange Tower
2 Harbour Exchange Square
London, E14 9GE
U.K.
+44 171 560 4120
www.worldarchitecture.com
Published 10 times a year by the Builder Group.

World of Interiors
Vogue House
Hanover Square
London W1S 1JU
U.K.
+44 020 7499 9080
www.worldofinteriors.co.uk
Published monthly by Conde Nast.

Did you know...

The top 11 architecture and design magazines, as chosen by U.S. architecture critics in a recent survey:

- Architecture
- Metropolis
- Architectural Record
- Dwell
- I.D.
- Nest
- Interiors
- Wallpaper
- ONE
- World of Interiors
- Architectural Digest

Source: The Architecture Critic, *National Arts Journalism Program, Columbia University*

Obituaries

In memory of the design and preservation
leaders and patrons who died between
October 1, 2000 and August 31, 2001.

Ellis LeRoy Armstrong, 86

Former national director of public roads, Ellis LeRoy Armstrong died January 26, 2001. As the U.S. director of public roads during the Eisenhower administration—from 1958 to 1961—he oversaw the rapidly expanding national highway system. Previously he served as Utah's highway director. From 1972 until 1974, he led the U.S. National Committee of World Energy Conference and subsequently the Committee of International Water Resources Association from 1976 until 1979. Following retirement, Armstrong lectured and published more than 150 articles on energy policy, water resource issues, and highway design.

Vladimir Basich, 66

Chicago architect Vladimir "Walter" Basich died October 16, 2000. During a 25-year career with A. Epstein & Sons, a Chicago-based industrial and commercial architecture firm, as an expert in managing the design and construction process, Basich supervised the design of such Chicago landmarks as the Hyatt Regency Hotel downtown and the award-winning guard towers at Cook County Jail. Other projects included the Cook County courts building and Curle High School on Chicago's South side. In the late 1980's Basich started his own firm, Basic Architecture. He was also a founder of the Croatian Cultural Center on Chicago's North side. Basich grew up in Zagreb, Croatia, graduating from the University of Zagreb with a degree in architecture. He came to the United States in 1961.

Sir Martyn Beckett, 82

A dedicated Neo-Georgian architect who specialized in adapting castles and country homes for modern living, Sir Martyn Beckett died August 5, 2001. A gentleman architect who served in the Second World War, Beckett is nonetheless remembered most for his controversial adaptation in King's College Chapel at Cambridge University. After Ruben's Adoration of the Magi was donated to the chapel in 1959, Beckett oversaw the changes needed to fit the enormous Baroque painting in the Gothic cathedral. While many thought the changes out of touch with the surroundings, others considered the over-all-effect of the subdued architecture with the painting a stunning achievement.

Eric Bedford, 91

Former chief architect for Britain's Ministry of Public Building and Works, Eric Bedford died July 28, 2001. His 1961 Post Office Tower, now the British Telecom Tower, is credited with altering London's skyline with its tall, slim profile and its exposed top floors. He also designed the British Embassy in Washington, D.C., and the British High Commission building in Ottawa, Canada (1964). In 1953, he designed the London decorations for Queen Elizabeth's coronation, including the ornamentation along the city's Mall in Hyde Park and around Westminster Abbey. In 1950, at the age of 41, he became the youngest chief architect in the history of the Ministry of Works.

Lachlan F. Blair, 81

Lachlan "Lock" Blair, FAIA, a pioneer in urban preservation and planning, died August 5, 2001. After working for the Providence City Planning Commission and the Rhode Island Development Council as chief of the planning division, Blair entered private practice, founding Blair Associates in 1957. In 1959 he produced *College Hill: A Demonstration Study of Historic Area Renewal*, the first urban renewal study to address historic preservation. The firm also produced the Vieux Carre district study for New Orleans. In 1966, Blair founded the Preservation Planning concentration at the University of Illinois Urbana-Champaign, where he taught until 1987. He also founded several local and state preservation organizations and served on the Illinois Historic Sites Advisory Council for 17 years. Blair studied at Western Reserve University (now Case Western) and the Massachusetts Institute of Technology.

Kevin Borland, 74

Australian architect and professor Kevin Borland died in November 2000. His career spanned more than 30 years. Following graduation from Melbourne University in 1947, he opened a practice with Peter McIntyre. His many projects included the Melbourne Olympic Swimming Pool (1956), the Harold Hot Pool in Malvern with Daryl Jackson (1969), Clyde Cameron Trade Union College in Wodonga (1975), and many others. He also served as an instructor at Deakin University in Melbourne and as head of the architects office in the West Australian government.

Gordon Bugbee, 66

Gordon Bugbee, an educator, author, and expert on the architecture of Detroit, died October 25, 2000. An associate professor at Lawrence Technological University in Detroit, Bugbee received two degrees from Harvard University, wrote the architectural specifications for the Pontiac Silverdome (1975) and authored a book about the Domino's Pizza headquarters (1985) near Ann Arbor, Michigan. He was widely considered a top expert on the architects and landmarks of Detroit. At the time of his death, Bugbee was working on a revised *American Institute of Architects' Guide to Detroit Architecture*.

Theodore A. Burtis III, 52

New York architect Theodore A. Burtis III died August 1, 2001. A founding partner of Buttrick White + Burtis, his projects ranged from Tower Records' New York flagship store and a redesign of over 40 Tower stores nationwide to educational commissions at Fordham University, the New School University, the Deaf Education Center for Mill Neck Manor on Long Island, and an expansion to the Brooklyn College Library with Shepley Bullfinch Richardson + Abbott. He was also active in the area of affordable housing, including the Carmel Apartments in Staten Island, the Edison Arms Apartments in the Bronx, and the Second Street Day Care Center in Park Slope, Brooklyn. Burtis received a M.Arch. degree from Harvard University in 1978.

**Fred Butner,
73**

North Carolina architect Fred Butner, FAIA, died January 6, 2001. He founded his own firm in 1952, and over the course of his career worked on over
300 projects throughout the Southeast. As a specialist in school and college
buildings, Butner designed over 100 such projects in Western North Carolina,
as well as other institutional facilities. He was named to the AIA College of
Fellows in 1974 and was a past president of both AIA North Carolina and of
the North Carolina Licensing Board for Architects.

**Richard C.
Clark, 72**

Richard C. Clark, a Manhattan architect and former head of the New York
World's Fair examination department, died January 22, 2001. He had been
president of his own firm, Taylor Clark Architects, and remained as a principal following the firm's merger with Swanke Hayden Connell in 2000. A recognized expert in the design of medical facilities and academic medical campuses, Clark directed a number of New York projects, including the New York
Presbyterian Hospital, the Brooklyn Hospital Center, Long Island College
Hospital, North Shore University Hospital, and the New York Hospital
Medical Center of Queens, for which he won a Pacesetter Award in 1998.

**Pamela
Cunningham
Copeland, 94**

Preservationist, noted gardener, collector, philanthropist, and widow of
Lammot du Pont Copeland, former president of Du Pont Company, Pamela
Cunningham Copeland died January 25, 2001. Her commitment to preserva-
tion extended from her own 240-acre Delaware estate, now the Mount Cuba
Center for the Study of Piedmont Flora, soon to be open to the public, to
Gunston Hall, the home of George Mason. She served as First Regent of
Gunston Hall from 1951 to 1960. For many years, Copeland was a benefactor
and trustee of the Henry Francis du Point Winterthur Museum and served on
the Committee for the Preservation of the White House, the council of the
American Association of Museums, and the board of the Historical Society of
Delaware. Copeland single-handedly funded the *Buildings of Delaware* project
in the Buildings of the United States program, a 50-book series on the architectural heritage of the U.S. states. In 2000, the National Trust for Historic
Preservation honored Copeland with its President's Award.

Paul E. Dietrich, 75

A founder of Boston's Cambridge Seven Associates, architect Paul E. Dietrich died June 2, 2001. The firm, renown for its innovate approach to unusual projects, was originally composed of seven artists, including architects, graphic designers, filmmakers and urban planners. Among Dietrich's projects at the firm were the New England Aquarium in Boston (1969), the U.S. Pavilion at Expo '67 in Montreal, the Basketball Hall of Fame in Springfield, Massachusetts (1968), the New Bedford (MA) Whaling Museum, and the master plan for the Massachusetts Bay Transportation Authority's station modernization. Before Cambridge Seven, Dietrich studied at Lazlo Moholy-Nagy's Institute of Design in Chicago and worked under mentor Alexander Girard in Santa Fe, NM. He received a Master's degree in architecture from Harvard University.

Carlos Diniz, 72

Carlos Diniz, an architectural renderer who worked with some of the world's leading architects, died July 18, 2001. Diniz studied industrial design and architecture at the Art Center College of Design in Los Angeles, now in Pasadena. In 1952 he joined Santa Monica-based Victor Gruen Associates and was later encouraged by Gruen to open his own rendering office, which he did in 1957. Diniz went on to produce drawings for architects such as Craig Ellwood, Cesar Pelli, Ricardo Legorreta, Ben Thompson, Frank Gehry, and many more. His most famous works are of high-profile buildings including New York's World Trade Center and London's Canary Wharf.

Antoinette F. Downing, 96

Famed Rhode Island preservationist Antoinette Forrester Downing died May 8, 2001. A scholar and activist, Downing began researching the history of the state in the 1930s, which eventually resulted in her book *Early Homes of Rhode Island*. Later she co-authored *The Architectural Heritage of Newport, Rhode Island* with Vincent Scully. However, it was her work in the 1950s to preserve Providence, RI's College Hill neighborhood that established her reputation as a preservation leader. Battling Brown University's plan to raze this historic neighborhood, Downing spearheaded a national model for community renewal through historic preservation. She later chaired the Rhode Island Preservation Commission, where she led a statewide survey of nearly 50,000 historic buildings, leading to the preservation and reuse of many structures. She also helped found the Providence Preservation Society and served as its chair. In 1986 she was honored with the Crowninshield Award, the highest honor granted by the National Trust for Historic Preservation, and in 1987 the Society for Architectural Historians established the Antoinette Forrester Downing Award, which each year honors outstanding publications in the field of historic preservation.

Rachel Coleman Duell, 100

Rachel Coleman Duell, co-founder of a firm that specialized in designing theme parks, died June 3, 2001. Among her many notable projects were Magic Mountain and the original Universal Studios Tour. Duell attended USC where she met her husband Randall Duell, the last MGM art director and architect. Duell and her husband founded R. Duell and Associates (later Duell Enterprises) in the 1950s. Their first big solo project, Six Flags Over Texas, established the firm as the premier creator of historic theme parks. Besides such groundbreaking parks as Magic Mountain and the original Universal Studios Tour, they were also responsible for the now-defunct Lion Country Safari in Irvine and the MGM Theme Park in Las Vegas. The firm also updated Hershey Park in Hershey, PA, created Opryland-USA in Nashville, Astroworld in Houston, and parks in France, Belgium and Brazil.

Daniel Dunham, 71

Daniel Dunham, an educator and specialist in city design in tropical regions, died December 19, 2000. Dunham served as a professor of architecture and city planning at Columbia University from 1972 to 1985 and from 1985 until his death as a professor of architecture at the City University of New York and associate director of the City College Architectural Center. His many notable designs include the Dhaka railway station in Bangladesh (1968), as well as several universities in that country. In India, he designed clinics and family planning facilities as well as government housing. Dunham was a consultant on projects for the United Nations, World Bank, United States Agency for International Development, and other aid agencies from the Caribbean to Sri Lanka to China and the author of numerous books and articles about building in developing countries. Dunham studied architecture at Harvard, city planning at Columbia, and tropical architecture at the School of Tropical Architecture in London.

Barbara Fealy, 97

Long considered the matriarch of landscape design in the Northwest, Barbara Fealy, FASLA, died December 30, 2000. After studying at the University of Illinois, she moved to Oregon in 1947 and soon became an expert in cultivating the natural beauty of the region. Her reputation spread through her numerous residential gardens, including the award winning Faber Lewis Garden, and her commercial work, including the Oregon College of Arts and Crafts and Timberline Lodge. Her designs have long been admired for their strong design sensibility characterized by simplicity of form, casual elegance, and timelessness. One of her signature works, the Salishan resort on the Oregon coast, won a prestigious Centennial Medallion from the American Society of Landscape Architects. Known for her positive and inspiring attitude, Fealy was a strong supporter of women landscape architects and an outspoken advocate of the idea that women can create success and personal satisfaction by raising a family while passionately pursuing a career.

Hermann Haviland Field, 90

Hermann Haviland Field, founder of Tufts University's graduate program in urban, social and environmental policy, died February 23, 2001, days away from being inducted as an American Institute of Certified Planners Fellow. Field was a practicing planner and architect as well as an educator and author. At Tufts, his philosophies on integrative and democratic planning are now recognized as a precursor to the sustainable development movement. While the director of planning at the New England Medical Center from 1961 to 1972, he oversaw the redesign of the hospital complex, later heralded as a model of neighborhood participation and transit-linked development. For many years, he also served on the planning commission of the Geneva-based World Conservation Union (IUCN).

Robert Barnard Fischer, 85

Robert Barnard Fischer, a landscape architect and horticulturist, died March 30, 2001. A graduate of the University of Massachusetts Amherst, he studied horticulture at the New York Botanical Garden before serving in the army during World War II. After his discharge in 1946, he managed the gardens and grounds of George Washington's Mount Vernon estate for 32 years, where his specialties included boxwood, English ivy, rhododendron, and mountain laurel, among others.

Bob J. Fowler, 67

Building codes champion Bob J. Fowler, FAIA, died August 1, 2001. As an architect, engineer, and building official, Fowler contributed his expertise to the advancement of building codes. He was a long-time member of the national Building Codes and Standards Committee, serving as its chair in 1989, and the International Conference of Building Officials, serving as its first architect chairman. He was also instrumental in the development of the AIA's 1991 "One Code" resolution, which ultimately led to the development of the International Building Code in 2000. Fowler had been the chief building official for Pasadena, California, since 1995. He earned a B.Arch. from Texas Technological University.

William Beye Fyfe, 90

Architect and student of Frank Lloyd Wright, William Beye Fyfe, died May 7, 2001. As a child, Fyfe was inspired by Wright's work in his home town of Oak Park. In 1932, after graduating from the Yale School of Architecture, he became one of Wright's first apprentices at Taliesin in Spring Green, Wisconsin. Although he left disenchanted two years later, Fyfe continued to practice many tenants he learned from Wright in his house, schools and library designs for the Chicago area. His most personally gratifying and important work was the master plan and design for all but one of the buildings for Calvin College in Grand Rapids, Michigan (1957-71). In 1975 Fyfe retired from Chicago's Perkins & Will, where he had worked since 1957.

John C. Gaillard, 62

John Gaillard, the director of meeting planning and events for The American Institute of Architects (AIA), died June 2, 2001. A native of Mobile, Alabama, he earned a bachelor's in architecture from Auburn University and a master's in regional and city planning from the University of Oklahoma. Gaillard began his career with the AIA in 1972 as the director of the design committee and the regional and urban design committee. Most notable, Gaillard served as the director of the last 18 AIA national conventions, which has become the largest annual event in architecture. He was also an associate professor of urban planning at George Washington University in Washington, D.C.

Paul Genecki, 61

Paul Genecki, retired senior vice president with Victor O. Schinnerer & Co., died in late 2000. Genecki was best known for his dedicated service to the design professions and his leadership within the Victor O. Schinnerer & Co. insurance company. Under Genecki's direction, Schinnerer set the standard for A/E professional liability insurers by focusing on risk management strategies rather than on risk avoidance. These included an extensive investment in educating design professionals. He retired in 1998.

Harmon Goldstone, 89

Harmon Goldstone, a New York architect dedicated to historic preservation, died February 21, 2001. After receiving an architecture degree from Columbia University in 1936, he joined the firm of Harrison & Fouiloux, where he helped design the centerpiece for New York's 1939 World's Fair, the World of Tomorrow. He later planned the space requirements for the United Nations and, with his own firm, redesigned New York's Christie's auction house (1977). He is best known, however, as the moving force behind the New York City Landmarks Preservation Commission, where he served as commissioner from 1968 to 1973. His firm hand led to the rejection of two plans for office towers over Grand Central Station, thus saving one of America's great architectural landmarks. During his tenure, 7,271 buildings were designated for preservation, including Greenwich Village and a large section of SoHo, as well as landscapes and interiors.

Alan Gowans, 77

A prominent architectural historian, educator, and author of more than 20 books, many of them classic texts still used in college courses, Alan Gowans died August 19, 2001. His specialty was vernacular architecture, a field which explored the beauty, uses, and cultural importance of durable but often critically berated buildings such as gas stations, bungalows, mail order houses, and road side attractions. He is credited with popularizing the term "foursquare" to describe the early 20th century boxy homes with four rooms upstairs and four downstairs. In 1994, he donated 25,000 slides of mostly unloved buildings, amassed during decades of research, to the National Gallery of Art's slide library. He served as chairman of the art history department at the University of Delaware and the University of British Columbia and was a former president of the Society of Architectural Historians. Gowans attended the University of Toronto, where he received a master's degree in art history. He also studied at Princeton University, earning a master's degree in fine arts and a doctorate in art history.

Aaron Green, 84

Architect Aaron Green, a former apprentice of Frank Lloyd Wright and a collaborator with Wright on more than 30 West coast projects, died June 5, 2001. Green was an associate architect with Wright in the design of the Marin County Civic Center in San Rafael, California, completing the building following Wright's death in 1959. Following study at The Cooper Union in New York City, Green apprenticed with Wright at Taliesin from 1940 – 1943. He went on to collaborate with his mentor on the V.C. Morris Store in San Francisco, as well as other projects, opening a Bay Area office for himself and Wright in 1951. In 1997, Green supervised the restoration of the 1949 Morris Store, then called The Maiden Lane Gallery, returning it to Wright's original vision. Green's book, *An Architecture for Democracy*, details his work on the Marin County Civic Center with Wright. In honor of a half-century of work in the Bay Area, he was awarded the first Gold Medal of the Frank Lloyd Wright Foundation. On his own, Green completed hundreds of design projects, including the Union City (CA) Civic Center and Public Library, the Newark (CA) Public Library and Community Center, and the Water Street Medical Plaza, Santa Cruz, CA.

Byron Hanke, 88

Byron Hanke, Chief Land Planner of the Architectural Division of the Federal Housing Authority (FHA) from 1945 to 1972, died October 3, 2000. A graduate of the Harvard Graduate School of Design, Hanke revolutionized the planning and governance of new communities in the decades following World War II. Through his pioneering work at the FHA in the 1950s and his seminal book, *The Homes Association Handbook* (1964), he created the concepts and standards that moved the housing industry away from residential buildings on strict grids to clustered community developments on curvilinear streets with strong neighborhood associations and locally owned and operated community facilities. In 1962, when research began on Hanke's groundbreaking study, there were only 500 such communities in the United States; by the year 2000, there were over 200,000.

George Hasslein, 83

Founding dean of California Polytechnic State University, San Luis Obispo's School of Architecture and Environmental Design, George Hasslein, FAIA, died August 24, 2001. A native of Los Angeles, Hasslein earned an architecture degree from the University of Southern California. In 1950 he joined the faculty of Cal Poly San Luis Obispo and was named the head of the new architectural engineering department the following year. A staunch advocate of multidisciplinary design, he was the founding dean of Cal Poly's School of Architecture and Environmental Design in 1968, which offers instruction in architecture, architectural engineering, city and regional planning, construction management, and landscape architecture.

William C. Hedrich, 89

The architectural photographer best known for his stunning photo of Fallingwater taken downstream looking upwards towards the house, William C. Hedrich, died August 31, 2001. A world-renowned photographer, he has been described as a "messenger of modernism." Throughout his career, Hedrich worked with such modern masters as Ludwig Mies van der Rohe and Bertrand Goldberg. He began working for his brother, Ken Hedrich, co-founder of the Chicago photography firm Hedrich Blessing, in 1931. In order to capture his famous Fallingwater photograph, his first important solo assignment, he stood in the stream wearing waders, a composition few have been able to recreate. Hedrich, who retired in 1984, received a medal for his architectural photography from The American Institute of Architects in 1967.

Interiors magazine, 113

One of the design industry's leading publications, in operation since 1888, *Interiors* magazine, ceased operation with its June 2001 issue. Most recently owned by Bill Communications, where it was part of their Real Estate and Design Group, *Interiors* received seven Society of Professional Designers awards in the last year alone. Officials cited changing market conditions as the reason for this decision. Some of *Interiors'* more innovative programs, most notably the Designer of the Year Awards, the annual Applied Brilliance conference, and the *Interiors'* Annual Design Awards, will continue under the leadership of other Bill Communications' publications.

Steven Izenour, 61

Famed Philadelphia architect known for his celebration of commonplace American buildings, Steven Izenour, AIA, died August 21, 2001. A member of Venturi, Scott Brown and Associates since 1969 and later partner, his first acclaim came in 1972 with the publication of *Learning from Las Vegas* with Robert Venturi and Denise Scott Brown, a book that celebrated the American commercial strip and encouraged architects to broaden their acceptance of the tastes and values of ordinary people. Izenour's special interest in the road-side vernacular extended to his many campaigns to save unappreciated neon signs and hamburger joints. He also infused his designs with this aesthetic, as in the 1978 BASCO showroom in Philadelphia and the 1999 Children's Garden in Camden, NJ. Most recently he convinced the beach town of Wildwood, NJ, that its dense concentration of 1950s and 1960s doo-wop style architecture was worthy of preservation. Izenour attended Swarthmore College and graduated from the architecture program at the University of Pennsylvania in 1965. He received a master's in architecture from Yale University in 1969.

Bruce G. Kulik, 61

Bruce G. Kulik, FASLA, a landscape architect that specialized in ecology, concept development, and design details, died March 15, 2001. He had extensive knowledge of native and exotic plants, which he utilized in numerous corporate office campus projects and international work. As a principal in Miceli Kulik Williams and Associates, P.C., a landscape architecture and urban design firm, some of Kulik's recent work includes award-winning gardens for KPMG Peat Marwick, revitalization of Journal Square in Jersey City, and several new waterfront developments for Jersey City. His designs have earned many national, regional, and state awards. Kulik received a bachelor's in landscape architecture from Michigan State University.

Clay Lancaster, 83

A major figure in architectural history and preservation, Clay Lancaster died December 25, 2000. He was born and educated in Kentucky, and his early works included writings about 19th century Kentucky architect John McMurtry. Throughout his career he wrote many papers and books on the architecture of his home state, all illustrated in his own distinctive pen and ink drawings. After a move to New York City, he wrote nationally recognized books on, among others, the American bungalow, New York brownstones, Brooklyn Heights, and Olmsted's Prospect Park, where he served as curator. His book, *Old Brooklyn Heights: New York's First Suburb*, provided the intellectual ammunition for Brooklyn Heights to be named New York City's first historic district in 1965, launching the historic district movement across the country. In addition to writing, Lancaster was an award-winning teacher and scholar both in New York and his native Kentucky.

Morris Lapidus, 98

Morris Lapidus, the architect of 1950s and 1960s kitschy Miami hotels which have only recently rebounded from decades of criticism, died January 18, 2001. His most well-known creations were the Fountainebleau (1954), Americana, and Eden Roc (1955) hotels, all in Miami Beach. Lapidus created a uniquely individual "modern French-chateau" style with ornate details and lots of color, the antithesis of the prevailing stripped-down Modernism. Although his buildings were a popular success, he was shunned by architects and architecture critics, and he finally retired in disgust in 1984. More recently his buildings have seen a renaissance with the restoration of many across the country. He collaborated with Miami architect Deborah Desilets to design the Aura restaurant in Miami and received an American Originals award from the Smithsonian's Cooper-Hewitt National Design Museum's inaugural National Design Awards in 2000. He published his autobiography, *Too Much Is Never Enough*, in 1996.

Denys Lasdun, 86

Sir Denys Lasdun, a central figure in European mid-century modernism whose buildings still inspire strong passions, died January 12, 2001. Inspired by Le Corbusier and his experience at many forward-looking firms at the onset of his career, Lasdun's fascination with concrete and organic forms made him a vastly influential figure in his native Britain and abroad. His Bethnal Green (1955) project in London transformed public housing after World War II. His other successes include such notable buildings as the Royal College of Physicians (1959) and Christ College in Cambridge (1966). He is most well-known, however, for the Royal National Theatre (1976) in London, his brutalist gray concrete masterpiece on the South Banks of the Thames. The Theatre, with its stratified terraces and foyers, is a perfect example of Lasdun's sculptural approach to design and his belief in building elements of an urban landscape. Greeted with mixed reviews upon completion in 1976, the building is now considered an indispensable London landmark.

Sarah Tomerlin Lee, 90

A leading proponent of "romantic modernism," both in fashion and interior design, Sarah Tomerlin Lee died April 15, 2001. After moving to New York in 1936, she began a career in design and fashion magazines, eventually becoming editor in chief of *House Beautiful* from 1965 to 1971. When her husband died in 1971, she took over his interior design firm, Tom Lee Ltd., and completed contracts for the Four Season Hotel in Toronto and the Plaza Hotel in New York. Over the next three decades, she became renowned as a hotel designer, specializing in the restoration of many signature hotels in a romantic but efficient style. Her works include New York City's Helmsley Palace and Parker Meridian, as well as the Pursuit of Happiness, a groundbreaking discotheque in the New York Hilton. In 1993, Lee merged her firm with Beyer Blinder Belle, becoming head of interior design until her retirement in 1997. She was also a co-founder of the New York Landmarks Conservancy, a trustee of the New York School of Interior Design, and a president of the Decorators Club in 1995-1997.

Derek Lovejoy, 75

British landscape architect Derek Lovejoy died November 3, 2000. After growing up in London's East End, Lovejoy studied architecture and urban planning at Harvard University before opening his own landscape architecture firm, The Derek Lovejoy Partnership, in 1959. In 1971, at age 45, he became the youngest president in the history of the Institute of Landscape Architects. A specialist in environmental design, his commissions included work in Islamabad, Pakistan; Dodoma, Tanzania; Morocco; Bermuda; and the Middle East. His designs won more than 80 national and international design awards.

Robert Marvin, 81

Internationally acclaimed South Carolina landscape architect Robert Marvin died June 25, 2001. Dedicated to preserving the beauty of his native South, Marvin encouraged all parties – potential clients, architects, engineers, developers, policy makers and his own staff – to tread lightly on the land. His many projects – including the Cecil B. Day Butterfly Center and John A. Sibley Horticultural Center at Callaway Gardens in Georgia, the Southern Progress Corp. in Birmingham, Alabama, and the Jones Bridge Headquarters of Simmons Co. in Atlanta, Georgia – were designed to fit into the existing landscape. In May 2001, Marvin was awarded the American Society of Landscape Architects' highest honor, the ASLA Medal, for his outstanding lifetime achievement. In addition to numerous local, regional and national awards, he received two of South Carolina's highest honors as a 2001 inductee into the South Carolina Hall of Fame and a 2000 recipient of the South Carolina Order of Palmetto. In the 1950s, Marvin prepared the following statement of purpose for his new firm: "The dominant reason for the existence of Robert E. Marvin and Associates shall be to create and design an environment in which each individual within it can grow and develop to be a full human being as God intended him to be."

Ian L. McHarg, 80

Environmentalist, educator, and author Ian McHarg, FASLA, died March 5, 2001. McHarg was founder and, for over 30 years, chairman of the Department of Landscape Architecture and Regional Planning at the University of Pennsylvania. His 1969 book *Design With Nature* inspired the first Earth Day, and his landmark course "Man and Environment" inspired the 1960's CBS television series *The House We Live In*. He was a principal in the firm of Wallace, McHarg, Roberts and Todd and the author of *To Heal the Earth* and *A Quest for Life*. McHarg was a principal on over 60 projects, including the 1962 Plan for the Valleys in Baltimore County, Maryland, the Inner Harbor in Baltimore, and The Woodlands in Houston, Texas. His 1972 project for the U.S. Environmental Protection Agency and its resulting report, "Toward a Comprehensive Plan for Environmental Quality," pioneered a conservation approach that formed the basis of future environmental impact assessments. McHarg was awarded the Harvard Lifetime Achievement Award, National Medal of Art, Thomas Jefferson Foundation Medal in Architecture, American Society of Landscape Architects' Medal, Japan Prize for Urban Planning, and many others.

Tuula-Maria Merivuori, 53

Finnish landscape architect and educator Tuula-Maria Merivuori died December 18, 2000. Merivuori studied horticulture briefly at the Faculty of Agriculture and Forestry at the University of Helsinki. After several apprenticeships in Germany and Denmark, she joined Hannover University of Technology, where she earned her Diploma-Ingenieur in Landscape Architecture in 1975. She then joined the faculty at the Helsinki University of Technology and later received her postgraduate degree from that same school. In 1994 she became a full professor at the university. She was also a devoted member of the International Federation of Landscape Architects (IFLA) since 1979, for which she served in many capacities including vice president of the central region and secretary-general.

Marshall Meyers, 70

Marshall Meyers, an architect who worked many years in the office of Louis Kahn and contributed to nearly all of Kahn's major projects, died August 12, 2001. His projects with Kahn included the Richards Medical Building at the University of Philadelphia (1956-65) and the Salk Institute for Biological Studies in La Jolla, California (1959-65). Meyers was project manager for the Kimbell Art Museum in Ft. Worth, Texas (1966-72). Following Kahn's death, Meyers oversaw the completion of his Center for British Art at Yale University. In 1985, Meyers joined Bower Lewis Thrower Architects, where he was project manager for the design of the Cone Wing of the Baltimore Museum of Art. He joined the Pasadena office of Perkins & Will in 1999.

Henry Michel, 76

A globe-trotting engineer and construction leader, Henry Michel, died May 23, 2001. Michel was born in Europe and worked on British airbases during World War II before founding his own engineering firm in Rome. When he moved to New York in 1965 he joined Parsons Brinckerhoff, the Manhattan construction firm that built the original IRT subway line in New York City. Michel oversaw the firm's work on large-scale transportation projects, such as Atlanta's rapid transit system and systems in Venezuela and Taiwan. In 1975 he became the reorganized company's first president, assuming chief executive role in 1990. Under his leadership, the company grew to 4,000 employees with offices in eight countries. After stepping down, he became a co-owner of Pegasus Consulting, which advises companies on large overseas investments.

Alfred Moen, 84

A burned hand led to a moment of inspiration and a billion dollar business for Alfred Moen, who died April 17, 2001. While working to pay his tuition at the University of Washington, where he was pursuing a mechanical engineering degree, Moen accidentally burned his hand on a conventional two-handled faucet. His injury led him to invent a double-valve faucet, eventually leading to the creation of Moen Inc., one of the world's leading producers of plumbing products. A compulsive refiner and developer of plumbing devices with more than 200 patents to his name, Moen was head of research and development at his company until he retired in 1982.

Francesco Montana, 89

Former architecture chairman at the University of Notre Dame, Francesco "Frank" Montana, died February 16, 2001. A native of Naro, Italy, Montana earned architecture degrees from New York University and the École des Beaux-Arts in 1933 and 1939, respectively. He joined the University of Notre Dame architecture faculty in 1939, serving as the architecture chairman from 1950-72. He founded the school's Rome Studies Program in 1969, directing it in 1972-75 and 1980-86, when he retired. In 1999 he made a $1 million gift to Notre Dame in support of the Rome Studies Program, the only year-long international study program among American architecture schools required for all students. Montana also designed numerous buildings on the Notre Dame campus and its Institute for Ecumenical Studies in Israel.

William J. Mouton Jr., 70

Structural engineer William J. Mouton, Jr. died June 30, 2001. In his native New Orleans, Mouton was most well-known for developing a technique for driving deep pilings through that city's soft ground and anchoring them in the hard ground deep below. This was first utilized in the 45-story Plaza Tower Building, which he built in the early 1960s and was the first building in the city able to soar to this height. He also held over 20 patents, including one for erosion control concepts for Louisiana's wetlands. Part of his work was shown in the "Engineers of the Century" exhibit at the Georges Pompidou Center in Paris in 1997. He received his bachelor's and master's degrees in civil engineering from Tulane University, where he also was a professor until 1998.

Ibsen Nelsen, 81

Architect of Seattle's Museum of Flight, Ibsen Nelsen, died July 19, 2001. In addition to his architecture work, for over 30-years Nelsen was instrumental in the preservation of many of Seattle's historic landmarks, including Pike Place Market and Pioneer Square. His firm Ibsen Nelsen and Associates designed many notable buildings in the Northwest, including the Inn at the Market, buildings at Western Washington University-Bellingham, the governor's mansion restoration, and the Merrill Court Townhouses. He was also active as a leader in the Seattle community as president of Allied Arts and chairman of the Seattle Art Commission. He earned an architecture degree from the University of Oregon.

George Nolte Sr.

George Nolte Sr., founder of Nolte Associates, a California-based engineering, planning and surveying firm with over a dozen offices in the West, died November 11, 2000. A registered engineer and licensed land surveyor, Nolte founded the firm in 1949, growing it to over 350 employees who worked in the U.S. and Mexico. Former U.S. Congressman Norman Mineta once credited Nolte with building the "foundation" of Silicon Valley. Nolte was a lifetime member of the American Society of Civil Engineers and an inductee of the Silicon Valley Engineering Hall of Fame. Nolte graduated with a degree in civil engineer from the Polytechnic College of Engineering in Oakland, California, in 1940.

M. Meade Palmer, 85

M. Meade Palmer, FASLA, died July 16, 2001. Palmer is best known for his design of the Lyndon B. Johnson Memorial Grove next to George Washington Memorial Parkway in Washington, D.C. In private practice since 1948, his work focused strongly on the Virginia, Maryland, and Washington, D.C. region, including the Washington National Cathedral, Bull Run National Park, Carters Grove, James Madison University, and Mason Neck State Park. In 1991 Palmer received the ASLA medal, the highest honor given by the American Society of Landscape Architecture, as well as numerous national design awards. He was also a distinguished professor at the University of Virginia for more than 30 years where he taught plant identifications and design courses. He graduated from Cornell University in 1939.

John A. Parker, 91

John A. "Jack" Parker, founder of the Department of City and Regional Planning at the University of North Carolina, died March 18, 2001. When the department opened in 1946, it was the only planning program with its principle university base in the social sciences instead of landscape design, architecture, or engineering. He served as department chairman for almost 30 years until his retirement in 1974. A lifelong educator, Parker won numerous awards and honors for his academic achievements, including the Distinguished Educator Award from the Association of Collegiate Schools of Planning in 1994. Parker earned two architecture degrees and a master's of city planning from the Massachusetts Institute of Technology.

Owen Harley Peters, 77

Owen Harley Peters, FASLA, a landscape architect and past president of the American Society of Landscape Architects (ASLA), died October 26, 2000. Peters designed many notable projects, including the Pacific Asia Museum, City of Westminster Complex, Parker-Hannifin Corporate Headquarters, Linda Isle Entry and Streetscapes, Pasadena First Baptist Church, various projects at the University of California, Irvine, and numerous private gardens. He graduated from Iowa State University in 1949 with a bachelor's degree in landscape architecture. After moving to Pasadena, California, that same year, he formed the firm Eriksson, Peters, and Thoms, now EPT. Aside from his professional work, Peters served on many committees and boards, including the California State Board of Landscape Architects, Southern California Chapter of the ASLA, College of Environmental Design, California State Polytechnic University in Pomona, and the ASLA at the national level.

Richardson Pratt Jr., 78

Richardson Pratt Jr., a former president of the Pratt Institute in Brooklyn and chairman of Charles Pratt & Company, died May 1, 2001. Pratt was the great-grandson of the Pratt Institute's founder, Charles Pratt, who was a partner with John D. Rockefeller in the Standard Oil Company. Pratt earned a master's degree from the Harvard Business School before joining Standard Oil (now Exxon Mobil). In 1971 he joined Charles Pratt & Company, which was established in 1891 to oversee the Pratt family interests, and retired in 2000. He also served as the president of Pratt Institute from 1972-1990.

Adele Quinn, 89

Adele Faulkner Quinn, FASID, the first woman to be named a fellow by the American Society of Interior Designers (ASID), died October 22, 2000. The diverse portfolio of her company, which she ran for 50 years, was a veritable history of Los Angeles. She designed the city's first penthouse condominium (1958), as well as the homes of many famous business leaders and entertainment personalities. Quinn taught interior design at UCLA for 17 years and, for the last twenty years of her life, was an active and inspirational member of the board of Orange County's Interval Crisis Shelters for battered women and children.

Frederick Rath Jr., 87

Frederick Rath Jr., the first director of the National Trust for Historic Preservation, died April 1, 2001. An early specialist in the field of historic preservation, Rath received degrees in American History from Dartmouth College and Harvard University. He joined the National Park Service before becoming Executive Secretary of the National Council for Historic Sites and Buildings, which was organized as the National Trust in 1949. Upon leaving the Trust in 1956, Rath became active in New York state historical preservation activities. He was a Vice Director of the New York State Historical Association and Adjunct Professor for the Cooperstown Graduate Program in History Museum Studies. He also chaired the Cooperstown (NY) Planning Commission and helped develop the first comprehensive plan for the city. In 1972, he became deputy commissioner in the New York State Office of Parks, Recreation, and Historic Preservation, setting up a program for all state historic sites and landmarks. Rath helped found the Eastern National Park and Monument Association, dedicated to developing and disseminating interpretive materials throughout the park system, and was its chief executive officer from 1979 to 1987. He held many advisories and chairmanships throughout his career. Rath was awarded a Bronze Star medal, the Conservation Service Award of the U.S. Department of the Interior, the Crowinshield Award from the National Trust, an honorary Doctor of Human Letters Award from the State University of New York, and many other accolades.

Lloyd Schwan, 45

Lloyd Schwan, an American furniture and interior designer who helped create a fertile atmosphere for design in New York City in the 1980s, died in January 2001. After studying at the Chicago Art Institute, he founded GodleySchwan Design in 1984 with his then-wife Lyn Godsey. At a time when Italians dominated the world of modern furniture design, GodleySchwan's expressionistic, colorful, pop-influenced pieces dominated Milan's Salon di Mobile in 1988 and brought excitement back to American design. His Crinkle Lamp (1996), a steel lamp with a crushed-vinyl light shade, is in the design collection of the Museum of Modern Art.

Fred Scott, 58

A radical furniture designer whose work focused on the human form, Fred Scott, died January 31, 2001. As a young man, he apprenticed with a traditional British furniture maker before winning a furniture scholarship to the Royal College of Art in 1963. In 1974, he designed a revolutionary folding chair that, although praised for elegance and innovation, was criticized for comfort. His subsequent five-year quest for comfort resulted in the creation of his Supporto range, which revolutionized office furniture. The 1979 line, made of cast aluminum with a tall slender backrest and arm supports, won the Design Council Award and is considered a classic of 20th Century design.

Philip A. Shipley, 88

Landscape architect for celebrities like Clark Gable, Walt Disney and Steven Spielberg, Philip A. Shipley, died July 5, 2001. Shipley earned a degree in landscape architecture from UC Berkeley in 1933, subsequently opening a practice in Southern California. His simple but unusual designs earned him many notable commissions, including Las Vegas' Tropicana Hotel, Los Angeles' Sheraton Universal Studios, and the Eldorado Country Club in Palm Springs. He also worked for many entertainers—Lew Wasserman, Jules Stein, Frank Sinatra, King Vidor, Kirk and Michael Douglas, Aaron Spelling, and Norton Simon – and Presidents Ronald Reagan and Richard Nixon.

Valerie Sivinski, 49

Architect, preservationist, and educator Valerie Sivinski died October 17, 2000. Sivinski oversaw the restoration of numerous Tacoma, Washington, historic buildings. She held a degree in building conservation from the University of York in England and a master's in architecture from the University of New Mexico. She taught preservation methods at the University of Washington and served as Tacoma's historic preservation officer. In 1998 she opened her own architectural consulting and design firm, Artifacts Consulting, Inc.

Ignasi de Solà-Morales, 58

Noted Spanish architect Ignasi de Solà-Morales died March 12, 2001. Solà-Morales was best known for his reconstructions of Mies van der Rohe's Barcelona Pavilion in 1986 and of Barcelona's Liceu Opera House in 1999. A professor at the Barcelona School of Architecture since 1978, he was an influential critic and historian whose books included *Gaudí* (1983), *Jujol* (1990) and *Difference: A Topography of Contemporary Architecture* (1995). He died while attending the jury deliberations for the European Union's Mies van der Rohe Prize, a biannual architectural prize that he helped create.

Martin Stern Jr., 84

Martin Stern Jr., a pioneer of Googie architecture—mid-century, space-age buildings with clever signage—died July 28, 2001. Stern began his career designing three Ships coffee shops in Los Angeles in 1956 and 1957. He subsequently brought his exuberant vision to Las Vegas with a series of commissions. His projects there include numerous additions to the Sahara Hotel, including a skyscraper and convention center; a 1964 cylindrical, sculpted tower for the Sands Hotel; the 1969 Hotel International (later the Hilton); and, in 1973, the MGM Grand (now Bally's).

Rosemary Verey, 82

Garden advisor to Prince Charles, Rosemary Verey, died May 31, 2001. When Verey was injured in a riding accident in the 1950s, her husband gave her a book on plants that sparked a life-long passion. The result was a magnificent four-acre garden at her Barnsley House, a 17th century rectory near Gloucester England, that almost single-handedly re-established the formal English garden. Opened to the public in 1970, it draws 30,000 visitors a year, especially to its famed Knot Garden of clipped boxwood and phillyrea hedges that resemble an embroidery pattern. A frequent lecturer and author of 15 books, Verey created gardens for Prince Charles, Elton John, New York's Botanical Garden, and many others. She received numerous horticultural awards, including, in 1999, the Royal Horticultural Society's highest award, the Victoria Medal of Honor.

Richard K. Webel, 100

Richard K. Webel, FASLA, died November 1, 2000. After immigrating from Germany, Webel studied at Harvard College, where he received a bachelor's degree in 1923 and subsequently earned a master's degree in landscape architecture from the Harvard Graduate School of Design. He studied in Europe as a fellow at the American Academy in Rome from 1926-29 and served as an assistant professor of the Harvard School of Design from 1929-39. In 1931 he formed Webel and Innocenti with Umberto Innocenti, now run by Webel's son, Richard C. Webel. Their numerous projects include the American Military Cemetery, Neuville, Belgium; Frick Park, Pittsburgh, Pennsylvania; MacAllister College, St. Paul, Minnesota; and racetracks in New York and Kentucky. Webel also served as a member of New York City's Fine Arts Commission and the Public Advisory Panel on Architectural Services, General Services Administration.

Sidney R. Yates, 91

Sidney Yates, one of Congress' most ardent supporters of the arts for almost 50 years, died October 5, 2000. In 1965, Yates pushed for the legislation that established the National Endowment for the Arts (NEA). As chairman of the House Appropriations subcommittee, he defended the NEA against conservative critics and others who tried to curtail funding or eliminate the program all together. In 2000, he retired from the House after serving 24 terms.

Marco Zanuso, 85

Prominent Italian architect and industrial designer, Marco Zanuso, died July 11, 2001. He is best known for his Olivetti factory in Argentina (1954). Other major commissions include IBM office buildings in Milan and Rome and a new theater in Rome. After earning an engineering degree and serving in World War II, he developed a sleek, understated style, which he brought to everyday objects like bathroom scales and televisions. His 1964 radio design for the Brionvega company, "TS502," was typical of his aesthetic with its use of plastic, simple colors, and a clamshell-like cover.

NAME INDEX

Alma-Taderna, Sir L., 150
Almeida, Flavia Augusta, 518
Almond, Killis P., Jr., 285
Almquist, Norman G., 280
Alper Ladd, Inc., 128
Alpert, Estelle, 311
Alpha Rho Chi, 516, 517–518
Alpha Rho Chi Bronze Medal, 517–518
Alschuler, Alfred S., 285
Alsentzer, Zacharias Karl, 518
Alsobrook, Jerry R., 311
Altes Museum, 254
Althouse, Edward S., Jr., 544
Altitude, 103
Altoon, Ronald A., 285, 341
Alvar Aalto Museum, 239
Alvares, Alfred V., 329
Alvarez, Jose, 329
Alvarez, Mario R., 329
Alvine, Raymond G., 280
Amaco Construction Ltd., 175
Amaral, Jesus E., 285
Amato, Julie, 515
American Academy in Rome, 47, 274–277, 666
American Academy of Arts and Letters, 56, 57, 62
American Academy of Arts & Sciences, 278–279
American Arbitration Association, 226
American Architectural Foundation, 116, 193, 259, 543–548
American Architectural Manufacturers Association, 226
American Association of Nurserymen, 226
American Association of School Administrators, 89
American Center for Design, 226
American Collegiate Schools of Architecture, 560
American Concrete Insititue, 226
American Consulting Engineers Council, 84–86, 194, 280–284
American Gas Association, 226
American Horticultural Society, 226
American Institute of Architects (AIA)
  awards/honors given by, 2, 3–6, 8, 9–12, 38, 39, 40, 41–45, 42, 44, 46–49, 50, 51, 52, 60, 61, 74, 83, 89, 119, 170, 171, 180, 188, 404, 405, 543–548, 560
  awards/honors given to, 160, 424
  Chancellors, 273
  Committee on Architecture forn Education, 155
  Continuing Education System, 444
  Fellows, 285–307
  Honorary Fellows, 329–331
  Honorary Members, 332–335
  library, 635
  organizational information, 195
  Presidents, 341
  publications, 639
  related organizations, 207

See also AIA entries; American Architectural Foundation
American Institute of Architecture Students, 97, 519, 553–554
American Institute of Building Design, 226
American Institute of Certified Planners, 130, 133, 196, 308–310, 514, 515
American Institute of Steel Construction, 226
American InterContinental University, 526
American Intercontinental University, 529
American Library Association, 119
American Museum of Natural History, 120, 148
American National Standards Institute, 227
American Planning Association, 58, 130, 133, 196, 514, 525
American Resort Development Association, 227
American Society for Testing & Materials, 227
American Society of Architectural Illustrators, 98
American Society of Architectural Perspectives, 48
American Society of Civil Engineers, 227
American Society of Consulting Arborists, 226
American Society of Golf Course Architects, 227
American Society of Heating, Refrigerating & Air-Conditioning Engineers, 227
American Society of Horticulture Science, 227
American Society of Interior Designers
  awards given by, 78, 81, 551
  Fellows, 311–313
  organizational information, 197, 525, 626
  Presidents, 342
  publications, 639
American Society of Landscape Architects (ASLA)
  awards/honors given by, 64, 65–68, 66, 114, 523–524
  Fellows, 314–319
  Honorary Members, 336
  organizational information, 198, 627
  Presidents, 343
  publications, 640
  student chapter, 525
American Society of Mechanical Engineers, 227
American Society of Plumbing Engineers, 227
American Society of Professional Estimators, 227
American Textile Manufacturers Institute, 227
AmericaOne Identity, 157
Ames, Anthony, 274
Amisano, Joseph, 274, 285
Amtrak, 100
Ancher, Sydney Edward, 144

Ander, Gregg, 285
Anderson, Al (Colorado), 280
Anderson, Al (Wisconsin), 280
Anderson, Amy, 274
Anderson, Dorman D., 285
Anderson, Harry F., 285
Anderson, Harry G., 280
Anderson, Hilary, 515
Anderson, J. Macvicar, 350
Anderson, J. Robert, 314
Anderson, J. Timothy, 285
Anderson, John C., 320, 346
Anderson, John D., 285, 341
Anderson, John E., 308
Anderson, Joseph Horatio, 392
Anderson, Lawrence, 344, 560
Anderson, Mark, 136
Anderson, Richard, 285
Anderson, Richard T., 308
Anderson, Robert O., 340
Anderson, Ross S., 274
Anderson, Samuel A., 285
Anderson, Sir Robert Rowand, 150
Anderson, Stephen C., 280
Anderson, Vickie L., 547
Anderson, William L., 285
Anderson Independent-Mail, 58
Ando, Dr. Yoichi, 48
Ando, Tadao
  awards/honors, 62, 75, 108, 138, 141, 151, 329
  quotes by, 181
Andreu, Paul, 37
Andrews, Frank Mills, 390, 392
Andrews, J. Philip, 285
Andrews, John Hamilton, 62, 144, 329
Andrews, Lavone D., 285
Andrews, Martha P., 285
Andrews, Peter N., 280
Andrews, Simon, 328
Andrews, William F., 311
Andrews University, 517, 532, 543
Andropogon Associates, Ltd., 65
Andros, Stephen John, 320
Angel, Truman, 436
Angell, Ellen, 311
Angle, Robert H., 311
Angotti, Thomas, 277
Ankrom Moisan Associated Architects, 70, 92, 495
Ann Beha Associates, Inc., 483
Annese, Domenico, 314
Anselevicius, George, 285, 344, 512
Ansell, W. H., 350
Anshen + Allen, 97
Anstis, James H., 285
Antoinette Forrester Downing Award, 422, 423, 650
Antonakakis, Suzana, 362
Anton and Associates, 483
Antonelli, Paola, 122, 342
Antuñez, Ellis L., 314
Antunovich Associates, 41
APA Journalism Award, 58

Baum, Joseph H., 48
Baum, Richard T., 280
Baume, Henry B., 346
Baumgarten, Howard R., 314
Baumschlager & Eberle, 185
Bausman, Karen, 277
Bauzeit Architekten GmbH, 38
Bavaro, Joseph D., 286
Bawa, Geoffrey M., 329
Baxter, Augustus, Sr., 332
Baxter, Clifton R., 280
Bay Engineering, 128
Bazer-Schwartz, Jeannine, 311
Bazzle, Tamara A., 311
BBC Pacific Quay, 251
B & B Italia, 105
Beach, Carrie, 515
Beal, Louis M. S., 339
Beal, Roy F., 311
Beale, John Craig, 286
Beall, Burtch W., Jr., 286
Beals, Ashley Elizabeth, 546
Bean, Leroy E., 286
Beard, Alan J., 286
Beardsley Design Associates, 371
Bearsch, Lee P., 286
Beasley, Ellen, 277
Beatty Harvey & Associates, 371
Beaty, William H., 286
Beaubien, Brad, 514
Beaudouin, Eugene, 329
Bechhoefer, William B., 286
Bechtel, Riley P., 125
Bechtel, Stephen D., Jr., 125
Bechtel Group, 125
Beck, Eldon W., 314
Beck, George, 323
Becker, Lee, 286
Becker, Nathaniel, 323
Becker, Ralph W., 280
Becker, Rex L., 286
Becker, Robert W., 308
Becket, Welton, 387
Beckett, Sir Martyn, 647
Beckhard, Herbert, 286
Beckley, Robert M., 286, 345
BecVar, Arthur N., 323
Bedell, Marjorie A., 311
Bedford, Eric, 647
Bedford-Stuyvesant Restoration, 46
Bednar, Michael, 286
Bee, Carmi, 286
Beeah Group Consultants, 35
Beer, David W., 286
Beers/Davison, 129
Beery, Edgar C., 286
Befu, Yoshiro, 314
Begay, Richard K., Jr., 518
Beggs, Arthur G., 314
Beha, Ann M., 286
Behnke, William A., 314, 343
Behre, Robert, 355
Beinecke, Walter, Jr., 424
Beishline, Robert, 548

Belcher, John, 150, 350
Bell, Byron, 286
Bell, C. E., 393
Bell, Frederic, 286
Bell, James G., 280
Bell, James R., 308, 314
Bell, M. E., 390, 391
Bell, M. Wayne, 286
Bell, Richard C., 276, 314
Bell, Theodore T., 280
Bellafiore, Vincent, 314, 343
Bell and Kent, 392
Belle, John, 286
Bellini, Atelier, 99
Belluschi, Pietro, 39, 135, 168, 171, 397
Belmont, Karleen, 328
Belmont Technical College, 535
Belt, Lemman and Lo, 390
Bender, Ralph C., 286
Benedek, Armand, 314
Benepe, Barry, 286
Benisch, G., 69
Benjamin Thompson & Associates, 60
Benktzon, Maria, 108
Bennet, H., 160
Bennett, Claire R., 314, 343
Bennett, Daniel D., 286
Bennett, David J., 286
Bennett, Edward H., 133
Bennett, Ralph, 512
Bennett, Stephen M., 332
Bennett, Ward, 47, 339
Bennett, Wells, 344
Benoit, Gerard, 329
Benson, John, 46, 139
Bentel, Frederick R., 286
Bentel, Maria A., 286
Bentsen, Kenneth E., 286
Bentz, Frederick J., 286
Benz, Christian Glauser, 545
Beranek, Leo L., 332
Berenson, Bertram, 344
Bereuter, Hon. Douglas, 336
Berg, Karl A., 286
Berg, Raymond, 144
Berg, Shary Page, 314
Bergen Record, 355
Berggren & Woll, Architects, 483
Bergman, Elaine, 332
Bergman, Teree L., 308
Bergmann, Paul A., 308
Bergmann, Richard R., 286
Bergmeyer Associates Inc., 109
Bergquist, Lloyd F., 286
Bergson, Maria, 339
Bergstedt, Milton V., 180
Bergstrom, Edwin, 341
Berkebile, Robert J., 286
Berkoff, Marlene J., 286
Berlage, Dr. Hendrik Petrus, 151
Berners, Edgar H., 349
Berners/Schober Associates, Inc., 371
Bernhardt, Richard C., 308
Bernheim, Anthony N., 286

Bernstein, Phillip, 286
Berry, Barbara, 339
Berry, Frank Lee, 311
Berry, K. Norman, 286
Berry, Tana, 523
Bertman, Richard J., 286
Bertone, Ronald P., 286
Bertram, Frederic A., 286
Bertsch, Dale F., 308
Berube, Claude, 325
Bess, Dave E., 308
Best, Melvin H., 323
BE-ST Bellevuestrae Development GmbH, 177
Best of Seniors' Housing Award, 70–71
Bethune, Louise Blanchard, 364
Bettman, Alfred, 133
Betts, Gary A., 320
Betts, Hobart, 286
Betts, Richard J., 351
Beuys, Joseph, 18
Bevins, William, 349
Beyer, John H., 286
Beyer, William, 286
Beyer Blinder Belle, 60, 139, 658
Bhalla, Jai R., 329
Biallas, Randall, 336
Bialosky + Partners, Architects, 483
Bialosky Piekert Architects, 70
Bice, Lawrence, 515
Bickel, John H., 286
Biddle, James, 332
Biderman, George R., 328
Bidwill, J., 332
Biebesheimer, Frederick C., III, 286
Bierman, Bruce, 339
Bigger, William I., 280
Biggs, T. J., 286
Bill Burton and Associates, 175
Billian, John Carlos, 355
Binder, Rebecca L., 286
Binger, Wilson V., 280
Binkley, James, 286
Binswanger, Christine, 15, 17
Birch, Eugenie Ladner, 308
Birchfield, Hal F. B., 311
Bird, Lance L., 286
Birge, John R., 286
Birk, Sherry, 332
Birkerts, Gunnar, 62, 168, 286, 511
Birnbaum, Charles A., 314
Birtles, Sarah, 547
Bischoff, Stan, 356
Bishir, Catherine W., 413, 422
Bishop, Calvin T., 314, 343
Bishop, James A., 286
Bishop, Walter F., 320
Bissell, George, 286
Bitter, Adriana, 311
Bitter, Edwin, 311
Bizios, Georgia, 286
BJ Krivanek Art + Design, 157
Björn and Björn Design, 33
BJSS Duarte Bryant, 505

Daewoo & Partners, 395
Daft, Jack R., 315
Daggett, Jeffrey M., 280
Dagit, Charles E., Jr., 289
Dahan, Fernand W., 289
Dahl, Taffy, 49
Dahlin Group, 71
Daileda, David A., 289
Daileda, Kathleen L., 332
Dailey, Donald E., 323
DaimlerChrysler Corporation, 76, 100, 101
Daky, Thomas Kennedy, 546
Dale, Curt, 289
Dale, P. A., 311
Daley, Honorable Richard M., 116
Daley, Royston T., 274
Dalhousie University, 517, 546
Dalland, Todd, 289
Dallas Morning News, 356
Daltas, Spero, 274
Dalton, J. E., 289
Dalton, Melissa, 517
Daly, Cesar, 150
Daly, Leo A., III, 83, 289
D'Amato, Alfonse M., 332
Damaz, Paul, 289
Damian Farrell Design Group, 148
Damianos, Sylvester, 83, 289, 341
Damon, Henry Eugene, 280
Damora, Robert, 289
Damuck, Walter E., 320
Dandan, Christine, 325
Danforth, George E., 289
Dangermond, Peter, Jr., 315
Daniel, Mann, Johnson & Mendenhall, 491, 501, 506
Danielian, Arthur C., 289
Daniel P. Coffey and Associates, 175
Daniels, Dwayne, 547
Daniels, Eugene, 325
Daniels, George N., 289
Daniels, Stanley L., 289
Danish Center for Architecture, 247
Danish Design Center, 48, 248
Danna, Doris Andrews, 289
Darby, Robert F., 289
Darby, Samuel N., 290
D'Arcy, Barbara, 81, 339
Darden, Douglas, 274
Darden, Edwin S., 289
Dare, Robert Harold, 545
Darling, Frank, 150
Darmer, Ben R., 289
Daroff Design Inc. and DDI Architects, 504
DaSilva, Carlos E., 329
DaSilva Black Calcagni Chesser Architects, 484
Dattner, Richard, 170, 289
Daugherty, Edward L., 315
Daumet, Honore, 150
David, Theoharis L., 289
David, Thomas, 323
David Berg Inc., 383
David Evans and Associates, Inc., 86
David Furman/Architecture, 50

David J. Katz & Associates, Inc., 483
David M. Schwarz Architectural Services, 375, 381, 389
David Morrison Books, 635
Davidoff, Paul, 133
Davidson, Ann, 332
Davidson, Colin H., 512
Davidson, D. G., 289
Davidson, David L., 280
Davidson, David S., 289
Davidson, Edward W., 280
Davidson, G. Robert, 280
Davidson, John M., 329
Davidson, Kent, 553
Davidson, Robert I., 289
David Wisdom and Associates, 35
Davies, David Y., 329
D'Avignon, Fay, 553
Davis, Albert J., 289
Davis, Ansel L., 281
Davis, Arthur Q., 289
Davis, Brent L., 332
Davis, Brody & Associates, 60
Davis, Charles M., 289
Davis, Clark A., 290
Davis, Clark, 289
Davis, Edward T., 281
Davis, Hortense, 311
Davis, James N., 320
Davis, Jerry A, 289
Davis, John M., 289
Davis, Lewis, 62, 170, 289
Davis, Linda Lund, 308
Davis, Nicholas, 290
Davis, Patric, 553
Davis, Paul, 277
Davis, Ray H., 281
Davis, Robert S., 277
Davis, Steven M., 289
Davis, W. T., 289
Davis Brody Bond Architects, 74, 106, 139, 183, 483
Davis-Kane, Architects, 484
Dawber, Sir Guy, 151, 350
Dawson, Clive, 484
Dawson, Stuart C., 64
Dawson, Stuart O., 315
Dawson, Thomas L., 274
Day, Clare Henry, 289
Day, Dennis J., 315
Day, Douglas W., 320
Day, Frank M., 341
Day, Frederic L., 289
Day, Jeffrey L., 183
Day, Mabel S., 332
Day and Associated Architects, 483
Daylor, Susan R., 328
Dayton Daily News, 356
DAZ Architects, 35
Deakin University, 648
Deal, Jerry H., 96
Deam, E. L., 289
Dean, Andrea O., 274
Dean, Francis H., 315

Dean, Kathryn, 274
Dean, Larry Craig, 320, 346
Dean, Lillian Frost, 308
Dean, Neil J., 315
Dean, Robert C., 289
Dean, Robert John, 311, 342
Dean Robert Camlin & Associates, Inc., 484
Deasy, C. M., 289
DeBartolo, Jack, Jr., 273, 289
De Blois, Natalie, 289
DeBoer, Roy H., 114, 315
Debra Nichols Design, 158
De Carlo, Giancarlo, 151, 160, 161, 181
Decavalla, Costantin N., 329
DeChellis, Rudolph V., 289
Deck, Ken, 311
Decker, Howard S., 289
Dedeaux, Edwin K., 281
Dee, Richard K., 315
Deefe Associates Inc., 485
Deems, Ward W., 289
Deep Foundations Institute, 229
Deering, Robert B., 315
Dees, Bruce, 315
Deets, Bradley, 514
De Fuccio, Robert, 277
Degenhardt, C. Christopher, 315
De Grinberg, Sara T., 329
Dehaan, Norman, 81
De Haas, John Neff, Jr., 289
DeHann, Norman, 342
Dehar, Allan J., 289
Dehn, Raymond H., 553
Deierlein, Matthew, 545
De La Hoz, Rafael, 329
Delano, Frederic Adrian, 39, 133
Delano, William Adams, 57
Delap, Kenneth L., 281
de la Reza, Rey, 289
De La Tour, S. D., 329
Delawie, Homer T., 289
DeLeuw, Cather & Co., 139
Delgado, Christopher G., 320
Della Vale + Bernheimer Design, Inc., 94
Delmar, Eugene A., 289
Delmonte, Ignacio M., 329
Delongchamps, Frederic J., 392
Delphenich, Pamela J., 290
Del Rio, Jorge, 289
del Sol, Germán, 186
Delson, Sidney L., 289
Delta Airlines DC-3, 441
Deluca, Fred R., 332
Del Webb Corporation, 71
DeMars, Vernon, 289
DeMattia & Associates, 484
DeMay, Kenneth, 289
De Mello, Eduardo, 329
Demetriou, Olvia, 289
de Meuron, Pierre, 14, 15–19, 141, 245
DeMoll, Louis, 289, 341
Demopulos, Chris, 281
Dempsey, Donna M., 544
Denisac, Charles M., Jr., 320

Dennis T. Su, AIA, Architects and
  Consultants, 486
Deno, William, 290
Denver Post, 356
De Pace, Joseph, 274
DePaul University, 175
DeRemer, Joseph B., 392
Desbiens, Hughes, 544
De Serio, James N., 320
Deshayes, Jos. Robert, 290
Design: M|W, 99
Design Alliance Architects, 484
Design and Construction Group, 33
Design Book Review, 639
Design-Build Institute of America, 127, 203
Design Collaborative, 71
Design Collective, 175, 176
Designer of Distinction Award, 81
Design for Humanity Award, 78
Design for Transportation National Awards,
  79–80
Design Futures Council, 204, 558, 559
Design History Foundation, 643
Design Institute of San Diego, 527
DesignIntelligence, 204, 368, 558, 559
Design Management Institute, 205
Design Management Journal, 205
Design Museum, 249
Design Workshop, Inc., 51
Desilets, Deborah, 657
Desmond, G. Henri, 392
Desmond, Gary L., 290
Desmond, John J., 290
Despont, Thierry W., 339
DeStefano, J. R., 290
DeStefano and Partners, 43, 44, 501
Dettmer Architecture, 484
Detwiler, M. S., 393
Dev, Gita, 290
Devaney, F. John, 308
DeVaris, Panayotis E., 290
De Vido, Alfredo, 289
Dewberry & Davis, 484
DeWeese, Roger, 315
DeYoung, Daniel J., 281
D/I + A, 484
Diadalos, 642
Diamant, Robert, 290
Diamond, A. J., 329
Diamond, J. J. J., 290
Diamond, Jack, 145
Diamond, Katherine, 290
Diaz, Horacio, 290
Diaz, James R., 290
Diaz-Azcuy, Orlando, 164, 339
Diaz-Morales, Ignacio, 329
DiBenedetto, A. P., 290
Dibner, David R., 290
Dickenson, H. Boyd, 281
Dickenson, Russell E., 336
Dicker, Bruce, 290
Di Donno Associates Architects, 484
Diehl, Gerald G., 290
Diekema/Hamann/Architects, Inc., 484

Dietrich, Paul E., 290, 650
Dietsch, Deborah, 332
Dietz, Robert H., 290
Diffrient, Niels, 48, 76, 323
Di Geronimo, Suzanne, 290
Dike, P. Woodward, 315
Dikis, William M., 290
DiLaura, Eugene L., 290
DiLeonardo, 493
Diller, Elizabeth, 76
Diller + Scofidio, 111
DiLullo, Clauss, Ostroski & Partners, 379,
  387
Di Maio, Judith, 274
Di Mambro, Antonio, 290
Dimensions Inc., 484
Dimery Associates Architects, 484
Dimond, F. Christopher, 315
Dimster, Frank, 290
DiNardo, John A., 332
Dines, Nicholas T., 315
Diniz, Carlos, 333, 650
Dinsmore, Philip, 290
Dioxiadis, G., 160
Dirsmith, Ronald L., 274
Disrud, Carol, 325
Ditchy, Clair W., 341
Diuven, Scott, 514
Dixon, David D., 290
Dixon, F. Dail, Jr., 290
Dixon, John M., 290
Dixon, Michael A., 290
DLR Group
  awards/honors, 128
  company profile/ranking, 484, 491, 492,
    493, 494, 502, 504, 505
DMJM Phillips Reister, 139
Doane, Jonathan, 392
Doane, Lawrence S., 290
Doblin, Jay, 323
Doche, Jim C., 290
DOCOMOMO, 425
DOCOMOMO Journal, 425
Dodge, Carlton T., 315
Dodge, Peter H., 290
Dodge Detroit Auto Show, 158
Dohr, Joy, 550
Dolginoff, Wesley J., 320
Dolim, George S., 290
Dombeck, Harold, 281
Domingue, Emery, 281
Dominick, Peter Hoyt, Jr., 290
Domus, 642
Donaldson, Milford W., 290
Donaldson, Thomas L., 150, 350
Donald W. McIntosh Associates, Inc., 177
Don Belford Associates, 175
Don Dommer Associates, 484
Donelin, Dan W., 315
Donelson, Janet, 290
Doner, H. Creston, 323
Donghia, Angelo, 339
Donkervoet, Richard C., 290
Donley, Wallace L., 281

Donnell, William S., 48
Donnelly, Marian C., 327, 351
Donovan, Justin T., 543
Door & Hardware Institute, 229
Dore, Stephen E., 281
Dorius, Kermit P., 290
Dorman, Albert A., 281, 290
Dorman, Richard L., 290
Dorpfeld, Wilhelm, 150
Dorsey, Robert W., 290
Doshi, Balkrishna V., 36, 329
Doss, Darwin V., 290
Doty, Walter L., 336
Dougherty, Betsey O., 290
Dougherty, Brian P., 290
Dougherty, Joanna, 276
Douglas, Frank F., 290
Douglas, Ian Harry, 518
Douglass, H. Robert, 290
Dove, C. R. George, 290
Dove, Knight and Whitehurst Architects,
  484
Dowling, John L., 340
Downing, Antoinette Forrester, 47, 53, 424,
  650
Downing Architects, 483
Downton, Diana Marie, 514
Dowson, Sir Philip, 151, 329
Doxiadis, Dr. Constantinos, 145, 311
Doyle, Gerald A., 290
Doyle, J. Edward, 281
Doyle, Peter G., 290
Doytchev, Kiril, 329
Dozen Distinctive Destinations, 426
DP Architects, 397
Drake, Paul W., 349
Dramov, Boris, 290
Drapeau, Mayor Jean, 145
Draper, Dede, 311
Draper, Earle S., 133
Dreiling, Helene, 290
Dresdner Bank AG, 177
Drew, Jane Beverly, 363
Drew, Roy M., 290
Drexel University, 517, 536, 544, 558
Drexler, Arthur, 46
Dreyer, Carl Theodor, 279
Dreyer, Ian Alexander, 547
Dreyfuss, Albert M., 290
Dreyfuss, Henry, 323, 347
Dripps, Robert D., 512
Drnevich, Ronald J., 281
Drummond, Jo, 320
Drummond, Robert Wayne, 290, 345
Drury University, 517, 533, 544, 553
Duany, Andres M., 290, 365
Duany Plater-Zyberk & Company, 365
Dubai International Award for Best
  Practices, 82
Dubin, Martin David, 290
Dubois, G. M., 329
Dubuffet, Jean, 47
Duc, Joseph Louis, 150
Dudley, George A., 290

Dudok, Willem Marinus, 151
Duell, Rachel Coleman, 651
Duell, Randall, 651
Duell Enterprises, 651
Duffendack, J. Paul, 290
Duffus, Allan F., 329
Duffy, Frank, 350
Duford, Dominic, 514
Dufour, Kelly, 514
Dujarric, Patrick, 37
Dumke, Rae, 333
Dunbar, Jack, 339
Dunbar, Thomas R., 315, 343
Duncan, Herbert E., Jr., 83, 290
Duncan, Jacqueline, 325
Duncan, James B., 308
Duncan, James R., 281
Duncan, William Cross, 517
Dundes, Lester, 164, 340
Dunham, Daniel, 651
Dunlop, Beth, 48, 143
Dunn, Lamar, 281
Dunne, William P., 320
Dunnette, Lee, 98
Dunwiddie, Foster W., 290
Dunwody, Eugene C., 290
Dupont, Henry Francis, 424
Duquette, Tony, 339
Duquette, William L., 290
Durband, Donovan, 515
Durham, Jerry W., 320
Durham, Robert L., 83, 273, 341
Durkee, Almon J., 290
Durning, Marvin, 333, 336
Durrant Group, 494, 504
D'Urso, Joseph Paul, 277, 339
Durst, Cheryl, 338
Dutcher, William R., 290
Duttman, Werner, 329
Dutzi, Howard C., 281
Duvall, Cheryl, 325
Duvall, J. Sprigg, 333
Dvorak, Robert Regis, 277
Dwell, 639, 643
Dwore, Donald J., 290
Dwork, Debórah, 163
Dwork, Melvin, 290
Dworsky, Daniel L., 290
Dworsky Associates, 139
Dyas, Robert W., 315
Dyckman, John, 513
Dyrness, Christina, 357
Dziersk, Mark, 323, 347

E

E. Cube, Inc., 96
E. I. Du Pont de Nemours & Company, 78
Ealy, Robert P., 315
Eames, Charles, 151, 164, 171, 206, 267
Eames, Ray, 151, 164, 171, 267, 337
Eames, William S., 341
Earl Walls Associates, 48
Easley, V. Gail, 308

East, Hilda M., 311, 325
East Carolina University, 535
Easterling, R. Grant, 320
Eastern Michigan University, 532
Eastern Washington University, 539
Eastman, Mary Jean, 290
Easton, David, 339
Easton, John Murray, 151
Easton, Robert, 48
Eber, Hayley, 543
Eberhard, John P., 290
Ebert, Carl J., 346
Ebert, H. Gerard, 311
Ebitz, Linda J., 333
Ebstein, Barbara, 311
Eck, Jeremiah, 290
Eckbo, Garrett, 64, 68, 311, 315
Eckels, Robert T., 484
Eckles Architecture, 371
Eckstut, Stanton, 290
Ecochard, Michel, 34
Ecole D'Architecture De L'Universite Laval,
    544
Ecole de l'Union Centrale des Arts
    Décoratifs, 365
École des Beaux-Arts, 660
Edbrooke, Frank E., 390
Edbrooke & Brunham, 390
Eddington, Thane M, 547
Eddy, Robert N., 290
Ede, Arlis, 311
Edelman, A. M., 349
Edelman, Judith, 290
Edelstein, Karen, 515
Edison, Thomas Alva, 436
Edison Electric Institute, 229
Edith Cherry/D. James See Architects, 484
Edlund, Paul, 320
Edmondson, F. W., 276
Edmonson, Allen R., 315
Edmunds, Frances R., 424
Edmunds, Graham, 389
Edmunds, James R., Jr., 341
Edward C. Kemper Award, 83
Edward Larrabee Barnes Associates, 60,
    278
Edward Pinckney and Associates, 177
Edwards, Arthur A., 281
Edwards, David A., 517
Edwards, David J., Jr., 290
Edwards, David W., 329
Edwards, Jared I., 290
Edwards, Joseph H., 320
Edwards, Judy A., 333
Edwards, Kevin M., 547
Edwards, Richard H., II, 320
Edwards, Samuel, 546
Efron, Albert, 290
Egan, M. David, 333, 512
Egender, Karl, 268
Eggers, David L., 290
Egnell, Stig, 33
Egyptian Antiquities Organization, 34
Ehmann, Richard C., 320

Ehrenkrantz, Ezra D., 290
Ehrig, John P., 290
Ehrlich, Joseph, 290
Ehrlich, Steven D., 45, 290, 484
Eichbaum, Thomas N., 290
Eid, Yehya M., 329
Eiden, Carl, 281
Eidlitz, Leopold, 392
Eifler, John A., 290
EIFS Industry Members Association, 229
Eight Inc., 104
Einhorn, Steven L., 290
Einhorn Yaffee Prescott, 106, 146, 494,
    496, 507
Eiriksson, Halldor, 518
Eisenman, Peter D., 62, 168, 278, 290
Eisenman Architects, 278
Eisenshtat, Sidney H., 290
Eisner, Michael D., 125
Eisner, Richard Karl, 290
Eisner, Simon, 133
Eizenberg, Julie, 218
Ekuan, Kenji, 108
Elam, Merrill, 56, 76
Elbasani, Barry P., 290
El Centro College, 537
Eldem, Sedad Hakki, 34
Eldredge, Joseph L., 290
Electrical Power Research Institute, 229
Eley, Charles N., 290
Elinoff, Martin, 311
Eliot, Charles W., II, 64
Elizondo, Juan Gil, 160
Elkerton, Stanley D., 281
Elkus, Howard F., 290
Elkus/Manfredi Architects, 124, 500
Ellen Wilson Community Development,
    177
Ellenzweig, Harry, 290
Ellerbe Becket
    awards/honors, 97, 186, 187
    company profile/ranking, 491, 493,
        494, 496, 502
    works/projects, 372, 377, 379, 381, 383,
        387, 389, 395
Ellerthorpe, Robin M., 290
Ellickson, Dale R., 290
Ellinoff, Martin, 342
Ellinwood Design Associates Ltd., 484
Elliot Contracting Corporation, 128
Elliot Dudnik + Associates, 484
Elliot & Elliot Architecture, 119
Elliott, Benjamin P., 290
Elliott, Rand L., 290
Elliott + Associates Architects, 45
Ellis, Donna A., 517
Ellis, James R., 333
Ellis, John M., 290
Ellis, Prof. Margaret Holben, 276
Ellison, James E., 290
Elmer, Frank L., 290
Elmo, John, 311
Elmore, James W., 290
El Wakil, Abdel W., 329

Ferris, Robert D., 291
Ferris Architects, 111
Ferro, M. L., 291
Ferro, Pablo, 77
Ferry, Donald E., 291
FFKR Architecture/Planning/Interior Design, 381
Fickel, Michael T., 291
Field, David W., 333
Field, Hermann Haviland, 291, 308, 652
Field, John L., 291
Fielden, Robert A., 291, 349
Fieldman, Michael M., 291
Fields, Jon J., 311
Filarski, Kenneth J., 291
Filer, R. Jerome, 291
Fillpot, Bob G., 291
Filson, Ronald C., 274, 291
Finch, Curtis, 291
Finch, James H., 291
Findlay, Robert A., 291
Fine, Steven, 137
Finegold, Maurice N., 291
Fine Homebuilding, 639
Finger, Harold B., 333
Fink, Ira S., 291
Finn, James F., 281
Finney, Garrett S., 274
Finrow, Jerry V., 291, 345
Finta, Jozsef, 330
Firestone, Charles E., 349
First National Bank of Maryland, 175
Firth, Ian J. W., 315
Fischer, Michael A., 188
Fischer, Robert Barnard, 652
Fish, Frank, 308
Fisher, A. Robert, 291
Fisher, Carol J., 543
Fisher, James Herschel, 291
Fisher, John L., 291
Fisher, Karen, 340
Fisher, Larry G., 320
Fisher Marantz Renfro Stone, Inc., 139
Fisher Marantz Stone, Inc., 120, 121
Fisk, Hollye C., 291
Fitch, James Marston, 46, 333, 424, 511
Fitch Worldwide, 103, 110
Fitts, Michael A., 291
Fitzgerald, Darrell A., 291
Fitzgerald, James T., 291
Fitzgerald, Joseph F., 291
Fitzgerald, Richard A., 291
FitzPatrick, Thomas, 344
FJ Clark Incorporated, 484
Flack + Kurtz Consulting Engineers, 186, 187
Flad, Joseph H., 291
Flad & Associates, 483
Flansburgh, Earl Robert, 291
Flapjack Interactive, 101
Flato, Ted, 291
Fleck, John C., 320, 346
Fleischer, Joseph L., 291
Fleischman, Richard J., 291

Fleming, David E., 281
Flesher, Thomas H., Jr., 349
Fletcher, Norman C., 168, 291
Fletcher, Shelley, 276
Fletcher, Sir Banister, 350
Fletcher Farr Ayotte, 50, 148, 149
Flicker, Eric L., 281
Flight, Harold E., 281
Flood, David J., 291
Florance, Colden R., 291
Flores, Antonio F., 330
Flores, Cesar X., 330
Flores, Phillip E., 315
Flores-Dumont, Luis, 291
Florian Nagler Architekt, 122
Florida A&M University, 517, 529, 544, 547
Florida Atlantic University, 514, 529, 544
Florida International University, 529
Florida State University, 514, 529, 540, 541
Flory, Robert C., 281
Flournoy, William L., Jr., 315
Floyd, J. Chadwick P., 291
Floyd, Richard F., 291
Floyd, W. Jeff, Jr., 291
Fly, Everett L., 315
Flynn, Ligon B., 291
Flynn, Michael, 291
Flynn-Heapes, Ellen, 328
Flynt, Henry N., 424
Flynt, Mrs. Henry N., 424
Focke, John W., 291
Foerster, Bernd, 291, 511
Fogg, George E., 315
Foit-Albert Associates, Architecture, Engineering & Surveying, PC, 484
Follett, James, 291
Fontenot, Lyn, 311
Foor & Associates, 371
Foote, Fred L., 291
Foote, Stephen M., 291
Foote, Vincent M., 323, 549
Forbes, John D., 333, 351
Forbes, Peter, 291
Ford, George Burdett, 133
Ford, John G., 311
Ford, O'Neil, 168
Ford, Robert M., 291
Ford Motor Company, 166
Forester, Russell, 291
Forgey, Benjamin, 48, 358
Forma, 175
Form Zero Architectural Books + Gallery, 633
Fornoles, Domingo, 547
Forrest, Deborah Lloyd, 311
Fort, William S., 333
Fort-Brescia, Bernardo, 291, 339, 366
Foss Associates, 371
Foster, James R., 291
Foster, John H., 281
Foster, Maelee Thomson, 512
Foster, Mark M., 274
Foster, Richard, 291
Foster, Ronald D., 281

Foster, Sir Norman Robert
  awards/honors, 39, 62, 108, 141, 151, 178, 219, 279, 330
  works/projects, 178, 284
  See also Foster & Partners; Norman Foster & Partners; Sir Norman Foster & Partners
Foster and Associates, 279
Foster & Partners, 178, 185. See also Foster, Sir Norman Robert; Norman Foster & Partners; Sir Norman Foster & Partners
Foundation for Architecture, Philadelphia, 48
Foundation for Interior Design Education Research, 339, 542, 558
Fowell, Joseph Charles, 144
Fowle, Bruce S., 291
Fowler, Bob J., 291, 652
Fowler, Charles A., 330
Fowler, Don W., 321
Fowler, Thomas, IV, 553
Fowles, Dorothy L., 311, 325
Fowlkes, Marion L., 291
Fox, Arthur J., Jr., 333
Fox, Cathy, 355
Fox, Donald Mark, 315
Fox, Kathleen M., 315
Fox, Robert, 553
Fox, Sheldon, 291
Fox & Fowle Architects, 41, 397, 503
Fraker, Harrison, 291
Frampton, Kenneth B., 47, 168, 278, 560
Francesco Borromini International Award for Architecture, 91
Francis, Billy W., 339
Francis, Cauffman, Foley, Hoffman, 504
Francis, Edward D., 291
Francis, Mark, 315
Frank, Jay E., 291
Frank, Morton, 291
Frank, Nikolaus, 100
Frank, Richard C., 291
Frank, Thomas, 311
Frankel, Neil P., 291, 325, 339, 348
Frank L. Hope and Associates, 383
Franklin, Carol L., 315
Franklin, Daniel B., 315
Franklin, James R., 83, 291
Frank Lloyd Wright School of Architecture, 145, 526
Frank O. Gehry and Associates, Inc., 72, 278. See also Gehry, Frank O.
Franta, Gregory, 291
Frantzen, Jason, 544
Franz Bader Bookstore, 633
Franzen, John P., 291
Franzen, Ulrich J., 62, 291
Frasca, Robert J., 291
Fraser, Charles E., 336
Frazee, Troy A., 547
Frazer, Robert L., 316
Frazier, Glenn G., 321
FRCH Design Worldwide, 494
Fredericks, Marshall M., 336

Hamel, Mylene, 518
Hamer, Hardt Walther, 161
Hamill, Robert L., Jr., 293
Hamilton, Calvin S., 316
Hamilton, D. K., 293
Hamilton, Diana M., 321
Hamilton, E. G., Jr., 293, 349
Hamilton, Mel, 339
Hamilton, William D., 312
Hamilton-Wentworth Vision 2020, 82
Hamlin, Talbot, 53
Hamline, Steve, 94
Hammel, Green and Abrahamson, Inc.
  (HGA), 493, 494, 502
Hammer, P., 333
Hammer, Theodore S., 293
Hammond, Charles H., 341
Hammond, Gerald S., 293
Hammond, John Hyatt, 293
Hammond, Wilton N., 281
Hamner, W. Easley, 293
Hampton, A. Niolon, 312
Hampton, Mark G., 293, 339
Hampton, Philip M., 281
Hampton University, 517, 538, 544
Hanamoto, Asa, 316
Hanbury, John Paul C., 293
Hanbury Evans Newill Vlattas & Company,
  155
Hancock, Marga Rose, 333
Hand, Irving, 308
Hand, Peter H., 293
Haney, Craig K., 321
Hangen, Richard E., 281
Hanke, Byron R., 316, 655
Hanna, Robert Mitchell, 276
Hannah, Bruce, 549
Hannover University of Technology, 659
Hansen, J. Paul, 293
Hansen, James G., 323
Hansen, Richard F., 293
Hansen, Robert E., 293
Hansens, Fritz, 108
Hanson, Becca, 316
Hanson, Richard E., 316
Hanson, Walter E., 281
Hantman, Alan M., 293, 393
Happold, Buro, 37
Hara, Ernest H., 293
Hara, John M., 293
Harboe, P. Thomas M., 188
Harbour, Antony, 339
Harby, Steven, 274
Harder, Dellas H., 293
Hardesty, Nancy M., 316
Hardin, James B., 321
Hardison, Donald L., 273, 293
Hardwick, Philip, 150
Hardwood Plywood & Veneer Association,
  229
Hardy, Hugh, 62, 293, 339
Hardy, Tom, 139
Hardy Holzman Pfeiffer Associates
  awards/honors, 43, 45, 60, 92, 93, 107,
  119

company profile/ranking, 494
Hare, Henry Thomas, 350
Hare, S. Herbert, 133, 343
Hare, Sid J., 133
Hargreaves, George, 316
Hargreaves Associates, 65
Hariri Pontarini Architects, 183
Harkness, John C., 293
Harkness, Sarah P., 293
Harkness, Terence G., 316
HarleyEllis, 494
Harmon, Frank, 183, 293
Harmon, Harry W., 83, 293
Harmon-Vaughan, Beth, 325, 348
Harmsworth Associates, 175
Haro, John C., 293
Harper, Angela N., 308
Harper, Charles F., 83, 293
Harper, David M., 293
Harper, Irving, 324
Harper, Robert L., 293
Harper, Terrell R., 346
Harrell, James W., 293
Harrell, Janeen A., 544
Harrell, Thomas B., 281
Harriman Associates, 371
Harrington, Robert W., 321
Harrington Institute of Interior Design, 558
Harris, Britton, 308, 513
Harris, Charles W., 316
Harris, Cyril M., 46
Harris, David A., 293
Harris, Donald M., 336
Harris, Edwin F., Jr., 293
Harris, Emanuel Vincent, 151
Harris, Harwell Hamilton, 511
Harris, James Martin, 293
Harris, John, 137
Harris, Richard, 415
Harris, Robert S., 293, 344, 511, 553
Harris, Ryan, 515
Harris, William M., Sr., 308
Harrison, Marc, 549
Harrison, Michael S., 308
Harrison, Partrick K., 333
Harrison, Robert V. M., 293, 321
Harrison, Sara, 545
Harrison, Shawna, 523
Harrison, Syd, 485
Harrison, Wallace K., 39
Harrison & Abramovitz, 397
Harrison & Fouiloux, 653
Harrover, Roy P., 293
Harry Weese & Associates, 60, 139
Hart, Arthur A., 333
Hart, Dianne, 333
Hart, Timothy, 548
Hartigan, Michael J., 281
Hartman, Craig W., 293
Hartman, Douglas C., 293, 321
Hartman, George E., 274, 293
Hartman, Morton, 293
Hartman-Cox Architects, 60
Hartmann, William E., 293

Hartray, John F., Jr., 83, 293
Hartung, Arthur F., 281
Hartung, Timothy, 293
Hartzog, George B., Jr., 336
Harvard Design Magazine, 640
Harvard University
  awards/honors given by, 178
  campus, 368
  degree programs, 532, 540, 541
  publications, 640
  school ranking, 559
  Sever Hall, 369
  staff, 279, 363, 511, 524, 560
  students, 107, 363, 544, 648, 650, 651,
    655, 658, 666
Harvey, Eugene C., 281
Harvey, Patricia, 312
Harvey, Robert R., 316
Hasbrouck, Wilbert R., 293, 364
Hashimoto, Lori M., 517
Haskell, Dennis E., 293
Haskell, Douglas, 46
Haskell, John G., 390
Haskins, Albert L., Jr., 293
Hass, Dr. F. Otto, 333
Hasselman, Peter M., 293
Hassid, Sami, 293
Hasslein, George J., 293, 655
Hastings, Hubert de Cronin, 151
Hastings, James M., 281
Hastings, Judith, 325, 348
Hastings, L. Jane, 273, 293
Hastings, Robert F., 341
Hastings, Thomas, 151
Hastings & Chivetta Architects, Inc., 128,
  506
Hatami, Marvin, 293
Hatchell, Susan M., 316
Hattery, Donald, 281
Hauf, Harold D., 293
Haugerud, Amy J., 281
Hauntaniemi, Danielle, 515
Haus, Stephen C., 276
Hauschild-Baron, Beverly E., 333
Hauser, Inc., 103
Hauser, Jon W., 323
Hauser, Stephen G., 323
Hausner, Robert O., 293
Hautau, Richard G., 316
Havekost, Daniel J., 293
Havens, William H., 316
Haverson Architecture and Design, 92
Haviland, David S., 48
Haviland, Perry A., 293
Hawes, Velpeau E., Jr., 293
Hawkins, Dale H., 276
Hawkins, H. Ralph, 293
Hawkins, Jasper Stillwell, 293
Hawkins, William J., III, 293
Hawkins Development Company, 485
Hawkinson, Laurie, 62, 63
Hawks, Richard S., 316
Hawley, William R., 293

Jackson, Mike, 294
Jackson, R. D., 330
Jackson, R. Graham, 294, 321
Jackson, Ralph T., 294
Jackson, Seth, 321
Jacob, Bernard, 294
Jacob, David J., 274
Jacobs, Allan B., 274
Jacobs, Barbara L., 312
Jacobs, Bernard, 316
Jacobs, Harry M., 294
Jacobs, Jane, 145, 179
Jacobs, Peter D. A., 316
Jacobs, Stephen B., 294
Jacobsen, Arne, 105, 248
Jacobsen, Hugh Newell, 294
Jacobsen, W. L., 321
Jacobs Facilities Inc., 506
Jacobson, Phillip L., 294
Jacobson, Roger L., 281
Jacobson, Susan L. B., 316
Jacobson, Timothy, 544
Jacobson, Victoria Tatna, 188
Jacoby, Helmut, 242
Jacoby, J. P., 294
Jaconetti, Daniel, Jr., 517, 545
Jaeger, Dale G. M., 316
Jaffe, Dr. Christopher, 49
Jahn, Helmut, 62, 294
Jain Malkin, Inc., 97
James, Dr. Frank D., 276
James, Harlean, 133
James, Jennifer L., 514
James, Vincent, 56
James Baird Company, 393
James Beard Restaurant Design Award, 111
James Cutler Architects, 45, 183
James Lynch & Associates Architects &
    Planners, 485
James Madison University, 538
James McHugh Construction Co., 128
James N. Gray Company, 127
James Oleg Kruhly + Associates, 485
James Stewart Polshek and Partners, 60,
    393
Jamieson, Douglas E., 98
Jamieson, Timm, 295
Jandl, Henry A., 295
Janka, Martin J., 321
Japan Architect, 642
Japan Art Association, 138
Japan Design Foundation, 108
Japan Institute of Architects, 213
Jarmusch, Ann, 357
Jarratt, William Robert, 273, 295
Jarrett, James R., 274
Jarvis, Frederick D., 316
Jary, Lloyd, 295
Jáuregui, Jorge Mario, 178
JB2 Dorius, 71
JBZ Architectural + Planning, 71
Jeanneret, Pierre, 365
Jeanneret-Gris, Charles Edouard. *See* Le
    Corbusier

Jeans, Mackenzie Miller, 518
Jean Tschumi Prize, 113
Jefferson, Bryan, 350
Jefferson, Peter, 295
Jefferson, Thomas, 39, 369, 370, 393, 436
Jelks, Jordan O., 295
Jellicoe, Sir Geoffrey, 64
Jenkins, J. Edward, 281
Jenkins, Leerie T., Jr., 316
Jenkins, Sarah B., 312
Jenkins Group, Inc., 485
Jennewein, J. J., 295
Jenney, William Le Baron, 194
Jennings, Richard W., 295
Jenrette, Richard H., 424
Jensen, Bruce H., 295
Jensen, Charlotte, 312
Jensen, Jan Olav, 37
Jensen, Robert, 277
Jensen and Halstead Ltd., 371
Jepson, David, 295
Jerde, Jon Adams, 295
Jerde Partnership International, 485, 493,
    501
Jewell, Linda Lee, 316
JG Johnson Architecture, 146
JH Group Architects, 483
Jickling, John W., 295
Jiricna, Eva, 339
JMP Architects Inc., 485
João Álvaro Rocha, Arquitectos Lda., 38
Joaquim de Meio Siza, Alvaro, 330
Johannes, Connie, 312
Johansen, John M., 62, 295
John, Georgy, 546
John & Bolles, 385
John Gill & Sons, 392
John Martin Associates, 485
John Portman and Associates, Inc., 396
Johns, Anthony N., Jr., 295
Johns Hopkins University, 513
Johnson, Addie M., 517
Johnson, Ahkilah, 544
Johnson, Arthur D., 295
Johnson, Atelier, 96
Johnson, Bethany, 515
Johnson, Bill, 377
Johnson, Carl D., 64, 316
Johnson, Carol R., 64, 316
Johnson, Cary D., 325, 348
Johnson, Christina, 325
Johnson, Clifford W., 281
Johnson, Danie, 295
Johnson, Dean A., 276, 316
Johnson, Derrell E., 281
Johnson, Dr. Joseph E., 333
Johnson, Edmund G., 281
Johnson, Edwin J., 295, 321
Johnson, Eric B., 295
Johnson, Floyd Elmer, 295
Johnson, Harry L., Jr., 321
Johnson, J. B., 333
Johnson, James A., 125
Johnson, James H., 295

Johnson, Jed V., 295, 339
Johnson, Lady Bird, 47, 125, 333
Johnson, Mark W., 316
Johnson, Marvin R., 295
Johnson, Morris E., 309
Johnson, P. N., 330
Johnson, Philip C.
    anecdote, 5–6
    awards/honors, 5–6, 39, 57, 108, 141,
        171, 278, 295
    quote by, 57, 75
    works/projects, 171, 405
Johnson, Pres. Lyndon B., 336
Johnson, Prof. Richard Norman, 144
Johnson, Ralph E., 295
Johnson, Reginald D., 171
Johnson, Robert W., 321, 346
Johnson, Scott, 295
Johnson, T. H., 392
Johnson, Walker C., 295
Johnson, Wilbur L., 321
Johnson, William J., 64, 316
Johnson, Yandell, 295
Johnson Braund Design Group, Inc., 485
Johnson/Burgee Architects, 396, 397, 398
Johnson McAdams Firm, 485
Johnston, Norman J., 295
Johnston Architects, 183
Johnstone, B. Kenneth, 344
Jolley, Dr. Harley, 336
Jonason, Wallace R., 312, 342
Jonassen, James O., 295
Jonathan Speirs and Associates Ltd., 120
Jones, Arthur E., 295
Jones, Barclay Gibbs, 513
Jones, Bernard I., 295
Jones, Carol, 325, 348
Jones, Charles, 323, 553
Jones, Dale C., 328
Jones, E. Fay, 39, 168, 274, 295, 369, 406,
    511
Jones, Gerre, 333
Jones, Grant R., 316
Jones, Ilze, 316
Jones, J. Delaine, 295
Jones, Jack B., 295
Jones, Johnpaul, 295
Jones, Margo, 325
Jones, Marnie, 323
Jones, Mary Margaret, 276
Jones, Melvin E., 281
Jones, Owen, 150
Jones, Paul Duane, 295
Jones, Renis, 295
Jones, Richard W., 312, 342
Jones, Robert Lawton, 295
Jones, Robert Trent, Sr., 316
Jones, Roy Childs, 344
Jones, Rudard Artaban, 295
Jones, Sir Horace, 350
Jones, Susan B., 523
Jones, Wesley, 274
Jones and Jones Architects & Landscape
    Architects, Ltd., 68, 404

692

Jones & Emmons, 60
Jones Group, 129
Jong, Bendrew G., 295
Jongejan, Dirk, 316
Jon R. Jurgens & Associates, Inc., 485
Jordan, Henry, 312
Jordan, Joe J., 295
Jordan, June Meyer, 277
Jordan, V., Jr., 333
Jordani, David A., 295
Jordan Parnass Digital Architecture, 106
Jordan Urban Development Department, 36
Jordy, William H., 47
Jorge Mario Jáuregui Architects, 178
Jorgensen, Roberta W., 295
Joseph, Wendy Evans, 274
Joseph Passonneau & Partners, 139
Joseph Wong Design Associates, Inc., 486
Joslyn Castle Institute for Sustainable
  Communities, 214
Josyln Art Museum, 214
Jot D. Carpenter Medal, 114
Journal of American Planning Association,
  640
Journal of Architectural Education, 640
Journal of Architecture, 642
Journal of Interior Design, 640
*Journal of the Society of Architectural
  Historians,* 640
Journal of Urban Design, 642
Jouzy and Partners, 36
Jova, Henri B., 275
Jova, Henri V., 275, 295, 312
Joy, McCoola & Zilch Architects and
  Planners, PC, 485
JPC Architects, 505
JPJ Architects, 396
Judd, Bruce D., 295
Judd, H. A., 333
Judson, Franklin S., 312
Judson College, 530
Juhasz, Nicholas D., 545
Juhlin, Sven-Eric, 108
Jules Fisher & Paul Marantz, Inc., 47
Jumsai, Sumet, 330
Jung, Yu Sing, 295
Jung/Brannen Associates, Inc., 492
Junius, Ralph W., 281
Juster, Howard H., 295
Juster, Robert J., 309
Justice, Lorraine, 323
JVP Engineers, 94

K

K. M. G. Architects & Engineers, 397
K. Y. Cheung Design Associates, 394
Kaelber, Carl F., Jr., 295
Kaeyer, Garment & Davidson, Architects,
  PC, 485
Kaeyer, Richard E., 295
Kagan, Gerald, 295
Kagermeier, Jeffry Lee, 188
Kahan, Richard A., 170
Kahane, Melanie, 339

Kahler, David T., 295
Kahn, Charles H., 295
Kahn, Louis I.
  awards/honors, 39, 57, 62, 151, 171, 173
  quotes by, 168
  students/staff, 366, 659
  works/projects, 35, 171, 173, 369, 406
Kahn, Robert, 275
Kahn, Vivian, 309
Kain Jitin, 514
Kainlauri, Eino O., 295
Kaiser, C. Hayden, 282
Kaiser, Edward, 309
Kaiser, Lloyd, 333
Kajima Construction Services, Inc., 127
Kale, Harry, 295
Kaleidoscope, 101
Kalin, Mark, 295
Kallmann, Gerhard Michael, 278, 295
Kallmann, McKinnell & Wood, 45, 60, 278,
  485
Kalman, Tibor, 76
Kamber, Dennis, 282
Kamekura, Yusaku, 108
Kamin, Blair, xiii–xvii, 49, 143, 355
Kamm & Associates, 72
Kamphoefner, Henry, 344, 560
Kampung Kebalen Community, 35
Kane, Janet E., 312
Kanmacher and Dengi, 390
Kanner, Stephen H., 295
Kansas City Art Institute, 533
Kansas State University
  degree programs, 531
  school ranking, 558
  staff, 344, 511
  students, 514, 517, 523
Kanto Gakuin University, 364
Kanvinde, Achyut P., 330
Kaplan, Gary Y., 295
Kaplan, Richard H., 295
Kaplan, Wendy, 277
Kaplan McLaughlin Diaz, 128, 492, 493
Kappe, Raymond L., 295, 560
Kappe, Shelly, 333
Kapsch, Robert J., 333
Karfik, Vladimir, 330
Karim Rashid Inc., 101, 102
Karlyn Group, 101
Karner, Gary E., 316
Karr, Joseph P., 316
Karr Poole and Lum, 392
Kasimer, Joseph H., 321
Kaskey, Raymond J., 295
Kass, Spence, 275
Kass, Thomas, 512
Kassabaum, George Edward, 273, 341
Kassner, John J., 282
Kast, Miller I., 349
Katherine, Todd, 76
Kauffman, Jerome L., 309
Kaufman, Donald, 49
Kaufman, Edward, 137
Kaufman Meeks & Partners, 70

Kaufmann, Edgar, Jr., 337
Kautz, Barbara, 309
Kavanagh, Jean Stephans, 316
Kawaguchi, Stan, 282
Kawahigashi, Theodore S., 282
Kawasaki, Frank H., 316
Kawneer Company Inc., 101
Kayden, Jerold S., 68
Kaye, Walter R., 321
KBJ Architects, 494
KCM International, 84
Keahey, Kirby M., 295
Keally, Francis, 393
Keane, Gustave R., 295
Keane, Jan, 295
Kean University, 534
Keating, Richard C., 295
Keay, Sir Lancelot, 350
Keefe, Lloyed, 309
Keefe, Moses P., 393
Keenan, Sharon K. Sommerlad, 551
Keeter, James E., 316
Keffer/Overton Architects, 371
Kehm, Walter H., 316
Kehrt, Allan, 295
Kelbaugh, Douglas S., 295
Kell, Duane A., 295
Kell, John H., 295
Kellenberger, Mary Gordon Latham, 424
Kellenyi, Bernard, 295
Keller, Charles W., 282
Keller, Genevieve Pace, 336
Keller, J. Timothy, 317
Keller, John, 309
Keller, Larry J., 295
Keller, Suzanne, 333
Kellett, Anna Starr, 543
Kelley, David M., 77
Kelly, Eric Damian, 309
Kelly, Frank S., 295
Kelly, Nathan B., 393
Kelly, Philip E., 340
Kelsey, Chester C., 282
Kelsey, F. L., 295
Kemp, Diane Legge, 295
Kendall, Edward H., 341
Kendall, Henry H., 341
Kendall, Taylor & Company, Inc., 371
Kendall, William D., 295
Kendall College of Art and Design, 532
Kender, Dorothy, 333
Keniston Architects, 485
Kennard, Robert, 180
Kennedy, David D., 282
Kennedy, Hon. Edward M., 336
Kennedy, Raymond, 342
Kennedy, Rhoda, 545
Kennedy, Robert N., 295, 325
Kennedy, Roger G., 333
Kennedy, Tessa, 295
Kennedy/Jenks Consultants, 86
Kenner, Todd J., 282
Kenneth Bensen & Associates, 381
Kenneth F. Brown Asia Pacific Culture &
  Architecture Design Award, 115

Kent, T. J., Jr., 133
Kent State University, 517, 536, 544
Kenzo Tange Associates, 396, 397, 398. *See also* Tange, Kenzo
Keough, Matthew, 515
Kerbis, Gertrude L., 295
Kerns, Thomas L., 295
Kerr, Leslie A., 317
Kershaw, Jeffrey T., 543
Kesler, Gary B., 317
Kessels DiBoll Kessels & Associates, 371
Kessler, George Edward, 133
Kessler, William H., 295
Ketcham, Herbert A., 295
Ketchum, Morris, Jr., 273, 341
Keune, Russell V., 295
Kevin Roche John Dinkeloo & Associates, 60, 173, 395
KeyBank, 177
Keyes, A. H., Jr., 295
Keystone Award, 116
Khalsa, Guru Dev Kaur, 545
Khan, Fazlur, 47
Khariakov, A., 398
KHR AS Arkitekten, 69
Kidder, Bradley P., 83
Kido, Neal M., 518, 545
Kienle, Peter J., 328
Kieran, Stephen J., 275, 295
Kilbourn, Lee F., 295, 321
Kiley, Daniel Urban, 62, 135
Kilgust Mechanical Inc., 72
Killebrew, James R., 295
Killingsworth, Edward A., 295
Kim, Janette, 517, 547
Kim, Tai Soo, 295
Kimball, Thomas R., 341
Kimble, Angela M., 328
Kimm, Jong S., 295
Kimsey, J. Windom, 188
King, Clarence H., Jr., 321
King, David R. H., 295
King, Dennis M., 295
King, Donald, 295
King, Frederick D. A., 282
King, Gordon L., 295
King, J. Bertram, 295
King, Jonathan, 333
King, Leland, 295
King, Michael J., 321
King, Perry, 248
King, Ronette, 339
King, Sol, 295
King & King Architects, 371
Kingston, M. Ray, 295
Kinnison, Paul, Jr., 295
Kinoshita, Masao, 317
Kinstlinger, Jack, 282
Kin Wai Hong, Jeffrey, 543
Kips Bay Decorator Show House, 340
KIP Technical Unit, 34
Kirchoff, Andre, 547
Kirchoff, Roger C., 349
Kirgis, George, 282

Kirjassoff, Gordon L., 282
Kirk, Ballard H. T., 295, 349
Kirk, D. W., Jr., 295
Kirk, Stephen J., 295
Kirke, William F., 392
Kirkegaard, R. Lawrence, 333
Kirkland, J. Michael, 277
Kirkpatrick, John F., 276
Kirkpatrick, Robert C., 282
Kirksey, John M., 295
Kirsch, Peter A., 336
Kirven, Peyton E., 295
Kitadai, Reiichiro, 330
Kitchell Constructors Inc. of Arizona, 129
Kitchell S.A. de C.V., 129
Kitchen, Robert S., 276, 295
Kitchin, Alexander, 275
Kito, Azusa, 330
Kitutake, Kiyonori, 69
Kivett and Meyers, 383
KJWW Engineering Consultants, 127
KKE Architects, 502
Klancher, Robert, 553
Klebe Donald F., 282
Kleier Associates, 485
Kleihues, Josef P., 330
Klein, Henry, 295
Klein, J. Arvid, 295
Klein, Stephen Marc, 550
Kleinman, Kent, 136
Klein McCarthy & Company, Ltd. Architects Inc., 485
Kleinschmidt, Robert, 339
Klemeyer, Frederick J., Jr., 321
Kletting, Richard K. A., 393
Kliment, Robert M., 295
Kliment, Stephen A., 295
Klindtworth, Kenneth F., 295
Kline, Donald H., 282
Kline, Lee B., 295
Kling, Vincent G., 168, 295
Kling Lindquist, 491, 503
Klinkhamer, Paul, 325
Klipp Colussy Jenks DuBois Architects, 119
Klontz, Matthias, 91
Klopfer, Mark, 276
KM Development Corp., 70
KMR Architects, 381
Knackstedt, Mary V., 312, 325
Knight, Charles L., 317
Knight, James F., 295
Knight, Roy F., 296
Knight, William H., 296
Knight Associates Inc., 485
Knoll, Florence, 364
Knoll, Hans, 364
Knoll International, 47, 364
Knoop, Stuart, 296
Knoops, Johannes M. P., 275
Knowles, Geno P., Jr., 518
Knowles, Ralph, 512
Knudsen, Dag I., 282
Knudson Gloss Architects Planners, 485
Kobayashi, Harold, 317

Kobayaski, Grace R., 275
Kober, Charles M., 296
Koch, Carl, 296
Koch, Kenneth J., 282
Kochlefl, Scott, 101, 102
Kodama, Steven Y., 296
KodamaDiseno, 71
Kodet, Edward J., Jr., 296
Koenig, Pierre F., 168, 296, 483
Koerner, Brad, 107
Koetter, Alfred H., 296
Kogan, Belle, 323
Kohler, John D., 485
Kohn, A. Eugene, 296
Kohn, Robert D., 341
Kohn Pedersen Fox Associates, 60, 395, 396, 397, 492, 493, 503
Kolatan McDonald Studio, 136
Kolb, Keith R., 296
Kolb, Nathaniel K., Jr., 296
Kolejka, Michael, 518
Kolman, Ronald, 296
Komatsu, S. Richard, 296
Komendant, Dr. August, 46
Kommers, Peter, 275
Koncelik, Joseph, 549
Koning, Hendrik, 296
Konkel, James H., 282
Kontz, D. Edward, Jr., 485
Koolhaas, Rem, xvii, 17–18, 141, 364
Koonce, Norman L., 83, 296
Koppelman, Lee E., 333
Kopplin, Charles W., 282
Korab, Balthazar, 336
Kordish, Emil, 282
Kortan, James F., 296
Korte Company, 129
Korte Design, 129
Kosmak, George, 323
Kostak Associates Architects, 485
Kostellow, Rowena Reed, 323
Kostmayer, Peter H., 333
Kostof, Spiro, 47, 351, 560
Koulermos, Panos G., 296, 511
Kouzmanoff, Alexander, 296
KPFF Consulting Engineers, 86
Krabbenhoft, Ken R., 317
Kraich, Norbert, 336
Kramer, Binnie, 312
Kramer, Gerhardt, 296
Kramer, Robert, 277, 296
Kramer/Marks Architects, 485
Krank, Mabel, 334
Krannitz, Michael E., 282
Krasnow, Peter, 296
Krause, George, 277
Krause, M. Stanley, Jr., 296
Krautheimer, Richard, 53, 54
Kray, Lili, 325
Krebs, Paul B., 282
Kremer, Eugene, 296, 344
Kremer, J. Richard, 296
Kress, Jerrily R., 296
Kreutzfeld, Gayle, 312

Lee, Robin, 334
Lee, Sarah Tomerlin, 340, 658
Lee, Sing-Sing, 545
Lee, Y. H., 50, 51
Leedy, Gene, 296
Leefe, James M., 296
Leers, Andrea P., 296
Leers Weinzapfel Associates Architects, 41
Lee Stout Inc., 110
Leff, Naomi, 340
Lefferts, Gillet, 296
Lefkovits, Peter, 545
Lefkowitz, Andrew, 544
Leger Wanaselja Architecture, 404
Legorreta, Ricardo, 39, 168, 174, 279
Lehigh University, 202
Lehman Architectural Partnership, 371
Lehmann, Phyllis Williams, 54
Lehman-Smith, Debra, 340
Lehtinen, Rauno, 185
Leibrock, Cynthia, 338
Leigh & Orange, 186
Leighton, Lord, 150
Leigh Whitehead Associates, 139
Leineweber, Spencer A., 296
Leira, Eduardo, 160
Leis, Lawrence J., 296
Leiserowitz, Nila, 312
Leitch, Richard, 296
Leiviskä, Juha Ilmari, 75, 330
Lembcke, Herbert, 296
Lembo, Joseph, 340
Le Messurier, William J., 334
LeMond, Robert, 296
Lems, Jay J., 518
Lenci, Sergio, 330
Lendrum, James T., 296
Lendrum, Peter A., 296
Lendrum Architecture, 71
L'Enfant, Pierre Charles, 133
Lentz, Kay, 328
Leo A. Daly, 491, 493, 494, 504, 506
Leobl Schlossman Dart & Hackl, 395
Leonard, Eason H., 296
Leonard, Paul, 338
Leong, Sacha H., 543
Leplastrier, Richard, 144
Lepper, Robert, 549
Lepsius, C. R., 150
Le Ricolais, Robert, 46
Lerner, Jaime, 330
Lerner, Lawrence, 340
Lerner, Ralph, 296
Lerner-Miller, Fola, 325
LeRoy, Glen S., 296, 309
Leroy Adventures, 111
Lescher & Mahoney Sports, 375
Lesko, Nicholas, 296
Leslie, Donald W., 317, 343
Lessard Group, 71
Lesueur, J. B., 150
Lethaby, W. R., 116
Lethbridge, Francis D., 296
Levenson, Conrad, 296

Levin, Brenda A., 296
Levin, Jack, 325
Levine, Aaron, 317, 334
Levis, Calvin E., 282
Levison, Robert H., 83
Levitas, E. H., 334
Levitt, Mitchel R., 328
Levy, Alan G., 296
Levy, Eugene P., 296
Levy, Herbert W., 296
Levy, Morton L., 296
Levy, Raoul L., 282
Levy, Toby S., 296
Lewin, Wendy, 115
Lewis, Anne McCutcheon, 296
Lewis, Brian J., 282
Lewis, Calvin F., 296
Lewis, David, 83, 296
Lewis, Diane, 275
Lewis, George B., 296
Lewis, Howarth, Jr., 296
Lewis, Jack R., 346
Lewis, Lawrence, Jr., 334
Lewis, Neville, 325, 340
Lewis, Paul, 275
Lewis, Philip H., Jr., 64, 317
Lewis, Prof. Walter H., 296, 336
Lewis, Richard L., 296
Lewis, Roger K., 296
Lewis, Roy W., 275
Lewis, Sally Sirkin, 340
Lewis, Thomas E., 321
Lewis, Tom, Jr., 296
Lewis, William D., 282
Lewis Mumford Prize, 117
LeWitt, Sol, 46
Lew & Patnaude, Inc., 483
Lezénés, Gilbert, 35
LG Electronics Inc., 100
L_H_R_S Architects, Inc., 371
Li, Wei, 98
Liaigre, Christian, 340
Liang Yong, Wu, 330
Libeskind, Daniel, xvi, 56
Library Buildings Awards, 118, 119
Library of American Landscape History, 68
Library of Congress, 424
Licht, George T., 275
Licko, Zuzane, 76
Liddle, Alan C., 296
Lieber, J. Roland, 317
Liebhardt, Frederick, 296
Liebman, Theodore, 275, 296
Lienau, Detlef, 220
Liff, Bernard J., 296
Light Guage Steel Engineers Association, 230
The Lighthouse: Scotland's Centre for Architecture, Design and the City, 251
Lighting Design Awards, 120–121
Lighting Practice, 110
Liguori, Nicholas, 514
Lillard, David H., 282
Lillie, Richard R., 309

Lily Auchincloss Study Center for Architecture and Design, 254
Lim, Jimmy C. S., 37
Lin, Maya, 56, 369
Lin, T. Y., 47
L.inc design, 101
Lincoln, Frank L., 282
Lincolne Scott & Kohloss, 129
Lind, John H., 297
Lindbloom, Leon J., 282
Lindemon Wincklemann Deupree Martin and Associates PC, 485
Lindenfeld, Sarah, 518
Lindenthal, Robert S., 312
Linders, Howard D., 282
Lindgren, Armas, 253
Lindhult, Mark S., 317
Lindquist & Associates, 485
Lindsey, David, 297
Lindsey, Gail A., 297
Lindsey, Patricia F., 551
Lindström, Joe, 33
Lindström, Sune, 33
Link, Theodore C., 392
Link & Hare, 392
Linley, Viscount David, 338
Linn, Karl, 317
Linnard, Lawrence G., 343
Lins de Mello, Luciana, 546
Linzay, Kristopher Paul, 544
Lipchak, Paul Joseph, 545
Lippincott, H. Mather, Jr., 297
Lipscomb, Joseph, 282
Lisec & Biederman Ltd., 485
Liskamm, William H., 297
Lister, James M., 276
Lit, Steve, 356
Little, Bertram R., 424
Little, Mrs. Bertram R., 424
Little, Robert A., 297
Little, Susan P., 317
Little & Associates, 492, 494
Littleton, Charles, 325
Litton, R. Burton, Jr., 317
Liu, Dr. Binyi, 336
Livesey, Robert S., 275, 297
Livingston, Stanley C., 297
Livingston, Thomas W., 297
Livingston, Walter R., Jr., 297
Livingstone, Bruce, 282
Lizon, Peter, 297
Lloveras, Carolina, 545
Lloyd & Jones, 381
LMN Architects, 41, 72, 492, 494, 505
Lobell, John, 161
Loch, Emil, 349
Lockard, W. Kirby, 297
Lockett, Thomas A., 317
Lockheed Martin Missiles & Space, 100
Lock Lomond National Park, 251
Lockwood, LeGrand, 220
Lockwood Greene, 371
Lodging, 92
Loeb Fellowship in Advanced Environmental Studies, 47

Loebl Schlossman Dart & Hackl, 396
Loebl Schlossman & Hackl, 501
Loendorf, Boyd L., 312
Loewy, Raymond, 323
Loftis, James L., 297
Logan, Donn, 297
Logue, Tim, 515
Lohan, Dirk, 297
Lohan Associates Inc., 495, 501
Lohmann, William T., 321
Lollini, Thomas E., 297
Lomax, Jerrold E., 297
Londono, Juan Carlos, 515
London's Architectural Association, 363
Long, Nimrod W. E., III, 317
Long Island University, 155
Longstreth, Richard, 117, 163, 351, 415
Loo, Kington, 330
Looney, J. Carson, 297
Looney Ricks Kiss, 148
Loope, R. Nicholas, 297
Loquasto, Santo, 340
Lorant, Gabor, 297
Lorch, Emil, 344
Lord, Larry, 297
Lord, W. H., 349
Lorenzini, David E., 321
Lorenzo, Aldana E., 330
Lorenzo-Torres, Jose, 545
Lorenz + Williams Incorporated, 483
Lortz, C. Richard, 282
Los Angeles Times, 356
Loschky, George H., 297
Lose, David O., 317
Loss, John C., 297
Lotery, Rex, 297
Louie, William C., 297
Louisiana State University, 512, 517, 523,
    531, 544
Louisiana Tech University, 517, 531, 544
Louisville Courier-Journal, 356
Lounsbury, Carl, 413, 415
Louvain la Neuve, 160
Love, John A., 336
Love, Michael, 312
Love, William, 297
LoVecchio, Joseph, 312
Lovejoy, Derek, 658
Lovelace, Eldridge, 317
Lovelace, Richard, 98
Lovell, Tom, 390
Love-Stanley, Ivenue, 297
Lovett, Wendell H., 297
Lowe, LeRoy, 485
Lowe, Peter E., 323
Lowe, Rick, 116
Lowery, Jack, 342
Lowrie, Charles N., 343
Lowry, Particia, 357
Loy, LeRoy D., 282
Loza, Serapio P., 330
LPK, 100
LS3P Associates, 494
Lu, Paul C. K., 317

Lu, Weiming, 334
Lubben, Ronald, 325
Lubetkin, Berthold, 151
Lucas, Frank E., 297
Lucas, Frederick Bruce, 144
Lucas, Thomas J., 297
Lucey, Lenore M., 297
Lucien Lagrange, 397
Luckenbach, Carl F., 297
Luckett & Farley Architects, Engineers and
    Construction Managers, Inc., 124, 371
Luckman, Charles, 379, 387
Luder, Owen, 350
Ludman Frank, Dianne, 328
Lueck, Odette, 312
Luers, Julie G., 328
Luhn, Graham B., 297
Lukermann, Barbara, 309
Lumsden, Anthony J., 297
Lunar Design, 103
Lund, Kjell, 330
Lunde, Frithjof, 297
Lunden, Samuel E., 83
Lundgren, Ray, 282
Lundoff and Bicknell, 392
Lundwall, Phillip, 297
Lundy, Victor A., 297
Lunz, Bradly T., 517
Luo, Tianjin, 545
Lupia, Major General Eugene, 334
Lupton, Ellen, 76
Lutes, Donald H., 297
Lutyens, Sir Edwin Land*seer*, 39, 151
Lye, Eric Kumchew, 113
Lyle, John, 64
Lyman, Frederic P., 297
Lynch, Kevin, 133
Lynch, Robert Dale, 297
Lynch, Robert J., 297
Lyndon, Donlyn, 297, 344, 560
Lyndon, Maynard, 297
Lynford, Ruth K., 312, 340
Lynn, David, 393
Lynn, Kathy, 514
Lyon, Peter A., 328
Lyons, Eric, 350

M

M. A. Mortenson Company, 128
M. D. Fotheringham, Landscape Architects,
    Inc., 68
Maas, Jane, 334
Maas, Michael, 297
Mabe, R. Doss, 297
MacAlister, Paul, 323
MacAllister, John E., 297
Macaulay, David A., 46
Macchi, A. J., 282
MacCormac, Richard C., 350
MacCready, Dr. Paul B., 76, 126
MacDonald, Donald, 297
MacDonald, Lee, 336
MacDonald, Virginia B., 297

MacDonald, William J., 55
MacDonald, William L., 54
MacDonald & Mack Architects, Ltd., 485
MacDougall, Carlin, 21–23
MacDougall, Elisabeth Blair, 327, 351
MacDougall, Prof. E. Bruce, 336
MacEwen, H. A., 297
MacFadyen, John H., 275
MacFarlane, J. L., 282
Machado, Rodolfo, 56
Machida, Hiroko, 325
Mack, Linda, 356
Mack, Robert C., 297
MacKaye, Benton, 133
MacKay-Lyons, Brian, 330
Mackay Mitchell Associates, 506
MacKenzie, Candace, 325
Mackey, Eugene J., III, 297
Mackey, Howard Hamilton, Sr., 180
MacKinlay, Ian, 297
Mackintosh, Charles Rennie, 251
Mackintosh Interpretation Centre, 251
MacLachlan, Cornelius & Filoni, Inc., 371
MacMahon, Charles H., 297
MacMillan, Kyle, 356
MacMinn, Strother, 549
MacPhee, James Daniel, 543
Macris, Marjorie, 309
Macsai, John, 297
Macy, J. Douglas, 317
Madawick, Tucker P., 323, 347
Maddox, Diane, 334
Maddox, Eva L., 164, 340
Madigan, Colin Frederick, 144
Madison, Robert P., 297
Madsen, Peter E., 297
Mae, Fannie, 125
Maeda, John, 77
Maffitt, Theodore S., Jr., 297
Magaziner, Henry J., 297
Maginnis, Charles Donagh, 39, 341
Maguire Group, 128
Maguire Thomas Partners, 48
Mahaffey, Gary, 297
Mahayni, Riad G., 309
Maheux, Anne Frances, 277
Mahler, Victor C., 297
Mahlum, 505
Mahlum, John E., 297
Mai, Zi, 544
Maibach, Sheryl, 328
Mains, Lendall W., 321
Maiwald, C. R., 297
Majekodunmi, Olufemi, 330
Maki, Fumihiko
    awards/honors, 62, 108, 138, 141, 174,
        178, 181, 279, 330
    works, 178
Mäki, Pekka, 185
Maki and Associates, 279
Makinen, Matti K., 330
Makinson, Randell Lee, 334
Malaj, 330
Malassigné, Pascal, 323

McCulley, Earl Byron, 317
McCurry, Margaret, 298, 340
McCutcheon, Sir Osborn, 144
McDermott, Patricia M., 517
McDermott, Terrence M., 334
McDermott, Vincent C., 317
McDonald, John J., 275
McDonald, Kenneth, 392
McDonough, William A., 298
McEldowney, H. Clay, 282
McEldowney, Robert, 282
McErlane, Roger B., 317
McFall, James D., 282
McFarland, Connie S., 298
McFarland, Donald, 323
MCG Architecture, 483, 494, 501
McGaughan, A. S., 298
McGill University, 512, 547
McGinnis, Joseph A., 346
McGinty, John M., 298, 341
McGinty, Milton B., 298
McGinty, Richard A., 298
McGlenn, John C., 282
McGough, John W., 298
McGough Construction Co., Inc., 65, 73
McGowan, Sandra, 312
McGrail, Rose-Anne, 515
McGranahan, James R., 298
McGrath, Evelyn B., 334
McGrath, Inc., 128
McGrath, Norman, 47
McGraw, Harold, 125
McGraw, Terry, 125
McGraw-Hill Bookstore, 634
McGraw-Hill Companies, 125
McGuire, Charles E., 321
McGuire, Joseph J., 321
McHarg, Ian Lennox, 64, 133, 135, 168, 317, 334, 659
McInstry and Company, 177
McIntosh, James E., 312
McInturff, Mark, 298
McIntyre, Prof. Peter, 144, 648
McIntyre, Robert Peter, 330
McKay, Ronald, 49
McKee, Larry A., 282
McKellar, Chris, 338
cKellin, J. Nelson, III, 485
McKenzie, Robert W., 282
McKim, Charles Follen, 39, 150, 341
McKim, Herbert P., 282, 298, 349
McKim, Mead and White, 393, 436
McKinley, David A., 298
McKinnell, Noel Michael, 62, 278, 298
McKinney, Arthur W., 282
McKinstry and Company, 177
McKittrick, Thomas L., 298
McKnight-Thalden, Kathryn E., 317
McKown, Zack, 340
McLarand, Vasquez and Partners, Inc., 50, 175
McLaughlin, Charles C., 336
McLaughlin, H. Roll, 298
McLean, C. Andrew, II, 298

McManus, James M., 298
McManus, Robert L., 321, 346
McMath, George A., 298
McMinn, William G., 275, 298, 511
McMurtry, John, 657
McNall, Cameron, 275
McNamara, Kevin, 340
McNaughton, E. Eean, Jr., 298
McNeal, David A., 317
McNulty, Carrell S., Jr., 298
McPheeters, E. Keith, 298, 511
McRae, John M., 298, 345
McReynolds, Charles B., 298
McShane, Patricia, 76
McSherry, Laurel, 276
Mead, Christopher, 351
Mead, Franklin, 298
Mead, William Rutherford, 57
Means, George C., Jr., 298, 511
Meathe, Philip J., 83, 273, 298
Meck, Stuart, 309
Meckel, David, 298
Meckley, Todd A., 546
Medary, Milton Bennett, 39, 341
MEDIUM, 245
Medrano, Jose, 325
Mee, Joy, 309
Meeks, Carroll L. V., 53, 351
Meeks, Everett, 344
Meem, John Gaw, 392
Mehrotra, Rahul, 115
Meier, Hans W., 321
Meier, Henry G., 298
Meier, Richard
    awards/honors, 39, 62, 138, 141, 151, 168, 278, 298, 340
    works/projects, 405
    See also Richard Meier & Partners
Meigs, Montgomery C., 255
Meinhardt, Carl R., 298
Meisel, Donald D., 321, 346
Meisner, Gary W., 317
Mejia-Andrion, Rodrigo, 330
Melander, A. Reinhold, 349
Melanson, Sara K., 546
Melbourne University, 648
Melchior, Adrianna M., 518, 545
Meléndrez Design Partners, 67
Melillo, Cheri C., 334
Melillo, Lawrence P., 298
Mellem, Roger C., 298
Mellergaard, Ruth, 325
Mellon, Paul, 334
Melnick, Robert Z., 68, 317, 422, 423
Melting, R. Alan, 277, 298
Mendler, Sandra, 166, 167
Mendoza, Rolando J., 517
ME Productions Inc., 109
Meredith College, 535
Merivuori, Tuula-Maria, 659
Merriam, Dee S., 317
Merricksmith, James, 81
Merrill, John, 309
Merrill, John O., 298

Merrill, Vincent N., 317
Merrill, William Dickey, 298
Merriman, Dwight, 309
Mertz, Stuart M., 276, 317
Mesa Verde National Park, 47
MESH Architectures, 106
Messer, Raymond F., 282
Messersmith, David R., 298
Mestre, Hector, 330
Metal Building Manufacturers Association, 231
Metcalf, Robert C., 298
Metcalf, William H., 298
Metcalf & Eddy of New York, Inc., 84
Metrius Trade Show Booth, 157
Metro-North Railroad, 139
Metropolis, 640, 643
Metropolitan Mechanical Contractors, Inc., 128
Metropolitan State College of Denver, 528
Metter, Andrew, 298
Metz Construction Company, 392
Metzger, David, 298
Metzger, Robert, 340
Meunier, John, 345
Meyer, Betty H., 334
Meyer, Borgman and Johnson, 73
Meyer, C. Richard, 298
Meyer, Charles A., 282
Meyer, Darrell C., 309
Meyer, David, 276
Meyer, James H., 298
Meyer, John T., 298
Meyer, Kurt W., 298
Meyer, Richard C., 298
Meyer, Scherer and Rockcastle Architects, 72, 148
Meyer, Vernon F., 282
Meyer, William O., 82
Meyers, Marshall D., 298, 659
Meyers, Richard J., 317
Meyer Scherer & Rockcastle, 494
Meyerson, Martin, 309, 513
Mezrano, James, 312
Miami-Dade Art in Public Places, 49
Miami University, 517, 536, 547
Miao, Nancy A., 298
Miceli, Luciano, 317
Miceli Kulik Williams and Associates, 656
Michael, Linda H., 298
Michael Bell Architecture, 136
Michael Fancher & Associates, 484
Michael Graves & Associates, Inc., 119
Michaelides, Constantine E., 298
Michael Rice and Co., 33
Michael Tatum Excellence in Education Award, 550
Michael W. Hyland Associates, PA, 485
Michaud Cooley Erickson, 73
Michel, Henry L., 282, 660
Michel, Jack, 413
Michelangelo, 331
Michelson, Valerius Leo, 298
Michigan Department of Transportation, 67

Michigan State University, 533, 541, 656
Mickel, E. P., 334
Microsoft Corp., 103
Middle East Technical University, 37
Middle Tennessee State University, 537
Middleton, D. Blake, 275
Mielke, William J., 282
Mies van der Rohe, Ludwig, 266
  awards/honors, 39, 57, 151, 171, 173
  museum collections and exhibitions,
    241, 244, 245, 254, 267
  students, 364
  works/projects, 171, 173, 369, 406
Mies van der Rohe Award for European
  Architecture, 122
Mies van der Rohe Award for Latin
  American Architecture, 123
Mies van der Rohe Foundation, 122, 123
Miklos, Robert, 298
Mikon, Arnold, 298
Milan Polytechnic School of Architecture,
  362
Milburn, Frank P., 393
Mildenberg, Juanita M., 298
Mileff, Melissa, 554
Miles, Don C., 298
Miles and Horne, 390
Mill Creek Studios, Ltd., 485
Millen, Daniel R., Jr., 298
Miller, Albert H., 282
Miller, Arthur J., 321, 346
Miller, Campbell E., 64, 343
Miller, Courtney E., 553
Miller, David E., 298
Miller, E. Lynn, 317
Miller, Eric Preston, 517
Miller, Ewing H., 298
Miller, Garen D., 553
Miller, George H., 298
Miller, Harold V., 133
Miller, Henry F., 298
Miller, Hugh C., 298, 336
Miller, J. Abbot, 76
Miller, J. Irwin, 125, 334
Miller, James Edward, 547
Miller, James W., 298
Miller, John F., 298
Miller, John Richard, 312
Miller, Joseph, 298
Miller, L. Kirk, 298
Miller, Leon Gordon, 323
Miller, Leroy B., 298
Miller, Martha P., 334
Miller, Michael A., 547
Miller, Patrick A., 317
Miller, Raymond T., 282
Miller, Richard B., 334
Miller, Richard, 298
Miller, R., 334
Miller, Steven, 298
Miller, Thomas H., 312
Miller, Warren D., 349
Miller, William C., 298
MIllett, Larry, 358

Milliken, Roger, 334
Millon, Henry Armand, 278, 327, 351
Mills, Edward I., 298
Mills, Elaine A., 523
Mills, Gordon E., 298
Mills, Michael, 298
Mills, Willis N., Jr., 298
Milovsoroff, Ann, 317
Milwaukee Institute of Art and Design, 539
Milwaukee Journal Sentinel, 356
Minale, Tattersfield, Bryce & Partners, 156
Minarik, Douglas, 544
Mindel, Lee, 298, 340
Minneapolis Star-Tribune, 356
Minnesota Life Insurance Co., 73
Minta, Lassina, 34
Mintier, J. Laurence, 309
Minton, Joseph, 81
Miralles, Adolfo E., 298
Miranda, Santiago, 248
Mirick, Henry D., 275, 298
Miss, Mary, 48
Mississippi State University, 345, 512, 517,
  533, 544
Mital, Vijay, 309
Mitchell, Cynthia, 424
Mitchell, Dan S., 298
Mitchell, Debra L., 317, 343
Mitchell, Ehrman B., Jr., 298, 341
Mitchell, George, 424
Mitchell, Hermine, 334
Mitchell, Melvin L., 298
Mitchell, O. Jack, 344
Mitchell, Robert D., 282
Mitchell, William, 278
Mitchell and Ritchie, 387
Mitchell/Giurgola Architects, 60, 155
Mithun, 147, 149, 404, 505
Mithun, Carter & Burgess, 494
MIT Press, 47
Mitrofanoff, Wladimir, 330
Mitsui, Mori, 321
Mittelstadt, Robert, 275
Mitzel & Scroggs Architects, Inc., 485
Miyabara, Michael T., 317
Miyake, Issey, 108
Mocine, Corwin R., 133
Mockbee, Samuel, 59
Modernization Awards, 124
Moeller, Sally, 25–28
Moen, Alfred, 660
Moen Inc., 660
Moe's Art & Antiquarian Books, 633
Moger, Richard R., 298
Mohammad, Rais Ghazi, 35
Mohler, Thomas E., 282
Moholy-Nagy, Lazlo, 650
Mokkhavesa, Sutana, 548
Mole, Susan I., 312
Moline, Lawrence R., 317
Moline, Ronald L., 298
Molnar, Donald J., 317
Molseed, Robert B., 298, 321, 346
Molzan, Lynn H., 298

Molzen, Dayton, 282
Monacelli Press, 49
Monchek, Marci, 514
Moneo, Jose Rafael, 62, 122, 141, 174, 279,
  330
Monical, R. Duane, 282
Monson, Neumann, 485
Montague, Jeffrey Neil, 545
Montana, Frank, 298
Montana, "Frank" Francesco, 660
Montana State University, 517, 533, 544, 553
Montero, Thomas D., 321
Monterose, Peter J., 321
Montgomery, Kathy Ford, 312, 342
Montgomery, Martha Barber, 334
Montgomery Watson, 86
Monticciolo, Joseph D., 83, 298
Montoya, Juan, 340
Montreal Metro System, 46
Moody, Curtis J., 180, 298
Moon, Thomas B., 298
Moore, Arthur C., 39, 298
Moore, Barry M., 298
Moore, Charles W., 62, 168, 511, 560
Moore, Diana K., 96
Moore, Gene, 340
Moore, James B., 346
Moore, Kenneth J., 321
Moore, Lynn A., 317
Moore, Maurine, 551
Moore, Patrick C., 317
Moore, Richard A., 317
Moore, Robert C., 282
Moore, Terry, 309
Moore, William B., Jr., 334
Moore College of Art and Design, 536
Moore Lyndon Turnbull Whitaker, 173
Moore Ruble Yudell Architects & Planners,
  485
Moorhead, Gerald L., 298
Moreira, Ricardo Muniz, 546
Morelli, Jill K., 299
Morey, Warren, 385
Morgan, Arthur Ernest, 133
Morgan, Jeffrey L., 546
Morgan, Jesse O., Jr., 299
Morgan, Julia, 310, 364, 405, 436
Morgan, Keith N., 351
Morgan, Robert Lee, 299, 554
Morgan, Sherely, 344
Morgan, William N., 49, 299
Morgan State University, 514, 532, 547
Morgridge, Howard H., 299
Moriarty, Stacy T., 276
Morin, Robert J., 321
Moris, Lamberto G., 299
Moriyama, Raymond, 145, 330
Morphett, John, 144
Morphosis, 56, 106
Morris, John W., 334
Morris, Paul F., 317, 343
Morris, Philip A., 334, 336
Morris, Seth I., 299
Morris Architects, 493, 495

Northeastern University, 532
Northwest Architectural Co., 89
Northwest Associates Architecture, 486
Northwestern University, 540
Norton, Charles Dyer, 133
Norton, Charles McKim, 133
Norton, Perry, 309
Norvell, Shirley J., 334
Norwegian Museum of Architecture, 258
Norwich, John Julius, 48
Norwich University, 517, 538, 544
Notkin Engineers, 72
Notman, John, 392
Nott, John, 243
Notter, George M., Jr., 299, 341
Nourse, Roger A., 321
Nouvel, Jean, 35, 91, 138, 151, 330
Novack, John M., 299
Novick, David, 282
Nowicki, Stanislawa, 46, 511
Noyes, Frederick, 299
NSSN: A National Resource for Global
    Standards, 232
NTT Power and Building Facilities, Inc.,
    398
Nugent, Barbara, 312
Nunn, Jimmie R., 299
Nurmesniemi, Antti, 108
Nussbaum, Bruce, 337
Nussberger, Hans Jörg, 161
Nutt, James W., 518
Nuzum, Dwayne, 344
Nycz, Shelley Joyce, 545
Nyfeler, John, 299
Nype, Diantha, 340
Nyren, Carl J. A., 330

O

O. Ahlborg & Sons, 128
Oakley, Charles W., 299
Obata, Gyo, 299, 336
Oberlander, Cornelia A., 318
Oberlin College, 368
Oberste Baubehörde, 161
Oblinger, Warren J., 318
O'Boyle, Robert L., 318
O'Brien, John "Mel," Jr., 349
O'Brien, W. L., Jr., 299
Ochsner, Jeffrey K., 299
O'Connor, Thomas, 299
The Octagon, 259
Odell, A. Gould, Jr., 341
Odell Associates Inc., 379, 385, 387, 486
Odenwald, Neil, 318
Odermatt, Robert A., 273, 299
O'Donnell, L. J., 299
O'Donnell, Patricia M., 318
O'Donnell Wicklund Pigozzi & Peterson,
    492, 493, 495, 500
Oehme, Wolfgang W., 318
Oehme van Sweden and Associates, Inc.,
    177
Oehrlein, Mary L., 299

Oenslager, Donald, 277
Ogawa/Depardon Architects, 111
O'Gorman, James F., 137, 351
Ögün, Emine, 36
Ögün, Mehmet, 36
OH & CO, 100
Ohio State University
    degree programs, 536, 540, 541, 547
    staff, 344, 549
    students, 514, 517
Ohio University, 536
Ohlhausen, Rolf H., 299
OHO Joint Venture, 37
Oishi, Satoshi, 282
Ojeda-O'Neill, Pablo, 277
Okada, ShinIchi, 330
Okeke, Nnadozie, 543
Oklahoma State University, 512, 517, 536
Olcott, Richard M., 299
Oldenburg, Claes, 46
Old House Journal, 640
Old Post Office Landmark Committee, 424
Olds, Andrew S., 543
Old Sturbridge Village, 413
Oldziey, Edward A., 299
O'Leary, Arthur F., 299
O'Leary, Patricia, 512
O'Leary, William A., 318
Oles, Paul Stevenson, 47, 98, 299
Olin, H. B., 299
Olin, Laurie D., 56, 276, 318, 334
Olin, Peter J., 318
Olinger, Edward J., 318
Oliver, Kevin Andrew, 517
Olko, Stephen M., 282
Olmsted, Frederick Law, Jr., 133, 343, 524
Olmsted, Frederick Law, Sr., 57, 133, 392
Olmsted, John C., 343
Olsen, Donald E., 299
Olsen, Harold L., 321
Olsen, O. H., 393
Olsen & Associates Architects, 486
Olshavsky, Carole J., 299
Olson, Don H., 276, 318
Olson, James W., 299
Olson, Julie, 328
Olumyiwa, Oluwole O., 330
Olympiad Games XXIII, 47
O'More College of Design, 537
Omrania, 37, 395
Omura Casey Morel, Inc., 486
Onblahd, G., 160
ONE, 640, 643
O'Neal, Paul Murff, Jr., 299
Oppenheimer, Herbert B., 299
"Oppositions," 47
Opus Architects/Engineers, 502
Orange County Public Schools, 177
Oregon State University, 541
Oremen, Edward L., 299
Oringdulph, Robert E., 299, 349
Orland, Brian, 318
Orland, Jerome I., 321
Orlando, City of, 177

Orlando Regional Healthcare System, 177
Orlando Sentinel, 58
Orleans, Peter, 486
Orlov, Georgui M., 331
Orlov, Iosif Bronislavovitch, 160
Orr, Douglas W., 341
Orr, Gordon D., Jr., 299
Ortiz-Santiago, Pedro J., 282
Osborne, Dutch, 545
Osborne Engineering Company, 375
O'Shea, Peter, 276
Osler, David William, 299
Osler, Peter, 276
Oslund, Thomas R., 276
Osman, Mary E., 334
Osmundson, Theodore O., 64, 318, 343
Ossipoff, Vladimir, 273
Östberg, Ragnar, 39, 151, 406
Ostergaard, Paul, 282
Otak Architects, 51, 140
Otis Elevator Company, 98
Otsuji, Dennis Y., 318, 343
Ottagono, 643
Otto, Atelier Frei, 33, 37, 69, 108, 181
Oudens, G. F., 300
Ouroussoff, Nicolai, 356
"Outdoor Circle," 133
Ove Arup & Partners, 48
Over, R. Stanton, 282
Overall, Sir John Wallace, 144
Overby, Osmund, 327, 351
Overland Partners, Inc., 147
Ovresat, Raymond C., 300
Owen, Michael T., Sr., 322
Owens, Hubert B., 64, 343
Owens, Kenneth, Jr., 300
Owings, Nathaniel A., 39
Ownby, J. Steve, 318
OWP&P. *See* O'Donnell Wicklund Pigozzi
    & Peterson
Oxford University, 368

P

Paavilainen, Käpy, 364–365
P/A Awards, 136
Paderewski, C. J. "Pat," III, 300, 349
Padjen, Elizabeth Seward, 300
Paepcke, Elizabeth, 78
Page, Max, 162, 163
PageSoutherlandPage, 371
Page & Steele, 398
Pahl, Pahl, Pahl Architects, 127
Pahlman, William, 81
Painter, Michael, 318
Pairo, Edwin T., 322, 346
Palacious, Jose Luis, 188
Palermo, Gregory, 300
Paley, Albert, 48
Palladino, Michael, 277
Pallasmaa, Juhani, 113, 331
Pallay, Ross D., 336
Palmer, J. Hambleton, 282
Palmer, M. Meade, 64, 318, 662

Perron, Robert, 318
Perry, Charles O., 275
Perry, Clarence Arthur, 133
Perry, Isaac G., 392
Perry, John Gray, 300
Perry, Michael D., 334
Perry, Robert C., Jr., 318
Persky, Seymour H., 327
Perspective, 641
Perttula, Norman K., 300
Pertz, Stuart K., 300
Peter Cavanough and Son, 392
Peter Kewittand Sons, 392
Peter Miller Architecture and Design
  Books, 635
Peters, Charles E., 46
Peters, Leo F., 283
Peters, Owen H., 318, 343, 662
Peters, Phillip D., 309
Peters, Richard C., 344, 512
Peters, Robert W., 300
Peterson, Anna Maria, 544
Peterson, BJ, 312, 342
Peterson, Carolyn S., 300
Peterson, Charles Emil, 170, 300, 327, 351,
  424
Peterson, Fred W., 415
Peterson, Leonard A., 300
Peterson, R. Max, 336
Peterson, Warren A., 275
Peting, Donald, 277
Petkus, Janie, 325
Petrazio, Edward G., 300
Petrie, Paul, 325
Pettengill, G. E., 334
Pettersen, Eleanore, 300
Petterson, Robert L., 322
Pettitt, Jay S., Jr., 300
Pevsner, Sir Nikolaus, 47, 151
Pfaller, Mark A., 300
Pfeiffer, Norman, 62, 300, 340
Pfister, Charles, 340
Pfluger, J. D., 300
Phelps, Barton, 300
Phelps, Boyd W., 283
Phelps, William, 336
Phibbs, H. Albert, 312, 342
Phifer, Thomas M., 275
Philadelphia Art Museum, 503
Philadelphia Inquirer, 357
Philadelphia University, 536, 545
Philadelphia Zoological Society, 48
Philip Johnson Architects, 278
Philip Johnson Award, 137
Philips International BV, 99
Phillips, Barret, Hillier, Jones & Partners,
  389
Phillips, Frederick F., 300
Phillips, Karen A., 318
Phillips, Preston, 486
Phillips, W. Irving, Jr., 300
Phillips Farevaag Smallenberg, 67
Phillips Group, 492
Piano, Renzo, 62, 138, 141, 151, 279, 284

Piano & Rogers, 69
Pichler, Walter, 240
Pickens, Buford L., 344, 351
Pierce, J. Almont, 300
Pierce, John Allen, 300
Pierce, Taylor James, 518
Pierce, Walter S., 300
Pierce Goodwin Alexander & Linville, 494
Pierson, Robert W., 318
Pierson, William H., Jr., 327
Pietila, Reima, 174, 331
Pigozzi, Raymond A., 300
Pike, Janet D., 334
Pilgrim, Dianne H., 312, 340
Pillo, Amanda L., 544
Pillorge, George J., 300
Pillsbury, Philip W., Jr., 334
Pina, Antonio, 517
Pinckney, J. Edward, 318
Pine, Joseph, Jr., xxiii
Pinero, E. Pinez, 69
Pinto, John, 55
Piper, Robert J., 300, 309
Piquenard, Alfred H., 390, *391*
Pirkl, James J., 323, 549
Pirscher, Carl W., 300
Pisetzner, Emanuel, 283
Piske, Richard, 283
Pissarski, Methodi A., 331
Pitman, John W., 300
Pitman, Karin M., 188
Pitts, Joe H., 283
Pittsburgh History & Landmarks
  Foundation, 46
Pittsburgh Post-Gazette, 357
Pitz, Marjorie E., 318
Piven, Peter A., 300
Places, 641
Placzek, Adolph Kurt, 47, 327, 351
Plan Architects Co., 395
Planning Accreditation Board, 542
Plater-Zyberk, Elizabeth, 300, 365
Platner, Warren, 275, 340
Platt, Charles Adams, 57, 300
Platt, Kalvin J., 300
Plautz, William H., 283
Pless, Rex T., 283
PLEX GmbH, 156
Plimpton, Bill, 553
Plischke, Ernst A., 331
Plosser, G. Gray, Jr., 300
Plumb, William L., 277, 324
Plumbing Manufacturers Institute, 232
Plunkett Raysich Architects, 371
Poche', James M., 283
Pocius, Gerald, 413
Poggemeyer, Lester H., 283
Pointe Design Architects PC, 486
Poirot, James W., 283
Pokorny, Jan Hird, 300
Polakowski, Kenneth J., 318
Poley, Lincoln A., 486
Polisano, Lee A., 300
Politis, Timothy, 518

Polk, William M., 300
Polk Stanley Yeary Architects, Ltd., 486
Pollack, Peter M., 276, 318
Pollack, Richard N., 325, 348
Pollock, Randlek, 328
Pollock, Wilson, 300
Pollom, Erik, 514
Polshek, James Stewart, 300
Polshek Partnership, 41, 45, 74
Polsky, Norman, 312, 338
Polsky Academic Achievement Award,
  551–552
Polyengineering, Inc., 86
Polytechnic College of Engineering, 661
Polytechnic University of Puerto Rico, 545
Pomerance, Ralph, 300
Pomeroy, Leason F., III, 300
Pomeroy, Lee H., 300
Pomeroy, Lynn S., 300
Pommer, Richard, 53
Pond, Irving K., 341
Ponti, Gio, 249
Pontier, H. A., 283
Pook, Gerrard S., 300
Poole, Gabriel, 144
Pooley, F. B., 350
Pope, Richard, Sr., 336
Popham Walter Burford Architects, 486
Popkin, Samuel D., 300
Poppino, Allen, 283
Porter, Harry W., 318
Porter, Joe A., 318
Porter, William L., 300
Porterfield, Neil H., 318
Portland Oregonian, 357
Portland State University, 536, 541
Portman, David J., 309
Portman, John C., Jr., 46, 300
Portzamparc, Christian de, 141, 331
Posedly, Penny H., 300
Posener, Julius, 113
Post, George Browne, 39, 341
Post, Raymond G. "Skipper," Jr., 300, 341
Postiglione, Michael A., 283
Potee, Milton C., 322
Potter, Alfred K., 328
Potter, Roy Wilson, 309
Potter & Cox Architects, 486
Powell, Artiss L., III, 545
Powell, Boone, 300
Powell, Donald D., 340
Powell, Gen. Colin, 336
Powell, Kelly D., 275
Powell & Moya, 151
Powell Todd, Gwendolyn L., 328
Power, James Owen, 322
Powers, Lois, 338
Praeger, Captain Emil, 377
Praeger, Richard Q., 283
Praeger-Kavanaugh-Waterbury, 377
Praemium Imperiale, 138
Prairie Avenue Bookshop, 634
Prairie View A&M University, 512, 517, 537,
  545

Pran, Peter, 300
Pratt, Candace J., 544
Pratt, James, 300
Pratt, Richardson, Jr., 663
Pratt Institute
  degree programs, 534
  School of Architecture building, 43
  school ranking, 558
  staff, 344, 511, 549, 550, 663
  students, 553
Pray, James Sturgis, 343
Precast/Prestressed Concrete Institute, 232
Predock, Antoine S., 275, 300
Preiss/Breismeister PC Architects, 486
Prendiville, Paul W., 283
Preservation, 641
Preservation of Architectural Records
  Committee, 46
Preservation Resource Center, 78
Preservation Society of Charleston, 48
Preservation Trades Network, Inc., 232
Presidential Design Awards, 138
Presnell, David G., 283
Press, Manuel, 322
Pressley, Marion, 318
Pressley, William, 318
Preston, Jerry W., 322
Preston, Steven A., 309
Price, Edison, 47
Price, Rae L., 318
Price, Thomas D., 276
Price, William, 255
Priestley, William T., 300
Priestman Goode, 101
Prigmore Krievins Haines Limon
  Architects, PA, 483
Prima, Arnold J., Jr., 300
Princeton Architectural Press, 48
Princeton University
  Blair & Buyers Residence Hall, 146
  Board of Trustees, Officers and Office
    of Physical Planning, 48
  degree programs, 534, 540, 541, 547
  staff, 3, 344, 560
  students, 365, 517, 553, 654
Prinsloo, Ivor C., 331
Prinz, Harold E., 300
Pritchard, Shirley, 325
Pritchard, Walter F., II, 334
Pritzker, Cindy, 125, 141
Pritzker, Jay A., 125, 141, 334
Pritzker Architecture Prize, 14, 15–19, 141,
  142
Procopio, Paul N., 318
Proctor, Katherine S., 322
Professional Construction Estimators
  Association of America, 232
Professional Management Services, Inc.,
  486
Progressive Architecture, 136
Progressive Architecture Awards Program,
  46
Proppe, Jody, 334
Propp + Guerin, 157
Prosse, Rev. Richard McClure, 180
Prouvé, Jean, 69, 365

Providence Journal, 357
Providence Preservation Society Revolving
  Fund, 442
Provine, Loring, 344
Prowler, Donald, 300
Prudon, Theodore H. M., 425
Prus, Victor M., 331
Pryce, Edward L., 318
PT Griyantara Architects, 35
PT Triaco, 35
Public Welfare Foundation, 422
Puckett, Hal, 283
Puderbaugh, Homer L., 300
Pueblos de Taos, 48
Pugh, David Arthur, 273, 300
Pugh, David L., 309
Pugh, Mary Joan, 309
Pugh + Scarpa, 43, 106
Pugh Scarpa Kodama, 51
Pulgram, William L., 300, 340
Pulitzer Prize for Architectural Criticism,
  143
Pulliam, James G., 300
Pulos, Arthur J., 108, 324, 347, 549
Purdue University, 531
Purintan, Jacquelyn, 551
Pursell, Joe T., 300
Purves, Edmund R., 83
Purvis, Betty J., 312
Pushelberg, Yabu, 109, 111
Putman, Andrée, 164, 165, 340
Pyatok, Michael, 50, 300
Pyatok Associates, 50, 51, 148

Q

Quackenbush, Helen M., 318
Quantrill, Malcolm, 511
Quarry, Neville, 113, 144
Quatman, G. William, 301
Quay, Ray, 309
Quebe, Jerry L., 301
Quebe, Lisbeth, 328
Queen, Andrew, 548
Quennell, Nicholas, 318
Queral, George L., 275
Quesada, Luis M., 331
Quigley, Herbert, 390
Quigley, Robert W., 301
Quimby, Marcel, 301
Quinn, Adele, 663
Quinn, Anthony, 516
Quinn, Michael L., 301
Quinn, Patrick J., 275, 345
Quinn, Richard W., 301, 349

R

R. Duell and Associates, 651
R. M. Kliment & Frances Halsband
  Architects, 45, 60
R. S. Means, 360
Raab, Martin D., 301

Rabun, F. Truitt, Jr., 318
Race, Bruce A., 301
Racker, David C., 318
Radius Product Development, Inc., 101
Rae, Andrew D., 322
Raeber, John A., 301, 322
Rafferty, Craig E., 301
Rafferty, Richard J., 301
Ragan, Sandra, 325
Ragold, Richard E., 283
Rahenkamp, John, 318
RAIA Gold Medal, 144
RAIC Gold Medal, 145
Rainer, Leslie, 277
Raitz, Karl B., 422
Raleigh News & Observer, 357
Ralph Appelbaum Associates Incorporated,
  101, 156, 157, 159
Rama, Angel, 543
Ramesh, Jyothsna, 515
Ramirez Vazquez, P., 113
Ramos, Jason H., 275
Ramos, Lemuel, 301
Rampy, Gil, 136
Ramsey, Jonathan, 544
Ranalli, George, 486
Rand, Peter A., 301
Rand, Sidney A., 334
Raney, Vincent G., 322
Rankin, Stan L., 283
Rankine, Terry, 301
Rann Haight, 381
Raphael, Bettina A., 277
Raphael Architects, 486
Rapp, Charles A., 276
Rapp, Raymond R., 301
Rapson, Ralph, 301, 511, 560
Rapuano, Michael, 276
Rasco, Howard Terry, 301
Rashid, Karim, xxiv, 77, 99
Rasmussen, Peter T., 301
Rasmussen, Steen Eiler, 46
Rassegna, 643
Rast, Joel, 117
Rath, Frederick, Jr., 424, 663
Ratliff, William R., 283
Rauch, John K., Jr., 301
Rauma, John G., 301
Raven, Peter H., 336
Ravereau, André, 33
Rawls, Sandra K., 551
Rawn, William L., 301
Rawson, Catharine G., 312
Ray, William Dunn, 312
Rayle, Martha Garriott, 312, 342
Ray Letkeman Architect Ltd., 175
Raymond, Charles, 325
Raymond, George, 309
Raymond, Larry T., 322
Rayner, Chessy, 340
Raytheon Systems Co., 100
RBB Architects Inc., 483
RD Installations Inc., 129
Read, Anice Barber, 424

Roche, Kevin, 39, 57, 62, 141, 278, 301
Rochester Institute of Technology, 534, 549
Rock, David, 350
Rock, Michael, 277
Rockcastle, Garth, 301
Rockefeller, Laurance S., 334, 336
Rockefeller Family, 125
Rockrise, George T., 301
Rockwell, Burton L., 301
Rockwell Group, 106, 139, 157
Rocky Mountain News, 357
Rodes, Elmer O., 283
Rodgers, Joseph Lee, 309
Rodman, Mark, 515
Rodrigues, Kenneth A., 301
Rodriguez, Barbara J., 334
Rodriguez, Pedro, 312
Rodriguez, Sergio, 309
Rodwin, Lloyd, 513
Roebling, John Augustus, 370
Roehling, Carl D., 301
Roemer, Chester E., 301
Roeseler, Wolfgang G., 309
Roesling, Ralph J., II, 301
Roessner, R. G., 301
Rogers, Agnes H., 312
Rogers, Archibald C., 301, 341
Rogers, James G., III, 301
Rogers, John B., 301
Rogers, John D., 301
Rogers, John I., 343
Rogers, Sir Richard H., 62, 138, 151, 219,
    318
Rogers Marvel Architects, 43, 106
Roger Williams University, 537, 545, 553
Rogoway, Lawrence P., 283
Rohde, Jane, 325
Roland, Craig W., 301
Rolland, Larry, 350
Rolland, Peter G., 48, 276, 318
Rollins, Ron, 356
Romanowitz, B. F., 301
Rome, James G., 301
Rome Prize, 274
Romieniec, Edward, 511
Ron Hobbs Architects, 485
Rook, Benjamin T., 301
Roos, Sigmund, 283
Root, John Wellborn, 39
Root, Robert W., 301
Roper, Laura Wood, 54
Ropes, George, 390
Rosa, Richard, 275
Rosan, Richard M., 301
Rose, Charles, 188
Rose, Kari E., 518
Rose, Peter, 245
Rose, William A., Jr., 273, 301
Rosen, Alan, 301
Rosen, Alan R., 301
Rosen, Harold J., 322
Rosen, Manuel M., 301
Rosen, Martin J., 336
Rosenblatt, Arthur, 170, 301

Rosenblum, Robert, 278
Rosene, Robert W., 283
Rosenfeld, Myra Nan, 54
Rosenfeld, Norman, 301
Rosenman, Marvin E., 512
Rosenstein, Steven, 518
Rosenthal, Steve, 47
Rosenzweig, Roy, 415
Ross, Donald E., 283
Ross, Donald K., 283
Ross, Edgar B., 301
Ross, John R., 349
Rossant, James S., 301
Ross & Associates Architects, 483
Ross Barney + Janowski, Inc., 94
Rosser Fabrap International, 86
Rossetti, Louis A., 301
Rossetti Associates/Architects Planners,
    379, 387
Rossi, Aldo A., 15–16, 141, 331, 405
Rostenberg, Bill, 301
Roth, Harold, 273, 301
Roth, Richard, Jr., 301
Rothe, Edward N., 301
Rothman, Martha L., 301
Rothman, Richard, 301
Rothman, Robert S., 188
Rothschild, Bernard B., 83, 273, 301, 322
Rothzeid, Bernard, 302
Rotival, Maurice, 302
Rotondi, Michael, 56, 302
Rottet, Lauren L., 302, 340
Rotz Engineers Inc., 72
Roudnev, L., 398
Rougerie, J., 69
Rounds Vanduzer Architects, 486
Rountree, Gini, 334
Rouse, James W., 125, 133
Rouse Company, 46
Rowan, Robert J., 553
Rowe, Colin, 47, 151, 560
Rowe, David T., 283
Rowe, Judith L., 302
Rowland, Ralph T., 302
Rowland, Robert D., 283
Roy, Clarence, 318
Roy, Jennifer L., 545
Royal Academy, 262
Royal Architectural Institute of Canada
    (RAIC), 145, 217
Royal Australian Institute of Architects
    (RAIA), 144, 218, 641
Royal College of Art, 664
Royal Gold Medal, 219
Royal Institute of British Architects (RIBA),
    150, 219, 260, 350, 642
Royoung Bookseller, 634
Royston, Robert N., 46, 64, 318
RPGA Design Group, 148
RSP Architects, 502
RTKL International, Inc.
    awards/honors, 50, 157
    company profile/ranking, 491, 492,
        493, 494, 495, 496, 502, 507
    works/projects, 50, 157, 375

Rubeling, Albert W., Jr., 302
Rubenstein, Harvey M., 318
Rubenstein, Michael, 486
Ruble, John, 302
Ruby & Associates, 127
Rucker, Della Gott, 514
Rucker, J. Ronald, 302
Rucker, Robert H., 318
Rudd, J. W., 302
Rudofsky, Bernard, 46
Rudolph, Paul, 62
Rudy Bruner Award for Urban Excellence,
    152
Ruedig, Adam Joseph, 546
Ruehl, Gordon E., 302
Ruffcorn, Evett J., 302
Ruffo, John A., 302
Ruga, Wayne, 78, 312, 326
Ruggiero, Janet M., 309
Ruhnau, Herman O., 302
Ruiz, Michael, 544
Ruiz-Fernandez, Maria del Pilar, 546
Rumbold, Charlotte, 133
Rumpel, Peter L., 302
Rundell Ernstberger Associates, 65
Rupe, William W., 302
Rupnik, Megan, 515
Rural Heritage Program, 451
Russel Wright Award, 153, 154
Russell, Beverly, 164
Russell, Earnest J., 341
Russell, John A., 145
Russell, T. T., 302
Russell, Virginia Lockett, 318
Russell Scott Steedle & capone Architects
    Inc., 486
Rutan, Burt, 76
Rutes, Walter A., 302
Rutgers, The State University of New
    Jersey, 514, 523, 534, 540, 541
Ruth, H. Mark, 302
Ruth, Jessica, 544
Ruthazer, Jack G., 312
Rutledge, Harry R., 302
Ryan, James, 324, 347
Ryan, Leslie A., 276
Ryan, Roger N., 302
Ryan, Terry Warriner, 318
Rybczynski, Witold, 331
Rydeen, James E., 302
Ryder, Donald P., 302
Rykwert, Joseph, 55
Rylan, Elizabeth, 551
Ryohin Keikaku Co., Ltd., 108

S

Saarinen, Eero, 39, 151, 171, 369, 405
Saarinen, Eliel, 39, 171, 253
Saarinen, Saarinen & Associates, 171, 173
Sabo, Werner, 302
Sabouni, Ikhlas, 512
Sacasa, Ana Paola, 547
Sachs Electric, 128

Schwartz, Irving D., 313, 342
Schwartz, Joel, 117
Schwartz, Kenneth E., 302
Schwartz, Robert, 302
Schwartzman, Alan, 302
Schwartzman, Daniel, 83
Schwartzman, Paul D., 277
Schwartz/Silver Architects, 41
Schwarz & Van Hoefen, Associated, 377
Schwengel, Frederick D., 335
Schwengels, Suzanne K., 335
Schwietz, Lawrence E., 322
Schwing, Charles E., 302, 341
Sclater, Alan D., 302
Sclater Partners Architects, 70
Scofidio, Ric, 76
Scogin, Mack, 56
Scogins, Mack, 76
Scott, David M., 302
Scott, Douglas, 108
Scott, Fred, 664
Scott, Mel, 134
Scott, Michael, 151, 331
Scott, Paul G., 283
Scott, Sir George G. Gilbert, 150
Scott, Sir Gilbert G., 350
Scott, Sir Giles Gilbert, 151, 350
Scott, Suzanne Benedict, 551
Scott Brown, Denise, 135, 168, 278, 340,
   366, 511, 560, 656
Scouten, Rex, 335
Scully, Daniel V., 275
Scully, Sunny Jung, 318
Scully, Vincent, 53, 278, 650
Scully, Vincent, J., Jr., 46, 168, 179, 560
SCUP/AIA-CAE Excellence in Planning
   Awards, 155
Scutt, Der, 302
Seablom, Seth H., 276
Sealy, Jim W., 302
Searl, Kenneth L., 322
Searl, Linda, 302
Sears, Bradford G., 318
Sears, Stephen, 276
Sears, William T., 436
Sease, Catherine, 277
Seaside, 48
Seattle Times, 357
Seavitt, Catherine, 275
Seay, Seay & Litchfield Architects/Interior
   Designers, PC, 486
Sebastian, B., 335
Sedgewick, Thomas J., 302, 349
Sedway, Paul H., 309
Seelye Stevenson, Value & Knecht, 139
Segal, George, 139
Segal, Paul, 302
SEGD Design Awards, 156–158, 159
Segoe, Ladislas, 134
Segrue, Lawrence P., 302
Seiberling, Hon. John F., 47, 336
Seibert, E. J., 302
Seidel, Alexander, 302
Seidler, Harry, 144, 151, 331

Seiferth, Solis, 349
Sekler, Eduard Franz, 48, 113
Selbert Perkins Design, 99, 156
Self, Larry D., 302
Seligmann, Werner, 275, 560
Seligson, Theodore, 302
Sellen Construction Company, 177
Sellery, Bruce M., 302
Sellman, C. G., 392
Selva, Bayardo, 518
Selzer, Dale E., 302
Semans, James H., 335
Seminole Community College, 529
Senhauser, John C., 302
Senseman, Ronald S., 302
Seracuse, Jerome M., 302
Serber, Diane, 302
Serrano, J. Francisco, 331
Serrill, Julian B., 335
Sert, Jackson and Associates, 60
Sert, Joseph Luis, 39
Settecase, Phillip K., 302
Setter Leach & Lindstrom, 502
Severance, H. Craig, 396
Sewell Jones, Elaine K., 335
Seydler-Hepworth, Betty Lee, 302
Seymour, Jonathan G., 318
Sgoutas, Vassilis C., 331
Shackleton, Polly E., 335
Shadbolt, Douglas, 145, 511
Shaffer, Marshall, 83
Shaivitz, Allan, 326
Shakespeare, William, 178
Shalom Baranes Associates, 94, 492, 494
Shambob Brick Producers Co-operative, 82
Shanis, Carole Price, 325
Shannon & Wilson, 128
Sharky, Bruce, 318
Sharoun, H., 69
Sharp, Dennis, 113
Sharpe, Edmund, 150
Sharpe, Richard S., 302
Sharpe, Sumner, 309
Sharratt, John A., 302
Shaver Architects, 486
Shaw, Howard Van Doren, 39
Shaw, Otho S., 313
Shaw, Paul, 277
Shaw, William V., 277
Shay, James L., 302
Shea, Leo G., 302
Shearer-Swink, Juanita D., 319
Sheehy, John P., 302
Sheffield, Jaymie, 515
Sheldon, George C., 302
Shellhorn, Ruth P., 319
Shelly, Alice Elizabeth, 322
Shelmire, W. Overton, 302
Shelor, Michele A., 523
Shelton, Mindel & Associates, 45, 106
Shelton, Peter, 340
Shemro Engineering, 72
Shen, Carol, 302
Shen, Haigo T. H., 331

Sheoris, John V., 302
Shepard, Herschel E., 302
Shepheard, Sir Peter F., 331, 350
Shepley, Henry R., 57
Shepley, Hugh, 303
Shepley Bulfinch Richardson & Abbott, 60,
   371, 493, 494, 500, 648
Sherman, Donald, 326
Sherman, Patricia C., 303
Sherman, Rayne, 326
Sherrill, Berry, 340
SHG Inc., 373, 375
Shi, Junkun, 546
Shida, Takashi, 303
Shiel, Gail, 326
Shiels, Roger D., 303
Shigemura, Dr. Tsutomu, 331
Shigeru Ban Architects, 185
Shim-Sutcliffe Architects, Inc., 182, 183
Shinohara, Kazuo, 331
Shipley, Philip A., 664
Shirley, Edward H., 303
Shirley Cooper Award, 89, 90
Shirvani, Dr. Hamid, 319
Shive, Philip A., 303
Shive-Hattery Inc., 124
Shive/Spinellli/Perantoni & Associates, 371
Shivler, James F., 283
Shofner Evans Architects/Interiors, 184
Shojaardalan, Roujanou, 545
SHoP/Sharples Holden Pasquarelli, 56
Shopsin, William C., 303
Short, Ronald N., 309
Short, William E., 283
Short Elliott Hendrickson, Inc., 483
Shrack, J. Kipp, 319
Shreve, Lamb & Harmon, 370, 394, 405
Shreve, Richmond H., 341
Shu, Evan H., 303
Shubin + Donaldson Architects, 74
Shuler, Wayne F., 283
Shulman, Julius, 335
Shupee, George Whiteside, 303
Shurcliff, Arthur A., 343, 524
Shurtleff, Flavel, 134
Shutts, Peter G., 486
SHW Group, Inc., 89, 90
Siddiqui, Tasneem Ahmed, 36
Sidener, Jack T., 303
Sidhu, Devindar S., 283
Sieben, Paul G., 303
Siebold, Sydow & Elfanbaum, Inc., 65
Siegel, Alan, 313
Siegel, Arthur S., 46
Siegel, Jeffrey L., 319
Siegel, Lloyd H., 303
Siegel, Robert H., 303, 340
Sieger, Charles M., 303
Siff, Joseph, 553
Silenus, Otto Friedrich, 37
Silling Associates Inc Architects/Planners,
   486
Silloway, Thomas W., 393
Silva, Thomas, 275

Washington Metropolitan Area Transit
Authority, 47
Washington Partners, 177
Washington Post, 358
Washington State University, 518, 539, 541,
546, 553
Washington University, 344, 511, 533
Washtenaw Engineering Company, 67
Wassef, Ramses Wissa, 34
Wasserman, Barry L., 305
Wasserman, Joseph, 305
Watanabi, Michelle, 517
Waterfront Center, 87, 233
Waterhouse, Alfred, 150
Waterhouse, Michael T., 350
Waterhouse, Paul, 350
Waterleaf Architecture & Interiors, 483
Watershouse, Alfred, 350
Watkins, David H., 305
Watkins College of Art & Design, 537
Watson, Donald R., 305
Watson, J. Stroud, 512
Watson, Kent E., 319
Watson, Raymond L., 305
Watson, Stoud, 170
Watson, Wayne N., 322
Watson, William J., 305
Wattenbarger Architects, 70
Watterson, Joseph, 83
Watts, Larry W., 310
Waymon, E. Ernest, 322
Wayne State University, 533
WBRC Architects/Engineers, 483
WD Partners, 494
W.E. O'Neil Construction Company, 175
Weatherby, Richard T., 322
Weatherford, Dwight W., 319
Weatherly, E. Neal, Jr., 319
Weave Plan, 101
Weaver, Francis X., 517
Webb, John L., 305
Webb, Sir Aston, 39, 150, 350
Webber, Melvin M., 513
Webber, P. R., 305
Webb Zerafa Menkes Housden
Partnership, 396
Webcor Builders, 127
Webel, Richard C., 666
Webel, Richard K., 276, 319, 666
Webel and Innocenti, 666
Weber, Arthur M., 305
Weber, F. Spencer, 283
Weber, G. F., 313
Webster, Frederick S., 305
Webster, William W., 283
Wedding, C. R., 305
Weese, Benjamin H., 305
Weese, Cynthia, 305
Weese, Harry, 62, 168
Weese Langley Weese Architects Ltd., 486
Weeter, Gary K., 305
Wegener, Jeffrey, 515
Wegerer, Vernon M., 283
Wegner, Hans J., 108

Wegner, Robert, Sr., 310
Weidlinger, Paul, 335
Weidlinger Associates Inc., 47
Weidmann, Victor, 283
Weigand, Bryce Adair, 305
Weigel, Paul, 344
Weihe Design Group, 148
Weikert, James P., 544
Weilenman, Joe Neal, 305
Wein, Frank B., 310
Weinberg, Scott S., 319
Weingardt, Richard, 283
Weingarten, Nicholas H., 305
Weinmayr, V. Michael, 319
Weinstein, Amy, 305
Weinstein, Edward, 305
Weinstein and Associates, 177
Weinstein Copeland Architects, 183
Weintraub, Lee, 65
Weinzapfel, Jane, 305
Weir, John P., 284
Weir, Maurice, 313
Weisbach, Gerald G., 305
Weisberg, Sarelle T., 305
Weiss, Dryfous and Seiferth, 392
Weiss, Steven F., 305
Weisz, Sandor, 324
Welborne, Martha L., 305
Welch, Frank D., 305
Welch, John A., 305
Welch, Paul W., Jr., 335
Welch, Scot Alan, 547
Welcome, Roger T., 322
Weller, Louis L., 180, 305
WeLL Industrial Design BV, 99
Wells, Roger, 319
Wells Brothers Company, 392
Wemple, Emmet L., 48, 335
Wendel, Delia, 517
Wenger, Vicki, 313
Wenk, William E., 319
Wenk Associates, Inc., 67
Wenzler, William P., 305
Weppner, Robert A., Jr., 275
Werden, Robert G., 284
Werner, David, 523
Wertz, Matthew, 101
Wescoat, Prof. James L., 276
Wesselink, Robert D., 284
West, Daniel Morgen, 518
West, Derek T odd, 548
West, John, 338
West, Lewis H., 284
West, William R., 393
Westbrook, Parker, 440, 441
Westby, Katie, 335
Westdeutsche Immobilienbank, 177
Westermann, Helge, 305
Western Carolina University, 535
Western Michigan University, 533
Western Reserve University. *See* Case
Western Reserve University
Western Washington University, 539
Westlake, Merle T., 305

Westlake, Paul E., Jr., 305
Westmoreland, Carl B., 424
Weston, I. Donald, 306
West Valley College, 528
West Virginia University, 539
Wethey, Harold, 53
Wetmore, James A., 390
Wetmore, Louis B., 310
Wetzel, Richard B., 284
Wexler, Allan, 76
Wexner Center Bookstore, 635
Wexner Prize, 119, 138
Weyenberg, Andrew J., 544
Weygand, Robert A., 319
Weyrauch, Andrew, 517
Whalen, Frank J., Jr., 335
Whalen, Molly Katherine, 514
Whalley, Raymond, 322
Wheat, James D., 319
Wheatley, Charles H., 306
Wheatley, John, 436
Wheeler, C. Herbert, 306
Wheeler, Daniel H., 306
Wheeler, Dr. George, 277
Wheeler, Ezra Ingvald, 546
Wheeler, Gary E., 81, 313, 340, 342
Wheeler, James H., Jr., 306
Wheeler, Kenneth D., 306
Wheeler, Nick, 47
Wheeler, Richard H., 306
Wheelock, Morgan Dix, 319
Whelan, Miriam, 323
Whichcord, John, 350
Whiffen, Marcus, 53
Whipsaw, Inc., 101
Whisnant, Murray, 306
Whiston, Brian R., 284
Whitaker, Elliott, 344
White, Allison Carll, 326
White, Arthur B., 306
White, David Eli, 514
White, George F., Jr., 322
White, George Malcolm, 170, 306, 393
White, H. Kenneth, 284
White, Harry K., 393
White, James M., 349
White, Janet Rothberg, 306
White, Norval C., 306
White, Robert F., 319
White, Ronald R., 284
White, Samuel G., 306
White, Sara Jane, 310
White, Stanford, 436
Whitefield, William, 331
Whitener-Rohe, Inc., 486
Whitescarver, Charles K., 284
Whiteside, Emily M., 277
Whitfield, James F., 322
Whitley, David, 515
Whitlow, Heather, 514
Whitnall, Gordon, 134
Whitney, Stephen Q., 306
Whitney M. Young, Jr. Award, 180
Whitney-Whyte, Ron, 326

Woods, Lebbeus, 48, 76
Woodsen, Riley D., 284
Woods & Starr Associates, Inc., 483
Woodward, Thomas E., 306
Woodward, William McKenzie, 422
Wooldridge, Joel C., 310
Wooley, David L., 306
Woollen, Evans, 306
Woolley, Kenneth Frank, 144
Woolley/Morris Architects, 70
Woolpert Design, 67
Wooten, J. R., 306
World Architecture, 185, 643
World Architecture Awards, 185–186, 187
World Conservation Union, 433
World Heritage Committee, 433, 461
World Heritage List, 433, 461–470
World Monuments Fund, 48, 471
World Monuments Watch Fund, 471
World of Interiors, 643
World's 100 Most Endangered Sites, 471–475
Wormley, Edward J., 81
Wornum, George Grey, 151
Worsley, John C., 306
Worth, Jack, III, 553
Worth, Ronald D., 328
Worthington, Sir Percy Scott, 151
Wosser, Thomas D., 284
WPa, Inc., 157
Wragg, Francis R., 346
Wrenn, Tony P., 335
Wright, David G., 319
Wright, David H., 306
Wright, Derek, 94
Wright, Frank Lloyd
    awards/honors, 39, 57, 151, 171, 173
    museum collections and exhibitions, 241
    quotes by, 519, 548
    students, 516, 652, 654
    works/projects, 171, 173, 246, 369, 370, 405, 406, 436, 444
Wright, George S., 306
Wright, Henry, 134
Wright, Henry L., 306, 341
Wright, John L., 306
Wright, Kenneth R., 284
Wright, Marcellus, Jr., 306
Wright, Porteous & Lowe/Bonar, 371
Wright, Robert G., 284
Wright, Rodney H., 306
Wright, Russel, 153, 246
Wright, St. Clair, 424
Wright Runstad and Company, 177
Wriston, Barbara, 351
Wu, Liangyong, 113
Wuellner, Cynthia, 306
Wurman, Richard Saul, 76
Wurster, Bernardi & Emmons, 60
Wurster, William Wilson, 39
Wyatt, Julie M., 313
Wyatt, Scott W., 306
Wyatt, Sir M. Digby, 150

Wyatt, Thomas Henry, 150, 350
Wyckoff, Mark A., 310
Wynn, Forbes, Lord, Feldberg & Schmidt, 389
Wynne, Brian J., 337
Wynne, Theodore E., 284
Wyss, Patrick H., 319

Y

Yale University
    campus, 368
    degree programs, 528, 540, 546
    school ranking, 559
    staff, 279, 344, 560
    students, 365, 518, 652, 656
    Yale University Art Gallery, 171
Yamada, Joseph Y., 319
Yamasaki, Minoru, 62, 394
Yang, Yizhao, 515
Yardley, Jack R., 306
Yates, Honorable Sidney, 335
Yates, L. Carl, 284
Yates, Nadine R., 328
Yates, Sidney R., 666
Yaw, John L., 306
Yazdani, Mehrdad, 94
Ye, Rutang, 331
Yeang, Ken, 69
Yeates, Zeno Lanier, 306
Yeaton, Alan H., 486
Yegul, Fikret, 55
Yeh, Raymond W., 306
Yen, Yung-Ning, 547
Yener, Ertur, 33
Yeo, Ronald W., 306
Yeomans, Jill D., 335
Yeon, John, 62
Yerkes, David N., 83, 306
Yim, Raymon, 523
Yoder, Bruce T., 310
Yokoyama, Minoru, 326
Yost, William R., 306
Young, Clayton, 306
Young, George, Jr., 344
Young, Janice, 326
Young, Joseph L., 306
Young, Norbert, Jr., 306
Young, Richard, 331
Young, Theodore J., 306
Young, Thomas I., 322, 346
Young, Whitney M., 180
Young Architects Award, 188
Yowell, Linda, 306
Yu, Wai-Ki Tracy, 543
Yuasa, Hachiro, 306
Yudell, Robert J., 306

Z

Zabel, Steven C., 543
Zabludovsky, Abraham, 331
Zach, Leon, 343
Zachary Taylor Davis, 377

Zago, Andrew, 136
Zagorski, Edward J., 324, 549
Zahn, James, 307
Zaik, Saul, 307
Zaleski, Serge, 98
Zanuso, Marco, 666
Zapatka, Christian, 276
Zaragoza, Jose M., 331
Zarillo, Mark J., 319
Zarina, Astra, 276
Zarnikow, Werner Edwin, 322
Zaugg, Rémy, 16
Zeaman, John, 355
Zednik, Tristen Marie, 546
Zeidler, Eberhard Heinrich, 145, 331
Zeidler Roberts Partnership, Inc., 371, 397
Zeigel, H. Alan, 307
Zeisel, Eva, 107
Zemanek, J., 307
Zenon, Golden J., Jr., 307
Zevaco, Jean-François, 33
Zevi, Bruno, 47
Zhou, Yufang, 547
ZIBA Design, 100, 101, 103
Zickler, Lou, 328
Ziegelman, Robert L., 307
Ziegler, Arthur P., Jr., 424
Ziegler, Raymond, 307
Ziegler Cooper Architects, 486
Zilm, Frank, 307
Zils, John J., 307
Zimmer Gunsul Frasca Partnership, 45, 60, 140, 177, 493, 494, 505
Zimmerman, Bernard B., 307
Zimmerman, Floyd W., 319
Zimmerman, Gary V., 307
Zimmerman, Thomas A., 307
Zimmermann, Philip, 76
Zimmers, Hugh M., 307
Zion, Robert L., 319
Zion National Park, 65
Zolomij, Robert W., 319
Zube, Prof. Ervin H., 64, 276, 319
Zuck, Alfred C., 284
Zucker, Paul, 310
Zuelke, Laurence W., 319
Zukowsky, John, 137, 335
Zumthor, Peter, 75, 122
Zurich Museum of Design, 268
Zweifel, K. Richard, 319
Zweig, Janet, 277
Zweig, Peter Jay, 307
Zyla, Chad Allan, 545
Zyscovich, Inc., 486

SITE INDEX

NOTE: This is an index of architectural projects, sites and works. Locations that are not an architectual site per se – for example, universities – can be found in the NAME INDEX on page 669. Pages in italics refer to illustrations.

Osmania Women's College (Hyderabad), 473
Pattadakal Monuments, 464
Pitampura TV Tower (New Dehli), 402
Qutb Minar and Monuments (Delhi), 465
Sanchi Buddhist Monuments, 464
Shanti, A Weekend House (Alibaug, Maharashtra), 115
Sun Temple (Konarak), 464
Taj Mahal (Agra), 464
TV Tower (Bombay), 401
Vidhan Bhavan (Bhopal), 37

INDONESIA
BNI City Tower (Jakarta), 397
Borobudur Temple Compounds (Java), 465
Citra Niaga Urban Development (Samarinda), 35
Indosat Telkom Tower (Jakarta), 399
Kampung Improvement Program (Jakarta), 34
Kampung Kali Cho-de (Yogyakarta), 36
Kampung Kebalen Improvement (Surabaya), 35
National Archives Building (Jakarta), 458, 459
Omo Hada, Nias (North Sumatra), 473
Pondok Pesantren Pabelan (Central Java), 34
Prambanan Temple Compounds (Java), 465
Saïd Naum Mosque (Jakarta), 35
Soekarno-Hatta Airport Landscaping Integration (Cengkareng),
    37

IRAN
Ali Qapu, Chehel Sutan and Hasht Behesht (Isfahan), 34
Meidan Emam (Esfahan), 465
Persepolis, 465
Shushtar New Town, 35
Tchogha Zanbil, 465
Tehran Telecommunications Tower, 399

IRAQ
Erbil Citadel (Kurdish Automonous Region), 473
Hatra, 465
Ninevah and Nimrud Palaces (near Mosul), 473
Saddam Tower (Bagdad), 403

IRELAND. *See* **UNITED KINGDOM**

ISRAEL
Bet She-arim Archaeological Site (Kiryat Tiv'on), 473
al-Haram al-Sharif (Jerusalem), 34

ITALY
Agrigento Archaeological Areas, 465
Aqueduct of Vanvitelli (Caserta), 465
Aquileia Archaeological Area and Patriarchal Basilica, 465
Assisi, 465
Basilica of San Francesco, 465
Bridge of Chains (Bagni di Lucca), 473
Caserta Royal Palace, 465
Castel de Monte (Andria), 465
Certosa di Padula, 465
Cilento and Vallo di Diano National Park, 465
Cinque Terre (Liguria), 465, 473
Costiera Amalfitana, 465
Crespi d'Adda, 465
Ferrara, 465
Florence Historic Centre, 465
Herculaneum Archaeological Area, 465
I Sassi di Matera, 465
Jil Sander Milan Showroom, 104
Modena Cathedral, Torre Civica and Piazza Grande, 465
Naples Historic Centre, 465
Orto Botanico (Padua), 465
Paestum Archaeological Site, 465

Palmaria Island, 465
Pantheon dome (Rome), 359
Piazza del Duomo (Pisa), 465
Pienza Historic Centre, 465
Pompeii, 465
Port of Trajan Archaeological Park (Fiumicino), 473
Portovenere, 465
Ravenna Early Christian Monuments, 465
Rome Historic Centre, 465
Royal House of Savoy, 465
St. Peter's Basilica (Rome), 331, 351
San Gimignano Historic Centre, 465
San Leucio Complex (Caserta), 465
San Paolo Fuori le Mura, 465
Santa Maria delle Grazie Church and Dominican Convent, 465
Siena Historic Centre, 465
Su Nuraxi di Barumini, 465
Tinetto Island, 465
Tino Island, 465
Torre Annunziata Archaeological Area, 465
Trulli of Alberobello, 465
Urbino Historic Centre, 465
Vatican City, 464
Vatican (Rome), 331, 351
Velia Archaeological Site, 465
Veneto Palladian Villas, 465
Venice and Lagoon, 465
Verona, 465
Vicenza, 465
Villa Adriana, 465
Villa Romana del Casale, 465

J

JAMAICA
Falmouth (Parish of Trelawny), 473

JAPAN
Ancient Kyoto Historic Monuments, 465
Ancient Nara Historic Monuments, 465
Fukuoka Prefectural and International Hall, 74
Fukuoka Tower, 402
Gokayama Historic Village, 465
Gusuku Sites (Kingdom of Ryukyu), 465
Hillside Terrace Complex (Tokyo), 178
Himeji-jo, 465
Horyu-ji Area Buddhist Monuments, 465
Il Palazzo Hotel (Fukuota), 405
Itsukushima Shinto Shrine, 465
JR Central Towers (Nagoya), 397
Kansai International Airport (Osaka), 284, 368
Landmark Tower (Yokohama), 395
Nikko Kirifuri Resort (Nikko City), 65
Nikko Shrines and Temples, 465
Opera City Tower (Tokyo), 398
Osaka World Trade Center, 397
Rinku Gate Tower (Osaka), 397
Saitama Super Arena, 186, 187
Shinjuku Park Tower (Tokyo), 398
Shirakawa-go Historic Village, 465
Tokyo City Hall, 406
Tokyo Metropolitan Government, 397, 407
Tokyo Tower, 401
Tomo Port Town (Fukuyama), 473

East Carson Street Business District (Pittsburgh), 427
Eastern State Penitentiary (Philadelphia), 456
Fallingwater (Mill Run), 369, 405, 436
First Union Center (Philadelphia), 378, 386
Fulton Building (Renaissance Pittsburgh Hotel), 146
Gallatin (Albert) House (Point Marion), 456
Gettysburg, historic, 421
Harrisburg Station and Train Shed, 456
Heinz Architectural Center (Pittsburgh), 250
Honey Hollow Watershed (New Hope), 456
Hotel Hershey (Hershey), 448
Independence Hall (Philadelphia), 469
Inglis Gardens at Eastwick (Philadelphia), 51
Leola Village Inn & Suites (Leola), 448
Meason House (Dunbar Township), 456
Mellon Arena (Pittsburgh), 386
Mellon Bank Center (Philadelphia), 397
Mount Union, historic, 421
Nittany Lion Inn (State College), 448
Ohio & Erie Canal National Heritage Corridor, 439
One Liberty Plaza (Philadelphia), 395, 408
Paint, historic, 421
Park Hyatt Philadelphia at the Bellevue, 448
Penncrest High School (Media), 89
Philadelphia, 131
Philadelphia International Airport Runway 8-26, 86
PNC Firstside Center (Pittsburgh), 404
PNC Park (Pittsburgh), 376
POD Restaurant (Philadelphia), 157
Rhys Carpenter Library, Bryn Mawr College, 119
Ritz-Carlton Hotel (Philadelphia), 146
Skytop Lodge (Skytop), 448
Southwestern Pennsylvania Industrial Heritage Route, 439
State Capitol (Harrisburg), 393
Three Rivers Stadium (Pittsburgh), 382
Two Liberty Place (Philadelphia), 397
University of Pennsylvania Modular VII Chiller Plant
    (Philadelphia), 41, 120
US Naval Asylum (Philadelphia), 456
US Post Office and Courthouse (Pittsburgh), 94
USX Tower (Pittsburgh), 397
Veterans Stadium (Philadelphia), 376, 384
Village of Arts and Humanities (Philadelphia), 152
William J. Nealon Federal Building and US Courthouse
    (Scranton), 94
Woodlands (Philadelphia), 456
Yale University campus, 368
York, 427
Yorktowne Hotel (York), 448

Rhode Island
Aqueduct Improvement (Cranston), 129
The Breakers (Newport), 436
College Hill, 131
Fort Adams (Newport), 456
Freeman Residence (Bristol), 148
Hotel Viking (Newport), 448
Inn at Newport Beach (Middletown), 448
Marble House (Newport), 436
McCoy Baseball Stadium (Pawtucket), 128
Newport, historic, 421
River Relocation (Providence), 79
Rosecliff (Newport), 436
State Capitol (Providence), 393
Westerly, historic, 421
Woonsocket, historic, 419, 421

South Carolina
Ahold Information Services Headquarters (Greenville), 72
Beaufort, 426
Bennettsville, historic, 421
Chapelle Administration Building (Columbia), 456
Charleston Historic District, 131
Chester, historic, 421
Fort Hill/John C. Calhoun House (Clemson), 456
John Rutledge House Inn (Charleston), 448
Kings Courtyard Inn (Charleston), 448
South Carolina National Heritage Corridor, 439
Spring Island (Beaufort County), 177
State Capitol (Columbia), 393
Union, historic, 421
Westin Francis Marion Hotel (Charleston), 448

South Dakota
Deadwood, historic, 419, 421
Frawley Ranch Historic District (Spearfish), 457
Rapid City, historic, 421
State Capitol (Pierre), 393
Waterford at All Saints (Sioux Falls), 70
Yankton, historic, 421

Tennessee
Adelphia Coliseum (Nashville), 382
Brenthaven (Brentwood), 148
Chickasaw Bluffs Conservancy (Memphis), 87
Columbia, historic, 421
Franklin, 427
Gaylord Entertainment Center (Nashville), 388
Graceland (Memphis), 436
The Hermitage (Hermitage), 436
Hermitage Hotel (Nashville), 448
Jack Daniels Visitor Center Enhancements (Lynchburg), 157
Nashville/Davidson County, 131
Norris, 131
Oak Ridge, historic, 421
The Peabody (Memphis), 448
Pittman Center, 426
Shelbyville, historic, 421
State Capitol (Nashville), 393
Storybook Farm (Bedford County), 184
Tennessee Civil War Heritage Area, 439
Tennessee Valley Authority, 131

Texas
Addison Circle (Addison), 50
Alamodome (San Antonio), 380
American Airlines Center (Dallas), 380, 388
Ballpark (Arlington), 374
Bank of America Plaza (Dallas), 396, 407
Bank One Center (Dallas), 398
Bastrop, historic, 421
Bat Dome Culvert (Laredo), 79
Brenham, historic, 421
Camino Real Hotel (El Paso), 448
Chase Tower (Houston), 395, 407
Compaq Center (Houston), 380
Cuero, historic, 421
Dallas Area Rapid Transit, 79
Denton, 427
Dredged Materials Environmental Resources (Houston), 86
The Driskill (Austin), 448
Enron Field (Houston), 86, 376
First Union Financial Center (Dallas), 398
Fort Brown (Brownsville), 457

Washington, DC
Fitch/O'Rourke Residence, 43
Lucent Technologies - Government Business Solutions, 43
MCI Center, 378, 386
National Gallery, East Wing, 369, 405
The Octagon, 193, 259
Pension Bureau Building, 255
Ronald Regan National Airport, 368
Terminal B/C, Ronald Reagan Washington National Airport, 79
True Reformer Building, 422
US Capitol, 369, 393
Vietnam Veterans Memorial, 369

West Virginia
Elkins Coal and Coke (Bretz), 457
The Greenbrier (White Sulphur Springs), 449
IRS Computing Center Works of Art Brochure (Martinsburg), 96
Martinsburg, historic, 421
Memorial Tunnelx Fire Ventilation (Charleston), 79
Morgantown, 427
National Coal Heritage Area, 439
Parkersburg, historic, 421
Philippi Bridge (Barbour County), 435
State Capitol (Charleston), 393
Weston Hospital Main Building (Weston), 457
Wheeling, historic, 419, 421
Windyridge (Keyser), 148

Wisconsin
American Club (Kohler), 449
Block 89 (Madison), 72
Bradley Center (Milwaukee), 378
Cable Natural History Museum (Cable), 136
Chippewa Falls, 426, 427
Greendale, 132
Harbour House (Greendale), 70
Hotel Metro (Milwaukee), 449
Lambeau Field (Green Bay), 384
Linwood and Howard Avenue Ozonation Facilities (Milwaukee), 128
Miller Park (Milwaukee), 376
Mineral Point, historic, 421
Pfister Hotel (Milwaukee), 449
Racine Downtown, 43
S.C. Johnson & Son Administration Building (Racine), 171, 369, 370, 406
Sentry Foods (Madison), 110
Sheboygan Falls, 427
State Capitol (Madison), 393
Sturgeon Bay, historic, 421
Watertown, historic, 421

Wyoming
Cheyenne, historic, 421
Moose, historic, 421
Rawlins, historic, 421
State Capitol (Cheyenne), 393
Swan Land and Cattle Company (Chugwater), 457
Tom Sun Ranch (Casper), 457
Yellowstone National Park, 131

URUGUAY
Colonia del Sacramento Historic Quarter, 469
UZBEKISTAN
Bukhara Historic Centre/Old City, 36, 469
Itchan Kala (Khiva), 469
Shakhrisyabz Historic Centre, 469
Tashkent Tower, 399

V

VENEZUELA
Ciudad Universitaria de Caracas, 469
Coro and its Port, 469
Office Towers (Caracas), 398
VIET NAM
Hoi An, 469
Hué Monuments, 469
My Son Sanctuary (Duy Phu Commune), 469

Y

YEMEN
Old Sana's Restoration, 36
Sana'a, 469
Shibam, 469
Tarim, Tarim and Wadi Hadramaut, 475
Zabid, 469
YUGOSLAVIA
Belgrade Tower, 403
Kotor Natural and Culturo-Historical Region, 470
Pec and Decani Monasteries (Kosovo and Metohiha), 475
Prizren Historic Centre (Kosovo), 475
Stari Ras, 470
Studenica Monastery (Kraljevo), 470
Subotica Synagogue (Subotica), 475

Z

ZIMBABWE
Khami Ruins National Monument, 470

2003 ORDER FORM

We welcome you to order the upcoming 2002 edition of the *Almanac of Architecture & Design*. Please return this form to us at the address listed below. You may pay by credit card or check. Volume discounts are available, call 1.800.726.8603 for information.

Almanac of Architecture and Design $37.50

Price	Quantity	Total
$37.50		
	Shipping	$4.95
	Order Total	

☐ **Check**   ☐ **Credit card**

Card #   Expiration Date

Signature

Contact Information

Name

Address

City   State   Zip

Telephone

Fax

Email

Please return this form to:
Greenway Consulting
ATTN: Almanac
30 Technology Parkway South, Suite 200
Norcross, GA 30092
Tel 770.209.3770
Fax 770.209.3778

Or email us at almanac@greenwayconsulting.com

COMMENT FORM

Invitation For Comments and Suggestions

Please include any ideas, comments, or suggestions for the *Almanac of Architecture & Design.*

Suggestions and Comments

_____

_____

_____

_____

_____

_____

_____

_____

_____

Contact Information

Name _____

Address _____

City _____ State _____ Zip _____

Telephone _____

Fax _____

Email _____

Please return this form to:
Greenway Consulting
ATTN: Almanac
30 Technology Parkway South, Suite 200
Norcross, GA 30092
Tel 770.209.3770
Fax 770.209.3778

Or email us at almanac@greenwayconsulting.com

CMD Group
CMD is a leading worldwide provider of quality construction information products and services designed to advance the businesses of its customers with timely, accurate and actionable project, plans & specifications, building product, and cost data. CMD collects, adds value to, and distributes construction industry information through print and online references and resources for architects, engineers, contractors, manufacturers and other professionals in the construction industry. Founded in 1975, CMD is an active participant in the construction industry, partnering with its customers and industry associations to meet customer information needs. CMD is a division of Cahners Business Information, a part of Reed Elsevier plc.

Greenway Consulting
Greenway Consulting is a management consulting firm that specializes in research and strategic advisory services. Greenway Consulting works with clients toward making design and construction a more efficient and profitable business. Services include executive coaching, goal setting, growth planning, strategic direction, futures forecasting, industry research, and business modeling for the design professions and the construction industry. The firm publishes *DesignIntelligence*, a strategic change bulletin and letter 12 times a year, as well as dozens of custom and limited circulation research reports for the design professions, product manufacturers, and construction industry. Greenway firm commitment to helping organizations grow faster and healthier through knowledge sharing and strategic decision support.

James Cramer
James Cramer is the founder and chairman of Greenway Consulting and adjunct professor of architecture at the University of Hawaii. He researches, consults, and gives seminars for leading professional firms around the world. He is the author of 135 articles and several books, including the critically acclaimed *Design + Enterprise, Seeking a New Reality in Architecture*. He is co-author of the upcoming *How Firms Succeed, A Field Guide to Management Solutions*. Cramer is the former chief executive of The American Institute of Architects in Washington D.C. and is the former president of the American Architectural Foundation. The recipient of over eighty awards and honors, he was presented the University of Minnesota's Distinguished Service Medal for his work advocating the value of good design into the mainstream of corporate America. He is currently the co-chair of the Washington D.C.-based think-tank, the Design Futures Council. An educator, futurist, and business advisor, he is currently leading workshops on technology advancements and pending value migration changes in the design professions.

Jennifer Evans Yankopolus
Jennifer Evans Yankopolus is the co-editor of the *Almanac of Architecture & Design* and an architectural historian. She is also the editor of the Archidek series of collectable, educational architecture trading cards. She has a Master's degree in architecture history from the Georgia Institute of Technology. She also studied at Drake University, where she received her B.S. in business administration and earned a Master's Degree in heritage preservation at Georgia State University. As a researcher, architectural historian, and project director, she leads Greenway's initiatives that bring historical perspective and fresh insight to futures invention assignments.

Robert Campbell

Robert Campbell is a writer and architect. In 1996 he received the Pulitzer Prize for Distinguished Criticism for his work as the *Boston Globe's* architecture critic. He is a contributing editor of the magazines *Architectural Record* and *Preservation*. He is also the author of a book, *Cityscapes of Boston: An American City Through Time*, a collaboration with photographer Peter Vanderwarker. Since 1975, he has been in private practice as an architect, chiefly as a consultant for the improvement or expansion of cultural institutions, and as an urban design consultant to cities. Campbell is also a Fellow of The American Institute of Architects and a recipient of the AIA's Medal for Criticism. He is a graduate of Harvard College, the Columbia Graduate School of Journalism, and the Harvard Graduate School of Design. He has lectured at more than 40 colleges and universities and has taught at the Harvard Graduate School of Design, the Boston Architectural Center, the University of North Carolina, the University of South Florida and the University of Michigan.